The Foreign Policy of Hitler's Germany

the foreign policy

Gerhard L. Weinberg

# of hitler's germany

Diplomatic Revolution in Europe 1933-36

The University of Chicago Press
Chicago and London

Chapter 1, "The World Through Hitler's Eyes," appeared in somewhat different form in *Midway,* Spring 1970, © 1970 by The University of Chicago.

THE UNIVERSITY OF CHICAGO PRESS, CHICAGO 60637
THE UNIVERSITY OF CHICAGO PRESS, LTD., LONDON

Paperback edition 1983
Printed in the United States of America

90 89 88 87 86 85 84 83   2 3 4 5 6

LCN: 70-124733
ISBN: 0-226-88509-7 (cloth)
0-226-88513-5 (paper)

Contents

Preface

Thirty years after the outbreak of World War II, the literature about the background of that conflict is enormous and constantly growing, but there is no comprehensive study that attempts to do what Sidney B. Fay, Pierre Renouvin, Bernadotte Schmitt, Alfred Wegerer, and Luigi Albertini had done within a similar period about the origins of World War I. Many factors may be adduced to explain this phenomenon: the absence, on the whole, of a controversy similar to the "war guilt" argument that stimulated a whole generation of scholars in the interwar years, a declining interest in diplomatic history that has accompanied the apparent decline of diplomacy as the main instrument for the conduct of international relations, the trend in historical scholarship that emphasizes monographic treatment of specific episodes for the benefit of other scholars at the expense of broader treatments of interest to a wider public, and a recognition that any account that deals only with diplomacy in the traditional manner but ignores other factors cannot be adequate for an understanding of the origins of World War II.[1]

One factor of a less philosophical but no less effective character in restraining scholars may be the very flood of evidence that threatens to overwhelm every attempt at synthesis. It is easy to forget that those who wrote on the outbreak of World War I were restricted almost totally to the use of memoirs supplemented by collections of documents published by the various European governments. With all its advantages and disadvantages, and in spite of its bulk and complexity, this material was subject to finite restrictions of volume, if little else. In addi-

1. See the provocative essay by Raymond J. Sontag, "The Origins of the Second World War," *Review of Politics,* 25, No. 4 (Oct. 1963), 497–508.

tion to a somewhat similar deluge of printed materials, the post-World War II generation of students is both blessed and cursed with the veritable Himalayas of paper left behind by National Socialist Germany as well as relatively full access to American archives. Furthermore, though too recently for full consideration in this work, the British Foreign Office records for the early and mid 1930s are now accessible. In the face of this plethora of riches, despair comes easily.

If the available material presents great difficulties by its sheer bulk, to say nothing of other problems, the question of organization is solved more readily. Whatever the conflicting ambitions, rivalries, and ideologies of the world's powers in the 1920s and 1930s, it is safe to assert that, with the solitary exception of Germany, no European nation considered another world war as a conceivable answer to whatever problems confronted it. Local wars and conflicts, specific aggressive moves or attempts at subversion, miscalculations leading to hostilities—all these were conceivable, and most of them occurred. But without German initiative another world-wide holocaust was inconceivable to contemporaries in all countries and is unimaginable retrospectively for the historian. Accordingly, the course of German foreign policy provides the obvious organizing principle for any account of the origins of World War II. This is not to assert that no other power or other factor bears any substantial share of the responsibility for the outbreak of that war or the developments leading up to it but rather to suggest that a complex question is perhaps best studied by examining its core.

Since Erich Kordt's preliminary survey in 1947[2] there has been no comprehensive attempt to examine the course and development of German foreign policy in the National Socialist era. There have been many monographs dealing with specific crises or issues, especially of the later 1930s, as well as episodes and figures in the history of other powers during those years, and such studies have been used where appropriate, but the author is not aware of any other over-all account. The able German scholar Hans-Adolf Jacobsen has worked at length on the internal structural development of the mechanisms for the control and implementation of foreign policy within National Socialist Germany;[3] we have discussed our respective endeavors to assure a minimum of overlapping.

In the course of preparing this study, it became evident that the path to war consisted of two rather different stages, stages which in the international sphere paralleled the internal development of Germany. The years from the beginning of 1933 to the end of 1936 saw a diplomatic revolution in Europe. From a barely accepted equal on the European stage, Germany became the dominant power on the Continent. With the remilitarization of the Rhineland, the stalemate in the Spanish civil war, the forming of the Axis, and the

2. Erich Kordt, *Wahn und Wirklichkeit, Die Aussenpolitik des Dritten Reiches* (Stuttgart: Union Deutsche Verlagsgesellschaft, 1947; 2d ed., 1948).

3. Hans-Adolf Jacobsen, *Nationalsozialistische Aussenpolitik, 1933–1938* (Frankfurt/M: Metzner, 1968).

signing of the Anti-Comintern Pact, this phase was completed. The diplomatic initiative in the world belonged to Germany and its partners. This volume attempts to show how and why this dramatic transformation of the world scene was accomplished—I say world scene because, perhaps for the last time, a purely European power initiated events that impinged dramatically on the whole globe. Once this phase had been completed, Germany's determination for war became the central issue in world diplomacy. The question now became, when, how, and under what circumstances did Hitler launch the first of his wars and what had been the course and effect of the attempts to keep him from doing so? That story will be the focus of another work.

In writing this book, I have become indebted to numerous individuals and institutions. Dr. Fritz T. Epstein read and commented on substantial portions of the manuscript; my colleagues Albert Feuerwerker, Sidney Fine, and Glen Waggoner also read chapters. Hans-Adolf Jacobsen not only discussed the relationship of our respective probes of National Socialist foreign policy but provided some useful documents. Joseph Anderle, George Kent, and Howard Smyth helped on special points.

The family of the late William E. Dodd permitted access to the Dodd papers; the papers of Jay Pierrepont Moffat are used and quoted with the permission of his widow, Mrs. Albert Lévitt. The Houghton Library of Harvard University allowed access to the William Phillips papers, and the University of Delaware Library permitted use of the George S. Messersmith papers. The Manuscript Division of the Library of Congress and the U. S. National Archives were both kind hosts during my lengthy stays. I am grateful for assistance from the Departmental Records Branch of the Adjutant General's Office—now the Modern Military Records Division of the National Archives—the Foreign Studies Branch of the Office of the Chief of Military History, the Historical Office of the Department of State, the Franklin D. Roosevelt Library at Hyde Park, the Wiener Library in London, the Public Record Office, the West German Federal Archives in Koblenz, and the Institute for Contemporary History in Munich. The reference librarians at the University of Michigan have been most patient and helpful.

My work has been greatly aided by grants from the Kentucky Research Foundation of the University of Kentucky, the International Relations Program of the Rockefeller Foundation, the Social Science Research Council, the American Council of Learned Societies, and the Horace R. Rackham School of Graduate Studies of the University of Michigan.

For over a decade my concern with this project has imposed itself on the patience of my wife Wilma.

Whatever I may owe to fellow scholars, all errors of fact and judgment are my responsibility.

Ann Arbor, Michigan
September 1969

1 The World through Hitler's Eyes

hen Adolf Hitler became chancellor of Germany at the age of forty-three in 1933, he had held no previous position of authority in government. He had neither read intensively nor traveled extensively. He knew no foreign language. Yet he had a clearly formulated set of ideas on major issues of foreign policy, and these ideas were intimately interwoven with his concepts of domestic affairs. It is essential for an understanding of world history since 1933 that these ideas be examined in some detail, for a great part of the impact of Hitler on Germany—and of Germany on the world—lies precisely in the fact that by exertion of his will and the response it elicited inside Germany, Hitler was to be able to impress his ideas on events rather than allow events and realities to reshape his ideas. It is true that the effort failed in the end. Realities that did not conform to Hitler's visions proved stronger even than his fanatic will and the mighty energies and resources the German people harnessed to it. But the great burst of activity in Germany in the 1930s that soon spilled over Europe and affected the whole globe was no random excitement, no accidental explosion.

There have been those who argue that Hitler was a pure opportunist, a manipulator of power, without guideposts. The shifts in the pattern of his alliances—now with the center of world communism, now with one of the sources of the so-called Yellow Peril—have suggested to some that plan, pattern, and ideological considerations of continuing influence must have been absent from the National Socialist scene. Recent efforts to rehabilitate Hitler's diplomatic reputation tend to be based on such a view. Alan J. P. Taylor has attempted to convert Hitler into an eighteenth-century diplomat, striving for revision of the most recent treaty in the same way Maria Theresa attempted to recover Silesia for Austria from the Prussia of Frederick the Great.[1] David Hoggan[2] and Philip Fabry[3] present Hitler in somewhat similar terms, only they show him victimized by unscrupulous opponents, Lord Halifax in one case, Josef Stalin in the other.

The available evidence, however, shows that Hitler had some very definite, fixed ideas on foreign policy before he came to power. This evidence comes primarily from his speeches and writings, a not unnatural source in the case of a man who devoted his full time to political agitation and who did not hesitate to include in his published views ideas he knew to be unpopular alongside others likely to elicit frenetic applause. The evidence also indicates that during the years from 1933 to 1939 Hitler kept these ideas very much in mind in the actual conduct of affairs, though he tended to reserve oral and written expression of them to the privacy of the conference room or the circle of his associates. The opportunism to which some have pointed as the essence of Hitler's policy was in fact an integral part of his long-term theory of political action, and many of the most extravagant and perplexing instances will be seen to fit most precisely into his general view.

The objection might be raised, of course, that those who see a plan in Hitler's steps will be tempted to read the evidence in a manner that supports their interpretation; but the unanswerable fact remains that new evidence, as it comes to light, not only fits into but in astonishing ways underlines the accuracy of that view. Thus the publication in 1961 of what can only be called an apologia for Field Marshal Keitel, who was executed at Nuremberg, includes an instance of a revelation of war plans by Hitler in a 1935 military gathering that moved the editor to comment on this new indication of Hitler's real policy at a time when peaceful liquidation of the Versailles Treaty was the officially proclaimed policy of the German government.[4] A number of other new examples of this kind will be cited in the course of the narrative, while the proponents of contrary interpretations have based them, not on the discovery of new evidence, but on attempts to explain away or disregard the obvious meaning of documents long known.[5]

In 1933 Hitler's ideology consisted primarily of two related systems of ideas, acquired and developed in chronological sequence. The doctrine of race took form first and is clearly delineated by 1923; the partly derivative

1. Alan J. P. Taylor, *The Origins of the Second World War* (London: Hamilton, 1961).

2. David L. Hoggan, *Der Erzwungene Krieg* (Tübingen: Verlag der Deutschen Hochschullehrerzeitung, 1961).

3. Philip W. Fabry, *Der Hitler-Stalin-Pakt, 1939–1941* (Darmstadt: Fundus, 1962).

4. Walter Görlitz (ed.), *Generalfeldmarschall Keitel, Verbrecher oder Offizier?* (Göttingen: Musterschmidt, 1961), p. 81, n. 89. The question posed in the title, "Criminal or Officer?" suggesting that Keitel could not have been both, indicates the general tenor of the book.

5. A particularly good demolition of such attempts may be found in Walter Hofer, *Die Entfesselung des Zweiten Weltkrieges, Eine Studie über die internationalen Beziehungen im Sommer 1939,* 3d ed. (Frankfurt/M.: S. Fischer, 1964), pp. 419–75, 503f.

doctrine of space came to be defined, in the formulation to which Hitler continued to adhere, in the immediately following years.

Hitler's conception of foreign policy in his first years of political activity, that is until November 1923, can be summarized as follows:[6] Germany was not defeated in World War I but stabbed in the back by Jews and those inspired by Jews. These same elements now controlled Germany internally and maintained themselves in part by their subservience to those foreign powers who had been made the victors by that stab in the back. A preliminary to any successful foreign policy therefore must be an internal change, in fact a revolution. A nationally conscious group must assume power, ruthlessly eradicate whatever steps toward democratic government had been taken inside Germany, and rearm to provide the tools for an aggressive foreign policy. Such a policy must be directed primarily against France, Germany's eternal enemy. This might mean an alignment with Italy since that power was also opposed to French hegemony in Europe. The inclusion of postwar Austria in a greater Germany was also required; and other territories, not very clearly defined, would be annexed. War was an unavoidable step on the road to national recovery, and would be victorious, as there would be no repetition of the home-front laxness responsible for Germany's recent defeat.

These views were based on Hitler's doctrine of race,[7] a vulgarized version of Social Darwinism that found increasing acceptance in Germany both in supposedly learned circles and, especially in the years between 1900 and 1914, among the masses.[8] According to this doctrine, the history of mankind can be understood in terms of racial analysis, that is, in terms of the supposed racial components of different societies. The rise or fall of civilizations is due to their success or failure in maintaining racial purity; the internal divisions of society are racially determined; and the cultural achievements of some are the result of their racial characteristics. The rise and fall of Rome can thus be understood as the products of the racial purity of early Roman and the racial mixture of later Roman society. The political division of France in the age of the French Revolution reflects the division between the Romanic, i.e., racially "Westic" lower classes, and the Nordic descend-

6. A fine survey of the subject is found in Günter Schubert, *Anfänge Nationalsozialistischer Aussenpolitik* (Cologne: Verlag Wissenschaft und Politik, 1963).

7. The most important sources for Hitler's views in this period may be found in Ernst Deuerlein (ed.), "Hitlers Eintritt in die Politik und die Reichswehr," *Vierteljahrshefte für Zeitgeschichte,* 7 (1959), 177–227; Reginald H. Phelps (ed.), "Hitler als Parteiredner im Jahre 1920," *Vierteljahrshefte für Zeitgeschichte,* 11 (1963), 274–330; Ernst Boepple (ed.), *Adolf Hitlers Reden* (Munich: Deutscher Volksverlag, 1934); Otto von Kursell (ed.), *Adolf Hitlers Reden* (Munich: Deutscher Volksverlag, 1925); Alexander Schilling, *Dr. Walter Riehl und die Geschichte des Nationalsozialismus* (Leipzig: Forum, 1933); and the *Völkischer Beobachter*. The major studies, in addition to Schubert, are Konrad Heiden, *Adolf Hitler* (Zurich: Europa, 1936); Franz Jetzinger, *Hitlers Jugend* (Vienna: Europa, 1956); Wilfried Daim, *Der Mann, der Hitler die Ideen gab* (Munich: Isar, 1958).

8. See Peter G. J. Pulzer, *The Rise of Political Anti-Semitism in Germany and Austria* (New York: Wiley, 1965).

ants of the Franks who had unified and organized the country. The cultural accomplishments of civilizations are the product of their racial composition —the great artists of Renaissance times were all Nordics whose works reflect their own appearance, while the monstrosities of modern art only mirror the appearance of their creators. Botticelli must have been as slim as his famous Venus, Rubens must have been as corpulent as the figures he painted, and Picasso presumably has three eyes.[9]

An especially significant facet of the racialist doctrine was its rejection of the biblical distinction between man and other creatures. With the most drastic implications—assuming that one was prepared to follow them to their logical conclusion—the new paganism argued that racial purity and selective breeding are the necessary instruments of progress in the human as in the animal world and insisted that social policy be oriented accordingly. The elimination of categories of people, like the elimination of categories of insects or plants, could be judged solely by standards of utility, not morality. It was within this framework that the allegedly alien racial stock represented by the Jews was particularly dangerous because of their wide distribution and imagined influence as well as the progress which their assimilation had made, especially in Germany.[10]

The racial element also provides a basis for Germany's hope. Its defeat in the war was due not to its inherent weakness; on the contrary, its ability to hold out for so long against a world of foes was in part a reflection of its inherent racial superiority. A full recognition of this superiority and the willingness to draw from it the necessary conclusions for domestic policy would combine to produce a different outcome next time. That this "next time" would come was beyond question. France was the great enemy. In Hitler's view, however, the enmity of Germany and France was based on more than the obvious reasons of recent war and contemporary (1920–23) French hegemony. There was a racial angle of special virulence that greatly affected Hitler's perception of France and his policies toward that country.

A key element in National Socialist hostility to France was the role of the latter as the European home of the concept of human equality, and especially the extension of *Égalité* to the Negro. Because racialism in Germany focused most directly on the Jews, it has generally been overlooked that the next great danger to European racial purity was supposed to be the Negro, introduced into Europe and sponsored by France. Unquestionably the experience of the world war had intensified, if it did not create, this

9. Anyone who considers this summary an unfair satire is urged to examine Paul Schultze-Naumburg's *Kunst und Rasse* (Munich: Lehmann, 1928, 2d ed. 1935), since the illustrations convey its message to anyone who does not read German.

10. It is true that in his speeches Hitler particularly emphasized the least assimilated Jews, i.e., those who had recently immigrated into Germany, as a sure way to stir up his audiences. But he also left no doubt that his attacks were directed against *all* the Jews, as when he explained to a cheering crowd on 6 April 1920 his determination "to pull up the evil by its roots and exterminate it completely" (das Übel an der Wurzel zu packen und mit Stumpf und Stiel auszurotten). Schubert, p. 16.

concern. The large-scale deployment on European battlefields of soldiers recruited in Africa had made a major impact on German thinking. Partly because so many Negroes had been included in the French army, and partly because of the presence of colored units among the French forces stationed in the Rhineland, this whole process came to be associated with France in German eyes. National Socialist publications of the 1920s were filled with attacks on the supposed negroidization of France, and Hitler found ways to connect this directly with the "Jewish menace."[11] Thus enmity for France was ordained by more than political or territorial factors.[12]

Hitler's views of other countries in these first years of his political activity were not yet as systematized as they were to become in the mid-1920s.[13] In his writings and speeches of these years his doctrine of space, built on that of race, was to provide a whole series of prescriptions for foreign policy in general and for policies toward certain countries in particular. This principle of space therefore requires scrutiny.[14]

Space, in Hitler's thinking, always referred to agriculturally usable land; the word is regularly employed in connection with the raising of food for the support of the population living on it. Hitler had no confidence in the

11. Hitler speech of 16 December 1921, *Völkischer Beobachter,* 21 December 1921; Schubert, p. 29; Adolf Hitler, *Mein Kampf* (Munich: Eher, 1933), 1:357 and 2:730. See the detailed exposition in Alfred Rosenberg, *Der Zukunftsweg einer deutschen Aussenpolitik* (Munich: Eher, 1927), pp. 36–39.

12. It will be seen how this racial factor led Hitler to a low estimate of French military power; and in a subsequent book on the war years the author will show how it reinforced Hitler's unwillingness to develop a policy of real cooperation with France after the armistice of June 1940. See also Eberhard Jäckel, *Frankreich in Hitlers Europa* (Stuttgart: Deutsche Verlags-Anstalt, 1966), pp. 13–24; Fritz T. Epstein, "National Socialism and French Colonialism," *Journal of Central European Affairs,* 3, No. 1 (April 1943), 52–64.

13. The contrast can be seen most clearly if Hitler's speeches in 1920–23 are compared with those after his release from jail. In the former, the focus is on the Treaty of Versailles, the Jews, the evils of the Weimar Republic, and the interrelation of these three topics. The speeches of the middle and late 1920s continue with these topics, but with constant emphasis on the problem of living space. This is most striking in Hitler's comments on Russia: his speech of 13 April 1923 explains that before 1914 there was no conflict of interest between Germany and Russia at all; the Jews urged each country to fight the other and then staged a revolution in each. Thus both are the innocent victims of an international conspiracy that created artificial differences between them and used each to help destroy the other (Boepple, pp. 43–50). The contrast is obvious between this and his later view, to be discussed in the text, that the Bolshevik Revolution was a stroke of good luck for Germany because it weakened the country that Germany had to fight for space.

14. The main sources for this period are *Mein Kampf;* the *Völkischer Beobachter;* Gerhard L. Weinberg (ed.), *Hitlers zweites Buch, Ein Dokument aus dem Jahr 1928* (Stuttgart: Deutsche Verlags-Anstalt, 1961); Norman H. Baynes (ed.), *The Speeches of Adolf Hitler, April 1922–August 1939,* 2 vols. (London: Oxford University Press, 1942); Heinz Preiss (ed.), *Adolf Hitler in Franken, Reden aus der Kampfzeit* (Nuremberg, 1939). Important studies are Alan Bullock, *Hitler, A Study in Tyranny* (London: Odhams Press, 1952, and later eds.); Hugh R. Trevor-Roper, "Hitlers Kriegsziele," *Vierteljahrshefte für Zeitgeschichte,* 8 (1960), 121–33. In a category by itself, because written years later, Hermann Rauschning, *The Voice of Destruction* (New York: Putnam, 1940).

possibility of increasing food production from available land. The struggle for existence in which the races of the world engaged, the basic element of life on earth, was fundamentally a struggle for space. In this struggle the stronger won, took the space, proliferated on that space, and then fought for additional space. Racial vitality and spatial expansion were directly related. A people always faced the question of bringing about a proper relationship between the space on which it lived and its population. In his view, a people could choose between adjusting the population to a given space or adjusting space to population. The adjustment of population to a fixed space meant emigration, birth control, abortion, and suicide—all leading to eventual racial decay as each occurred with higher frequency among the racially superior elements of the population. Furthermore, this course generally involved dependence on others, because of the need to import food, even for the population that had been intentionally held down. Only a weak people would choose this course, and they would become weaker in the process.

The desirable alternative course, which Hitler consistently advocated in *Mein Kampf* and his political speeches from 1925 on, was the adjustment of space to population by the conquest of additional land areas whose native population would be expelled or exterminated, not assimilated. The availability of such land areas would in turn encourage the good, healthy Nordic couples settled on them to raise large families that would both make up for the casualties incurred in the conquest of the territory and assure adequate military manpower for subsequent wars *they* would need to wage.

Two facets of this last point need emphasis. Wars cost casualties—Hitler knew this as well as his audiences—but this did not mean that wars should be avoided. They were the only way to gain the land required for racial survival, and therefore necessary. But they should be fought for an adequate purpose: an amount of land believed worth the casualties in a calculation that applied to the prospective German dead the same extreme instrumentalization Hitler applied to all.[15] In Hitler's calculation, the German borders of 1914 were not such an adequate purpose and were not worth the sacrifices their recovery would require. Until 1933, therefore, he never ceased to attack as a ridiculously inadequate objective the idea of trying to regain the borders of 1914. In his second book, Hitler mentioned 500,000 square kilometers of additional space in Europe as his first goal.[16] Since Germany's European territorial losses in the war had slightly exceeded 70,000 square kilometers, it is no wonder that he wrote in *Mein Kampf:* "The borders of the year 1914 mean absolutely nothing for the future of the German

15. For examples of this type of "casualty mathematics" before Hitler came to power see *Mein Kampf,* 2:738–40; and *Hitlers zweites Buch,* p. 48, where the editor has also noted an example from the World War II period.

16. *Hitlers zweites Buch,* p. 102.

nation."[17] The foreign policy Hitler advocated thus promised war for new land beyond Germany's prewar borders, and further specified that the land would be settled by German farmers.[18]

The second aspect of this expansionist program requiring attention is its potentially limitless character. The specific and immediate conclusions Hitler drew from his theories of race and space will be reviewed in detail, but first this inherent long-term trend toward world conquest must be noted. Clearly, if space is to be adjusted to an expanded population by conquest, and such conquest again enables the population to expand and facilitates further conquest, the only possible limitations are utter defeat on the one hand or total occupation of the globe on the other. A gifted German scholar, Günter Moltmann, has already called attention to the tendencies in this direction to be found in *Mein Kampf* and has suggested that the more explicit statements of 1932–34, attributed to Hitler by Hermann Rauschning, may be accepted as consistent with them.[19] Evidence that has come to light since Moltmann wrote shows that in the years between the periods reflected by *Mein Kampf* and by Rauschning's report Hitler himself recognized these implications. Rudolf Hess in 1927 informed Walter Hewel, who had been in Landsberg prison together with Hess and Hitler, that Hitler was of the opinion that world peace could come only "when one power, the racially best one, has attained complete and uncontested supremacy." It would then establish a world police and assure itself "the necessary living space. . . . The lower races will have to restrict themselves accordingly."[20] The process was described aptly by Hitler himself in 1928: "We consider our [anticipated] sacrifices, weigh the size of the possible success, and will go on the attack, regardless of whether it will come to a stop 10 or 1,000 kilometers beyond the present lines. For wherever our success may end, that will always be only the starting point of a new fight."[21]

The combined doctrines of race and space had significant implications for the day-to-day conduct of foreign affairs. Hitler was publicly explicit about these before 1933; their influence will be apparent in his record

17. *Mein Kampf,* 2:738.

18. On the attendant problems of resettlement commissions, expelling the local inhabitants and so forth, see *Mein Kampf,* 2:448–49; *Hitlers zweites Buch,* p. 81.

19. "Weltherrschaftsideen Hitlers," in *Europa und Übersee, Festschrift für Egmont Zechlin* (Hamburg: Hans Bredow-Institut, 1961), pp. 197–240.

20. Gerhard L. Weinberg (ed.), "National Socialist Organization and Foreign Policy Aims in 1927," *Journal of Modern History,* 36 (1964), 432. Hitler expressed similar world-wide ambitions to Otto Strasser in May 1930; see Strasser's brochure, *Ministersessel oder Revolution* (Berlin: Kampf-Verlag, 1930), reprinted in his *Aufbau des deutschen Sozialismus* (2d ed.; Prague: Heinrich Grunov, 1936), pp. 122–24, 132.

21. *Hitlers zweites Buch,* p. 77. Examples of references by Hitler to repeated wars leading to world-wide conquest from the period of World War II are quite numerous; many are listed by Moltmann. The point here has been to document the conscious recognition of the idea in the period before 1933.

after 1933, although he no longer discussed them quite so publicly. It has already been shown that war was to be a key instrument of policy; not the last resort, but in some instances the preferred approach. This role of war as a deliberate prior choice, not the *ultima ratio,* was to have a profound influence on German diplomacy. It meant, for example, that if you decided that your opponent must give in absolutely or you would go to war, the process of negotiations would be one in which your demands would be constantly raised as deadlock approached, not reduced as the parties move toward a compromise.

A second way in which the doctrines affected the handling of international relations was their import for treaties. If treaties are to serve the struggle for space, their primary objective would be either the immediate gain of space by the partitioning of third countries or the postponement of troubles considered dangerous at the moment until they could be faced with safety. In either case, treaties were temporary instruments to be broken as soon as they were no longer useful in the struggle for space. Hitler assumed that there could be no alliance except on the basis of such gains for both parties. Once the prospect of gain was gone, or even obstructed by the treaty, it had to be dropped.[22]

With this view of treaties in mind, one can readily understand National Socialist opposition to all multilateral treaty commitments. It is easier to make and break a treaty with one partner than to join and subsequently disengage oneself from a complicated multilateral structure. For this reason, as well as opposition to the doctrine of the equality of states, the National Socialists did not approve Germany's adherence to the Locarno Pact and the Kellogg Pact and were strongly opposed to Germany's entrance into the League of Nations. Hitler's repeated public denunciations of the League were paralleled by the frequent introduction of resolutions calling on Germany to leave Geneva by the National Socialist members of the Reichstag.[23] As will be seen, after 1933 Hitler not only took Germany out of the League and tore up the Locarno Pact at what seemed to him the earliest possible moments, but he was to avoid most carefully any new type of multilateral commitment.

Still another way in which the doctrines of race and space affected Hitler's view of international affairs was their relation to the traditional diplomatic service. Specific evidence of Hitler's attitude toward diplomats before 1933,

22. *Mein Kampf,* 1:154–55; *Hitlers zweites Buch,* pp. 94f. Hitler further assumed that every other country made its treaties on the same basis (*Hitlers zweites Buch,* p. 82).

23. As Hitler's views on war were publicly expressed, so the N.S.D.A.P.'s Reichstag opposition to the League and all measures for world peace was not concealed but made the proud subject of National Socialist propaganda. A compendium of the positions taken by the National Socialist delegation in the Reichstag was issued by its chairman, Wilhelm Frick, in 1928 as No. 4 in the *Nationalsozialistische Bibliothek* and reissued in up-to-date form as No. 37 in 1932 (*Die Nationalsozialisten im Reichstag,* Munich: Eher).

as contrasted with the subsequent period, is slight. His denunciations of the elements of German society who controlled the government in the prewar, wartime, and postwar periods, however, presumably included the diplomats. Certainly there was nothing to distinguish the German foreign service from what might be called the German establishment, and all efforts to change that service during the Weimar period were largely frustrated.[24] The prewar German policy of alliances which Hitler denounced was a product of their activities; they were implicated in the allegedly weak and defeatist wartime government; and they implemented, willingly or unwillingly, the foreign policy of Weimar Germany that Hitler considered treasonable in nature. Hitler's comments on Count Johann Heinrich Bernstorff, former German ambassador to the United States who in 1928 represented Germany in the disarmament negotiations, may serve as an indication of his assessment: "This man . . . was a typical representative of Germany's prewar foreign policy, just as he is a typical representative of the German foreign policy of the [Weimar] Republic. This character [*Subjekt*], who would have been hung by order of a state tribunal in every other country, is Germany's representative at the League of Nations in Geneva. These men bear the guilt and responsibility for the collapse of Germany."[25]

The diplomatic service Hitler inherited in 1933 consisted almost entirely of men whose background, education, and general orientation precluded full acceptance of Hitler's doctrines, although it will be seen that the vast majority were in agreement with the policies Hitler used to implement his own ideas in his first years in power. The long-term personnel problem this would present to the National Socialist regime will appear subsequently, but traces of it may be recognized when one considers the three men who in a way constituted the foreign service of the party before 1933: Alfred Rosenberg, Kurt Lüdecke, and Ernst (Putzi) Hanfstaengl.

Alfred Rosenberg was born in Riga, studied in Moscow, and had done some other traveling before settling in postwar Munich as a professional agitator for anti-Semitic causes. He became both one of the National Socialist party's leading theoreticians and the foreign policy expert of its Reichstag delegation. His interests in international affairs were concentrated on Eastern Europe and somewhat influenced Hitler's ideas; but his efforts to play a key role in foreign affairs after January 1933 were, generally, a failure. Rosenberg's unsuitability as a diplomat was at least partially apparent to Hitler before 1933. Rosenberg was simply a dedicated theoretician with no organizational talent. It was for precisely this reason that Hitler while in jail had placed him temporarily in charge of the party, certain that he could take over again once released from Landsberg. Even if Rosenberg could be given a diplomatic assignment for a short time, he was obviously

24. For a brief, reliable survey see Paul Seabury, *The Wilhelmstrasse* (Berkeley: University of California Press, 1954), chap. 1.

25. *Hitlers zweites Buch,* p. 215.

no man to recruit or organize a foreign service or any other sort of diplomatic apparatus, a judgment that his later efforts in this direction proved correct.[26]

Kurt Lüdecke was an international adventurer and gambler who joined Hitler in 1922. Anti-Semitism was a key element in his original adherence to national socialism, and he continued to preach the doctrines of racial purity between amorous adventures with women of rather varied origins of which he boasts in his memoirs.[27] Lüdecke's relevance to a study of Hitler's foreign policy lies in the fact that he was one of the very few early members of the party to have some experience of the world outside Germany and some knowledge of foreign languages.[28] He represented Hitler in his "diplomatic" contact with the Hungarian Gömbös[29] and with Mussolini,[30] and was delegated to raise funds for the party in the United States. Lüdecke represented precisely the type of ideologically oriented adventurer Hitler could employ for diplomatic missions that would serve the new Germany; and the men who played this role in the 1930s—Ribbentrop, Heye, Kleist, Veesenmayer, Bernhardt, to name a few—bear a startling resemblance to Lüdecke. But Lüdecke's ideology was too doctrinaire for Hitler, who was more willing to be opportunistic in his means; and Lüdecke was not only frustrated in his hopes for a great diplomatic career after assumption of power by the National Socialists but found himself arrested for his pains. Though even his memoirs, published in 1937 after his escape to the United States, reveal his continued faith in national socialism, and though he tried

26. The *Aussenpolitische Amt* of Rosenberg will be discussed in later chapters. For Rosenberg's pre-1933 role see Schubert, pp. 99–138. His subsequent administrative failure in the field of ideological training is carefully explained in a University of Michigan Ph.D. dissertation by Herbert Rothfeder, "Alfred Rosenberg's Office for the Ideological Training of the Nazi Party." His similar failure as minister for the occupied Eastern territories is ably recounted in Alexander Dallin, *German Rule in Russia, 1941–1945* (New York: St. Martin's Press, 1957).

27. Kurt G. W. Lüdecke, *I Knew Hitler* (New York: Scribner's, 1937). A careful assessment of Lüdecke may be found in Schubert, pp. 138–67. In addition to references to Lüdecke cited elsewhere in this book, information not used by Schubert may be found in two documents in the Centre de Documentation Juive Contemporaine in Paris under the file No. 129-a-120 (Joseph Billig, *Alfred Rosenberg dans l'action idéologique, politique et administrative du Reich hitlérien* [Paris: Centre, 1963], pp. 314f.); and in an excerpt from a report on National Socialist groups in the United States by Carl-Heinrich Nolle of the *Auslandsamt* of the *Stahlhelm* published in *Der deutsche Imperialismus und der zweite Weltkrieg* (Berlin: Rütten & Loening, 1961), 2:301. See also Jacobsen, p. 68, n. 3.

28. It is worth noting that years later Hitler remembered Lüdecke as a man who spoke French, English, Spanish, and Italian like a native and by implication as a man who could be depended on to seduce the right women. Hugh R. Trevor-Roper (ed.), *Hitler's Table Talk,* 30 October 1941 (London: Weidenfeld and Nicholson, 1953), p. 102.

29. Lüdecke, pp. 128, 261–66.

30. See also Alan Cassels, "Mussolini and German Nationalism, 1922–25," *Journal of Modern History,* 35 (1963), 137–57; Klaus-Peter Hoepke, *Die deutsche Rechte und der italienische Faschismus* (Düsseldorf: Droste, 1968), Part 5; Ernst Deuerlein (ed.), *Der Hitler-Putsch* (Stuttgart: Deutsche Verlags-Anstalt, 1962), pp. 543–47.

in 1939 to return to Hitler's fold,[31] the model National Socialist diplomat had to observe the Third Reich from the sidelines.

The same fate overtook Ernst Hanfstaengl, whose personal quarrels and rivalry with Lüdecke must not be allowed to obscure the similarity in their outlook, careers, and relation to Hitler. The Harvard graduate, and member of a respected Munich family, joined Hitler in 1922, to a large extent drawn by a common intensity of anti-Semitic feelings.[32] In addition to introducing Hitler to members of Munich society, Hanfstaengl entertained Hitler by his jokes and piano playing, serving as a kind of court jester. Hanfstaengl's travels abroad made him an expert on international affairs among the beerhall politicians, and Hitler used him in his dealings with foreign journalists.[33] Hanfstaengl became the foreign press chief of the party, and his activities in that capacity will be recorded. Like Lüdecke, however, he was an independent-minded adventurer; he was rather too intent on chasing skirts;[34] and his openly voiced criticisms of some of Hitler's associates and temporary departures from the true doctrine made it impossible for him to fit in. As Lüdecke had fled in 1934, so Hanfstaengl was to flee in 1937; and again like Lüdecke, he failed in his efforts to return to the Reich in 1939.[35]

Rosenberg, Lüdecke, and Hanfstaengl were all greatly concerned about getting the outside world to understand and appreciate Hitler's ideas. Rosenberg was prepared to accept whatever Hitler did and said; his experience was to prove that it would be impossible to arouse enthusiasm in the out-

31. On Lüdecke's efforts to rejoin the National Socialists in 1939 through Fritz Wiedemann, then German consul general in San Francisco, see the interrogation of Wiedemann of 10 November 1945 in the Nuremberg Trials Material, U. S. National Archives. On L.'s care in his speeches see the 2 May 1935 note by Leibbrandt of the APA, in EAP 250-d-18-05/5, T-81, Roll 11, Serial 32.

32. There is no study of Hanfstaengl's role in the history of national socialism, but see his memoirs, *Hitler, The Missing Years* (London: Eyre & Spottiswoode, 1957). As Lüdecke's anti-Semitism survived his escape to America, as can be seen in his memoirs, so Hanfstaengl's survived World War II, as may be seen in his memoirs (e.g. pp. 31f., 80f.).

33. Hitler's subsequent reference to this in his *Table Talk* of 6 July 1942 was related to his memory of Hanfstaengl's alleged avarice (Trevor-Roper edition, No. 252; Picker edition, No. 171; Ritter edition, No. 230).

34. See the memorandum on Hanfstaengl in the unpublished memoirs of George S. Messersmith (then U. S. consul general in Berlin) in the University of Delaware Library. For Hanfstaengl's assessment of Hitler, heavily stressing the sexual aspects, see, in addition to his memoirs, the long memorandum on Hitler of 3 December 1942 in the Franklin D. Roosevelt Library, Hyde Park, P.P.F. 5780 (the "Dr. Sedgwick" of this memorandum is Hanfstaengl).

35. The story as told by Hanfstaengl in his memoirs (p. 290) is contradicted by the contemporary record to be found in the memorandum of the British government accompanying a letter by Sir Ronald Campbell to John Franklin Carter of 23 June 1942 in the Henry Field papers, Franklin D. Roosevelt Library. I am indebted to Dr. Field for permission to use this document. See also the reference to a letter, Bormann to Hanfstaengl, 15 August 1939, in Joseph Wulf, *Literatur und Dichtung im Dritten Reich* (Rowohlt, 1966), p. 413.

side world; but since he never attempted to change anything, Hitler rewarded his loyalty by allowing him to continue in office. Lüdecke and Hanfstaengl, however, sought to have Hitler make minor modifications in his tactics in order to enhance his reputation abroad. For such men there was no room in Nationalist Socialist diplomacy, and soon they were succeeded by men who shared their interest in international intrigue and their lack of responsibility but were careful to keep to themselves their own opinions of tactical details.

One other National Socialist figure who dabbled in foreign affairs before 1933 was Hermann Göring. He, too, had some international adventure behind him, and he was already representing Hitler in some external negotiations, in Danzig for example.[36] He was to continue to play a role in the German-Danzig-Polish complex as well as some other aspects of foreign affairs after 1933; but his numerous offices in the Third Reich were to direct most of his extensive energies to domestic affairs.

Upon Hitler's accession to power there was no ready-made apparatus to replace the established diplomatic service as the chosen implement of new policies.[37] Hitler would have to utilize the old while experimenting with the new. The first was to prove much simpler and the second much more difficult than might have been anticipated.

The doctrines of race and space were not limited in their implications to general considerations of foreign policy aims and methods but had very specific import for the policies to be followed toward individual countries. The space Germany needed was to be found primarily in the East, in Russia. The major theme of the foreign policy sections of *Mein Kampf* and of most of Hitler's second book was this insistence on the conquest of territory toward the Urals. This theme, constantly reiterated in his speeches before 1933, was one in which Hitler's perception of Russia, primarily in terms of his doctrine of race, seemed to fit most precisely with the requirements of space policy. The land area the Germanic farmers would be settled on was inhabited by Slavs, an inherently inferior group. They were incapable of organizing a state or developing a culture. The only state organization ever successfully imposed on these inferior people had been established and maintained by individuals of Germanic racial stock whose russification had been no more real in the racial sense than the supposed germanization of Poles and Czechs had made real Germans of these groups. This stratum of good racial stock, however, had been weakened even in prewar Russia by political attacks from the developing Slavic bourgeoisie with its Pan-Slavic and anti-German ideology. The world war had drastically depleted the Germanic group: war always bears most heavily on the racially best elements who serve at the front while the racially inferior attempt to escape service.

36. See Ernst Ziehm, *Aus meiner politischen Arbeit in Danzig, 1914–1939* (Marburg: Herder-Institut, 1960), pp. 143–45. See also Hoepke, pp. 310–13.
37. Jacobsen, pp. 13–15.

The enormous casualties Russia had suffered thus decimated the Germanic stock, especially in the officer corps in which they were heavily represented. The final blow came during the Bolshevik Revolution in which the last remnants were exterminated.

This process of elimination of the Germanic element in Russia had left behind an amorphous block of Slavs, ruled and exploited for the benefit of world capitalism by the Jews. Inherently, the Jews were even less capable of organizing and maintaining a state than the Slavs, and would in any case be destroyed on the triumph of Pan-Slavism among the Russian people. The remaining Slavic population, however, would constitute a permanently feeble and unstable society. The "Slavs have no organizational ability whatever," and a purely Slavic Russia would have no power; in fact, it would fall into dissolution. That recent events—World War I and the Bolshevik Revolution—had so weakened Russia, therefore, constituted a piece of "good luck" for the future of a Germany that would know how to profit from it.[38] The vast number of Russians presented no problem in itself: Germany had defeated the great Russian armies in the war,[39] and space and numbers alone were not important. Nobody, Hitler maintained, would ever arrive at the idea that there was any danger of Russian hegemony in the world, because there was no inner value—meaning no racial value—in the Russian population, however numerous.[40] Since the reduction of the Russian population by slaughter and expulsion was implicit in his policies, it is not surprising that Hitler referred to the rural areas of Eastern Europe, notoriously suffering from overpopulation, as being thinly settled.[41] Territorial conquest eastward was thus both necessary and simple, and the major areas to be conquered lay in Russia.

If Germany were to conquer Russian territory, it had to concern itself with the tier of new states that had gained their independence after the first world war because all the great powers of Eastern Europe had been defeated in that conflict. Poland was the largest of these states. It should be noted that Hitler did not pay nearly as much attention to Poland as many of his German contemporaries. To them, regardless of political orientation, Poland was an abomination, temporary but most irritating.[42] The Poles were, in German eyes, an Eastern European species of cockroach; their state was generally referred to as a *Saisonstaat*—a country just for a season;

38. The clearest presentation of Hitler's views, summarized above, from which the quotations are taken, is in *Hitlers zweites Buch,* pp. 155–59.

39. See Hitler's comments in *Mein Kampf,* 1:215.

40. *Hitlers zweites Buch*, p. 128. This would not, of course, preclude the convenient use of the Russian or Bolshevik menace as a tool, first of domestic and later of foreign propaganda, by the National Socialists. Hitler explained to his associates that this was a device for the consumption of others; his own policy was based on the gross underestimation of Russian power described in the text.

41. *Hitlers zweites Buch*, p. 102.

42. See Christian Höltzle, *Die Weimarer Republik und das Ostlocarno-Problem, 1919–1934* (Würzburg: Holzner, 1955).

and the expression *polnische Wirtschaft*—Polish economy—was a phrase commonly applied to any hopeless mess. The general orientation of German foreign policy with its goal of a return to the borders of 1914, at least in the East, hoped for a new partition of Poland, probably in cooperation with the Soviet Union. There is no evidence to suggest that anyone who occupied a leading position in Weimar Germany recognized that the existence of a strong and independent Poland might have great advantages for Germany. Until the Germans had broken what were commonly known as the "chains of Versailles," they did not notice that the same chains had bound Soviet Russia. Official German policy called for permanent hostility to Poland, manifested in a trade war as well as constant friction over questions of minorities and revisionist propaganda.[43]

In the Weimar period, German policy toward Russia was influenced to a great extent by the priority of revisionist hopes against Poland; in Hitler's view, policy toward Poland was incidental and subordinated to his aim of territorial aggrandizement at the expense of the Soviet Union. This certainly did not make him any friendlier toward the Poles than his predecessors, but he did not share their fixed objectives because he thought them inadequate. His desire for enormous territory rather than border revision automatically diminished the long-term importance of Poland and freed from rigid preconceptions Hitler's short-term tactics toward that country.[44] He assumed Polish hostility toward Germany, understood Poland's close ties with France, and was aware of the possibility of a Polish preventive war against Germany; but in the conduct of relations with Poland, Hitler could proceed pragmatically, subordinating everything to the tactical requirements of other policies.

If the doctrine of space led Hitler to seek territorial expansion eastward, the presumptive increase in strength that would accrue to Germany from such expansion added yet another reason to the many existing ones making for enmity between Germany and France. Surely France would do anything to prevent such an enormous increase in German might. On this assumption, it seemed safer to defeat France first, that is, before moving East, so that Germany would not have a dangerous enemy at its back while engaged in the great enterprise. The first great war Germany would fight, therefore, would be against France; the second would be against Russia. In fact, Hitler now asserted that in the long run the first war would prove useless unless it paved the way for the second.[45]

As the concept of space reinforced enmity for France, so it accentuated a hitherto only slightly apparent difference in Hitler's attitude toward Eng-

43. See the important dissertation of Gaines Post, Jr., "German Foreign Policy and Military Planning, The Polish Question, 1924–1929" (Stanford, 1969).

44. The same interpretation, with slight differences in emphasis, may be found in Martin Broszat, *Nationalsozialistische Polenpolitik, 1939–1945* (Stuttgart: Deutsche Verlags-Anstalt, 1961), pp. 9–11.

45. *Mein Kampf*, 2:741.

land. Until about 1923, England was regularly included with France among Germany's present and future enemies, but with greater emphasis on the enmity of France.[46] Perhaps British opposition to the French occupation of the Ruhr stimulated a more fundamental differentiation between the two powers.[47] England now appears in Hitler's view of the world in a separate category. His new attitude toward Great Britain was a mixture of admiration and hate, never entirely untangled. He thought he recognized in the British upper classes the product of a process of selective breeding not entirely unlike what he hoped to accomplish in Germany. Similarly, he often referred to the ability of a small number of Englishmen to control the Indian subcontinent as a model for his own vast schemes of conquered areas and subdued peoples.[48] On the other hand, Jews were allowed to play a part in British society, Britain had a democratic form of government, and the people of England were oriented more toward trade and industry than toward agriculture. The Jews were imagined to have all sorts of great influence; by definition democracy destroyed responsibility and leadership in a society; and trade and industry were not only not as healthy occupations as agriculture but had a debilitating effect on the social structure. Nevertheless, the hegemony of France, apparently created by the Paris peace settlement, would strengthen France in world competition for trade and empire and was thus against the interests of Great Britain.[49] Opposition to the strongest power on the continent in defense of the European balance would logically place England alongside Germany in its conflict with France—even if that conflict eventually produced a Germany so strong that England would again turn against Germany,[50] at a time when, presumably, it would be too late.

In Hitler's eyes, the only thing required to persuade England of the wisdom of an alliance with Germany would be the abandonment of Germany's world trade and naval ambitions. These had threatened England before the war, and he believed them responsible for British entrance into an alliance with her former enemies France and Russia against Germany. The new eastward-directed space policy that Hitler projected for Germany would entail finding food for Germany's people by competition for land in Europe instead of competition for trade in the world and would thus remove any basis for hostility between Germany and England. Furthermore, if France was one

46. See the source collections of Deuerlein, Phelps, and Boepple which concentrate on this period, and A. V. N. van Woerden, "Hitler Faces England: Theories, Images and Policies," *Acta Historiae Neerlandica,* 3 (1968), 145–46.

47. Schubert, pp. 74–75.

48. It never occurred to Hitler that the small number of Englishmen in India might be related in any way to their success; had the British attempted the sort of large-scale settlement accompanied by the equally large slaughter of the indigenous population Hitler projected for his own empire, India would not have been nearly as quiet as Hitler, already somewhat erroneously, imagined it to be.

49. *Mein Kampf,* 1:699; *Hitlers zweites Buch,* p. 173.

50. *Hitlers zweites Buch,* pp. 167, 174.

great danger to England, Russia with its expansionist possibilities in the oil-rich Near East and toward India was a second danger, while the rising trade empire of the United States was a third.[51] With no cause for enmity with Germany, therefore, and with a shared hostility to France and Russia, there was no reason why England should not become an ally of Germany, at least temporarily. As has been mentioned, there are explicit hints in Hitler's second book that such an alliance might subsequently give way to renewed enmity, but that was a distant future in which Germany would have acquired the territory needed to take care of itself.

The new emphasis on *Lebensraum* strengthened the apparent wisdom of a German alliance with Italy. Hitler had favored such an alliance on purely pragmatic grounds: Italy's ambitions in the Mediterranean clashed with those of France, and this common hostility to France could furnish the basis for joint action.[52] Hitler's plans for expansion eastward would upset France but not Italy. The divergent expansions of Italy and Germany constituted a potential tie between them; they would not bring the two powers in conflict with each other, but both could be achieved only over the opposition of France. The alliance between Germany and Italy that appeared to be the logical deduction from this set of facts was confronted by a negative factor in the form of a potential division between the two powers and a positive factor in the form of a potential additional tie. The potential tie was the ideological affinity of Italian fascism and national socialism; the potentially divisive factor was the question of South Tirol.

Hitler was an early and continuing admirer of Mussolini and his program. The fascist seizure of power in Italy seemed to him a harbinger of his own success. The attacks upon the Fascist leader by the liberal newspapers in Germany and elsewhere confirmed Hitler's assessment of their spiritual kinship. Personal admiration for Mussolini played an undoubted part in this, and the curious type of friendship Hitler developed for his distant hero was to outlast shocks that would have sundered most personal relationships. In the period before 1933 the actual dictator of Italy and the prospective dictator of Germany dealt with each other by unofficial emissaries; Lüdecke performing this role for Hitler, while Major Giuseppe Renzetti acted in a similar capacity for Mussolini. Lüdecke merely made a few brief trips to Rome, but Renzetti as president of the Italian Chamber of Commerce in Berlin and later as Italian consul general provided a means of regular contact. While it is known from Lüdecke's memoirs that he made his first trip to Italy for Hitler in 1922, Renzetti first appears in the documents in 1931, referred to in a letter to Rosenberg as "our friend."[53] The earliest available

51. Ibid., pp. 172–74.

52. Walter Werner Pese, "Hitler und Italien, 1920–1926," *Vierteljahrshefte für Zeitgeschichte,* 3 (1955), 113–26, has shown that Hitler favored common action with Italy before Mussolini's march on Rome.

53. Arno Schickedanz to Rosenberg, 13 January 1931, Nuremberg document 1146–PS (U. S. National Archives). Referring to a recent statement by Mussolini about Göring, Schickedanz wrote: "The Duce surely received this understanding through our friend Renzetti."

reports prepared by Renzetti for Il Duce are those of 15 October and 20 November 1931.[54] The latter records that Renzetti brought Hitler some political advice from Mussolini and reports on Hitler's great desire to make a trip to Rome to see the Italian leader. At that time, as during all of 1932, the ardent hopes of Hitler for a meeting with Mussolini came to naught,[55] but the contact remained and would provide a continuing means of direct communication outside regular diplomatic channels even after Hitler came to power.[56]

The very first contact between the two leaders in 1922 was used by Mussolini to bring home to Hitler the danger to German-Italian relations in the question of South Tirol. The German agitation for revision of the peace treaties constantly called attention to those people of German background who had been transferred from Austria to Italy by the Treaty of St. Germain and were being subjected to a process of italianization.[57] In the 1920s, the German minority in South Tirol was probably the one most subject to repression of their original nationality and thus a plausible object for attention by those German parties that claimed a monopoly in national patriotism. Italian insistence on the maintenance of the existing border on the Brenner made revision here incompatible with German-Italian friendship, and Hitler promptly decided that the question of South Tirol must be sacrificed to the vastly greater interest in a German-Italian alliance.[58] Although this was a most unpopular stand in Germany, where in any case public opinion was very anti-Italian because of Italy's alleged unfaithfulness to its alliance with the Central Powers, Hitler publicly defended a renunciation of South Tirol. The relevant portion of the second volume of *Mein Kampf* was published as a separate brochure in 1926, and the impetus for Hitler to prepare (though never to publish) a second book in the summer of 1928 was closely related to the problem that the unpopularity of his position on this issue created for him in German domestic politics.

The National Socialists constantly tried to deprecate the importance

54. Renzetti to Mussolini, 15 October and 20 November 1931, National Archives Microcopy T–586, container 491, frames 050253–56. On R.'s career in Germany see Hoepke, pp. 248, n. 20, 258, 307–8. For Mussolini's use of R. to contact liberals and socialists see Eugen Schiffer, *Ein Leben für den Liberalismus* (Berlin: Herbig, 1951), p. 227.

55. See Renzetti's reports to Mussolini of 12 January, 9 June, and 30 June 1932, T–586, container 491, frames 050259–265; Hoepke, pp. 316–17.

56. Some known examples of such contacts will be referred to subsequently. The published Italian diplomatic documents indicate that this channel remained in use for many years and was not unknown to the Italian diplomatic service. Attolico to Ciano, 14 June 1939, *I Documenti diplomatici Italiani*, 8th series, Vol. 12, No. 231; 2 September 1939, ibid., Vol. 13, No. 607. See also Winfried Schmitz-Esser, "Hitler-Mussolini: Das Südtiroler Abkommen von 1939," *Aussenpolitik*, 13, No. 6 (June 1962), p. 327.

57. The discussion of South Tirol here, except where otherwise noted, is based on the author's introduction to *Hitlers zweites Buch*, pp. 21–25, 34f., and Conrad F. Latour, *Südtirol und die Achse Berlin-Rom, 1938–1945* (Stuttgart: Deutsche Verlags-Anstalt, 1962).

58. The chronology of this reversal is carefully traced in Schubert, pp. 76–81. See also *I Documenti diplomatici Italiani*, 7th series, Vol. 1, No. 131.

of the South Tirol issue and to point to the agitation over it in Germany and Austria as simply a convenient pretext for Jews, Marxists, Freemasons, and others to attack Mussolini. Within the party, Hitler defended his position on South Tirol as essential for Germany if it were to regain its position of power and influence, a position it could secure only by alliance with Italy and England.[59] To Mussolini, Hitler reaffirmed his renunciation through Ettore Tolomei, the leading proponent of the policy of italianization of South Tirol.[60] Of course, this should not be taken to mean that other circumstances might not lead to other perspectives. Hitler would refrain from a ruthless drive for colonies and world trade as a tactical sacrifice to secure the assistance of England, but that would not keep him from grandiose colonial plans when England failed to fulfil his expectations. He would ignore the South Tirol question as a tactical sacrifice to the needed alliance with Italy, but that would not prevent him from seizing that area, plus other large portions of northern Italy, once Italy had left the Axis. In few other areas is the relationship between Hitler's long-term aims and short-term opportunism more clearly revealed.

There was still one other potential source of difficulty between Germany and Italy, and on it Hitler was not prepared to make concessions so readily —the annexation of Austria.[61] Hitler always argued that Austria and Germany should be joined in one country and never ceased to make this opinion public. The very fact that tactical considerations led him to renounce claims to South Tirol probably made him all the more obdurate in regard to the *Anschluss.* It is clear from his writings—and later acts—that this desire was not due to any great love for the land of his birth. Rather, it was the desire to expand the racial base of the forthcoming German empire. He hoped that his renunciation of South Tirol would ease Italy's objections to the *Anschluss,* and that the time would come when Italy would see no more reason to oppose a union of Austria with an anti-French Germany.[62] Subsequent developments unveiled by events quite early in the years of his rule were to prove this a miscalculation, but the policy which produced that abrupt confrontation of his illusions with the real world around him can be understood only if the illusions and their place in his thinking are kept in mind.

If Austria was to be swallowed up completely, Hungary was another

59. See the report on a conference in the National Socialist party headquarters in Munich on 31 March 1932, quoted in *Der deutsche Imperialismus und der zweite Weltkrieg,* 2:478. See also Hoepke, pp. 165ff.

60. The draft of Tolomei's report to Mussolini of 30 September 1928 on his meeting with Hitler on 14 August 1928 has been published in Karl Heinz Ritschel, *Diplomatie um Südtirol, Politische Hintergründe eines europäischen Versagens* (Stuttgart: Seewald, 1966), pp. 133–37. (Hoepke is mistaken in setting the date as mid-August 1929 [p. 165].) It should be noted that the Hitler-Tolomei meeting took place a few weeks after Hitler wrote his second book.

61. The questions of South Tirol and the *Anschluss* were closely related. Italy had little to fear as long as the agitation emanated from a small and weak Austria. If Austria ever joined Germany, Italy would face a neighbor both large and strong.

62. *Hitlers zweites Buch,* pp. 208f. To Tolomei, Hitler described the *Anschluss* as certain but in the distant future (Ritschel, p. 137).

potential ally, even if not a very important one.[63] A revisionist power opposed to Yugoslavia, which was backed by France and in turn opposed by Italy, Hungary might be fitted into the German alliance system.[64] The National Socialists and other extremist groups in Bavaria had been in contact with similarly oriented elements in Hungary in the years before 1923, and there had been talks about simultaneous revolutions in both locations in November of that year.[65] Lüdecke had been in Hungary as Hitler's emissary, and a similar role had been played by another international adventurer, Max Erwin von Scheubner-Richter, whose career was ended by death in the putsch of 9 November 1923.[66] It was to Scheubner-Richter as their intermediary of a decade before that the leader of the Hungarian rightists, Julius Gömbös, referred when, having become prime minister of Hungary, he sent greetings immediately after Hitler became chancellor of Germany.[67]

Another Central European country that figured in Hitler's perceptions and plans was Czechoslovakia.[68] His analysis of prewar Austria dealt very extensively with the growing power of the Czechs in both Bohemia and Vienna itself, his attacks on the Habsburg dynasty were phrased to a great extent in terms of their failure to combat this trend, and his praise of the Pan-German movement was based heavily on the anti-Czech element in Georg von Schönerer's program.[69] In Hitler's eyes, the nationality problem in Bohemia

63. It is striking how few references there are to Hungary and to the Magyars in Hitler's various written and oral comments, especially on the Habsburg empire. The converse is his emphasis, in a very negative way, on the Czechs. Perhaps this reflects the narrow nationalistic concerns of his Vienna days where Czechs were numerous and Magyars more distant.

64. *Hitlers zweites Buch*, p. 217. Hungary is here grouped with Spain, another country which had scarcely attracted Hitler's attention.

65. These relations are reviewed in Schubert, pp. 168–80. See also the letter of Ludendorff to Horthy in Miklós Szinai and László Szücs (eds.), "Horthy's Secret Correspondence with Hitler," *New Hungarian Quarterly*, 4, No. 11 (1963), 176f.; Hans Bleyer, "Die ungarländische Deutschtumsfrage im Spiegel der diplomatischen Gespräche zwischen Budapest und Berlin," in *Gedenkschrift für Harold Steinacker* (Munich: Oldenbourg, 1966), pp. 303–05.

66. There is no reference to Scheubner-Richter's Hungarian contacts in the adulatory biography by Paul Leverkuehn, *Posten auf ewiger Wache* (Essen: Essener Verlagsanstalt, 1938), pp. 191–94. This book does provide considerable information on this shadowy figure, however, including his connection with White Russian émigrés and his trip to Wrangel's army in the Crimea. The assertion that Scheubner-Richter was a Russian agent in World War I has never been substantiated and is most unlikely. On his role in the early NSDAP see Walter Laqueur, *Russia and Germany, A Century of Conflict* (London: Weidenfeld and Nicolson, 1965), pp. 58–68.

67. The instructions of Gömbös to Kálman de Kánya, then Hungarian minister to Germany, of 1 February 1933 are quoted in Elek Karsai (ed.), "The Meeting of Gömbös and Hitler in 1933," *New Hungarian Quarterly*, 3, No. 5 (1962), 172. The message as delivered to Hitler on 7 February 1933 is in *Documents on German Foreign Policy, 1918–1945*, Series C, Vol. 1, No. 15.

68. On this subject see the author's paper, "Czechoslovakia and Germany, 1933–1945," in Miloslav Rechcigl, Jr. (ed.), *Czechoslovakia Past and Present*, 1 (The Hague: Mouton, 1969), pp. 760–69.

69. On the key role that the nationality conflict with the Czechs played in the origins of national socialism see Andrew G. Whiteside, *Austrian National Socialism before 1918* (The Hague: Nijhoff, 1962).

was the presence of Czechs in an area he believed appropriate solely for German settlement.[70] He assumed that the Czech state would be hostile to Germany, and he kept in contact with sympathetically inclined elements among the German population of Czechoslovakia.[71] When the time came, they were to be the tool of far-reaching schemes.

Yugoslavia appeared in Hitler's mental world primarily in two ways. First, he thought of Yugoslavia as an enemy of Italy and friend of France and thus as a possible partner of France in a war against Mussolini's Italy; and second, as the country of the Serbs who had followed their national interest realistically and persistently by working for the destruction of Austria-Hungary. It should be noted that in Hitler's assessment of people in terms of their racial awareness and value, this point constituted something of a plus mark for the Serbs. Hitler was, of course, aware of the struggle over the border between Austria and Yugoslavia in Carinthia, but there is nothing on his part to suggest any special interest in that issue. Other European countries appear to have played little part in Hitler's thinking before 1933; what references to them can be found will be mentioned in the context of their later relations with Germany.

Outside the European continent and its colonial extensions, the major areas of importance for German foreign policy were the Far East and the United States. Hitler's vision was primarily continental, and he paid very little attention to either area, a habit that was to continue until 1945. He was not especially interested in the Far East, a fact that was to be reflected in a more than usual confusion in German policies toward that area after 1933. Three facets of Hitler's perspective on Far Eastern affairs deserve mention. In the first place, there can be no question that he shared in some way the aversion to the people of Eastern Asia expressed in references to the Yellow Peril, widespread in those early years of the twentieth century when so many of Hitler's ideas were formed.[72] His own racist orientation, of course, served only to intensify this attitude. Second, Hitler did not share the sinophilism current in the Germany of his day as a counterweight to the "Yellow Peril" fears. In the third place, he had somewhat kindlier feelings toward Japan.[73] Though of "racially uncreative stock," the Japanese were at any rate very clever; and their aggressive moves in the Far East, which

70. *Hitlers zweites Buch*, pp. 78f.; Rauschning, *Voice of Destruction*, pp. 37–38.

71. In view of the post–1933 contacts between Sudeten German National Socialists and the German government, in which the latter helped finance the former, it is ironic to see the signatures of two Sudeten German members of the Czech parliament, Rudolf Jung and Hans Knirsch, on the letter authorizing Kurt Lüdecke to collect money for the *Nationalsozialistische Partei Grossdeutschlands* in the United States after Hitler's arrest in 1923. Lüdecke, photograph facing p. 191.

72. See Heinz Gollwitzer, *Die Gelbe Gefahr, Geschichte eines Schlagwortes* (Göttingen: Vandenhoeck & Ruprecht, 1962).

73. Ernst L. Presseisen, *Germany and Japan, A Study in Totalitarian Diplomacy, 1933–1941* (The Hague: Nijhoff, 1958), pp. 2–5; Theo Sommer, *Deutschland und Japan zwischen den Mächten, 1935–1940* (Tübingen: Mohr, 1962), pp. 8f.

brought down upon them the attacks of the liberal press, were to their merit in Hitler's eyes.[74]

The United States originally drew very little attention from Hitler.[75] In his political speeches and writings Hitler echoed the denunciations of the United States in general and President Wilson in particular that were then current in Germany. He was sure that Jewish influence had been responsible for America's entrance into the war, but his references to the United States were few indeed. His interest was aroused, however, by American immigration legislation and by the very considerable importation of American automobiles into Germany. This latter fact drew Hitler's attention to the advantages of a large domestic living space, and thus market, for industrial as well as agricultural purposes. This evidence of American strength was related, in Hitler's eyes, to American immigration legislation. These laws seemed to Hitler, not without reason, to be basically racist in orientation. They reinforced a tendency he believed inherent in the process of migration from Europe to America: the best and most enterprising members of each community, i.e., the Nordics, emigrated to America. The United States was, therefore, not the melting pot of the American imagination but the great meeting place of the Nordics who maintained their racial purity by strict immigration laws. This gathering of the finest Nordic racial stock from each European country explained why the Americans had made such good use of their living space. With a racial headstart over the others—especially the European countries drained of their best blood by the same process that had made America strong—and with a vast area on which to proliferate, the American people were exceedingly dangerous and a real threat to German predominance in the world. Only a Eurasian empire under German domination could hope to cope with this menace successfully. A third big war was added to the original two; after the wars against France and Russia would come the war against the United States. One of the major tasks of the National Socialists would be the preparation of Germany for this conflict.

This assessment of the United States was to give way in the early 1930s to a far different one.[76] Under the impact of the world depression and its effect on the United States—an effect Hitler thought permanent—Hitler concluded that the United States was really a very weak country. Turning again to a racial explanation, he came to believe that America was a racial mixture after all, a mixture that included Negroes and Jews. Such a mongrel society, in which "the scum naturally floated to the top," could not construct

74. Hitler's speech of 23 May 1928, *Völkischer Beobachter*, 25 May 1928; cf. *Hitlers zweites Buch*, p. 25.

75. The following is summarized from the author's article, "Hitler's Image of the United States," *American Historical Review*, 69 (1964), 1006–11. In addition to the evidence cited there see Hitler's speech of 4 August 1929 in Preiss (ed.), *Adolf Hitler in Franken*, p. 114.

76. Weinberg, "Hitler's Image of the United States," pp. 1010–13.

a sound economy, create an indigenous culture, or establish a successful political system. America was a weak country whose hope for strength had been destroyed in the past by the victory of the wrong side in the Civil War and whose hope for the future, if there were any, lay with the German-Americans. In any case, the United States could not interfere with Hitler's plans which, in confidential discussions, were now said to include Mexico and much of Latin America. Thus Hitler was to go forward in the 1930s, unconcerned about the United States and generally uninterested in it. The basic hostility remained, but concern about America's racial strength had vanished.

It should be noted that, with insignificant exceptions, the general nature of Hitler's views as summarized in the preceding pages was readily recognizable before his assumption of power.[77] In fact, the rise of the National Socialist party was financed to a considerable extent by the thousands and thousands of Germans who paid admission to public meetings at which Hitler publicly proclaimed his belief in these ideas and policies. He tried to leave his audiences in no doubt about his meaning; on the contrary, he repeated the same ideas and even phrases over and over again. He assured them that, if granted power, he would ruthlessly and brutally establish a dictatorship in Germany, build up Germany's military might after its republican institutions and ideas had been swept away, and then proceed to lead his country as its absolute dictator in a series of wars. In promising a ruthless dictatorship, he did not hesitate to say explicitly that it would be like that of Italy and of Soviet Russia.[78] In promising war, he was always personal and specific: "I believe that I have enough energy to lead our people whither it must shed its blood [*zum blutigen Einsatz*], not for an adjustment of its boundaries, but to save it into the most distant future by securing so much land and space that the future receives back many times the blood shed," Hitler said on 23 May 1928.[79]

Why did millions of Germans respond so enthusiastically to these appeals? Certainly the terrible cost of the war had left many Germans disillusioned with war and fearful of its repetition. But it should be noted that the disillusionment in Germany was not quite like that in Western countries. There were books expressing such sentiments as characterized Erich Maria Remarque's *All Quiet on the Western Front* in other countries than Germany, but one would find it exceedingly difficult to match outside Germany the literature glorifying war that was typified by the works of Ernst Jünger and

77. The author has been careful to avoid using evidence from a later period. It is true that practically none of Hitler's opinions on the subjects discussed here ever changed, but reliance on material of the pre-1933 period minimizes the danger of later events or documents influencing the interpretation.

78. An example of 28 February 1926 in Werner Jochmann (ed.), *Im Kampf um die Macht, Hitlers Rede vor dem Hamburger Nationalklub von 1919* (Frankfurt/M: Europäische Verlagsanstalt, 1960), p. 103.

79. *Völkischer Beobachter*, 25 May 1928.

was applied to the postwar period by the members of the Free Corps.[80]

More important, perhaps, than this survival of militaristic attitudes was the psychological disorganization produced by defeat. Unaware of the real situation, the German people had seen their hopes tumble from the vision of victory to the reality of collapse in a few months of 1918. After the glory of a powerful state, after the immense sacrifices of war, their world had crashed down around them. In the preceding decades, while the peoples of England and France were painfully learning to govern themselves, the German people had been trained to think that this was neither possible nor desirable for them. In the chaos and despair of a defeated country, it was easier for many to mock the brave few who tried hard to reconstruct a self-respecting society than to take a hand in the difficult task of rebuilding. It was simpler to put one's faith in one man who would take care of everything than to assume a share of the responsibility for the agonizing choices to be made in daily political life. Those who agreed that one man was to lead and decide while they would obey and follow could not thereby escape the responsibility for his decisions; they simply accepted that responsibility in advance.[81]

A further factor of great significance was the widespread acceptance of racial ideology among the people of Germany. Whether or not willing to agree to all its horrible implications, vast numbers were prepared to accept its premises.[82] It is significant that in a country where academic persons were high in prestige, the pseudoscience of racism had made very rapid inroads in the academic community. Furthermore, it is clear from all accounts of National Socialist gatherings that anti-Semitism was the most popular part of Hitler's appeal to his audiences. If so many followed, it was in part that they were enthusiastic about the direction he wanted to take.

Certainly one should not overlook the belief of many that the National Socialists did not necessarily mean precisely what they said; that Hitler's more extreme ideas should not be taken seriously; that, once in power, the

80. For illuminating samples and comments see Robert G. L. Waite, *Vanguard of Nazism, The Free Corps Movement in Postwar Germany, 1918–1923* (Cambridge, Mass.: Harvard University Press, 1952). Note Waite's defense of his extensive quotations: "Had I relied on paraphrase, it seems probable that I would not have been believed" (p. ix).

81. An instructive illustration of this may be found in Dietrich Orlov's University of Michigan Ph.D. dissertation on the Southeast Europe Society (Südost-Europa Gesellschaft), *The Nazis in the Balkans* (Pittsburgh: University of Pittsburgh Press, 1968). This organization, with no directives from Hitler and quite possibly without his even being aware of its existence, carried forward a comprehensive program for the establishment of the National Socialist New Order in Southeast Europe. Much of the time after 1933 Hitler did not have to point the way; consensus in Germany was sufficiently widespread for many to proceed on their own within a framework that was generally understood.

82. An excellent introduction to the subject is found in George L. Mosse, *The Crisis of German Ideology, The Intellectual Origins of the Third Reich* (New York: Grosset & Dunlap, 1964). See also Hermann Glaser, *Spiesser-Ideologie, Von der Zerstörung des deutschen Geistes im 19. und 20. Jahrhundert* (Freiburg: Rombach, 1964).

movement would find itself forced into a more reasonable course by the impact of responsibility and reality. Many of those who deluded themselves in this opinion were to argue after World War II that Hitler had deluded them. But he had not lied to them; they had misled themselves. In many instances this self-delusion was greatly facilitated by the hope that Hitler *did* mean what he said about destroying the Social Democratic Party and the trade unions, regardless of the methods used and the purposes for which this might be done.[83] There was also the hope of some of the older generation of German leaders that the dynamism of national socialism could be harnessed to their own more limited goals. But above all there was the opposition of millions to the Weimar Republic, its ideals and its practices, and the whole tradition of liberalism and humanism to which they were related. The German people was to be the new all-powerful god and Hitler the all-powerful prophet; and already in January 1933 there were many who identified the two.[84] He could lead Germany back to strength; he could overcome the psychological depression of past defeat and the economic depression of Germany's contemporary situation.

Many in Germany opposed Hitler's rise to power, some of them recognizing clearly the implications of his policies, especially in the field of foreign affairs.[85] Before 1933 the millions who pushed Hitler forward, and the small clique who installed him in office, by no means constituted the whole population. But there were vast reservoirs of support for the new leader to draw on, and for many years the support was to increase rather than lessen. The national acceptance of the leadership principle implied the unconditional surrender of the country to the will of a leader who had explained for years what he would do with power when he secured it. His people were not to be disappointed. They would get all the wars he had promised, and he would remain faithful to the ideas he had preached until the bitter end.

83. A local case study illustrating this process is in William S. Allen, *The Nazi Seizure of Power, The Experience of a Single German Town, 1930–1935* (Chicago: Quadrangle Books, Inc., 1965).

84. See the thoughtful summary in Karl Dietrich Bracher, Wolfgang Sauer, and Gerhard Schulz, *Die nationalsozialistische Machtergreifung* (2d ed.; Cologne: Westdeutscher Verlag, 1962), pp. 22–27.

85. A startlingly accurate pre-1933 analysis may be found in Theodor Heuss, *Hitlers Weg, Eine historisch-politische Studie über den Nationalsozialismus* (Stuttgart: Union Deutsche Verlagsgesellschaft, 1932), pp. 96–105. This book by the late president of the West German Federal Republic has now been reprinted.

2 First Steps of the New Regime

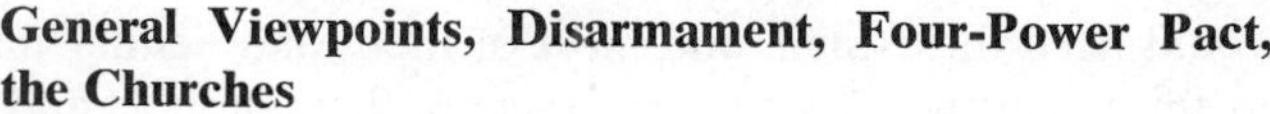

General Viewpoints, Disarmament, Four-Power Pact, the Churches

The conduct of foreign policy in the first months of Hitler's chancellorship may be seen as the double interaction between his plans and hopes on the one hand and on the other the existing realities in Germany's domestic and international situation. Characteristic of this period is the constancy of Hitler's plans; their execution, however, involved some adjustment to the exigencies of the contemporary scene.

The economic difficulties of a nation at the depths of the great depression and the loss of the considerable worldwide esteem attained by the Weimar Republic might appear to have placed obstacles in Hitler's path, but in fact these appearances of adversity were provided for in the general concept of policy Hitler had projected. He had never argued for a policy of advance by negotiation on a step-by-step basis. He had joked about the advances made during the Weimar period when he had not attacked them as intrinsically bad. He believed that the prerequisite for success in foreign affairs was a revolutionary change in the domestic situation in Germany, and he had never pretended that this would not take considerable time. The whole structure of Germany must change, the opposition parties be crushed, democratic and pacifist thought extirpated, and a large new military force built on an ideologically unified basis. It would be that new force from that new base that would enable Hitler to guide German foreign policy along new lines. He had spelled this out in *Mein Kampf* and his second book; he had publicly reaffirmed it in his famous speech to German industrialists on 27 January 1932.[1] After becoming chancellor, Hitler could no longer proclaim

1. The speech was published at the time by the Eher-Verlag, "Vortrag Hitlers vor westdeutschen Wirtschaftlern im Industrie-Klub zu Düsseldorf." See also Domarus, 1:68–90.

these objectives quite so publicly—for reasons he perceived in a manner to be described subsequently—but he was perfectly willing to voice them in private. For this we have not only the recollections of Hermann Rauschning[2] but the contemporary record of Hitler's comments to key elements in Germany whose support was at that stage essential to the realization of his aims.

On the evening of 3 February 1933, Hitler had an opportunity to meet and address the leading German generals and admirals as guest of General Kurt von Hammerstein, the commander in chief of the German army. Hitler would need these men, and most of them had neither met him nor read his writings. This was his chance to secure their support and allegiance, to show them how their interests coincided with his. He knew that they were the only ones who could stop him if they would; he would point out the common road ahead. Hitler spoke for two hours, and he was as explicit in private as he had hitherto been in public.[3]

In his presentation, Hitler explained the need for domestic change as the first order for a new and mighty Germany. Democracy, Marxism, and pacifism must disappear from the scene. "Internal unity is the prerequisite for every state. We failed in 1918 because we had not been politically trained for insight and unity, because class conflicts counted for more than the fatherland." "Democracy is the most disastrous thing there is. Only one person can and should give orders." "The population must learn to think nationalistically and thus be welded together. This cannot be done by intellectual means alone, but only by force. Whoever will not accept [our] insight must be forced."[4]

2. Rauschning, *Voice of Destruction.*

3. Brief accounts in Herbert Rosinski, *The German Army* (London: Hogarth, 1940), p. 215; Hermann Foertsch, *Schuld und Verhängnis* (Stuttgart: Deutsche Verlags-Anstalt, 1951), p. 33; John W. Wheeler-Bennett, *The Nemesis of Power* (London: Macmillan, 1954), p. 291. The main sources are "Aufzeichnung Liebmann" (hereafter cited as Liebmann Notes), *Vierteljahrshefte für Zeitgeschichte,* 2, No. 4 (Oct. 1954), 434–35; Mellenthin to Foertsch, 4 June 1951 and enclosure, "Hitler vor der führenden Generalität in der Bendlerstrasse, Febr. 1933," [4 February 1933] (hereafter cited as Mellenthin Notes), Munich, Institut für Zeitgeschichte, Z.S. 105; notes by Eugen Ott commenting on Mellenthin Notes, February 1952, Institut für Zeitgeschichte, Z.S. 279, pp. 18–19.

Admiral Raeder's account in his memoirs, *Mein Leben* (Tübingen-Neckar: Schlichtenmayer, 1956), 1:280–81, directly contradicts the independently prepared contemporary records of Liebmann and Mellenthin. Since the actual construction program of the German navy from 1933 on, as will be shown, was based on the policies ascribed to Hitler by the Liebmann and Mellenthin notes, one may safely assume that at the time the commander in chief of the German navy understood Hitler very well but subsequently found reasons for revising his memory. Raeder always proudly referred to his honorary doctorate, conferred in recognition of his historical work on German cruiser warfare in World War I. In general, he remembered more about cruiser warfare than the canons of historical accuracy.

4. Mellenthin Notes. The Liebmann Notes contain the same thoughts in more abbreviated form. But compare the last sentence in the quotation, "Wer nicht einsehen will, muss gebeugt werden," with Liebmann's version, "Wer sich nicht bekehren lässt, muss gebeugt werden."

The economy of Germany could be saved only by an expansion of its land base. This could be accomplished only by the army when it was drawn from a country that had been properly indoctrinated. He and his party would take care of the domestic consolidation and indoctrination, and it would be the generals' task to build up the army. This process would, however, take time.[5] During that time, Germany would have to do some negotiating at Geneva under the pretense of equality of arms with other powers but secretly prepare a much greater force.[6] This would be the time of greatest danger, because it would be during this period, while a weak Germany prepared to attack her neighbors, that France—if it had any statesmen at all—would launch a preventive war against Germany.[7] What would Germany's new military might be used for? Hitler left his audience in no doubt: *"Lebensraum* for the surplus population," one of those present noted. Another quotes Hitler as calling for the "conquest of *Lebensraum* in the East and its ruthless germanization."[8]

Key themes in this presentation will be discussed in connection with their relation to the conduct of foreign affairs in 1933–34, but first they should be compared with Hitler's explanation of his policies to a group of industrialists soon after, on 20 February. If Hitler needed the passivity of the generals while consolidating his absolute power in Germany, he needed money from the industrialists for his party's campaign in the election then in progress, an integral part of that consolidation. He promised the generals a vast program of rearmament and conscription, militaristic indoctrination of the nation, and removal of the danger that civil commotion might require army involvement in domestic conflict.[9] The industrial leaders of Germany

5. The Liebmann Notes refer simply to "time" (*Zeit*); the Mellenthin Notes to "many years" (*viele Jahre*).

6. On Hitler's attitude toward the Geneva negotiations see pp. 43 ff., below.

7. The phraseology of the two records differs on this point in detail but not in substance. Liebmann: "The most dangerous time is that of the build up of the armed forces. There we will see whether France has statesmen; if it does, it will not allow us the time but will attack us (presumably with its eastern satellites)." Mellenthin: "The path which I have explained to you will take up many years. If France has capable statesmen, it will attack us during the period of [our] preparations; not itself, but probably through its vassals in the east." The allies of France that Hitler refers to are Poland and Czechoslovakia.

8. The first quotation is from the Mellenthin Notes, the second from the Liebmann Notes. Eugen Ott, one of those present at the meeting, commented after the war: "I remember the speech as having the character of a sharp offensive; the plan to secure new *Lebensraum* in the East seemed to me at the time a crucial declaration. Fritsch [then commander of *Wehrkreis* III, the military district that included Berlin] and Fromm [Ott's successor as chief of the *Wehramt*] shared this impression and were both alarmed, but Fromm tried to reassure Fritsch that these boundless schemes would be halted by the strength of reality and restricted to a reasonable basis." Institut für Zeitgeschichte, Z.S. 279, p. 19.

9. For a fine analysis of the generals' reaction and their apparent willingness to accept Hitler's word on domestic affairs while disregarding his prognosis of aggressive war see Karl Dietrich Bracher, Wolfgang Sauer, and Gerhard Schulz, *Die nationalsozialistische Machtergreifung* (Cologne: Westdeutscher Verlag, 1962) (hereafter cited as Bracher, *Machtergreifung*), pp. 732–43.

were promised very much the same thing; but with his great political and oratorical talent, Hitler was careful to attune his presentation to their orientation.[10] He would protect private property against bolshevism—that was why democracy had to be terminated. If the generals had been told that the people must be unified on the subject of military service, the industrialists were assured that it must be unified on the subject of private property. The new ideology is similarly defined as requiring an end to pacifism and a rejection of the concept of reconciliation between peoples.[11] Domestic political consolidation would be followed by economic progress. The consolidation, moreover, would come after the election in which the National Socialists would try to increase their hold on the country; but if the election turned out poorly, "the battle would be fought with other weapons." Only in a consolidated Germany could rearmament take place; the decision on that subject would be made in Germany, not in Geneva. The immediate role of the industrialists in all this was to provide money for the election campaign. They could contribute generously in a situation where, as Hermann Göring explained, "there would be no more elections for at least ten but more probably a hundred years." If Hitler did not elaborate further on this occasion, it may have been in part due to the fact that his audience included individuals, and represented the same group, to whom he had spoken at greater length a year before at Düsseldorf. Then he had tied the identical themes to future conquests; now he wanted only to draw their attention to the immediate needs of the election campaign. Hjalmar Schacht collected the funds for that campaign; he would soon be providing it for others.

The election itself, the enormous propaganda effort accompanying it, the suppression of all civil liberties during the campaign through the Reichstag fire decrees,[12] and the weak opposition or more frequently complete cooperation of the ministers who were not National Socialists enabled Hitler to proceed at a tremendous speed with the consolidation of his regime in February and March 1933.[13] Hitler was doing in domestic affairs what he had said he would do, and with consummate skill.[14] Sometimes he could move directly:

10. The text is printed as Nuremberg document 203–D in *Trial of the Major War Criminals* (Nuremberg, 1946–1948) (hereafter cited as *TMWC*), 35:42–47; Göring's speech at the same occasion in ibid., pp. 47–48; Krupp's note of 22 February on his reply on behalf of those present is 204–D, ibid., p. 48. See also Bullock, pp. 334f.

11. The German is "Ablehnung der Volksversöhnung."

12. The most recent research suggests that the fire could conceivably have been set by Marinus van der Lubbe, unassisted. Historically the most significant point is that with the approval of President Hindenburg and the cabinet, Hitler used the welcome pretext provided by the fire to suspend the constitutional rights of all Germans for the duration of his rule. The decrees of 28 February, not the Enabling Act, were the basis of the totalitarian system installed by the National Socialists.

13. A superb account of this whole process may be found in Bracher, *Machtergreifung*.

14. It should be noted parenthetically that the incredibly low intellectual and political level of most of those who thought they might restrain Hitler by serving in the same cabinet with him rarely put Hitler's abilities to any severe test. Much of the opposition in this period was created only in the post–1945 period by imaginative memoir writers like Franz von Papen. His *Der Wahrheit eine Gasse* (Munich: Paul List, 1952) is mainly fiction.

on 3 February he had promised the generals that anything considered treason would be punished by death; one paragraph of the 28 February 1933 emergency decrees so provided. In other respects Hitler had to temporize and compromise, but that had the advantage of making the revolution appear less abrupt. Whatever elements in German society could be used in the process of consolidation would be used, even at the cost of temporary compromise. This procedure combined the advantage of lessening opposition at the moment with the advantage of preparing the way for the subsequent absorption or destruction of that element. Years before, when he himself was in jail after the 1923 putsch, Hitler had explained this approach for the benefit of some followers involved in ideological and organizational hairsplitting. "According to Hitler, the available time is too short to make the people ready for action [*frontreif*] only with the National Socialist ideology. We must therefore be satisfied with making the people nationalistic, so that they are ready for action, in alliance with other nationalist groups. To do this, it will even be necessary to make some compromises." The author of this description continued by comparing Hitler's expressed need for compromise with his own earlier ideological intransigence: "Today, when Hitler for the first time placed major considerations of foreign policy on the scales, I really had my first doubts whether we have been completely correct in our position. I am absolutely convinced that Hitler will never deviate one iota from his National Socialist ideals . . . but when that sometimes seems to be the case, it happens because of greater aims."[15]

The first major measures of the new chancellor were, accordingly, directed toward domestic concerns. In the first cabinet meetings, practically nothing was said about foreign affairs. Consolidation of his internal position was Hitler's main and most immediate concern, and the records of the cabinet meetings reflect this clearly.[16] The firm establishment of totalitarian rule, however, has been shown to be an integral part of Hitler's foreign policy plans, just as the perpetual territorial expansion that was the essence of his foreign policy was an integral part of his perception of the nature and needs of German society as defined in racial terms. The traditional distinction between domestic and foreign policy, and the related question as to the priority of one over the other, is thus largely irrelevant to an analysis of German politics in this period. Nowhere is this more obvious in the first years of National Socialist rule than in matters of economic and budgetary policy.

The world depression had hit Germany hard, even if the self-centered German public then—and since—failed to recognize that there were other countries either as badly hit or in an even worse situation. Hitler never expounded any detailed economic program in public, but he made his views known in the cabinet the first time budgetary problems arose. A proposal

15. Hermann Fobke to Ludolf Haase, 21 August 1924, in Werner Jochmann (ed.), *Nationalsozialismus und Revolution, Ursprung und Geschichte der NSDAP in Hamburg, 1922–1933* (Frankfurt/M.: Europäische Verlagsgesellschaft, 1963), pp. 132–35.

16. Protocols of cabinet meetings of 30 January 1933, *TMWC,* 25:372–76; 31 January, *Documents on German Foreign Policy, 1918–1945,* Series C (hereafter cited as *G. D.,* C), 1, No. 3; 1 February, ibid., No. 7; 2 February, ibid., No. 8.

for the construction of a reservoir triggered Hitler's exposition of policy. Nothing demonstrates the relationship between economic and foreign policy in Hitler's thinking more dramatically than the protocol of the cabinet meeting of 8 February 1933. "The Reich Chancellor stated that in judging the request . . . another decisive consideration had to be taken into account. Germany was now negotiating with foreign countries about her military equality of rights. But Germany could not content itself with that. . . . The next five years in Germany had to be devoted to rendering the German people again capable of bearing arms. Every publicly sponsored measure to create employment had to be considered from [this] point of view. . . . This had to be the dominant thought, always and everywhere." While some ministers stressed the military importance of waterways and highways—neither of which were to be overlooked in later years—the defense minister expressed his full agreement with Hitler, who "again stressed that for the next four/five years the main principle must be: everything for the armed forces. Germany's position in the world was decisively conditioned upon the position of the German armed forces.[17] The position of the German economy in the world was also dependent on that." The decision of the cabinet was to look at the whole budget, to see what could be done for the armed forces, and "finally to see what funds were left" for such projects as the reservoir that had sparked the discussion.[18] In a similar vein, on the following day Hitler informed a conference on government measures to increase employment that the program in this field inaugurated under his predecessor, Chancellor Kurt von Schleicher, should now be converted to projects of military importance. Hitler held that the public label previously given to this employment program was especially suited to the concealment of its new character as a part of his own rearmament policy.[19]

This account of Hitler's views of priorities in the economic field shows that, paradoxically, the depressed nature of the German economy in 1933 would be of great advantage to him. It meant that the rearmament he wanted, in its initial stages, would not have to compete for labor and resources with other economic activities, a competition that would have raised the danger of the inflation Hitler wished to avoid, at least in its more obvious manifestations, because of the German public's horrendous memories of the runaway inflation of 1923. Rearmament would mean employment for work-

17. It should be noted that Ambassador Nadolny recorded in his memoirs that at their first meeting after 30 January 1933 Hitler told him that he first had to make all of Germany National Socialist. This would take four years, and only then would he turn to foreign policy. Rudolf Nadolny, *Mein Beitrag* (Wiesbaden: Limes, 1955), p. 130.

18. *G. D.,* C, 1, No. 16. The record has been quoted at length to demonstrate that the tie of rearmament to economic policy was present from the beginning. This is recognized in Bracher, *Machtergreifung,* p. 785. A good survey may be found in Arthur Schweitzer, *Big Business in the Third Reich* (Bloomington: Indiana University Press, 1964), chap. 7.

19. See the quotation in Dieter Petzina, "Hauptprobleme der deutschen Wirtschaftspolitik, 1932–1933," *Vierteljahrshefte für Zeitgeschichte,* 15, No. 1 (Jan. 1967), p. 43.

ers and profits for employers; once the economy was reactivated by this stimulus, secondary effects could be headed off by controls. As soon as full employment was reached, drastic measures would hold the needed workers and resources in the public portion of the economy, but by then the regime would be sufficiently established to cope with a problem that might have been quite difficult in 1933. In one important respect, however, Hitler would have to overcome some resistance right away. The rearmament policy required enormous state expenditures. This meant large-scale deficit financing and a break with the moderate fiscal policy of the von Papen and von Schleicher regimes that had followed and partially modified the rigidly deflationary policies of Chancellor Brüning. If vast schemes of rearmament were to be financed, there would have to be a drastic change in the policy of the Reichsbank.

The president of the Reichsbank was Hans Luther, a man who prided himself, not without considerable justification, on trying to aid the economy of a depression-ridden country without resorting to remedies likely to be more dangerous than the disease. When Hitler asked him for the credits needed to finance rearmament, Luther offered one hundred million marks, the legal limit of the Reichsbank.[20] Hitler, of course, expected to spend billions and later claimed that he first thought he had misunderstood Luther. But he had heard correctly, and Luther was promptly replaced by a man who was in full agreement with the creation of limitless amounts of credit instruments as a procedure for financing rearmament. The new man was Hjalmar Schacht, who had probably been promised the Reichsbank presidency in any case and who on assuming that position on 17 March 1933 inaugurated a new fiscal policy.[21] He converted the device of "employment creation bills" (*Arbeitsbeschaffungswechsel*) originated by Luther into an unlimited credit program, using bills drawn on what was essentially a dummy corporation, the Metallurgische Forschungs-G.m.b.H., created by the government and several private firms. These bills, the "Mefo-bills," functioned as a concealed form of money; twelve billion marks' worth had been issued by 1938 when the government turned to other methods of financing rearmament.

It is with this dramatic change in fiscal policy that one can see at the beginning of National Socialist rule the interrelation of the rearmament

20. On this controversy see Bracher, *Machtergreifung,* p. 786; Earl R. Beck, *Verdict on Schacht* (Tallahassee: Florida State University, 1955), pp. 36–37; Hans Luther, *Vor dem Abgrund, 1930–1933, Reichsbankpräsident in Krisenzeiten* (Berlin: Propyläen Verlag, 1964), pp. 304–306. Hitler's subsequent account of the incident in the *Table Talk,* Trevor-Roper edition, No. 193; Picker edition, No. 83 (text and commentary in the Ritter edition, No. 64, are quite unreliable).

21. According to Kliefoth of the American embassy in Berlin, on the evening of 1 February Schacht told him that Hitler had wanted him to take over the Ministry of Finance but that he had urged the retention of Schwerin von Krosigk in that position while asking for the presidency of the Reichsbank for himself so that Luther could be pushed out (Kliefoth to Hull, 2 February 1933, Dodd Papers, Folder 1933 Germany).

program, the hope for recovery from depression at home, and the aspiration for conquest abroad. The newly appointed Reich Commissar for Air, Hermann Göring, could now tell Ernst Heinkel that the new air force would be built as he had predicted.[22] As early as February the German navy received its first big installment of extra money, followed by even more in March.[23] If there was any money left over, the Minister of Transport—who was to become the only cabinet member ever to defy Hitler to his face—could build reservoirs.[24] Such financial questions must be viewed apart from the details of rearmament policy and disarmament negotiations because of the time interval between the authorization and the expenditure of the large sums involved. The focus of many students of National Socialist Germany on expenditure for arms, delivery of weapons, and the actual size of Germany's forces has obscured the fact that a rise in these, however significant in itself, reflects decisions made some time before. This is especially true in the case of air and naval armaments in which the interval between the planning and delivery of warships in the one case and the development and mass-production of aircraft in the other is particularly great. Thus the eighty million extra marks allotted to the German navy on 1 May 1933 was used to start work on the *Scharnhorst,*[25] a ship publicly announced as 26,000 tons but really 31,300 tons,[26] which was launched on 3 October 1936 and put into service on 7 January 1939.[27] The time lag in this instance was six years; the varying budgetary allocations for the *Scharnhorst* during that period reflected construction stages, not policy decisions.

If the need for domestic consolidation involved temporary postponement of the more ambitious foreign policy plans of the new chancellor—even though the period of postponement would be utilized for rearmament—other not entirely unrelated factors postponed changes in the personnel who would actually conduct Germany's relations with foreign countries. Only Friedrich W. von Prittwitz und Gaffron, the German ambassador to the United States, decided that he could not in good conscience serve the new masters of Germany,[28] and this provided Hitler with a conveniently distant post to which he could send Hans Luther as a consolation prize after forcing his resignation from the Reichsbank. There is considerable evidence that Hitler had originally planned to make Alfred Rosenberg his foreign

22. Ernst Heinkel, *Stürmisches Leben* (Stuttgart: Mundus-Verlag, 1953), pp. 270, 287ff.

23. *TMWC,* 35: 590–91.

24. Freiherr von Eltz-Rübenach refused to accept a golden party badge from Hitler at a cabinet meeting in 1937 and thereupon resigned.

25. *TMWC,* 35: 591.

26. Ibid., 34:188.

27. See the useful compilation in Rolf Bensel, *Die deutsche Flottenpolitik von 1933 bis 1939* (Beiheft 3 der *Marine-Rundschau*) (Frankfurt/M.: Mittler, 1958), pp. 71–77.

28. *G. D.*, C, 1, No. 75.

minister, or at least state secretary in the foreign ministry—the second highest post in that agency.[29] This was prevented, however, by the insistence of President Paul von Hindenburg that Constantin von Neurath remain as foreign minister, thereby practically excluding Rosenberg from the other position as well. Von Neurath knew of Hitler's original intention,[30] which may help to explain the confidence he displayed when recounting to the British ambassador President Hindenburg's insistence that he be retained.[31]

Hitler himself regretted his inability to reorganize the foreign ministry immediately with suitable personnel. When he summoned Mussolini's special contact man, Giuseppe Renzetti, to the Chancellory on 31 January to thank him for Mussolini's congratulations of the day before, Hitler asked Renzetti to assure Il Duce that Neurath would follow his wishes, and that while he could not reshape the foreign ministry as quickly as he wished because of a lack of qualified personnel, he hoped in time to surround himself with faithful followers.[32]

Both as a consolation prize for Rosenberg, and as a possible means of preparing for later changes in the diplomatic service, Hitler authorized the creation of a foreign policy office of the National Socialist party, the *Aussenpolitische Amt* or APA. He had been persuaded of the wisdom of this idea by Kurt Lüdecke in the middle of March, and the agency was formally established on 1 April 1933 with Rosenberg as its chief.[33] The new organization began to develop in the spring of 1933 as a potential base for a future reorganization of the foreign service. Its subsequent escapades in various fields will be examined in their chronological and geographical context, but the initial period which is relevant here proved to be singularly inauspicious. Efforts to recruit individuals with diplomatic experience failed.[34] Lüdecke himself, who thought of the agency he helped establish as an organization for foreign propaganda as much as policy, wanted to be press attaché in Washington while simultaneously strengthening the power base of the APA in Berlin. Both of these efforts seemed to make headway at first. He apparently at one point secured Hitler's agreement to his appointment.[35] He also had some initial success in setting up a fund-

29. There is a good summary of this subject in Schubert, pp. 220–26.

30. Interrogation of von Neurath, 12 November 1945, Nuremberg Trials Materials in the National Archives.

31. *Documents on British Foreign Policy 1919–1939,* Second Series (hereafter cited as *B. D.*, 2d), 4, No. 235.

32. Renzetti to Mussolini, 31 January 1933, in National Archives T–586, container 491, frames 050275–76.

33. Seabury, pp. 33ff.; Schubert, pp. 226–32; Jacobsen, pp. 45–89. Only sources not cited in these books are noted below.

34. See the strange story in Werner Otto von Hentig, *Mein Leben eine Dienstreise* (Göttingen: Vandenhoeck & Ruprecht, 1962), pp. 292–95.

35. Memorandum by Bülow, 24 April 1933, Microcopy T–120, container 2371, Serial 4601, frames E 188728–29. (Documents from National Archives microfilm will be cited hereafter by T number with other identifying numbers separated only by a "/".)

raising luncheon among German bankers and industrialists.[36] In his eagerness to have the world receive only good news from Germany, however, Lüdecke overreached himself by demanding, in Rosenberg's name, the recall from Germany of a prominent American correspondent, H. R. Knickerbocker. The resulting protests from America were utilized by Lüdecke's enemies in the party, especially Ernst Hanfstaengl, to have him jailed.[37] Though later released, Lüdecke was soon rearrested and then escaped abroad. His first arrest had occurred while Rosenberg was in London on a trip that was such a fiasco it greatly reduced the prospects of Rosenberg becoming a key figure in National Socialist diplomacy and the APA one of its major agencies.

There is some evidence that Hitler and Rosenberg had discussed the possibility of a trip abroad by Rosenberg early in April 1933 to try to persuade the horrified Western world of the beneficence of national socialism.[38] Rosenberg decided to go to London early in May, while his rival in the field of foreign propaganda, Joseph Goebbels, who had been made Minister of Propaganda on 13 March, wanted to go on a similar trip to the United States.[39] Goebbels gave up his plan and thus saved himself a great deal of embarrassment that would surely have accompanied any trip undertaken immediately after the great book-burning in Berlin,[40] but Rosenberg was determined to go on his mission. He had been in England before, in 1931,[41] and he apparently hoped that an explanation of Germany's do-

36. In addition to Lüdecke's memoirs, see Bülow's note of 22 April 1933, T–120, 2376/4606/E 193047 and the letter of Fritz Bülow to his uncle, Bernhard von Bülow, 25 April 1933, ibid., frame E 193048.

37. Messersmith dispatch 1303 of 12 May 1933. Part of this is printed in *Foreign Relations of the United States, 1933* (hereafter cited as U. S. 1933), 2: 400–402; the rest, with additional information on Lüdecke, is in the National Archives, State Department Decimal file (hereafter cited as State), 811.91262/112. See also von Neurath's note RM 278 of 3 March 1933, T–120, 1493/3087/D 621755–56; Diary of Jay Pierrepont Moffat, 8 May 1933, Houghton Library, Moffat Papers, Vol. 33. Another scheme of Lüdecke's shortly before had been an invitation to visit Germany extended to the American racialist author Lothrop Stoddard (Moffat Diary, 26 April 1933, ibid.). Rosenberg's own recollection of Lüdecke is in Serge Lang and Ernst von Schenck (eds.), *Memoirs of Alfred Rosenberg* (trans. by Eric Posselt, Chicago: Ziff-Davis, 1949), pp. 60–61 (the edition of this work by Heinrich Härtle under the title *Letzte Aufzeichnungen, Ideale und Idole der nationalsozialistischen Revolution* [Göttingen: Plesse Verlag, 1955], is tendentiously distorted).

38. When Walther Funk, then head of the Reich Press Bureau, talked with Hitler on 10 April about Roosevelt's invitation to the preliminary economic talks in Washington, Hitler mentioned Rosenberg as one possible person to send (*G. D.*, C, 1, No. 149). Schacht went instead.

39. Gordon (Berlin) tel. 72 of 1 May 1933, State 033.6211 Goebbels, Joseph/1; *New York Times,* 7 May 1933, p. 13.

40. Messersmith dispatch 1305 of 12 May 1933, State 862.00/2984. According to Werner Stephan, *Joseph Goebbels* (Stuttgart: Union Deutsche Verlagsgesellschaft, 1949), pp. 185–86, Hitler turned down the idea. According to Helmut Heiber, *Joseph Goebbels* (Berlin: Colloquium, 1962), p. 248, Hitler forbade the trip after Rosenberg had allowed the plan to leak out.

41. Testimony of Rosenberg, *TMWC,* 11: 453–54; see also the reference to the prior meeting of Rosenberg with Lord Hailsham in Hoesch's tel. 132 of 15 May 1933, *G. D.,* C, 1, No. 237.

mestic policies would reduce the strong shift of British public opinion following upon the National Socialists' assumption of power. This, in turn, might strengthen his claim with Hitler to a key role in foreign affairs (as the Anglo-German naval treaty was to do for Ribbentrop).

The course and outcome of the Rosenberg visit, however, were the opposite of what had been intended.[42] The British foreign secretary, Sir John Simon, and the undersecretary, Sir Robert Vansittart, were unimpressed by Rosenberg's defense of the persecution of the Jews, suppression of constitutional freedoms, and establishment of concentration camps in Germany. Prime Minister Ramsay MacDonald and the Conservative party leader Stanley Baldwin declined to see the itinerant propagandist, while the swastika-bedecked wreath that Rosenberg left at the Cenotaph, the British war memorial, was unceremoniously removed. Negative comments in the press publicly signaled the failure of Rosenberg's mission, and he found it expedient to cut short his trip and return to Germany, much sadder but little wiser. The obvious rebuff he had suffered greatly reduced the effectiveness and prestige of the APA, though Hitler allowed it to continue in operation. This was apparently due to three factors: Hitler's personal loyalty to Rosenberg as to other associates of his struggle for power, regardless of their political and personal failings; the occasional successes of the APA, such as arranging in the month after the London debacle the first visit of the head of a foreign government—Julius Gömbös of Hungary—to National Socialist Germany; and the associated prospect of eventually using the APA in some manner to reorganize the foreign service after all, or at least to keep it in line by the threat of competition. But Rosenberg himself would have to wait until 1941 for a ministerial appointment; Hitler would continue to work with the foreign ministry which by that time had been entrusted to another of his followers.[43]

Hitler's utilization of von Neurath and the other officials of the foreign ministry had the advantage of making it seem that no radical changes in German foreign policy were intended during those first years of his rule when the danger of foreign intervention seemed most acute to him. Few German diplomats were better suited for such a role than Constantin von Neurath. His appearance was as distinguished as his career. He had held several important diplomatic posts before being recalled by Hindenburg from the embassy in London in 1932 to serve as foreign minister. The German ambassador to Italy, Ulrich von Hassell, and the chief of the German delegation to the disarmament conference in Geneva, Rudolf

42. Schubert, pp. 230, 232–35. In addition to the sources cited there see Lord Vansittart, *The Mist Procession* (London: Hutchinson, 1958), p. 475; Atherton (London) for Norman Davis to Hull, tel. 114 of 9 May 1933, State 500.A 15 A 4/1850; Jan Masaryk report 13 of 16 May 1933, Czech document in T–120, 1316/2376/D 497012–14 (on these Czech documents see the bibliographic note). There is a more positive evaluation of Rosenberg's London trip in Jacobsen, pp. 74–75.

43. Rosenberg's letter recounting his disappointment when von Ribbentrop was appointed foreign minister in 1938 (Schubert, p. 235, n. 4) has been published in Theodor R. Emessen (ed.), *Aus Görings Schreibtisch* (Berlin: Allgemeiner Deutscher Verlag, 1947), No. 29.

Nadolny, had been considered his competitors for the post of foreign minister in 1932,[44] and Neurath's friction with both men in 1933 reflects more an anxiety over the secureness of his own position than a concern for the fate of his country. A jovial person, often inclined to take his vacations more seriously than his official responsibilities, Neurath was no hindrance to Hitler's ambitions.[45] He put up no resistance to the consolidation of Hitler's power in domestic affairs; if no anti-Semitic rowdy, he did not hesitate to move into a house expropriated from a Jew. There were occasions when he tried to temper the headlong rush of National Socialist foreign policy with greater finesse of execution, but pride of place long repressed any serious doubts he might have.[46] The rumors of his imminent departure soon died down; and late in May 1933 the American chargé d'affaires in Berlin aptly concluded: "Baron von Neurath has shown such a remarkable capacity for submitting to what in normal times could only be considered as affronts and indignities on the part of the Nazis, that it is still quite a possibility that the latter should be content to have him remain as a figurehead for some time yet."[47]

This "some time yet" would include the first period of intensive rearmament, which in Hitler's own terms had been described as one of four or five years. The new budget plans were agreed on early in April; at the same time the navy was told to replace its one-front mobilization plan (against Poland) with a two-front plan by 1 April 1934 and to be ready for action within the framework of the whole armed forces within five years.[48] Though these time estimates must not be taken too literally, they do suggest that there was a short-term concern with preventive war waged by Poland and France and a long-term expectation that in the late 1930s Germany would be ready to move on its own. The problem, as General Wilhelm Adam, who held a position equivalent to chief of staff of the army, put it in a memorandum of 15 March 1933, was how to rearm without provoking a preventive attack Germany could not resist.[49] Putting the issue in diplomatic terms, Mussolini explained to von Hassell on the same day that the question was how Germany could secure through negotiations the time it needed to rearm without French interference.[50] For an examination of how Hitler hoped to cope with

44. *TMWC,* 40: 462; Nadolny, p. 121.

45. Seabury, pp. 27–28; Jacobsen, pp. 28–33. A biography of von Neurath by John L. Heineman may be expected soon.

46. When the Enabling Act was discussed in the cabinet on 15 March 1933, von Neurath first suggested and then quickly withdrew the idea of leaving with the Reichstag the power to ratify treaties (*TMWC,* 31: 402–9). He was as willing to leave uncontrolled power in Hitler's hands in foreign as in domestic affairs.

47. Gordon dispatch 2428 of 22 May 1933, State 862.00/2985.

48. *TMWC,* 34: 473; Bracher, *Machtergreifung,* p. 796, n. 212 and p. 797, n. 222.

49. Affidavit of General Wilhelm Adam, 5 March 1948, Nuremberg documents, Krupp Nr. 105; cf. *Table Talk,* Picker edition, No. 12, Trevor-Roper edition, No. 112.

50. *G. D.*, C, 1, No. 87. For an earlier, similar, warning see von Hassell's report I 395 of 25 February 1933, T–120, 2700/5737/H 028639–41.

this problem one must turn to Germany's position in the disarmament negotiations then in progress in Geneva.[51]

Germany's international position clearly suffered from Hitler's domestic victory. Under the Weimar Republic, Germany had attained status in three ways, each related to the other. The German state had secured a measure of international standing by its participation on an equal basis in the Locarno treaties and by the allocation to it of a permanent seat on the council of the League of Nations. Hitler certainly did not look upon these attainments as desirable, and any attenuation of them could only be welcome to him as an opponent of both Locarno and the League. The Weimar Republic had also developed relatively good relations with Russia, Austria, and Italy. The first two of these countries Hitler soon alienated, intentionally at that, while the last was to be a friend with some reservations. The third, and in the long run though intangible perhaps the most important international asset, was the recovery of a substantial measure of international goodwill for Germany, especially in Great Britain and the United States, but in a special way also in France. There was the growing feeling that the peace treaties that had ended the world war had been excessively harsh on Germany, that the many modifications since made in Germany's favor had been too few and too late, and that in some areas further concessions might well be appropriate. It is not necessary to examine here either the origin or the wisdom of these attitudes, but their existence provides a significant part of the background for the events of 1933. The import of this situation for specific developments will be reviewed where relevant; it will suffice to point out one illustration of Germany's new position in the world that is not without ironic ramifications. Included in the five-member Lytton Commission, established by the League in cooperation with the United States to investigate the situation arising out of Japan's seizure of Manchuria in the fall of 1931, was a representative of Germany, Heinrich Schnee, the last governor of German East Africa. The changing tides are personified by his role. From 1924 to 1932 he had served in the Reichstag as a member of the German People's party (DVP), the party of Gustav Stresemann. In view of his participation in the unanimous verdict of the Lytton Commission against Japan's aggression, the German government found its hands tied.[52] In spite of a special request from the Japanese government that Germany at least abstain, a vote was cast on 24 February 1933, in support of the report which precipitated Japan's withdrawal from Geneva.[53] In October 1933 Germany itself broke with the League, and in the combined

51. Hitler's worry in 1933 may be contrasted with his confident assertion five years later, on 18 June 1938, that no danger of a preventive war against Germany existed (*TMWC,* 35: 445).

52. Von Neurath had endorsed the report in November 1932; see U. S. 1932, 4: 362.

53. *G. D.*, C, 1, No. 28; see the reports from Keller in Geneva on the League discussions in the German foreign minister's file "China, Bd. 5, Jan. 1933–Juni 1935," T–120, 1522/3086/passim; *Documents diplomatiques français,* 1st. Series, Vol. 2 (hereafter cited as *D. D. F.*, 1st, 2), No. 278.

election and plebiscite that followed, Schnee returned to the Reichstag, now on the National Socialist ticket. He would still be there on 20 February 1938 to hear Hitler repudiate Germany's vote of almost exactly five years earlier.

The reaction of the outside world to the new German government was to a great extent the result of domestic events in Germany. The brutal suppression of civil liberties and the opposition parties, the vehement attacks on the Jews, the dismissal of prominent university professors, the suppression of the trade unions, the public burning of books, the incipient church struggle, and the pitiful stories told by the first refugees to escape abroad all combined to bring about a drastic reversal of the rising world esteem for Germany. This was particularly significant because in several countries political movements inclined to the Left had been the most vehement advocates of treaty revisions in favor of Germany; these same groups were most drastically affronted by the policies of the new regime.[54] At the same time, the hooliganism in the streets and the policy of extreme reaction proclaimed in public by the new regime were unlikely to inspire confidence among more conservative elements in countries like Great Britain and the United States. The strongly negative reaction abroad to the Hitler government did not go entirely unnoticed in Germany. Some members of the government were alarmed by the possible impact on Germany's foreign relations and foreign trade, while Hitler and Göring were incensed at the publicly aired charges that they themselves had set fire to the Reichstag.[55]

Specific incidents emphasized the problem. Diplomats and other foreigners in Germany were repeatedly assaulted on the streets for imagined insults of one sort or another, as the police looked on benignly.[56] While inci-

54. For a thoughtful report on this process in France, see Tyrrell's report of 20 March 1933, in *B. D.*, 2d, 4, No. 266; see also Otto Abetz, *Das offene Problem* (Cologne: Greven Verlag, 1951), p. 36.

On the same process in England see the report of the Czech chargé in London, No. 3 of 21 March 1933, Czech document in T–120, 1316/2376/D 496992–97 (tendentiously selected excerpts in Friedrich Berber [ed.], *Europäische Politik 1933–1938 im Spiegel der Prager Akten* [3d ed., Essen: Essener Verlagsanstalt, 1942] [hereafter cited as Berber, *Prager Akten*], No. 5); and compare *B. D.*, 2d, 5, No. 69 and *G. D.*, C, 1, Nos. 146, 152, 193. The British ambassador to Berlin, Sir Horace Rumbold, was instructed to inform Hitler at their first meeting that in two months Germany had lost the sympathy it had gained in the preceding ten years (*B. D.*, 2d, 5, Nos. 126, 139; *G. D.*, C, 1, No. 223). For some acute observations on this turn in British opinion see the entry for 5 May 1933 in Harry Graf Kessler, *Tagebücher 1918–1937* (Frankfurt/M.: Insel-Verlag, 1961), pp. 716–17. Von Neurath wrote to Hindenburg about this subject from the London Economic Conference on 19 June 1933 (*TMWC*, 40: 465–68), and reported on it to the cabinet on his return (*G. D.*, C, 1, No. 335; cf., ibid., No. 406). The most recent treatment is in Charles Bloch, *Hitler und die europäischen Mächte 1933–34, Kontinuität oder Bruch* (Hamburg: Europäische Verlagsanstalt, 1966), chap. 2.

55. Conference of ministers on 2 March 1933, *G. D.*, C, 1, No. 44.

56. The documentation on these incidents is almost endless; von Neurath sent a brief list to Göring with a request for some action on 10 March 1933, T–120, 2382/4619/E 197637–39.

dents in the demilitarized zone in the Rhineland excited the French,[57] a wild speech by Göring on air rearmament alarmed the British.[58] The persecution of the Jews, generally viewed as the most spectacular sign of Germany's intentional relapse into barbarism, aroused especially strong reactions abroad. The outgoing administration of President Herbert Hoover as well as the incoming one of Franklin Delano Roosevelt warned the German government of the disastrous effects of these activities on American public opinion.[59] The British government was similarly alarmed and used Rosenberg's visit to try to convey their concern to the highest quarters in Berlin. Even the Italians became concerned about the violence of their new-found friends. Italian fascism, as the National Socialists had regretfully noted in the 1920s, had not adopted the anti-Semitic line so prominent a part of German fascism; and Mussolini was apparently genuinely shocked at what he considered a temporary aberration in German conduct.[60] His efforts to restrain the German government in this program of persecution were given greater emphasis by the personal feelings of Vittorio Cerruti, the Italian ambassador to Germany, who was outspoken on this subject and whose wife was Jewish.[61] The Italian government thus joined the American and British governments in their efforts to prevent or at least restrain the great anti-Jewish boycott scheduled to start on 1 April 1933, which was in fact held but restricted to that day.[62] This restriction was imposed partially in response to the outside pressure and the intervention of Hindenburg, brought about by von Neurath.

The regime thus modified its actions slightly in the face of the rising tide of anti-German sentiment abroad. It also made some efforts to influence foreign opinion by overt and covert propaganda.[63] To reduce foreign fear of German rearmament, news stories and pictures of militaristic activities

57. *G. D.*, C, 1, Nos. 69, 70; *D. D. F.*, 1st, 2, Nos. 354, 402, 408.

58. Von Neurath Memorandum RM 238 of 14 March 1933, T–120, 2382/4619/E 197641.

59. Some documents on this have been published in U. S. 1933, 2: 320, 322, 327, 330–33.

60. Graham to Vansittart, 24 March 1933, *B. D.*, 2d, 5, No. 52.

61. See Elisabetta Cerruti, *Ambassador's Wife* (New York: Macmillan, 1953).

62. Relevant documents have been published in U. S. 1933, 2:337ff. See further von Neurath to Hitler, 2 April 1933, *TMWC*, 35: 523–24 (the copy of this document in T–120, 784/1556/377615 carries the notation that it was submitted to Hitler); Memorandum by Moffat, "Record of Events in Connection with the Situation of the Jews in Germany beginning March 30, 1933," 1 April 1933, State 862.4016/516; Gordon dispatch 2297 of 10 April 1933, State 862.4016/619; Dertinger, "Informationsbericht vom 31. März 1933," Bundesarchiv Koblenz, Sammlung Brammer (hereafter cited as Bundesarchiv, Brammer), Z.Sg. 101/26, f. 225.

63. On the covert propaganda abroad see the secret memorandum of 20 April 1933 by the Aufklärungs-Ausschuss Hamburg-Bremen (organized in 1923 and controlled by the German foreign ministry), with a covering letter to Alfred Rosenberg, Nuremberg document 134–PS. See also *G. D.*, C, 1, Nos. 261, 359. The Aufklärungs-Ausschuss came under the control of the propaganda ministry; for an interesting, if not entirely reliable, account see Emil Helfferich, *1932–1946 Tatsachen,* pp. 65–71.

in Germany were restricted;[64] furthermore, a transparently fake incident involving the dropping of leaflets from airplanes was staged over Berlin to convince the world that Germany indeed needed warplanes to defend itself.[65] In this and some other minor gestures made early in 1933, Hitler revealed some concern about opinion abroad;[66] but on the broad measures of domestic policy, there would be no change, and hence a continued negative response in the world.

An area where the question of Germany's position in the world was most immediately at issue in 1933 was the disarmament conference at Geneva. In the period just before Hitler came to power, Germany's temporary withdrawal from the conference had ended with a statement by France, Germany, Italy, the United Kingdom, and the United States that Germany and others disarmed under the peace settlement should be granted "equality of rights in a system which would provide security for all nations" provided Germany agreed to return to the conference to discuss the method of implementing this equality of rights.[67] The bureau of the conference met again on 23 January and the general commission on 2 February 1933. The issues facing the disarmament conference had been difficult enough; they were greatly complicated by the change of government in Germany.

The Germans had been required to disarm to a level set by the Treaty of Versailles. Although they had violated the specifications in various ways, the effective strength of the German armed forces was in fact so close to the treaty provisions that in comparison with the military strengths of other countries it was not unreasonable to take the treaty's figures as a basis for comparison. It was the contention of the Germans that the other powers had an obligation to reduce their arms to a level commensurate with their own, both in size and in nature of armament. If the other powers were unwilling to do so, then they could not insist that Germany remain disarmed unilaterally—its disarmament had originally been intended as a prelude to the general disarmament thought necessary for peace; Germany's remaining the only major power that had disarmed, however, was in fact an invitation to attack. By implication, therefore, Germany's demand for equal rights

64. See the circular of the Ministry of the Interior of 6 July 1933 in T–120, 1783/3650/D 813082–87; and the SA order of 25 July 1933, *TMWC,* 35: 6–7.

65. For this incident and the ensuing argument over German air rearmament, see *B. D.*, 2d, 5, Nos. 179, 219, 222, 231, 233, 256, 259, 261, 262, 265, 267, 268, 275, 294, 277, 278, 280, 281, 282, 284, 286, 287, 289, 327; *G. D.*, C, 1, Nos. 359, 380; Gordon dispatch 2499 of 26 June 1933, State 862.00/3018.

66. This is probably the context for the account of an effort to use a member of a German nationalistic labor organization to calm the labor unions in France (Albert Krebs, *Tendenzen und Gestalten der NSDAP* [Stuttgart: Deutsche Verlags-Anstalt, 1959], p. 148) and the attempt to use a Social Democratic member of the Reichstag to restrain the Social Democratic press in Scandinavia (Richthofen [Copenhagen] report 101.P of 26 March 1933, T–120, 1517/3124/D 648903–4). See also *B. D.*, 2d, 4, No. 248.

67. Five-Power Declaration of 11 December 1932, in U. S. 1932, 1: 527–28.

meant that the others would have to disarm or Germany would be entitled to rearm.

Both the realities of the world situation and the view other powers took of the situation were quite different. The fact was that the former enemies of Germany had disarmed to a very considerable extent. They had not only participated in a number of international naval disarmament arrangements, but they had drastically reduced their land forces as well. England and the United States, to all intents and purposes, had dissolved the huge continental armies they had built up in the world war. The American army in 1933 numbered 135,000; the British army had been reduced to about the same size. In both countries the vast armaments factories that once poured forth a flood of war materials had been either dismantled or converted to peacetime use. Only the olive-drab color of America's mailboxes reminded the knowledgeable that its productivity had once outpaced the war's seemingly insatiable requirements. In Eastern Europe, the great armies of the czar which Germany had once faced were no more. Several hundred miles further east, the Soviet Union was struggling to rebuild a military force, but dangers in the Far East were likely to keep it preoccupied for years. If three of the four great armies that had brought down imperial Germany had either vanished or been drastically reoriented, the Germans were not much interested in this fact, focusing their attention on the fourth army—that of France—and the new forces of France's allies, Poland and Czechoslovakia.

The French army had also been reduced substantially from its wartime level, the term of service reduced, and its equipment neglected. Perhaps more important in the long run was the nearly total mental ossification of its leadership. The burden of the war had been far greater for France than for Germany; its psychological aftermath was by no means over. The defensive mentality of the French would hang like lead weights on all their policies; the knowledge that their allies of the great war had left them would make France alternately stubborn and fearful; and the news they received of Germany's secret rearmament, paramilitary formations, and agitation for further revisions in the peace treaties made them look to the future with apprehension. The Germans, however, saw a very different picture. They saw that the French armed forces were several times the size of their own, that behind that French army stood large numbers of trained men who had passed through the army in the years when the long-term service requirement of the Treaty of Versailles had precluded a build-up of equivalent German reserves, that the French had heavy artillery and other weapons denied to them, and that their own frontier facing that formidable French army lay as open to invasion because of enforced demilitarization as it had at the time of the Ruhr occupation of 1923. In retrospect, it is clear that Germany was no more threatened by the French army of 1933 than were Luxembourg or Andorra—neighbors of France even weaker than Germany—but few people in Germany at the time recognized this fact. Added to the apparent preponderance, and hence in German eyes danger, of French military power was the military strength of the two neighbors of Germany who were allied to France, Czechoslovakia and Poland.

The Czech army was about the size of Germany's, but with larger trained reserves. Nothing suggests that the Germans were concerned about it, except in combination with other potential enemies. Czech-German relations in earlier years generally had been untroubled, and there was no expectation in Germany that any change would be initiated by the Czechs. There was greater apprehension about Poland. The Polish army was approximately twice the size of Germany's and could call upon extensive trained reserves. Furthermore, the exposed position of East Prussia, the experience of the Polish uprising in Upper Silesia, and the continuing friction over trade and minorities questions predisposed Germany to look for trouble from that quarter. The rising tide of nationalist agitation in Germany seemed to find an almost equally vehement echo in Poland, and the size of Poland's forces —in spite of the dangers from Russia on Poland's eastern frontier— obviously worried members of the German government. The relationship of this concern to the development of German-Polish relations will be reviewed in the next chapter, but it certainly also formed an element in Germany's view of the disarmament conference.

The general German negotiating position in the disarmament conference, that unless the other powers disarmed to Germany's level or below it—in view of their alliances with each other—Germany ought to be allowed some increase in its forces, had met with increasing sympathy, a sympathy reinforced by the general disillusionment with war in general that had followed the years of war and upheaval. Such attitudes had been given an immediate and pragmatic turn by the desire of most governments during the depression to save the money being spent on armaments. The five-power declaration of 11 December 1932 was a symptom of this closing of the gap between Germany and the other powers, and the plans proposed at Geneva in January and March 1933 may be understood as further steps along this road. Hitler's rise to power in Germany, however, initiated a drastic change in the situation.[68]

The other powers, especially France, were immediately alarmed by the new German regime. The bellicose tones of the new leaders, their past agitation against international reconciliation, the reports on an increase in the level of secret rearmament,[69] all reinforced the reluctance of France to make concessions to the German point of view, especially in the absence

68. Important for this subject are Gerhard Meinck, *Hitler und die deutsche Aufrüstung, 1933–1937* (Wiesbaden: Steiner, 1959); and Burkhart Mueller-Hillebrand, *Des Heer 1933–1945,* Vol. 1, *Das Heer bis zum Kriegsbeginn* (Darmstadt: Mittler, 1954).

69. See Georges Castellan, *Le réarmement clandestin du Reich 1930–1935* (Paris: Plon, 1954); and General Gauché, *Le deuxième bureau au travail (1935–1940)* (Paris: Amiot-Dumont, 1953).

of guarantees from Britain of support against future German aggression. The stiffening of the powers against Germany was also due to their reaction to the sight and sound of marching in Germany. The military value of the SA and other paramilitary formations so conspicuous on the German scene was undoubtedly exaggerated—even if sincerely feared—by Germany's neighbors, but those fears cannot simply be dismissed as unrealistic. If the hundreds of thousands who marched on Germany's streets were not yet trained reservists, this was obviously not because they lacked the will.[70]

How did Hitler view the Geneva negotiations? For Germany to leave again when it had just returned was obviously too risky. Because it would publicly reveal the real aims of the new regime, such a step could provoke the preventive action of other powers that Hitler most feared. On the other hand, Hitler had repeatedly explained before 1933 his belief that the improvements Germany could expect to make in its armed forces as a result of international negotiations would be quite useless. The pocket battleships of which Admiral Raeder was so proud were "little boats" good only for training.[71] Hitler's speech to the industrialists on 27 January 1932 had been very pointed. If Germany "wanted to solve its space problem," it would have to build up its strength. "That can never be accomplished by introducing a motion in the Reichstag to negotiate for the acquisition of a couple of heavy batteries, eight or ten tanks, twelve airplanes, or for all I care even a few squadrons—that doesn't add up to anything at all."[72] It should be noted that the weapons mentioned were precisely those prohibited to Germany by the Treaty of Versailles. One can see here Hitler's real attitude toward the subject of allowing Germany "samples" of these weapons, a matter discussed at great length in the disarmament negotiations in 1933. His attitude on this was consistent with his general outlook. He did not want a few weapons of the types prohibited Germany by the peace treaty because others had them, or because he thought Germany's honor was at stake. He knew that Germany would eventually need vast quantities of these weapons to win wars. The previously quoted comments of Hitler on the Geneva negotiations, made right after his accession to power, show that he understood that what he wanted could obviously not be attained in those negotiations. Similarly, his expressed plans for the reintroduction of conscription pointed in an entirely different direction from the aims of the disarmament conference. How then to proceed on the diplomatic stage where Germany was caught by the circumstances of the moment?

The answer to this question is more likely to be obscured than found by tracing the actual course of the conversations and negotiations in Geneva and the various capitals through the tedious months that preceded

70. See Heinrich Bennecke, *Die Reichswehr und der "Röhm-Putsch"* (Munich: Olzog, 1964).

71. *Hitlers zweites Buch,* p. 147 and n. 1.

72. Domarus, 1: 85–86.

the final failure of the disarmament conference.[73] The nature of German policy can best be understood if the directives issued to the German delegation to Geneva are examined against the double background of German rearmament policy and the international setting. From the beginning, there were present in the instructions given to the German delegation certain elements that pointed to an eagerness to leave the discussions altogether. A revealing indication of this tendency was the instruction sent to Geneva on 25 February to walk out of the committee dealing with air force questions if it discussed a French proposal to internationalize civil aviation ahead of disarmament schemes. The delegation immediately replied from Geneva that these instructions were not in accord with established German policy and would produce an unfavorable reaction. A lengthy telegraphic and telephonic hassle produced a compromise; but the exchange, in which Göring and defense minister von Blomberg played important parts, shows that the inclination to walk out was very strong indeed.[74] In this instance, as in the instructions given to the delegation for their conduct in general, the emphasis was not on attempting to prevent a break or on finding solutions but on the purely propagandistic aspect. At the cabinet meeting of 8 February, at which Hitler had explained that rearmament had the first priority for the next four to five years, von Neurath and von Blomberg briefly discussed the expiring arms truce established by the disarmament conference. Every effort was to be made to avoid extension of the truce, but if no other power took this position, "we must not be the only ones to do so, since our intention to rearm would thereby be manifested too soon."[75] Similarly von Neurath wrote to Nadolny on 15 February 1933 that "if a failure of the conference really proves inevitable, the lack of an intention to disarm on the part of France must appear as the cause."[76]

The specific terms of the various disarmament schemes therefore were examined from the point of view of how much they would hinder or favor the rearmament program that the German government had decided upon in any case. The proposal for standardizing armies, for example, was accepted eventually by Germany—with due publicity stressing the great concession thus made—because it could be made to fit into Berlin's plan to change the recruitment policy of the German army, depending less on long-term service by professionals than upon short-term service by conscripts. As Nadolny expressed it: "The statements of [French air minister]

73. Key documents on these negotiations have been published in *B. D.*, 2d, Vols. 4, 5, and 6; *G. D.*, C, Vols. 1 and 2; U. S. 1933, 1 and 1934, 1; *D. D. F.*, 1st, Vols. 2 and 3. Until the Italian documents are published, a key source is Pompeo Aloisi, *Journal (25 juillet 1932–14 juin 1936)* (trans. by Maurice Vaussard, Paris: Plon, 1957).

74. The exchange of messages, starting with the instruction No. 96 of 25 February 1933, is in T–120, 1557/3154/D 668575–593. Cf. the account in Paul Schmidt, *Statist auf diplomatischer Bühne 1923–45* (Bonn: Athenäum-Verlag, 1950), pp. 259–61.

75. *G. D.*, C, 1, No. 17.

76. Ibid., No. 20. Serial 7668, named as the source of this document, is not identified; for another copy, see T–120, 1557/3154/D 668508–11.

Pierre Cot make it appear possible that the framework proposed for standardization will be so developed and transformed through negotiations that it will permit the measures deemed necessary by us."[77] On the other hand, any specific proposal that might seriously interfere with rearmament had to be avoided. An example of this was budget limitations. Obviously, an agreed budget limitation system, combined with widely publicized budgets, would automatically call the attention of the world to Germany's real intentions as the stream of money poured into rearmament broke whatever limits might conceivably be established. On this subject there could be no compromise; and, although again the sharp tone of the instructions was slightly modified as a result of exchanges between the delegation and Berlin,[78] the views Hitler expressed on 15 March 1933 were explicit and never repudiated, namely that Germany must avoid any limitation or control of the military budget.[79]

The attitude of the German government can also be recognized in its handling of two other aspects of the disarmament conference early in 1933: the question of sending a cabinet member to Geneva and the possible reaffirmation of the Locarno Pact. The first of these may seem insignificant unless it is remembered that meetings at Geneva of prime ministers and foreign ministers had become an accepted part of the conduct of international relations. It is true that von Neurath finally did go to Geneva in September, but by then much had changed. In March, when the British decided to make one more great effort to secure an agreement, the British prime minister, Ramsay MacDonald, and the foreign secretary, Sir John Simon, went to Geneva, hoping to meet there with von Neurath or possibly Hitler. Neither would go, to the great disappointment of the other powers.[80] Since several other attempts to arrange high-level personal contact with Hitler and von Neurath also failed in the spring of 1933,[81] one may be permitted to conclude that the German government was reluctant to give importance to negotiations it considered unlikely to produce agreements sufficiently favorable to itself, particularly if they threatened to lead to commitments it would prefer to break. This was especially obvious in

77. Telephone message from Nadolny, 18 February 1933, *G. D.*, C, 1, No. 23; cf. the resulting directive to the delegation of 19 February, ibid., No. 26.

78. Ibid., Nos. 97, 106.

79. "A limitation on the budget is to be refused categorically," Memorandum of Kreutzwald, 15 March 1933, T–120, 1557/3154/D 668746. See also *G. D.*, C, 1, No. 94, and Werner Freiherr von Rheinbaben, *Viermal Deutschland* (Berlin: Argon Verlag, 1954), pp. 272–76 (Rheinbaben had been recalled to Berlin especially for the purpose of receiving instructions [von Neurath to Nadolny, tel. 124 of 7 March 1933, T–120, 1557/3154/D 668645].).

80. *B. D.*, 2d, 4, Nos. 257, 285, 288, 289, 295; *G. D.*, C, 1, Nos. 46, 49, 54, 56, 76; *D. D. F.*, 1st, 2, No. 377; U. S. 1933, 1:22–25; the draft of Bülow to Köster, telegram 114 of 15 March 1933, T–120, 1388/2784/D 540153.

81. *G. D.*, C, 1, Nos. 79, 92, 142, 255; *B. D.*, 2d, 5, Nos. 134, 162, 163, 164, 169, 188, 191; U. S. 1933, 1: 410–11, 165, 165–66, 182; Memorandum of Bülow, 21 May 1933, T–120, 2371/4602/E 189067.

the issue, incidental to other questions at the time but indicative as a harbinger of German policy, of including a reaffirmation of the Locarno agreements in the text of a no-force declaration discussed at Geneva. German wishes were respected in the formula finally adopted, and the documents show that in excluding a reference to Locarno the German government was trying to avoid reaffirming its obligations with regard to the demilitarization of the Rhineland before Germany was ready to demand "a material change in the Locarno provisions."[82]

Determined to rearm, the Germans used the negotiations to secure whatever advantages they could without committing themselves to agreements they would have to break conspicuously and quickly. Care was exercised, however, that Germany not give the appearance of sabotaging the conference: "Work for a positive conclusion is to be preferred to rearmament without a treaty."[83] The developments of the spring and summer of 1933, however, made the other powers increasingly reluctant to consent to the ever-growing German demands. Since neither Britain nor France was willing to take military action, Germany could continue to rearm secretly while publicly making concessions from time to time and offering promises of peace and friendship to all. Once Germany's position seemed to allow more drastic steps, this policy would give way to an even bolder one; in the meantime, the other powers faced the difficult problem of salvaging something from a conference on which so many hopes were centered.

The British thought it best to get some kind of agreement, hoping thereby to set at least some limit to German rearmament. They argued for this position consistently in 1933 and 1934. The French, on the other hand, insisted that the new developments inside Germany that had given rise to increasingly extravagant demands both precluded further French disarmament and made concessions to German rearmament all the more dangerous.[84] This divergence in policies could not be bridged. The ingenuity exercised by the United States in trying to find a way out was of no help either.[85] The agonizing search for an answer to the dilemna continued unsuccessfully for months.

In 1933 one major effort to break the deadlock was made inside the conference, and one was made outside—the former by Britain, the latter by Italy. The effort within the conference was launched by the British government when Ramsay Macdonald on 16 March presented a plan for disarmament that included specific figures for the size of the army of each country as well as a number of other specific proposals.[86] This last comprehensive attempt to meet as far as possible both the general desire for disarmament and the point of view of the various participants to the

82. Neurath to Nadolny, 24 February 1933, *G. D.*, C, 1, No. 37. See also ibid., Nos. 36, 38; *B. D.*, 2d, 4, No. 282; U. S. 1933, 1:14–16.

83. *G. D.*, C, 1, No. 94.

84. These two approaches are well defined in *B. D.*, 2d, 4, No. 299, and 5, No. 161.

85. *B. D.*, 2d, 4, No. 294; U. S. 1933, 1:36.

86. *B. D.*, 2d, 4, Appendix IV; U. S. 1933, 1:43–54.

conference failed of general acceptance. As Eduard Beneš, the Czech foreign minister, accurately predicted, each power tried to change that part of the MacDonald plan it did not like, thus making it worse for all the others.[87] The new plan postponed but did not avert a crisis in the conference.

Brought forward at almost the same time as the MacDonald plan for disarmament at Geneva was Mussolini's project for a pact between the four powers, Italy, Britain, France, and Germany, to settle certain key issues among themselves—and thus to some extent at least outside the League. Before this proposal, which came to be known as the Four-Power Pact, can be described, its place in Mussolini's policy toward revision of the peace treaties in general and toward Germany in particular first must be assessed.[88]

The Italian leader was inclined to be impulsive and to place an intrinsic value on action, whether or not objectively warranted by the circumstances. This tendency gave to Italian foreign policy an erratic quality, an alternation of calmer periods with sudden experiments and extravagances. Perhaps this could be termed the outward manifestation of the inner conflict between Italy's desire for great power status and its recognition of its lack of resources for this role, a conflict accentuated in the person of Mussolini by an emotional commitment to activism, a hope of glory and power, and a mind that was shrewd and calculating and not without insights when Il Duce was willing to use it. In the early 1930s, few would have guessed that his impulses would lead to disaster for his country and himself; most were impressed by the apparent success of his effort to provide Italy with a stable government that allowed for some opportunity of internal development and international respect. His previous adventures, like the Corfu incident of 1923, had alarmed the world just as his repressive domestic policies had antagonized liberals everywhere; but Mussolini's voice was heard in the world with respect, though not with affection.[89]

Mussolini hoped that in a changing world Italy's power and prestige would grow. The settlement of 1919 had left it dissatisfied in Africa and the

87. Beneš telegram to Czech foreign ministry, 20 March 1933, Czech document in T–120, 1041/1809/413891–92 (excerpt in Berber, *Prager Akten,* No. 4). For other reactions to the MacDonald plan, see *B. D.*, 2d, 4, No. 310; *G. D.*, C, 1, Nos. 103, 106; Hoesch to Neurath telegram 69 of 25 March 1933, T–120, 1558/3154/D 668859–60; Major-General Arthur C. Temperley, *The Whispering Gallery of Europe* (London: Collins, 1938), chap. 12.

88. A summary of the negotiations on the basis of the published documents in Lothar Krecker, "Die diplomatischen Verhandlungen über den Viererpakt vom 15. Juli 1933," *Die Welt als Geschichte,* 21 (1961), 227–37; a more detailed account in Konrad H. Jarausch, *The Four-Power Pact 1933* (Madison: State Historical Society of Wisconsin, 1965); added details from the Aloisi papers in Fulvio d'Amoja, *Declino e prima crisi dell' Europa di Versailles* (Milan: D. A. Giuffré, 1967), chap. 4.

89. It might be said that this picture of Il Duce is unduly generous, as he had expressed himself as clearly in favor of war—which would ruin Italy—as Hitler; but given Mussolini's more cautious policies, one may be allowed to wonder if he would have taken the plunge had Hitler not provided the opportunity. Even in the Ethiopian venture, he might well not have run the risks he did if it had not been for his knowledge that Britain and France were worried about Germany. But then the historian may be influenced by the fact that Mussolini is somehow a less unattractive figure in comparison with Hitler.

Adriatic. He was, therefore, not interested in the maintenance of the European status quo. If there were changes in that status quo, Italy as one of the great powers would benefit, provided certain conditions obtained. Of these the most important was that the changes could not be determined exclusively by the League of Nations. In that body, the doctrine of the equality of states and the combined pressures of the small would inhibit the aggrandizement of the great. Any changes should be the product of negotiations among the major powers, of which Italy was clearly one. The more fluid the situation, the better for Italy, and hence the support Mussolini extended to elements striving for a revision of the peace settlement. Here lay the origin of his contacts with the nationalist movement in Hungary in the 1920s, his support of Croatian terrorists and of the IMRO (Internal Macedonian Revolutionary Organization), and his relations with the nationalist right in Germany.

There is considerable evidence, some of which will be reviewed chronologically, that Mussolini was afraid that unlimited German rearmament and unlimited German strength would be dangerous to Italian interests not only in regard to the Austrian and South Tirol questions but also for Italy's ambitions in Southeast Europe generally. On the other hand, he was also convinced that a stronger Germany would make a more adequate counterweight to France, the backer of the Little Entente, and would enhance the value of Italy's friendship to both France and England. Mussolini was therefore willing to sponsor a degree of German rearmament as well as territorial revision in its favor.

That the Hitler movement might provide a government aggressive in its foreign policy and more congenial to him in its domestic politics than the Weimar Republic had long been evident to Mussolini. If the National Socialists argued for the *Anschluss* of Austria like most other Germans, they at least differed from the general position of German nationalist groups on the subject of South Tirol. Contacts with the National Socialist movement dated back many years, as has already been shown. Although the plans for a meeting between Mussolini and Hitler had never been realized, Mussolini had met other prominent National Socialists. At the time the von Papen government fell in November 1932, Göring, Rosenberg, and the rightist veterans' leader Franz Seldte were in Rome. Mussolini immediately conferred with Göring and provided him with a plane to return to Germany.[90] Mussolini's special contact man to the National Socialists, Giuseppe Renzetti, congratulated Hitler on his appointment as chancellor on behalf of Il Duce right after Hitler had seen Hindenburg on 30 January; and Hitler summoned Renzetti to the Chancellery on the next day.[91] Hitler asked the

90. Von Hassell telegram 248 of 18 November 1932, T–120, 2700/5737/H 028592; Schubert, pp. 222–23.

91. Renzetti to Mussolini, 31 January 1933, T–586, container 491, frames 050275–76; the first page of Renzetti's report to Mussolini of 30 January is missing from the film, the other two pages are on the next two frames.

Italian to tell Mussolini that he would follow a policy of friendship for Italy and wanted to talk to him personally, perhaps flying to Rome for a private visit. Renzetti replied that Mussolini had watched Hitler's rise to power with favor and pleasure, and that Italy's foreign policy was simple—cooperation of the four great powers. Italy, Germany, and Britain could get together with or without France, but cooperation would be impossible if any single one of them concluded an agreement with France.[92] This reference to four-power cooperation reflected earlier pronouncements by Mussolini, echoed a speech Rosenberg had made in Rome with Hitler's approval at the time of his visit the previous November,[93] and was to become a major theme of European diplomatic discussion in the first half of 1933.

When the German ambassador to Italy, Ulrich von Hassell, saw Mussolini on 6 February, in reply to the special greetings sent the German chancellor,[94] Il Duce expressed his pleasure at the formation of the new government and his anticipation that Germany and Italy would coordinate their policies closely after the German elections, scheduled for early March, had strengthened the newly formed coalition. These initial exchanges of greetings and congratulations were followed by several weeks during which there was some cooperation between the German and Italian delegations at the disarmament conference, but the main emphasis was on other matters. The Germans were not quite sure how closely to tie themselves to Italy; there was considerable internal division of opinion that appears not to have led to any clear conclusion[95] and in which Hitler was not directly involved, perhaps because he was concentrating on the election campaign. At this time the German advocate of closer cooperation between the two powers was von Hassell, while the foreign ministry was more cautious. A conservative whose subsequent break with the Hitler regime should not obscure his extreme nationalistic leanings,[96] von Hassell wanted a closer relationship with Italy based on interests the two nations had in common but without entering into an explicit alliance. He was thus at first ahead and later behind official German policy. He was ahead at first because the German foreign ministry still had considerable influence on the conduct of current diplomatic relations and was unwilling to agree to what von Hassell suggested, in part

92. Renzetti went to Rome to transmit this message to Mussolini in person (Aloisi, *Journal,* 13 February 1933, p. 62). Almost simultaneously, Cerruti tried to get this unofficial contact ended, now that Hitler had secured power and could be dealt with through official channels (ibid., 14 February, p. 63).

93. See Schubert, p. 223.

94. *G. D.,* C, 1, No. 12, note 3 states that no record of the Berlin instructions for this has been found; the instructions are in T–120, 1388/2784/D.540129.

95. *G. D.,* C, 1, Nos. 14, 27, 35, 40, 64.

96. He belonged to the German Nationalist party (DNVP) in 1918–19 and later joined the NSDAP. In December 1937, shortly before his dismissal, he was smuggling antiques out of Italy for Göring via the diplomatic pouch (Emessen, pp. 28–32)! Until far into World War II, he wanted to keep most of Hitler's conquests for a post-Hitler Germany. See the apt characterization in H. R. Trevor-Roper, "Hitlers Kriegsziele," *Vierteljahrshefte für Zeitgeschichte,* 8, No. 2 (April 1960), 126–28.

apparently precisely because he was the man who suggested it.[97] He would be behind later when the two dictators wanted to make the ties closer than von Hassell thought wise. In this early stage, however, other issues came to the fore. Discussion of a meeting between Hitler and Mussolini continued without definite result.[98] The new initiative this time came from Mussolini.

In the first days of March 1933, Mussolini decided to come forward with a plan that would simultaneously settle what appeared to be the most pressing and dangerous European problems and at the same time provide a mechanism for handling international disputes in the future. In the absence of the relevant Italian documents, it is not possible to present Mussolini's plan in full detail, but quite enough is known to give a picture entirely adequate for an understanding of German policy and reactions to it.[99] The problems that seemed to call for immediate solution were certain demands of Hungary and Germany. Hungary was to receive forthwith certain territories of solid Magyar population that had been assigned to other countries by the peace treaty of Trianon. Germany was to receive a narrow strip, five to ten miles wide, along the Baltic coast—including the city of Danzig—in order to provide East Prussia with a land connection to the rest of Germany, for which Poland was to receive some undefined compensation.[100] For the future handling of international disputes Mussolini visualized a sort of four-power directory, revising the peace treaties, arranging for German

97. The documents are filled with quarrels between the foreign ministry, especially von Neurath himself, and von Hassell; see, e.g. *G. D.*, C, 1, No. 64, n. 2, p. 385, n. 3, No. 241, n. 4. After years of work in the files, the author cannot avoid the impression that personal rivalry played an important part in this; von Neurath looked on von Hassell as his rival for the post of foreign minister, while von Hassell felt that he knew more about the proper policy to follow toward Italy (where von Neurath had once served). It is ironic that von Hassell and von Neurath were sacked on the same day in 1938; von Neurath had been a hardly innocent bystander when his other rival, Nadolny, was unceremoniously dumped in the summer of 1934.

98. *G. D.*, C, 1, No. 64; Köster to Bülow No. 167 of 15 March 1933, T–120, 1388/2784/D 540152; Bülow to Köster No. 114 of 15 March 1933, ibid., frame D 540153; *D. D. F.*, 1st, 2, Nos. 332, 339, 354, 424.

99. The account of Mussolini's initial project is based on the following sources: *B. D.*, 2d, 5, Nos. 37, 44, 45, 216; *G. D.*, C, 1, Nos. 68, 83, 109; U. S. 1933, 1:396–98; *D. D. F.*, 1st, 2, Nos. 368, 382, 391; Aloisi, *Journal*, 4 March 1933, pp. 77–80; Garrett (Rome) telegram 14 of 20 March 1933, telegram 17 of 21 March and dispatch 1853 of 24 March, State 740.0011 Four-Power Pact/5, 9, 24. Jarausch does not attempt to analyze the earliest aspects of Mussolini's plan. For the British government's reaction to the project, see the notes on *B. D.*, 2d, 5, No. 37, in the Foreign Office records in the Public Record Office (hereafter cited as Foreign Office), C 2148/175/22.

100. It should be noted that Mussolini's idea of a strip no more than 10–15 kilometers deep would have included the cities of Danzig, Langfuhr, Oliva, and Zoppot (to use the 1933 names) as well as the Polish port of Gdynia within the area to be ceded to Germany, but excluded at least half the territory of the free city as defined by the peace treaty. This scheme for partitioning the free city of Danzig meant drawing the border East-West, as contrasted with the North-South lines considered in 1938–39 (Gerhard L. Weinberg, "A Proposed Compromise over Danzig in 1939?" *Journal of Central European Affairs*, 14, No. 4 (Jan. 1955), pp. 334–38). For geographical data see Nikolaus Creutzberg, *Atlas der Freien Stadt Danzig* (Danzig: Danziger Verlagsgesellschaft, 1936).

equality of arms by stages, and generally cooperating in extra-European matters—such as the colonial question—as well as intra-European issues. All this was to be accomplished within the framework of the League; Mussolini apparently assumed that once the four great powers were in agreement, the other countries would have no alternative but to acquiesce in their decisions.

Mussolini broached these ideas, still in a tentative form, to the French by 2 March 1933[101] and told the Germans about them on 10 March;[102] but even as he prepared the proposals in draft form, he began to have doubts about the proposals relating to immediate territorial revision. The first days of March 1933 brought a crisis in German-Polish relations in which it became quite evident that Poland would fight rather than allow revision. It is at least possible that the Westerplatte incident of 6 March was in part the Polish answer to Mussolini's territorial scheme.[103] In any case, although he instructed the Italian delegation at Geneva to support the Germans on the Westerplatte incident,[104] Mussolini began to think of deferring territorial change for some time, "since Germany was at present not even a match for the Polish army," as he had his ambassador explain to von Neurath.[105] During the Rome visit of MacDonald and Sir John Simon, therefore, the plans for territorial change were first briefly touched on and then dropped from the discussion. This suited the Germans as well as the Poles, since Germany was not interested in any territorial compromise. "Territorial revisions can be broached only when Germany has become strong militarily, politically, and financially. . . . Our main objective remains revision of the eastern border. Only a total solution comes into question. Interim and partial solutions are to be rejected. Likewise a special solution for Danzig should be rejected," von Neurath told the cabinet on 7 April.[106] Because of Mussolini's changed approach, the Germans were not required in 1933 to explain their position publicly. Privately they had already waved off a slightly more generous French proposal. It was simply not yet time for Germany to get all it wanted: "there will be only one more partition of Poland."[107]

101. *B. D.*, 2d, 5, No. 37.

102. *G. D.*, C, 1, No. 68.

103. Until more evidence from the French, Italian, and Polish archives becomes available, it will not be possible to state with any assurance how soon Mussolini's scheme for the cession of a coastal strip became known in Warsaw. The Westerplatte, of course, would have been included in such a strip. Cf. *G. D.*, C, 1, No. 34. No reference to this facet of the issue is made in the articles on the Westerplatte incident and on the Four-Power Pact by Jósef Lipski, reprinted in translation in Waclaw Jedrzejewicz (ed.), *Diplomat in Berlin, 1933–1939, Papers and Memoirs of Jósef Lipski, Ambassador of Poland* (New York: Columbia University Press, 1968) (hereafter cited as *Lipski Papers*), pp. 46–70. See also *D. D. F.*, 1st, 2, Nos. 227, 384; Hassell report I 170 (on Szembek's January 1933 visit to Rome), 25 January 1933, T–120, 3404/8820/E 614069–075.

104. Aloisi, *Journal,* 10 March 1933, p. 86.

105. *G. D.*, C, 1, No. 83.

106. Ibid., No. 142.

107. Ibid., No. 18; cf. ibid., No. 19, with its reference to similar views of Hitler.

The other portion of Mussolini's program was to suffer a similar fate, though more slowly. The proposed text of a Four-Power Pact drafted by Mussolini himself referred explicitly to cooperation for revision of the peace treaties, equality of arms for Germany by stages, and cooperation in regard to colonies. The Germans wanted to remove the limitations on revision implicit in tying it to the League, and also to remove French influence on the stages of their rearmament.[108] The British argued for removing the reference to colonies, while the French were skeptical about the whole project and, in part in response to pressure from the Little Entente, insisted on modifications in the sections on revision and disarmament.[109] The period between mid-March and early June therefore was one in which complicated negotiations led to a continuing redrafting of the pact, slowly reducing its significance, until the four powers signed a collection of generalities that was neither ratified nor applied. The French government had insisted on changes that tied the pact to the League and the sanctity of treaties; and the Germans —at times under pressure from Italy—found it expedient to agree to a text that promised them little.[110] Mussolini's prestige was at stake, and he therefore pressed for some conclusion, however devoid of concrete meaning. The negotiations themselves had an advantage for Germany, at least in Mussolini's view, by providing it with time to rearm unmolested.[111] During the same period, Italy was also becoming stronger.[112] The difficulties of reaching agreement, however, precluded the meeting of the four heads of government mooted earlier in the negotiations. By the time the tortuous negotiations led to a conclusion in July, international attention had long since shifted elsewhere.[113]

Another area in which Germany signed a treaty in the summer of 1933 was also one in which Mussolini had strongly urged Hitler to be conciliatory. In this case, consideration of domestic rather than foreign problems dominated German policy. The first major break in the atmosphere of hostility that surrounded Hitler's Germany in its initial phase was the concordat signed by Cardinal Secretary of State Pacelli and Vice-Chancellor von

108. Ibid., No. 84.

109. The negotiations are summarized in Jarausch, chaps. III, IV, and V. Additional documents not published are von Neurath's memorandum RM 490 of 7 April 1933, T–120, 2382/4619/E 197654 and the telegrams of Štefan Osuský, Czech minister in Paris, to Prague of 19 March and 21 March 1933, Czech documents in T–120, 1041/1809/413889 and 413894–95.

Important information on Rumania's role in the negotiations may be found in I. M. Oprea, *Nicolae Titulescu's Diplomatic Activity* (trans. by Andrei Bantas; Bucharest: Academy of the Socialist Republic of Romania, 1968), pp. 116–19.

110. The analysis of Dertinger's "Informationsbericht Nr. 18 vom 10. Juni 1933," stresses the concessions made to avoid the isolation of Germany if she refused to sign. The German foreign ministry assumed that the pact was to be taken seriously, hence its reluctance during the negotiations. Bundesarchiv, Brammer, Z.Sg. 101/26, f. 429–33.

111. *G. D.,* C, 1, Nos. 87, 151.

112. Ibid., No. 122.

113. This point is obscured by the narrow focus of Jarausch's book.

Papen on 20 July 1933, following three and a half months of negotiations.[114] These negotiations took place while the Hitler regime was primarily interested in consolidating its hold on power inside Germany. The prior opposition to national socialism on religious grounds of the bulk of German Catholics posed a major obstacle to the enthusiastic enrollment of a large portion of the German population into what was to become the new mainstream of German life. The Center party and its Bavarian relative, the Bavarian People's party, provided for the political representation and organization of Catholic interests. Hitler mounted an exceedingly clever attack on this potential source of opposition, weakening possible arguments against his movement on ideological grounds by pretending to support Christianity as well as undermining all political parties by a combination of terror and persuasion.[115]

The negotiations for a concordat with the Vatican were initiated by the German government following the beginnings of a rapprochement between the new regime and the Catholic church inside Germany in late March. By promising concessions based on prior drafts but going beyond those the Weimar Republic had been willing to make, Hitler hoped to have Vatican backing withdrawn from the Center party. The removal of the Catholic clergy from any role in German political life would aid in the suppression of Catholic political parties, parties that could not yet be subjected openly to all the terrorist methods applied to Marxist parties. Once the Catholics had been deprived of the political organizations that might provide them with a potential defense against the government, whatever concessions might be made to the clergy in Germany and the Vatican in Rome could be vitiated in practice by an all-powerful regime.[116] The interest of Hitler in an agreement that would help him toward this goal is obvious; the intents and hopes of the Vatican are not nearly so clear.

In the years of the Weimar Republic, the Vatican had signed concordats with the three German states having the largest Catholic populations—Prussia, Bavaria, and Baden—and the overwhelming majority of German Catholics thus already had whatever protection concordats might provide.

114. Summaries of the situation and negotiations leading to the concordat may be found in William M. Harrigan, "Nazi Germany and the Holy See, 1933–1936: The Historical Background of *Mit brennender Sorge*," *Catholic Historical Review*, 47, No. 2 (July 1961), 164–73; Bracher, *Machtergreifung*, pp. 341–45; Karl Otmar Freiherr von Aretin, "Kaas, Papen und das Konkordat von 1933," *Vierteljahrshefte für Zeitgeschichte*, 14, No. 3 (July 1966), 252–79. Ernst Deuerlein, *Das Reichskonkordat* (Düsseldorf: Patmos-Verlag, 1956) is especially useful for its background material and for showing how the 1933 negotiations must be related to the prior efforts at a concordat between the Vatican and the Weimar Republic.

115. It should be noted that similar motives had suggested to Hitler his earlier attempted contact with the Vatican in 1931. See Deuerlein, p. 107, for a summary of this episode, and pp. 294–95 for the text of the report of the Bavarian minister to the Vatican of 11 May 1931 on Göring's visit to Rome shortly before.

116. In the process, von Papen no doubt hoped to strengthen his position in the government by a diplomatic triumph and to take revenge on the Center party for its disdain of his imagined abilities.

There were, however, other considerations and possibilities. Any refusal on the part of the Vatican to sign with the new regime a national concordat on what seemed very favorable terms, based on a draft worked out years before in negotiations with the government of the republic, might lead to the denunciation of the existing concordats. This must have seemed an especially dangerous possibility because the National Socialists had voted against the ratification of those concordats in the respective state legislatures. Furthermore, there was the real possibility that the new government of Germany would embark immediately on a violent campaign against the Catholic Church. An agreement signed by the new government itself might restrain such a campaign, or at least provide German Catholics with a clear position to defend. And, of course, there was no way of knowing how long the new regime would last.

There can have been few illusions in the Vatican about Hitler's willingness to adhere to the terms of treaty commitments. Attached to the concordat was a secret protocol that has not received the attention it deserves, not so much for its specific terms as for its basic nature.[117] It provided certain exemptions for German divinity students and other special arrangements in "the event of a reorganization of the present German military system by the introduction of general military service." The secret protocol of 20 July 1933 thus dealt with the contingency of Germany breaking its treaty commitment prohibiting conscription, an indication that the Vatican must have had a rather clear view of the new government's lack of good faith. If the concordat was signed nevertheless, it may be taken as a measure of the desperation with which the Vatican hoped to protect the continued existence of the religious institutions of Catholicism in Germany so that they might keep the sacramental structure available to the faithful.[118] The same issue was to recur with increasing acuteness in later years; it would play an important role in the question of euthanasia in the winter of 1939–40 and the extermination of the Jews beginning in 1941, but here the Church faced it for the first time.[119]

The Hitler government, from its point of view, correctly thought the concordat its first major diplomatic triumph that both made Germany appear more respectable abroad and helped clear the way to total power inside Germany.[120] The government, as Cardinal Pacelli had anticipated, began to violate the terms of the concordat immediately; and the subsequent his-

117. Text in *G. D.*, C, 1, pp. 678–79. This aspect of the concordat was praised to the German cabinet by von Papen as one of its great advantages (ibid., No. 362); there were discussions about the protocol in 1935 when conscription was introduced (T–120, 2673/5575/passim) and in 1939 when Germany mobilized for the attack on Poland (*G. D.*, D, 7, No. 432). The British and French governments both found out about the protocol in 1933 (Foreign Office C 7995 and C 9602/3244/18).

118. *B. D.*, 2d, 5, No. 342.

119. The best brief survey at present is Guenter Lewy, *The Catholic Church and Nazi Germany* (New York: McGraw-Hill, 1964).

120. See Hitler's explanation to the cabinet in *G. D.*, C, 1, No. 362.

tory of German-Vatican relations is one of continuing friction, in which the Vatican based its protests on the written promises of the German government. The growing intensity of the National Socialist struggle against the Catholic Church inside Germany was restrained temporarily in 1934 by the approaching plebiscite in the predominantly Catholic Saar territory; but once the Catholic clergy and laity there had done what Hitler wanted them to do, swelling the vote for a return to Germany, the barriers were down. The years 1935 and 1936 were a time of rising tension accompanying the increasing number of attacks on the institutions, organizations, and doctrines of German Catholicism. The possibility of a public protest by Pope Pius XI against the persecution of the Catholic Church and the advance of the neo-pagan movement in Germany had been ventilated as early as December 1933, but was postponed as efforts were made toward negotiations to relieve the situation.[121] Repeated efforts by Mussolini, starting with a long talk at their first meeting in June 1934, failed to dissuade Hitler from his course.[122] The National Socialist regime was no more restrained in its religious policy by a treaty it had signed than in its rearmament policy in the absence of a treaty. As the tension within Germany mounted, the pope became increasingly alarmed. Pius XI was not a man to remain quiet indefinitely. In agreement with the German Catholic clergy, he decided to call public attention to the persecutions and their meaning for all Catholics in and outside Germany. Using a draft prepared mainly by Cardinal Faulhaber of Munich and Cardinal Pacelli, Pius XI issued the encyclical *Mit brennender Sorge* (With burning concern), which was read from the pulpit in all Catholic churches in Germany on 21 March 1937.[123]

If Germany's relations with the Vatican were clouded in spite of the concordat, its relations with Protestant countries, especially England and the Scandinavian nations, were gravely affected by the struggle within the German Protestant community.[124] The National Socialist effort to integrate the German Protestants into one essentially anti-Christian system at first appeared to have considerable success. In church elections on 23 July 1933 two-thirds of the Protestants voting heeded the call of the nominal Catholic

121. Harrigan, pp. 173–98.

122. For this aspect of the Hitler-Mussolini conversations see Mussolini to De Vecchi, 22 June 1934, T–586, container 491, frames 050279–80.

123. Two useful collections of material on this subject are Johann Neuhäusler, *Kreuz und Hakenkreuz* (2 vols. in one, Munich: Katholische Kirche, 1946) and [Walter Mariaux (ed.)], *The Persecution of the Catholic Church in the Third Reich* (New York: Longmans Green, 1942) (on this publication see Max Beloff [ed.], *On the Track of Tyranny* [London: Vallentine Mitchell, 1960], pp. 212ff.; and Ludwig Volk, "Anonymous no Longer," *Wiener Library Bulletin*, 18 [1964], 17). The diplomatic correspondence between the Vatican and the German government for 1933–37 has been published in Dieter Albert (ed.), *Der Notenwechsel zwischen dem Heiligen Stuhl und der Deutschen Reichsregierung*, 1, *Von der Ratifizierung des Reichskonkordats bis zur Enzyklika "Mit brennender Sorge"* (Mainz: Matthias-Grünewald-Verlag, 1965).

124. A good introduction to the domestic aspect in Bracher, *Machtergreifung*, pp. 326–41.

Hitler by voting for the neo-pagan candidates to take over the Protestant churches. Opposition among the Protestant clergy was however, beginning to be heard; and this opposition received further impetus from a great rally of the "Religious Association of Germanic Christians" (*Glaubensbewegung Deutsche Christen*) in Berlin in November 1933, when the public denunciation of the Old Testament, the demand for the removal of Paul from the New Testament, and the recasting of Jesus into a Germanic war hero opened the eyes of many who had hitherto kept them firmly closed. The resulting accentuation of the divisions in German Protestantism and the attendant persecution of those ministers who formed the confessional church had widespread international repercussions.

As the land of Luther, Germany was a center of attention for all Protestants, but especially those in Scandinavia and England who looked to the German Reformation for their immediate spiritual origins. In these countries the reaction to the church conflict in Germany was most negative; the semi-open character of German society, readily accessible to travelers and reporters, and the international ties of the various national Protestant churches assured widespread knowledge of the developing situation.[125] The German foreign ministry used reports on the impact abroad of religious persecution at home in attempts to influence Hitler to moderate the struggle with the church.[126] Because the international uproar threatened to interfere with foreign acquiescence in German rearmament, Hitler made a tactical adjustment in the struggle with the Protestant churches late in 1934.[127] The public image was changed; the most offensive of the government's new clerical appointees were dropped. Instead, the party now pretended neutrality in the internal affairs of the Protestant churches, and while continuing to persecute the confessional church, the National Socialists placed their main emphasis on the undermining of Christianity by quietly furthering the neo-pagan movement and restricting the religious training of the young. Such methods were less conspicuous and therefore less offensive to the outside world, but all the more effective at home.[128] After the Saar plebiscite of 1935, the road to new measures was open here as well, and the regard of the government for opinion abroad steadily lessened.

125. For reports on such foreign reactions see *G. D.,* C, 3, Nos. 18, 211, 218, 246.

126. Ibid., Nos. 15, 213, 225.

127. Ibid., Nos. 251, 252, 276, 279, 282; Bracher, *Machtergreifung,* pp. 338–39. The role of foreign policy considerations in Hitler's decision is made very clear in Klaus Scholder, "Die evangelische Kirche in der Sicht der nationalsozialistischen Führung bis zum Kriegsausbruch," *Vierteljahrshefte für Zeitgeschichte,* 16, No. 1 (Jan. 1968), 23–25, and Ernst C. Helmreich, "The Arrest and Freeing of the Protestant Bishops of Württemberg and Bavaria, September–October 1934," *Central European History,* 2, No. 2 (June, 1969), 159–69.

128. Hitler apparently explained this course to the leaders of the party at a meeting on 23 November 1934. See Sekretär des Führers, "Daten aus alten Notizbüchern," entry for 23.11.1934 on p. 3 (Library of Congress, Manuscript Division), and the reference in Hans-Günther Seraphim (ed.), *Das politische Tagebuch Alfred Rosenbergs 1934/35 und 1939/40* (Munich: Deutscher Taschenbuch Verlag, 1964) (hereafter cited as Rosenberg, *Tagebuch*), entry under 24 February 1935, p. 72.

3 Eastern Europe

German Policy toward Poland, the Soviet Union, Lithuania, and the Ukraine in 1933

Aspects of German-Polish relations in the early months of 1933 have already been referred to several times. Contemporaries, not without reason, looked upon them as particularly likely to touch off a new war. Much of the post-World War II research on this subject has been oriented around the question of whether or not the Polish leader, Marshal Pilsudski, considered or planned a preventive war on Germany in early March and late April 1933 and was held back by the reluctance of France to offer support.[1] This is, of course, a question of great intrinsic importance, but for an understanding of German policy in and after 1933 it must be viewed in a wider context. The German attitude toward Poland before 1933 has already been sketched. The propaganda for a change in the German-Polish border had gained substantial support elsewhere, and there were signs by the end of 1932 and the beginning of 1933 that the possibility of territorial revision in favor of Germany was being given serious consideration in France and Italy. The German government, as has been shown, was not yet interested, because the revision that might be attained was likely to be both limited and final. Nevertheless, the possibility of international pressure for some

1. The most detailed argument that there was such an intention on Pilsudski's part is found in Hans Roos, "Die Präventivkriegspläne Pilsudskis von 1933," *Vierteljahrshefte für Zeitgeschichte,* 3, No. 4 (Oct. 1955), pp. 344–63, and the same author's, *Polen und Europa, Studien zur polnischen Aussenpolitik 1931–1939* (Tübingen: Mohr, 1957), pp. 65–71. The opposing position is taken in Boris Čelovsky, "Pilsudskis Präventivkrieg gegen das nationalsozialistische Deutschland (Entstehung, Verbreitung und Widerlegung einer Legende)," *Die Welt als Geschichte,* 14, No. 1 (1954), pp. 53–70, and by Zygmunt J. Gasiorowski, "Did Pilsudski Attempt to Initiate a Preventive War in 1933?" *Journal of Modern History,* 27, No. 2 (June 1955), pp. 135–51. These articles contain extensive footnotes to sources on the subject, and these are generally *not* cited again here.

revision was sufficiently dangerous in Polish eyes to lead to a willingness to try new policies there; while at the same time Germany's new government was headed by a man whose views on relations with Poland were, as has been explained, somewhat different from those of his predecessors.

The Polish government had begun a reorientation of its foreign policy even before Hitler came to power. The relaxation of tension between Poland and the Soviet Union, signalized by their non-aggression pact of 25 July 1932, reflected the greater danger Poland seemed to face from Germany and the threat the Soviet Union appeared to face from Japan. Simultaneously, Poland began to conduct its foreign policy more independently of France, in part fearful of being let down by France, in part because of national pride, in part because the position of Poland was automatically strengthened by the weakening of Russia's European position due to domestic travail in the early stages of industrialization and collectivization and the threat of Japan.[2] The loosening of Polish ties with France was personified by the new Minister of Foreign Affairs, Josef Beck, who moved up from the post of state secretary in that ministry on 2 November 1932. Young, vain, and with the reputation of having a slippery tongue, Beck was a coldly opportunistic follower of Pilsudski. His alignment with Germany was to leave him with a pro-German reputation, but this does not do justice to his views or his policy. Like Pilsudski, he wanted Poland to observe a balance in its relations with Germany and Russia—trying to keep its two neighbors from becoming so friendly that they might agree to divide Poland between them, or so hostile that they might force Poland to side with one against the other. Beck wanted Poland to play the part of a great power—which he would represent on the international scene—and thought it possible to do so in the face of a Germany determined to redraw the map of Europe. Unwilling to recognize that the peace settlement following World War I could not be abrogated so soon without damage to Poland, he tried to work out Poland's relations with Germany independent of other countries and institutions. If he has been condemned as blind, he might have pleaded that blindness was epidemic in Europe in the thirties and that Poland, vulnerable as it was, had fewer choices than France and Britain. There can be no doubt, on the other hand, that Beck had a special anti-French bias, in part related to his own expulsion from that country a decade earlier as *persona non grata,* and this bias accentuated the cooling of relations between France and Poland.[3]

Although there are indications that Pilsudski and Beck thought Hitler as a man of Austrian background less immediately dangerous than his traditionally anti-Polish predecessors, they were certainly worried observers of

2. For the "new course" in Polish foreign policy see Roos *Polen und Europa,* pp. 27–43; Roman Debicki, *Foreign Policy of Poland 1919–1939* (New York: Praeger, 1962), pp. 63–70.

3. For reports on this process by the Czech Minister to Poland see his report No. 10 of 2 February 1933 and No. 22 of 18 February, Czech documents in T–120, 1316/2376/D 497184–85 and D 49188–89.

the change of government in Germany.[4] At first there appeared to be good reason for concern. The election campaign that raged in Germany during February and early March saw the parties trying to outdo each other in appeals to nationalism and in these, the question of the eastern borders of Germany always played a major role. In the middle of the campaign, the London *Sunday Express* of 13 February reported an interview Hitler had given on 6 February in which he claimed that the whole area of the Polish Corridor should be returned to Germany. The German government immediately denied the accuracy of the report and insisted that Hitler had referred to the corridor merely as a great injustice to Germany, but the denials were not particularly convincing.[5] On the same day that Beck replied to the Hitler interview in a moderate speech, the government of the free city of Danzig denounced the Danzig-Polish agreement about the harbor police.[6] The combination of this action with National Socialist agitation in Danzig and the demonstrations of the S. A. near the border during the German election obviously alarmed the Polish government. Rumors of imminent border revision were being spread among Germans within Poland, and these of course came to the attention of the authorities. The German state secretary, Bernhard Wilhelm von Bülow, worried about the danger of Polish action, suggested an explanation for the origin of the rumors that reveals additional possible causes of Polish alarm. "Furthermore, I have the impression that some of the people assigned by us or on our behalf by the ministry of defense to collect information on possible ways to draw the boundaries in the future may not have kept complete security. It would be well to halt this collection of information entirely as long as the present tension continues."[7] The possibility of agreement to proceed to territorial revision by the four powers of Western and Central Europe may also have stimulated Warsaw to action. Under these circumstances, the Polish government decided to demonstrate its firmness on the Danzig—and by implication the corridor—issue.

On the morning of 3 March, two days before the German election, the Polish commissioner general in Danzig told the high commissioner of the League of Nations at Danzig, Helmer Rosting, that to protect the Polish

4. The Polish minister in Berlin told von Bülow on 30 January that he had been called six times that day from Warsaw and Geneva with questions about the policy of the new government (Memorandum of Bülow, 30 January 1933, T–120, 1430/2945/D 575807).

5. *G. D.*, C, 1, No. 22; Domarus, 1:201–2; Sackett (Berlin) dispatch 2194 of 14 February 1933, State 762.00/65.

6. On the Danzig issue see Hans L. Leonhardt, *Nazi Conquest of Danzig* (Chicago: University of Chicago Press, 1942); John Brown Mason, *The Danzig Dilemma* (Stanford: Stanford University Press, 1946); Ludwig Denne, *Das Danzig-Problem in der deutschen Aussenpolitik 1934–39* (Bonn: Röhrscheid, 1959); Ernst Ziehm, *Aus meiner politischen Arbeit in Danzig 1914–1939* (2d ed., Marburg/Lahn: Herder-Institut, 1960); Christoph M. Kimmich, *The Free City, Danzig and German Foreign Policy, 1919–1934* (New Haven: Yale University Press, 1968).

7. Memorandum by Bülow, 25 April 1933, T–120, 2371/4601/E 188730–31. See also the note of 30 June 1933, no author or file number, T–120, 2906/6176/E 463446.

position in the free city the Polish garrison at the Westerplatte, the depot at the harbor entrance, would be increased from 88 to about 200—clearly a token demonstration. This plan was carried out on 6 March over the objections of Rosting and the protests of the free city.[8] The issue was taken to Geneva, where the Polish government, under general pressure from the other states, agreed to withdraw its reinforcements. On 16 March this step was accomplished, and the Danzig government simultaneously agreed to revoke its action in regard to the harbor police. The Poles had made their point: they had shown their determination to defend their position in principle; in practice, of course, one hundred additional soldiers at the Westerplatte would have made no difference whatsoever.

It was at this time, in the middle of March, that Pilsudski supposedly consulted France about a possible preventive military action against Germany. That he himself considered the possibility and discussed it with several Polish officials is certain; that he suggested it to the French is in dispute.[9] The action against Germany, if one was seriously considered, was not a preventive war in the form of a general attack on Germany, but the occupation of parts of Germany to make it conform to the provisions of the peace treaty, including disarmament; in other words, a repetition of the action of France in 1920 and 1923. If the proposal was in fact made, it was rejected in Paris, but whether made or not, the possibility of such a Polish move became known in Germany; and it may be that the motive behind whatever Pilsudski actually did was to let the German government know that the possibility existed. In that case they would have to decide on the policy to follow: accommodation to the status quo, at least temporarily, or war. The Westerplatte incident would fit into such a strategy by showing Germany that Poland would not tacitly accept a National Socialist coup in Danzig or any other *fait accompli,* while simultaneously showing its willingness to accept—but not provoke—broader risks.

Hitler had to decide what to do in the face of this situation. He was at that time preoccupied with domestic developments in Germany right after the election—a period in which he took a series of drastic steps for the consolidation of his control, particularly the seizure of power in the German

8. In addition to the sources listed in n. 6 see *Lipski Papers*, pp. 46–59; Joseph Beck, *Dernier rapport* (Neuchatel: Éditions de la Baconnière, 1951), p. 25; Jules Laroche, *La Pologne de Pilsudski* (Paris: Flammarion, 1953), pp. 120–21; Richard Breyer, *Das Deutsche Reich und Polen 1932–1937* (Würzburg: Holzner, 1955), pp. 71–76; *Zweites Weissbuch der Deutschen Regierung* (Basel: Birkhäuser, 1939) (hereafter cited as *German White Book*), Nos. 21, 22, 24; *G. D.*, C, 1 (those documents initialed by Hindenburg are marked with an asterisk), Nos. 52*, 57, 59, 60*, 61, 65*, 71, 74, 82, 91; Thermann tel. 6 of 6 March 1933, T–120, 1468/3015/D 598248; Meyer tel. 258* of 15 March, T–120, 2954/6208/E 469483–84; *D. D. F.*, 1st, 2, Nos. 376, 380, 407, 414; Gilbert (Geneva) dispatch 836 of 7 March 1933, State 760c.6212/31.

The dates usually given for the Westerplatte incident which place the initial Polish consultation with Rosting on 5 March are incorrect. Papée, the Polish commissioner general, raised the matter orally on 3 March and in writing on 4 March (Papée to Rosting, 4 March 1933, T–120, 2954/6208/E 469389).

9. Vansittart, *Mist Procession*, pp. 468f., 536.

states of Bavaria, Baden, Saxony, and Württemberg between 5 March and 10 March.[10] While other German military and political leaders worried about the military dangers of a Polish attack, dangers they feared Germany could not cope with successfully,[11] Hitler's attention was soon after drawn to the Danzig issue as a result of developments growing out of the political coordination just completed in the German states. The National Socialist gauleiter for Danzig, Albert Forster, saw Hitler on 10 March, just before the head of the Danzig government, Ernst Ziehm;[12] and while there is no record of their conversation, it apparently gave Forster the idea of moving forward with National Socialist agitation in Danzig, perhaps with the possibility of a take-over like those just accomplished in the German states. Immediately on Forster's return to Danzig—while Ziehm was negotiating about the Westerplatte incident in Geneva—troubles started in the free city. There was a series of incidents, started by the National Socialists, in which the German consul general in Danzig, Edmund Thermann, intervened on behalf of the National Socialists and against the Danzig government which was trying to keep things quiet during the Geneva talks.[13] At this point the situation threatened to get out of hand and provoke Poland. Hitler immediately gave instructions that the party was to maintain the greatest reserve and was also not to push for a reorganization of the government, a subject Thermann[14] and Forster had apparently been pushing.[15] Göring gave orders to the S. A. near the Polish borders to avoid any provocative actions; and Ziehm, on his visit to Berlin en route from Geneva to Danzig, found Hitler both more interested and cooperative.[16] The party in Danzig was temporarily restrained, but it was evident that only the danger of foreign compli-

10. This is the explanation for the discrepancy between President Hindenburg's close following of the Westerplatte incident (see n. 8) and Hitler's lecture to the astonished Danzig senate president, Ernst Ziehm, on 10 March about Martin Luther, the wars of liberation against Napoleon, and the nature of the National Socialist revolution (Ziehm, pp. 178–83). Ziehm was on the way to Geneva to defend Danzig's position before the League council; Hitler was busy with the Prussian municipal elections scheduled for 12 March, getting Hindenburg's approval for the unconstitutional change in Germany's national flag, and breaking his promise to keep the 30 January coalition unchanged by adding Joseph Goebbels as another National Socialist to the cabinet. The subjective honesty of Ziehm's memoirs is obvious at this point: fifteen years after the end of World War II he still did not understand that on 10 March Hitler was rehearsing his 11 March speech for the municipal elections; while Ziehm, naturally, was thinking about the free city's presentation at Geneva.

11. Ziehm, pp. 164–66; Meinck, pp. 14–16, 19.

12. Ziehm, p. 179.

13. Thermann was acting without instructions from Berlin (memorandum of Bülow, 24 March 1933, T–120, 2373/4603/E 190912–13). He was kicked upstairs in July 1933 by being sent as minister to Argentina (*G. D.*, C, 1, No. 384). Kimmich (p. 133) claims that Thermann was acting on orders from Berlin, but cites no such orders.

14. *G. D.*, C, 1, No. 58.

15. The most spectacular of the incidents in Danzig was the raising of a swastika flag on 13 March; on 15 March Hitler told von Neurath that he had given the stated instructions to Forster (ibid., No. 85).

16. Göring at the cabinet meeting of 20 March 1933 (*TMWC*, 31:415); Ziehm saw Hitler on 22 March (Ziehm, pp. 184–87).

cations had restrained Hitler. The pressure for an internal change in the Danzig government immediately resumed, but in behind-the-scenes political negotiations, not street demonstrations.[17] These negotiations culminated in the collapse of the political arrangement supporting the Ziehm government and the holding of new elections. When public agitation in the election campaign threatened to bring on international complications,[18] Hitler again intervened to calm the situation; but nothing was to prevent the National Socialists from actually taking power in Danzig. The new government of the free city, however, was to assume power under circumstances and with policies far different from those of the crisis-laden days of early March.

During March and April 1933, the German government received conflicting reports about a possible military move on the part of Poland, but it is not necessarily of great importance for an understanding of German policy whether the stories were true, false, or intentionally planted by the Poles. There can be no doubt that the reports came in and that the German government took them seriously in spite of the fact that the German minister to Poland thought there was no serious danger.[19] Hitler, as has been shown, first toned down the Nationalist Socialist agitation in Danzig and postponed the take-over of the Danzig government from the middle of March—right after the analogous action in the German states—until a few weeks later. Second, he reexamined the whole problem of Germany's relations with Poland. Knowing that Germany was not ready for war, he decided to consider the possibility of a temporary rapprochement, perhaps impressed by the very determination Pilsudski had shown. In the last days of March there were signs of just such a reorientation in Hitler's thinking, publicly reflected in the broad sweep of his appeal for peace with all of Germany's neighbors in his speech of 23 March.[20] At a cabinet meeting on 7 April, von Neurath argued for good relations with Russia while asserting that "an understanding with Poland is neither possible nor desirable."[21] Hitler made no comment at the meeting, but his policy was to be just the opposite of von Neurath's recommendation. The basis of von Neurath's intended policy, as is clear from his presentation and his other comments, was that only continued agitation for revision would secure for Germany a return of lands lost to Poland after the war. As the German foreign ministry argued, there could be only one more partition of Poland; all of Germany's territorial aims in the East must, therefore, be attained at one time; and these could be secured only if world opinion were prepared for such a revision while Germany built up its own

17. Ziehm, pp. 189–91; *G. D.*, C, 1, Nos. 96, 116, 127, 131. Hitler and Forster met again on 30 March (*Völkischer Beobachter,* 31 March 1933).

18. *G. D.*, C, 1, No. 155.

19. Ibid., Nos. 77, 183, n. 3, 177, 180, 183, 184. It should be noted that at the cabinet meeting of 25 April von Neurath distorted the reports from von Moltke to make the situation appear more critical than it really was (compare No. 184, n. 2, with No. 183).

20. Roos, *Polen und Europa,* p. 71.

21. *G. D.*, C, 1, No. 142.

strength and supported the German elements inside Poland.[22] In this framework, the 1914 borders of Germany, with the exception of the Poznan area, were the ultimate aims, and a concern for the people of German background living in Danzig and parts of the areas ceded to Poland may have been a genuine factor, at least in part.[23] Hitler's territorial ambitions and ideas for the fate of the Poles, by contrast, went far beyond von Neurath's wildest dreams, and his attitude toward the Germans involved was entirely different: they would be used or sacrificed at will.

If Hitler was prepared to consider a new relationship with Poland, Pilsudski was interested in exploring the possibility of a rapprochement with Germany.[24] At the beginning of April, Pilsudski decided to send to Berlin Count Jan Szembek, who had had a considerable diplomatic career before assuming the post of Secretary of State in the Polish foreign ministry in November 1932.[25] He was to see Hitler in person, without going through von Neurath, an idea inspired by Pilsudski's accurate impression of von Neurath's views, but immediately ruled out as impossible by Alfred Wysocki, since early 1931 the Polish minister in Berlin. Instead of sending a special emissary, therefore, the Polish government instructed Wysocki to seek an interview with Hitler, discuss the situation in Danzig, warn of possible complications if agreement could not be reached, and suggest a public statement of some kind upholding Polish rights in the free city.[26] The Polish minister thereupon began asking for a meeting with Hitler,[27] while feelers were put out by Beck in a talk with Hans Adolf von Moltke, the German minister to Warsaw, in a conversation on 12 April.[28] Hitler delayed the requested meeting but evidently came to the conclusion that the meeting Wysocki had asked for was meant to improve relations between the two countries and that the Polish intentions were sincere.[29] He agreed to see the Polish

22. Ibid.; Memorandum "IV Po 4070" of 26 April 1933, T–120, 2906/6176/E 463413–14.

23. The suggested boundary described by von Neurath in his letter to von Papen of 9 February 1933 (*G. D.,* C, 1, No. 18), is very similar to that outlined in von Dirksen's memorandum of 29 December 1925 (*G. D.,* B, 2, Part 1, No. 21 and map at end of volume). It should be noted that on this subject von Neurath's views resemble those expressed by Gustav Stresemann (*G. D.,* B, 2, Part 1, No. 150).

24. Roos (pp. 80–82) mentions only those Polish measures in April that pointed to military action; the feelers for a rapprochement put out by Poland during the same period must be mentioned to complete the picture.

25. Jean Szembek, *Journal 1933–1939* (Paris: Plon, 1952). A more complete edition of the Szembek diary is being prepared by Tytus Komarnicki; the volumes for 1935 and 1936 have appeared. The title of the French edition is misleading in that there are only a few documents, not a diary, for the period before 1935.

26. Gasiorowski, "The German-Polish Nonaggression Pact of 1934," *Journal of Central European Affairs,* 15, No. 1 (April 1955), pp. 9–10.

27. *G. D.,* C, 1, No. 168.

28. Ibid., No. 167.

29. *Lipski Papers,* p. 76. There is no record of a Hitler-von Moltke talk before the Hitler-Wysocki meeting of 2 May. The account in Roos (p. 82) is based on information supplied to that author by Otto Meissner, then chief of the Presidential Chancel-

minister, and their conference was finally scheduled for 2 May 1933.[30]

In their conversation, the Polish minister stressed the concern of his government over the possibility of trouble about Danzig. Hitler declined to recognize any special position of Poland in Danzig beyond that specified in the peace treaty but explained at length that, regardless of the mistakes made at Versailles, these could not be corrected by war. He insisted that the German government had no intention of taking Polish territory by force.[31] He agreed to the release of a press communiqué about the meeting, though striking a reference to Poland's rights and interests in Danzig. As it stood, therefore, the communiqué mentioned Hitler's intention of keeping the attitudes and conduct of the German government strictly within the limits of the existing treaties and expressed his wish that "both countries might review and deal with their common interests dispassionately." Von Neurath was clearly unhappy about this outcome, but his efforts at obstruction resulted only in agreement to defer release of the communiqué until von Moltke had seen Beck and a similar communiqué could be released in Warsaw.[32]

These conversations and communiqués inaugurated a period during which German-Polish relations were quiet and unspectacular, a prelude to more dramatic events later in the year. Conversations between German and

---

lery. Meissner's version is in conflict with the contemporary evidence on von Moltke's views. Von Moltke reported that on balance he did *not* think Poland would turn to preventive war on 23 April (*G. D.*, C, 1, No. 180), 25 April (ibid., No. 183), and 26 April (ibid., No. 192). The last of these reports was shown to Hitler, and von Moltke must have reckoned with the possibility that all of them would. He could not know that von Neurath would distort his views (see n. 19, above). Von Moltke believed that the Poles were trying to influence the League and the disarmament conference and urged that Germany exercise restraint and rearm quietly. It is very probable that von Moltke in fact did not go to Berlin before the Hitler-Wysocki meeting at all, and that Meissner's reference to such a trip reflects a confusion with von Moltke's visit to Berlin right after his meeting with Beck on 3 May (Laroche, p. 128; *G. D.*, C, 1, No. 253).

For a supposed 27 April meeting between Hindenburg, Hitler, von Blomberg, von Neurath, von Papen, and Göring on the defense of the eastern border against any possible Polish attack see Dertinger's "Informationsbericht Nr. 8 vom 27. April 1933," Bundesarchiv, Brammer, Z.Sg. 101/26, f. 303.

30. *Weissbuch der Polnischen Regierung* (Basel: Birkhäuser, 1939) (hereafter cited as *Polish White Book*), No. 1; *Lipski Papers,* Nos. 11, 12; *G. D.*, C, 1, No. 201; *B. D.*, 2d, 5, Nos. 116, 128; Laroche, pp. 127–28; Mastný report 32 of 4 May 1933, Czech document in T–120, 1041/1809/413941–42.

31. According to both the German and Polish accounts, Hitler insisted that he would never try to deprive any foreign nationality of its language and customs. This statement—excised in the *German White Book*—was a predecessor of his 1938 statement that Germany wanted no Czechs. It could be read to mean that Germany repudiated foreign conquests and the forced assimilation of non-Germans, and this was the way it was generally interpreted at the time. It could mean something entirely different, as anyone who had read *Mein Kampf* would know, namely that Germany would conquer land but expel or exterminate its non-German population. Hitler's antiassimilationist views were a part of his racialist doctrines, and when he voiced them he spoke the truth, but not the whole truth.

32. *Lipski Papers,* No. 13; *G. D.*, C, 1, No. 206; note by von Bülow, 2 May 1933, T–120, 1431/2945/D 575841.

Polish diplomats were civil, and Germany's first military attaché to Poland was promptly received in audience by Pilsudski.[33] In spite of German fears, the Polish government made no attempt to intervene in the election campaign in Danzig as the Danzig National Socialist leaders followed Berlin's instructions to keep the situation reasonably quiet.[34] The Poles were willing to stand by while the National Socialists took over the property of the trade unions in Danzig;[35] they were ready to give the new leaders a chance to prove their adherence to the promise to respect the status quo in the free city if power came to them as a result of the election.[36] Hitler himself spoke to the people of Danzig on the day before the voting which brought the NSDAP a bare majority of the popular vote.[37] Warsaw now calmly observed the accession of the National Socialists to power in Danzig, not only because of reassuring words from Hitler, but also because the person and views of the new president of the Danzig government were taken as tokens of Hitler's sincerity.

In his foreign policy speech to the Reichstag on 17 May, Hitler had referred publicly to Poland in words similar to those used with Wysocki two weeks before.[38] The new German government was opposed to forcible germanization, and while the eastern borders drawn at Versailles were bad, they could not be improved by war. The simultaneous avowal of a peaceful foreign policy, willingness to sign non-aggression pacts, denunciation of the idea of sanctions, and threat to leave the League of Nations and the disarmament conference if Germany were outvoted summarized the policy Hitler was to follow in 1933 and the immediately following years. While preparing for subsequent acts of aggression, the German government would proclaim its peaceful inclinations to reassure skeptics at home and abroad, and would substitute bilateral for multilateral obligations in the meantime.

Not only the references to Poland in the speech but other evidence of the time points to Hitler's willingness to think of Poland as a possible partner in a bilateral arrangement. Late in May 1933, the German ambassador in Moscow, Herbert von Dirksen, was in Berlin, trying to persuade the German government to keep relations with the Soviet Union on tolerable terms. Von Dirksen was a vain and pompous man who believed strongly in German cooperation with whatever country he was assigned to at the moment.[39] His

33. *G. D.,* C, 1, No. 221; *Lipski Papers,* No. 14; Gasiorowski, "German-Polish Nonaggression Pact," p. 15. See also Antoni Szymánski, "Als politischer Militärattaché in Berlin (1932–1939)," *Politische Studien,* 13, No. 141 (1962), pp. 42–51.

34. *G. D.,* C, 1, Nos. 213, 216, 253 (see also Wirth to von Bülow, 4 May 1933, T–120, 2832/6077/E 450643–45); Laroche, p. 127.

35. Leonhardt, pp. 49–50.

36. Ibid., p. 57.

37. On German intervention in the campaign see ibid., pp. 47–50, 57–58; *G. D.,* C, 1, Nos. 205, 216; Baynes, 2:1060–62; Domarus, 1:279. It should be noted that the National Socialist percentage of the vote in Danzig was lower than in adjacent East Prussia in the March election.

38. Domarus, 1:270–79.

39. See the essay on von Dirksen in Lewis Namier, *In the Nazi Era* (London: Macmillan, 1952), pp. 44–62.

memory was sometimes poor,[40] and his predictions frequently erroneous,[41] but his observations on the situation in countries to which he was accredited were generally accurate. Hitler told von Dirksen that he wanted to come to an agreement with Pilsudski, a suggestion von Dirksen countered with the argument that this meant recognizing the border with Poland, something all Germans had rejected since 1919. Like von Neurath, von Dirksen wanted to maintain tension with Poland to push for revision; Hitler preferred to wait until he was ready for wider schemes. Students of National Socialist Germany have too often suggested that Hitler first tried for revision of the Treaty of Versailles and thereafter moved on to bolder plans of conquest. This is only a half-truth, and grossly misleading. Where his hopes for ultimate conquests and short-term revision collided, Hitler was quite capable of opposing revision. In the only recorded instance before 1933 in which Hitler mentioned a specific size for the additional land area Germany could well use, that area was substantially greater than the *total* territory of Poland.[42] The trifling adjustments von Neurath and von Dirksen were thinking about were therefore irrelevant to Hitler's plans. In the short run, the traditional diplomats seem more radical than Hitler, whose soaring ambitions required postponement.[43] In Danzig, postponement meant temporary quiet, and the man to keep Danzig quiet was Hermann Rauschning, the man elected to succeed Ziehm as president of the Senate.

Rauschning had studied the nationality conflict in western Poland, bought a small estate in Danzig in 1927, and became a leader of the Danzig *Landbund* which he took with him into the National Socialist party.[44] A conservative nationalist, Rauschning was to break with the National Socialists when he realized that their aims and methods were incompatible with his own, which included a genuine effort at cooperation with Poland.[45] When Rauschning was in Berlin at the end of May and the first days of June 1933, he received instructions from Hitler appropriate to the sentiments the latter had expressed publicly to the Reichstag and privately to von Dirksen.[46]

40. The trip to Berlin at the end of May was moved up to March or April in his memoirs (Herbert von Dirksen, *Moskau Tokio London* [Stuttgart: Kohlhammer, 1950], pp. 122–23; cf. *G. D.,* C, 1, No. 284, n. 3). This has confused authors who relied on von Dirksen's memory.

41. This point will be discussed in connection with Germany's Far Eastern policy.

42. *Hitlers zweites Buch,* p. 102.

43. The superficial anomaly of the National Socialists in the cabinet representing the more moderate course in domestic affairs and, with the exception of Austria, in foreign policy as well is described with insight and accuracy in Dertinger's "Informationsbericht Nr. 16 vom 31. Mai 1933," Bundesarchiv, Brammer, Z.Sg. 101/26, f. 403–409.

44. See the biography of Rauschning prepared before his 1 November 1933 audience with Hindenburg, T–120, 2787/6023/H 044553–54.

45. Note Beck's comment on the "attitude conciliante envers la Pologne" of the new Danzig government (*Dernier rapport,* p. 27).

46. On Rauschning's meeting with Hitler and his other conferences in Berlin on this trip see G. D., C, 1, No. 273; Rauschning, *Voice of Destruction,* pp. 86–88; Hermann Rauschning, *Die Revolution des Nihilismus* (Zurich: Europa-Verlag, 1938), p. 440;

Hitler told Rauschning and Forster that the solution of the Danzig and corridor questions was a problem for Germany, not Danzig, to solve. They should work quietly in Danzig in a manner that would spare Germany international complications during the coming years. He was determined to get along with Poland; he would sign any treaty that might ease Germany's position. The Danzig government should help in this by operating in a manner that maintained the German character of the city with a minimum of excitement. As for the immediate future, the German government would help Danzig with financial assistance to meet its deficits and would try to release a specialist to aid the officials of the free city in their trade and economic negotiations with Poland.

The new National Socialist government in Danzig accordingly initiated a policy of settling the outstanding difficulties with Poland by direct negotiations rather than complaints to the League as had been the prior custom.[47] The new policy was announced publicly in Danzig by Gauleiter Forster when the new Senate assumed power on 20 June, with Rauschning making similar comments three days later.[48] While consolidating their rule in Danzig, the new government began talks with Poland. These were conducted during July, and included a visit of Rauschning and Artur Greiser, vice-president of the Senate, to Warsaw on 5 July.[49] With a real desire for agreement on both sides, negotiations moved forward rapidly. To prevent interference with the course of the talks, the German press was directed to avoid all polemics that might unfavorably affect Danzig-Polish relations.[50] The imminent change at the Polish legation in Berlin provided Hitler with an opportunity to stress his desire for peaceful relations with Poland to the departing minister, Wysocki, on 13 July.[51] He told Wysocki that he had seen to it that there would be no trouble between Danzig and Poland and intimated that the fine atmosphere created there would have good results

---

Rauschning to the Minister of Finance, 2 June 1933, T–120, 2954/6211/E 469613–14.

Rauschning's memory of the chronology is correct. Contemporary evidence dates his meeting with Hitler to 1 June. In the *Voice of Destruction,* p. 86, he tells of Hitler's attacks on Austria at the same meeting and states that this was just after the German currency barrier to travel in Austria had been instituted. That event, examined in chap. 4, had taken place on 27 May. The material in *Voice of Destruction,* p. 102, may also refer to this period.

47. The opposition in Danzig henceforth had to complain to the League high commissioner, so that the complaints that reached the League from Danzig hereafter were against, instead of from, the government of the free city.

48. *Schulthess europäischer Geschichtskalender 1933*, p. 262.

49. On these negotiations see Beck, p. 27; Breyer, pp. 90–91; Leonhardt, p. 65; and the dispatches from the U. S. vice-consul in Danzig, Johnson, and chargé in Warsaw, Crosby, of July 1933, State 760c.60K/279–284 *passim.*

50. "Mitteilungen an die Redaktionen," 29 June 1933, Bundesarchiv, Brammer, Z.Sg. 101/1, f. 37.

51. The agrément for the new minister, Jósef Lipski, had been granted on 3 July. On the Hitler-Wysocki meeting of 13 July see *Polish White Book,* No. 4; *Lipski Papers,* p. 90; Mastný report 55 of 17 July 1933, Czech document in T–120, 1041/1809/ 413946–48.

elsewhere. These good results would come later, but the immediate effects were soon evident.

A series of agreements between Danzig and Poland was initialed on 5 August and ratified on 8 August. These dealt with a variety of questions, of which the volume of Polish trade to be routed through Danzig and the position of the Polish minority in Danzig were the most important.[52] Not all in the German government agreed with this course,[53] but Hitler was firm.[54] The Polish government was satisfied that there was a real improvement in Danzig-Polish relations, that Hitler had in fact given orders for the Danzig government to be conciliatory—while he concentrated on the annexation of Austria—and that under these circumstances Poland could make some real concessions to the free city.[55] That the Poles felt that Hitler with his Austrian background might be more interested in the *Anschluss* than the corridor is borne out by other evidence.[56] The Polish policy may, therefore, be considered the converse of Italy's emphasis on revision in the corridor to divert the Germans from Austria. With both Danzig and Poland willing to make concessions, agreements could be reached; and on 18 September the preliminary agreements of early August were included in a comprehensive settlement of the issues outstanding between the two governments.[57] By this time the rapprochement between the free city and Poland had advanced to a point where it definitely influenced the prospect of better relations between Germany and Poland. On 30 August, for example, von Moltke urged Berlin that the trade and tariff war between the two countries, then more than eight years old, might well be ended.[58]

52. *Schulthess 1933,* pp. 263–64; Leonhardt, p. 65; Roos, pp. 100–01; Breyer, p. 91; *German White Book,* No. 179; Johnson (Danzig) dispatch 298 of 22 August 1933, State 760c.60K/288.

53. See the comment of Consul-General Thermann in his report I.G. 1118/33 of 10 August 1933, T–120, 1315/2371/D 495617–21.

54. On 8 August, the day of the Danzig-Polish agreement, Schacht was informed that Hitler wanted foreign exchange transferred to Danzig in spite of the large amount involved (*G. D.,* C, 1, No. 387). About 30 million Reichsmark were needed (Schaefer [Bank of Danzig] to Schacht, 10 August 1933, T–120, 2915/6203/E 468423–31; Reich Minister of Finance to the Senate of the free city of Danzig, 18 August 1933, ibid., frames E 468434–37).

55. See the comments of Count Michal Lubiénski, chief of the Danzig section of the Polish Ministry of Foreign Affairs, to a member of the U. S. legation in Warsaw on 14 August (Cosby dispatch 320 of 16 August 1933, State 760c.60K/287).

56. Laroche, pp. 134–35.

57. Again the German foreign ministry had been doubtful, but since Rauschning saw Hitler before signing, it may be assumed that the latter approved (*G. D.,* C, 1, No. 417). See also Breyer, p. 91; Leonhardt, p. 65; Kimmich, pp. 142–46; Johnson (Danzig) dispatches 316 of 25 September 1933 and 322 of 7 October 1933, State 760c.60K/293 and 300; "Informationsbericht Nr. 25 vom 24. August 1933," Bundesarchiv, Brammer, Z.Sg. 101/26, f. 533.

58. *German White Book,* No. 30. It should be remembered that the original German purpose in this economic struggle had been to weaken Poland to such an extent as to force territorial revision as a condition for relaxation of trade barriers and German participation in the international economic assistance to Poland that would thereafter be feasible because of the reduced danger to Poland's economic safety.

The German government's decision to go forward with economic negotiations with Poland as von Moltke suggested was closely related to the development of the international situation in September and October 1933, to be discussed subsequently. The progress, or rather lack of progress, in the disarmament negotiations was about to lead to a major crisis in Geneva; and under these circumstances it would make sense to develop better relations, or at least reduce tension, with Poland to offset any possible danger in the West. While von Neurath was preparing to go to Geneva for the League meeting, von Moltke was in Berlin, and the German government then decided to go forward with negotiations for an end of the trade war and the conclusion of a trade agreement with Poland.[59] The Polish government simultaneously reexamined its international position with the possibility of reorientation very much in mind.[60] At Geneva, the German and Polish foreign ministers met in a friendly conversation followed by one in which the German propaganda minister, Joseph Goebbels, also participated.[61] There was agreement that direct negotiations about matters of common concern and controversy provided the best approach to improved German-Polish relations, and the peaceful handling of Danzig questions at this League session illustrated the new atmosphere that such a course could generate.[62] The beginning of serious economic negotiations early in October gave each side an opportunity to assess the intentions and to test the sincerity of the other; the dramatic developments of mid-October would lead both powers to quick decisions on the basis of the assessments just made.[63]

The German government's announcement on 14 October that it was leaving both the disarmament conference and the League of Nations placed the developing rapprochement between Germany and Poland in a new light. While efforts would be made from Berlin to befuddle the French by suggestions of bilateral talks, the danger of foreign action against Germany was considered by Hitler; and the available information suggests that it helped lead him to the decision for an agreement with Poland. At a meeting with von Neurath and Rauschning on 17 October, Hitler strongly urged Rauschning to arrive at an understanding with Poland while deferring,

59. "Sitzung des Handelspolitischen Ausschusses vom 21. September 1933," T–120, 2612/5650/H 003731–33. The formal instructions of von Bülow of 25 September (*German White Book,* No. 31) grew out of this conference.

60. Beck, p. 29; Gasiorowski, "German-Polish Nonaggression Pact," pp. 17–19.

61. *G. D.,* C, 1, Nos. 449, 451; Beck, pp. 30–31. Beck, who identified von Neurath (a Württemberger) with the traditions of Prussia, told the Belgian foreign minister, "j'aime mieux Goebbels que Neurath" (*Documents diplomatiques belges 1920–1940,* 3 [Brussels: Académie royale, 1964] [hereafter cited as *D. D. B.*], No. 55).

62. Breyer, pp. 93–94. It should be noted that the German foreign ministry was still reluctant to agree to Rauschning's conciliatory course (*G. D.*, C, 1, Nos. 491, 492).

63. On the economic negotiations in October see "Sitzung des Handelspolitischen Ausschusses vom 5. Oktober 1933," T–120, 2612/5650/H 003737–40; Cudahy (Warsaw) dispatch 52 of 18 October 1933 and Vice-Consul Hugh C. Fox (Berlin) report 1107 of 18 January 1934, State 660c.6231/193 and 203.

though not rejecting, Rauschning's suggestion that Hitler himself meet with Marshal Pilsudski.[64] On the same day, the new Polish minister to Berlin, Jósef Lipski, had a most friendly talk with von Neurath who expatiated at length on the need to settle all outstanding problems.[65] The next day, Hitler told the leaders of his party at a closed meeting that he would sign any treaty of any sort to postpone war until he was ready for it, and subsequently told Rauschning that he wanted a treaty with Poland—it could be broken at a convenient moment later.[66]

If, in the crisis precipitated by its departure from Geneva, the German government was ready for an agreement with Poland, the same event led to the same conclusion in Warsaw. Pilsudski and his associates canvassed the situation created by what they believed to be a weakening of Poland's international position. Though he was anything but fond of the League, Pilsudski did value the minimal protection it had afforded Poland; he doubted that France would take any action against Germany; and he did not believe that Germany was really dangerous as yet. There was, however, always the possibility that the other powers would come to an agreement at Poland's expense, as the Four-Power Pact negotiations had demonstrated all too clearly; and agreement with Germany might deflect its aggression elsewhere.[67] Early in November, Pilsudski instructed Lipski to sound out Hitler about some substitute for the security the League had previously provided,[68] and this possibility was discussed at the meeting between Lipski, Hitler, and von Neurath on 15 November.[69] Hitler responded to Lipski's presentation of the Polish point of view by an extended discourse on the futility of war and the advisability as well as possibility of bilateral peaceful settlement of all differences. He welcomed Pilsudski's initiative and agreed to the immediate release of a press communiqué expressing the intention of the two powers to take up the questions affecting them by direct negotiations and renouncing the use of force in their relations with each other. The subsequent fate of the direct negotiations and of the no-force declaration showed to what extent the two powers were willing to give substance to their public professions.

In late October, an impasse in regard to the subject of coal threatened the success of all German-Polish economic negotiations. Although John

64. *G. D.*, C, 2, No. 11.

65. *Polish White Book,* No. 5.

66. Rauschning, *Voice of Destruction,* pp. 104–10; Breyer, p. 98; Domarus, 1: 317.

67. Szembek, pp. 1–2; Breyer, p. 99; Laroche, pp. 136–37; Roos, pp. 106–07.

68. *Lipski Papers,* pp. 94–98.

69. *Polish White Book,* No. 6; *Lipski Papers,* p. 99; Mastný report 78 of 16 November 1933, Czech document in T–120, 1041/1809/413957; *G. D.,* C, 2, No. 69; Cudahy dispatch 87 of 18 November and Crosby (Warsaw) dispatch 88 of 21 November 1933, State 760c.62/214 and 215. The German briefing paper for von Neurath for this talk deals with the economic and minorities issues that were in fact not touched upon (IV Po 8250 of 14 November 1933, T–120, 2906/6174/E 462948–50).

Maynard Keynes had once predicted that the German economy could not function without Upper Silesian coal, the Germans had in fact made the exclusion of coal imports from Poland the key element in their trade war against that country. The Poles now insisted, for both economic and psychological reasons, that Germany annually accept a minimum quantity of Polish coal, and the Germans recognized that some concession on this point would have to be made if they wanted an agreement.[70] Hitler met with several of his ministers on the evening of 16 November 1933, the day after the Hitler-Lipski talk; and it was decided to accord Poland a coal quota if that were needed for the conclusion of an economic treaty.[71] Some technical questions remained, but the road was now open to a treaty ending the many years of trade war between Germany and Poland.[72]

The same conference that removed the major obstacle to an economic agreement also produced a decision to pursue in specific terms the suggestion Hitler himself had originally mentioned to Lipski, that the agreement of the two powers not to use force be embodied in a treaty.[73] Work on this subject was immediately initiated in the German foreign ministry.[74] In that office, in spite of the misgivings about any settlement with Poland, the assumption was that Germany would consider itself bound by any nonaggression treaty; a renunciation of the use of force in treaty form was, therefore, advocated as the most desirable procedure. Hitler quickly agreed to this idea, and von Moltke was instructed to present it to Pilsudski with Hitler's greetings, care being taken to keep the plan secret and to present it to the Poles before they could come up with a draft of their own.[75] Pilsudski received von Moltke promptly, promised a favorable but careful examination of the German proposal, and stressed his desire for a settlement with Germany. Calling attention frankly to the anti-German tradition in Poland, Pilsudski explained that all this would take some time. Another delaying factor, not mentioned quite so explicitly, was the special relationship of Poland to France. The very fact that the Polish government kept

70. Von Moltke discussed these issues in Berlin; see the minutes of the *Handelspolitische Ausschuss* (Foreign Trade Policy Committee, H. P. A.) of 30 October, 2 November, and 9 November 1933, T–120, 2612/5650/H 003746–55; *G. D.*, C, 2, Nos. 38, 52, 58.

71. *G. D.*, C, 2, No. 73; H. P. A. meeting of 20 November 1933, T–120, 2612/5650/H 003761–62; Memorandum by Ritter, 20 November 1933, T–120, 1431/2945/D 575884.

72. The treaty was signed on 7 March 1934 (Berthold Puchert, *Der Wirtschaftskrieg des deutschen Imperialismus gegen Polen 1925–1934* [Berlin: Akademie-Verlag, 1963], p. 176), but led to only a minor increase in trade (Berthold Puchert, "Die deutsch-polnische Nichtangriffserklärung und die Aussenwirtschaftspolitik des deutschen Imperialismus gegenüber Polen bis 1939," *Jahrbuch für Geschichte der UdSSR. und der volksdemokratischen Länder Europas,* 12 [1968], 346–47).

73. *G. D.*, C, 2, No. 70, n. 4.

74. *B. D.*, 2d, 6, No. 59, n. 1.

75. *G. D.*, C, 2, Nos. 77, 79, 81, 82, 84, 87, 88, 90; *Lipski Papers,* No. 15.

important parts of the negotiations with Berlin secret from France, however, shows the serious intentions of Pilsudski.[76] The French government's own negotiations with the Germans at this time showed that country's willingness to come to an agreement with Germany itself; and Hitler could play off the two allies against each other by manipulating the sincere but uncoordinated desire of each to secure peace.[77]

There were discussions of the provisions of the German draft during December, but the signal event in the negotiations was a meeting between Rauschning and Pilsudski in Warsaw on 11 December. Shortly before, there had been a dispute between Rauschning and Forster over the handling of affairs in Danzig, and both had gone to Berlin for a settlement of the issue. This had been decided in Rauschning's favor on 8 December, and on the same day there had been other discussions of the policy to be followed toward Poland. When Rauschning went to Warsaw, therefore, he had a clear picture of Hitler's wishes.[78] The conversation between Pilsudski and Rauschning was frank and detailed. They canvassed the outstanding problems in Danzig-Polish and German-Polish relations; and it became clear that while some cooperation was possible and Pilsudski was willing to recognize the German character of the free city, certain more far-reaching proposals that Rauschning had planned to raise were inopportune. Pilsudski was evidently of the opinion that any meeting between himself and Hitler would have to wait some time. Pilsudski knew that Hitler would be preoccupied with domestic affairs for several years. Combined with the need for security and a desire for a stronger position in world diplomacy, this factor contributed to Pilsudski's willingness to come to a settlement with Germany. He was also, however, quite explicit on one point that the Germans for many years refused to accept as a fundament of Polish policy, namely that Poland would not ally itself with Germany against the Soviet Union for the obvious reason that it would then lose its independence to Germany. As Rauschning reported on his return to Berlin, "Pilsudski also brought up in the conversation that Poland would never under any circumstances respond to any German attempts to turn Polish efforts toward the Russian Ukraine."[79]

76. Laroche, pp. 138–45; see also *B. D.*, 2d, 6, No. 59; Vereker (Warsaw) telegram 45 of 10 November 1933, Foreign Office C 9895/9895/18.

77. The German-French negotiations are examined in chap. 7. The release by the Quai d'Orsay in late November 1933 of secret German documents revealing the real aspirations of Germany may have been designed to warn the Polish government. This incident is discussed in the same chapter. The first of those documents refers to the fact that "Germany has assumed a conciliatory attitude toward Poland for the time being because special efforts are being made in this direction to secure the attainment of the German demands by other means. These demands have, of course, not been given up in any way any more than the demand for the return of at least part of the former German colonies overseas."

78. *G. D.*, C, 2, Nos. 102, 109; Memorandum by Meyer, 8 December 1933, T–120, 2915/6203/E 468615–17 and a note by Rauschning of the same date in ibid., frames E 468618–21.

79. German foreign ministry Memorandum IV Po 9133 of 14 December 1933 (ini-

The subject of a German-Polish alliance against Russia was, as we know from Rauschning, on Hitler's mind at the time, but it was not formally raised again by the Germans until later.[80] The promising beginning that had been made on the immediate proposal for a treaty renouncing the use of force was carried forward relatively rapidly, considering the legacy of controversies and suspicions in the past. A new atmosphere was discernible in Berlin. As Lipski wrote to the director of Beck's cabinet on 3 December, "As if by orders from the top, a change of front toward us is taking place all along the line. In Hitlerite spheres they talk about the new Polish-German friendship."[81] Agreement was reached on 26 January 1934. With a reservation that covered Poland's obligations under its League membership and treaties with France, the two powers promised to settle all problems that might arise between them by direct negotiations and without recourse to force. The agreement was to run for ten years, subject to extension as long as this was mutually agreeable.[82]

Poland had secured a degree of temporary security; Hitler had broken the ring of French alliances around Germany, both by the agreement itself and by the deliberate secrecy with which it was prepared.[83] The first major settlement, except for the concordat, that Germany had signed was with the very country it was generally expected to be most likely to attack. At home and abroad the Hitler government could point to this diplomatic triumph as a sign of its peaceful intentions, while the Polish government reinforced the weakness of France that had contributed to Warsaw's willingness to sign with Germany in the first place. There might be skepticism among both German and Polish diplomats. One diplomat with reservations, the French ambassador in Washington, saw the meaning of the pact clearly: Germany merely wanted peace in the East for a few years to strengthen its position at home so that it might then dominate Europe.[84] The Italian ambassador to Berlin feared that the agreement might be accompanied by more far-reaching German-Polish understandings, would be followed by the annexation of Austria and a subsequent turning against Czechoslovakia

---

tialed by von Lieres), T–120, 3024/6601/E 495072–77. For additional information on the Pilsudski-Rauschning meeting see Rauschning, *Die Revolution des Nihilismus,* pp. 428–32; Breyer, p. 94; Moltke telegram 79 of 13 December, T–120, 2915/6204/E 468613–14 (submitted to Hitler on 14 December, 1468/3015/D 598307); Crosby (Warsaw) dispatch 126 of 19 December 1933, State 760c.60K/304.

80. Rauschning, *Voice of Destruction,* pp. 117–19.

81. *Lipski Papers,* p. 105.

82. On the course of the final negotiations see *G. D.,* C, 2, Nos. 131, 168, 169, 186, 203, 211, 217–19; *Lipski Papers,* Nos. 17–24; Cudahy dispatch 141 of 3 January 1934, State 660c.6231/202; Gilbert (Geneva) dispatch 836 of 7 March 1934, and Cudahy dispatch 410 of 6 September 1934, State 760c.6212/31 and 38.

83. For a good picture of the secrecy and of the lies Lipski told under instructions from Beck see Mastný's telegram of 27 January and his report 6 of 29 January 1934, Czech documents in T–120, 1041/1809/413689 and 413589–93.

84. Memorandum of Under Secretary William Phillips on a conversation with French Ambassador de Laboulaye on 27 January 1934, State 760c.6212/10.

that would produce a Germany most difficult "for any coalition, however powerful, to deal with without enormous sacrifice of life."[85] There can be no doubt, however, about the psychological and political impact at the time of a treaty that seemed to reconcile two countries most Europeans thought irreconcilable. The relations between Germany and Poland were henceforth by no means untroubled, but their alignment with each other drastically altered the situation in Europe.

If Germany's policy toward Poland moved in new directions in 1933, its attitude toward the Soviet Union was also full of surprises. German-Russian relations when Hitler came to power were by no means as good as they had been some years earlier. In the last years of the Weimar Republic, relations between the two powers had deteriorated for a number of reasons, among which the apparent rapprochement between Germany and the Western Powers was of special importance. The Russians feared that a German-French rapprochement might well lead to an alliance against itself, a fear that was exaggerated though not entirely unjustified. As Russia, therefore, drew a trifle closer to France and Poland, signing non-aggression pacts with both countries, German interest in close relations with the Soviets decreased, and this in turn reinforced Russia's desire to strengthen its ties, or at least ease tension, with France. Furthermore, the long-term prospects for German-Russian cooperation were lessened by changes affecting precisely those fields of practical cooperation that had done much to bring them together: military and trade relations.

In the military field, Germany and the Soviet Union had long cooperated to the benefit of both and the worry of others.[86] The moves toward rearmament in Germany, however, that were already under way before Hitler came to power, would make Germany less dependent on Soviet aid; while the emergence of the new cadres and leaders of the Red Army reduced Russian interest in attendance at German training courses. In 1932 these trends were already bringing about a reduction in the level of military cooperation and hints that the German military training and experiment stations in the Soviet Union would be closed.[87] Similarly, the build-up of

85. Phipps (Berlin) telegram 30–Saving of 7 February 1934, Foreign Office C 929/138/18. The comment on this by Mr. Perowne in the British Foreign Office deserves quoting: "Signor Cerruti's prognostications . . . may well be fulfilled; but it may be hoped that the process of digestion will be longer and more difficult than he seems to fear. But the dynamism of the present rulers of Germany is something quite out of the common; and ordinary yardsticks are useless where they are concerned. Moreover this is a clear case where 'L'appetit vient en mangeant.' "

86. The best summary is in Hans W. Gatzke, "Russian-German Military Collaboration during the Weimar Republic," *American Historical Review,* 63, No. 3 (April 1958), pp. 565–97.

87. The waning of German-Soviet military cooperation as a continuing phenomenon of the period 1932–33, without any significant acceleration as a result of Hitler's coming to power, is a main theme of chap. IX of Karlheinz Niclauss, *Die Sowjetunion und Hitlers Machtergreifung* (Bonn: Röhrscheid, 1966). A document dated 26 January 1933, published in Karl-Heinz Voelker, *Dokumente und Dokumentarfotos zur Ge-*

Soviet industry had implications both for their interest in the skills of German technicians and the eventual level of German-Soviet trade. The economic partnership of the two countries was at least partially self-liquidating as the end of the first Five-Year Plan inclined the Russians to reduce the role of German technicians.[88] Any large-scale armament boom in Germany, on the other hand, would reduce German interest in Russia as an export market for machinery and other goods produced in factories that but for Russian orders would have been idled by the depression. Whatever new policies the two nations might adopt toward each other, the basis of their earlier association was already weakening.

Hitler's attitude toward Russia has already been discussed. He intended to take as much territory as he could and as soon as possible, and he was of the opinion that the rule of the Communists in Russia was advantageous for Germany in that it simultaneously weakened Russia's powers of resistance and provided him with an excellent basis for propaganda inside and outside Germany. The realization of his ambitions, however, had to be deferred beyond the period of domestic consolidation and rearmament. During that period, Germany need have no fixed attitude toward Russia as long as relations were neither too close nor too hostile. For domestic political reasons and because of his personal preferences, Hitler did not want the relationship to be very close, and he was to forestall all efforts on the part of either his own diplomats or occasional feelers from the other side to make them so. On the other hand, because of his low estimate of Soviet strength, Hitler was not particularly worried about Soviet hostility, though he would keep it within bounds if no great concessions were needed. This description of Hitler's attitude toward the Soviet Union in the years from 1933 until the spring of 1939 is not based so much on explicit statements by Hitler as on a survey of the series of decisions about relations with Russia made by the German government in that period.[89] The subject of German-Russian relations in those years was of far greater interest to the German professional diplomats than to Hitler. It may be that the foregoing description of his attitudes systematizes Hitler's views to an unwarranted degree, but at least there is no evidence to suggest alternative general perspectives.

Certainly the inauguration of the new regime in Berlin boded ill for relations with the Soviet Union. Hitler's views on expansion eastward, his

---

schichte der deutschen Luftwaffe (Stuttgart: Deutsche Verlags-Anstalt, 1968), pp. 78–79, indicates that the German air force station at Lipetsk was scheduled to be closed down in the fall of 1933; at the beginning of 1933, the German military attaché in Moscow was told that the stations would be closed down and he himself was to resign as of 1 March (Hermann Teske, *General Ernst Köstring* [Frankfurt/M: Mittler, 1966], pp. 69–70).

88. Von Dirksen, p. 125.

89. For a general treatment see Jean-Baptiste Duroselle (ed.), *Les relations germano-soviétiques de 1933 à 1939* (Paris: Armand Colin, 1954). This book is now partially replaced by the work of Niclauss.

publicly proclaimed and promptly implemented policy of suppressing the German Communist party, his close association with Alfred Rosenberg, all could be considered symbols of an anti-Russian policy. Nevertheless, the Soviet Union was at first quite cautious in the face of the new regime, partly for ideological, partly for practical reasons. The ideological reasons were similar to the miscalculation made by the German Communist party, namely that Hitler's policy of destroying the republic, the Social Democratic party, and the trade unions would drive the German workers into the Communist fold and thus, by making the class conflict in Germany more acute, make the revolution and Communist triumph more nearly imminent.[90] It was also believed that the National Socialist regime would not last long and would hasten the collapse of capitalism in Germany.

The practical reasons for Soviet reluctance to turn to new policies were of a different sort. In the first place, the Soviet, like many German soldiers and diplomats, hoped for a continuation of that cooperation between the two countries which had proved so advantageous for both and to which individuals on both sides would hark back nostalgically for years to come. Neither the German nor the Soviet "Rapallo generation" of soldiers and diplomats had any illusions about the domestic policies of the other country, but separated as they were by what they considered to be the common enemy of Poland, each felt able to deal with any domestic advocates of the other's social and political system. In this regard, the National Socialist regime looked to the Soviets simply more vehement and ruthless than its predecessors. Such a situation had not prevented the Soviet Union from having good relations with Turkey and Italy, as German diplomats in Moscow were to be reminded quite frequently. In a similar way, the Moscow government was quite willing to give considerable aid to Chiang Kai-shek and the Chinese Nationalists both before and after the Nationalists attempted to suppress the Chinese Communist party. As will be seen, there was one important difference between these apparently analogous situations. The Soviet regime did not fear the military potential of Turkey or Italy. Once it had forcibly asserted its rights in Manchuria in 1929, it did not fear any action that might be taken by a China dominated by the Kuomintang. But Germany was different. As the Soviet leaders knew all too well, Germany had been capable of occupying huge stretches of Russian territory in World War I, and there was always the possibility that a rearmed Germany might try to do so again, perhaps with the tacit or even active support of the Western powers. That prospect, however frightening, lay in an uncertain future. In the meantime there were good reasons why Germany might follow a more moderate policy, of which the support given to the German economy by Russian orders formed a significant part.

It was with reference to the interest in Russian orders evidenced by

90. Niclauss (pp. 96–100) holds the contrary view that the opinions expressed by Soviet and Comintern leaders to this effect were purely camouflage for Russian quiescence in the face of the destruction of the German Communist party.

German industrialists, whom the Soviet leaders thought in charge of the new government, that they reassured themselves about the intentions of the Hitler regime.[91] This illusory assessment of what the Russians believed to be the realities of the situation was probably more important than the hasty reassurances voiced by German diplomats.[92] As violent incidents against Soviet nationals and institutions in Germany increased, however, and as the election campaign brought forth a torrent of anti-Communist and anti-Russian oratory, the leaders of the Soviet government became worried and insisted that the private words of diplomats be matched by a public pronouncement from the new chancellor.[93]

The public repetition of Hitler's assurance to von Neurath that he wanted to maintain "our previous political, economic-political, and military-political line" and would "not allow any sort of changes to occur in German policy toward Russia"[94] had to wait until after the election, as would the equally spectacular gesture of ratifying the 1931 protocol extending the Berlin treaty that had never been submitted to the Reichstag. A vehement anti-Communist political campaign inside Germany, designed to help secure National Socialist control of the government, was obviously not the time for Hitler to make speeches assuring the Soviet Union of his goodwill.[95] The one gesture that could be made as an earnest of German intentions was a quiet extension—with Hitler's approval—of a special credit of 140 million reichsmark, deferring repayment of a portion of earlier credits granted by Germany to Russia.[96] Otherwise the Germans temporarily parried Soviet worries by referring to their own concern about Russia's closer relations with France.[97] Continued incidents within Germany, however, exacerbated the situation. The Soviet regime, with its extensive experience in organizing "spontaneous" demonstrations, was not easily convinced that the attacks on Soviet citizens in Germany were without government authorization. This was particularly true in regard to the interference with the operations of DEROP (Deutsche Vertriebsgesellschaft für

91. Thus Krestinskii to the Czech chargé-d'affaires ad interim in Moscow on 4 February 1933 (Košek report 6, Czech document in T–120, 1316/2376/D 497059).

92. *G. D.*, C, 1, Nos. 6, 10; Meyer to von Dirksen tel. 17 of 9 February 1933, T–120, 2789/6025/H 045372; Niclauss, p. 86.

93. *G. D.*, C, 1, Nos. 29, 41, 55; von Dirksen note of 7 March 1933, T–120, 1071/1908/429509–18; *D. D. F.*, 1st, 2, Nos. 398, 416.

94. *G. D.*, C, 1, No. 10, n. 5.

95. Ibid., No. 43.

96. Ibid., n. 7; von Dirksen, p. 122; Niclauss, pp. 87–88; Gustav Hilger, *Wir und der Kreml* (Bonn: Athenäum, 1964), p. 269; Sackett (Berlin) tel. 34 of 11 March 1933, State 661.6231/132. Alfred W. Kliefoth of the American embassy in Berlin recorded on 7 March that Consul General Schlesinger had informed him that the Germans had told the Russians that they would take as security gold to be mined that year, "furs on the backs of the foxes still running wild in the forests of Siberia," and "uncaught fish from the Volga" (State 661.6231/134).

It is not known whether the Soviet request for this credit extension was the result of financial necessity or a test of German intentions; Niclauss assumes the former.

97. *G. D.*, C, 1, Nos, 29, 33, 41, 73.

russische Ölprodukte A.G.), the agency that sold all over Germany petroleum products imported from Russia and formed a key element in the structure of German-Soviet trade. These and other types of difficulties created for Soviet nationals and institutions in Germany were to provide a continuous source of aggravation in the coming months.[98]

The German government eventually did make a public effort to keep relations with Russia on a reasonable basis. In his speech to the Reichstag on 23 March, Hitler followed a text recommended by the foreign ministry with the exception of a reference to the Berlin treaty. He promised the continuation of a mutually profitable policy of friendship, more easily conducted by a nationalistic regime, and in no way affected by the fight against communism inside Germany, which was a purely internal affair.[99] Furthermore, the German government tried to reassure Moscow about the Four-Power Pact negotiations and promised that the passage of the Enabling Act would now empower the German government to proceed to ratification of the protocol extending the Berlin treaty.

This step was finally agreed to by the cabinet on 4 April but was not announced for some time while minor questions were being settled. An additional delay before Hitler saw the Soviet ambassador, Leo Khinchuk, on 28 April and until ratifications were exchanged on 5 May undermined the value of any such gesture.[100] Nevertheless, there was at least a temporary relaxation in response to the German action. The constant recriminations about incidents involving harassment of Soviet nationals, however, showed that the Russians were by no means entirely reassured by Hitler's soothing words to Khinchuk. More important in keeping the Soviet Union from completely turning its back upon Germany were Russian troubles with Japan and the strain imposed on Anglo-Soviet relations by the Metropolitan-Vickers trial then in progress.[101] Simultaneously, moreover, the Soviet leaders looked more closely at their relations with Poland and France. As to Poland, the publicity attendant on the Hitler-Wysocki conver-

98. Ibid., Nos. 43, n. 3, 104, 134, 137, 140, 157, 166 (the missing words can be supplied from the copy in T–120, 2372/4602/E 189416), 197, n. 4, 186; Note by von Bülow, 16 March 1933, T–120, 2372/4602/E 189414; Niclauss, pp. 100–05. As a man whose interests were in the economic field, Khinchuk was especially concerned about DEROP (see Lionel Kochan, *Russia and the Weimar Republic* [Cambridge: Bowes & Bowes, 1954], p. 149). In retaliation for the German actions against DEROP, the Soviet government forced the closing of DRUSAG, the German agricultural concession in the North Caucasus (von Dirksen, p. 124).

99. The speech is in Domarus, 1: 229–37; the foreign ministry draft of 18 March 1933, in T–120, 2789/6025/H 045451.

100. *G. D.,* C, 1, Nos. 121, n. 6, 136, 140, 147, 166, 194, 197, 198; Hilger, p. 255; Niclauss, pp. 88–89.

The Italians had been urging Berlin to try for better relations with Russia (*G. D.,* C, 1, No. 403; von Dirksen note of 6 April 1933, T–120, 1071/1908/429581; von Bülow memorandum of19[?] April 1933, T–120, 2371/4602/E 189237).

101. *G. D.,* C, 1, Nos. 204, 212, 232; Czech chargé a.i. Moscow report 23 of 15 May 1933, Czech document in T–120, 1316/2376/D 497081–82.

sation of 2 May suggested to Moscow the possibility that Germany might reverse its traditional alignment with Russia against Poland.[102] In regard to France, for the first time since Russia left its world war alliance, a French military attaché arrived in the Soviet capital on 8 April 1933.[103] German-Soviet military contacts were still continuing, but in April and May serious rifts were discernible.[104] The Soviet Union was publicizing a change in its official line on the Treaty of Versailles, arguing now that revision meant war.[105] Hitler told von Dirksen at the end of May that he still wanted friendly relations with the Soviet Union; but the continuation of incidents in Germany and the mission of Rosenberg to London, which indicated that the apostle of eastward expansion was still in Hitler's favor, left the Russians doubtful and suspicious.[106]

If Rosenberg's London mission in May touched a sensitive Russian nerve, the London memorandum of Alfred Hugenberg in June was to have even greater repercussions on German-Soviet relations. Hugenberg, who had been a bitter opponent of the Weimar Republic, played a key role in aiding Hitler's rise to power. He had imagined that with the backing of President Hindenburg and the army he would exercise great influence in the new government; but his abilities did not match his imagination, and he received no support from the army, the president, or the other non-National Socialist members in the cabinet who were all willing to go along with Hitler even when slightly unhappy about some aspects of his policies. Holding several ministerial portfolios in the economic field, Hugenberg went as a member of the German delegation to the World Economic Conference which opened in London on 12 June 1933, while inside Germany the National Socialists were rapidly demolishing Hugenberg's political party, the German Nationalists (DNVP).[107] For short-term advantages, Hugenberg was pushing a foreign trade policy even more isolationist than that of Hitler and Schacht, and he presented his ideas to the conference in the form of a memorandum. With its demand for high protective tariffs, its call for continued struggle against the *Untermensch* for colonies and living space for Germany and an end to existing conditions in Russia, the mem-

102. *G. D.,* C, 1, No. 342.

103. William E. Scott, *Alliance against Hitler* (Durham, N. C.: Duke University Press, 1962), p. 106.

104. *G. D.,* C, 1, Nos. 147, 197, 252; U. S. 1933, 1: 120; Hilger, pp. 256–57.

105. *G. D.,* C, 1, Nos. 212, 232, 245.

106. Ibid., Nos. 232, 245, 284; von Dirksen, pp. 122–23.

107. The best summary is in Bracher, *Machtergreifung,* pp. 208–14; important, but strongly apologetic in tone, is Anton Ritthaler (ed.), "Eine Etappe auf Hitlers Weg zur ungeteilten Macht, Hugenbergs Rücktritt als Reichsminister," *Vierteljahrshefte für Zeitgeschichte,* 8, No. 2 (April 1960), 193–219; a very detailed account is in John L. Heineman, "Constantin von Neurath and German Policy at the London Economic Conference of 1933: Backgrounds to the Resignation of Alfred Hugenberg," *Journal of Modern History,* 41, No. 2 (June 1969), 160–88; cf. Niclauss, pp. 115–17; Klaus Hildebrand, *Vom Reich zum Weltreich* (Munich: Wilhelm Fink, 1969), pp. 301–14.

orandum did not have the full support of the German delegation but did have a deplorable effect on world opinion.[108] It provided the occasion for Hitler to rid himself of a partner he no longer needed, but it also created new problems in Germany's relations with Russia. Most of what Hugenberg had said could be subscribed to by his colleagues and by Hitler, but it was certainly inopportune to flaunt such ideas in public.

The Russian government had been suspicious of Hugenberg from the beginning, and they found it hard to believe that his statements had been made without at least the tacit authorization of Hitler.[109] Soviet fears were aroused; and though Hugenberg really was acting on his own, the suspicion that he voiced actual German aspirations was quite warranted. It was the inopportune publicity that Hitler found inexpedient. There was a considerable uproar in Moscow, and the Germans were to find it difficult indeed to dispel the doubts that this incident left behind. The fear in Soviet circles was real.[110] The German military bases in Russia were closed, and visits by Soviet officers to Germany were canceled.[111] To justify these actions, the Russians asserted that von Papen had told the French about German-Soviet military cooperation,[112] but in fact by this time the Russians themselves were already receiving French officers.[113] The German government was interested in keeping the situation from getting out of hand, and the press was instructed to refrain from attacking the Soviet regime on 5 July.[114] Contacts between the two countries in the summer of 1933 show a continued interest in preventing an excessive deterioration of their relations.[115] There was evidence of this in the friendly tones and fond farewells accompanying the closing of the German bases in the Soviet Union,[116] and in the efforts made, though unsuccessfully, to reach some agreement on the current prob-

108. *G. D.*, C, 1, Nos. 312, 335, 338; Hey to von Dirksen, 20 June 1933, T–120, 3082/6609/E 497091; Schmidt, pp. 266–67. Important details on the attendant intrigues within the German delegation, especially by the National Socialists to discredit Hugenberg, are to be found in a series of reports of 17–21 June 1933, in Bundesarchiv, Brammer, Z.Sg. 101/26, f. 463–79. Hanfstaengl is characteristically silent on this matter in his memoirs (p. 212).

109. *G. D.*, C, 1, No. 6; von Dirksen, p. 127.

110. *G. D.*, C, 1, Nos. 325, 327, 331, 336, 361; von Dirksen report A/1245 of 22 June 1933, T–120, 2789/6025/H 045811–16; Memorandum of von Dirksen, 22 June 1933, T–120, 1071/1908/429650–60; Memorandum of von Neurath RM 903 of 30 June 1933, ibid., frames 429673–74; Report of the Czech legation Moscow for April, May, June 1933 of 30 June 1933, Czech document in T–120, 1316/2376/D 497091–96.

111. *G. D.*, C, 1, Nos. 439 (p. 822), 339. The Germans replied in kind (Hartmann report 154/33 of 1 August 1933, T–120, 2760/5892/E 432509).

112. *G. D.*, C, 1, No. 403.

113. German Military Attaché Hartmann, "Beilage IV zu Bericht 6/35," 11 February 1935, T–120, 2760/5892/E 432986–89.

114. Bundesarchiv, Brammer, Z.Sg. 101/1, f. 44.

115. *G. D.*, C, 1, Nos. 389, 404; von Dirksen to von Bülow, 17 August 1933, T–120, 1071/1908/429729–36.

116. *G. D.*, C, 1, Nos. 409, 439, 460; Hartmann report 164 of 17 October 1933, T–120, 2760/5892/E 432697.

lems in German-Russian trade.[117] Clearly there was great reluctance over the parting of the ways in both Berlin and Moscow.

A further attempt was made to reopen the possibility of good relations between the two powers by arranging a meeting in late October between Hitler and Nikolai Krestinskii, the Soviet deputy commissar for foreign affairs, former Soviet ambassador to Germany, and a man considered by the German embassy in Moscow to be a continuing advocate of close relations between the Soviet Union and Germany. The efforts of the German embassy staff, supported by the German foreign ministry, came to naught.[118] The failure to hold the meeting could be blamed formally on the Russians, since Hitler did finally agree reluctantly that he would receive Krestinskii; but a series of new incidents, clearly provoked by the German government itself, was both responsible for the failure of this effort and an obvious indication that Hitler did not want a rapprochement. The most serious of these incidents, the threatened rupture of press relations between the two nations arising out of the arrest of the representatives of Tass and *Izvestia* when they tried to cover the Reichstag fire trial in Leipzig, was the result of orders Hitler himself had given.[119] As this and other related questions were placed before him, Hitler stated categorically that "a restoration of the German-Russian relationship would be impossible."[120] He was willing to receive Krestinskii, and he did not favor breaking off relations with Russia or providing the Russians with a pretext for doing so; but he made it clear that the steps he was willing to take to meet complaints about incidents were of a tactical and temporary nature.[121] Whatever hints the Russians might give, this policy line provided merely a framework for reducing unnecessary tension but no basis whatever for a new rapprochment.[122]

It is not surprising that under these circumstances, and in view of the German-Polish rapprochement, the Soviet Union should have continued its search for potential allies elsewhere. In the summer of 1933, Soviet rela-

117. *G. D.,* C, 1, No. 421; Minutes of the H. P. A. for 12 and 13 July 1933, T–120, 2612/5650/H 003695–96 and H 003699; Dodd (Berlin) dispatch 37 of 29 July 1933, State 861.51 German credits/36. For a valuable analysis of one key element in German-Soviet trade see U. S. Consul John H. Morgan (Berlin), "The Tendency of the Import of Soviet Oil into Germany to Decline during 1933 and the Possible Significance of this Decline with Regard to General German-Russian Trade Relations," 21 December 1933, State 662.61/10.

118. Twardowski to Hey, 22 August 1933, T–120, 2790/6025/H 046103; *G. D.,* C, 1, No. 438; Dirksen, p. 128.

119. *G. D.,* C, 1, Nos. 428, 455, 458, 467, 476, 477; German press instruction of 26 September 1933, Bundesarchiv, Brammer, Z.Sg. 101/1, f. 110. The incident over the Leipzig trial was settled by the direct intervention of Göring (the most recent account in Niclauss, pp. 142–46).

120. *G. D.,* C, 1, No. 457.

121. Ibid., No. 456.

122. Ibid., 1, Nos. 461, 462, 470, 487; 2, Nos. 12, 14; Hilger, p. 261; von Dirksen, p. 130; Niclauss, pp. 134–41. Von Dirksen's transfer from Moscow at this time appears not to have been related to Hitler's policy decision.

tions with Poland improved, and feelers for an alliance were extended to France.[123] Former French prime minister Edouard Herriot and French air minister Pierre Cot were greeted in the Soviet Union with much emphasis and publicity in August and September.[124] The crisis in German-Soviet relations brought on by the September incidents gave the Soviet government the opportunity to warn Germany that it was obliged to turn to France and Poland in the face of Berlin's policy. As these warnings and the friendly farewells to the Germans who had run German military installations in the Soviet Union indicate, the Russians were still interested in cooperation, but under the circumstances Germany would have had to take the initiative in mending the fences.[125] Any such step was precluded by Hitler's policy directives.

Two other East European areas with which German policy was directly concerned in 1933 and the following year were the state of Lithuania and the movement for Ukrainian independence. As an immediate neighbor of Germany, as a country exercising control over the Memel territory lost by Germany at the end of the war, and as a neighbor of Poland, Lithuania was a country whose importance for German diplomacy in the 1920s and 1930s was vastly greater than that of any of the other Baltic countries carved out of Czarist Russia.[126] German concern over the treatment of the German population in the Memel area, and in particular, Lithuanian observance, or rather frequent non-observance, of the statute governing that territory were continuing factors in German-Lithuanian relations. The possible strain imposed on their relations was generally outweighed by the fact that Poland's occupation of the Vilna area led Lithuania to share Germany's enmity to Poland and thereby forged an anti-Polish triangle with Russia.[127] In addition to the Memel dispute, an occasional shadow was thrown over German-Lithuanian relations by periodic talk of an arrangement under which Poland would yield to Germany Danzig and the Polish Corridor, or at least the northern part of the corridor, and would secure an alternative outlet to the sea by gaining control over Lithuania.[128]

123. *G. D.*, C, 1, No. 379; Scott, p. 121.

124. In part this was probably for the benefit of the Germans as well as the French (*G. D.*, C, 1, No. 439); but Germany's departure from the League in October would make the French receptive to the alliance suggested by Moscow (Scott, pp. 134ff.).

125. *G. D.*, C, 1, Nos. 444, 460.

126. There are no satisfactory treatments of German-Lithuanian relations in this period. Two important studies based on archival materials are Felix-Heinrich Gentzen, "Die Rolle der 'Deutschen Stiftung' bei der Vorbereitung der Annexion des Memellandes im März 1939," *Jahrbuch für Geschichte der UdSSR und der Volksdemokratischen Länder,* 5 (1961), 71–94; and Ernst-Albrecht Plieg, *Das Memelland 1920–1939* (Würzburg: Holzner, 1962). The first of these is limited to the perspectives then authorized in the Soviet zone of Germany; the second reads like a Pan-German propaganda tract.

127. For an interesting report on the nature and history of this triangle see *G. D.*, C, 2, No. 125.

128. References to this plan recur from time to time in the sources, but there is no

There is nothing to suggest that Hitler was in any special way concerned about Lithuania before 1933, and he was to pay relatively little attention to it thereafter. In his eyes, it was included in the areas suitable for Germany's *Lebensraum*—Russia and its border states[129]—but that was a project for the future. In the first years of National Socialist rule, German-Lithuanian relations were affected by two developments. The improvement of Germany's relations with Poland and the deterioration of its relations with Russia removed a significant tie between the two neighbors, but the impact of this change was felt slowly and did not manifest itself clearly for over a year. In the meantime, Germany tried to keep relations from deteriorating, even at the expense of some economic concessions to Lithuania, especially in regard to the pig exports that were of great importance to the Lithuanian economy.[130] While Hitler wanted no publicly conspicuous agreement with Lithuania, he did approve trade concessions and authorized an informal agreement on the handling of other current problems in August 1933.[131]

The second factor, which was to have more dramatic implications for German-Lithuanian relations, was the interaction between the activities of the new movements of a National Socialist character among the Germans of the Memel area and the interference with the rights of the Germans by the central government of Lithuania, partly in continued pursuance of national aims, partly in response to German agitation.[132] In 1933 two National Socialist parties competed with each other in Memel.[133] The first was the "Christlich-Soziale Arbeitsgemeinschaft" (CSA) of Theodor von Sass. This was the pre–1933 Memel National Socialist party, appearing publicly for the first time in the municipal elections of May 1933. The personal peculiarities of von Sass and the extreme character of CSA agitation threatened to discredit national socialism and provoke Lithuanian reprisals against which Germany could not yet defend the Memel Germans. Some groups within the Memel area, with the support of state and party offices inside Germany, thereupon organized another National Socialist party, the "Sozialistische Volksgemeinschaft" (Sovog) of Ernst Neumann. There was a short but noisy struggle between the two parties, in which the Sovog won out.[134]

---

indication that it was ever considered seriously. A good summary of the whole idea is in a report of the Czech minister in Warsaw of 26 January 1933, Czech document in T–120, 1316/2376/D 497176–82.

129. *Mein Kampf,* 2:742.

130. *G. D.,* C, 1, Nos. 45, 47, 48, 354, 373; Memorandum by Meyer, 17 July 1933, T–120, 1466/3015/D 596290–91.

131. *G. D.,* C, 1, Nos. 281, 405; Memorandum by von Bülow, 1 June 1933, T–120, 1466/3015/D 596287.

132. Of the two studies cited in n. 126, above, that of Gentzen concentrates on the German agitation, that of Plieg on the Lithuanian measures of repression.

133. A brief summary by Martin Broszat in *Gutachten des Instituts für Zeitgeschichte,* 1 (Munich: Selbtsverlag, 1958), 395–400.

134. Gentzen, pp. 76–79; Plieg, pp. 108–15. Most of the documents seized by the

Von Sass had appealed to Hitler himself, as well as to his party friends in adjacent East Prussia, but the German National Socialist party including its foreign policy office (APA) and the agencies of the German government sided with Neumann and, in fact, helped finance his party almost from its formation in the middle of June.[135] Such taking of sides between rival National Socialist groups may well have been an indication of a policy decision, that the less frenetic appeal of Neumann's Sovog better suited the long-term aims of the National Socialist regime. This choice should be considered analogous to Hitler's previously examined instructions to the Danzig National Socialists at about the same time that they avoid complications with Poland and to his initial siding with Rauschning against the more impulsive Forster; the ultimate settlement of the Memel issue, like the Danzig issue, would come not from the local National Socialists but from a rearmed Germany.

The Lithuanian government, however, was disturbed by the appearance of these National Socialist movements, whatever their tactics and orientation. In the face of the rising nationalistic agitation in Germany, more rigorous measures were taken against the Memel Germans. In the fall of 1933 and the following winter, a series of steps ranging from the dismissal of officials to the arrest of many leaders of both National Socialist groups created resentment in the Memel territory, aroused objections in Berlin, and led the German government to take economic reprisals.[136] Neither these reprisals nor the diplomatic warnings of Great Britain and the other powers that had signed the Memel Convention restrained the Lithuanian government from more drastic action.[137] The president of the Memel Directorate

Lithuanian authorities and used as evidence in the later trial of Memel Germans grew out of this feud between the two National Socialist movements. French translations of a group of these documents are in Foreign Office N 3515/96/59. Extensive German documentation on the trial may be found in T–120, 3475/8923/E 625227–798 and 3498/8959/E 628124–206.

135. Plieg (p. 111) cites the founding proclamation from a Memel newspaper of 18 June 1933. The earliest reference to financial support from the German Foreign Ministry that I have been able to locate is a marginal note, referring to a payment of 3,000 Reichsmark on 15 July 1933, on telegram 47 of 4 September 1933, from the German Consul General Toepke in Memel (T–120, 3070/6606/E 496448). The telegram requests a further installment out of a previously established fund, so that the decision to support the Neumann party must have been made in the German foreign ministry at least by the middle of July. It is noteworthy that just as Gentzen cannot find evidence of Lithuanian violations of the Memel Statute, Plieg's research in the German foreign ministry archives failed to turn up any of the numerous telegrams on Neumann's financial support (ibid., frames E 496449–53). That these payments represented a clear choice, not simply the financing of another German group abroad, is shown by the intended use of a subsequent payment "Special action against the *Volkskurier,*" the newspaper of the CSA (Halem [Vice-Consul Memel] telegram 61 of 25 September 1933, ibid., frame E 496450; cf. Plieg, p. 114).

136. *G. D.,* C, 1, No. 405, n. 3; 2, Nos. 142, 214, 215, 348; Stafford (U. S. chargé a.i. Kovno) dispatch 6 of 9 January 1934, State 760M.62/92.

137. Stafford dispatch 281 of 16 October 1933, State 860M.01-Memel/251; *G. D.,* C, 2, No. 388; Preston (British chargé Kovno) dispatches 158 of 1 September 1933 and 178 of 12 October 1933, Foreign Office N 6955 and N 7691/541/59.

was dismissed on 28 June, and the National Socialist parties were prohibited on 13 July 1934. In December, the trial of those National Socialist leaders arrested in February was begun in Kovno. There was, as a result, continued friction between Germany and Lithuania. Having left the League and thus without a direct basis of intervention, Germany repeatedly asked the signatories of the Memel Convention to intervene with the Lithuanian government. In spite of repeated warnings, especially from Great Britain, the Lithuanians proceeded on their course, and beyond the maintenance of their economic reprisals—which hurt the Memellanders too—there was little that the German government could do. Until the crisis in 1935, there would be little change.[138]

The other East European area of significance for early National Socialist diplomacy was the Ukraine. A people divided territorially in 1933 between the Soviet Union, Poland, Czechoslovakia, and Rumania, the Ukrainians were represented in Germany by several varieties of feuding nationalist organizations, some of which maintained close contact with right-wing circles.[139] Some of these groups were in touch with the National Socialists, especially with Rosenberg, whose vision of an alliance between Germany and the Ukraine after the disappearance of Poland and the destruction of the U.S.S.R. seemed congenial to Ukrainian nationalist agitation.[140] The ideological affinity toward national socialism of the integral nationalism of many Ukrainian émigrés appears to have blinded them to the fact that Hitler's agrarian expansionism was in reality the gravest threat to any and

138. On the difficulties in German-Lithuanian relations in 1934 and the interventions of the signatory powers in Kovno see *G. D.*, C, 3, Nos. 67, 75, 68, 80, 131, 142, 144, 193, 196, 199, 203, 205, 209, 219, 230, n. 7, 266, n. 9, 312, 314, 381, n. 2, 384; Dodd dispatch 1064 of 23 July 1934, State 860M.01-Memel/293; Stafford dispatch 133 of 26 September, 1934, ibid., /308; Stafford dispatch 155 of 4 December 1934, ibid., /323; Memorandum by von Bülow, 22 December 1934, T–120, 2372/4602/E 189935–936; Speaight (British Foreign Office), "Memorandum respecting the Situation in Memel," 13 March 1934, Foreign Office N 1618/96/59; Memorandum by Collier (London), 6 April 1934, and Sir John Simon to Knatchbull-Hugessen (Riga), 11 April 1934, Foreign Office N 2146/96/59; Memorandum by Collier, 6 October 1934, Foreign Office N 5658/96/59; Note by Grey (London), "Situation in Memel," 4 December 1934, Foreign Office N 6735/96/59.

From the records it is evident that the British government made the most determined efforts to find a settlement, while France hung back and Italy—annoyed with Germany over Austria—gave little support to the protests. Japan, the fourth signatory power, was still represented by Britain in the October 1933 protests and made some inquiries in July 1934 (British Foreign Office Minutes of 25–26 October 1934, N 6084/96/59; Plieg, p. 157).

139. The best survey of Ukrainian nationalist activities and organizations is John A. Armstrong, *Ukrainian Nationalism 1939–1945* (2d. ed., New York: Colombia University Press, 1966).

140. Alfred Rosenberg, *Der Zukunftsweg einer deutschen Aussenpolitik* (Munich: Eher, 1927), pp. 97–98; Jacobsen, pp. 449–50; Niclauss, p. 109. It should be noted that Rosenberg's quarrels with Erich Koch as Reich commissar for the Ukraine during World War II have often led to an exaggerated estimate of his positive attitude toward the Ukrainians. Rosenberg's own candidate for the position had been Fritz Sauckel, an equally ruthless fanatic whose slave-labor program was to be one of the main sources of Ukrainian suffering.

all Ukrainian aspirations. Their naïve belief that this expansionism could be diverted from the rich farm lands of the Ukraine to the food deficit areas further north is otherwise difficult to understand. The first disappointment of the Ukrainian nationalists—though it did not disillusion them entirely—came in 1933. By the summer of that year, they recognized the signs of a detente in German-Polish relations. Since the bulk of Ukrainian nationalist activity at this time was directed against Poland, hopes for help from Germany were evidently premature.[141] Through Rosenberg and the army, however, the German government maintained contact with several émigré groups, expecting to use them at the appropriate time against either Poland or the Soviet Union or both. The Ukrainians in turn hoped to use the Germans. As in the case of Memel, major policy developments lay in an uncertain future. Meanwhile, the National Socialist contact with Ukrainian groups was unlikely to ease suspicions of Germany in the Soviet Union, the country in which the vast majority of Ukrainians lived.

Hitler's policy toward Eastern Europe in the first year of National Socialist rule is thus a more coherent whole than might appear at first sight. The reversal in the relationships with Poland and the Soviet Union as well as the soft-pedaling of German interests in Memel and the Ukraine fall into a general pattern, a pattern in which relaxation in the present and immediate future could lay the groundwork for an attempt at extensive conquests later, in contrast to the previously well-established German policy of operating with current tensions for immediate but limited gains. The old policy fitted into a vision of an Eastern Europe in which Germany played a greater part; the new policy was designed to provide the basis for an Eastern Europe under German domination. The implication of revisionist agitation was change, significant but measured; short-term quiescence, on the other hand, might lay the groundwork for later revolutionary upheaval.

141. There is a useful summary in Roos, pp. 89–94. It is based heavily on intelligence reports of the Polish government, which was obviously well informed about the activities of Ukrainian nationalist groups. See also *Lipski Papers,* pp. 135–36, for evidence that German army intelligence warned Poland of a planned assassination attempt by Ukrainian nationalists in June 1934.

4 Austria, Czechoslovakia, Southeast Europe

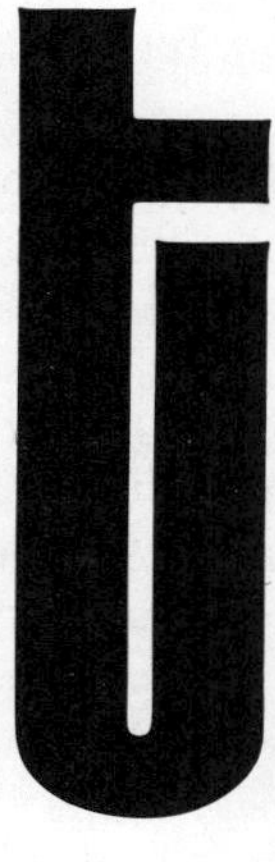

Austria

he policy of Hitler's Germany toward Austria was, at the beginning, significantly different from the treatment accorded other countries and problems. Hitler himself came from Austria, planned to include it in Germany, and in the meantime included the National Socialist party of Austria in his own. Austrian sentiment for a union with Germany had been strong since the Habsburg empire fell apart in the closing weeks of the first world war, and these feelings had been reciprocated in Germany.[1] The coming to power of the National Socialist regime in Germany increased the German but decreased the Austrian interest in the *Anschluss*, as inclusion of Austria in Germany had generally come to be known. Hitler proceeded as if little had changed. He applied his concept of consolidating power to Austria in terms of domestic politics similar to the procedures he had already followed in Germany. Election campaigns alternating with negotiations for government coalitions would increase the size and role of the Austrian National Socialists until by pseudolegal means a position of growing authority in the government could be exploited for the subsequent attainment of total power. This would later enable Hitler to effect the *Anschluss* at whatever moment seemed opportune and reasonably safe. It should be noted that this policy was opportunistic as to means, and could be carried forward with disclaimers about expansionist intent for some time but had a clearly defined ultimate goal.

On the road to the eventual goal of annexation, the methods Hitler had used in Germany could be applied, modified by two characteristics of the Austrian situation that differed from the German experience. The first dif-

1. Though hardly definitive, the most useful summary is Jürgen Gehl, *Austria, Germany, and the Anschluss, 1931–38* (London: Oxford University Press, 1963).

ference was, of course, the very fact that there was already a National Socialist government in Berlin in a position to exercise influence and pressure from the outside. Hitler had explained two years earlier to Waldemar Pabst,[2] a key figure in organizing coups of all sorts in Austria, that when he himself came to power in Germany he would send his best speakers and plenty of money in order to attain the same success in Austria.[3] One of the major characteristics of the struggle for control of Austria's destiny, therefore, was to be Germany's controlled intervention into that struggle. The second difference related to the general nature of politicians and the political process in Austria. Among the leaders or would-be leaders of the right—the Christian Socials, the fascist-oriented Heimwehr, the Greater German party, and the Peasants' party (*Landbund*)—there was a general belief that politics consisted of betraying your friends and associates at every opportune moment. There were a few individuals in the groups named who did not share this belief, otherwise acted upon with vigor and frequency, but it certainly was a key tenet of the Austrian National Socialists. The history of the Austrian party from 1933 to 1938 is to a very large extent a tedious record of factional struggles, mutual betrayals, and endless recriminations. After the *Anschluss,* many of the Austrian National Socialists were to have plenty of leisure to continue these recriminations, and the apologias produced in that process provide a substantial proportion of the interesting, if not always reliable, evidence on the events of the 1930s.

The government of Chancellor Engelbert Dollfuss, in power in Vienna at the beginning of 1933, was based on a coalition of parties and groups with a bare majority of one vote in parliament.[4] Because local elections in 1932 had shown an increase in National Socialist votes, and because events in Germany suggested that more gains were coming, the Austrian National Socialists and their German mentors insisted on the holding of new elec-

2. Waldemar Pabst was an international adventurer who had been involved in efforts to bolshevize Poland so that Germany could demand a larger army (Wilhelm Breucker, *Die Tragik Ludendorffs* [Stollham: Rauschenbusch, 1953], p. 179, n. 3); represented Gustav Stresemann in various illegal activities in Austria (Hans Gatzke, *Stresemann and the Rearmament of Germany* [Baltimore: Johns Hopkins Press, 1954], pp. 51–53; *Der Deutsche Imperialismus und der zweite Weltkrieg,* 2:465–68); and played a key role in right-wing politics in Austria in spite of a temporary deportation (*G. D.,* C, 1, No. 357; 2, No. 289; 3, No. 124). For his part in establishing a society for the study of fascism in Berlin see Hoepke, pp. 297–303, and Carl Eduard Herzog von Coburg und Gotha to von Neurath, 15 November 1933, T–120, 2700/5737/H 028781–86. For his role in the Heimwehr see Lajos Kerekes, *Abenddämmerung einer Demokratie* (trans. by Johanna Till, Vienna: Europa Verlag, 1966) (hereafter cited as Kerekes, *Abenddämmerung*).

3. Memorandum [by Gábor Apor], 25 January 1931, Lajos Kerekes (ed.), "Akten zu den geheimen Verbindungen zwischen der Bethlen-Regierung und der österreichischen Heimwehrbewegung," *Acta Historica,* 11, Nos. 1–4 (1965), p. 338; cf. Apor's note of 15 December 1930, ibid., p. 331. Pabst also recounted that Hitler told him he expected to come to power in the framework of a coalition, would never leave office, and would either subdue or force out his coalition partners.

4. Helpful, though somewhat biased in favor of Dollfuss, is Gordon Brook-Shepherd, *Dollfuss* (London: Macmillan, 1961).

tions and participation in the governing coalition with or without such elections. The Social Democratic opposition also expected gains from new elections and did what it could to embarrass the government, including the revelation of Italian arms shipments through Austria to Hungary and to Austria for its Heimwehr opponents. The uproar over this incident, the Hirtenberg arms affair, was soon settled by clever maneuvering,[5] and in March the Dollfuss government dispensed with parliament altogether by taking advantage of a procedural technicality. But if the Social Democratic opposition could be put on the defensive so easily, the National Socialists could not.

The agitation of the National Socialist party in Austria increased as it, as well as the Greater German party, received support from Germany.[6] The German National Socialist leadership, from the fragmentary evidence available, appears to have thought that the process of *Gleichschaltung,* political coordination, that was being applied to the German state governments early in March 1933 might be applied to Austria just as it would be applied, with some delay, to Danzig. Thus Hans Frank, the new minister of justice of the National Socialist regime installed by Franz Ritter von Epp's coup in Bavaria on 9 March, warned the Austrian government not to suppress the National Socialist movement in that country, lest their German comrades "take upon themselves the task of assuring the freedom of their fellow Germans in Austria."[7] The Austrian protests against this speech were met with a variety of excuses, but no regrets. Protests entered by the Italian government were no more successful.[8]

Il Duce was concerned about the danger of an *Anschluss* as it would affect Italy's interests in southeastern Europe as well as South Tirol and wanted the Berlin government to give support to Dollfuss. Similar pleas for support of Dollfuss were made by the Hungarian prime minister, Julius Gömbös.[9] This was, of course, the one thing the Hitler regime was not prepared to do. Hitler would not support Dollfuss in Austria any more than he had supported the von Papen government in Germany. What he wanted was a major role for the Austrian National Socialists in the government, and in view of his own concept of that role, he could safely tell the Italians that he did not wish the *Anschluss* at that time.[10] Some caution was indicated, how-

5. *G. D.,* C, 1, No. 81; *B. D.,* 2d, 5, No. 38, n. 1; Gehl, pp. 48–49.

6. *G. D.,* C, 1, No. 25; *D. D. F.,* 1st, 2, No. 267.

7. The German official text is in *Beiträge zur Vorgeschichte und Geschichte der Julirevolte* (Vienna: Bundeskommissariat für Heimatdienst, 1934) (hereafter cited as *Beiträge*), p. 20. This official brochure published by the Austrian government is accurate as far as it goes but leaves out a great deal to avoid incriminating certain Austrians and some Germans.

8. *G. D.,* C, 1, No. 112.

9. Kerekes, *Abenddämmerung,* pp. 131–37.

10. *G. D.,* C, 1, Nos. 112, 128, 206; von Neurath to von Hassell, 27 March 1933, and von Neurath's memorandum RM 411 of same date, T–120, 2832/6077/E 450623 and E 450629.

ever. Clearly internal steps leading to National Socialist seizure of power in Austria were less dangerous than excessively obvious external pressures that could only lead to foreign intervention. But this could be applied to official state, not party, affairs. The "channels opened up by the ideological and organizational bonds between the National Socialist movements in the Reich and in Austria" would have to be sufficient.[11]

In mid-April, both the National Socialists and Dollfuss tried to get support for their policies from Mussolini. The German emissaries, von Papen and Göring, accompanied by Renzetti, discussed the whole range of international subjects with Il Duce and also took a hand in the concordat negotiations with the Vatican. Mussolini replied to Germany urging for a National Socialist government in Austria with warnings against the *Anschluss,* while he promised Dollfuss support in his struggle for Austrian independence if he would seriously begin the transformation of his country into a Fascist state on the Italian model.[12] Dollfuss, who preferred reasonably good relations with Germany if that were possible, took advantage of the opportunity to send to Berlin via von Papen an indication that he was willing to come to Berlin himself to sign a German-Austrian trade agreement. Such an agreement had been under discussion for some time, and Dollfuss was willing to make the concessions necessary to bring about a conclusion.[13] In spite of the economic advantages to Germany, the German government decided not to conclude an economic agreement with the Dollfuss government and most assuredly did not wish to welcome Dollfuss himself to Berlin.[14]

Far from being willing to consider an economic agreement, Hitler was in fact examining ways to put the Austrian government under economic pressure. When he raged at the Austrian minister to Berlin on 10 May over the audacity of Austria in protesting German press slanders of Dollfuss, Hitler warned that Germany might stop all tourist traffic to Austria.[15] This plan for greater German pressure was related to the failure of negotiations between Dollfuss's Christian Socials and the National Socialists led by Theo Habicht, a German Reichstag deputy whom Hitler had placed in charge of the Austrian branch of the NSDAP.[16] Action on the German plan was pre-

11. *G. D.,* C, 1, No. 107; see also Memorandum by Köpke, II Oe 342, 28 March 1933, T–120, 2832/6077/E 450845–47.

12. For information on these conferences see *G. D.,* C, 1, Nos. 154, 162, 164, 171, 173, 176, 403; 4, No. 61, p. 106; *B. D.,* 2d, 5, Nos. 73, 75, 77, 80 81, 85, 89, 90; for background on Göring's mission to Rome see the documents in T–120, 1388/2784/D 540156–60.

13. Note by von Bülow, 20 April 1933, T–120, 2373/4603/E 190930.

14. *G. D.,* C, 1, Nos. 187, 191; Dieter Ross, *Hitler und Dollfuss* (Hamburg: Leibniz-Verlag, 1966), pp. 31–32.

15. *G. D.,* C, 1, No. 219; *B. D.,* 2d, 5, No. 147; *Beiträge,* p. 22. It should be noted that the evidence of the British documents here leaves no doubt that the subject was under active consideration before Frank's trip to Austria on 13 May.

16. Gehl, pp. 55–56; Ross, pp. 34–36.

cipitated by an incident provoked by Frank. Together with such judicial luminaries as the Prussian minister of justice, Hanns Kerrl, and the state secretary, Roland Freisler, Frank flew to Austria to bring messages of greeting to the local National Socialists and voice threats against the Dollfuss government. The Dollfuss government indicated its displeasure at the beginning of the visit and strongly urged a more speedy termination near its end.[17] Hitler saw no reason for restraint at this point and decided to use the occasion for the next blow. While Göring was in Rome again, reassuring Mussolini about Germany's Austrian policy,[18] new measures against Austria were under consideration in Berlin. Although there was some reluctance on both measures in the foreign ministry, the German government took two major steps.[19] The first of these was a tourist boycott of Austria, arranged by charging Germans the prohibitive sum of 1,000 marks for a visa to Austria. It was assumed that this measure would strike such a blow to the Austrian economy, already weakened by the depression, as to force the Dollfuss regime into line very quickly. Hitler expressed the opinion that the Dollfuss government would collapse and that new elections would follow. These elections, for which the NSDAP would make tremendous propaganda, would bring about the *Gleichschaltung* of Austria and thereby obviate the need for an *Anschluss*. There would be economic costs for Germany as well, but not for long; before the end of the summer the contest would be decided. This explanation, which Hitler gave to his ministers on 26 May, was repeated to Rauschning and another delegate from Danzig a few days later.[20] Hitler thought the decisive moment was imminent; success would follow the tourist boycott. He brushed aside efforts at mediation as he aimed for a National Socialist takeover in Vienna. The procedure in Bavaria that had so alarmed the Austrians would soon be applied to them.[21]

At the same time as the tourist boycott was to bring down the Dollfuss government, Hitler was counting on another measure to provide a way of capitalizing on that situation. Habicht himself, together with an assistant, was to be made a member of the staff of the German legation in Vienna. This step, of which the Austrian government was informed on the same day as the 1,000-mark rule was promulgated,[22] can be understood only if it is assumed that Habicht was to play in Vienna the role that von Epp had per-

17. The account in the memoirs of Hans Frank, *Im Angesicht des Galgens* (Munich: Friedrich Alfred Beck Verlag, 1953), pp. 284–89, is interesting but quite unreliable. See *G. D.,* C, 1, Nos. 234, 249; *B. D.,* 2d, 5, No. 147; *Beiträge,* pp. 20–21; U. S. 1933, 1:428–32; Ross, pp. 38–40; Note [by Menshausen?], RM 698, 18 May 1933, T–120, 2832/6077/E 450689.

18. *G. D.,* C, 1, No. 258.

19. On the internal discussions see ibid., Nos. 249, 256, 262; Memorandum by Ritter, 20 May 1933, T–120, 2832/6077/E 450707–10; Ross, pp. 43–49.

20. Rauschning, *Voice of Destruction,* pp. 86–88.

21. *G. D.,* C, 1, No. 270; cf. ibid., No. 130.

22. Ibid., No. 267; *Beiträge,* p. 23; Ross, pp. 41–43, 51–53.

formed in Munich and that Rauschning and Forster were about to play in Danzig—as the representative of Hitler whose task it was to set up locally a government entirely subservient to the dictates of Berlin. The Austrian government, to the great annoyance of Berlin, declined to accept its executioners as diplomats. In fact, they searched Habicht's apartment and began to talk about deporting him.[23] Following some terroristic acts in Austria, the authorities arrested Habicht and his associate and proceeded to ship Habicht back to Germany. Hitler retaliated by ordering the arrest and subsequent expulsion of the press attaché at the Austrian legation in Berlin, the significant difference being that the attaché really did have diplomatic immunity.[24] The resulting international uproar was accentuated by the fact that Dollfuss and von Neurath were both in London at the time for the World Economic Conference, so that the whole issue was immediately placed on the world stage where Germany was already both despised and isolated.[25] The possibility of international intervention increased the danger for Germany; the Austrian government felt able to act. On 19 June 1933 the Austrian National Socialist party was outlawed, and the struggle became more bitter than ever.

The great propaganda campaign Hitler had planned was now launched, and Habicht with the full confidence of his master directed it from Munich.[26] In speeches on the radio and in leaflets dropped by plane over Austria, the Dollfuss regime was assailed and the Austrian people were called on to rise against a government which would soon collapse.[27] All Austrian protests were rejected; so were last-minute Austrian efforts to improve relations.[28] To make certain there could be no smoothing out of the conflict, the German minister to Vienna was instructed not to meet Dollfuss for the time being at all.[29]

As the situation became more critical, Dollfuss looked to other powers for backing. The Italian government was increasingly concerned and began to demonstrate its displeasure at Germany's actions by reducing its support of the German negotiating position in Geneva, a shift that was becoming

23. It was not until 22 June, more than a month after Hitler had decided to appoint Habicht, that von Bülow learned of a 1927 decision by Germany's highest court, the Reichsgericht, that a diplomat acquired immunity and extraterritoriality only *after* he had received the agrément (Note by von Bülow, 22 June 1933, T–120, 2374/4603/E 190961). In the meantime, the German minister in Vienna was dreaming up ingenious schemes to forestall Habicht's deportation (Rieth report A.603 of 3 June 1933, T–120, 2494/4938/E 268337).

24. *G. D.,* C, 1, Nos. 298, 305, 306, 307; *Beiträge,* p. 24; *B. D.,* 2c, 5, No. 215.

25. *G. D.,* C, 1, Nos. 310, 313; von Neurath to von Bülow, 14 June 1933, T–120, 2383/4619/E 197687.

26. Waldeck note for Köpke, 19 June 1933, T–120, 2836/6111/E 452501.

27. Heinz Pohle, *Der Rundfunk als Instrument der Politik* (Hamburg: Hans Bredow-Institut, 1955), pp. 400ff.; *Beiträge,* pp. 26–30. See also the leaflets enclosed with Stockton's (Vienna) dispatch 905 of 12 September 1933, State 762.63/114.

28. *G. D.,* C, 1, No. 346; *Beiträge,* pp. 46-48; Ross, pp. 57–59.

29. *G. D.,* C, 1, Nos. 364, n. 10, and 376, n. 7; *Beiträge,* p. 29.

evident by 11 May.[30] In spite of reassurances from Berlin, Mussolini took a growing interest in aiding Dollfuss.[31] He promised Dollfuss his support and tried to have the Hungarian leader Gömbös do likewise.[32] If Dollfuss would suppress the Social Democrats and thus deprive the National Socialists of the anti-Marxist argument, he would strengthen his position at home and be in a better situation to arrive at a settlement with Germany. If this advice from the Italian dictator pointed in one direction, the other possible sources of support—Britain and France—were unlikely to be pleased by further repression of the democratic forces in Austria. Dollfuss, therefore, informed Mussolini that he would have to move toward a corporative state at his own speed,[33] while he tried to secure assistance from the League, Britain, and France.[34] As the German campaign continued, international alarm increased; and Britain and France considered joint intervention with Italy in Berlin.[35] The Italian government, wishing to maintain good relations with Germany while still defending Austria, told the Germans of the forthcoming demarche in which they themselves refused to participate. The German government made some vague promises to Italy, rudely rejected the 7 August intervention of Britain and France, and proceeded on its own course.

In the face of continued firm and successful resistance by the Austrian government and the threat of further foreign intervention, the German government in late July and early August 1933 did find it necessary to reformulate its policies, or at least its procedures. The struggle had not ended as quickly as Hitler had anticipated, but he was not prepared to call it off. He made it perfectly clear that Germany would not deal with the Dollfuss government. Furthermore, even though he promised the Italians to tone down Habicht's campaign, he allowed Habicht to continue broadcasting attacks on Austria from the Munich radio, rejecting all Italian protests against such speeches, and also declining to provide a written renunciation of an *Anschluss*. There was, in other words, to be no basic change in policy. Certain limitations on the campaign against Dollfuss, however, seemed wise. Hitler did not want to give either Italy or other powers any more opportunity to intervene than necessary, and he did not relish the prospect of

30. Nadolny to von Neurath No. 358 of 11 May 1933, T–120, 1558/3154/D 669074; Wilson (Geneva) to Hull, 11 May 1933, U. S. 1933, 1:136–38; *G. D.*, C, 1, No. 239, p. 439 and n. 13.

31. *G. D.*, C, 1, No. 343.

32. Mussolini to Dollfuss, 1 July 1933, in Julius Braunthal, *The Tragedy of Austria* (London: Gollancz, 1948), pp. 184–87; *B. D.*, 2d, 5, No. 246; Mussolini to Gömbös, 8 July 1933, excerpt in Lajos Kerekes (ed.), "Akten des ungarischen Ministeriums des Äusseren zur Annexion Österreichs," *Acta Historica*, 7, No. 3–4 (1960) (hereafter cited as "Akten zur Annexion Österreichs"), 361.

Gömbös, whose previous visit to Berlin had disturbed Dollfuss, visited Vienna on 9 July (*B. D.*, 2d, 5, No. 245; *G. D.*, C, 1, No. 363).

33. Dollfuss to Mussolini, 22 July 1933, Braunthal, pp. 187–92; Ross, pp. 55–56.

34. *B. D.*, 2d, 5, Nos. 210, 211, 213, 214, 233, 236, 237, 245, 260.

35. Summaries in Gehl, pp. 62–68, and Ross, pp. 68–69.

having the dispute brought before the League. As the state secretary, von Bülow, explained to Habicht, Germany was reluctant to use on the Austrian question the threat of leaving the League that it preferred to save for more important issues—disarmament or the Saar.[36] The dropping of leaflets from airplanes was accordingly halted, Habicht was told to tone down his speeches a little, and some controls were imposed on the Austrian legion, a paramilitary organization of Austrian cutthroats who had found it expedient to seek refuge in Germany and were encamped not far from the German-Austrian border.[37] But with such limitations, pressure on Austria was to continue until the Dollfuss government yielded or collapsed.[38] Tension rose during August and September as incidents near the border suggested that a coup by the Austrian legion might be imminent.[39] The National Socialist party in Austria had been declared illegal in June; it continued its activities underground. On 14 August the Austrian government, through a brochure issued by the semiofficial newspaper *Reichspost,* published a number of documents on that illegal activity and plans for a coup, documents that implicated the foreign policy office (APA) of the NSDAP as well as the German foreign ministry.[40] Little had changed.

In the face of this situation, Dollfuss tied himself more closely to Italy. Having covered himself with the *Reichspost* revelations, he saw Mussolini again on 19–20 August.[41] Il Duce made it clear to Dollfuss that in return for continued support he expected him to reorganize his government with a greater role for the Heimwehr, followed by crushing of the Social Democrats. Under continued pressure from Mussolini, Dollfuss did rearrange his government and move in the direction of a corporative state, but he was

36. Memorandum by von Heeren, 31 July 1933, T–120, 2838/5113/E 453737–42.

37. The Austrian National Socialist who was to become most notorious after his flight to Germany was Adolf Eichmann. There is extensive material on the legion in *Beiträge,* pp. 30–39; see also *B. D.,* 2d, 5, No. 398; *G. D.,* C, 1, No. 427; Memorandum by Hüffer, II Oe 1470 of 23 September 1933, T–120, 2890/6115/E 454769–70.

38. For evidence on German policy at this time see *G. D.,* C, 1, Nos. 385, 390, 391, 398, 401, 402, 407, 411; *Beiträge,* pp. 27–29; *B. D.,* 2d, 5, Nos. 308, 309; U. S. 1933, 1:443–46; Ross, pp. 70–76; Memorandum by von Bülow, 27 July 1933, T–120, 2372/4602/E 189333–35; Smend (Rome) to the foreign ministry No. 199 of 12 August 1933, 778/1549/376403–04; Lammers to the foreign ministry, 16 August 1933, 2700/5737/H 028711.

39. *B. D.,* 2d, 5, Nos. 335, 338, 339, 340, 343, 349, 355, 363, 377.

40. A copy of the brochure was attached to a report of the U. S. legation in Vienna of 28 August 1933, and is in State 762.63/119: "Die Verschwörung gegen Österreich, Dokumente und Akten." See also *B. D.,* 2d, 5, No. 345; *G. D.,* C, 1, No. 407. The foreign ministry had just stopped allowing the Austrian party to use its diplomatic pouch (Rieth to von Bülow, 19 August 1933, T–120, 2836/6111/E 452517–24).

While the Austrians had access to German documents, the Germans were reading many Austrian ones. The German military attaché in Vienna regularly saw the reports of the Austrian military attaché in Berlin; see the supplement to Muff report 47 of 16 August 1933, T–120, 2695/5705/E 414183.

41. U. S. 1933, 1: 437, 439–40, 442; *B. D.,* 2d, 5, Nos. 353, 354, 365, 367, 374; *G. D.,* C, 1, Nos. 398, 408; Braunthal, pp. 192–94; Brook-Shepherd, pp. 203–206; Ross, pp. 77–81.

still reluctant to go all the way in meeting Mussolini's and the Heimwehr's demands, knowing that he would then be totally dependent upon Italy.[42] Dollfuss therefore decided to try negotiations with the National Socialists for a coalition in which he hoped to balance them against the Heimwehr while he himself remained in control. There can, furthermore, be little doubt that the strong German feelings of Dollfuss were an important factor in leading him to make one more attempt at a rapprochement with Germany before throwing himself completely on the mercy of the Heimwehr. Simultaneously, the inability of the Austrian National Socialists to topple the Vienna government as rapidly as they had hoped, the decreasing prospect of success, and the fear of a Heimwehr dictatorship inclined at least some elements in the Austrian NSDAP to the idea of an accommodation. In the fall of 1933, therefore, a variety of feelers were put out to Germany from Vienna, some directly through diplomatic channels and some through individual members of Austrian political movements outside the government. These complicated maneuvers, punctuated by the mutual betrayals characteristic of Austrian politics of the day, led to no concrete results; but they do serve to shed some light on German policy toward Austria in the critical period just before and after Germany's departure from the League.[43]

Hitler continued to back Habicht. He insisted on Habicht as his own representative against other National Socialists like Hanfstaengl who wanted to dabble in German-Austrian relations. Similarly he insisted to Dollfuss as well as other Austrians trying to negotiate alongside Dollfuss or behind his back that Habicht was the man they were to deal with. Under these circumstances, Habicht's demands, which included half the cabinet for his associates and the vice-chancellorship for himself, must be assumed to have had Hitler's backing.[44] To hold the office he demanded, Habicht would have had to become a naturalized Austrian citizen, a form of poetic justice in view of the ex-Austrian Hitler's naturalization in Germany the preceding year.[45] Clearly Hitler was still pushing toward *Gleichschaltung* in Austria through internal change supported by outside pressure. Since victory had not come as quickly in the summer as Hitler had predicted, he was now willing to have Habicht ask for less than some months earlier, even though these demands still seemed outrageous to Dollfuss. Hitler, furthermore, was firm in

42. *B. D.*, 2d, 5, No. 414; Braunthal, pp. 195–98, 210–12; Gehl, pp. 70–73.

43. Summary of the evidence in Gehl, pp. 72–77, and Ross, chap. 2.

44. It should be noted that in late October or early November 1933, Hitler was informed of plans for a National Socialist coup in Austria, originally scheduled for 15 October but then postponed. Hitler refused to approve the action (Ludwig Jedlicka [ed.], *Die Erhebung der österreichischen Nationalsozialisten im Juli 1934, Bericht der Historischen Kommission des Reichsführers SS* [Vienna: Europa Verlag, 1965] [hereafter cited as *Die Erhebung*], p. 67).

45. A closer analogy would perhaps be Forster, like Habicht a member of the German Reichstag, who had been made gauleiter of the party in Danzig though not a Danzig resident. A semiofficial biography is Wilhelm Löbsack, *Gauleiter Albert Forster, Der deutsche Angestelltenführer* (Hamburg: Hanseatische Verlagsgesellschaft, 1934).

insisting that the National Socialist party must again be legalized in Austria,[46] but he could reassure Mussolini that the *Anschluss* was not imminent.[47]

When the Italian undersecretary of state in the foreign ministry, Fulvio Suvich, who had been born in Trieste, met Hitler on 13 December, the two ex-Austrians discussed the present situation in Austria, agreeing that it should not be allowed to harm relations between the two great powers.[48] Hitler, nevertheless, was insistent on drastic changes in Austria and on Habicht as his man to have those changes made, just as his own representative had made them in Danzig. Since Suvich was scheduled to go to Vienna in the middle of January, Dollfuss had to use the time left before that visit to make the best bargain he could with the National Socialists or find himself obliged to go along with whatever the Italians desired. Reluctantly, Dollfuss now agreed to see Habicht to negotiate a settlement in person. Habicht, on the other hand, saw in negotiations with Dollfuss an opportunity to reassert his own role in the face of a possible German-Italian agreement to push the dispute over Austria into the background, while the Austrian National Socialist movement drifted into desperation or oblivion.

With Hitler's approval, it was agreed that Habicht should fly to Vienna and confer with Dollfuss on 8 January 1934. When information about this got out in Vienna, direct pressure from the Italian government, as well as indirect pressure through the Heimwehr, forced Dollfuss to cancel the planned meeting. Only a radio call with an order from Hitler caused Habicht to have his plane turn back before landing in Austria.[49] Habicht was disappointed and angry at his failure to make direct contact with the Austrian government; and with the approval of both Hitler and von Neurath, Prince Josias von Waldeck und Pyrmont of the German foreign ministry went to Vienna without notification to the Austrian government to confer with Austrian National Socialist leaders on the next steps. Those with whom Waldeck conferred were arrested; he himself was politely encouraged to return to Germany.[50] As terrorist incidents in Austria increased, the Dollfuss gov-

46. See the meeting of Hitler and François-Poncet on 24 November 1933, in *G. D.*, C, 1, No. 86; *B. D.*, 2d, 6, No. 79; Mastný's report of 29 November 1933, Czech document in T–120, 1041/1809/413961–62.

47. For Mussolini's attitudes see especially *B. D.*, 2d, 5, No. 417; *G. D.*, C, 2, No. 3, p. 5; U. S. 1933, 1:253–55. Göring reassured Mussolini while in Rome on 6 November 1933 (*G. D.*, C, 2, Nos. 50, 78; *B. D.*, 2d, 6, Nos. 10, 20, 29).

The Germans had the report of the Austrian military attaché in Berlin (Jansa) of 21 September 1933, asserting that the German army knew Italy would fight if the Germans or the legion invaded Austria, but Britain and France would not (Muff report 64 of 16 October, T–120, 2695/5705/E 414200–06).

48. This visit will also be discussed in connection with other aspects of German foreign policy in the winter of 1933–34. For references to the subject of Austria see *G. D.*, C, 2, Nos. 126, 145; *B. D.*, 2d, 6, Nos. 137, 142, 143, 144; Ross, pp. 131–33; Dertinger's "Informationsbericht Nr. 31 vom 31. Dezember 1933," Bundesarchiv, Brammer, Z.Sg. 101/26, f. 619–21.

49. *Beiträge,* pp. 18, 50–51; *G. D.*, C, 2, Nos. 160, 166; Ross, pp. 140–53; Kerekes, *Abenddämmerung,* pp. 174–76.

50. *G. D.*, C, 2, Nos. 167, 179; *Beiträge,* pp. 52–53.

ernment threatened to take the issue to the League, while the German government continued to profess its own anger over the cancellation of the Dollfuss-Habicht meeting.[51] By now time had run out for Dollfuss's maneuvers. The 8 January incident had already shown how limited his freedom of action really was. When Suvich came to Vienna on 18 January, he reminded the Austrian chancellor of his promise to crush the Social Democrats and move closer to Hungary as well.[52]

Dollfuss still tried to secure some support from the League powers other than Italy and to keep up contacts with the Germans. But there was no strength in the League, and all he could get from the Western powers was a platonic statement of interest in the maintenance of Austrian independence.[53] By the time this statement was issued on 17 February 1934 by England, France, and Italy, the situation had been changed by events inside Austria. Dollfuss allowed the Heimwehr to incite a violent campaign against the Social Democrats which culminated in the destruction of the Social Democratic stronghold in Vienna under the thunder of Austrian artillery and Heimwehr bullets. The policy of the German government and the Austrian National Socialists in the face of the Austrian civil war of 12–14 February was to stand aside while the Dollfuss government destroyed one of the main bastions defending the country against the National Socialists. The National Socialists hoped that the stress of civil war would push many of the workers into their camp and perhaps force Dollfuss into a coalition with themselves. They indicated a willingness to enter the government under the conditions set forth in the preceding year; but although Dollfuss maintained contact with the Austrian National Socialists, he had neither the inclination nor, after the new triumph of the Heimwehr, the opportunity to agree to Habicht as vice-chancellor.[54]

While Dollfuss did what he could to secure support for his position by closer ties with Italy and Hungary,[55] the National Socialists made a final effort to pressure him into negotiations. Berlin continued to adhere to the view that there could be no direct negotiations between the German and Austrian governments as long as Austria suppressed the NSDAP.[56] Habicht maintained pressure on the regime by means of spoken threats over the Munich radio alternating with acts of terror inside Austria.[57] As the Aus-

51. *G. D.*, C, 2, No. 188; *Beiträge,* p. 27; *B. D.*, 2d, 6, Nos. 186, 201; Memorandum by von Neurath RM 41, 11 January 1934, T–120, 778/1549/37643–46.

52. *B. D.*, 2d, 6, Nos. 194, 205; *G. D.*, C, 2, No. 225; Braunthal, pp. 199–201, 203–4; Ross, pp. 166–68. For the role of M. M. Rost van Tonningen as intermediary between Dollfuss and Mussolini in 1934 see the excerpts from his diary in *Correspondentie van M. M. Rost van Tonningen,* 1 ('s-Gravenhage: Nijhoff, 1967), 288–97.

53. *B. D.*, 2d, 6, Nos. 213, 221, 222, 238, 246, 254, 259, 261, 263, 265–70, 273, 274, 276, 277, 280, 282–84, 288–90; *G. D.*, C, 2, Nos. 213, 242, 255, 261.

54. *G. D.*, C, 2, Nos. 253, 254, 260, 263; 264; *B. D.*, 2d, 6, Nos. 275, 279, 286, 293, 294; Kerekes, *Abenddämmerung,* pp. 178–86.

55. *G. D.*, C, 2, Nos. 257, 296; *B. D.*, 2d, 6, Nos. 321, 332.

56. *G. D.*, C, 2, Nos. 282, 290; Memorandum of von Neurath RM 164, 9 February 1934, T–120, 2838/6113/E 453924–25.

57. *G. D.*, C, 2, No. 278, n. 3; *Beiträge,* pp. 12–13; "Bestellung aus der Pressekon-

trian government now refused to deal with him at all the whole situation became more critical. The rivalries within the Austrian National Socialist movement and within the Heimwehr led both to negotiations for agreement and plans for various types of coups in Vienna that were generally at cross-purposes with each other and also threatened to explode into open and large-scale violence.[58] There had been indications of this possibility earlier in the year.[59]

While the Austrian internal situation drifted more and more in the direction of a violent solution, what was Hitler's policy? In his Reichstag speech of 30 January, Hitler had attacked the Austrian government while denying any past and forswearing any future intervention in Austrian internal affairs.[60] There can be no question, however, that he continued to provide the Austrian National Socialists with support from Germany. As the plots and counterplots continued, Hitler adopted a stance of watchful waiting, allowing the situation to develop but not taking the lead himself.[61] Since the Rome meeting of Mussolini, Dollfuss, and Gömbös culminated in the consultative protocol of 17 March—as part of the so-called Rome protocols—caution was clearly indicated.[62] Hitler did not wish to push closer together the three countries they represented and was now inclined to think of the Austrian conflict in long-range terms. The party should build up its strength inside Austria; time was on its side.[63] He tried to restrain the exuberance of his Austrian party comrades[64] at the same time he hinted at restraint to those who wished to push the revolution in Germany more rapidly. Temporarily, he was becoming as reluctant to move quickly in Austria as he was in Germany; with many possibilities open, he preferred to await developments and then take advantage of those that came closest to combining the greatest probability of success with the least risk. Since the first year of pressure had failed to topple Dollfuss, Hitler was less sure of himself.

Hitler was particularly concerned about the drift of Italian policy which suggested that not merely the *Anschluss* but even a purely internal National Socialist takeover in Austria was totally unacceptable to Rome.[65] It was under these circumstances that talk of a Hitler-Mussolini meeting was re-

---

ferenz vom 20.2.34, Anweisung Nr. 293," Bundesarchiv, Brammer, Z.Sg. 101/3, f. 88, and Dr. Kausch, "Information über das Angebot Habichts," 20 February 1934, in ibid., Z.Sg. 101/27, f. 7.

58. Summary in Gehl, pp. 87–96. See also [Major Kaltenboeck?], "Der 4. Mai 1934, Starhemberg und die Nationalsozialisten," T–120, 2500/4939/E 272839–61.

59. *G. D.*, C, 2, No. 229; *TMWC*, 34:56.

60. Domarus, 1:358–59; the German foreign ministry had suggested a shorter and less violent passage (Hüffer note of 26 January 1934, T–120, 3836/6111/E 452704).

61. *G. D.*, C, 2, No. 247.

62. See Gehl, pp. 84–86, for background on the Rome protocols.

63. *G. D.*, C, 2, No. 328.

64. See also the account by Habicht on 7 March 1934, in Bundesarchiv, Brammer, Z.Sg. 101/27, f. 35–39.

65. *G. D.*, C, 2, No. 258.

vived and eventually led to their coming together in Venice.[66] In part, the motive for this meeting from Berlin's perspective was to offset the three-power meeting in Rome that had alarmed the German government, even though the Hungarians, at least, looked forward to Germany joining the three in one grouping.[67] While the German foreign minister recommended that the economic struggle with Austria be settled before any Hitler-Mussolini meeting, Hitler himself preferred a continuation of the tourist boycott and the addition of other economic pressures, with only more drastic measures being postponed for some time.[68] This meant, in effect, that Hitler would tolerate the continued excesses of Habicht's followers in Austria, though public displays and demonstrations were to be reduced. The clearest indication of the general thrust of Hitler's policy was his refusal, in spite of both internal and external urging, to take action to restrain the Austrian legion in Germany or to remove its units from camps in the vicinity of the Austrian border.[69] The increased terror campaign against the Austrian government in May 1934 must therefore be regarded as tolerated, if not directly authorized, by Hitler. The repercussions of this policy worried the German foreign ministry, but the evidence shows that even von Neurath's personal interest in the subject failed to produce any results.[70] While German economic measures weakened the Austrian economy in some areas, terroristic acts to scare off non-German tourists were expected to undermine the Dollfuss government even more.[71]

The available evidence on German policy toward Austria in the eight weeks from the end of May to the July uprising is fragmentary. There were plans for the Hitler-Mussolini meeting, which was finally held on 14 June. There were the murders of 30 June that Hitler ordered to forestall any future challenge to his authority from the SA—by literally beheading that body—and from the army by implicating it in the beheading process. Other

66. See the account in Hanfstaengl, pp. 35–39; cf. William E. Dodd, Jr., and Martha Dodd (eds.), *Ambassador Dodd's Diary* (New York: Harcourt, Brace, 1941) (hereafter cited as *Dodd Diary*), pp. 132–33.

67. See the excerpt from the record of the Gömbös-Mussolini meeting, in Kerekes, "Akten zur Annexion Österreichs," p. 361. For German reaction to the meeting, see *G. D.*, C, 2, Nos. 333, 334, 338, 339, 344.

68. *G. D.*, C, 2, Nos. 389, 393, 409, 431, 451, 479.

69. On the problems presented by the Austrian legion at this time see Wehrkreis VII, Ic (Adam), "Nr. 2172g.K. an Reichskriegsministerium, Betr.: Österreichische SA," 30 March 1934, T–79, roll 207, frames 489–90; *G. D.*, C, 2, No. 394.

70. *G. D.*, C, 2, Nos. 462, 492; von Neurath to Frick, 24 May 1934, T–120, 778/1549/376560–63; *G. D.*, C, 3, No. 3 (n. 9 to this document shows that as of 22 June the situation on the German side of the border had not changed). To the Austrians, of course, all the incidents were denied (Memorandum of Renthe-Fink, 2 June 1934, T–120, 2890/6115/E 454864–66). See also *B. D.*, 2d, 6, No. 449; U. S. 1934, 2:26–27; *G. D.*, C, 2, No. 501; Ross, pp. 166ff., 212–14.

The account in Ross, pp. 189ff., assumes that Hitler seriously wanted to restrain all acts of terror but fails to reconcile this with his attitude toward the Austrian legion.

71. *Beiträge*, p. 14; U. S. 1934, 2:25; von Hassell report I 580, 11 May 1934, T–120, 2836/6111/E 452828–29 (which was submitted to Hitler).

foreign policy aspects of that event remain to be considered; its relation to the Austrian issue was its deepening of the split between the Austrian SA, led by Hermann Reschny, and the Austrian SS and party administration headed by Habicht. Then, on 25 July, an attempted coup in Vienna led to the murder of Dollfuss but failed to establish a National Socialist regime.

It is clear that during this period the situation was coming to a head. Many of the National Socialists in Austria felt abandoned by Berlin and were becoming increasingly desperate. Their acts of violence were bringing on strong police reactions from the Austrian government, and these in turn brought further acts of terror. Under these circumstances, Habicht and one of his chief assistants went to Berlin at the end of May. Habicht saw Hitler both then and on 6 June.[72] Since the date for the meeting between Hitler and Mussolini had been fixed for the following week, and because it was understood that the Austrian problem would be one of the main subjects discussed, one may speculate in the absence of any evidence on the Hitler-Habicht meetings that no new decisions were communicated to Habicht. Clearly the outcome of the meeting with Mussolini would provide Hitler with a basis for new guidelines. Before the meeting, Mussolini had been informed by Renzetti that the alternatives in regard to Austria might well be a German-Italian agreement for a new government in Austria under Anton Rintelen and with National Socialist participation—or a revolution.[73] Rintelen had been sent to Rome as Austrian minister in August 1933 because of his hostility to Dollfuss, and he had continued plotting against his own government from the new post.[74] He was in close and continuing contact with emissaries of Habicht, was scheduled to be the head of a government in which the National Socialists would be included, and was to play a key role in the abortive July coup. Though unnamed, he also figured in the Hitler-Mussolini talks on 19 June.

In his meeting with Mussolini in Venice, Hitler asserted that the *Anschluss* was not an acute question. He insisted that a person not tied to any political party should head the Austrian government; Rintelen was not named, but he was apparently the person meant. The new government would call for elections and then take the National Socialists into the government in proportion to their showing in the election Germany and Italy would handle their economic relations with Austria in close consultation. Hitler further asked Mussolini to withdraw his protecting hand from Austria.[75] It is quite obvious from the evidence now available that the two men left the meeting with a very different understanding as to their respective views on this subject. Hitler was convinced—and apparently sincerely so—that Mussolini had been in general agreement with his position and that there would be no trouble with Italy as long as there was neither an *An-*

72. *G. D.*, C, 2, No. 469; Memorandum by Köpke, 31 May 1934, *TMWC*, 35:617–19.
73. Renzetti to Mussolini, 12 June 1934, T–586, container 419, frame 009466.
74. *G. D.*, C, 1, No. 416; 2, No. 308; Ross, pp. 197–99, 208–09.
75. *G. D.*, C, 3, Nos. 5, 7; Ross, pp. 223–25.

schluss nor an entirely National Socialist government in Vienna.[76] This meant, in other words, that he could continue to support Habicht's pressure on the Dollfuss regime, and even that regime's replacement, provided that there was neither an immediate *Anschluss* nor a full National Socialist government as a result of that replacement. Mussolini, on the other hand, as well as Suvich, were of the opinion that it had been made clear to Hitler that negotiations to accomplish what Hitler had postulated were not to come during the present conditions of conflict in Austria, during which Italy still backed Dollfuss. If there were to be changes, they lay in an indefinite future.[77]

The German government became aware of this difference in interpretation, but Hitler preferred not to have the difference clarified.[78] He gave as reason that there was no urgency in the Austrian question, but subsequent events suggest that he preferred to confront Mussolini with a *fait accompli,* or at least to avoid any precise commitment. The drift toward open conflict in Vienna, therefore, continued. Dollfuss tried to strengthen his own position, maneuvering between the two rival Heimwehr leaders, Emil Fey and Ernst Rüdiger von Starhemberg, both of whom from time to time had also been negotiating with the National Socialists.[79] Simultaneously, the terror campaign against the Austrian government continued with the aim of forcing Dollfuss to resign; the Austrian government retaliated and threatened drastic punishment, including the death penalty.[80] When Hitler was informed by his minister in Austria that this process might well lead to an explosion, the conspirators planning the coup had already met to set the fuse.[81]

76. Of key importance is an entry in the diary of Alfred Rosenberg in which he records Hitler's version of the conversation (Rosenberg, *Tagebuch,* pp. 39–41). The Hitler-Rosenberg meeting recorded in the diary must have taken place on 19 June, for on that day the *Völkische Beobachter* carried Rosenberg's answer to von Papen's speech at Marburg. Hitler refers to Rosenberg's article as appearing "today" (*heute*). On 20 June, Hitler went to Neudeck; the announced reason was to report on the Venice meeting to Hindenburg (*Völkischer Beobachter*, 22 June 1934). See also *G. D.*, C, 3, Nos. 5, 7, 10.

77. See von Hassell's report I 729 of 21 June 1934, *G. D.,* C, 3, No. 26; cf. ibid., No. 62.

78. See *G. D.*, C, 3, p. 68, n. 12 and p. 132, nn. 3 and 4. On the probability that Mussolini's insistence that his German was good enough to enable him to talk with Hitler without an interpreter being responsible for any possible misunderstanding see Ernst Wiedemann, *Der Mann, der Feldherr werden wollte* ([Dortmund?]: Blick und Bild Verlag, 1964), pp. 63–64. The account of the Venice meeting given by the German foreign ministry to the Polish minister also reflects the discrepancies between the German and Italian views (*Lipski Papers,* No. 28, p. 145).

79. Fey was in touch with the National Socialists at this time (*G. D.*, C, 3, No. 112, n. 7 and p. 226; *Die Erhebung,* p. 111; Ross, p. 200). Starhemberg was then, as so often, occupied elsewhere with female companionship. While Fey played a most dubious role in Vienna between the insurgents and the government on 25 July, Starhemberg was flying back to the city from more pleasant company on the Lido at Venice.

80. See Rieth report 1691, 16 June 1934, T–120, 2838/6112/E 453454–57; *G. D.,* C, 3, Nos. 34, n. 6, 56, 89, 109, n. 17, 116, n. 7.

81. See the note by Lammers of 27 June on Rieth's report 1695 of 21 June 1934, T–120, 2838/6112/E 453474–76.

The last days of June and much of July were taken up in preparations for a seizure of power in Vienna by a regiment of former soldiers who had joined the National Socialists, SS *Standarte* 89. The plan was simultaneously to seize the members of the government at a cabinet meeting, capture the Vienna radio station, and kidnap Wilhelm Miklas, the president of Austria. A new government under Rintelen would be proclaimed. Some support from within the Austrian army was expected; there were plenty of National Socialist spies in the Austrian police; and it was by no means unlikely that some parts of the Heimwehr might cooperate.[82] The timing of the operation was determined mainly by Rintelen, the would-be chancellor, who warned the conspirators to act before Dollfuss's next visit to Mussolini, planned for the end of July.[83] Rintelen himself arranged his leave so that he could conveniently be in Vienna when the conspirators struck. He returned to the Austrian capital on 23 July and the coup was scheduled for the following day. A last-minute postponement of the cabinet meeting led to a similar postponement of the coup to 25 July.

It is by no means entirely clear at what point and who in the German government knew of the scheduled events. It is, however, certain that while the German minister Rieth did not know what was coming,[84] some of his subordinates, and in particular the counselor of legation, Günther Altenburg, did. Altenburg was assigned to the German legation in Vienna from February to September 1934, worked closely with the conspirators, and was informed of the details of the planned coup.[85] His involvement is especially

82. The best, though certainly not definitive, account is in Brooke-Shepherd, pp. 231–84. See also Hellmuth Auerbach (ed.), "Eine Nationalsozialistische Stimme zum Wiener Putsch vom 25. Juli 1934," *Vierteljahrshefte für Zeitgeschichte,* 12, No. 2 (April, 1964), pp. 201–18. The editor's introduction is apologetic and unreliable, but the document itself is important. An excellent contemporary report in Messersmith (Vienna) to Phillips, 1 August 1934, U. S. 1934, 2:35–47.

83. Rudolf Weydenhammer, "Bericht über die Erhebung der Nationalsozialisten am 25. Juli 1934 in Wien," 1938, p. 6, NSDAP Hauptarchiv folder 634, Hoover Institution Reel 33 (hereafter cited as Weydenhammer, "Bericht").

84. *G. D.,* C, 3, No. 369.

85. Weydenhammer, "Bericht," p. 14: "Between 5 and 7 P.M. [on July 24] Wächter and I revised the proclamations and announcements for the next day in the private residence of Counsellor of Legation Altenburg, whom I had visited briefly at the legation in the morning and who had been of great assistance to me since the beginning of his assignment in Vienna." *Die Erhebung,* p. 80, is derived from this statement. There are several references to Altenburg in the account of Wächter, published by Auerbach (n. 82, above). In another connection Wächter refers to "Herren der deutschen Gesandtschaft" (Auerbach, p. 216). (It should be noted that Altenburg was most careful to provide no information on his stay in Vienna to Ulrich Eichstädt for his *Von Dollfuss zu Hitler* [Wiesbaden: Steiner, 1955], and that Ross in his monograph ignores all references to Altenburg in the sources he used.) Weydenhammer's reference to Altenburg should be contrasted with his comment (p. 23) about Minister Rieth: "I immediately [afternoon of 25 July] drove to the legation and explained the situation to the German Minister Rieth with whom I had maintained contact regularly in the preceding months." For obvious reasons, there are few contemporary documents on Altenburg's activities in Vienna, but see his letter to Hüffer of 30 May 1934, T–120, 3395/8675/E 606963–964.

The German army was providing weapons and explosives to the terrorists in Aus-

important in that those who still argue that Hitler was indeed surprised by events in Vienna, and not simply by the failure of the coup, have to assume that a subordinate official of the German legation in Vienna—perhaps as a matter of routine?—was prepared to assist in the murder of the chief of government, seizure of the cabinet, and kidnapping of the president of the country to which he was accredited, to say nothing of editing the pronunciamentos to be read over the radio, all without authorization from the highest German authority.

In addition to whoever provided Altenburg with authority to collaborate with the conspirators, some individuals at party headquarters in Munich knew what was planned; several of the key meetings were held there, and at least one of the leaks to the Austrians appears to have originated there also. Furthermore, in Berlin several offices subordinate to the propaganda ministry knew beforehand. The German official news agency on 25 July released a series of reports on the situation that clearly reveal inside information on the planned coup and were, therefore, withdrawn when the coup failed and these reports proved incriminating.[86] Even more convincing evidence was the issuance in Berlin of pictures of the supposed events in Vienna by a newspaper picture service (Deutsche Presseklischee-Dienst) under the date 22 July.[87] Both forms of release included the assertion that Rintelen was negotiating the formation of a new government, a piece of information requiring prior knowledge of the plot because Rintelen in fact never had the opportunity to negotiate anything. While being celebrated as the new chancellor in Berlin, Rintelen was in fact trying to commit suicide over the coup's failure in Vienna.[88]

It would be difficult to argue that four weeks after the blood purge had shown all Germans what to expect from Hitler in case of suspected or imagined disobedience, Habicht, who repeatedly discussed the Austrian situation with Hitler, could have organized a revolt in Vienna coordinated with appropriate publicity in Berlin, assisted from within the German legation in Vienna, and implemented by a substantial group of his followers, without some prior indication of Hitler's approval. The indirect evidence is overwhelming, the subsequent events will be seen to fit the pattern, and Hitler's interpretation of his meeting with Mussolini gave him grounds to

---

tria, but apparently had no prior knowledge of the coup (*G. D.*, C, 2, No. 459; 3, No. 125, n. 3).

86. *B. D.*, 2d, 6, No. 540; *Dodd Diary*, p. 133 (Dodd sent a copy of the German News Agency report to Washington). See also the press directives of 25 July 1934, in Bundesarchiv, Brammer, Z.Sg. 101/4, f. 35.

87. The text is reproduced as annex 6 in *Beiträge* and also in *Red-White-Red-Book* (Vienna: Austrian State Printing House, 1947), p. 53.

88. For a detailed and perceptive report on Rintelen's trial after he recovered from his self-inflicted wound, see Messersmith dispatch 358, 15 March 1935, State 863.00/1161. Rintelen disappeared from public view after the *Anschluss*, except for the appearance of his memoirs, *Erinnerungen an Österreichs Weg* (Munich: Bruckmann, 1941).

assume that all would be well if the coup succeeded. In the absence of even the slightest evidence to the contrary, therefore, it may be assumed that the coup was launched with the knowledge and at least tacit approval of Hitler.[89] Whether the murder of Dollfuss had been taken up with Hitler is another question, but really not a very important one. The murder was one of the contingencies included in the planning as is known from the prearranged code to be used during the coup, in which "Dollfuss †" was a parallel contingency for "Rintelen Chancellor."[90] There would have been no need to clear such an action with a German chancellor who had just arranged the murder of his own predecessor. As Hitler claims to have told Mussolini in Venice, "Dollfuss is a traitor; in Austria he himself would also be working with bombs and grenades."[91]

In Vienna, the conspirators worked with bombs and grenades in the weeks before the coup but relied on pistols and rifles on 25 July. Betrayal from within their ranks gave Fey the opportunity to play both sides on the fatal day; he gave Dollfuss enough information to dismiss most of his cabinet members, but not enough to save himself. When the plotters struck, therefore, they caught and killed the chancellor; but the coup failed as other cabinet members took counteraction, the army remained loyal, and the attempt to kidnap the president miscarried. The president appointed Kurt von Schuschnigg chancellor; the Heimwehr stayed with the government; and the SA stood by as the SS coup was defeated. Four years later, after the Anschluss, the anniversary of the coup was celebrated by a reenactment in which those who had seized the chancellory again moved through the streets of Vienna as those who had marched in Munich in November 1923 annually repeated their procession. Hitler's deputy, Rudolf Hess, gave a commemorative address, and a plaque was unveiled which memorialized the heroes of the occasion: Otto Planetta, the murderer of Dollfuss, and six of his associates, who had been tried and executed by the Austrian authorities.[92]

It was in connection with the fate of the conspirators that Rieth, the

89. The testimony of Göring that Habicht secured Hitler's approval on the basis of misinformation about the favorable attitude of the Austrian army (*TMWC*, 9:294–95) should not be accepted uncritically. In the same context Göring claims not to have known beforehand of the 1,000-mark visa rule; yet he participated in the cabinet meeting that decided on this (*G. D.*, C, 1, p. 490). The Weydenhammer "Bericht" (p. 7) simply says that Habicht conducted the final discussions in the second half of July with the agencies concerned ("zuständigen Stellen"). Ross takes Göring's testimony at face value (pp. 234–36).

90. *Beiträge*, p. 56. It should be noted that Austrian police action on 25 July was in part confused because of information, secured either by betrayal or as an intentional diversion, of another National Socialist scheme to kill Dollfuss in his car with hand grenades when he left the cabinet meeting (*Die Erhebung*, pp. 44–46, 86, 263). The fact that Dollfuss was shot a second time after falling from the first shot discredits all subsequent efforts to make the murder appear accidental or unintentional.

91. Rosenberg, *Tagebuch*, p. 39.

92. Wiley (Vienna) dispatch 344 of 26 July 1938, *TMWC*, 38:94–96; picture of the plaque in *TMWC*, 31:421.

German minister, became involved. He was persuaded to play a part in securing a rather questionable safe-conduct for the conspirators in the chancellory when it was clear that the plot had failed. This involvement was innocent on his part; he neither knew of the plot nor wanted to be drawn in on 25 July but yielded to those who appealed to him to save lives. In Hitler's eyes, of course, he was thereby guilty—of making it appear that the German government was implicated in the murder—and he was promptly recalled. Once he had explained himself to Hitler, he was placed on the inactive list, not to be recalled until World War II when he was put in charge of the German consulate general in Tangier.[93] But while Rieth was banished for what Hitler considered clumsiness, the member of the Vienna legation really implicated in the plot, Günther Altenburg, who on the fatal evening quietly sheltered in his home some of the conspirators who had not been caught and escorted one of them over the border personally,[94] was rewarded by increasingly influential positions as the "Balkan expert" of the German foreign ministry.

There were more spectacular repercussions in other quarters. As word of the attempted coup spread around the world, there was great excitement, heightened by the distaste aroused by the recent German purge.[95] Most affected was Mussolini. Members of Dollfuss's family were already with him, and instead of welcoming the Austrian chancellor, Mussolini had to break the sad news to his widow. Several Italian divisions were moved to the border, and this fact became generally known; but they did not move into Austria, partly because the Italian government quickly found out that the coup had failed, partly out of concern that Yugoslavia would then send its troops into Carinthia.[96] Although military complications were thus avoided, Italian policy for a time turned sharply against Germany, and this was made most obvious by bitter polemics in the government-directed Italian press. It would take considerable time for Italian press attacks to die down.[97]

In the face of international repercussions, the German government took drastic action to disclaim any connection with the coup. While no one outside Germany believed the denials about the past policy of Berlin, there was a real change in the policy Hitler intended to follow thereafter. Once the

93. Von Neurath to Köpke, 28 July 1934, *TMWC,* 40:500–01; Memorandum by von Bülow, 27 July 1934, T–120, 1488/3086/D 617280. By 1942 Rieth had overcome any scruples he had and was working with the SD in Tangier (1095/2072/passim). For American doubts about Rieth, dating to Herbert Hoover's experience with him in the World War I Belgian relief effort, see Moffat (Washington) to Earle (Vienna), 7 December 1933, Houghton Library, Moffat Papers, Vol. 2.

94. Weydenhammer, "Bericht," p. 28.

95. See the comment by Neville Chamberlain, in Keith Feiling, *The Life of Neville Chamberlain* (London: Macmillan, 1946), p. 253.

96. *G. D.,* C, 3, No. 128; Fischer (German military attaché Rome) report 21, 2 August 1934, T–120, 2676/5609/E 402126–30, and report 24 of 31 August, ibid., frames E 402139–47; Memorandum by Kordt, 27 July 1934, T–120, 1488/3086/D 617271.

97. *G. D.,* C, 3, pp. 242–43, No. 122, n. 6; *B. D.,* 2d, 6, No. 530.

initial shock and excitement had worn off,[98] Hitler formulated a new policy toward Austria. Both Göring and Goebbels were with Hitler at Bayreuth at this time, and von Neurath even interrupted his vacation to join them briefly. Hitler decided to drop Habicht, dissolve the headquarters of the Austrian NSDAP in Munich, hold down the Austrian legion, and tell the National Socialists in Austria to behave with more restraint in the future.[99] The effort at a takeover as in Danzig had failed in 1933; the attempt to seize power by force had failed in 1934; clearly the concept of treating the Austrian situation like a part of the German domestic scene would not work. The role of the Austrian party henceforth would not be to take over power inside the country but to provide a vehicle for taking over from the outside by force or under the threat of force. Such an approach meant postponement.

Hitler has been quoted as explaining in 1933 that foreign expansion would come only after four or five years of rearmament. He had hoped to exclude Austria from the timetable, but now realized that this could not be done. While Poland had been willing to let the National Socialists take control of the government of Danzig, Italy was unwilling to see the National Socialists follow the same route in Austria. Instead, Italy supported other elements in Austria, and change would therefore have to await the strengthening of Germany until it could impose a solution from the outside. The interval would be a difficult one, and in the interim Hitler had just the man to send to Vienna to carry out the necessary intrigues: Franz von Papen.

Von Papen's assistants had been murdered on 30 June, and he had barely escaped death himself. A schemer without much talent, a bother to Hitler as vice-chancellor, and a professing Catholic, he was just the man for the job of bamboozling the Austrians until they could be pressured or intrigued into the Reich. Hitler was so thrilled with this brilliant solution to the twin problems of how to get rid of von Papen—who was still asking embarrassing questions about 30 June—and who should replace the hapless Rieth that he announced the new appointment before asking the Austrian government for its agrément.[100] The Vienna authorities were by no means pleased by the appointment itself or the curious circumstances surrounding it but yielded to German pressure to receive the special and extraordinary envoy.[101] While in Germany the press campaign against both Austria and Italy was toned down, the new envoy went to his mission in Vienna.[102] As

98. Hanfstaengl, pp. 259–62.

99. *G. D.,* C, 3, Nos. 122, 134, 149; *TMWC,* 40: 500–01; Memorandum of von Bülow, 26 July 1934, T–120, 909/1575/381293–94; Gehl, pp. 101–104.

100. *G. D.,* C, 3, Nos. 123, 167, enclosure 2. Von Papen later claimed that on 15 July Hitler had offered him the German embassy at the Vatican (*Der Hochverratsprozess gegen Dr. Guido Schmidt vor dem Wiener Volksgericht* [Vienna: Österreichische Staatsdruckerei, 1947] [hereafter cited as *Guido Schmidt Trial*], p. 351).

101. *B. D.,* 2d, 6, No. 539; *G. D.,* C, 3, Nos. 136, 146; Memorandum of von Neurath, RM 893, 4 August 1934, T–120, 778/1549/376621–22.

102. "Bestellungen aus der Pressekonferenz vom 1.8.34," and "vom 17.8.34," Bundesarchiv, Brammer, Z.Sg. 101/4, f. 45, 62; *G. D.,* C, 3, No. 151; Renzetti to Mussolini, 3 August 1934, T–586, container 419, frames 009479–80.

the American minister records him as explaining, "It was his business to see that the *Anschluss* was brought about peacefully."[103] That program would take several years.

Czechoslovakia

Germany's relations with Czechoslovakia had been reasonably good in the years of the Weimar Republic.[104] There were, however, two related sources of potential conflict and both of these were eventually to cast their shadow over the future of the two countries. These were the geographic relationship of Czechoslovakia, and especially its Bohemian portion, to Germany, and the presence inside Czechoslovakia of over three million people of German descent who since the seventeenth century had looked upon themselves as the ruling nationality in the Bohemian lands of the Habsburgs. The maintenance of the historic borders of Bohemia when the boundaries of Czechoslovakia were established at the Paris peace conference left these people in a state ruled by the Czechs.[105]

The policies followed by the predominant Czech element toward their German-speaking fellow nationals in the following years were at times almost as short-sighted as those pursued toward the Czechs by the Germans for most of the preceding two and a half centuries. There were, however, several exceedingly important differences in the situation. In the first place, Czechoslovakia was a democracy in which the cultural rights of the Germans were largely respected and their political wishes could receive public expression as long as they were not clearly treasonous. Secondly, with the reduction of the great Habsburg empire to a small Austrian state, the Germans in Czechoslovakia would look increasingly to Berlin rather than to Vienna. Finally, and perhaps most important of all, the concept of national self-determination which provided the justification for creating a Czech state on the ruins of the Habsburg empire constituted a challenge to the leaders of the new state that included millions of non-Czechs within its borders. They did not master this challenge in the 1920s, and they could not master it in the 1930s. The failure in the 1920s was partly due to the obduracy of the Germans but to a considerable extent their own responsibility; that in the 1930s a result of German policy which took full advantage of the difficulty of Czechoslovakia in reconciling to the new state those it had insisted should be included in its territory.

By 1933 the Germans of Czechoslovakia, later often called Sudeten Germans after a mountain range between Bohemia and Silesia, were to a considerable extent dissatisfied with their lot, a dissatisfaction that was

103. George S. Messersmith, "Conversations with von Papen in Vienna," p. 4, University of Delaware Library, Messersmith Papers.

104. The most comprehensive survey is in Johann W. Brügel, *Tschechen und Deutsche, 1918–1938* (Munich: Nymphenburger Verlagshandlung, 1967).

105. There is a fine review of this problem in Dagmar H. Perman, *The Shaping of the Czechoslovak State* (Leyden: Brill, 1962).

greatly intensified by the depression which hit their industries particularly hard. Even those elements among them who had cooperated actively in the government of Czechoslovakia and hence were called "activists" were increasingly disillusioned, while many of their followers were inclined to desert them for other movements. Included among the other groups of Sudeten Germans were a National Socialist party and several additional right-wing organizations. With the growth of the National Socialist party in Germany, these movements became more attractive to young Sudeten Germans and more obviously dangerous to the Czech state. In the fall of 1932 the Czech government had begun legal proceedings against some leaders of these groups, and the sentences issued in that trial were to be one focus of discussion between Germany and Czechoslovakia in 1933.

The German government was aware of the military and diplomatic strength of Czechoslovakia; the former embodied in its army and fortifications, the latter in its alliances with France and the Little Entente. From the very beginning, therefore, Czechoslovakia—unlike Austria—belonged in the category of those areas that Germany could do little about for several years until it had rearmed. That meant that although German-Czech relations after 30 January 1933 were no longer as friendly as they had once been, the time of danger still lay in the future. There was a considerable amount of discussion about the trials of German nationals and people of German descent in Czechoslovakia, about the arrests of Czechs in Germany, about press attacks on each other, and about the activities of the numerous refugees from Hitler's Germany who escaped to Czechoslovakia, but all such matters caused no major tensions.[106] The disruption of the Sudeten German National Socialist party, culminating in its almost simultaneous self-dissolution and banning by the government in October 1933, opened the way for a new organization among the Sudeten Germans. Out of the urging of some former members of the National Socialist party, a small elitist group of ultra-rightist advocates of a dictatorship called the *Kameradschaftsbund,* and some independent elements, a new movement emerged, known originally as the Sudeten German Home Front and eventually as the Sudeten German party. This new party was led by Konrad Henlein.[107] The man who was eventually to lead the Sudeten Germans home into the Reich in a manner none of them anticipated was a thirty-five-year-

106. *G. D.,* C, 1, Nos. 31, 334, 364, 366, 429; 2, No. 56; Domarus, 1: 275; Mastný report no. 9 of 9 February 1933, Czech document in T–120, 1040/1809/413928–930 (part in Berber, *Prager Akten,* No. 2), Mastný report 13 of 16 February, ibid., frame 413931, Mastný report 19 of 22 February, ibid., frame 413932, Mastný report 27 of 25 March, ibid., frames 413933–935 (excerpts in Berger, *Prager Akten,* No. 6), Mastný report 39 of 23 May, ibid., frames 413943–944, Mastný report 55 of 17 July, ibid., frames 413946–948; Memorandum of Köpke, 15 July 1933, T–120, 1488/3086/D 618260–61; Cermák (Berlin) report of 18 August 1933, in Koloman Gajan and Robert Kvaček (eds.), *Germany and Czechoslovakia, 1918–1945* (Prague: Orbis, 1965), No. 18.

107. Boris Čelovsky, *Das Münchener Abkommen von 1938* (Stuttgart: Deutsche Verlags-Anstalt, 1958), pp. 108–11; Brügel, chap. 12.

old veteran of the war who had achieved prominence in a racist athletic organization in the Sudeten area. He now rallied around himself a motley assortment of elements that were long involved in internal feuds but were eventually to be uniformly utilized by Berlin to bring disaster upon the Czech state as well as themselves.

The new government of Germany was unwilling to take inside Czechoslovakia the risks they readily took in Austria. Hitler's directive to the Sudeten German National Socialists as conveyed to one of their longtime leaders, Hans Knirsch, before his death in December 1933 was that they "should make their own policy; the Reich could not help them for a long time."[108] Berlin, therefore, at first stayed out of the internal problems of the Sudeten Germans.[109] At Hitler's insistence, some financial assistance was provided to individual Sudeten National Socialists and members of their families affected by prosecution under the Czech law for the defense of the republic, great efforts being made to avoid compromising the recipients of such aid.[110] The contacts of the Sudeten Germans with Germany were to be controlled by a new organization, the *Volksdeutsche Rat,* a council supervised by Hitler's deputy Rudolf Hess who tried to restrain from rash actions the Sudeten Germans and their supporters inside Germany.[111] There was plenty of time for them to work out their internal difficulties.

The last months of 1933 and the first half of 1934, in fact, saw a reduction in the incidents affecting German-Czech relations. In this period there were soundings for a no-force declaration or nonaggression pact analogous to that concluded in the same months between Germany and Poland. The evidence on these soundings remains tenuous, but beyond the fact that they led to no agreements, certain conclusions can be drawn.[112] There was an interest on both sides in a reduction of both incidents and tension.[113] The feelers for a nonaggression pact were handled by National Socialist party officials outside diplomatic channels and, whether authorized by Hitler or not,[114] were neither welcomed by the Czechs nor pursued seriously by Berlin. The proposal was not welcomed in Prague because the Czechs were

108. *G. D.,* C, 2, No. 132.

109. Ibid., 1, Nos. 110, 326, 483; 2, No. 51.

110. Ibid., 2, Nos. 128, 132, 137.

111. Ibid., No. 180. On the *Volksdeutsche Rat,* see ibid., Nos. 31, 140, 330; Jacobsen, pp. 160ff.; Robert Ernst, *Rechenschaftsbericht eines Elsässers* (2d ed.; Berlin: Bernard & Graefe, 1955), pp. 191ff.

112. Čelovsky, p. 88, n. 3; Brügel, pp. 348–49; *G. D.,* C, 2, Nos. 15, 68, 83, n. 3, 293; *B. D.,* 2d, 6, No. 70; Benton (Prague) dispatches 50 of 7 December 1933, and 119 of 20 March 1934, State 760F.6211/1 and 4; Mastný report of 29 November 1933, Czech document in T–120, 1041/1809/413961–962, and report 46 of 25 June 1934, ibid., frames 413614–615; "Bestellungen aus der Pressekonferenz vom 31. Januar 1934," Bundesarchiv, Brammer, Z.Sg. 101/3, f. 48.

113. Note by Waldeck, II Ts 1678 of 8 December 1933, T–120, 2899/6143/E 459515; *G. D.,* C, 2, No. 355.

114. One of the intermediaries, Hohen-Aesten, was put in a concentration camp for his troubles.

reluctant at this time to replace multilateral agreements with a bilateral arrangement. The German government, as von Neurath explained to Vojtěch Mastný, the Czech minister in Berlin, did not think that the time was ripe for a German-Czech nonaggression pact.[115]

By March 1934 the German government felt sufficiently secure to look for any excuse to avert future Czech soundings for a treaty.[116] During the remainder of 1934, Berlin quietly observed developments in Czechoslovakia, keeping in touch with the Sudeten Germans but without as yet engaging German policy directly in their affairs.[117] There was some friction over the attacks on Germany by the émigré press in Czechoslovakia,[118] while the Czech government was already of the opinion that Henlein was supported financially by Berlin.[119] On key issues, the two countries would stay at arm's length, as was particularly obvious in Germany's unwillingness to join Czechoslovakia and other countries in the proposed Eastern Locarno Pact, to be discussed subsequently.[120] Certainly Germany would assume no commitments to a Czech state that Hitler planned to include within his empire and to transform into an area of purely German settlement. As the British minister in Prague suggested in March 1934, the Czechs were aware of the fact that their turn would come after the *Anschluss,* that then only the aid of France could avert disaster, and that when the time came, such aid might well not be forthcoming.[121] Until that moment, the Czech government could only wait and hope.

Hungary

With the exception of Italy, there was no country with which Germany's relations in the 1930s were both as close and as difficult as Hungary. Germany and Hungary, allies in World War I, both objected violently to the peace treaties imposed upon them by the victors. Beyond this tie, there were several others. Both countries looked protectively to their respective national minorities within Czechoslovakia, and these minorities were located at different ends of the Czech state. In 1933, both countries were ruled by

115. *G. D.,* C, 2, No. 83; Mastný report 93 of 30 December 1933, Czech document in T–120, 1041/1809/413973–974.

116. Memorandum of von Bülow, 22 March 1934, T–120, 909/1574/381247.

117. *G. D.,* C, 2, No. 361; 3, No. 16; Mastný report 22 of 25 February 1934, Czech document in T–120, 1041/1809/413601–603 (excerpts in Berber, *Prager Akten,* No. 20).

118. *G. D.,* C, 2, No. 453. Large numbers of Germans had fled from the National Socialist terror into Czechoslovakia; one would have thought that their reports might have suggested to those of German descent in that country that they were best off where they were. See Bohumil Černý, "Der Parteivorstand der SPD im tschechoslowakischen Asyl (1933–1938)," *Historica,* 14 (1967), 175–218.

119. See the note on Beneš's views attached to a memorandum of 15 May 1934 from the chancellery of the Czech president, in Václav Král (ed.), *Die Deutschen in der Tschechoslowakei, 1933–1947* (Prague: Nakladatelstvo Československé Akademie Věd, 1964) (hereafter cited as Král, *Die Deutschen*), No. 10.

120. *G. D.,* C, 3, No. 33.

121. *B. D.,* 2d, 6, No. 328.

rightist regimes which stressed their ideological affinities, though the government of Julius Gömbös had muted in practice its publicly pronounced anti-Semitism. There were, furthermore, at least potentially important economic ties between the two countries. Their trade with each other had been small, but the possibility of expanding an exchange of agricultural for industrial products was certainly present.

There were, on the other hand, several sources of potential difficulty. Tactical considerations in the expansionist policies of Germany at any particular point might involve a sacrifice of Hungary's ambitions, a sacrifice easier for Germany than Hungary. In other situations, in pursuit of similar interests, Germany might well take risks that Hungary could not afford, a complication that was to arise in 1938. The economic policies of the new German government had a strongly autarchic character, especially emphasized in its first months by Hugenberg, that could spell trouble for Hungary's trade. The German minority inside Hungary constituted an additional source of possible friction. Their resistance to magyarization received a powerful stimulus from the National Socialist rise to power, while the emphasis the new regime in Berlin placed on racial ties of kinship across state borders accentuated Hungarian fears. Especially annoying to the Hungarians in connection with this issue was the obvious reluctance of the German minorities in territories Hungary had lost to the sucessor states to join in revisionist agitation for a return to Hungarian rule. Whatever their difficulties in the face of the nationalism of the new states of Southeast Europe, nothing in prior or contemporary Magyar practice suggested that they would be better off if returned to control from Budapest.[122] These considerations, both positive and negative—revision of the 1919 borders, ideological affinity, trade relations, the German minorities in Hungary and the successor states—would be the themes of German-Hungarian relations.

In his letter to Hitler congratulating him on his assumption of power, Gömbös alluded to their "common principles" and "common ideology"; urged closer trade relations, especially a greater German willingness to accept Hungarian agricultural products; and asked Hitler to bring about closer cooperation between the German and Magyar minorities in the successor states.[123] Simultaneously, National Socialist party circles in Berlin were intimating that the German element in Hungary would not be allowed to disturb German-Hungarian relations.[124] In Gömbös's eyes, agreements on

122. See *G. D.*, C, 1, No. 345. For a detailed account see G. C. Paikert, *The Danube Swabians, German Populations in Hungary, Rumania and Yugoslavia and Hitler's Impact on their Patterns* (The Hague: Nijhoff, 1967).

123. Gömbös to Kanya, 1 February 1933, Elek Karsai, "The Meeting of Gömbös and Hitler 1933," *New Hungarian Quarterly*, 3, No. 5 (Jan.–Mar. 1962), p. 172; *G. D.*, C, 1, No. 15.

124. [German foreign ministry, Abteilung VI, A], "Aufzeichnung über die Frage der deutschen Minderheit in Ungarn," 6 March 1933, T–120, 1435/2980/D 580453. These comments were made to Kanya before he left Berlin in February to become Hungarian foreign minister.

the two subjects of trade relations and minorities problems were the prerequisites for any political cooperation.[125] He appealed to Hitler to help Hungary market its surplus agricultural products, an appeal that met with a ready response whose implementation was delayed only because of the intransigence of Hugenberg.[126] Trade and compensation agreements were concluded on 2 June 1933; they constituted the first small step toward a new German economic policy toward Hungary and all of Southeast Europe. Before further measures in that economic policy can be examined, two facets of the economic negotiations of the spring of 1933 require special attention.

It should be noted that economic considerations played an important role in Hungary's policy toward the *Anschluss* question. Not only close personal and political relations with the Dollfuss government, but also the fear that the *Anschluss* might lead to the exclusion of Hungary from the Austrian market, which was of such great importance for it, made the Hungarian government sensitive to any possible upheaval in Vienna.[127] Partly for this reason, partly out of regard for the views of their Italian friends, the Hungarian government had vainly urged Hitler to direct the Austrian National Socialists to support the Dollfuss regime. Hungarian efforts to improve German-Austrian relations were to recur subsequently, though never with any greater results. A second aspect of the economic negotiations was the appearance on the scene of one of the many curious figures of National Socialist diplomacy, Werner Daitz. Active in the party since 1931, he found representing the city of Lübeck in Berlin an insufficient use of his diplomatic talents and became head of the foreign trade section of Rosenberg's APA. More prolific than lucid, he poured forth articles explaining how the living space of various peoples ought or ought not to be organized, with special emphasis on the economic sphere in which regional autarchy should replace world trade and interdependence.[128] Such ideas provided a perfect framework for a lecture Daitz delivered to an attentive audience of Hun-

125. See the comments of Gömbös at the Hungarian cabinet meeting of 18 March 1933, in Miklós Szinai and László Szücs (eds.), *The Confidential Papers of Admiral Horthy* (Budapest: Corvina Press, 1965) (hereafter cited as *Horthy Papers*), No. 15, p. 63.

126. *G. D.*, C, 1, Nos. 179, 195, 247; "Sitzung des Handelspolitischen Ausschusses vom 8. Mai 1933," T–120, 2612/5650/H 003665.

127. Carlile A. Macartney, *October Fifteenth, A History of Modern Hungary* (Edinburgh: University Press, 1956), 1:137; Schoen (Budapest) to Köpke, II Oe 448 of 17 April 1933, T–120, 2832/6077/E 450635–642.

128. The ideas of Daitz were certainly similar to those of Hitler (*Hitlers zweites Buch*, p. 219), but he appears not to have been personally close to his leader. There is as yet no study of Daitz's career in the secondary literature. Lothar Gruchmann, *Nationalsozialistische Grossraumordnung* (Stuttgart: Deutsche Verlags-Anstalt, 1962) only touches on his work. There is a collection of articles by Daitz from the files of the APA in T–81, roll 11, serial 32, item 250–d–18–05/5. Documents pertaining to Daitz's diplomatic ventures will be cited where relevant. Publications containing collections of his pieces are *Der Weg zur völkischen Wirtschaft und zur europäischen Grossraumwirtschaft* (Dresden: Meinhold, 1938 and 1943); *Lebensraum und gerechte Weltordnung* (Amsterdam: De Amsterdamsche Keurkamer, 1943); *Wieder-*

garian officials in Budapest on 29 May 1933.[129] His advocacy of the reorientation of Germany's trade from overseas to Southeast Europe gained him an extended audience with Gömbös in which a visit by Gömbös to Hitler was discussed.[130] The possibility of a trip by Gömbös to Berlin had arisen even before Hitler came to power.[131] Now that the two governments were on the same ideological track the idea was even more attractive, and direct contact between Gömbös and Hitler, so it seemed, could be arranged quietly through party rather than diplomatic channels, with András Mecsér, once Hungarian military attaché in Berlin, playing the role of contact man for Gömbös that Daitz played for Hitler.[132] An unofficial trip to Germany was arranged for Gömbös, and Hitler was to receive on 17–18 June the first head of a foreign government. In the meantime, with the help of Daitz, the economic agreements of 2 June had been signed, and other questions could be discussed by the two chiefs of government.

The public trappings surrounding Gömbös's June visit were unimpressive and confused, a result of the unofficial character of the trip which, furthermore, was arranged by a party agency whose chief, Rosenberg, wanted to make up for his May fiasco in London but had not increased the administrative competence of his office.[133] The talks themselves, however, provide some very important insights into the conduct of German foreign policy not only in 1933 but also in subsequent years as Hitler, partly in response to questions raised by Gömbös, explained his view of present problems and future prospects. Gömbös was concerned about the tension in German-Austrian relations, the development of German-Italian relations, the further improvement of German-Hungarian trade, the activities of the German minorities in Hungary and the sucessor states, and the basic problem of peaceful or violent change in the status quo. In response to such questions, Hitler explained his views with considerable frankness. He made some

---

geburt Europas durch europäischen Sozialismus (Amsterdam: De Amsterdamsche Keurkamer, 1944); and the yearbooks and reports of Daitz's Gesellschaft für europäische Wirtschaftsplanung und Grossraumwirtschaft published by Meinhold, Dresden, 1940–1943. There is a thoughtful but purely theoretical analysis of Daitz's ideas in the 1962 Erlangen-Nuremberg dissertation of Achim Bay, *Der nationalsozialistische Gedanke der Grossraumwirtschaft und seine ideologischen Grundlagen, Darstellung und Kritik*. See also Jacobsen, pp. 61–62.

129. Karsai, pp. 172–73.

130. Schoen telegram 22 of 1 June 1933, T–120, 1435/2980/D 580455; *G. D.*, C, 1, No. 280.

131. Memorandum by von Bülow, 28 January 1933, T–120, 2371/4602/E 189155.

132. *G. D.*, C, 1, No. 329; Macartney, 1: 112, 138. Mecsér eventually served as minister in Berlin when the Germans installed the Arrow Cross party in Budapest in 1944.

133. The most useful source on the visit is the collection of Hungarian documents published by Karsai. See also *G. D.*, C, 1, Nos. 324, 329, 330, 344; *D. D. F.*, 1st, 2, No. 395; Gordon (Berlin) dispatch 2497 of 24 June 1933, State 864.001/11; Williamson (Budapest) dispatch 459 of 5 July 1933, State 762.64/14; Jörg K. Hoensch, *Der ungarische Revisionismus und die Zerschlagung der Tschechoslowakei* (Tübingen: J. C. B. Mohr, 1967), pp. 29–31.

general promises but no specific commitments on the economic and minorities questions; these practical issues would recur in German-Hungarian talks during the following months. In regard to Austria, he explained to Gömbös his distaste for Dollfuss and his refusal to have anything to do with the Austrian chancellor. Hitler reassured his guest, however, that what he wanted was not an immediate *Anschluss* but a government in which the Austrian National Socialists would have the position to which they would be entitled as the result of new elections. As for revision of the peace treaties, this could come about only by force; there could be no peaceful solution. The evidence shows that Hitler was quite explicit that regardless of any concessions extorted without recourse to arms, his real aims required war, which, at that time, he tied to the destruction of Czechoslovakia.

Hitler knew that Hungarian and German revisionist aims coincided most closely in regard to Czechoslovakia and began at this time an effort to have Hungary give priority over all others to revisionist claims on the Czechs, a policy he was to follow consistently until the fall of 1938. The war Hitler's plans envisioned was, of course, to be fought against France: "I shall utterly crush France," Hitler vowed.[134] Gömbös, suitably impressed, returned to Hungary to face an uproar in the press and parliament over his trip and with the necessity to reassure Mussolini and Dollfuss; Hitler was pleased by the demonstration that Germany was not entirely isolated in the world, and retained a favorable memory of the Hungarian leader who had had the courage to make the gesture.[135]

The visit of Hungary's prime minister was returned by the German vice-chancellor, Franz von Papen, who made an unofficial trip to Budapest in the middle of September. The reception given him was most friendly,[136] but its warmth was insufficient to resolve one important subject discussed, that concerning the German minorities in pre- and post-Trianon Hungary.[137] To avoid embarrassing German-Hungarian relations, the German minority in Hungary was instructed to refrain from public hostility to the

134. "Ich werde Frankreich zermalen" is the phrase recorded by Gömbös published in Karsai, p. 193. Baron Gábor Apor, then chief of the political department of the Hungarian Ministry of Foreign Affairs, remembered the phrase after the war as "ich werde Frankreich zermalmen" (Macartney, 1: 139, n. 6).

135. There is no evidence for Hitler's comments on Gömbös that compares with his extensive recorded comments on Mussolini. Hitler's obsession with his own and Mussolini's age and possible death was of great importance in 1938 and 1939. One cannot help speculating whether Gömbös's death at the age of 50 while under medical care in Germany in 1936 contributed to this preoccupation.

136. Von Papen to Hitler, 21 September 1933, in Budapest telegram 48, T–120, 1436/2980/D 586488.

137. Subsequent references to his conversation with von Papen by Gömbös show that the latter considered this one of the key topics discussed at the time (*G. D.*, C, 2, Nos. 129, 252). The marginal note by Gömbös that he discussed with von Papen the procedure for taking up such matters (Karsai, p. 193) may well have been made by him in this connection. The American minister in Budapest noted that von Papen met with Jacob Bleyer, the leader of the German minority in Hungary (Montgomery dispatch 24 of 4 October 1933, State 762.64/17).

Hungarian government; Germany sympathized with them but would not exert pressure on their behalf.[138] Nevertheless, this issue remained an irritant in the relations between Berlin and Budapest. Repeatedly in late 1933 and early 1934 the Hungarians urged the German government to instruct the German minorities in the successor states to cooperate with the Hungarian minorities, and—in partial contradiction—to end the contacts between the German minority in Hungary and the *Volksbund für das Deutschtum im Ausland* (VDA), an agency through which cultural and political ties were maintained with German minorities in other countries. Just as frequently, the Germans countered by suggesting that the Hungarian government make concessions to its German and other minorities in order to reconcile them and to make Hungarian rule attractive to those living in the lands Hungary wished to recover.[139] Continued difficulties over this issue contributed to Germany's unwillingness to commit itself to Hungary in the winter of 1933–34 when the Hungarians anxiously inquired about the rumors of German nonaggression pacts with Czechoslovakia and Yugoslavia.[140] When Gömbös finally wrote Hitler a long letter on the subject, the German government after considerable delay finally decided not to answer at all.[141]

If the problem of national minorities provided a continuing irritant, in the area of economic relations a series of negotiations, trips of experts, and policy conferences led to agreements that marked a significant step in a new direction. The desire to preclude a customs union between Hungary and Austria or Hungary, Austria, and Italy; the desire to strengthen Hungary vis-à-vis the Little Entente as well as French and Italian ambitions in the Balkans; and some hard economic realities all contributed to Germany's development of a trade policy later applied to other countries of Southeast Europe.[142] On 21 February 1934 the two countries signed a group of agreements, most of them kept secret, by which they exchanged trade concessions worked out to circumvent the most-favored nation clause still embodied in many of their trade treaties with other countries. Germany would acept more Hungarian agricultural products at prices above those of the world market, while Hungary would take more German manufactured goods.[143] The special preferences, some leading to an increase in trade, some simply diverting trade at the expense of other countries such as the United States, would tie Germany and Hungary more closely together.

138. *G. D.,* C, 1, No. 400.

139. Ibid., No. 440; 2, Nos. 42, 129; cf. Macartney, 1: 168–71.

140. *G. D.,* C, 2, Nos. 95, 175, 192, 216.

141. Ibid., Nos. 252, 288, 371; 3, No. 400.

142. The negotiations may be traced in ibid., 1, No. 464; 2, Nos. 175, 182, 189; Williamson (Budapest) dispatch 467 of 17 July 1933, State 762.63/90; "Sitzung des Handelspolitischen Ausschusses vom 23. Januar 1934," ". . . vom 25. Januar 1934," ". . . vom 13. Februar 1934," T–120, 2612/5650/H 003818–819, 822–823, 836–838; Memorandum of von Bülow, 15 February 1934, T–120, 909/1574/381236.

143. *G. D.,* C, 2, No. 322; 3, No. 13, p. 36.

This process of economic integration continued in subsequent years, was well advertised publicly, and had important political ramifications.[144] Germany's push toward hegemony over Southeast Europe was largely to follow pathways prepared by agreements in the economic field that tied those countries closely to it, a process greatly aided by the desperate situation of the Southeast European countries under the impact of the depression. Hungary was the first country to which this policy was applied, while Yugoslavia was soon to follow. It is, therefore, quite understandable that in looking back over past German trade policy toward the Danube area in November 1937, the German foreign ministry should point to the German-Hungarian secret arrangement of 21 February 1934 as the first major step on the new road.[145]

Yugoslavia

A similar step was soon to be taken in Germany's relations with Yugoslavia, but this required something of a reorientation in German policy. Hungary had been on Germany's side in World War I; the Serbian element dominating postwar Yugoslavia was essentially the same group that had led Serbia on the side of the Entente in the war. Furthermore, unlike Hungary, Yugoslavia had grown greatly as a result of the peace settlement, and this process of expansion had precipitated a conflict with Austria in Carinthia which received considerable public attention in Germany. The German government, nevertheless, was to follow a policy toward Yugoslavia that at least temporarily would improve relations between the two countries. This policy was designed to give Germany a foothold in the Little Entente of which Czechoslovakia was considered Germany's enemy, and Rumania, as will be explained, would be a dubious partner. German conflicts of interest with Yugoslavia were in fact few; and the Berlin government decided to move in this case, as had been done in regard to Hungary, in the economic sector. Major developments in the economic as well as political field were not to come until 1935 and 1936, but the first signs pointing in this direction could be noted earlier.

During 1933 there were no significant political issues dividing Germany and Yugoslavia, nor was Germany backing Hungarian revisionist aspirations against Yugoslavia, which in turn was less concerned about a possible *Anschluss* than other countries.[146] The German government, partly in response to Yugoslav requests, did inaugurate talks for better trade relations.[147] In March and April 1934 these negotiations were pushed by the

144. Macartney, 1: 141–42.

145. *Documents secrets du Ministère des affaires étrangères de l'Allemagne,* 2, *Hongrie, La politique allemande 1937–1943* (trans. by Madeleine and Michel Eristov, Paris, 1946), No. 1.

146. See *G. D.,* C, 1, Nos. 279, 345; *B. D.,* 2d, 6, No. 331.

147. *G. D.,* C, 2, No. 309 (parts of this document appeared in the German White Book No. 7, *Dokumente zum Konflikt mit Jugoslawien und Griechenland* [Berlin: Eher, 1941], as No. 14); see also U. S. 1933, 2: 478–79.

Germans, who were willing to make concessions "to obtain a strong trading base within the economic sphere of the Little Entente," and to block both Italian and French influence in Southeast Europe.[148] The treaty eventually signed on 1 May 1934 was designed to tie Yugoslavia more closely to Germany, and undoubtedly provided the Germans with political leverage in exchange for special arrangements for Yugoslav exports to Germany that were granted in secret supplements to the published agreement.[149] Furthermore, Germany gained new export possibilities of its own; and both these economic opportunities and bases for future pressure on Yugoslavia were expected, at least by the German government, to be susceptible of further development in later years.[150] As yet, there could be no clear political agreement between the two countries,[151] but marking both the new spirit in German-Yugoslav relations and pointing to his future special interest in this field, Hermann Göring visited Belgrade briefly in the middle of May 1934, leaving behind what King Alexander of Yugoslavia called "an agreeable impression."[152]

By early 1934, the German government had also taken steps to reduce the one area of possible friction in which the Yugoslavs were especially sensitive, the problem of Croatian émigrés. The terrorist Right-wing of the Croatian nationalist movement, Ante Pavelič's Ustasha, had small groups in various European cities engaged in activities directed against the government of Yugoslavia. Among these were some in Germany who had contacts with the German armed forces and with Rosenberg's APA.[153] The Yugoslav intelligence service had penetrated the Ustasha and was well-informed about its Berlin operations.[154] The Belgrade government accordingly protested to the Germans. In Berlin, the foreign ministry was opposed in its endeavor to restrain the Croatian émigrés by the APA which wished to continue political contacts with them and by the war ministry which wanted to keep open a source of intelligence and a potential ally in case of a future war in which Yugoslavia, it was assumed, would be on the other side. The problem was not unlike that of German dealings with the Ukrain-

148. *G. D.*, C, 2, No. 318. For details on the negotiations see "Sitzung des Handelspolitischen Ausschusses vom 10. März 1934," ". . . vom 24. März 1934," ". . . vom 29. März 1934," ". . . vom 19. April 1934," T–120, 2612/5650/H 003848–50, 861–63, 864, 868–69; "Bestellung aus der Pressekonferenz vom 15. März 1934," Bundesarchiv, Brammer Z.Sg. 101/3, f. 121.

149. *G. D.*, C, 3, No. 13; Jacob B. Hoptner, *Yugoslavia in Crisis, 1934–1941* (New York: Columbia University Press, 1962), pp. 101–102. A good summary of the political as well as economic significance of the treaty may be found in "Informationsbericht vom 5. Mai 1934, Der deutsch-jugoslawische Handelsvertrag," Bundesarchiv, Brammer Z.Sg. 101/27, f. 121–23.

150. *G. D.*, C, 3, No. 23.

151. Ibid., 2, No. 381.

152. Ibid., 3, No. 27.

153. Ladislaus Hory and Martin Broszat, *Der kroatische Ustascha-Staat, 1941–1945* (Stuttgart: Deutsche Verlags-Anstalt, 1964), pp. 22, 26.

154. Vladeta Miličevič, *Der Königsmord von Marseille* (Bad Godesberg: Hohwacht, 1959), pp. 43–44.

ian nationalists, with the difference that the Yugoslav government raised the question in official channels. Hitler decided that as long as German interests demanded friendly relations with Yugoslavia, there should be no active intervention in its internal affairs. Ustasha newspapers that had been published in Germany were now banned, and what contacts remained were maintained without public fanfare.[155] The Ustasha's role in German policy toward Yugoslavia was temporarily relegated to the background. The short-run advantages were all on the side of building up a good relationship with the existing authorities in Belgrade.

Rumania

If Germany's relations with Yugoslavia began to develop along new lines of cooperation, its relations with Rumania were tenuous in spite of attempts at a rapprochement. Having broken its ties with Germany in the war, Rumania gathered a rich harvest from the collapse of the Central Powers, and its policy was directed primarily toward keeping what it had won by good fortune more than military prowess. In spite of the obvious interest of Germany in a revision of the peace settlement, the Rumanian government made a number of efforts toward a closer relationship with Germany in 1933. Perhaps the old ties to Germany of the ruling dynasty, the fear that Germany might back Hungarian revisionist aspirations in Transylvania, and the hope for better trade relations in the face of depression contributed to this policy. Whatever the motives, repeated soundings were made by Rumania.[156] The German government was not convinced that the Rumanians were sincere; the policies of the Rumanian foreign minister, Nicolae Titulescu, were too obviously anti-German. Parallel efforts to build on the ideological affinity between the National Socialists of Germany and similar movements in Rumania did produce some contacts. Hitler met the Rumanian National Socialist leaders Stefan Tatarescu and Octavian Goga, but little came of this except for pleasant memories for Goga to recall when he was prime minister for six weeks in the winter of 1937–38.[157] For the time being it seemed too dangerous for Germany to dabble in internal Rumanian politics, and not only was the idea of financing Rumanian National Socialist politicians abandoned, but the National Socialists among the German minority in the country were instructed to be most cautious.[158]

The Rumanians were not put off entirely, however. The need to export their products to Germany led them to press Berlin repeatedly on this

155. On this issue see *G. D.,* C, 2, Nos. 43, 72, 91, 92; Schumann (APA) to Lammers, 15 December 1933, Nuremberg document 006–PS.

156. *G. D.,* C, 1, Nos. 32, 118, 189, 264, 328, 395. The soundings had included a scheme, promoted by Rosenberg, for a private meeting between Hitler and Titulescu analogous to that between Hitler and Gömbös.

157. *G. D.,* C, 1, Nos. 468, 496; D, 5, No. 157; *Rosenberg Tagebuch,* 29 May 1934, p. 36.

158. *G. D.,* C, 2, No. 36; Jacobsen, pp. 80–83.

subject; and for a whole year, from May 1933 to June 1934, they tried to convince the German government that a trade agreement would be mutually beneficial. The Germans were skeptical, partly for economic, partly for political reasons.[159] In spite of these difficulties, limited agreements were reached. In the summer of 1933, the great German chemical trust, I. G. Farben, arranged a trade contract involving Rumanian grain and oil seed exports in return for imports of I. G. Farben products and political contributions inside Rumania.[160] Furthermore, on 5 June 1934, a German-Rumanian trade agreement was signed.[161] It was restricted to a relatively small scale—five million marks—but would set a precedent as well as an encouragement for later expansion.

The other countries of Southeast Europe—Albania, Greece, Bulgaria, and Turkey—played no great role in German foreign policy in the first year of National Socialist rule. Germany was interested in promoting its economic position in these countries,[162] and for sentimental as well as practical reasons maintained good relations with its wartime ally, Bulgaria,[163] but none of this was as yet of special importance. On only one subject was Germany clear in its perception of policy toward all the countries of Southeast Europe: it wanted no regional grouping that included all of them, for any such grouping might exclude Germany from pursuing a policy of economic and political penetration.[164]

159. On these talks, see *G. D.*, C, 1, No. 264; 2, Nos. 468, n. 3, 486; 3, No. 285, n. 1; Memorandum of von Bülow, 8 June 1933, T–120, 1437/2980/D 581383–84; Schulenburg (Bucharest) telegram 25 of 11 July 1933, ibid., frame D 581380; Memorandum of von Neurath RM 1016 of 13 July 1933, ibid., frames D 581390–91; Memoranda of von Bülow of 13 October and 28 November 1933, ibid., frames D 581392–97.

160. *G. D.*, C, 1, Nos. 414, 415.

161. Ibid., 2, No. 468, n. 5; 3, No. 285, n. 1.

162. An interesting document on a German effort early in 1934 to gain control of the Turkish copper mining industry, in Office of Military Government for Germany (U. S.), "Report on the Investigation of the Deutsche Bank," November 1946, Exhibit, 111.

163. On Turkey see *G. D.*, C, 2, No. 22, n. 7; 3, No. 371, n. 1; Lothar Krecker, *Deutschland und die Türkei im Zweiten Weltkrieg* (Frankfurt/M: Klostermann, 1964), p. 23; "Sitzung des Handelspolitischen Ausschusses vom 14. April 1934," T–120, 2612/5650/H 003866–67. On Bulgaria see *G. D.*, C, 2, Nos. 22, 291, 411; Bentinck (Sofia) dispatch 75, 10 April 1934, Foreign Office R 2113/112/7; Balfour (Sofia) dispatch 228, 14 September 1934, Foreign Office R 5148/1400/7; Bentinck dispatch 283, 24 November 1934, R 6740/112/7. On Greece see *G. D.*, C, 2, No. 289.

164. *G. D.*, C, 1, No. 5; 2, No. 246.

5 The Far East to the Summer of 1935

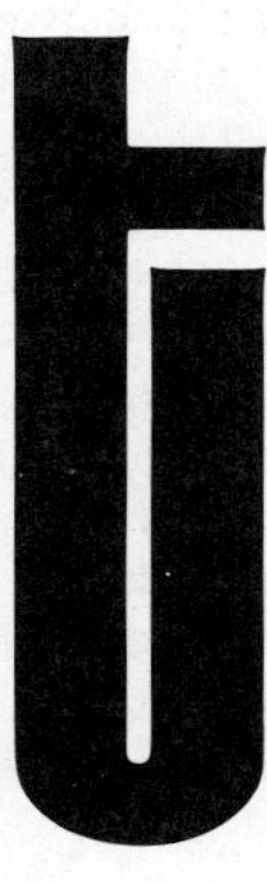

he Far Eastern crisis precipitated by the Japanese occupation of Manchuria had commanded a large share of the world's attention before 1933, but this was by no means true for Germany's new leaders. The new rulers of Germany were neither systematic in their work habits nor comprehensive in their interests, with the result that attention was given to the Far East only sporadically.[1] This lack of interest meant that the initiative of enterprising individuals and the frequently differing policies advocated by different German officials or agencies were allowed an astounding opportunity to move forward without much plan or coordination. In a regime that has been very aptly characterized as an "authoritarian anarchy,"[2] the area furthest removed from the center of authority in Berlin was to provide some of the most extraordinary crosscurrents. The initial stages of the crosscurrents will be described in this chapter, but it should be made clear at the outset that until 1938 there was no general plan or policy whatever. The contradictions that may have looked like the surface manifestations of some grand design, all the more dangerous because its nature was concealed from view, were in fact something quite undramatic: the pet schemes of various individuals and organizations, occasionally brought into temporary harmony either when they threatened other interests of the regime or when the conflicts between them became too extreme for Hitler to tolerate.

An immediate problem created for Germany by the advent of national socialism was inherent in the public

1. In some respects the ignorance of the National Socialist leaders may have been a blessing in disguise; what if they had known that the Ainu, the primitive people of Japan, were white?

2. Walter Petwaidic, *Die autoritäre Anarchie* (Hamburg: Hoffman und Campe, 1946).

ideology of the new government. The loudly proclaimed racialist ideology of national socialism was certain to arouse hostility to Germany in Asia, just as it would reinforce preoccupation with the "Yellow Peril" in Germany itself.[3] This problem arose in 1933 and was to plague the German government from then on. Proposals for a reform of the German penal code to prohibit interracial marriage and even social contact produced an especially violent reaction in the Far East.[4] As a symbol of Germany's evaluation of the peoples of Asia, these proposals precipitated very strong complaints from the Chinese and Japanese governments.[5] These complaints in turn led to instructions to the German press not to refer to the "Yellow Peril,"[6] and a public statement designed to reassure the offended countries was issued by the German government.[7]

Efforts to persuade foreign diplomats that Germany's official differentiation between races should not be construed as a value judgment did not, however, persuade everyone. Incidents involving Orientals in Germany periodically revived the issue on which the Japanese were especially sensitive. Attempts were made to reduce the negative impact on German foreign policy by providing for special treatment of cases involving Orientals (as contrasted with Jews and Negroes), but the difficulties continued.[8] Nor were these restricted to foreign reactions to German racial policies. The National Socialists themselves were uneasy about the matter, and as the idea of an alignment with Japan developed, the racial contradictions implicit in it would trouble many in Germany.

Germany's economic and political interests in the Far East at the beginning of Hitler's chancellorship, however, were heavily concentrated on

3. The discussion in chaps. 1 and 3 of Ernst L. Presseisen, *Germany and Japan, A Study in Totalitarian Diplomacy, 1933–1941* (The Hague: Nijhoff, 1958), refers only to Japan; but much of it is applicable to Asia as a whole.

4. Hanns Kerrl, *Nationalsozialistisches Strafrecht, Denkschrift des Preussischen Justizministers* (Berlin: Decker, 1933). To the embarrassment of the Germans, news of these proposals came out just when the German cruiser *Koeln* was visiting Colombo; an uproar over the social functions for the crew planned by the German consul immediately ensued (Buell [Colombo] dispatch No. 20 of 10 October 1933, with numerous clippings attached, State 862.4016/1318).

5. For reports on the excitement in Japan and Japanese protests see Memorandum of von Bülow, 11 October 1933, T–120, 1520/3080/D 623166; Voretzsch (Tokyo) telegram 108 of 20 October, ibid., frame D 623165; Memorandum of Völckers (Berlin), 20 October, ibid., frame D 623164. For Chinese complaints see the protest of 2 November 1933, in T–120, 2787/6022/H 044372; and *G. D.*, C, 2, No. 48.

6. "Bestellungen aus der Pressekonferenz vom 1. November 1933," Bundesarchiv, Brammer, Z.Sg. 101/2, f. 24; the topic was apparently so popular that these instructions had to be repeated on 4 February 1934 (ibid., 101/5, f. 30).

7. *G. D.*, C, 2, No. 123. It should be noted that this document was prepared in response to an expression of concern by President Hindenburg; the reference to Ceylon presumably covers the incident mentioned in n. 4, above.

8. *G. D.*, C, 3, Nos. 182, 331, 486; 4, No. 69; John P. Fox, "Japanese Reactions to Nazi Germany's Racial Legislation," *Wiener Library Bulletin*, Vol. 23, Nos. 2 & 3 (1969), 46–50.

China.[9] Germany had made a substantial comeback in the China trade during the 1920s. In spite of internal dissension in China, the opportunities for the continued expansion of that trade looked good. A significant facet of Germany's economic relations with China was its possible relationship to the German military advisers to Chiang Kai-shek.[10] This group of German officers was working under individual contracts to help train and organize the Chinese army; they were at this time under the command of General Wetzell, who had succeeded another World War I assistant of General Erich Ludendorff, Max Bauer. The Chinese had tried to replace Wetzell in 1932 with the former German minister of defense, General Groener; in view of his declination, they were now interested in General von Seeckt, the man who had played a key part in rebuilding the German army in the early 1920s. Von Seeckt did go to China in the summer of 1933, conferred with some of the German officers there, met General and Madame Chiang Kai-shek, and left behind a detailed memorandum on the reorganization of China's army.[11] The question of von Seeckt taking charge of the German military advisers was not formally raised until after he had returned to Germany; but while in China, von Seeckt had already become involved in a project that was to play a major, and by no means entirely happy, role in German-Chinese relations.

Before leaving Germany, von Seeckt had been visited by a representative of the South China military regime centered on Canton.[12] During his stay in China, von Seeckt stopped in Canton, meeting the local war lords in the company of two other Germans, Hans Klein, a businessman who had been active in Africa before 1914 and had shifted his interests to China, and Major Preu of the German Ministry of War.[13] With the support, apparently, of von Seeckt and the German war ministry, Klein and Preu developed elaborate plans for the construction of an arsenal and other military installations

9. A good survey, though now dated in parts, is Kurt Bloch, *German Interests and Policies in the Far East* (New York: Institute of Pacific Relations, 1940).

10. A useful folder on these advisers for the period 1923–34 is in the U. S. War Department Records, National Archives, File 2657–I–357. In connection with the possible replacement of General Wetzell as chief of the German group see the comment on him in Report 8517 of 27 February 1933, by the U. S. assistant military attaché in China (ibid.). Considerable insight into the life of the advisers may be secured from the memoirs of Fritz Lindemann, *Im Dienste Chinas, Erinnerungen aus den Jahren 1929 bis 1940* (Peking: Selbstverlag, 1940). For a survey of the activities and impact of the German military advisers in the development of the Chinese army see Chih-pu Liu, *A Military History of Modern China, 1924–1949* (Princeton: Princeton University Press, 1956), chaps. 7–10 passim.

11. Friedrich von Rabenau, *Seeckt, Aus seinem Leben, 1918–1936* (Leipzig: Hase & Koehler, 1940), pp. 677–701; Lindemann, p. 334; *G. D.*, C, 1, Nos. 156, 412; U. S. 1933, 2: 320; Hans Meier-Welcker, *Seeckt* (Frankfurt/M: Bernard & Graefe, 1967), pp. 649–66.

12. Rabenau, p. 687, n. 2. Meier-Welcker is most reticent on this aspect of von Seeckt's trip (see p. 658).

13. *G. D.,* C, 1, No. 436; Lindemann, pp. 386–87; Emil Helfferich, *1932–1946, Tatsachen* (Jever, Oldenbourg: C. L. Mettcker, 1968), pp. 111–12.

in the Canton area as well as for the detailing of German military advisers to the Canton regime. In view of Canton's tenuous relationship to the central government in Nanking, such projects created the prospect of German intervention into Chinese internal affairs against the government of Chiang Kai-shek. The German foreign ministry for political and economic reasons opposed this move, while the German army, partly to build up the arms export business, backed the scheme. The compromise reached in practice was that the military advisers were not sent but the construction work went ahead. Although the central government alternately objected and approved Klein's projects, one might fairly draw the conclusion that Chiang was not sorry to have Germany build up the resources of the Canton area that his regime would eventually swallow—as it did in 1936—as long as German activities did not unduly strengthen the local war lords in the interim. The endless correspondence on the subject certainly points in this direction, but it also shows that the German government was about as divided internally as the Chinese.[14]

In spite of all sorts of trouble both in China and Germany, Klein's project in Canton moved forward, no doubt aided by the fact that one of the three engineers supervising the work was a brother of General Walter von Reichenau, one of the most adamant sponsors of Klein in the Ministry of War.[15] In fact, in the summer of 1934, Klein made a series of new agreements with the Canton regime providing for the exchange of Chinese raw materials for German industrial products, and also made a similar agreement with the central government in Nanking.[16] These agreements, which opened a new chapter in German-Chinese relations, were negotiated by Klein under the supervision of von Seeckt himself. Both the latter's return to China and the steps in German-Chinese trade that paved the way for these agreements must first be explained.

The new regime in Germany was interested in building up its armaments industry and acquiring foreign exchange for the purchase of raw materials needed by the arms industry. The exportation of armaments looked like an ideal way to accomplish both objectives; the export contracts would lead to expanded capacity at home, the payments to greater purchasing power abroad. That such actions were illegal under Germany's treaties and domestic laws hindered no one; the oath German officers and officials took to uphold their country's laws rested very lightly on their consciences.

The visit of the Chinese minister of finance, T. V. Soong, to Germany in July 1933 provided an excellent opportunity to make arrangements for

14. For documentation on the original Klein project see *G. D.*, C, 2, Nos. 89, 235, 262; Lindemann, pp. 387–88; German legation Peking report 3 of 2 January 1935, T–120, 2988/6680/H 096053.

15. German consulate general Canton to legation Peking, report 856/34/4101 of 20 October 1934, T–120, 2991/6691/H 098359.

16. *G. D., C,* 3, No. 180.

arms exports to the government of Nationalist China. Although not all the details of Soong's negotiations with German firms and agencies are clear, the evidence indicates that he made several agreements with the Krupp arms firm and with Rheinmetall-Borsig, an armaments firm controlled by the Ministry of War and which in turn controlled a firm named Solothurn in Switzerland that could conveniently provide a cover for illegal or politically dubious transactions.[17] These schemes, and the related proposal that the German government guarantee the German suppliers against losses on the transactions, were viewed with great doubt by the German foreign ministry and strongly opposed by the German minister to China, Oskar Trautmann. In long arguments against the Ministry of War, where Reichenau continued to be the leading advocate of such projects, the foreign ministry for once secured a decision from Hitler somewhat favorable to its own position. By the time that decision was given in October 1934, however, the Chinese central government was growing so rapidly in strength that the foreign ministry withdrew its objections; and the project went forward after all.[18]

In this unusually clear example of how policy could be made in National Socialist Germany on a subject not directly engaging Hitler's interest, we can observe a lengthy dispute between several ministries in which the matter is referred to Hitler for a decision after more than a year of squabbling. Hitler makes his decision on the basis of the arguments presented; but when it comes to implementation, the situation has changed to such an extent that the original difference between the contending parties has disappeared. All now move forward in a direction *contrary* to that determined by Hitler's decision, evidently secure in the knowledge that as long as they agreed, he would not much care.

In the meantime von Seeckt had been asked to return to China, it being clearly understood that he would replace Wetzell as chief adviser.[19] When this question arose in October 1933, von Seeckt had first refused, partly in

17. On Soong's visit and the agreements made see *G. D.*, C, 1, Nos. 357, 373, 435, 463; Soong to Krupp von Bohlen, 24 July 1933, T–120, 2383/4619/E 197748–50; von Neurath memorandum RM 1307 of 16 September 1933, ibid., frame E 197747; Dodd (Berlin) dispatch 100 of 26 August 1933, State 693.6215/1; Newton (Berlin) dispatch 729, 21 July 1933, Foreign Office F 4997/2717/10.

18. The course of this argument may be followed in *G. D.*, C, 1, No. 410; 2, Nos. 412, 454; 3, Nos. 220, 232, 253, 258. The last of these documents deals with Hitler's decision; for information on the subsequent reversal of the foreign ministry's position and the cooperation of the German Ministries of Finance and Economics in carrying the project forward without reference back to Hitler see Memorandum by Kühlborn, 4 April 1935, T–120, 2991/6691/H 098419–420; Foreign ministry to Ministry of Economics, 18 April 1935, ibid., frame H 098440; Ministry of Economics to Foreign ministry, 1 November 1935, ibid., frame H 098572; cf. Peck (Nanking) dispatch D–588 of 23 January 1934, State 893.20/473.

It should be noted that Waldemar Pabst, while unable to plot the overthrow of the Austrian government because of his temporary deportation from that country, played a part in handling the Berlin end of the arms sales to China.

19. One concern of von Seeckt on his return from his first trip had been that he had not commanded Pharaoh's army at the time of Moses (Rabenau, p. 693)!

response to the German foreign ministry's worries about repercussions from Japan if so prominent an individual were assigned to the position. The first thoughts of a German-Japanese rapprochement in late 1933 soon evaporated, and Chiang's threat to replace the Germans with French military advisers helped persuade the German government to approve von Seeckt's trip. He therefore went out in March 1934; accompanying him was General Alexander von Falkenhausen who would succeed von Seeckt after what was anticipated would be only a short period of time.[20] The objections of Japan were not allowed to interfere with the maintenance of Germany's position in China.

While in China, von Seeckt worked with Chiang on the organization and training of the Chinese army. He was to prepare General von Falkenhausen to assume the role of chief military adviser, but in reality von Seeckt practically turned the military activities over to von Falkenhausen from the beginning of his mission while devoting his own time primarily to economic questions.[21] The major development in the economic field was a series of new agreements made by Klein with the Chinese authorities at Canton as well as the central government. These agreements foresaw the exchange of Chinese raw materials for German military and railway construction projects and for industrial products. Included in the provisions were promises by Klein to secure credits of two hundred million marks for Canton and one hundred million for the central government.[22] These commitments seemed to go too far for the German diplomats both in China and Berlin and gave rise to a controversy that continued for some time. Hitler had supposedly approved the idea—an argument often used in such disputes in the Third Reich—but the course of subsequent discussions in Germany suggests that such approval, if really given, was very limited in scope. The intricate negotiations with various groups in China and between the different agencies of the German government need not be recounted here, but their main themes and their outcome are revealing.[23] The German government was keenly interested in imports of tungsten, tin, and other ores; on this Hitler, Schacht, von Neurath, and the military were in full agreement. They were in disagreement on the amount of financial and political risk to take. The financial risks were eventually reduced to a very modest level, about twenty million marks to be exact. The political risks of antagonizing Japan and becoming involved in the difficulties between Nanking and Canton also operated as

20. *G. D.*, C, 2, Nos. 16, 48, 63, 80, 157, 199, 243, 323; Rabenau, pp. 701ff.; Liu, pp. 99ff; Meier-Welcker, pp. 667–84.

21. Rabenau, p. 705. Rabenau adds that "it is unfortunately impossible to cover the economic questions in detail." The year 1940—when Rabenau's book was published—was not the time to discuss the projected German loan to Chiang Kai-shek.

22. The relevant documents are in T–120, 2988/6680, with a summary in *G. D.*, C, 3, No. 180.

23. Key documents in T–120, 2988/6680. Published items in *G. D.*, C, 3, Nos. 301, 366, 472, 476, 488, 508, 504, 554; 4, Nos. 1, 40, 76; cf. Memorandum of General Thomas, 20 July 1945, Nuremberg document 436–PS. The account in Helfferich, pp. 107–40, is useful but one-sided.

restraining factors, and in this regard the German involvement was also held down, especially at Canton.[24]

In spite of the limitations imposed in Berlin, by the summer of 1935 German-Chinese trade had been increased, and the German military mission was supplemented by an air mission.[25] The air mission was especially interested in an airplane factory German industrialists had erected for Chiang near Hangchow, an installation that provided an additional focus for German influence in China.[26] Even if Klein had not been able to carry out all the extravagant schemes he had hoped for, German interests in China were clearly growing in 1934–35, in spite of Japanese objections.[27] Whatever the real economic benefit these interests might actually have had for Germany had war not subsequently broken out in the Far East, they did give Germany a stake in China sufficiently great to restrain the first venture into pro-Japanese policy that began to be advocated in some quarters, beginning in 1933.

Aside from publically expressed admiration extended to Japan by some elements in National Socialist Germany in 1933, the first real involvement of the two powers was to be occasioned by economic interests in a third area, namely Manchuria.[28] A key role in the Manchurian drama was to be played by a product Germany needed—soybeans—as well as by an adventurer who seemed perfectly suited to the new German government, Ferdinand Heye. Soybeans were imported into Germany to help meet the need for cattle fodder and vegetable oils. The threat to Germany's domestic economy by the scarcity of these staples had been brought dramatically home to the regime in World War I; at various times during the National Socialist period attempts were made to assure a steady supply. In addition to the episode taken up here, there were such other efforts as schemes to grow soybeans in Southeast Europe and, later, to obtain Soviet aid in

24. The reduction of Germany's involvement at Canton was in part the result of a direct plea from the German consul general at Shanghai, Hermann Kriebel, an associate of Hitler from the time of the Munich putsch (*G. D.*, C, 4, Nos. 94, 101; cf. the excerpts from von Falkenhausen's letter to Lt. Colonel Brinckmann, 19 May 1935, T–120, 2991/6691/H 098512–518).

25. In the margin of a report by General Streccius, the German air adviser, State Secretary von Bülow raised the question whether the German air ministry was now also making its own China policy (Trautmann report 497 of 16 May 1935, T–120, 2988/6680/H 096293). For information on a German naval officer in China see Foreign Office F 753/753/10.

26. This project was carried forward by the Junkers Works and by the industrialist Otto Wolff (*G. D.*, C, 3, Nos. 373, 379, 404; Memorandum by Frohwein, 8 June 1935, T–120, 2988/6680/H 096308). Otto Wolff was also to construct some railways and carry out other projects; see the excerpts from the letter of von Falkenhausen to Brinckmann, 13 March 1935, T–120, 2991/6691/H 098462–466; U. S. 1935, 3: 583.

27. *G. D.*, C, 2, No. 358.

28. On his return to Japan after walking out of the League over the vote to approve the report of the Lytton commission, Yosuke Matsuoka stopped in Berlin in March 1933 (*D. D. F.*, 1st, 2, No. 393; cf. ibid., No. 375); but there is no evidence that important matters were discussed.

transporting the precious product from Manchuria over the Trans-Siberian Railway in the years of the German-Soviet nonaggression pact.[29]

Ferdinand Heye was a German businessman who had been in Manchuria in 1925–27. The business activity in which he participated involved the smuggling of narcotics, led to the suicide of one member of the firm, and ended in bankruptcy following an embezzlement.[30] As early as 1931 Heye contacted Fritz Thyssen, a German industrialist who strongly supported the National Socialists at that time and who referred him to his friend Göring. In anticipation of a National Socialist takeover in Germany, Heye prepared some elaborate projects for German-Manchurian trade which, on Göring's advice, he took to the foreign ministry in March 1933.[31] Heye claimed the support of both Göring and Hitler and soon enlisted the aid of Rosenberg's foreign policy office, where Werner Daitz, the head of the APA's foreign trade office, came to be Heye's main party sponsor. The foreign ministry was most dubious about the whole project; but financed by Thyssen, and with some sort of government encouragement, Heye went to Manchuria in August 1933, returning to Germany in late September.[32]

Heye's stay in Germany coincided with the change in Germany's embassy in Tokyo and thus looked like an opportune moment for new departures in foreign policy. Heye saw the newly appointed German ambassador, Herbert von Dirksen, whom the foreign ministry promptly enlightened on Heye's background.[33] From here on, the conflict between the foreign ministry and Heye was to evolve until it wrecked the chances for the policy change that Heye (and the National Socialist circles behind him) wanted and that von Dirksen himself soon came to advocate, namely the recognition of the Japanese puppet state of Manchukuo as both a token of closer German-Japanese relations and an opening for a special German economic role in Manchuria.

Heye wanted to become special trade commissioner in Manchukuo with an appointment as consul-general there. He was supported in this by the APA as well as by Thyssen and, for a while, Hitler's special economic ad-

29. For early attempts to grow soybeans in Rumania and Bulgaria see Wilmowsky to Knoll, 10 July 1935, T–120, 3502/8987/E 630288–289; on transit across the Soviet Union see Gerhard L. Weinberg, *Germany and the Soviet Union, 1939–1941* (Leiden: Brill, 1954), pp. 72–73.

30. German consul Harbin to the foreign ministry, 10 March 1933, T–120, 2992/6693/H 098873–885. When Heye's background later became a subject of dispute in the German government, Karl Ritter of the foreign ministry could refer to Heye's own reference in the correspondence to 21 kilograms (about fifty pounds) of morphine (Memorandum of Ritter, 21 November 1933, ibid., frames H 098926–929).

31. *G. D.*, C, 1, No. 50. The correspondence referred to in ibid., n. 3, concerns Heye's earlier dealing with Göring and Thyssen going back to 1931. There are no references to the whole episode in Thyssen's memoirs, *I Paid Hitler* (New York: Farrar & Rinehart, 1941).

32. Erdmannsdorff (Tokyo) telegrams 89 of 28 August and 93 of 13 September 1933, T–120, 2992/6693/H 098898–899.

33. Von Dirksen, p. 159; Altenburg (Berlin) to von Dirksen (Moscow), 30 October 1933, T–120, 2992/6693/H 098894.

viser, Wilhelm Keppler. Hitler himself clearly became interested and for a while appears to have considered recognizing Manchukuo. The foreign ministry argued the danger of losing Germany's economic interests in a resentful China as against the doubtful prospect of advantages in Manchuria beyond those that could be secured through normal trade channels. Furthermore, it was argued that a Germany which had just pulled out of the League would be unwise to isolate itself still more by affronting the powers opposed to recognition of the puppet state. Unwittingly, Rosenberg himself was to provide Hitler with another argument against recognition by stressing that closer cooperation with Japan would alienate Britain, which Germany still hoped to woo. These arguments won the day—as they would continue to do for several years more. The decision was long-postponed, however, and in the interim other complications intervened. Since Heye had conducted several political discussions on his 1933 trip and continued to mix politics with trade on his second journey to the Far East, he soon came into personal conflict with von Dirksen, who in fact advocated a policy that otherwise closely paralleled Heye's.[34]

When von Dirksen talked with Hitler, von Blomberg, and others in mid-October 1933 before starting on his new assignment, the subject of German relations with Japan was naturally discussed.[35] Von Dirksen gained the impression that Hitler wanted closer relations with Japan and was prepared to recognize Manchukuo. When the Japanese foreign minister urged von Dirksen to make a trip to Manchuria at their first meeting on 18 December 1933, von Dirksen wanted to comply with this request. He argued, when confronted by the immediate opposition of the foreign ministry, that this was precisely what Hitler wanted. He thought that such a trip was the best way to prepare for recognition, the key step in his plan for close German-Japanese relations. The foreign ministry maintained that von Dirksen had misunderstood Hitler, and pointed out the dangers to Germany's relations with China, the Soviet Union, England, and the United States if von Dirksen's adventurous course were followed. Von Dirksen had to content himself with sending his economic counselor to Manchuria, a step that promptly set off speculation that German recognition of the puppet state was imminent.[36]

34. Documents on this episode are in T–120, 2992/6693/passim. Published items are *G. D.*, C, 2, Nos. 97, 238, 241. On Hitler's interest see Memorandum by Ritter, IV Chi 2555 of 21 November 1933, frames H 098930–931; Rosenberg's report for Hitler of mid-October 1933, forwarded on 18 December 1933, Nuremberg document 048–PS in *Rosenberg Tagebuch*, p. 159.

35. At one point in his memoirs (p. 130) von Dirksen claims Hitler gave him no hints of his future policy toward Japan; at another (p. 156) he asserts that von Blomberg told him Hitler wanted better relations.

36. On this dispute see *G. D.*, C, 2, Nos. 7, 237, 138, 154, 158, 162, 174, 183, 198, 236, 256, 267; Memorandum by von Bülow, 8 February 1934, T–120, 2992/6692/H 098750; U. S. 1934, 3:8, 23, 43–44.

One cannot simply dismiss von Dirksen's repeated insistence that Hitler had authorized recognition in their conversation of 18 October as either a total misunder-

These rumors of impending recognition were furthered by Heye's appearance in the Far East. Hitler had decided on 16 February 1934 that Heye could negotiate a trade agreement with the Manchukuo authorities, but this action was not to constitute recognition. In view of the Chinese fears resulting from Heye's activities, Hitler had also authorized the publication of a communiqué denying that recognition was imminent, and a statement to this effect was communicated to the Chinese government.[37] In this policy of compromise, Hitler deferred to the foreign ministry's desire to avoid recognition with all its international political complications, while yielding to the wishes of Rosenberg, Thyssen, and Heye to try for the economic advantages that might be gained in Manchuria. If recognition seemed appropriate later, it might be accorded; but the moment when von Seeckt was about to go to China to take over direction of Chiang's military advisers seemed a poor time to come down too obviously on the side of Japan.

The new policy was defined by von Neurath to von Dirksen as one of watching the realities, skeptically seeing what might really be accomplished in Manchuria without pursuing the political question of recognition for the time being.[38] The instrument chosen to do the exploring, namely Ferdinand Heye, did not prove successful. He arrived in Manchuria late in February 1934 and began negotiations for greater German-Manchurian trade.[39] His activities produced an immediate and general uproar. He promised German recognition, advertised himself as the forthcoming German minister to Manchukuo, and offered to maintain German soybean imports at the 1933 level for three years. He proposed that all the payments for these imports be handled through an account in Germany and be used to pay for German industrial products, thereby short-circuiting all the German firms previously

---

standing or a reflection of von Dirksen's confusion about the realities of Far Eastern politics (he thought all the other powers were about to extend recognition). The origin of the misunderstanding might be seen in Hitler's excitement at the time about having left the League a few days earlier. In his thinking, the League was closely related to the non-recognition doctrine (see Gerhard L. Weinberg, "German Recognition of Manchoukuo," *World Affairs Quarterly,* 28, No. 2 [July 1957], p. 153 and n. 17), and Hitler may well have made some hasty reference to that doctrine if he reviewed for von Dirksen his most recent and most spectacular step. For evidence that the German foreign ministry thought Hitler might approve recognition see von Bülow to Meyer, 13 January 1934, T–120, 2992/6692/H 098730.

37. *G. D.,* C, 2, Nos. 238, 241, 269, 281, 285, 429, n. 6; von Neurath to von Bülow, 27 February 1934, T–120, 2383/4619/E 197898; von Neurath to Trautmann, telegram 24 of 8 March 1934, T–120, 2992/6692/H 098798. The confusion was compounded by the fact that Daitz was telling diplomats in Berlin that recognition was imminent, while Meyer, the head of the Eastern section of the German foreign ministry, was denying it (*G. D.,* C, 2, No. 353; U. S. 1934, 3:59; Ambassador Dodd could tell the difference, but many others could not).

38. *G. D.,* C, 2, No. 300.

39. Myers (Mukden) dispatch of 1 March 1934, State 762.93-Manchuria/1; see also the memorandum by Edmund Fuerholzer, head of the German news agency Transocean for the Far East, "Betrachtungen über die mandschurische Frage, Anfang April 1934," in T–81, roll 32, serial 53, frames 28814–818.

trading in the Far East and assuring a new firm—in which he and Thyssen played key roles—a general commission of 10 percent.[40] Since these proposals were put forward right after Berlin had published the communiqué of 24 February stating that Germany was not about to recognize Manchukuo, Heye was not received enthusiastically by the Manchukuo authorities, who politely declined his offer on 25 March 1934.

In the meantime, the political role Heye had assumed for himself had agitated von Dirksen and the German foreign ministry; his plan to cut all other German firms out of the Manchurian trade alarmed German businesses with interests there; and the implications of his dealings with the Manchukuo authorities terrified those German firms, often the same ones, whose position in China was likely to be imperiled by the Chinese reaction to the agreement Heye proposed.[41] There was an immediate re-examination of the situation in Berlin and the submission of the Heye problem to Rudolf Hess, Hitler's deputy, who was frequently called upon to untangle or to cut the Gordian knots with which the German government snarled itself.[42]

While Hess was trying to unravel the dispute between the APA and Thyssen on one side and the foreign ministry backed by the now-suspicious Japanese as well as the German firms with Far Eastern interests on the other, Heye proceeded with his negotiations in Manchuria. By the begining of June 1934 these negotiations had produced a provisional agreement that said practically nothing but still alarmed the Chinese government. When copies of the agreement finally became available in Berlin, it could be seen that the proposed treaty contained no substantive concessions by the Manchukuo authorities but provided them with some dubious assurances about German soybean import policies. The bureaucratic infighting in Germany continued, with the tone of the communications becoming increasingly bitter. For a while, the whole matter was stalled.[43] The Berlin agencies

40. Heye's proposals of 3 March 1934 are alluded to in various published documents; their text was attached to von Dirksen's report 1341 of 6 April 1934, T–120, 2992/6693/H 099291–292.

41. It should be remembered that Germany had lost its extraterritorial rights in China under articles 128–134 of the Treaty of Versailles, so that German firms in China were unusually vulnerable to reprisals.

42. For documents on this episode see *G. D.*, C, 2, Nos. 312, 324, 326, 353, 425, n. 5, 429, 438; 3, No. 24; Nuremberg document 049–PS in *Rosenberg Tagebuch*, pp. 163–67; Balser (Harbin) report 46 of 22 March 1934, T–120, 2992/6693/H 099213–217, and memorandum by Erdmannsdorff (Berlin), 27 March 1934, frame H 099044; von Dirksen to von Bülow, 7 April, T–120, 2998/6693/H 099355–359; Hess to von Neurath, 27 April, ibid., frame H 099393; von Neurath to Hess, 15 May, ibid., frames H 099397–400; Note by Ritter (Berlin), 26 May, ibid., frame H 099555.

43. *G. D.*, C, 2, Nos. 482, 489, 493, 494 (on the original copy of this document, the fact that the telegram from Heye to Thyssen's Stahlverein was number 61 of a series was underlined twice at the foreign ministry), 495; 3, Nos. 22, 24; Trautmann report 508 of 6 June 1934, T–120, 2787/6022/H 044381–384; von Dirksen telegram 82 of 11 June, T–120, 2998/6693/H 099668; von Dirksen telegram 83 of 12 June (containing the text of the agreement), ibid., frame H 099675; Daitz to von Neurath, 15 June, ibid., frames H 099683–684; Ritter to Daitz, 20 June, ibid., frames H 099686–687; Note by Ulrich (Berlin), 15 June, ibid., frames H 099698–699; Memorandum by Ritter, 21 June, ibid., frame H 099701; *Rosenberg Tagebuch*, pp. 38 (8 June), 41–43 (28 June), 49–51 (11 July).

slowly untangled themselves during July and August, eventually deciding to separate private from official business. Heye and his associates in the Far East as well as their backers in Germany would operate as a private concern, dealing in Manchuria like other German firms. The German government declared its willingness to have such trade governed by a compensation agreement that Heye would negotiate for the German-Manchukuo Export-Import Company.[44] By this time, however, Heye had been so discredited in Manchuria that he could not get an agreement. He thereupon became involved in a deal to sell a zeppelin to the Japanese as part of a soybean exchange, but soon that enterprise was similarly bogged down.[45]

Hitler finally withdrew his support of Heye in February 1935; a German-Manchukuo trade agreement was not to be signed until the end of April 1936—and then through regular diplomatic channels.[46] Efforts by the APA to replace Heye with another special commissioner failed, and the foreign section of the NSDAP was no more successful with its fancy schemes for trade with Inner Mongolia.[47] Party diplomacy in Far Eastern economic affairs had produced nothing but confusion. The main questions of policy remained: should Germany side with Japan at the expense of its position in China? Could Germany maintain the position it already held in China without offending Japan?

Through 1934 and the first half of 1935, Germany continued to balance its Far Eastern interests, with predominant emphasis still given to its relations with China.[48] A tentative effort by Germany to bring China and Japan together was fruitless, though the attempt would be repeated several times later.[49] As it balanced its commitments in the Far East, Germany maintained its military advisers in China in spite of Japanese objections;[50] on the other hand, it reassured the Japanese that it was not about to demand a return of its pre-World War I colonies in the Pacific.[51]

In the summer of 1935, Germany's Far Eastern policy seemed to reach a new stage. The dichotomy of interests in both China and Japan that had

44. *G. D.,* C, 3, Nos. 107, 172, 217; foreign ministry telegram to von Dirksen number 88 of 21 August 1934, T–120, 2998/6693/H 099714; and T–120, 3502/8987/E 630171–345 passim.

45. Noebel (Tokyo) telegram 137 of 20 November 1934, T–120, 2998/6693/H 099738–739; foreign ministry to Noebel telegram 120 of 23 November, ibid., frame H 099741; von Dirksen report 4404 of 8 December, ibid., frames H 099748–758; air ministry to foreign ministry, 16 March 1935, 3502/8986/E 630119–131.

46. *G. D.,* C, 3, No. 478.

47. Trautmann report 515 of 21 May, 1935, T–120, 2991/6691/H 098486–504.

48. *G. D.,* C, 2, Nos. 374, 403, 404; 3, Nos. 247, 350, 521; 4, No. 45. German economic interests in China may have looked especially good because of certain problems in Germany's trade with Japan, mainly as a result of Japan's deficit in that trade (*G. D.,* C, 2, No. 460; 3, Nos. 217, n. 3, 239; 4, No. 69).

49. *G. D.,* C, 3, Nos. 153, 157, 168, 288.

50. Ibid., No. 512.

51. On this subject see "Stichworte für die mündliche Information der Presse," 18 March 1933, T–120, 2998/6694/H 099788; German foreign ministry Memorandum, 25 April 1933, T–120, 3475/8925/E 625876–877; von Dirksen report 1169 of 29 March 1935, T–120, 2673/5575/E 400036–037; *G. D.,* C, 4, No. 173.

marked the years since Hitler came to power was continuing, but the level of German involvement in the Far East had increased considerably. In regard to China, this was signalized by the raising of the German legation in Peiping to an embassy in May 1935, followed by its transfer to Nanking in June, both at Chiang's urging.[52] At the same time, German-Japanese negotiations for a special agreement that was to become the Anti-Comintern Pact were inaugurated.[53] These steps ushered in a new period of Germany's dilemma. With a growing interest in the two Far Eastern powers that were often in conflict with each other, could Germany maintain good relations with both and draw from each what it needed: influence and economic advantage from China, and political support from Japan?

The possible turning of Germany to Japan because of Japan's conquest of Manchuria, a special focus of German economic interest in the Far East, had been temporarily thwarted by a combination of three factors: the resistance of the German foreign ministry, the development of greater interest in China by the German army, and the confusion of private profit with public policy in the Heye venture. The Manchurian question, however, would continue to play a significant role in Germany's Far Eastern policy. Moreover, the German ambassador to Japan, Herbert von Dirksen, would continue to predict a glowing future for Japan's imperial expansion and for the possibility that Germany might profit from it in spite of Japanese exclusiveness in the areas it controlled, an exclusiveness to which the opponents of an alignment with Japan repeatedly—and prophetically—pointed. For the time being, Hitler would not choose; his attention was focused on problems that seemed both more urgent and more important. The elements in the German government and the National Socialist party which were especially interested in that faraway portion of the world could work at cross-purposes for a while longer.

52. *G. D.*, C, 3, Nos. 239, 493; Rabenau, p. 713; Meyer to Trautmann, 4 December 1934, T–120, 2787/6022/H 044409–410; von Neurath Memoranda RM 417 of 17 May 1935, and RM 422 of 20 May, T–120, 1522/3088/D 624772 and D 624776.

53. Theo Sommer, *Deutschland und Japan zwischen den Mächten, 1935–1940* (Tübingen: J. C. B. Mohr, 1962), p. 25.

6 Germany and the Western Hemisphere, 1933-36

Before 1933, German-American relations had been improving steadily. The American revulsion against the peace settlement had turned public opinion in the United States against its former associates, especially France. This attitude was exacerbated by the insistence of the Americans and the reluctance of their former allies to proceed with the repayment of loans made to help win the war. The struggling German republic, on the other hand, was viewed with increasing sympathy in the United States as the anti-German hysteria of the war years gave way to strong animus against Britain and France.[1] In Germany, there had been some appreciation of the more positive attitude the United States had taken toward it, and the absence of major disputes between the two countries led many Germans to look across the Atlantic with increasingly friendly regard. No two major powers were on better terms with each other than Germany and the United States before 1933, and the destruction of that relationship must be considered one of the signal events of the 1930s.

The new German government at first took little interest in the United States, regarding that country as far off and of no immediate concern in the plans for European conquest that dominated Hitler's thoughts. Germany's ambassador to the United States withdrew from the foreign service, unwilling to serve the new masters of his country; and Hitler found Washington a conveniently distant place to which to consign Hans Luther whom he was eager to remove from the presidency of the Reichsbank. Shortly before, General Friedrich von Boetticher had been assigned as military attaché to

1. See Selig Adler, "The War-Guilt Question and American Disillusionment, 1918–1928," *Journal of Modern History,* 23, No. 1 (March 1951), 1–28.

Washington; he would serve there until 1941, his reports reinforcing Hitler's low estimate of American military power and potential.[2]

America's representation to Germany was a matter of replacing an incumbent ambassador who was returning home with an appointee of the new administration inaugurated in Washington in March 1933. President-elect Franklin D. Roosevelt evidently wished to maintain good relations between the two countries. William C. Bullitt, who was in Europe as Roosevelt's unofficial emissary before the inauguration, conveyed such a message to Berlin in late January 1933;[3] and, worried about the possible accession to power of Hitler, Roosevelt had urged Hanfstaengl, his one acquaintance among the National Socialists, to attempt to moderate Hitler's conduct.[4] Hitler came to power between the American election and the inauguration, and under these circumstances Roosevelt canvassed a number of possibilities before settling on the historian William E. Dodd as his ambassador. Roosevelt's first consideration of James M. Cox, the Democratic presidential candidate of 1920, Newton D. Baker, former secretary of war and Roosevelt's rival for the 1932 presidential nomination, and a number of other prominent men suggests the importance he attached to Berlin as a key diplomatic post in contrast to Hitler's use of Washington as a place of exile.[5] The man appointed was the incoming president of the American Historical Association, a distinguished man of letters who had also been active in Democratic politics and on whom Roosevelt counted as a representative of both the values of American society and the hopes of the new administration. Though subjected to considerable criticism, Dodd maintained the president's full confidence. While the German government, to its own ultimate misfortune, went forward along policy lines of which Dodd was openly critical, Roosevelt seemed to feel in him a kindred spirit. As

2. German embassy Washington to Secretary of State Stimson, 6 February 1933, State 701.6211/805. Boetticher had made a trip to the United States in 1922 while serving as chief of army intelligence. On his role, see Gerhard L. Weinberg, "Hitler's Image of the United States," *American Historical Review*, 69, No. 4 (July 1964), 1012. A naval attaché, Captain, later Rear-Admiral, Witthoeft was assigned to Washington as of 1 October 1933.

3. Note by von Bülow, 28 January 1933, T–120, 2371/4601/E 188719–721; documents in T–120, 3381/8594/E 603512–517; Bullitt to Roosevelt, 8 November 1936, Franklin D. Roosevelt Library, Hyde Park (hereafter cited as Hyde Park), P. S. F. France; Beatrice Farnsworth, *William C. Bullitt and the Soviet Union* (Bloomington: Indiana University Press, 1967), pp. 80–85.

4. Hanfstaengl, p. 188. Hanfstaengl and Roosevelt were acquainted from the time FDR was a New York State senator and Hanfstaengl managed the New York branch of his family's art reproduction business. Roosevelt was responsible for having Hanfstaengl transferred from internment in Canada to the United States in 1942.

5. Roosevelt to Cox, 9 March 1933, in Elliott Roosevelt (ed.), *F. D. R.: His Personal Letters, 1928–1945* (New York: Duell, Sloan, and Pearce, 1950), 1:337; Roosevelt to Hull, 20 April 1933, and Phillips to Roosevelt, 18 May 1933, Hyde Park, O. F. 198–B; Robert Dallek, *Democrat and Diplomat, The Life of William E. Dodd* (New York: Oxford University Press, 1968), pp. 187–90.

the president wrote in September 1935, in connection with an extended leave for Dodd, "I need him in Berlin."[6]

In view of the incipient deterioration in German-American relations in the spring of 1933, Roosevelt tried to establish direct contact with the new German government before his ambassador could arrive in Berlin in July. In mid-March, Roosevelt suggested to the departing German ambassador that he would like an opportunity for a personal meeting with one of the German leaders, perhaps foreign minister, von Neurath.[7] With the work of the disarmament conference set back by events in Germany, he decided to have the American delegate to the conference, Norman Davis, go to Berlin to discuss both disarmament and the forthcoming World Economic Conference in London with Hitler and other German officials, in spite of some advice to the contrary from the State Department.[8] At his meetings in Berlin, Davis received an impression of the revolutionary changes in progress in Germany and the intransigeance of Hitler in regard to the Jewish question and the need for territorial change, couched in terms of revision of the Versailles treaty.[9] Hitler's recorded impression of Norman Davis was entirely negative.[10] He would receive reinforcement of this evaluation of American leadership from the report of Hjalmar Schacht on his visit to Washington in May 1933 for preliminary bilateral talks preceding the World Economic Conference. Roosevelt had invited Germany to send Hitler or another special emissary to Washington, unless the German government preferred regu-

6. Roosevelt to R. Walton Moore, 11 September 1935, Hyde Park, O. F. 523 (*FDR and Foreign Affairs*, 3:6). On Dodd see his *Diary* (ed. by W. E. Dodd, Jr., and Martha Dodd) (New York: Harcourt, 1941); Gordon Craig and Felix Gilbert, *The Diplomats* (Princeton: Princeton University Press, 1953), pp. 447–60; and Arnold A. Offner's fine essay on Dodd in *The Historian,* 34 (Aug. 1962), 451–69. The book by Dallek, cited above, is useful; see pp. 373–75 on the Dodd diary. Important details in Offner's *American Appeasement, United States Foreign Policy and Germany, 1933–1938* (Cambridge: Harvard University Press, 1969). Through the courtesy of the Dodd family, I have had access to the W. E. Dodd papers in the Library of Congress. There is a very sensitive appreciation of Dodd in the papers of George S. Messersmith (at the University of Delaware), "Some observations on the appointment of Dr. William Dodd as Ambassador to Berlin." Messersmith, who was in a position to know, asserts that Roosevelt appointed Dodd because he wanted someone who knew Germany, would be unspectacular, and had the background to interpret events. Messersmith maintained that "there were very few men who realized what was happening in Germany more thoroughly" than Dodd, and that his ineffectiveness was due mainly to the fact that Dodd "was completely appalled by what was happening." I believe that the subject of effectiveness ought to be considered in a broader context: there is no evidence that any other ambassador to National Socialist Germany was more effective, even if some were more popular and others better informed (see also R. Walton Moore's letters to Dodd of 26 December 1936 and 13 December 1937 in the Dodd Papers, files 1936–M and 1937–M).

7. *G. D.*, C, 1, No. 93.

8. U. S. 1933, 1:79–81; Moffat diary, 4 April 1933, Moffat Papers, Vol. 33.

9. On the Davis trip to Berlin see *G. D.*, C, 1, Nos. 144, 148; U. S. 1933, 1:85–89; U. S. 1933, 2:216–20; *B. D.*, 2d, 5, No. 83.

10. *Hitlers Tischgespräche* (ed. Picker), p. 351.

lar diplomatic channels.[11] Hitler would not go; von Neurath was willing to go himself and suggested that otherwise Ambassador Luther conduct the talks,[12] but Hitler decided to send Schacht. Because of the avowed purpose of the Washington talks, Hitler's decision is easily understandable: he had not replaced Luther with Schacht at the Reichsbank so that Luther could have an important role in German economic policy.

By the time Schacht went to Washington early in May, the factors beginning to trouble German-American relations were becoming sufficiently distinct to form important subjects for discussion. Schacht himself was directly involved in one of these factors; it would provide the occasion for the most dramatic incident during his trip, and the failure to resolve the differences raised would poison German-American relations for years. This was the question of international payments. It included certain payments owed by Germany to the United States government, but the bulk of the problem involved the transfer to Americans of interest and amortization payments on German government, municipal, and corporation obligations sold in the United States during the 1920s. The German government was planning to stop the transfer of such payments, allegedly because of a lack of foreign exchange. Although German foreign exchange resources were indeed strained by both the general effects of the depression and its specific deficit in trade with the United States, these were not the only reasons—probably not even the main ones—for the impending moratorium. The specific trade problem with the United States was being greatly alleviated for Germany by the drastic drop in the prices of American commodities exported to Germany. As Schacht himself later reported, for example, Germany had paid 428 million Reichsmark to purchase 296,000 tons of American cotton in 1930, while in 1933 it could purchase 313,000 tons for as little as 217 million Reichsmark.[13]

The general lack of foreign exchange for payments in the United States, however, was as much artificial as real. Germany would not pay its obligations in the United States because it preferred to use its foreign exchange for other purposes, partly to subsidize political and propaganda operations abroad[14] but primarily in connection with its rearmament program. There

11. For this episode see the author's "Schachts Besuch in den USA im Jahre 1933," *Vierteljahrshefte für Zeitgeschichte,* 11, No. 2 (April 1963), 166–80. In general, documents cited there will not again be listed here.

12. Note by Völckers, 11 April 1933, T–120, 2382/4619/E 197658.

13. Schacht to Dodd, 20 February 1934, State 611.6231/384. It should be noted that this one item represented almost half of Germany's imports from the U. S., 5 percent of the total German imports in 1933, and more than its imports from any other country except Great Britain and the Netherlands (*Statistisches Jahrbuch für das Deutsche Reich 1936* [Berlin: Verlag für Sozialpolitik, 1936], p. 253).

14. Such use of foreign exchange was a continuing feature of the National Socialist period. Non-German governments who observed this, although they could not always be aware of its precise extent, were understandably skeptical when a government gave a lack of foreign exchange as the reason for its refusal to pay its debts and simultaneously used apparently limitless amounts of such foreign exchange to finance propa-

was no lack of foreign exchange for the purchase of American airplane parts;[15] as Franz Grueger, chief of the economic department of the government-owned *Reichskreditgesellschaft* (State Credit Agency), put it: "No obstacles have been placed in the way of those wishing to obtain foreign exchange for imports to be used in the process of armament construction."[16]

There were, furthermore, positive advantages to Germany in defaulting on the payments to American creditors. Refusal to transfer interest and amortization of the principal would lead to a drastic drop in the value of the securities in the American money market. Germans could then purchase them with the allegedly nonexistent foreign exchange at a fraction of their face value.[17] Moreover, by authorizing German exporters to use some of the dollar proceeds obtained from the sale of German goods in the United States for the purchase of these depreciated bonds in America, and the subsequent resale of the securities at face value to the original German debtor for Reichsmark, German exports could be subsidized at the expense of the American bondholder, the German exporter having lowered his price in anticipation of this arrangement. The bondholder was "given the choice of sacrificing a large part of his original investment in order to salvage a proportion of his capital, thereby subsidizing the German export trade at the expense of American manufacturers, or of hanging on to his bonds and foregoing most of his annual interest and risking the loss of his entire investment in the remote hope of eventually saving his principal."[18]

Some of this type of activity, in fact, had started before 1933,[19] but it was Schacht who, to Hitler's great delight, made a regular system out of this procedure.[20] Periodic changes in the regulations governing its operation would enable the German government to manipulate the system for immediate advantage. Germany's leaders so looked forward to the economic and political benefits to be derived from such manipulation of defaulted bonds as to reject any idea of trying to have them canceled. Hitler and Schacht

---

ganda or other activities within the same country's borders (see, *e.g.*, *G. D.*, C, 1, Nos. 96, 387).

15. Douglas Miller (acting commercial attaché in Berlin) to Willard Thorpe (director of the Bureau of Foreign and Domestic Commerce), 4 April 1934, State 611.6231/348. This report was shown to the U. S. Senate Special Committee on Investigation of the Munitions Industry (Nye Committee) and figures prominently, though anonymously, in the section "Participation by American Firms in the Rearming of Germany" of its report, *Munitions Industry*, 74th Congress, 2d Session, Senate Report No. 944, Part 3 (Washington: Government Printing Office, 1936), pp. 256–60.

16. Messersmith dispatch 2031 of 17 May 1934, State 862.50/806.

17. For a brief history of the bonds and their repatriation through 1933 see the Memorandum of the Finance and Investment Division of 20 March 1934, State 862.51/3946.

18. John G. Erhardt (U. S. consul general Hamburg) report of 10 January 1934, State 611.6231/306.

19. Memorandum of Sussdorf (State Department, Economic Affairs), 7 February 1933, State 462.00 R 296/5749½.

20. *Hitlers Tischgespräche* (ed. Picker), p. 287.

were secretly agreed that Germany "could not agree to a total concellation of the debt," against which they often directed public attacks.[21] The German government had originally intended to suspend transfer payments even before Schacht left for Washington but decided instead to let him explain the forthcoming measure, simultaneously authorizing him to put the moratorium into effect either after his return or even by telegram from Washington. Nevertheless, just before leaving Germany, Schacht confidentially promised the American government that no such policy would be adopted during his talks; and after his arrival he gave public expression to similar sentiments.[22]

Possibly because of a misunderstanding, Schacht did send the telegram from Washington to Berlin, authorizing the immediate publication of a moratorium and summoning the creditors to Berlin for talks. President Roosevelt was naturally horrified at what must have looked like a most unscrupulous trick: Schacht had announced publicly at the beginning of the talks that he was "absolutely opposed to any moratoriums" and then a few days later, while still in the American capital, authorized a step that would harm thousands of American bondholders. The obvious conclusion would be that the moratorium was an American idea, urged on the Germans in their talks with American officials, when in truth the facts were exactly the other way around.[23] Roosevelt and Secretary of State Cordell Hull arranged for Schacht to be told off in no uncertain terms in a carefully staged scene that Roosevelt subsequently recounted with great glee to Ambassador Dodd and which led Schacht to rescind his precipitate action.[24] The moratorium, accordingly, was postponed briefly, being instituted in June after Schacht's return to Germany.

In spite of promises Schacht had made while in Washington, special pro-

21. *G. D.*, C, 1, No. 182.

22. Gordon telegram 66 of 26 April 1933, State 550.S 1 Wash./220; *New York Times*, 6 May 1933, p. 2.

23. The diary of the chief of the State Department's Division of Western European Affairs reflects the feelings of the time: "Went in to see Bullitt, who told me at length of the talks with Schacht, including his attempt to put the President in an almost untenable position (an episode which cannot yet be put on paper) . . ." (Moffat diary 12 May 1933, Moffat Papers, Vol. 22).

24. This incident is presented in detail in the author's article on the Schacht visit. Hull's memorandum on his dressing-down of Schacht is in State 862.51/3988½; the appended draft of the presidential communication handed Schacht bears Roosevelt's handwritten corrections and initials (see also Cordell Hull, *Memoirs* [New York: Macmillan, 1948], 1:237–38). Roosevelt's account of the incident to Dodd is in the latter's *Diary*, 16 June 1933, pp. 4–5; reference to Roosevelt's later recounting of the incident to Henry Morgenthau, Jr., in John M. Blum (ed.), *From the Morgenthau Diaries*, 3: *Years of War 1941–1945* (Boston: Houghton Mifflin, 1967), p. 418. Herbert Feis's account is in his *1933, Characters in Crisis* (Boston: Little Brown, 1966), pp. 138–41.

The claim that this whole incident was invented by Hull and Dodd is typical of the distortions—and characteristic of the scholarship— of Charles C. Tansill's *Back Door to War: The Roosevelt Foreign Policy, 1933–1941* (Chicago: Regnery, 1952), pp. 46–48.

visions discriminating against American creditors were included in the moratorium procedures, and the American emphasis on at least preserving the principal, even though interest were scaled down, was disregarded. The different approaches were due to the basic difference in the aims of the two powers. The United States government wanted to find ways to ease the situation of the debtor and thereby protect both the debtor and the principal of the lender (as in the New Deal's domestic policy in regard to home mortgages);[25] the German government wanted to enrich the debtor at the creditor's expense. There was little prospect that these policies could be reconciled. The constant protests from Washington had little impact on the Germans, who joyfully proceeded with increasingly ingenious devices that amounted to making the American people subsidize German rearmament.[26] When the Germans excused themselves by referring to their shortage of dollars, the Americans angrily pointed to advertisements placed by Germans in American newspapers offering to purchase for dollars the securities whose prices had fallen because of the alleged absence of dollars to pay interest and amortization.[27] All warnings against the implications of such measures for German-American relations fell on deaf ears.[28] One should not overlook the fact that the victims of these defrauding operations were precisely those Americans who had backed up their faith and friendship for Germany with hard cash in the years when Germany rebuilt its economy in a world still largely hostile to that nation. The selection of precisely those individuals most friendly to Germany out of a population of about 125 million, so that by shady manipulations they might be turned to anti-German attitudes must be considered a masterstroke of perverted genius; no wonder Schacht was referred to as a wizard.

Another subject touched on during Schacht's Washington conversations was that of trade and tariffs. The American government had proposed a tariff truce until the World Economic Conference could deal with the subject. The German response was most unenthusiastic; after considerable delay and agitated internal debate, the German government sent an evasive answer. Hugenberg was the principal obstacle in Berlin. He had developed a bizarre scheme for a "debt reduction tariff" (*Entschuldungsabgabe*) that no one else inside or outside the German government could be persuaded to support but that he feared would be permanently ruled out by a tariff truce.[29] Schacht strongly urged acceptance of the American plan to avoid the total

25. *G. D.*, C, 1, No. 259.

26. U. S. 1933, 2:439–45, 452–53, 456–59; Hull, 1:238–40; *G. D.*, C, 1, No. 316; 2, Nos. 93, 103; "Sitzung des Handelspolitischen Ausschusses vom 12. Juli 1933," ". . . vom 15. September 1933," T–120, 2612/5650/H 003694–695, 729.

27. U. S. 1933, 2:459–60. Summaries of Schacht's procedures may be found in Earl R. Beck, *Verdict on Schacht* (Tallahassee: Florida State University Press, 1955), pp. 46–49; Arthur Schweitzer, "Die wirtschaftliche Wiederaufrüstung Deutschlands von 1934–1936," *Zeitschrift für die gesamte Staatswissenschaft,* 114 (1958), 622–23.

28. *G. D.*, C, 1, No. 294.

29. Ibid., No. 161.

isolation of Germany as other powers agreed to it. The objections of the German Minister of Economics were overcome only after the crisis in Washington produced by Schacht's action on the transfer moratorium made a concession to American wishes seem necessary.[30]

The German government, however, was in principle determined not only to maintain its basic tariff system but in fact planned to extend its scope.[31] Its tariff program consisted to a great extent of diverting German trade from the United States to other countries, and this required a variety of discriminatory measures against American products.[32] Here was the obverse of Germany's trade concessions to such areas as Southeast Europe; it led to immediate difficulties with the United States on two grounds. In the first place, the discrimination against American exports—at a time when the German government was engaging in the practices already mentioned to subsidize its own exports to the United States—was certain to arouse hostility in an American government struggling to lift its country out of the depression. Second, and perhaps more important in the long run, was the fact that the procedures involved in this tariff system were incompatible with Germany's treaty commitments to the United States and with Cordell Hull's belief in the freeing of world trade as a major avenue to both economic recovery and world peace.

The significance of this factor for the relations between Germany and the United States has not hitherto received the attention it deserves. His political career greatly influenced by the American tariff controversy, Cordell Hull as Secretary of State was dedicated to the belief that many of the world's ills were caused by excessive barriers to trade. He preached to all who would and many who would not listen that only an easing of these barriers on a broad, multilateral scale could raise the level of world trade and prosperity, while this in turn would ease world tensions in the political sphere. At a time when the New Deal was turning the monetary policy of the United States from an internationalistic to a nationalistic policy, American trade policy was moving from nationalism to internationalism.[33] German policy, however, was becoming extremely nationalistic on both counts, and this was to become a major cause of deterioration in the relations between the two countries. The strong personal dedication of the American Secretary of State to the policy of opening the channels of world trade, eventually symbolized by the reciprocal trade agreements, meant that the man who would play a key role in American foreign policy in the 1930s was continually and personally affronted by Germany's determination to

30. Ibid., Nos. 210, 224; "Sitzung des Handelspolitischen Ausschusses vom 3. Mai 1933," T–120, 2612/5650/H 003661.

31. *G. D.,* C, 1, No. 296.

32. U. S. 1933, 2:418–30, 480–83; "Sitzung des Handelspolitischen Ausschusses vom 18. Oktober 1933," T–120, 2612/5650/H 003742.

33. This is the essence of Arthur M. Schlesinger, Jr.'s, discussion in *The Age of Roosevelt,* 2: *The Coming of the New Deal* (Boston: Houghton Mifflin, 1959), esp. p. 260.

bend trade policy to the narrowest military and political considerations.[34]

A third major area of concern in German-American relations grew out of the fundamental clash between the ideology of the new regime in Germany and the ideals of the United States, ideals that were being emphasized increasingly by the new administration in Washington. The general hostility of national socialism to democracy and all its beliefs and practices may have won it many recruits inside Germany, but it certainly made no friends in a country self-consciously dedicated to democratic ideals. The attack of the new Germany on cultural and literary freedom struck at one of the main pillars of American respect for German attainments. The day Schacht arrived in New York, the American press carried lists of books to be burned by the National Socialists on 10 May. A related area of sensitivity was the persecution of Jews in Germany. One of the first manifestations of this in 1933 was the purge of the faculties of German universities—of the very universities that had long been a major factor in American admiration for Germany. One of Hull's first talks with Ambassador Luther was devoted to the persecution of the Jews;[35] the records of the Department of State for this period bulge with protests from American individuals and organizations of all kinds; and while Schacht was in Washington on 10 May, Major General O'Ryan of New York's 27th Division led a protest march of 100,000 people in New York City. The subject was touched on repeatedly in Schacht's conversations in Washington; just before leaving America, Schacht discussed Germany's persecution of the Jews with a group of prominent Christians and Jews in New York;[36] and he was sufficiently impressed by the strong reactions in the United States to take up the subject with Hitler on his return to Germany.[37]

There is no evidence that Schacht either had or wanted to have any sig-

34. I do not wish to underestimate Roosevelt's personal role in American foreign policy, but there has been a tendency to downgrade the influence of Hull. My research in the files of the State Department, Roosevelt's papers at Hyde Park, Hull's own papers in the Library of Congress, and numerous other collections of papers of American diplomats leaves me with the impression that the Secretary of State's role in key areas of foreign policy in the 1930s was generally a determining one. President Roosevelt maintained a personal and continuing interest in both the conduct and personnel of American foreign relations and formed his own impression of world events, sometimes on the basis of unofficial reports, but generally held to the lines of policy advocated by Hull. It should be noted that even for the later 1930s this view is also held by William L. Langer and S. Everett Gleason, *The Challenge to Isolation, 1937–1940* (New York: Harper, 1952), pp. 7–9.

35. U. S. 1933, 2:352–54; Hull, 1:236–37.

36. FDR to Irving Lehman, 18 May 1933 (printed in Edgar B. Nixon [ed.], *Franklin D. Roosevelt and Foreign Affairs* [Cambridge: Harvard University Press, 1969], 1:136), and Irving Lehman to FDR, 24 May 1933, Hyde Park, P.P.F. 436.

37. Schacht's statement to Irving Lehman, then associate judge of the New York Court of Appeals and brother of the governor of that state—both prominent Democrats and Jews—that Roosevelt "reminded me in every way of Hitler" suggests that Schacht was hardly an expert on American attitudes. For his comments in Berlin, see *G. D.*, C, 1, No. 262; note by Dieckhoff on a conversation with Schacht, 21 May 1933, T–120, 3508/9037/E 632853–854.

nificant impact on the anti-Jewish policy of the regime; in many areas of German life he wanted an anti-Semitic policy followed. His concern was only that it be orderly, comprehensive, and nonviolent.[38] From that perspective, all he might hope for was tactical adjustments in the application of anti-Jewish policies to the exigencies of Germany's foreign trade needs, and at times he did secure such modifications. In the summer of 1933, a retired American professor of German literature who had known Hitler in the 1920s, John F. Coar, attempted to impress on Hitler and his associates the negative impact Germany's anti-Semitic policies were having in the United States. He was treated by Hitler to an anti-Jewish diatribe, an attack on the boycott of German goods abroad, an assurance that Germany would absorb Austria, and an authorization to sound out President Roosevelt as to concessions that the United States would make if the anti-Jewish campaign in Germany were temporarily relaxed. Roosevelt indicated his willingness to meet Coar, but nothing came of the episode.[39] The attacks on religious liberty in Germany and the retaliatory boycott of German goods in the United States would continue to poison relations between the two countries.[40]

The one other subject discussed at length during Schacht's Washington visit was in some ways the most important: the issue of disarmament or German rearmament, then under debate at Geneva. The American government very much wanted the disarmament conference to succeed and did what it could to find a middle ground between the French and German positions.[41] While the new administration in Washington was willing to make a contribution to the negotiations by promising not to interfere with League economic sanctions against an aggressor or the provisions permitting inspection in compliance with disarmament agreements, and was further willing to support the Germans on procedural matters,[42] the president and all his advisers were very concerned about the prospect of German rearmament. Roosevelt put the issue to Schacht in the strongest possible terms, and this message was in fact conveyed to Berlin by Schacht, but with no discernable result.[43] President Roosevelt thereupon attempted to influence

38. Raul Hilberg, *The Destruction of the European Jews* (Chicago: Quadrangle Books, 1961), p. 22.

39. *Dodd Diary,* 5, 9, 16, 18 August 1933, pp. 20–24; Memorandum of Dodd, 16 August 1933, Dodd Papers, 1933 Folder D; Coar to FDR, 9 August, 2 September, and 21 September 1933 and related papers in Hyde Park, P.P.F. 3716 (*FDR and Foreign Affairs,* 1:352–53, 359, 384–85); Memorandum of Moffat, 14 and 19 September 1933, Moffat Papers, Vol. 22; Hull to Coar, 20 October 1933, Moffat Papers, Vol. 2. For Coar's later attempts to play a role in U. S.-German relations see *Dodd Diary,* 1 November 1934, p. 183; "Bestellungen aus der Pressekonferenz v. 13. Dezember 1934." Bundesarchiv, Brammer, Z.Sg. 101/4, f. 214; Memorandum by Moffat, 14 March 1935, Moffat Papers, Vol. 23; Memorandum by Moffat, 4 April 1935, State 611.0031/1925.

40. U. S. 1933, 2:357, 359; Hull, 1:240; Offner, *American Appeasement,* pp. 59–63.

41. U. S. 1933, 1:117; *G. D.,* C, 1, No. 239, p. 437; Offner, chap. 2.

42. U. S. 1933, 1:128; Moffat Diary 8 May 1933, Moffat Papers, Vol. 33.

43. U. S. 1933, 1:130–31; FDR to Hull, 6 May 1933, *Peace and War* (Washington: Government Printing Office, 1943), No. 14; *G. D.*, C, 1, Nos. 214, 233.

Hitler directly just before Hitler's Reichstag speech of 17 May 1933. Roosevelt's personal message may have contributed to the careful and moderate tone Hitler took in his speech.[44] As the evidence summarized shows, however, such sweet tones were designed only to lull Germany's neighbors until Hitler had his army ready.

It was precisely this possibility that some Americans feared. Jay Pierrepont Moffat, chief of the West European division in the State Department, had agreed with William C. Bullitt on the danger of German rearmament on the basis that "The Nazis want five years of peace in order the better to prepare for eventual war."[45] The United States chargé in Berlin warned that "Hitler's statement [in his 17 May speech] that no country stands to gain from a new war . . . is in marked contrast to the zeal with which pacifists are now being persecuted in the Third Reich for voicing similar views"; furthermore, he was hearing from Nazis in private conversations that in less than five years Hitler would be able to move forward along the lines laid down in *Mein Kampf*.[46] Hitler's conciliatory tone, probably inspired by British and French threats of sanctions, pleased Roosevelt but cannot have been very reassuring.[47] The president was beginning to receive along with the regular diplomatic papers a series of perceptive and alarming reports on the situation in Germany from Samuel R. Fuller, Jr. Fuller had worked with Roosevelt in the Navy Department during the war and made periodic trips to Europe to look after his own textile interests there.[48] In addition to meeting his business associates, he saw Schacht before his American trip and also briefly met Hitler. The picture Fuller painted then and later of a Germany revitalized and enthralled by Hitler, of signs of regimentation and militarization, of indications that the persecution of the Jews would continue, and of the probability that Hitler would start a war either influenced Roosevelt's view of Germany or was strikingly similar to what the president perceived on his own. If Hitler did not much care about the impression his Germany made in Washington, there was certainly deep concern in the American capital. Schacht's visit had done nothing to alleviate this discrepancy in attitude between Washington and Berlin. He reported

44. U. S. 1933, 1:139–45; Hull, 1:226–27; *G. D.*, C, 1, Nos. 243, 246; Nadolny, p. 133. Hitler initialed both the English and German texts of Roosevelt's message (T–120, 1783/3650/D 813103–111). See also *FDR and Foreign Affairs,* 1:395.

45. Moffat Diary, 2 May 1933, Moffat Papers, Vol. 33.

46. Gordon dispatch 2421 of 20 May 1933, U. S. 1933, 1:159–64.

47. *G. D.*, C, 1, No. 259.

48. The reports of Samuel R. Fuller, Jr. (1879–1966), on his trips are at Hyde Park, P. P. F. 2616. Roosevelt would lend these reports to the State Department, indicating his own belief in their great interest and requesting their return. After a trip in the fall of 1935, Roosevelt asked Fuller to speak to Hull (Fuller to FDR, 11 October 1935); it was on this occasion that Fuller left with Hull the copy of his talk with Schacht that thus came to be filed with the State Department records, was used against Schacht at the Nuremberg Trial, and is printed in U. S. 1935, 2:282–86. Correspondence of Roosevelt concerning Fuller's 1935 trip is also filed in Hyde Park, P. S. F. Dodd. Excerpts from this material have been published in *FDR and Foreign Affairs,* 1:172–76; 2:518, 541, 604; 3:23–25, 38, 69, 139, 166, 195, 291–94, 422, 459–60.

to Berlin that Hull was unfit for his post and the members of Roosevelt's cabinet men of no stature; a State Department official commented that there would be "universal relief" on Schacht's departure.[49]

The latter half of 1933 saw not only the friction over trade and transfer discrimination, the persecution of the Jews, and the evident determination of the Germans to rearm, but brought German-American relations close to the breaking point over the continuation of physical attacks on Americans in Germany. A series of incidents, frequently uninterrupted by the police and unpunished by the German government, excited American public opinion. The subject was raised in the cabinet in Washington, and serious measures, including a warning to Americans not to travel in Germany and even a temporary rupture of diplomatic relations, were contemplated. The new American ambassador made the strongest representations to Hitler at their first meeting, and warnings were issued both directly and indirectly of the grave steps the United States might be forced to take. By the end of the year, new and strict orders by the German government temporarily quelled this issue, but the crisis had been serious indeed, and the state of American opinion toward Germany had been deeply affected.[50]

As if the incidents involving Americans in Germany were not sufficiently disturbing, there was the problem of National Socialist activities within the United States. American opinion, which was particularly sensitive to foreign political agitation in the United States, was quickly aroused by signs of public activity on the part of National Socialist groups in America. This was to become an increasingly important subject of dispute in subsequent years, but its role in conditioning American opinion to a view of national socialism as a direct menace to the United States, not simply as an ideology that might be despicable but was at least remote, began as early as 1933.[51]

49. Note by Dieckhoff on a conversation with Schacht, 21 May 1933, T–120, 3508/9037/E 632853–854; *G. D.*, C, 1, No. 262; *Moffat Papers,* entry for 12 May 1933, p. 96.

50. The crisis over these incidents may be followed in U. S. 1933, 2:385–98; *Dodd Diary,* pp. 35–37, 47, 48–50; Memorandum of von Neurath, RM 1297 of 14 September 1933, T–120, 2383/4619/E 197740–741; Phillips to FDR, 23 August 1933, Hyde Park, O.F. 198 (*FDR and Foreign Affairs,* 1:374); Dodd to FDR, 28 October and FDR to Dodd, 13 November 1933, Hyde Park, P. P. F. 1043; Dodd to Hull, 14 September and Hull to Dodd, 5 October 1933, State 123 Dodd, W.E./48; Dodd report 147 of 14 September 1933, State 362.1113/10; and George S. Messersmith's 21 pp. memorandum in his papers, "Conversation with Goering on the break of relations."

51. The subject is examined at length in Alton Frye's, *Nazi Germany and the Western Hemisphere, 1933–1941* (New Haven: Yale University Press, 1967), esp. chaps. 3–4. The article by Joachim Remak, "'Friends of the New Germany': The Bund and German-American Relations," *Journal of Modern History,* 29, No. 1 (March 1957), 38–41, deals primarily with the later 1930s, as does the collection of German speeches, articles, excerpts from yearbooks, etc., *The German Reich and Americans of German Origin* (New York: Oxford University Press, 1938). See also Jacobsen, pp. 528–49. Important but fragmentary files pertaining to the German veterans organization *Stahlhelm* and its activities abroad, including the United States in 1934–35, form the basis of Heinzpeter Thümmler, "Die Auslandsorganisation des Stahlhelm im Dienst der Faschistischen Propaganda (1934/35)," *Der deutsche Imperialismus und der Zweite Weltkrieg,* 2:283–302.

The "Friends of the New Germany" and other National Socialist groups immediately attracted great public attention, became the object of a congressional investigation, and were observed most anxiously by the American government. While some German diplomats saw the danger of such antics to German-American relations, the National Socialist party in Germany continued to support the American groups; and since these activities were directed by Rudolf Hess, one must assume that they had Hitler's general approval. In any case, he was not sufficiently concerned to halt the waving of swastikas before the eyes of the American public.[52] Germany's withdrawal from both the League and the disarmament conference in October led the United States in turn to withdraw even more from European affairs, but it did nothing to increase regard for Germany.[53] The first year of relations between Hitler's regime and the United States ended with the German government still disinterested in America and the American government discouraged over what looked to many like steps toward a new world war.[54]

The themes of conflict that began to characterize German-American relations in 1933 continued thereafter. The documentation is voluminous and the details vary, but no significant changes mark the record of continued friction.[55] The blatant militarism of the German regime continued to offend the susceptibilities of the American public and to alarm the makers of policy. Reports reaching Washington pointed to great dangers in the future once Germany had rebuilt its economy and its army. There was no question in the minds of American diplomats in Berlin that Germany "would certainly rearm and definitely prepare to wage a war against Europe in general, which would change the course of history, if not of civilization, beyond what we even dream, if their supreme effort would be successful."[56] With great concern, the United States observed the failure of the disarmament negotiations,[57] and there are signs that President Roosevelt began to think

52. *G. D.*, C, 2, Nos. 5, 139. For the *Stahlhelm* representative Georg Schmidt referred to in the latter document see the memorandum of Moffat for Phillips of 9 November 1933, Moffat Papers, Vol. 22.

53. *Moffat Papers,* pp. 99–104; U. S. 1933, 1:273–76.

54. *War and Peace,* Nos. 20, 21.

55. The book by James V. Compton, *The Swastika and the Eagle; Hitler, the United States and the Origins of World War II* (Boston: Houghton Mifflin, 1967), adds little but errors to my articles on "Hitler's Image of the United States" and "German Colonial Plans and Policies, 1938–1942."

56. Geist (consul general Berlin) to Moffat, 9 June 1934, Moffat Papers, Vol. 5. See also Geist's perceptive letters of 10 August and 15 September 1934, ibid.

57. In June 1934, the German government through a member of the Military Policy Office of the National Socialist party (*Wehrpolitisches Amt*) acting for Disarmament Commissioner Ribbentrop made an unsuccessful effort to involve the United States in unofficial disarmament negotiations. The U. S. was willing to talk, but only through official channels and with the knowledge of Britain and France. On this incident, see U. S. 1934, 1:96, 119–20; Norman Davis telegram 897 of 12 June 1934, State 500.A 15 A 4 General Committee/977; Davis to FDR, 4 June 1934, Library of Congress, Norman H. Davis Papers, Official Correspondence 1934–35; Moffat Diary 12 June 1934, Moffat Papers, Vol. 35; see also *Dodd Diary,* 15 June 1934, pp. 110–11. I have been unable to locate any reference to this incident in the German archives.

in terms of isolating Germany, as eventually voiced in his "quarantine" speech of October 1937.[58] The isolation to which Roosevelt referred involved the very way in which, from an American perspective, Germany appeared to be isolating itself—in the field of international economic relations.

The decision of the German government to concentrate its resources on rearmament increasingly affected the extension of controls over Germany's domestic economy and foreign trade in 1934. In the summer, Schacht himself took over the Ministry of Economics; and in order to conserve all foreign exchange for politically and militarily important purposes he inaugurated what was called "The New Plan" for the control of international trade and payments.[59] The new policies precluded the availability of foreign exchange for the payment of German debts to American citizens, and this subject would provide a topic for continuing and acrimonious arguments between Germany and the United States, arguments in which the highest officials of both governments repeatedly participated in 1934 and 1935.[60] Although very minor concessions were occasionally made by Berlin in order to calm the Americans temporarily, the basic policy of the German government was directed toward a continuation of those manipulations developed in 1933 that were most offensive to Washington.[61] German claims that these measures were imposed on them by the shortage of foreign exchange were regularly met by American references to the purchase of war materials with the allegedly nonexistent dollars.[62] Schacht's argument that the German debt to the United States had been incurred for political purposes and was, therefore, no debt at all was countered by reference to the reconstruction of German industry and public services that had been financed with the proceeds from the loans.[63]

German trade policy continued to complement its debt manipulations.

58. U. S. 1934, 1:62, 70, 170–72; FDR to E. M. House, *Personal Letters 1928–1945,* 1:472–73. On the U. S. desire that Germany return to the disarmament negotiations see U. S. 1934, 1:98.

59. See *B. D.,* 2d, 6, No. 406; Bracher, *Machtergreifung,* p. 790; Schweitzer, *Big Business in the Third Reich,* pp. 436ff.; *G. D.,* C, 3, Nos. 13, 169, 207. An account that takes Schacht at face value is Allen T. Bonnell, *German Control over International Economic Relations, 1930–1940* (Urbana: University of Illinois Press, 1940).

60. The documentation on this debate is voluminous; see U. S. 1934, 2:331–99, 497–98; U. S. 1935, 2:428–38; *G. D.,* C, 2, Nos. 202, 205, 206; 3, Nos. 14, 76, 78, 79, 82, 83, 221, 237, 238, 664; 4, Nos. 284, 290; *Dodd Diary,* pp. 69–70, 73–74, 104–05, 112–13, 119–20, 129–30, 173–74; Moffat Diary, 19 January 1934, Moffat Papers, Vol. 35; "Sitzung des Handelspolitischen Ausschusses vom 12. August 1935," T–120, 2612/5650/H 004034–035; Memorandum of Livesay (State Department, Economic Affairs), "Treatment of the Kreuger Loan after July 1934," 14 November 1934, State 862.51 Bondholders/214.

61. *G. D.,* C, 2, No. 484.

62. Memorandum of Moffat, 6 July 1934, State 862.51/4109.

63. U. S. 1934, 2:356–63, 369–73; Moffat Diary, 17 March 1934, Moffat Papers, Vol. 35.

As already indicated, here was the other side of Germany's economic penetration of Southeast Europe. Discrimination against American exports and American firms in Germany, and the policy of transferring markets from the United States to other countries remained as constant irritants in German-American relations.[64]

Nevertheless, various efforts were made by the German government to maintain a modicum of trade with the United States, as long as it could be fitted with the new German trade policy. Schacht proposed several complicated schemes, including one in which the American government would repurchase depreciated bonds and then accept interest on the actual price it had paid in exchange for continued German purchase of American cotton. It is indicative of the fact that Hitler was not alone in his misassessment of the United States that the German economic wizard found it difficult to understand why the administration in Washington did not wish to participate in the defrauding of its citizens.[65] Another approach was to push barter deals between the two countries. Of these the most significant was one in which American cotton and possibly lard were to be exchanged for German wines. In the American administration, such arrangements had a strong supporter in George Peek, a special adviser on foreign trade to the president. After lengthy negotiations the cotton barter failed, however, because of the objections of the Department of State to an arrangement unlikely to increase cotton exports, but more importantly running directly counter to the international trade policy the administration was pushing in Congress and making the basis of its negotiations for reciprocal trade agreements with other countries. Furthermore, the intermediate credits to American exporters required by this proposal seemed singularly inappropriate to the United States government in the face of Germany's discriminatory policies and the resulting agitation of American public opinion.[66] Some trade was conducted by direct barter transactions between German and American businessmen nevertheless. A particularly good example of the

64. U. S. 1934, 2:409–14, 424–26, 458–60; U. S. 1935, 2:472–73; "Sitzung des Handelspolitischen Ausschusses vom 23. Januar 1934," T–120, 2612/5650/H 003818–819.

65. *Dodd Diary,* 20 February 1934, pp. 80–81; Schacht to Dodd, 20 February 1934, enclosure to State 611.6231/384; Strauss (Paris) telegram 190 of 13 March 1934, State 851.5151/113.

66. On these barter plans see U. S. 1934, 2:421–23 (appended to this document was a letter from James Mooney of General Motors Export Corporation to George Peek of 13 April 1934, State 611.6231/348); Mooney to Peek, 7 May 1934, enclosure to State 611.6231/345; Moffat to Livesey, 24 January 1934, Moffat Papers, Vol. 23; Moffat Diary, 1 June 1934, Moffat Papers, Vol. 35; Moffat to John C. White (Berlin), 20 December 1934, Moffat Papers, Vol. 7; Moffat to Messersmith (Vienna), 27 December 1934, Moffat Papers, Vol. 9; *FDR and Foreign Affairs,* 2:314–15, 319–22; Phillips Diary, 13–14 December 1934, Houghton Library, Papers of William Phillips, Vol. 6; Offner, pp. 99–102.

Werner Daitz of the APA was also thinking up new schemes at this time, Wiley (Berlin) to Dodd (in U. S.), 29 March 1934, Dodd Papers, 1934–W.

nature of Germany's exports and imports under such trade practices was the bartering of water-lice to feed tropical fish in exchange for American copper plate.[67]

Beyond such efforts to maintain a minimum level of trade by barter and other special arrangements, during 1934 and 1935 the German government attempted to place its whole economic relationship with the United States on a new basis. Germany hoped to persuade the United States to negotiate a new trade treaty that would regulate all the relevant questions on a purely bilateral basis, bring about a substantial increase in German exports to the United States, and end the application of the most-favored nation principle under which each power benefited from the concessions either nation made to other countries. The decision to move in this direction was made in Berlin in late February 1934; and it was the hope of the German government that major steps in the negotiations could be taken in March.[68] The American government was extremely dubious about negotiating with Germany on this basis while urging Congress to enact the Trade Agreements Act with its basically opposite world trade policy.[69] Once the act was passed, Washington preferred to negotiate the first of the reciprocal trade agreements with countries that agreed with Hull's nondiscrimination policies rather than work out with Germany a treaty that replaced the nondiscrimination clause in the existing German-United States commercial treaty by an arrangement more congenial to Berlin.[70]

As the moment came closer when the commercial treaty could be denounced under its own terms, the American government, after considerable deliberation, decided to take no initiative. There were few practical concessions to offer Germany; there was little hope that the Germans would abide by new trade agreements any more than the existing ones; and while the United States should not enter agreements that would further throttle world trade, it should also avoid starting a trade war with Germany.[71] The German government had decided in the meantime that it would under no circumstances pass up the 15 October 1934 opportunity to denounce the Treaty of Friendship, Commerce, and Consular Rights, hoping that during

67. Erhardt (consul general Hamburg) dispatch 294 of 28 January 1935, State 611. 6231/532. In another such barter reported by Erhardt on 15 April 1935, American cotton was received for I. G. Farben chemical exports to du Pont, with the foreign-exchange surplus for the Germans used to subsidize the export price through repurchase of depreciated bonds (611.6231/602).

68. *G. D.*, C, 2, No. 284; *Dodd Diary*, 28 February 1934, p. 83, and 6 March 1934, p. 87; "Sitzung des Handelspolitischen Ausschusses vom 26. Februar 1934," T–120, 2612/5650/H 003843.

69. *G. D.*, C, 2, No. 294; U. S. 1934, 2:218, 415–18, 420–21; Memorandum of Hull, 12 April 1934, State 611.6231/336.

70. *G. D.*, C, 2, No. 457; 3, No. 43; U. S. 1934, 2:426–30, 433–37.

71. U. S. 1934, 2:443–44, 448–53; Memorandum by Moffat, 14 September 1934, State 462.00 R 296/5865; Assistant Secretary Sayre to several State Department officials, 4 October 1934, State 611.6231/561.

the year it would continue to be in effect it could pressure the United States into a new treaty more favorable to Germany.[72] The step was taken as planned, but although it assured the Germans a legalized escape from the obligation to accord the United States most-favored nation treatment, the prospect that this would lead to the sort of treaty Germany wanted was slight indeed.[73] Ambassador Dodd correctly warned the Germans that their past discriminatory practices would make it very hard for the United States to accept a new trade arrangement but that even greater difficulty attached to any new formal agreement that might now be proposed. Once Germany had denounced the treaty, the prospect would be slight indeed of securing U. S. Senate ratification of a new treaty in the face of American public opinion alarmed by the belief that Germany planned a new war and disturbed by the domestic policies of the German government. When Dodd took new German proposals to Washington in December 1934, his view was immediately confirmed.[74]

Americans were increasingly perturbed by reports from Germany that stressed the militarization of German life, the persecution of the Jews, and the struggle against the Christian churches.[75] Anti-German movies, public demonstrations, and the boycott of German goods both reflected the sensitivity of Americans and furthered the spread of anti-German sentiments. The argument of Hitler that National Socialist propaganda in the United States to which Washington objected was really the product of the Jews did not impress the American government, and German protests against anti-German publicity in the United States were countered by the suggestion that such agitation would stop as soon as the reports of German actions that fed this publicity no longer had a basis in fact.[76] The murders on 30 June 1934 and the assassination of the Austrian chancellor Engelbert Dollfuss increased American alarm; and the American public continued to be

72. "Sitzung des Handelspolitischen Ausschusses vom 25. September 1934," T–120, 2612/5650/H 003944; U. S. 1934, 2:453–55; Douglas Jenkins (consul general Berlin) to Moffat, 20 October 1934, and Moffat to Jenkins, 21 November 1934, Moffat Papers, Vol. 8.

73. Moffat wrote in his diary for 13 and 14 October 1934: "Germany drove another nail into her economic coffin today when she denounced the most-favored nation treaty of 1924." Moffat Papers, Vol. 36. The Treaty of Friendship, Commerce, and Consular Rights had been signed on 8 December 1923; ratifications were exchanged on 14 October 1925 (text in U. S. 1923, 2:29).

74. *G. D.*, C, 3, Nos. 389, 390; *Dodd Diary,* 11 December 1934, pp. 203–04; Dodd to Schacht, 12 December 1934, Dodd Papers, 1934–S; U. S. 1934, 2:461–62; Offner, pp. 93–99.

75. In July 1934, James Perkins, chairman of the board of the National City Bank, sounded out von Ribbentrop on behalf of President Roosevelt on the possibility of lessening the persecution of the Jews and the churches, but nothing came of the effort. *Dodd Diary,* 24 July and 31 August 1934, pp. 131, 157; letter from Henry Mann (then with the National City Bank) to me, 25 October 1962.

76. *G. D.*, C, 2, Nos. 295, 297, 298, 302, 307, 315; *Dodd Diary,* 5 March 1934, pp. 86–87; *Moffat Papers,* 8 March 1934, p. 110.

unfavorably impressed by the activities of National Socialist organizations which suggested that the United States should follow the German model.[77] A vague message from Hitler to Roosevelt could hardly affect this situation,[78] nor did a most inept visit by Ernst Hanfstaengl to the United States in June 1934.[79] The German embassy in Washington reported to Berlin on the deteriorating situation, but as the policies that most exercised the Americans were precisely those intrinsically a part of National Socialist Germany—rearmament, racialism, and police terror—such reports had no substantial effect.[80]

A temporary calm in German-American relations in the spring of 1935 was quickly followed by renewed tension after a new wave of attacks on the Christian churches and the Jews in Germany that began in the summer and culminated in the fulminations of the National Socialist leaders at the party rally in Nuremberg.[81] The continuing growth of German power during 1935 made American officials increasingly apprehensive about Germany's future intentions. It was this apprehension, reinforced by accurate and alarming analyses received from official and unofficial American observers in Berlin,[82] that made the United States government reluctant to bless the visit of the British foreign secretary, Sir John Simon, to Berlin,[83] and dubious about the Anglo-German naval agreement that followed in June 1935.[84]

In view of this background, the failure of the negotiations conducted in

77. On the deteriorating political atmosphere see U. S. 1934, 2:530–31, 218–20, 516–20; *Dodd Diary*, 28 May and 4 June 1934, pp. 102–03, 106; *G. D.*, C, 2, Nos. 248, 259, 337, 347, 356, 359, 410; 3, Nos. 570, 571.

78. *Dodd Diary*, 7 and 23 March 1934, pp. 88–89, 93; Moffat Diary, 24 and 26 March 1934, Moffat Papers, Vol. 35; *G. D.*, C, 2, Nos. 319, 325, 367; *FDR and Foreign Affairs*, 2:27–28, 34, 35.

79. Hanfstaengl had hoped to come to the U. S. in the fall of 1933 (William Moore to Marguerite Le Hand, 17 September 1933, Hyde Park, O. F. 198–A), but actually came for the twenty-fifth reunion of the Harvard Class of 1909. On his visit and the attendant uproar see *Moffat Papers*, pp. 111–13; Hanfstaengl, pp. 242–46; Messersmith (Vienna) to Moffat, 13 June 1934, and Moffat to Messersmith, 27 June 1934, Moffat Papers, Vol. 6.

80. *G. D.*, C, 3, Nos. 250, 569.

81. U. S. 1935, 2:357–58, 483–85, 404–05, 487–89; *G. D.*, C, 2, No. 545; 4, Nos. 18, 67, 155, 184, 222, 237.

On the case of an American whose arrest and detention in Germany gave rise to much unfavorable publicity in the U. S. starting in July 1935 see U. S. 1936, 2:291–304; Luther telegram 183 of 28 July 1936, T–120, 3024/6600/E 494947.

For unofficial efforts to improve German-American relations in 1935 see Memorandum by Moffat, 4 April 1935, State 611.0031/1925; Jenkins dispatch 453 of 13 July 1935, State 862.51/4308.

82. Fuller was in Berlin in September 1935; his reports to President Roosevelt are in Hyde Park P. P. F. 2616, and U. S. 1935, 2:282–86 (see also *Dodd Diary*, 14 September 1935, p. 267). A very perceptive report by the U. S. military attaché in Berlin, "German Foreign Policy under Hitler," of 25 November 1935, is in State 762.00/122.

83. Memorandum of Moffat for Hull and Phillips, 21 March 1935, Moffat Papers, Vol. 23.

84. U. S. 1935, 1:163–65; Memorandum by Noel H. Field, "German Naval Proposals," 8 June 1935, State 862.34/146; Moffat to Atherton (London), 24 June 1935, Moffat Papers, Vol. 8.

1935 for a new German-American trade agreement is not particularly surprising. The German government was determined to avoid agreeing to a meaningful most-favored nation treatment clause in any new treaty—that, after all, was why it had denounced the old treaty—but it wanted to benefit from American concessions extended to other countries under the trade agreements acts. The inconsistency between these two positions came into sharp focus when Karl Ritter, director of the German foreign ministry's economic department, came to the United States in October 1935. In the face of German discrimination against American trade, the United States would not make immediate trade concessions to Germany in return for dubious promises that at some time in the future Germany would stop discriminating. In view of Germany's refusal to grant equality of treatment to American creditors at least during a short *modus vivendi*, there was no prospect that agreement could be reached before the expiration of the old treaty in mid-October 1935.[85]

Schacht and others in Berlin now regretted their earlier denunciation of the 1925 Treaty with the United States; their hope that they could pressure Washington into a new agreement that provided special advantages for Germany had proved a serious miscalculation.[86] The article of the treaty by which each party promised most-favored nation treatment to the other was formally annulled; Germany could continue its policies without being in technical violation of the treaty, but it could not enjoy the growing advantages it would otherwise have received as Hull's trade program developed. The threat of higher tariffs on American goods had not sufficed to force a new treaty on the American government. Furthermore, by the end of 1935 Germany was increasingly concerned that it was not only losing trade advantages in the American market but might soon find the United States retaliating by imposing on goods imported from Germany countervailing duties to compensate for the export subsidies that Germany was using to make up for not having joined in the devaluation of currencies.[87] The prospects on the political and economic horizons of German-American relations were dim at the end of 1935, but there is no evidence to suggest that Hitler was particularly alarmed.[88]

85. For documentation on these negotiations see U. S. 1935, 2:439–71; *G. D.*, C, 4, Nos. 174, 264, 331, 332, 340, 341; "Sitzung des Handelspolitischen Ausschusses vom 26. April 1935," ". . . vom 12. August 1935," ". . . vom 4. September 1935," ". . . vom 5. November 1935," T–120, 2612/5650/H 004016, 34–35, 41–42, 57–58; Schacht to Fuller, 24 September 1935, Hyde Park, P. P. F. 2616. A memorandum by R. E. Schoenfeld on a conference in the State Department on 1 October 1935, in which Hull, Phillips and other high officials participated, summarizes the American position very well (State 611.6231/727); this position was reported accurately to Berlin (joint telegram of Luther and Ritter, No. 228 of 7 October 1935, T–120, 3381/8597/E 603729–732).

86. *Dodd Diary,* 7 October 1935, p. 269; Memorandum by Schoenfeld, 9 September 1935, State 862.51/4336.

87. U. S. 1935, 2:473–77.

88. The German press, however, was instructed on 27 November 1935, not to attack

When the German foreign ministry warned in the summer of 1935 that the planned export subsidy program would surely lead to countervailing duties under the American tariff laws, Hitler allowed the ministry of economics to go ahead with its schemes anyway. In the hope of avoiding retaliation, the form of the new system would be changed slightly and the United States government given formal assurances that the new law did not provide what it in fact provided.[89] In the winter of 1935–36, however, the American government began to investigate the whole German export system to determine whether it violated the Tariff Act of 1930 that provided for extra import duties to offset export bounties of foreign countries.

The Germans became sufficiently alarmed about the prospect of countervailing duties to send on a special mission to Washington in February 1936 one of the directors of the Reichsbank and an official of the Ministry of Economics; but the legal aspects of the American Tariff Act, Cordell Hull's trade expansion program, and Germany's foreign trade practices simply could not be brought into harmony.[90] The special emissaries reinforced the concern in Berlin on their return, and some new proposals were worked out in an effort to avoid the further reduction in German-American trade that would surely follow the imposition of countervailing duties.[91] These proposals, however, failed to meet the main American concerns; and as Hans Leitner, the second man in the German embassy in Washington, left to be replaced by Hans Thomsen, hitherto an official in the chancellery in Berlin, Hull gave him a parting lecture on the iniquities of Germany's trade policies.[92] A month later, on 4 June 1936, the U. S. Treasury gave notice of the forthcoming imposition of countervailing duties.

The fact that German-American economic relations were heading for a crisis had been apparent to the German government for some time; as the situation deteriorated a new element entered the picture. As will be discussed in connection with the Four-Year Plan, Hermann Göring was entrusted with special responsibilities in the field of foreign exchange and raw materials in the spring of 1936; and this brought the problems in German-

---

foreign chiefs of state, including President Roosevelt (Bundesarchiv, Sammlung Brammer, Z.Sg. 101/6 f. 197).

89. *G. D.*, C, 4, Nos. 157, 174. The German assurances were given in December 1936 when the U. S. government made inquiries about the new system (U. S. 1936, 2:211).

90. On this question, see U. S. 1936, 2:210–41; *FDR and Foreign Affairs,* 3:308–09; John Morton Blum (ed.), *From the Morgenthau Diaries,* 1: *Years of Crisis, 1928–1938* (Boston: Houghton Mifflin, 1959), pp. 149–54. Offner (pp. 146–53) stresses the opposition of the State Department to countervailing duties

91. The report of the German emissaries, Puhl and Hartenstein, on their trip is in "Sitzung des Handelspolitischen Ausschusses vom 19. Februar 1936," T–120, 2612/5650/H 004068–69; the new plan agreed on is in "Sitzung . . . vom 28. März 1936," ibid., frames H 004074–77; it was presented to the U. S. on 30 March 1936 (U. S. 1936, 2:221–23). For related German schemes in regard to the interest on bonds see *G. D.*, C, 4, No. 290; Strauss (Paris) telegram 180 of 10 March 1936, reporting on a meeting of Merle Cochran with Schacht, State 462 R 296 B.I.S./501.

92. U. S. 1936, 2:225–27; Dodd telegram 114 of 18 April 1936, State 701.6211/934.

American economic relations to his attention. The specific issue on which Göring first became involved, as a result it would appear of a decision by Hitler, was the long-standing problem of remaining American claims growing out of German sabotage in the United States during World War I. In its handling of the claims cases before the U. S.-German Mixed Claims Commission, the German government had at first secured some success by a systematic policy of bribing witnesses; but as these unsavory practices came to light, the original impact of the sabotage incidents on public opinion in the United States was redoubled by the blatant bad faith of the procedures used to discredit true and to manufacture false evidence.[93] As the claimants pressed for settlement of their claims and the American government pushed for expeditious handling of the issue, Hitler turned the matter over to Göring after Schacht had proved unwilling to help Frederico Stallforth, a representative of American claimants.[94] Göring thereupon had a long conversation with Ferdinand Mayer, the American chargé in Berlin, on 6 May 1936, and suggested informal negotiations between unofficial German and American representatives both to settle the claims and as a step toward better economic and political relations.[95] Although there was some trouble with the German foreign ministry, Göring entrusted the talks to Captain Franz Pfeffer von Salomon (the former SA leader) who tried from the beginning, quite unsuccessfully, to have the sabotage claims tied to general German-American trade problems. The American announcement of countervailing duties burst into the middle of von Pfeffer's preliminary talks and demonstrated the urgency of the situation.[96]

At a meeting in Göring's office on 8 June the whole problem was discussed. It was clear that new steps were required. Another mission would be sent to Washington, and something would have to be done about the German measures that had given rise to countervailing duties; but the rivalry between Göring and the German foreign ministry would make every step difficult indeed.[97] Three German emissaries were sent to Washington in June 1936 to discuss the trade problems, while the U. S. Agent and counsel before the Mixed Claims Commission went to Germany. The Germans

93. This whole subject merits scholarly investigation; it is ignored in the secondary literature on this period. The concluding report of the American commissioner of 26 July 1941, is in Hyde Park, O. F. 198–C. It should be noted that the frauds had been perpetrated during the Weimar period. The facts came out during the National Socialist era, and as they became too obvious to be ignored, the Germans withdrew their commissioner in 1939 rather than either agree in the final awards or disagree in the face of incontrovertible evidence.

94. U. S. 1936, 2:256–60; Dodd telegram 104 of 7 April and Mayer telegram 115 of 21 April 1936, State 462.11 L 5232/555 and 558.

95. U. S. 1936, 2:260–62; Hull to Mayer, telegram 45 of 7 May 1936, State 462.11 L 5232/560.

96. U. S. 1936, 2:262–70; Mayer telegram 137 of 8 May 1936, State 462.11 L 5232/561; Phillips Diary, 14 May 1936, Phillips Papers, 10:1513.

97. Memorandum by Bodenschatz (of Göring's office), 9 June 1936, Nuremberg document PS–3875; U. S. 1936, 2:229–35; Phillips Diary, 15, 16, and 17 June 1936, Phillips Papers, 11:1578, 1579, 1581.

were received very pleasantly in Washington, and the Americans and von Pfeffer even came to an agreement in Munich; but eventually nothing would come of either set of negotiations.[98] The Germans decided to drop those practices that had provoked the countervailing duties but simultaneously took steps that in any case would further reduce German-American trade.

The new schemes proposed by the Germans in Washington did not meet the requirements of American trade policy; although the countervailing duties were lifted, no other American concessions were made. On the German side, this led first to postponement and finally a refusal to implement the agreement that had been reached by German and American negotiators in Munich. A final effort by von Pfeffer to salvage the broader goals of Göring's policy by sending still another special emissary, Dr. Karl Markau, to Washington in December failed because of the doubts of the German foreign ministry and embassy in Washington, as well as the American refusal to make trade concessions to Germany in exchange for German adherence to the signed agreement on the claims. More, rather than less, bitterness was the result, less rather than more satisfaction in economic relations.[99]

Göring and his assistant von Pfeffer were interested in agreement with the United States only if it provided an opportunity for immediate trade concessions; the Americans would not compromise their general trade agreements policy by making special and exceptional concessions to the one country whose trade policies ran most directly contrary to their own. The countervailing duty issue had been settled by changes in German practices—Berlin had backed down in the face of Washington's resolve. The basic differences in trade policy, however, remained. The German ambassador, Hans Luther, had indicated to his own government not only that this was in part

98. On the Munich negotiations see U. S. 1936, 2:272–76; Enclosure 4 of State 462.11 L 5232/630 (see ibid., p. 272) contains the minutes of the 10 July session in Munich with Dr. Karl Markau, who was later to come to Washington, joining von Pfeffer on the German side and with Hitler's old associate, Walter Hewel, acting as secretary.

On the talks in Washington, primarily with Brinkmann, Imhoff, and Baer, see U.S. 1936, 2:236–246; *G. D.*, C, 5, No. 469; Memorandum by Schoenfeld, 29 June 1936, State 611.6231/747; Memorandum by Schoenfeld, 6 July 1936, State 611.623/210.

Baer remained in the U. S. until the end of September 1936; see Phillips to Dodd dispatch 663 of 22 August 1936, State 611.623/225, and *G. D.*, C, 5, No. 503, n. 6.

99. The documentation on this episode is extensive. There were troubles between various groups of American claimants and holders of awards as well as on the German side. The published reports of the Mixed Claims Commission for the period 1933 to 1939 (Washington: Government Printing Office, 1940) and the *Final Report of H. H. Martin* (Washington: Government Printing Office, 1941) contain much relevant material. In addition see U. S. 1936, 2:246–50, 277–88; *Dodd Diary,* 20 October 1936, pp. 357–58; *G. D.,* C, 5, Nos. 503, 567; Phillips Diary, 7 August 1936, Phillips Papers, 11:1630; Memorandum by Robert W. Bonyinge (American agent), 11 August 1936, in R. Walton Moore Papers at Hyde Park; Adams (vice-consul Berlin) report 611 of 8 August 1936, State 611.6231/809; a series of documents, including the correspondence of von Pfeffer and Markau with Hull and Moore, for the period July-December 1936, in State 462.11 L 5232/645–798 passim; Memorandum by Gritzbach (of Göring's office), 20 November 1936, T–120, 2621/5482/E 381988. It should be noted that the Germans attempted to secure the assistance of the Senate majority leader, Joseph Robinson, referred to as *Senatspräsident* in the German documents.

Germany's own fault but that no other administration in Washington was likely to follow as liberal a trade policy as that of Franklin Roosevelt.[100] As Luther left for Berlin in late November, a bitter conversation with the assistant Secretary of State, Francis Sayre, showed him that no concessions could be expected from Washington.[101] When he returned in January 1937, his conversations had the same tone, and so did his final farewell in May.[102] Germany formally repudiated its agreement on the sabotage claims while making clear that it would not agree to a new trade arrangement with the United States on terms the Americans could accept.[103]

At the same time as German-American economic relations were evidencing signs of acrimonious deterioration, the failure of the West European powers in the Ethiopian crisis, the apparently growing danger of another war, the public impact of Senator Gerald Nye's investigation of the munitions industry, and the agitation of pacifist groups were accentuating the pressure toward isolationism in the United States.[104] In some ways there seemed to be a vicious circle: such developments as the Hoare-Laval Plan that seemed to sell out Ethiopia to Italy when Britain and France were supposedly defending it increased isolationist pressures in the United States, while knowledge that help could not be expected from America if war came only reinforced the willingness of Britain and France to make concessions that might avoid the danger of war.[105] The cause of peace was harmed in this fashion, for the absence of a vigorous American role encouraged Germany to greater risks. This in turn undermined the assumptions underlying the isolationist impulse by increasing the likelihood that if war came the United States would be involved in spite of its own preferences. The longer war was postponed, the more likely it was that German victories would threaten an extra-European power like the United States. The American minister to Vienna, George S. Messersmith, pointed this out after the Rhineland occupation of March 1936 in a letter to Undersecretary Phillips:

> I feel that we have a very great interest in this [British and French firmness] for if this question is settled now as it can be settled, the chances are 99 out of 100 that we can stay out of it [any war risked in the process] and that it will soon be over. If there is weakness and the Germans are allowed to fortify their western frontier, a war in a year or so hence is inevitable if the regime is able to hold on

100. *G. D.*, C, 5, No. 567.

101. U. S. 1936, 2:252–54; Luther's report on this talk will appear as *G. D.*, C, 6, No. 52. It was then already known in Washington that Hans Heinrich Dieckhoff would replace Luther; see Messersmith to Hull, 16 October 1936, Library of Congress, Cordell Hull Papers, Folder 93.

102. U. S. 1937, 2:328–29, 331.

103. Luther Memorandum of 17 April 1937, ibid., pp. 348–50; Jenkins dispatch 1491 of 15 April 1937, ibid., pp. 329–31; *Final Report of H. H. Martin*, p. 35.

104. A good summary of the situation is in Robert A. Divine, *The Illusion of Neutrality* (Chicago: University of Chicago Press, 1962), chaps. 4–5.

105. On the European view of this trend, see *D. D. F.*, 2d, 1, Nos. 13, 14, 26; 2, Nos. 341, 441; *G. D.*, C, 5, No. 514; Thomas Jones, *A Diary with Letters 1931–1950* (London: Oxford University Press, 1954), 14 September 1936, p. 266.

that long, and in that case the chances of our being able to stay out will certainly be less than 50–50, and in my opinion a good deal less, and this is the opinion, as you know, of one who believes so strongly that we should do everything to endeavor to stay out.[106]

These warnings were wise indeed and applied to those on both sides of the Atlantic. But the American public refused to consider the possibility that measures they imagined could have kept the United States out of World War I—such as refusal to sell weapons to the victims of aggression—might help to insure their involvement in World War II.

There are indications that in 1936 President Roosevelt's increasing concern about developments in Europe led him to have the possibility explored of some constructive American role in the search for peace by several of his ambassadors in Europe, especially Dodd in Berlin. Roosevelt had observed the growing dangers anxiously, continuing to use S. R. Fuller, Jr., to keep in informal contact with the situation. In this process, he had Fuller sound out the Germans in the spring about the possibility of leasing colonies as a means of dealing with the controversial colonial question without raising the question of sovereignty.[107] Later he authorized Dodd to check whether some kind of conference of the powers, called by American initiative, was likely to be at all helpful. The informal soundings Dodd made in Berlin confirmed the obvious fact that, given the situation in the fall of 1936 after the outbreak of the Spanish civil war, nothing could be done. By the end of the year, the plan had been dropped—though it would remain in Roosevelt's mind as a possibility to explore later.[108] In the meantime, the United States had to explain to the leaders of the Western powers as clearly as possible that they could not rely on American military help if it came to war with Germany.[109] Only in the economic field was there the possibility of cooperation, a possibility symbolized by the U. S.-British-French stabilization agreement of 25 September 1936.[110] No more effort on Germany's part was needed to antagonize the American public, but the possibility of future

106. Messersmith to Phillips, 13 March 1936, State 863.00/1279.

107. See Fuller's report on his talk with Schacht on 1 April 1936, in Hyde Park, P. P. F. 2616; cf. his talk with Schacht on 27 March, with Hitler and Schacht on 1 April, and his correspondence about prior and subsequent appointments with Roosevelt, in ibid. On the colonial issue see pp. 276–81, below.

108. On this episode see FDR to Dodd, 5 August 1936, *Personal Letters 1928–1945,* 1:605-06; Dodd to FDR, 19 August and 21 September 1936, Hyde Park, P. S. F. Dodd; *FDR and Foreign Affairs,* 3:373; *G. D.,* C, 5, Nos. 544, 611, 626; Anthony Eden, *Facing the Dictators* (Boston: Houghton Mifflin, 1962), pp. 595–96; Offner, pp. 171–72.

For indications that Roosevelt was dropping the idea at the end of 1936 see his letters to Cox of 9 December 1936, to Dodd of 9 January 1937, and to Cudahy of 15 January 1937, in *Personal Letters 1928–1945,* 1:638, 648–49, 652–53.

109. Bullitt (Paris) to Moore, 29 November 1936, quoted in Moore's letter to Sol Bloom of 23 January 1941, in Hyde Park, R. W. Moore Papers; and U. S. 1936, 1:586–87.

110. On the Tripartite Stabilization Agreement see U. S. 1936, 1:535–66; *D. D. F.,* 2d, 3, Nos. 240, 246, 288; Blum, *Morgenthau Diaries, Years of Crisis,* pp. 159–73; Fuller to FDR, 22 October 1936, Hyde Park, P. P. F. 2616.

danger was not yet clear either to Germany or the people of the United States.

The antagonism toward Germany that had been aroused in the United States was to become a factor of immense importance. The course of German-American diplomatic relations traced here necessarily stresses economic issues—and frictions with regard to them—for it was primarily in this area that Germany's day-to-day relations with the United States were in fact conducted during this period. Furthermore, from the German point of view, these economic issues were of considerable current significance; in Washington they played a part in turning American officials, and especially Secretary Cordell Hull himself, against the German government. Nevertheless, the factors most responsible for the developing hostility of American public opinion were not of an economic kind. There was genuine and widespread horror at the German relapse into barbarism, a horror fed by reports from Germany by prominent American correspondents and by refugees from German persecution who reached the United States. There was a self-conscious reaction against the vitriolic denunciations of democracy that poured out of the Third Reich. There was angry foreboding about a Germany which combined these developments with a glorification of war and the sponsorship of like-minded—or equally mindless—organizations on the American side of the Atlantic.

When at the end of 1934 the chief of the State Department's western European division confirmed the estimate of Ambassador Dodd that the United States should prefer to lose its markets in Germany rather than to make a new trade treaty agreeable to Berlin, he recalled that, contrary to the fears of the State Department, its successful opposition to the proposed cotton barter with Germany had not produced any avalanche of protests from the public.[111] The American people were greatly exercised about economic problems in the years of the great depression, but basic ideological challenges affected them more deeply still.

In Latin America, German activity in the period 1933–36 had been concentrated in two fields of endeavor. The foreign organization of the National Socialist party had taken control of the Germans and those of German descent living in South America, as well as their institutions and publications.[112] Of more immediate importance to Germany was the development of trade relations. In order to establish a framework that fitted in with the foreign trade policy of the new regime in Berlin, a special mission was sent to Latin America and a series of trade agreements signed.[113] Designed to increase German exports, these agreements also opened up avenues for po-

111. Moffat Diary, 28 December 1934, Moffat Papers, Vol. 36.

112. The most recent account is in Frye, chap. 5.

113. On the trade mission see *G. D.*, C, 3, Nos. 30, 492; 5, No. 511; "Sitzung des Handelspolitischen Ausschusses vom 27. Juni 1934" (with annexed instructions for the delegation), and ". . . vom 15. Oktober 1934," T–120, 2612/5650/H 003903–908, 960–961.

litical influence; but no major impact was evident before 1937. Only in Brazil, the country that was to be the scene of considerable excitement, were there indications of political repercussions by 1936.[114] The trend in German trade policy was by that time increasingly toward the export of armaments, the displacement of United States trade with South American countries, and the search for raw materials needed for preparations for war under the Four-Year Plan.[115] It would not have been difficult to predict that such activities were certain to have repercussions not only in Latin America but on Germany's relations with the United States as well. At the time, however, the main effect of German policy appears to have been to lend impetus to American attempts to convert the Monroe Doctrine into something resembling a defensive alliance against Germany. Ironically, and unintentionally, Germany was helping to bring together the nations of the Western hemisphere; but there is nothing to suggest that anyone in Berlin particularly cared.[116]

114. *D. D. F.*, 2d, 1, No. 479; 3, No. 449; *G. D.*, C, 5, No. 500

115. *G. D.*, C, 5, Nos. 569, 598; Deutsche Revisions- und Treuhand Aktiengesellschaft to the Reichsfinanzministerium, 2 June 1938, Bundesarchiv, Reichsfinanzministerium, R 2/27, f. 102.

116. Offner, pp. 168–71.

7 German Rearmament, Withdrawal from the League, and Relations with Britain and France

In order to develop the main themes in Germany's relations with some countries, it has been necessary to deal with certain events out of chronological order before returning to examine the circumstances under which Hitler took Germany out of the disarmament conference and the League of Nations in October 1933. The review of Hitler's general aims before he came to power documented his distaste for the League as an organization and the incompatibility of the policies he intended to follow with the obligations of membership in it. The discussion of German foreign policy in the first months of the new regime illustrated how the previously projected policies were in fact initiated in 1933. By the summer of that year, international reaction to events in Germany had made the disarmament negotiations in Geneva increasingly difficult at the same time as Germany's rearmament was actually getting under way. The British, French, Italian, and American governments continued to hope for agreement on a disarmament convention; but though the British were inclined to prefer an agreement that provided some limits on Germany to no agreement at all, the French were most reluctant to make concessions in the absence of new guarantees of their security if any new treaty were violated. The British, however, were unwilling to assume new responsibilities on the Continent and were, therefore, ready to listen to the Italian argument that concessions must be made to Germany since no power was willing to take steps to keep Germany from rearming.[1]

1. *B. D.*, 2d, 5, No. 383. The French ambassador to Rome summarized the Italian attitude in the same way: Germany will rearm anyway; no one will start a preventive war; action by the League will lead to a German withdrawal from that organization; therefore one should get Germany's signature on a treaty by allowing some rearmament (ibid., No. 393).

The negotiations in Geneva deadlocked in June, and the following months were devoted to exploring new plans. These plans, advanced in different versions by the British, French, and Italians, took varying views of allowing Germany a token supply of those types of weapons denied it by the peace treaty, including differing provisions for a preliminary period in which no basic changes would be made, followed by another period during which specific disarmament measures would be taken by France and other countries. These plans also provided for some forms of control to assure that whatever had been agreed upon would in fact be observed.[2] When the German foreign minister, von Neurath, met with the leaders of the other delegations at Geneva in the last week of September 1933, it became clear that there was a wide gap between the proposals Britain, Italy, France, and the United States would support and those Germany was willing to accept.[3] The British government thereupon began work on a compromise plan;[4] but before it could be formally presented, the British themselves abandoned it in the face of Germany's return to a position even more intransigent than the one taken in the September talks.[5] How had German policy reached this stage?

The actual progress of German rearmament in 1933 was slow. The new regime inherited from its predecessor some plans for an increase in the size of the army and basic preparations in certain areas forbidden to Germany—military aviation,[6] armored warfare, chemical warfare, and submarines.[7] Though adding very little to the actual strength of the German armed forces above the limits set by the Treaty of Versailles, these preparations did make it easier for Hitler to get his rearmament program under way, and had, by their illegitimate character, sufficiently undermined the moral susceptibilities of the German officer corps to make them willing and even eager participants in the military program of the new government.[8]

The German cabinet had established a National Defense Council (*Reichsverteidigungsrat*) by a secret decree on 4 April 1933, and this agency, to-

2. Documents on these schemes have been published in *B. D.*, 2d, 5; U. S. 1933, 1; *G. D.*, C, 1; *D. D. F.*, 1st., 3. The course of Italian policy is reflected in Aloisi's *Journal*. See also Eden, *Facing the Dictators*, p. 50.

3. *B. D.*, 2d, 5, No. 411; *G. D.*, C, 1, No. 447; U. S. 1933, 1:232–35; *D. D. B.*, 2, Nos. 47, 50, 53, 54, 56.

4. On the British compromise and German information about it see *B. D.*, 2d, 5, No. 440, n. 1; *G. D.*, C, 1, No. 478.

5. On the British cabinet meeting of 9 October 1933 at which the 3 October draft compromise was abandoned see *B. D.*, 2d, 5, Nos. 425, 440. The Germans were informed on 10 October (*G. D.*, C, 1, No. 486).

6. A useful summary is in Karl-Heinz Völker, "Die Entwicklung der militärischen Luftfahrt in Deutschland 1920–1933," *Beiträge zur Militär- und Kriegsgeschichte*, 3 (Stuttgart: Deutsche Verlags-Anstalt, 1962), 121–292.

7. Kapitän zur See Schüssler, *Der Kampf der Marine gegen Versailles 1919–1935* (Berlin: Oberkommando der Kriegsmarine, 1937), pp. 38–49, reprinted in *TMWC*, 34:565–78.

8. The best summary of the scope and meaning of the secret rearmament measures of the Weimar period is in Bracher, *Machtergreifung*, pp. 766–84.

gether with its subordinate but more regularly functioning working committee (*Arbeitsausschuss*), began the process of coordinating the activities of different government agencies toward military planning.[9] The initial steps in this process could be taken secretly, but substantial rearmament measures would sooner or later become known to the outside world which, because of the constant sight of marching SA paramilitary formations, was inclined to overestimate rather than underestimate German military might. At some point, the publicly visible process of rearmament would clash with the participation of Germany in the disarmament negotiations; if this clash was postponed until the fall of 1933, two factors were responsible. One was the reluctance of Hitler to provoke other powers too soon—he wanted to see whether they would in fact move toward preventive war in the face of German rearmament. The other was the necessarily slow beginning of the rearmament process itself: as other powers would learn later, the initial period of a rearmament program involves a great deal of planning, organizing, training, and contracting but produces little in the way of immediately apparent military power.[10] There was little doubt in the German government, however, that the time would come when the contradiction between internal rearmament and external disarmament negotiations would confront Berlin with new policy choices.

In late April 1933, the German delegate to the disarmament negotiations, Rudolf Nadolny, gave some German journalists a confidential briefing on German plans and prospects in the Geneva negotiations that deserves to be cited as an indication of Germany's real aims.[11] Nadolny explained that Germany hoped to secure legalization for a standing army of 600,000 but was in the process of building an army of that size anyway. Nadolny saw two possible dangers in Geneva: one was that the British and French might agree to a German army of 300,000, reduce their own forces a little, and then insist on an international control of the newly agreed levels. If the British and French were to insist on such a program, Germany would leave the conference and perhaps also leave the League. The second danger was that the other powers would in fact agree to disarm substantially and therefore refuse to allow Germany to rearm at all; this, too, would lead Germany to depart from the conference.

Since the two contingencies under which Germany would walk out—Germany being allowed to rearm to the level of the others, or the others disarming to Germany's level—were precisely the two alternatives that the German delegation consistently argued for in the Geneva talks, the mendac-

9. Burkhart Mueller-Hillebrand, *Das Heer 1933–1945,* 1: *Das Heer bis zum Kriegsbeginn* (Darmstadt: Mittler, 1954), 102–03. The earliest published minutes of a meeting of the working committee are those for the second session on 26 April 1933 (*TMWC,* 36:220–29). See Gerhard Meinck, "Der Reichsverteidigungsrat," *Wehrwissenschaftliche Rundschau*, 6, No. 8 (August 1956), pp. 411–15.

10. Bracher, *Machtergreifung,* p. 803.

11. Dr. Hans Joachim Kausch, "Informationsbericht Nr. 7 vom 22. April 1933," Bundesarchiv, Sammlung Brammer, Z.Sg. 101/26, f. 275–79.

ity of their negotiating position is obvious. Clearly an army of great size was needed to attain the aims of the regime in Berlin: doubling or tripling the existing 100,000-man army would be insufficient for great conquests, and international control would immediately reveal Germany's true aims to all. On the other hand, any substantial disarmament by the other powers as a basis for Germany keeping its army small would immediately destroy both at home and abroad, the propagandistic underpinnings of the whole rearmament program. No wonder Nadolny preferred to the dangers posed for Germany by agreement on a treaty at Geneva a third alternative, namely no agreement at all but negotiations continuing for months and even years while Germany rearmed. Nadolny was to adhere to this position even after Hitler had gone beyond it.

A crisis early in May led the German government to review its negotiating policy and to make a temporary conciliatory gesture in the form of a moderate speech by Hitler on 17 May.[12] This speech contained a threat to leave the League, but it did not reveal the extent of the German government's commitment to rearmament and to a rupture at Geneva. In a cabinet meeting preceding the speech, both von Neurath and war minister von Blomberg had argued that Germany should not continue to participate in the negotiations at Geneva; but Hitler had decided that Germany should stay while threatening to leave, meanwhile carefully rearming and always remaining fully aware of the fact that the issue would not be resolved at the conference table.[13] Hitler thus took the same line as Nadolny on the advantage of continuing to participate in negotiations, but with a greater willingness to pull out at whatever might look like an appropriate moment. The building up of Germany's armed forces, quietly but without regard for the negotiations at Geneva, was to continue as a matter of course; and von Blomberg explained this policy to an assemblage of German generals on 1 June.[14] A month later Hitler himself directed an expansion of the armed forces through a build-up of special border formations and the training of 250,000 reservists in the SA.[15] Germany thus preferred to let the disarmament discussions go forward in the summer of 1933 without publicly defining its own position

12. *B. D.*, 2d, 5, Nos. 141, nn. 1 and 3, 144; *G. D.*, C, 1, No. 239, p. 439.

13. *G. D.*, C, 1, No. 226. This was the reason for von Bülow's telling Habicht that Germany wanted to save the threat of leaving the League for the disarmament and Saar questions rather than using it on the Austrian issue (Memorandum of Heeren, 31 July 1933, T–120, 2838/6113/E 453737–42).

14. Liebmann Notes, Institut für Zeitgeschichte, E D 1, pp. 48–49 (main portions quoted in Meinck, *Hitler und die deutsche Aufrüstung*, pp. 31, 91). Although the policy of rearming during the negotiations was supposed to be kept secret, the German delegation in Geneva discussed it relatively freely with others. Rheinbaben told the counselor of the American delegation that he thought Germany ought just to rearm to the level authorized by the latest British draft proposal and then have the convention ratify this action (Wilson's unnumbered dispatch of 29 June 1933, State 500. A 15 A 4 Steering Committee/338).

15. Bracher, *Machtergreifung*, p. 797.

precisely;[16] whatever treaty violations it committed in the meantime could always be explained away somehow.[17]

On several occasions during the summer of 1933 Hitler reiterated in private the extravagantly aggressive schemes characteristic of his pre-1933 speeches and writing, schemes previously cited as a continuing element in his thought immediately after the National Socialist assumption of power at the beginning of the year. Some of the most extreme plans about expansion into the Western Hemisphere, the Far East, and Central Africa reported by Rauschning were voiced by Hitler during this period.[18] At the beginning of August, Hitler explained to two American visitors, Sosthenes Behn of International Telephone and Telegraph and Henry Mann, European vice-president of the National City Bank, that he hoped to annex Austria, the Polish Corridor, Alsace-Lorraine, and the German-inhabited sections of Denmark, Italy, Czechoslovakia, Yugoslavia, and Rumania—though he wanted to postpone war until Germany was completely prepared.[19] In examining the German drive to rearm while avoiding excessive provocation, the evidence of these consistently held aggressive intentions must be kept in mind by the analyst of Hitler's tactics in the disarmament negotiations.

As the fall meeting of the League of Nations Assembly and the resumption of formal disarmament negotiations in Geneva approached, the line to be taken by Germany was discussed in a conference of ministers. Von Neurath decided to go in person and to take along Joseph Goebbels to help counter the anti-German propaganda in Geneva.[20] At this point von Neurath still wanted to use the forum that the League provided for Germany, pulling out only after the collapse of the disarmament conference—which he took for granted—and the settlement of the Saar question.[21] Publicly he prepared the way by a speech denouncing the lack of progress at Geneva and a press interview denying that the new German government created a new international situation that could justify delay in agreement to Germany's ostensible demands.[22] Those demands were at one point to extend

16. See the note by von Bülow of 23 August on Schwendemann's memorandum "zu IIF Abr 2655," of 21 August 1933, T–120, 1629/7360/E 537258.

17. *TMWC,* 34:205–10; *G. D.,* C, 2, No. 39.

18. Rauschning, *Voice of Destruction,* pp. 61–72.

19. There is a brief reference to this meeting in the *New York Times,* 4 August 1933, p. 6. Henry Mann gave an account of the conversation to the American minister in Vienna, George H. Earle, who reported on it in his dispatch 9 of 11 October 1933 (State 862.00/3104). I am indebted to Mr. Mann for an oral report on this meeting on 17 July 1962 and a letter of 1 August 1962.

20. To make a more impressive showing of party leaders, von Neurath at one point also planned to have Rosenberg accompany him to Geneva (Reichschancellory document, "zu RK 11152/33 für den Vortrag beim Herrn Reichskanzler am 19. September 1933," Nuremberg document 2907–PS).

21. *G. D.,* C, 1, No. 426.

22. The texts may be found in Richard Schmidt and Adolf Grabowsky (eds.), *Disarmament and Equal Rights* (Berlin: Carl Heymanns, 1934), pp. 208–15.

to numerical equality with France in size of army and number and types of weapons during the first stage provided for in any convention, and superiority to France as a counterweight to France's eastern allies in the second stage; but the situation in Geneva showed that these demands would wreck the conference under circumstances in which Germany would be blamed.[23] The conference, it soon became apparent, could be wrecked without such a propaganda disadvantage to Germany.

In Geneva, von Neurath found himself confronted by a proposed two-stage convention that included a provision for controls and seemed to postpone realization of German equality of arms for several years. This looked like a much more promising basis for breaking up the negotiations, since it might be argued in public that the other powers had concerted together to deny Germany the "equality of rights in a system which would provide security for all nations" that they had promised in December 1932. Von Neurath told the leaders of the other delegations at Geneva that their proposals were hardly likely to be acceptable and that he would return to Berlin to confer with Hitler.[24] Under British pressure, the French thereupon agreed to inform the Germans of some additional concessions that they were prepared to make,[25] and the British themselves, as has already been mentioned, began to work on a compromise proposal. Hitler, however, decided that this was the time to leave the disarmament conference and the League of Nations.[26]

The reaction of foreign powers to Germany's activities, especially against Austria, in the summer of 1933 had shown that they were alarmed by the new regime and unwilling to make great concessions to it in the course of formal negotiations, but their reaction also showed that they were not willing to take military action against Germany unless they were literally forced to do so. There was neither the prospect of an agreement satisfactory to Germany nor the danger of military intervention against unilateral action. Some officials in Berlin argued for continued negotiations while Germany rearmed; Nadolny was among those who took this position, and he was therefore excluded from the decisive conferences in Berlin.[27] Goebbels, on the

23. This is a summary of the exchanges between Hitler, the German foreign ministry, the German Ministry of Defense, and the German delegation in Geneva on 25–30 September in T–120, 1629/7360/E 537463–471, 476–479, 499–501, 558–59.

24. *B. D.*, 2d, 5, No. 422; *G. D.*, C, 1, No. 469.

25. *B. D.*, 2d, 5, Nos. 420, 427; *G. D.*, C, 1, No. 472.

26. Meinck, *Hitler und die deutsche Aufrüstung,* pp. 38–48, gives a summary of these developments and their implications.

27. This is clear from the attendance at the key meetings in Berlin; from von Neurath's marginal comments on Nadolny's memorandum "IIF Abr 4106," of 4 October, T–120, 1629/7360/E 537585–590; and Nadolny's memoirs, *Mein Beitrag,* pp. 140–41. For an excellent exposition of the view that Germany had everything to gain and nothing to lose by continuing to talk at Geneva while rearming at home see Schwendemann's memorandum "II F Abr 3091," of 29 September 1933, 1629/7360/E 537514–516.

other hand, apparently influenced by his brief experience in Geneva, supported Hitler's inclination to take advantage of the impasse in the negotiations to broaden the differences and then leave altogether.[28] For a moment, Hitler appears to have considered further negotiations[29] but then decided to avoid them, lest Germany be pushed by the process of such talks into an agreement, as had been the case in the Four-Power Pact.

Fearing such an agreement, Hitler did not want the conference to break up either over Germany's rejection of controls or over its demands for rearmament, both dangerous grounds for Germany if publicized. He preferred to stiffen the German negotiating position, leave the conference and the League, and couple these steps with a public appeal to Germany and the world.[30] The beginning of October 1933 was in any case a time when Germany's armament program was scheduled to move into a new phase of acceleration. At the same time, Ludwig Beck was made chief of the army office which subsequently became that of the chief of the general staff of the army.[31] The prospect of a disarmament convention including the possibility of international controls must have been especially distasteful to Hitler under these circumstances.[32] Here was the time to remove Germany from the international forum that the National Socialists had always argued it should never have entered in the first place. Japan had left the League when it suited it; Germany would leave the League at the time when the breakup of the disarmament talks provided a convenient opportunity.

The tactics for leaving Geneva were quickly worked out in accordance with a suggestion by the state secretary, von Bülow. Although Hitler allowed himself an opportunity to review the decision at the last moment, the intervening days brought no change. On the contrary, the last German negotiating position was so great a step back to the original high demands that the British gave up their idea of a compromise, and the confrontation at the disarmament conference was, therefore, all the more dramatic.[33] A last-

28. On Goebbels's activities in Geneva and return to Berlin see Paul Schmidt, *Statist auf diplomatischer Bühne 1923–1945* (Bonn: Athenäum-Verlag, 1950), pp. 279–80; U. S. 1933, 1:303; *D. D. B.*, 3, No. 55; "Bestellungen vom Propagandaministerium vom 29.9.33," Bundesarchiv, Sammlung Brammer, Z.Sg. 101/1, f. 116; Messersmith to Phillips, 28 October 1933, State 862.00/3128. It should be noted that incidents arising out of a visit to Geneva of another prominent National Socialist, Robert Ley of the Labor Front, had precipitated Germany's departure from the International Labor Organization (von Bülow memoranda of 17 and 19 June 1933, T–120, 2374/4603/E 190958–960).

29. *G. D.*, C, 1, No. 475. The German proposals of 4 October (ibid., No. 480) were based on von Neurath's instructions after a talk with Hitler (RM 1374 of 30 September 1933, T–120, 1629/7360/E 537561).

30. *G. D.*, C, 1, No. 479.

31. Rudolf Absolon, *Wehrgesetz und Wehrdienst 1935–1945* (Boppard: Harald Boldt Verlag, 1959), p. 75; Wolfgang Foerster, *Ein General kämpft gegen den Krieg* (Munich: Münchener Dom-Verlag, 1949), p. 16.

32. See also *B. D.*, 2d, 5, No. 446.

33. *G. D.*, C, 1, Nos. 484, 480, n. 3, 489; *B. D.*, 2d, 5, Nos. 434, 435, 444.

minute effort by Mussolini to mediate the differences was rejected in Berlin;[34] Nadolny was recalled and, still protesting, left the negotiations for the last time.[35] For the first of many instances during the Third Reich, there was to be no diplomatic contact that might somehow lead to agreement while the German government was deliberately moving toward a break.

On 13 October 1933, the decision to leave Geneva, previously made by Hitler, supported by all of Germany's leading diplomats except Nadolny,[36] and approved by President Hindenburg, was agreed to by the German cabinet. Hitler explained that he did not fear any sanctions, that it would be a service to the world to strike a blow against the League, and that the German people would be given an opportunity to vote their enthusiastic support of the government's policy. This last step would provide the occasion to dissolve the Reichstag elected in March so that it could be replaced by one in which all the members were nominated by Hitler himself, as well as to dissolve permanently all the local legislatures.[37] On the following day, this decision was reviewed and confirmed and then made public. The government appealed to the German electorate, blaming the other powers for the failure of the negotiations, and calling for friendship with France, the one power whose reaction might have worried Hitler. The public response was most favorable; and though there were election irregularities to "improve" the returns of the 12 November plebiscite, the regime could point proudly to a demonstration of national solidarity.[38]

If the decision to leave the international forum of Geneva pleased the German public and enabled Hitler to consolidate his domestic position, its foreign repercussions were acrimonious though without great danger. The notification of Mussolini was handled in an exceptionally clumsy fashion and produced a temporary cooling in German-Italian relations, especially since it was coupled with Germany's refusal to invoke the Four-Power Pact or to accept the latest Italian proposals as a means out of the impasse.[39] The German attempt to blame Sir John Simon for the breach did nothing to improve German-British relations.[40] The French government had had no

34. U. S. 1933, 1:304, 258; *G. D.*, C, 1, No. 494; *B. D.*, 2d, 5, No. 450.

35. *G. D.*, C, 1, No. 495.

36. This point is appropriately stressed by Offner (pp. 50–52).

37. *G. D.*, C, 1, No. 499.

38. Bracher, *Machtergreifung*, pp. 351ff. It is not very likely that people in countries other than Germany were greatly impressed by the huge margins for Hitler's ticket returned by the inmates of Dachau concentration camp (*B. D.*, 2d, 6, No. 39; U. S. 1933, 2:265).

39. *G. D.*, C, 1, Nos. 498, 500, 502; 2, Nos. 2, 4, 18, 28; 4, p. 106; *B. D.*, 2d, 5, No. 476; U. S. 1933, 1:270. The Czech minister to Berlin suggested that the change in German-Italian relations reflected the strengthening and consolidation of German power which precluded Mussolini from influencing Germany as much as formerly, while at the same time the Germans liked the Italian ambassador Cerruti less and less (Mastný report 73 of 29 October 1933, Czech document in T–120, 1041/1809/413954–956).

40. *B. D.*, 2d, 5, Nos. 451, 462, 463, 466, 475, 501; *G. D.*, C, 2, Nos. 13, 19; Temperley, p. 257.

confidence that the Germans would in fact observe any disarmament agreement they might sign and were therefore not as disturbed as others by the rupture in the disarmament negotiations. Unwilling to take solitary action against Germany, they could neither stop German rearmament nor muster the needed domestic support for an adequate rearmament effort of their own in the face of an uncertain future.[41] Furthermore, Hitler quickly started a publicity campaign for a rapprochement with France, designed to undermine whatever spirit of opposition might still exist in France. This effort is reviewed below; it appears to have contributed to French acquiescence in the German moves in the fall of 1933.

Hitler could feel that his gamble had succeeded. The disarmament negotiations would proceed in a desultory and meaningless fashion for some months, but since no one had taken any action against Germany at this point it was unlikely that anyone would do so when the diplomatic united front that existed in Geneva at the beginning of October vanished.[42] Hitler could remind his cabinet of the correctness of his predictions and instruct the military to defend Germany against any foreign attack, knowing that Germany could not win—but also knowing that no attack would come.[43]

The failure of other nations to take action against Germany was certainly not due to the absence of warnings from perceptive observers. The British government was told what the future held not merely by newspaper reporters but by official observers. The British ambassador in Berlin, Sir Horace Rumbold, in summing up the first three months of the Hitler regime, called attention to the exactness with which Hitler was following the route set forth in *Mein Kampf*; noted that this meant domestic consolidation accompanied by rearmament; and warned that once these objectives had been attained, "it would be misleading to base any hopes on a return to sanity or a serious modification of the views of the chancellor and his entourage." Sir Horace argued that all this "can only end in one way" and concluded cautiously that Germany's neighbors had good reason to be vigilant.[44] The British military representative at the Geneva negotiations, Brigadier Arthur Temperley, provided his government with a similar analysis of the dangers. He suggested confronting Germany with threats now, while it "is powerless before the French army and our fleet," and maintaining pressure over subsequent years until Germany came to its senses. The alternative, to allow things to drift for another five years, would allow German rearmament to become an accomplished fact; and then, unless there were a change of heart in Germany, war would be inevitable. The alternatives were all grim, but "there is a mad dog abroad once more and we must resolutely combine

41. Joseph Paul-Boncour, *Entre deux guerres,* 2 (New York: Brentano's, 1946), pp. 386–87; U. S. 1933, 1:279–81; *B. D.*, 2d, 5, No. 508.

42. Documents on the continued disarmament negotiations may be found in *G. D.*, C, 2; *B. D.*, 2d, 5 and 6; U. S. 1933, 1 and 1934, 1.

43. *G. D.*, C, 2, Nos. 9, 39; *TMWC,* 34:487–91.

44. *B. D.*, 2d, 5, No. 36.

either to ensure its destruction or at least its confinement until the disease has run its course."[45] Both documents were circulated to the British cabinet with the concurring comments of the permanent undersecretary in the Foreign Office, Sir Robert Vansittart.[46] Such views could bring a temporary stiffening in the British negotiating position in Geneva and lengthy examinations of the legal obstacles to military action against Germany, but no warnings could move the British government to decisive steps.[47]

Prime Minister Ramsay MacDonald had long been a critic both of war as an instrument of policy and the Treaty of Versailles as a European settlement. Stanley Baldwin, leader of the Conservatives, the largest group supporting the British national government, was uninterested in foreign affairs, and though unwilling to let down France if a war did break out, had no inclination to accept new commitments for Great Britain.[48] Sir John Simon, the British foreign secretary, was a brilliant lawyer who yet managed to conceal from his contemporaries as well as the puzzled reader of his memoirs whatever firm views on foreign policy he may have held.[49] His keen powers of analysis were not matched by the vigor and passion that effective leadership requires. He commented on an incisive analysis of German foreign policy, its direction, and its dangers submitted by Sir Eric Phipps, the new British ambassador to Berlin, by saying "this is a most illuminating document—and terrifying";[50] but there is no evidence to suggest that he ever drew from such terrifying prospects the conclusion that his countrymen needed to be awakened to the danger. In spite of all warnings that Germany's leader did not want reconciliation, such reconciliation remained the laudable but unattainable goal of the British foreign secretary.[51]

In this fruitless endeavor, Sir John and his colleagues were supported by the temper of the British people. Distaste for arms and revulsion against war ran deep in the England of the early 1930s, and many still thought that the absence of guns guaranteed the remoteness of war, as a converse of the popular view that the accumulation of arms assured the imminence of war. A by-election at East Fulham on 25 October 1933, in which a Conservative seat was lost in a local Labour landslide on the issue of disarmament, both reflected the dominance of pacifist inclinations in Labour circles and frightened the national government by suggesting the political dangers

45. Memorandum by Temperley enclosed with ibid., No. 127.

46. See the quotation from the Vansittart papers in Ian Colvin, *None so blind* (New York: Harcourt, 1965), pp. 23–24.

47. *B. D.*, 2d, 5, Nos. 142, 185. See ibid., No. 253, and Colvin, pp. 26–29, for other warnings by Vansittart in July and August 1933.

48. See his comments on 22 September 1933, in *B. D.*, 2d, 5, No. 406, pp. 618–19.

49. *Retrospect* (London: Hutchinson, 1952).

50. *B. D.*, 2d, 6, No. 241.

51. See his letter to George V of 19 January 1935, in Harold Nicolson, *King George V* (London: Constable, 1952), p. 522. It should be noted that Sir John's effectiveness with the Germans was affected by their erroneous belief that he was Jewish.

of a firm policy.[52] For the next six years—until the summer of 1939—the Labour and Liberal parties would denounce as unnecessary all efforts to rebuild British military power; and those like Neville Chamberlain who were later to be reviled as weak-kneed, were attacked as militarists and warmongers for every halting step they took to rearm the country.[53]

The French government had, if anything, an exaggerated picture of the dangers ahead, but in Paris the discrepancy between insight and resolution was even greater than in London. The French intelligence service provided a reasonably accurate picture of the progress of Germany's rearmament, and its official representative in Berlin, Ambassador André François-Poncet, had a clear picture of both the situation at the time and the probable dangers ahead.[54] Nevertheless, the French government neither could nor would take drastic action. Internally divided, worried about the danger of a war with Germany, dubious about the assistance or even the moral support of Britain and the United States, the French observed the rise of German power with frightened indecision.[55] Its former allies pressed it to make concessions to Germany in precisely those years when the low birth-rate of the war period would automatically reduce the size of the annual class of conscripts for its army. Under these circumstances, France would turn to new international treaty arrangements rather than individual and drastic steps. As will be seen, Paris pushed the idea of a set of agreements covering Eastern Europe, the so-called Eastern Locarno Pact, and then turned to an alliance with Russia. In the meantime, its resolution was weakened further by the clever way in which the German government manipulated French hopes for peace by calling for a direct understanding between the two powers.

There had been occasional references to the possibility of a direct German-French understanding in 1933. Included in these soundings had been references to a mutual-assistance pact between the two countries.[56] There were soundings calling for high-level personal contacts, first between Édouard Daladier, president of the Council of Ministers, and von Neurath

52. Colvin, p. 31.

53. For an effort by the British Labour Party to enlist Franklin D. Roosevelt in the campaign against British rearmament, see Harld J. Laski's letter to FDR of 5 November 1935 and the latter's noncommittal reply of 18 November in *FDR and Foreign Affairs,* 3:53–54, 80.

54. Castellan's book is based on French intelligence reports. Many reports of François-Poncet for the first period of National Socialist rule have been published in the second and third volumes of series 2 of the French diplomatic documents. His observations are also often to be found in the reports of other diplomats, e.g., report 166 of the Hungarian minister to Berlin, Constantin de Masirevich, of 7 July 1933, in Elek Karsai "The Meeting of Gömbös and Hitler in 1933," *New Hungarian Quarterly,* 3, No. 5 (1962), 194–95.

55. *B. D.,* 2d, 5, Nos. 151, 154.

56. *G. D.,* C, 1, Nos. 9, 163, 165, 190, 360; Memorandum of von Bülow, 24 April 1933, T–120, 2371/4602/E 189182–184; Mastný report 31 of 24 April 1933, Czech document in T–120, 1041/1809/413939–940 (excerpt in Berber, *Prager Akten,* No. 9).

or von Papen,[57] and subsequently between Daladier and Hitler, but nothing came of all this.[58] There were also various semiofficial attempts to bring the two powers closer together,[59] but until the crisis in the disarmament negotiations developed in September-October 1933, the German government was not interested in pursuing talks that might reassure the French.

In September 1933, however, such reassurance was an urgent need of German policy, oriented now to keeping France quiet while Germany moved ahead unrestrained rather than nudging France into specific concessions in negotiations. By this time, Joachim von Ribbentrop, who was to play an increasingly important role in German foreign policy, was using for diplomatic purposes the contacts he had made in France as a champagne salesman. He had become familiar with Fernand de Brinon, an ardent advocate of Franco-German cooperation who soon became an equally ardent admirer of Adolf Hitler. With the knowledge of Daladier, von Ribbentrop arranged for a meeting between Hitler and de Brinon on 9 September 1933.[60] This meeting was kept secret, but it paved the way for an interview in November that was publicized and attracted general attention. Concurrently with first bringing Hitler and de Brinon together, von Ribbentrop was also inaugurating those contacts with French war veterans that were to become a major element in Germany's dealings with France.[61] In mid-September, Hitler personally reassured the French ambassador of Germany's peaceful intentions,[62] and in Geneva later that month, von Neurath urged on French foreign minister Joseph Paul-Boncour a direct German-French understanding as the deadlock in the disarmament negotiations came to a climax.[63] In Hitler's speech of 14 October, justifying his exit from the League, he included a most friendly reference to Daladier—in response to some friendly words from the latter—and to the possibility of German-French reconciliation.[64] He was eloquent on this subject at a time when he was still slightly concerned that his step might provoke a French reaction—and as he was turning more and more toward a treaty of some sort with

57. *G. D.*, C, 1, No. 92 (it should be noted that Daladier used Fernand de Brinon in this unofficial sounding). When von Neurath met Daladier at the London Economic Conference, nothing of consequence was discussed (ibid., No. 314).

58. *B. D.*, 2d., 5, Nos. 258, 266, 269; *G. D.*, C, 1, No. 374.

59. On attempts by the German General von Bredow see *G. D.*, C, 1, No. 114; for an approach in April 1933 by the self-styled French radical anti-Semite Robert Fabre-Luce see T–120, 2382/4619/E 197650–651.

60. De Brinon's record of the talk is in *Les procès de collaboration, Fernand de Brinon, Joseph Darnand, Jean Luchaire, compte rendu sténographique* (Paris: Albin Michel, 1948), pp. 78–80. On the background of this meeting see de Brinon's statements, ibid., pp. 53–55, 200–02, and Daladier's testimony, pp. 203–05.

61. *TMWC*, 35:134.

62. *G. D.*, C, 1, No. 430; André François-Poncet, *Als Botschafter in Berlin 1931–1938* (Erna Stübl, trans.; Mainz: Florian Kupferberg, 1949), pp. 154–55; Memorandum by Köpke, 20 September 1933, T–120, 2660/5669/H 014244.

63. *G. D.*, C, 1, No. 466.

64. Domarus, 1:311–12; see also *B. D.*, 2d, 5, No. 468; *G. D.*, C, 2, No. 8; U. S. 1933, 1:281–86.

Poland as the opportune complement to his pacific assurances to the West.[65]

While Hitler thought of bilateral negotiations with Poland and conceivably Czechoslovakia, the French government wanted Germany to return to Geneva coupled with an Eastern Locarno Pact and a promise to leave Austria alone as conditions for agreeing to German rearmament. The conflict between these two approaches was clear—Germany wanted bilateral agreements, to be broken at will without third-party interference; France wanted multilateral commitments in which the threat of third-power involvement would act as deterrent to any breach of treaty obligations or assure unified action against an aggressor if a violation did take place. This conflict became apparent as soon as the specifics of a German-French rapprochement were discussed in the first half of November.[66] As an impasse accordingly began to develop in these negotiations, Hitler attempted to help recreate confidence by publicizing his pacific intentions. On 15 November plans were made to use a newspaper under instructions from the German foreign ministry to push for a German-French rapprochement,[67] and on the following day Hitler granted de Brinon an interview, filled with pacific assurances, for publication in France.[68]

By the time this interview was published in Paris in *Le Matin* on 22 November, its effect in France was greatly undermined by the appearance in *Le Petit Parisien* (16–17 November and 22 November) of two secret German documents released to the political editor of that newspaper by the French foreign ministry, presumably with that purpose in mind.[69] The documents were, of course, denounced as forgeries by the German government, but there is no doubt of their authenticity.[70] One was a general instruction for German propaganda in the Western Hemisphere, issued by the

65. Hitler's talk to the National Socialist leaders is reported in Rauschning, *Voice of Destruction,* pp. 104–10, and Breyer, p. 98, as taking place on 14 October, but is almost certainly that of 18 October described in Domarus, 1:317.

66. See *G. D.*, C, 2, Nos. 54, 61, 62, 65; *B. D.*, 2d, 6, Nos. 43, 49.

67. Von Bülow to State Secretary Funk in the propaganda ministry and Pfundtner in the Ministry of Interior, "P10091," of 15 November 1933, T–120, 2660/5669/H 014386–388.

68. Fernand de Brinon, *Frankreich-Deutschland 1918–1934* (Albert Koerber, trans.; Essen: Essener Verlagsanstalt, 1935), pp. 145–52; Fernand de Brinon, *Mémoires* (Paris: n.d.), p. 28; Domarus, 1:332–34 (erroneously dated to 19 November); Phipps (Berlin) telegram 92, 23 November 1933, Foreign Office C 10276/320/18.

69. Marriner (U. S. chargé Paris) dispatch 412 of 28 November 1933, State 751.62/240. The full texts of the documents were subsequently published by the political editor, Albert Jullien, under the title *Le vrai visage des maîtres du IIIe Reich. Les instructions secrètes de la propagande allemande* (Paris: Petit Parisien, 1934). Discussion of this publication may be found in Ernst Kris, "German Propaganda Instructions of 1933," *Social Research,* 9, No. 1 (Feb. 1942), 46–81, and in Ernst Kris and Hans Speier, *German Radio Propaganda* (London: Oxford, 1949), pp. 95, 220. There is a detailed summary in Frye, pp. 21–31. The French government had communicated the texts to London on 9 November (Foreign Office C 9996/9848/18).

70. The internal evidence of the documents themselves is corroborated, at least in part, by von Bülow's memorandum of 28 July 1934, T–120, 909/1574/381306.

propaganda ministry in September 1933, and the other a shorter, special directive of late October concerning Germany's departure from the League. Both documents expressed with considerable clarity the continuing hostility of Germany for France, the desire to separate France from England, the aim of Germany to regain all territories with a German minority, and the rejection of any international control of armaments. German propaganda was to be directed to show that the failure of others to grant Germany's legitimate demands was responsible for the failure to bring about a peaceful reconciliation, so that at least a part of world opinion would blame the other powers when Germany eventually resorted to force. In the meantime, Germany needed time to rearm and thus would pose no threat to its neighbors. As its arms slowly increased, hints of strength would decrease any willingness on the part of others to take action against Germany.

Such revelations, believed in the French foreign ministry if nowhere else, combined with Hitler's statement, even in his interview with de Brinon, that Germany would not return to Geneva, dampened French enthusiasm for concessions to Germany. Discussion, therefore, continued tentatively in the winter of 1933–34 but without concrete results.[71] The Germans would make no concessions on the subject of either rearmament or participation in new multilateral agreements, and the French were unwilling to agree to a return of the Saar territory to Germany without a plebiscite, a subject that had been canvassed in the negotiations. By the time Hitler and François-Poncet met to review the negotiations on 11 December 1933, it was obvious that no basis for an agreement had been reached. It was equally clear, however, that France would take no drastic steps to prevent Germany from continuing quietly with her rearmament program, the scope of which was known in Paris with considerable accuracy.[72] The talks concerning both disarmament and direct German-French rapprochement continued for a time, but reached an impasse in the spring of 1934. The divergence persisted between the British desire to secure some sort of a treaty with the new German government at almost any cost and the French reluctance to concede publicly Germany's constantly increasing demands. Deadlock was reached in April and publicly admitted in June 1934.[73]

In the meantime, Germany reaffirmed its determination not to return

71. *G. D.*, C, 2, Nos. 86, 100, 101, 104, 105, 112, 113; *B. D.*, 2d, 6, Nos. 79, 89, 90, 104, 115, 116, 117; *D. D. B.*, 3, No. 87; Jules Laroche, *La Pologne de Pilsudski* (Paris: Flammarion, 1953), p. 144; Mastný telegram of 29 November 1933, Czech document in T–120, 1041/1809/413961–962; "Vertrauliche Mitteilung," 27 November 1933, Bundesarchiv, Brammer, Z.Sg. 101/2, f. 53.

72. *G. D.*, C, 2, No. 116; *B. D.*, 2d, 6, Nos. 130, 131; Mastný telegram of 12 December 1933, Czech document in T–120, 1041/1809/413965. For a December 1933 French estimate of German military strength, showing that there would be real danger by 1938 see *B. D.*, 2d, 6, No. 103. For Hitler's and Blomberg's view that France would accept German rearmament see the report on the military conferences of 15 and 18 January 1934, in the Liebmann Papers, Institut für Zeitgeschichte, ED 1, p. 51.

73. For unofficial soundings in France in early 1934 authorized by Hitler and con-

to the League[74] and continued to rearm, covering the process by building up friendship societies in France and Germany, led in France by Fernand de Brinon and in Germany by Otto Abetz.[75] It must be remembered that such organizations could and did draw upon substantial reservoirs of genuine belief in the need for reconciliation between the two countries growing out of a mutual respect for the courage of the other's armies in the last war and a horror of any possible repetition of the carnage of that conflict. Though willing to risk serious difficulties in trade relations with France, Hitler temporarily ordered that no insults to France be allowed to appear in Germany.[76] Reassurance and promises combined with an unwillingness to make substantive concessions characterized Germany's dealings with France, which were conducted, as State Secretary von Bülow explained, for the "purpose of restoring Germany's military freedom . . . the center and main goal of our foreign policy."[77]

The German concern that nothing interfere with the scheduled plebiscite and possible return of the Saar territory to Germany in 1935 operated to restrain Berlin for a while, but the obvious willingness of Britain to make greater concessions than France suggested to the Germans that the dangers to their hopes of recovering the Saar were slight indeed. In 1933 and early 1934, the German government worked toward the return of the Saar by politically coordinating all elements in that area into a united front, giving Vice-Chancellor von Papen a special role in handling Saar matters, and by making tactical concessions to assure an early and smooth transfer back to German control of the territory temporarily separated from Germany by the peace treaty. A tremendous propaganda campaign in and toward the Saar was launched by the German government. When it was clear that the effort to have France waive the requirement of a plebiscite had failed,[78]

---

ducted by Dr. von Brehmer, who happened to be a German cancer specialist, see Memorandum by von Rintelen, "zu II Fr 430 II," 8 March 1934, T–120, 2660/5669/H 014486–488. Documents on the official negotiations may be found in *G. D.,* C, 2; *B. D.*, 2d, 6; U. S. 1934, 1. The summary in Meinck, *Hitler und die deutsche Aufrüstung,* pp. 52–86, is helpful but overstates Hitler's willingness to come to an agreement.

74. This is especially clear in the talks of the Italian undersecretary for foreign affairs, Fulvio Suvich, when he visited Berlin in December 1933 and argued strongly but in vain for Germany's return (*G. D.,* C, 2, Nos. 120, 126, 145; Memorandum of von Neurath, RM 1735 of 16 December 1933, T–120, 2383/4619/E 197855).

75. Information on this may be found in the trial of de Brinon, cited in n. 60, above, and in Abetz's interesting, though unreliable, memoirs, *Das offene Problem* (Cologne: Greven Verlag, 1951).

76. Compare "Sitzung des Handelspolitischen Ausschusses vom 10. Januar 1934," and ". . . vom 17. Januar 1934," T–120, 2612/5650/H 003811–813, 815, with Memorandum by Marschall, "II Fr 1396," 14 April 1934, T–120, 2660/5669/H 014524–525.

77. *G. D.,* C, 2, No. 216.

78. In addition to the German-French diplomatic negotiations already mentioned, there was also an unofficial sounding in Paris on behalf of von Papen by Kurt Freiherr von Lersner, a retired German diplomat. See von Bülow to Köster, 6 March 1934, T–120, 2386/4620; Köster to von Bülow, 22 March 1934, *G. D.,* C, 2, No. 350.

attention was focused on holding the plebiscite as early as possible and attaining the highest possible number of votes for reunion with Germany. By the summer of 1934, the plebiscite date had been set for 13 January 1935, and the Germans were well prepared for the triumph they confidently expected.[79]

The greater willingness of Great Britain to make concessions to German arms demands came not only from the genuine desire to secure at least some limitation on a new arms race but also from the hope that the German government might adhere to an agreement that Hitler signed himself rather than one he had inherited from the earlier regime. As the other alternatives appeared to be a preventive war or the unlimited rearmament of Germany, the British even made some concessions to the French desire for guarantees in case Germany broke its commitments, but this obvious sign of the British desire for agreement only spurred on the Germans to further demands and more rapid steps toward rearmament. The February 1934 Berlin visit of the British Lord Privy Seal, Sir Anthony Eden, only clarified the previously mentioned trend to deadlock in the negotiations without suggesting to the British that prompt action on their part was desirable or to the Germans that further rearmament on their part would be particularly dangerous.[80] In the same period, as a parallel to the encouragement of unofficial German-French contacts, efforts were made to spur friendship between German and British war veterans as one way of improving the atmosphere between the two countries.[81] This improving atmosphere, or at least efforts in that direction, together with British eagerness to secure some sort of agreement eventually led to the Anglo-German naval agreement of 1935; but in the spring of 1934 few would have been so bold as to predict such an event.

79. On the Saar question in 1933–34 see *G. D.*, C, 1, Nos. 80, 169, 203, 207, 227, 235, 236, 240, 248, 423, 452, 482; 2, Nos. 94, 96, 114, 170, 185, 207, 223, 224, 249, 274, 303, 304, 397, 400, 428, 436, 442, 450, 470, 474, 475, 477, 481, 500; *B. D.*, 2d, 5, No. 490; 6, Nos. 182, 192, 426; U. S. 1934, 1:17; *D. D. F.*, 1st, 2, No. 287. A British Foreign Office memorandum summarizing the situation as of 27 November 1933 is in Foreign Office C 10451/2251/18.

On the German united front organization in the Saar, the *Deutsche Front,* see Institut für Zeitgeschichte, *Gutachten,* 1:403–04; on German propaganda directed to the Saar population see Pohle, pp. 408–13; on the internal problems in the Saar see the report of 20 February 1934, Bundesarchiv, Brammer, Z.Sg. 101/27, f. 9–15; for an example of von Papen's ruthless methods in the Saar see the report and attached documents of Heinrich Drehmer of 20 June 1945, Nuremberg document 1540–PS (National Archives).

80. Eden, pp. 69–75.

81. Graham Wootton, *The Official History of the British Legion* (London: Macdonald & Evans, 1956), p. 169; Phipps (Berlin) dispatch 375, 5 April 1934, Foreign Office C 2294/2294/18. Lord Rothermere, who was to play an influential part in British-German relations, also made his first overtures in 1934; see the draft of a letter from Hitler to Rothermere, 2 March 1934, T–120, 1802/3707/036560–562. For other early unofficial contacts to influence British opinion, see also Rosenberg, *Tagebuch,* pp. 28–29; Phipps telegram 88, 4 March 1934, Foreign Office W 2201/1/98; Dodd, *Diary,* pp. 40–41, 27–29 September 1933; and a seven-page untitled memorandum in the Messersmith papers, beginning with the phrase "The years that I spent in Germany after Hitler came into power . . ."

On the day after the last French memorandum on disarmament, 17 April 1934, Joachim von Ribbentrop was officially appointed by Hitler to the post of disarmament commissioner.[82] Hitler's decision to make this appointment at precisely this time cannot yet be explained, but the fact that questions had been raised about von Ribbentrop's status in his earlier travels to Britain and France must have suggested that something needed to be done; and the changed situation in the disarmament negotiations may have provided the occasion. With his formal appointment to this position, von Ribbentrop took a major step on the road to prominence in world diplomacy. An ambitious man, capable of great perseverance but little insight, von Ribbentrop must have seemed to Hitler the perfect embodiment of the kind of diplomat he needed. Von Ribbentrop's travels as a champagne salesman, his social contacts in Germany as a liquor importer, and the knowledge of foreign languages that went with these roles made him stand out in the National Socialist hierarchy. No old fighter for the party's causes, he had joined the National Socialist movement only in the 1930s, played a part in the intrigues that led to Hitler's appointment as chancellor, and quickly became close to Hitler whose every wish was his command—in part because he started with no foreign policy concepts of his own. Von Ribbentrop did eventually develop ideas and initiative in certain areas, especially in regard to German policy in the Far East; but for the most part he endeavored to find out what Hitler wanted and then confirmed the opinion of his master. His view of diplomacy was as primitive as Hitler's; the suggestion that the way to make Winston Churchill more friendly to Germany was to give him a substantial bribe reflects accurately the approach of both.[83] Von Ribbentrop's first major diplomatic mission for Hitler—to try for an adjournment of the disarmament conference—was a failure, but this in no way affected his standing.[84] His feuding with the German foreign ministry automatically endeared him to Hitler: failures could be attributed to foreign ministry sabotage, while success showed his superior abilities in overcoming all obstacles.

In order to carry forward his diplomatic efforts, von Ribbentrop had organized and now expanded a kind of foreign ministry of his own, the *Dienststelle Ribbentrop* or Ribbentrop office, staffed by ambitious young men who thought that they had found a back door into the realm of high-level diplomacy. This agency, an additional rival for the foreign ministry, was used by von Ribbentrop for both official diplomatic tasks assigned to

82. The appointment was announced publicly on 24 April; on this, see *G. D.*, C, 2, No. 405; *B. D.*, 2d, 6, No. 406; Dertinger's "Informationsbericht vom 24. April 1934, Die Ernennung des Herrn von Ribbentrop," Bundesarchiv, Brammer, Z.Sg. 101/27, f. 107–111.

83. Von Ribbentrop, "Notiz für den Führer," 29 October 1935, Nuremberg document 1169–PS (National Archives). This item is apparently from the Adjutantur des Führers, requesting the allocation of foreign exchange for this and similar purposes.

84. *G. D.*, C, 2, Nos. 443, 456; 3, No. 94; *B. D.*, 2d, 6, No. 421; Long dispatch 552 of 25 May 1934, State 500. A 15 A 4/2549.

him and for such semiofficial contacts as the German-French friendship societies by which the Third Reich manipulated sentiment for international reconciliation for its own purposes. The foreign ministry observed the growth of this competitor with a combination of alarm and disdain; a career foreign service officer was assigned to von Ribbentrop to keep an eye on his activities, and the hope was that, like Rosenberg, von Ribbentrop would soon discredit himself.[85] At the beginning, however, von Ribbentrop's appointment merely puzzled and intrigued the outside world. Even Stanley Baldwin, not generally greatly interested in such matters, expressed some concern. When his friend Thomas Jones complained about the pro-French attitude of the British Foreign Office on 28 April 1934, a few days after von Ribbentrop's appointment, Baldwin replied: "We don't know what Germany really intends. We do know and have long known that France is pacific. . . . We cannot say that about Germany."[86]

The part of German rearmament that was beginning to worry the British government was the growth of its air force. It may be argued retrospectively that this concern was slightly late and did not lead to a reaction commensurate with the danger, but the evidence shows that in London the meaning of German air power for the island kingdom was at least understood.[87] There was even better reason for this than almost anyone in the British capital realized. The German air force in 1934 embarked on a great construction program, initially for a goal of 4,000 planes, and in the same year began a program of secret military air reconnaissance over other countries.[88] At the same time, German rearmament in other categories was also moving forward. The navy, already above the strength allowed by the peace treaty, started a major expansion plan for the period April 1934 through March 1936.[89] In June 1934, Hitler and Admiral Erich Raeder, the com-

85. A full-length study of von Ribbentrop and his special office remains to be written. The most recent treatment is in Jacobsen, pp. 252–318. A good introduction is Paul Seabury, *The Wilhelmstrasse* (Berkeley: University of California Press, 1954), pp. 46–53. There are thoughtful comments on von Ribbentrop in Walter Petwaidic, *Die autoritäre Anarchie* (Hamburg: Hoffman und Campe, 1946), pp. 71–75. Of interest, though not always accurate, are the memoirs of the foreign ministry official assigned to von Ribbentrop, Erich Kordt, *Nicht aus den Akten* (Stuttgart: Union Deutsche Verlags-Gesellschaft, 1950), and of two former members of the *Dienststelle Ribbentrop,* Otto Abetz (see n. 75) and Bruno Peter Kleist, *Zwischen Hitler und Stalin* (Bonn: Athenäum, 1950). There is an interesting description by Alfred Leitgen in the Institut für Zeitgeschichte, Z.S. 262.

86. Thomas Jones, *A Diary with Letters 1931–1950* (London: Oxford, 1954), p. 129.

87. *B. D.,* 2d, 6, Nos. 308, 309, 311, 313. The German military attaché in London, General Geyr von Schweppenburg, was aware of this relation between British policy toward Germany and German air rearmament; see his reports for 1934–35 in T–120, 2673/5576/passim. The notes of various British Foreign Office officials on an air ministry assessment of German air strength of 6 June 1934 are most interesting (Foreign Office C 3511/31/18). The British Air Ministry continued to underestimate Germany for years (C 3228/55/18).

88. *G. D.,* C, 3:1125. Information on the special reconnaisance squadron of Colonel Rowehl is provided by Rudolf Holzhausen, 14 and 15 May 1955, Institut für Zeitgeschichte, Z.S. 595, p. 2.

89. *TMWC,* 35:583; ibid., 34:519–25.

mander-in-chief of the German navy, discussed the new warships, including a series of submarines, that Germany was building in violation of the peace treaty and agreed that the fleet—originally planned mainly with France and Poland in mind—would eventually have to be developed for use against England.[90] Thus, although the actual build-up of the German navy in the early years of the National Socialist regime was primarily directed toward a struggle for the oceanic supply routes across the North Atlantic in a war with France, the possibility of war with England was already being considered although it did not dominate German naval planning until early in 1938.[91]

These discussions about building up the German navy, in turn, emphasized heavily the need to safeguard Germany's own trade routes, especially for the import of iron ore from Sweden. Nor was this the only field in which the economic needs of a future war played an important part in the rearmament program in late 1933 and 1934. Germany's military effort would require great quantities of petroleum products, then almost entirely imported. By December 1933 the government had come to an agreement with the great chemical trust, I. G. Farben, assuring it of a market for synthetic gasoline. Since this product could not yet be produced at competitive prices, government subsidy was required for any application of the technical processes that had been invented in earlier years.[92] While this program was in its infancy, the German government began efforts to force foreign oil companies to maintain vast quantities of petroleum products in storage inside Germany, a project in which Werner Daitz of the APA and the oil magnate Sir Henry Deterding played active roles.[93] Hitler's own ideas about the Western Hemisphere were influenced by his interest in Mexico's oil resources,[94] but that vision looked to the distant future. In the hard present, the economic policies advocated by many National Socialists that have sometimes been referred to as "middle-class socialism" such as de-urbanization and the break-up of the large department stores, conflicted with the economic needs of rearmament; and the summer of 1934 would see the triumph of the latter needs over the remnants of the former.[95]

90. Ibid., 34:775. See also Raeder's note on his talk with Hitler on 2 November 1934, ibid., pp. 775–76.

91. A pioneering work on this subject, rigorously demolishing the apologetic distortions of much of the postwar German literature on the basis of careful research, is Carl-Axel Gemzell, *Raeder, Hitler und Skandinavien, Der Kampf für einen maritimen Operationsplan* (Lund: Gleerup, 1965). For the early 1930s see especially chap. 3. On the new financial requirements of the naval program see the report on the Hitler-Raeder talk of early August 1934 in *TMWC,* 35:592.

92. Bracher, *Machtergreifung,* pp. 819–20; see also chap. 13, below.

93. See Rosenberg, *Tagebuch,* pp. 163–67; U. S. 1934, 2:320ff.; Werner Daitz, "Aktennotiz für Herrn Reichsleiter Rosenberg, Erdöleinlagerung," 1 November 1934, Nuremberg document 1356–PS (National Archives).

94. Rauschning, *Voice of Destruction,* pp. 65–67.

95. This point is amply documented in Schweitzer, *Big Business in the Third Reich,* chaps. 4 and 5.

The main focus of German effort, naturally, was on the growth of its army. The new commander-in-chief and the chief of staff, Generals von Fritsch and Beck, worked hard to create a strong and well-trained force. If Beck had reservations about the speed at which Hitler and some military men wanted to move in the spring of 1934, there can be no doubt that these were as yet differences in detail rather than in principle.[96] Hitler was not yet interfering in the details of military administration; he merely told his generals to build up the largest and best army possible in the least amount of time, provided the means, and periodically urged greater speed. He also told them at the end of February 1934 that this army should be ready for a defensive war in five years and an offensive war in eight years, and that he planned to strike first in the West and subsequently in the East—precisely as he had once written in *Mein Kampf*.[97]

A more immediately pressing subject discussed in such conferences was the growing tension between the German army and the SA. Hitler needed the army as the nucleus of his military might; for the time being he still needed the SA to bluff the outside world, in spite of his own assessment that their military value was exceedingly small. For a while, he tried to keep the two groups in uneasy cooperation, restricting the exuberance of Ernst Röhm's Brownshirts where necessary in order to avoid excessive complications in international affairs.[98] While the SA was still dreaming of submerging the army in a brown flood, the military were pushing for the early announcement of a conscription system that Hitler had promised in February 1933 and that would give them full control of Germany's huge new military establishment. The conscription law was drafted and discussed in the summer of 1934, but its official adoption was postponed temporarily and was postponed yet again in the fall.[99] Ironically, these postponements were due to the horror aroused in the world by the large-scale murders during the purge on 30 June and by the killing of Dollfuss in the following month; but these events, together with the death of Hindenburg and Hitler's assumption of the presidency, put the final touch on the consolidation of National Socialist rule in Germany and the end of any threat to the army from the SA. The army, having provided the weapons for the murders, was now called by its leader, General Werner von Blomberg, to stand loyally

96. Compare Beck's memorandum of 20 May 1934, in Foerster, pp. 22–23, with the record of the National Defence Council Working Committee meeting chaired by Beck on 23 and 24 January 1934, in *TMWC,* 36:381–404.

97. On the conferences of 27 and 28 February 1934 see the analysis in Bracher, pp. 749–50, 804; Liebmann Notes, Institut für Zeitgeschichte, ED 1, pp. 54, 61. The authenticity of the key source is discussed in Bracher, p. 749, n. 14.

98. Ibid.; see also *TMWC*, 36:72–73; Blomberg to Hitler, 2 March 1934, and Röhm circular, "G 312/34," of 6 March 1934, Nuremberg document 846–PS (National Archives); *B. D.*, 2d, 6, No. 244.

99. See von Bülow to Beck, 18 June 1934, T–120, 2776/4603/E 192992–993; Memorandum by von Bülow, 8 August 1934, 909/1574/381317; Liebmann Notes on Fritsch's talk of 9 October 1934, Institut für Zeitgeschichte, ED 1, p. 74; *G. D.*, C, 3, Nos. 105, 165, n. 3, 126.

by its master.[100] The build-up of Germany's military forces could proceed apace, and the reintroduction of conscription would come in due time. The purge cleared the way for rearmament along the lines Hitler and his military advisers thought most effective at home, as the end of disarmament conversations had removed the possibility of newly imposed restrictions from abroad.

100. Blomberg's comments on 9 October 1934, Liebmann Notes, Institut für Zeitgeschichte, ED 1, p. 70. On the Röhm purge see Bracher, pp. 934ff.

8 Germany and the European Powers from the Proposed Eastern Pact to the Announcement of Conscription

hile Germany rearmed more intensively in the months following its departure from the League, the European diplomatic picture was rearranged in response to its moves. The German-Polish rapprochement was greeted by the British government with genuine pleasure because it appeared to remove from the international scene one controversial problem fraught with dangerous possibilities.[1] The French government, on the other hand, was concerned about the apparent unreliability of its ally in the East. Relief over the lessened danger of war mingled with doubts about the future policy of Poland and an increasing interest in the Soviet Union as a counterweight to Germany.[2] The Poles themselves wanted to make certain that their new relationship with Germany did not upset their delicately balanced policy between their two great neighbors. With suitable explanations to Berlin, the Polish foreign minister, Josef Beck, visited Moscow in February 1934 to maintain a semblance of good relations.[3] Germany's own relations with the Soviet Union, however, continued to deteriorate in spite of gestures from the Russian side and the urgings of some German diplomats.

After Germany left the League, it looked for a short time as if its relations with the Soviet Union might at least be kept from growing worse. The dispute over press relations that had grown out of incidents connected with the Reichstag fire trial was ended in late October 1933.[4] Starting about this time, Moscow began

1. *B. D.*, 2d, 6, Nos. 233, 237, 253.

2. Ibid., Nos. 167, 227.

3. Roos, pp. 136–39; *G. D.*, C, 2, Nos. 244, 275; "Informationsbericht Nr. 35 vom 13. Februar 1934," Bundesarchiv, Sammlung Brammer, Z.Sg. 101/27, f. 3.

4. Niclauss, pp. 146–48; *G. D.*, C, 2, Nos. 21, 25, 30, 34.

to hint to German diplomats that better relations were desired. The evidence suggests that many Soviet leaders were reluctant to leave the traditional policy of cooperation with Germany and to align themselves instead with France and the League. Certainly the military leaders of the Soviet Union were dubious of such a shift; and some of the political leaders were not yet convinced that the turn toward collective security that came to be advocated by Maxim Litvinov, the People's Commissar for Foreign Affairs, was either wise or safe. Perhaps the hope of securing a better bargain from the prospective ally played a part in the proceedings; the similarity to the situation in 1939 is most striking. In each instance, the Soviet government appeared to look back to past associates while preparing to sign with new friends—unless confronted with a really attractive offer. In both cases, the danger from Japan in the Far East made for Russian caution in Europe.[5] What was German policy in the face of these approaches?

The new German ambassador to the Soviet Union, Rudolf Nadolny, was a strong advocate of close German-Russian relations. His instructions, approved by Hitler personally, seemed inclined to a positive policy. They called for restoring a better atmosphere, redeveloping friendly relations, preventing the Soviet Union from joining any anti-German grouping, and maintaining good economic relations.[6] From the beginning of his stay in Moscow, however, Nadolny found his own government unwilling to respond to suggestions for steps to implement a policy along these lines. On the contrary, the two governments appeared to be drifting further apart.[7] The Germans, not surprisingly, were upset by the indications that the Soviet government was leaning toward an agreement with France but for some time could not bring themselves to look upon this as a serious contingency.[8] In his speech to the Reichstag on 31 January 1934, Hitler made a conciliatory reference to the Soviet Union, and Germany, as has been shown,[9] waved off any approaches from Japan to avoid feeding any Soviet apprehension of a German-Japanese alliance; but Hitler was clearly not prepared to go any further in approaches or offers. The agreement with Poland gave him the free hand he wanted, and all the urgings of Nadolny could not budge him.[10] He wanted no close relations with Russia and re-

5. On the Soviet soundings of this period, and the enthusiastic interpretations placed on them by German diplomats who themselves preferred a policy of alignment with Russia, see *G. D.*, C, 2, Nos. 24, 44, 47, 53, 130; Hartmann (German military attaché Moscow) report 167/33 of 7 November 1933, T–120, 2760/5892/E 432735–739.

6. *G. D.*, C, 2, No. 66.

7. Ibid., Nos. 75, 118, 119, 122, 127.

8. See U. S. 1933, 1:347–48 (von Neurath's memorandum on this talk, RM 1747, T–120, 2383/4619/E 197856, is very abbreviated); U. S. 1933, 2:830–31; *G. D.*, C, 2, Nos. 147, 148, 150, 161, 163, 165.

9. See above, pp. 128f.

10. It is obvious from Nadolny's careful analysis of the situation of the Soviet Union and of German-Russian relations that he was thinking of a policy looking toward a revision of the Versailles settlement, in contrast to Hitler's aim of *Lebensraum* in the

jected all proposals from either Nadolny or the Soviet government pointing in that direction.

The deterioration in German-Soviet relations had reached a point where a major new step to bring them together again was necessary to prevent the Soviet Union from turning elsewhere. Hitler rejected the new step and thus encouraged the Soviet search for a new ally. In this he had the support of von Neurath whose hostility to Nadolny as a person as well as to the policies he advocated was unchanged. As one student of the subject has pointed out, the foreign minister who had been placed in the cabinet especially to maintain the continuity of German foreign policy himself shifted to the new line.[11] Nadolny, who had long wanted to become foreign minister, left the diplomatic service when his advice was undermined by von Neurath and rejected by Hitler.[12] New ambassadors soon represented the two countries to each other, their relationship correct but without the closeness of prior years.[13]

The deterioration of German-Soviet political relations, however, was not allowed to interfere with the continuation of satisfactory economic ties. The changing economy of the Soviet Union after the First Five-Year Plan somewhat altered the details of the picture, especially in reducing Soviet imports, but the German-Soviet trade and credit protocol of 20 March 1934 provided for the smooth functioning of economic relations. The year 1934 was one in which the Soviet Union repaid a very large proportion of its outstanding debts to Germany, and these repayments substantially bolstered Germany's slim resources of foreign exchange.[14] As in all economic dealings between Germany and Russia, there were occasional specific points

---

East. Thus Nadolny dismisses as absurd all Soviet fears of a German offer to Poland that would exchange the Polish Corridor for the Ukraine after a successful joint war of Germany and Poland against Russia (*G. D.*, C, 2, No. 171). As will appear, this was almost precisely what Hitler was thinking about early in 1934 and what he had Göring propose to Poland early in 1935.

11. Niclauss, p. 169.

12. On the German decision not to make any agreement with Russia and the departure of Nadolny see *G. D.*, C, 2, Nos. 173, 176, 181, 191, 187, 190, 210, 227, 240, 251, 362, 364, 375, 382, 390, 391, 396, 398, 401, 414, 424, 447, 476, 488; Nadolny telegram 89 of 15 January 1934, T–120, 2791/6025/H 046583–584; Nadolny, *Mein Beitrag*, pp. 166–68.

On Nadolny's interest in becoming foreign minister see Aloisi, *Journal*, 13 March 1933, pp. 90–91, and 29 April 1933, pp. 117–18.

For Litvinov's comment on Nadolny's role in the negotiations see his statement to Anthony Eden on 28 March 1935, in Eden's *Facing the Dictators*, p. 164.

13. *G. D.*, C, 3, Nos. 265, 270, 271 (a note in the last document cited the pointed remark of von Bülow that "we feel that our Embassy in Moscow is now in good hands"). See also Niclauss, pp. 175–76.

14. *G. D.*, C, 2, Nos. 342, 433, 476, n. 7; Niclauss, p. 167; U. S., Soviet Union 1933–1939, p. 84; Bullitt dispatch 30 of 20 April 1934, State 861.51–German credits/44. An excellent review of German-Soviet trade in 1934 by U. S. Vice-Consul Fox in Berlin was sent by Geist (U. S. consul) on 19 August 1935, with his dispatch 515, State 661.6231/160.

of difference, but the evidence does not support the hypothesis that these were of political origin.[15]

The specific Soviet proposal for an agreement with Germany that had occasioned the final argument between Hitler and Nadolny in May 1934 had been a project for a joint protocol on the independence of the Baltic states. It would have provided an assurance of security in Eastern Europe for the Soviet Union, and since Russia could not secure it from Germany, it turned to France. The French government was interested in an agreement with Russia and, partly under pressure from Britain, discussed first what generally came to be known as an Eastern Locarno. This proposal, considered in various forms in 1934 and 1935, was a mutual security pact between France and the countries of Eastern Europe, which Germany would be invited to join. The special project of the French foreign minister, Louis Barthou, it was designed as a multilateral mutual-assistance pact to assure peace in Eastern Europe. It assumed the entrance of the Soviet Union into the League of Nations and gave Germany the alternative of tying its own hands against aggressive moves or for all practical purposes isolating itself in the face of a hostile coalition.[16] Germany could join a new multilateral system—and perhaps rejoin the League as well—have its rearmament recognized by France, and be protected against attack from any neighbor; but the price was the renunciation of aggressive moves unless it were prepared to face a group of powers pledged to assist each other. Germany's answer to this was definitely negative, and it continued to be negative through a lengthy series of negotiations, even though Berlin recognized that its refusal would lead to a mutual assistance treaty between France and the Soviet Union.[17] In some respects this outcome looked like an advantage to Hitler: it compromised the French government both internally and externally in the eyes of those hostile to Soviet Russia.[18]

15. U. S., Soviet Union 1933–1939, p. 126; *G. D.*, C, 3, Nos. 181, 359; Memorandum of von Bülow, 22 October 1934, T–120, 2372/4602/E 189817–818.

16. *B. D.*, 2d, 6, Nos. 428, 450, 457, 459, 460, 454, 455, 461, 465, 468, 472, 487–97, 499–501, 504, 510, 512, 515, 516, 523; *G. D.*, C, 2, Nos. 458, 486, 491, 502–505; 3, Nos. 1, 84–88, 92, 93, 95, 101–104, 106; U. S. 1934, 1:489, 117–18, 496–97; Niclauss, pp. 171–80; Parliamentary (Command) Papers: Cmd. 5143, *Correspondence showing the course of certain Diplomatic Discussions directed towards securing an European Settlement, June 1934 to March 1936,* Miscellaneous No. 3 (1936) (London: H. M. Stationery Office, 1936) (hereafter cited as Cmd. 5143), No. 2. Documents on these negotiations from Soviet archives may be found cited in M. Andreyeva and L. Vidyasova (eds.), "The Struggle of the U.S.S.R. for Collective Security in Europe during 1933–1935," *International Affairs* (Moscow), 9, Nos. 6, 7, 8, and 10 (June, July, Aug. and Oct., 1963). British Foreign Office memoranda of 17 October 1934 (C 6916/247/18) and 19 December 1934 (C 8797/247/18) are also very useful.

17. *G. D.*, C, 3, Nos. 11, 51, 57, 61, 74. There is a short but revealing summary of German tactics in von Bülow's letter to Köster of 28 July 1934 (T–120, 3401/8760/E 610917).

18. Rosenberg, *Tagebuch,* 8 June 1934, p. 38. Soviet entrance into the League would also provide the Germans with an additional excuse for staying out (Wilson [Geneva] telegram 916 of 30 June 1934, State 500.C 001/972).

Unwillingness to be associated with the Soviet Union itself and the benefits to be derived from having others associated with Russia instead were not the only reasons for Germany's unwillingness to participate in any form of Eastern Locarno. The opposition of the German regime to all multilateral commitments, especially when they involved promises of mutual assistance, was doubtless the most important one. There was, furthermore, the danger that any Eastern Locarno, in the process of providing international legal recognition of German rearmament, would set some fixed limits to that rearmament. Having already surpassed in actual rearmament the levels of military strength it had demanded in earlier negotiations, the German government was unwilling to accept limitations that would immediately force either a reduction in its military strength or an obvious public breach of a treaty that provided for mutual assistance among its adherents in case of violations.[19] Behind the final rejection of any new treaty commitment, decided in late August and announced in early September 1934, was one other supporting factor.[20] Germany believed that it could risk the seeming isolation in which rejection of the Eastern Pact would place it in part because Poland would also reject the proposal.

The Polish government was displeased by the Franco-Soviet rapprochement, even though it had contributed to it by drawing closer to Germany. Warsaw was unwilling to undertake any obligations to help its neighbors militarily or to accept the help of any of them against another. Poland's policy precluded both aiding another power against either Germany or Russia and accepting military aid from one of them against the other. Furthermore, Poland was quite uninterested in aiding either Czechoslovakia or Lithuania against anyone—it had territorial claims against the former and a long-standing quarrel with the latter. Temporarily secure in its agreement with Germany, Poland was no more interested in accepting the commitments of an Eastern Pact than was Germany, and the two powers repeatedly reassured each other of their negative attitude toward the whole concept.[21] Whatever modifications in the pact were proposed, Germany and Poland continued to oppose it and to work out arguments that would avert from either blame for the failure of the negotiations.[22] The strongest efforts of the French government failed to move Pilsudski and Beck. In April 1934, Barthou visited Warsaw to sound out the Polish leaders, and during the following months he vainly tried other ways to secure Polish support for a

19. This dilemma is well defined in von Bülow's letters to von Neurath of 23 July and 16 August 1934 (*G. D.,* C, 3, Nos. 109, 162).

20. On the German decision see *G. D.,* C, 3, Nos. 164, 188, 190, 191, 200, 201, and pp. 376 and 382.

21. *G. D.*, C, 2, No. 465; 3, Nos. 45, 77, n. 7, 92, 139, 177, 184, 194, 226, 379; Memorandum of von Neurath RM 817 of 13 July 1934, T–120, 1431/2945/D 575938; B. D., 2d, 6, Nos. 479, 484, 503, 519, 520, 534, 549, 564; *Lipski Papers,* Nos. 27–32, 34, 36–38.

22. *G. D.,* C, 3, No. 392.

pact.[23] After Barthou's assassination in October 1934, Pierre Laval, the new French foreign minister, made a final effort to attract Poland as well as Germany by further concessions but without success.[24]

It was not that the Poles had illusions about German aims; in November, Polish ambassador Lipski told William Dodd, the American ambassador in Berlin, that Germany intended "to re-annex Alsace-Lorraine and large parts of Poland as well as Austria and Czechoslovakia."[25] If the moment of German aggression ever did come, Poland would fight and call on its French ally; but in 1934 as in 1939 Poland was reluctant to do anything that might provoke this contingency, including forming an alliance with Russia, a country that had no greater and no lesser interest in Poland's territorial integrity than did Germany.

The outcome of these lengthy negotiations was one that had been long anticipated in the capitals of Europe. In December 1934, France and Soviet Russia signed an agreement, which Czechoslovakia joined, while Germany and Poland stood aside.[26] The import of this new development in international affairs and the related questions of French, British, and Italian policy toward Germany need to be examined, but first the relationship between Germany and Poland, which had contributed so much to the failure of the negotiations, must be scrutinized in greater detail.

Although the public posture of the two countries hitherto hostile but now reconciled was the aspect of German-Polish relations most important for European diplomacy in the mid-1930s, a closer look should also be taken at specific issues concerning the German-Polish relationship during those years. Such an examination will illuminate both the "calming" effect of their pact and the continuing difficulties that loomed in the background. The handling of these difficulties, in turn, sheds some light on the long-term policies of both powers.

In addition to the very obvious sign of a reduction of tension and joint opposition to the pact, there were other indications of a better atmosphere between Germany and Poland. Beyond mutual expressions of pleasure over the conclusion of their agreement in January 1934, and the attendant publicity that ensued, there was concrete progress in those public statements of loyalty that replaced earlier expressions of hostility and recrimination.[27] German newspapers and radio stations ceased attacking Poland, and the tone of the official Polish press changed drastically. Efforts were made to give the public in each country a more favorable image of the other and to

23. *G. D.*, C, 2, Nos. 423, 465, n. 1; 3, Nos. 5, 77; *B. D.*, 2d, 6, Nos. 413, 418, 421, 558, 559; Szembek, pp. 3–7.

24. See Scott, pp. 209–10.

25. Dodd, *Diary*, 17 November 1934, p. 192.

26. U. S. 1934, 1:523–24; *G. D.*, C, 3, No. 382.

27. *G. D.*, C, 2, Nos. 226, 230, 234, 244, n. 1; "Bestellungen aus der Pressekonferenz v. 17. 3. 34," Bundesarchiv, Brammer, Z.Sg. 101/3, f. 128; *Lipski Papers*, No. 51.

restrain in this manner the skepticism toward the new policy retained by many on both sides of the border. After preliminary soundings in May, Goebbels reciprocated the visit of some Polish journalists by going to Warsaw in mid-June for satisfactory talks with Pilsudski and Beck.[28] One practical result of this trip was the German-Polish radio agreement of 13 October 1934 and the resulting attempts to improve mutual understanding by friendly and informative broadcasts about each country.[29]

The economic sphere was another area in which concrete steps were taken to cement the new relationship. The treaty ending the trade and tariff war was followed by talks between German and Polish agricultural representatives, a series of negotiations in the summer of 1934, and eventually a supplementary trade and compensation agreement in the fall.[30] The development of German-Polish economic relations, however, was by no means perfectly smooth. The payments owed by Germany to Poland for railway traffic across the Polish Corridor were increasingly in arrears, and a serious dispute soon arose, eventually threatening to lead to political complications in late 1935 after the subject had been included in the purview of new trade negotiations.[31] Hitler had to insist on concessions to Poland in order to obtain a new agreement on 4 November 1935,[32] but the dispute over German arrears in railway payments dragged on into 1936, primarily because Germany preferred to use its foreign exchange for other purposes.[33]

28. *G. D.*, C, 2, No. 485; 4:1226–27; Memorandum by Meyer, 7 May 1934, T–120, 2906/6174/E 463044; Meyer to Moltke, 12 May 1934, ibid., frames E 463047–048; Cudahy dispatch 312 of 14 June 1934, State 760c.62/234.

There was also a proposal for von Ribbentrop to see Beck and Pilsudski in the summer of 1934, but this was postponed because of the latter's bad health (Moltke to von Ribbentrop, 31 July 1934, T–120, 2387/4620/E 200742). Von Ribbentrop eventually made a nonpolitical visit to Poland in October 1935 (Nielsen [U. S. chargé a.i. Warsaw] dispatch 863 of 8 October 1935, State 033.6260c/1). Later that year, Hans Frank made his first visit to Poland in connection with his work in the Academy for Germanic Law (Szembek, 10 December 1935, p. 139; Frank, pp. 400–01).

29. Pohle, *Der Rundfunk als Instrument der Politik,* pp. 397–98.

30. *G. D.,* C, 2, No. 431; "Sitzung des Handelspolitischen Ausschusses vom 30. April 1934," ". . . vom 24. Mai 1934," ". . . vom 4. Juni 1934," T–120, 2612/5650/H 003874, 890, 893; Rosenberg, *Tagebuch,* 13 July 1934, p. 42; Crosby (Warsaw) dispatch 384 of 14 August 1934, Jefferson Patterson (U. S. consul Breslau) dispatch 4 of 5 November 1934, and Cudahy dispatch 651 of 28 March 1935, State 660c.6231/221, 227, and 232.

31. The difficulties can be traced in *G. D.,* C, 3, Nos. 419, 487, 561; 4, Nos. 53, 192, 204, 217, 271, 301, 302, 390, 392, 409, 436, 455; Szembek, 26 October 1935, p. 123, 28 October, pp. 123–24, 22 November, pp. 133–34; *Lipski Papers,* No. 50; "Sitzung des Handelspolitischen Ausschusses vom 6. April 1935," ". . . vom 13. Juli 1935," ". . . vom 18. Juli 1935," ". . . vom 22. August 1935," T–120, 2612/5650/H 004014–015, 029–030, 036–040.

32. *G. D.,* C, 4, No. 390.

33. For the later stages of the Corridor railway payments issue, settled through the intervention of Hitler and Göring, see *G. D.,* C, 4, Nos. 470, 474, 521, 528, 537, 551, 567; 5, Nos. 22, 62, 82, 107, 151, 261, 264; Szembek, 13 December 1935, pp. 140–41, 8 January 1936, pp. 148–49, 25 January, p. 155, 10 February (?), p. 159; *Lipski Papers,* Nos. 52, 54, 56, pp. 248–50; Cudahy dispatch 989 of 30 January 1936, State 760c.62/310; U. S. vice consul Berlin Adams report sent as dispatch 593 of 13

In the meantime, however, the two powers had repeatedly exchanged expressions of goodwill and elevated their respective ministers to the status of ambassadors.[34]

Such international pleasantries did not remove all the difficulties on the path to German-Polish cooperation. From its inception the new relationship could not obviate serious policy clashes in some sensitive areas. In 1933 and 1934, the efforts of Germany to preserve, and of Poland to restrict, German influence in the control and management of key industrial and mining facilities in those parts of Upper Silesia ceded to Poland after World War I led to continued friction. The lengthy German struggle against the polonization of I. G. Kattowitz-Laura enterprises need not be reviewed here, but it reveals much more than the tendency of such German industrialists as Fritz Thyssen and Friedrich Flick to place profit above all national considerations. This issue, rather, showed that where specific material interests were concerned any number of goodwill trips were unlikely to ease differences when neither side was prepared to make major concessions unless forced to do so by the circumstances of the situation.[35] The suggestion of the American minister to Poland, John Cudahy, that in this instance Polish actions reflected continued mistrust of Germany was at least partially correct.[36] As von Bülow noted of German subsidies to Prince Pless, one of the most important German landholders in Upper Silesia, Germany was supporting the prince in expectation of eventually regaining territory in Upper Silesia—and for no other purpose.[37] In the face of the determination of Michal Grazýnski, the Polish governor (*voivod*) of Silesia, to eliminate all German influence, the conflict was certain to continue. Under the cover of the German-Polish agreement, and in spite of German protests and the warnings of the Polish foreign ministry, Grazýnski moved forward with increasing effectiveness.[38] For the time being, Berlin was prepared to sacrifice interests in Upper Silesia to the political advantages of the agreement with Poland, but there was no guarantee that this would always be the case.

July 1936, State 660c.6231/264; Lipski to Schacht, 26 February 1936, T–120, 2621/5482/E 382288; von Moltke to Göring with inclosure, 3 April 1936, ibid., frames E 382283–287.

34. *G. D.*, C, 3, No. 256; *Lipski Papers*, No. 30 .

35. On this problem see *G. D.*, C, 1, Nos. 359, 473; 2, Nos. 41, 52, 209, 217, 331, 340, 352, 372; 3, No. 401; Memorandum of von Bülow, 2 September 1933, T–120, 2371/4601/E 188746–747; von Moltke telegram 16 of 12 February 1934, T–120, 2954/6213/E 469926; "Bestellungen a.d. Pressekonferenz v. 6.3.34," Bundesarchiv, Brammer, Z.Sg. 101/3, f. 105. Correspondence of the APA for 1933–34 on this dispute is in folder EAP 250–d–18–20/1, T–81, Roll 17, Serial 38.

36. Cudahy dispatch 242 of 11 April 1934, State 760c.6212/35. The United States government observed this whole question with particular care because of the involvement of American (Harriman) interests in Upper Silesian industry.

37. Memorandum by von Bülow, 25 January 1934, T–120, 2371/4601/E 188764–766; see also von Neurath's memorandum RM 1223 of 31 October 1934, T–120, 1431/2945/D 575957.

38. *G. D.*, C, 3, Nos. 496, 498; Szembek, 17–18 April 1935, pp. 61–64.

The nationality struggle in Upper Silesia represented only an especially acute portion of the wider possibilities for friction inherent in the presence of the German minority in Poland. Their fate had been a primary focus of German-Polish difficulties in the Weimar period. The German government had often used its position in the League of Nations to attempt to protect the rights of this minority by insisting that Poland respect the obligations it had assumed when granted the territory in which they lived. The departure of Germany from the League provided the Polish government with the long-sought opportunity to be rid of international responsibilities in this regard. Berlin, having deprived itself of a forum for protest in Geneva, and having decided to maintain good relations with Poland, could only observe the Polish moves with quiet regret and occasional, unsuccessful appeals to Polish goodwill.[39] Germany might still speak up for the German minority in Poland, but only in a most limited way.[40] The long-range interest of the Reich in this minority could be maintained only by unofficial means. From the German side, the key agency was the League of Germans for the East (*Bund Deutscher Osten*), under the leadership of Theodor Oberländer, who had been associated with the National Socialists since 1923. It publicized inside Germany the racial struggle along the Polish and Czechoslovakian borders and acted as an agent for the financial and moral support of the German minority in Poland.[41] Within Poland, a lengthy internal struggle led to the nazification of the larger part of the German minority, although the group continued to be divided into separate organizations that feuded with each other and maintained contacts with rival agencies in Germany.[42] In this field, too, conflict between Germany and Poland was postponed rather than resolved.

The situation in Danzig, which had helped pave the way for the rapprochement between Germany and Poland, was troubled in many ways in 1934 and 1935, but neither nation allowed the complications in Danzig to disturb the maintenance of their new relationship. The problem of German financial support to maintain the budget of the free city so that it would not have to turn for help to Poland remained a constant worry for Berlin, especially be-

39. *German White Book,* No. 40; *G. D.,* C, 3, Nos. 8, 197, 210, 313, 325, 339; Szembek, 24 April 1935, pp. 66–67, 20 July 1935, p. 108. For a somewhat more optimistic report see "Informationsbericht 13," of 7 November 1934, Bundesarchiv, Brammer, Z.Sg. 101/27, f. 435–37. A useful summary is in Roos, pp. 170–74; see also Margarete Gärtner, *Botschafterin des guten Willens* (Bonn: Athenäum, 1955), pp. 274–75.

40. Von Moltke report 1046 of 16 October 1934, T–120, 2907/6177/E 464087–095.

41. Most interesting are two reports on a briefing given some German journalists by Oberländer in early March 1935. One account is in "Informationsbericht 31," of 7 March 1935, in Bundesarchiv, Brammer, Z.Sg. 101/28, f. 85–91; the other is in a letter by Kurt Metzger of 8 March 1935, in Bundesarchiv, Traub, Z.Sg. 110/1, f. 22–25. See also Jacobsen, pp. 69, 169.

42. See Institut für Zeitgeschichte *Gutachten,* 1:404–07; Jacobsen, pp. 580–97. The accounts in Breyer and in Theodor Bierschenk, *Die deutsche Volksgruppe in Polen* (Kitzingen: Holzner, 1954), are exceedingly apologetic in tone, the latter even more than the former. For the problem of German agencies' contacts with the organizations in Poland see *G. D.,* C, 4, No. 35.

cause of the great quantity of foreign exchange required for the process. On each occasion when the situation became acute, Hitler insisted that the essential minimum of foreign exchange be transferred in order to avoid forcing Danzig into concessions to Poland that would threaten its German character. Clearly he wanted a holding operation on the economic front.[43] This operation was aided slightly by the functioning of Rauschning's policy toward Poland. There was still occasional economic friction, but as long as a real will for cooperation reinforced the economic needs of both Danzig and Poland, some progress could be made. Both the atmosphere and the level of economic activity between Danzig and Poland improved.[44]

The improvement of Danzig-Polish relations was threatened from two sides, however. The Polish government was quite willing to use the cover of the German-Polish agreement to push harder for its own interests in the free city in a manner similar to its course in the minorities question inside Poland. Such pressure, of course, produced irritation as the Danzig authorities resisted. More dramatic was the political development within the free city where the National Socialist leader Forster wanted to push rapidly forward the nazification of the state in violation of the Danzig constitution. He was willing to take grave risks in the economic sphere to build up political support for his party. Once the National Socialists secured full power through successful elections, they could keep any subsequent economic crisis from having political repercussions—there would be no more elections. Furthermore, Forster objected to Rauschning's basic aim of a real rapprochement with Poland. In all of these areas, Forster's position was closer to Hitler's views than Rauschning's. It is, therefore, understandable that although Hitler supported Rauschning until the new relationship with Poland was firmly established, he dropped Rauschning in the fall of 1934 when it became evident that further cooperation between Rauschning and Forster was impossible. Others might advise against such a step—the foreign ministry apparently did, and the army may have—but Hitler sensed that Forster was really his man, while Rauschning had views of his own.[45]

43. *G. D.*, C, 2, Nos. 22, 407, 441; 3, Nos. 40, 96, 192, 223, 224, 259, 262, 327; Radowitz (Danzig) to Meyer telegram 5 of 24 January 1934, T–120, 2787/6023/H 044563; Meyer to Radowitz telegram 9 of 28 May 1934, T–120, 2915/6203/E 468473; Ministerialrat Mayer, Treuhänder für Danzig im Reichsfinanzministerium, to various ministries, 18 October 1934, 2787/6023/H 044587–588; Memorandum of von Neurath RM 1239 of 3 November 1934, and Note by Falkenberg of 29 January 1935, 1468/3015/D 598324–325. The beginnings of financial support of Danzig by Berlin during the Weimar period are traced in Christoph M. Kimmich, *The Free City: Danzig and German Foreign Policy, 1919–1934* (New Haven: Yale University Press, 1968), chaps. 2 and 3.

44. Breyer, p. 94; Leonhardt, p. 67; *G. D.*, C, 2, No. 40; "Informationsbericht" of Dertinger on a confidential report by Rauschning to a press conference on 17 April 1934, in Bundesarchiv, Brammer, Z.Sg. 101/27, f. 69–75; Bruins (U. S. consul Danzig) dispatches 391 of 17 March 1934 and 512 of 29 October 1934, State 760c.60K/311 and 321.

45. On the Rauschning-Forster dispute and its denouement see *G. D.*, C, 2, No. 439; 3, Nos. 224, 236, 243, 244, 248, 249, 308, 329; Hermann Rauschning, *The Conservative Revolution* (New York: Putnam, 1941), pp. 14–30. On the army's concern see the

Forster's new course was to put forward Arthur Greiser as senate president instead of Rauschning, and immediately increased tension over the internal development of the free city. The Forster-Greiser regime hoped to use the subsidies from Germany and an exuberantly extravagant internal economic policy to gain support in new elections, but these efforts did not bring the desired result: the National Socialists failed to secure the two-thirds vote needed to amend the constitution. Under these circumstances, Forster's policy implied violation of the Danzig constitution with increasing frequency and gravity. Neither the Polish government nor the League was willing to take action to uphold the democratic institutions of Danzig. Poland would not act as long as purely Polish interests within the free city were respected; as for the rights of individual Germans, Warsaw did not care. The League of Nations as guarantor of the constitution, and the high commissioner as the League's local representative tried—with neither vigor nor success—to restrain the onslaught of the National Socialist party upon the freedom of the people of Danzig.[46]

The internal action of the Forster regime that promptly drew the attention of the Polish government was one of a series of measures taken by the Danzig authorities in the summer of 1935 when they were forced to devaluate the currency in the wake of their own extravagant policies.[47] Since Danzig's economic situation deteriorated rapidly in the spring and summer of 1935, Berlin was obliged to choose between allowing Danzig to turn to Poland for help—with a resulting increase in Polish influence—and combining further aid from Germany with stringent economies and controls inside Danzig.[48] The latter course was adopted, and of the steps taken in Danzig under the accompanying program of restrictions the foreign-exchange control law of 11 June immediately touched off a crisis in Danzig-Polish relations. Considering themselves injured by this measure, the Poles

---

documents apparently sent by the Army Area Headquarters in East Prussia (*Wehrkreiskommando* I) to Berlin, one a report on a talk with Rauschning on 12 October 1934, and the other a report on the situation in Danzig on 15 October 1934, initialed by von Blomberg, von Fritsch, and Beck, and with a marginal note by von Fritsch on the outcome of the dispute, in the Bundesarchiv Koblenz, Nachlass Gen.Obst. Beck, H 08–28/1, f. 46–53.

46. On this subject see the accounts in Leonhardt, passim., and Ernst Sodeikat, "Der Nationalsozialismus und die Danziger Opposition," *Vierteljahrshefte für Zeitgeschichte*, 14, No. 2 (April 1966), 139–74. Published documents include *G. D.*, C, 3, Nos. 202, 391, 485, 500; 4, Nos. 4, 80, 86.

Sean Lester, the League High Commissioner in Danzig from the fall of 1933 to 1936, was at first welcomed by the officials at Danzig (U. S. consul Danzig, Heisler dispatch 333 of 6 November 1933, State 860K.01–High Commissioner/13), but later became unpopular with them because of his insistence on respect for the constitution.

47. See the interrogation of Karl Schaefer of the Bank of Danzig by John Brown Mason, 14 September 1945 (Office of the Chief of Military History, Foreign Studies Branch).

48. *G. D.*, C, 4, Nos. 65, 92, 97, 103, 112, 123, 126, 130, 133, 134, 143, 150; Szembek, p. 93; Gallman (U. S. consul Danzig) dispatch 129 of 11 September 1935, State 760K.62/46.

answered with restrictions on Danzig's trade, and Danzig in turn opened the customs border to East Prussia. For a moment it looked as if the whole Danzig question would suddenly cause a major dispute between Poland and Germany.

It was correctly assumed in Warsaw that Hitler had been willing to have the Danzig government try the currency control scheme, but it was hard for the Poles to know how far Germany was prepared to go. They were willing to fight but hoped that Germany did not really want war.[49] They were alarmed by the fact that Schacht and the head of the eastern section of the German foreign ministry, Richard Meyer, both known for their intransigent attitude toward Poland, were in Danzig, presumably instructing the authorities of the free city on the tactics to follow. In view of Göring's earlier role in German-Polish relations and the affairs of Danzig, the Polish government approached him; and Göring in turn directed the Danzig authorities to be conciliatory.[50] At a meeting in Berlin between Hitler and Beck on 3 July, the two agreed that Danzig would not be allowed to affect the good relations between the two countries.[51] Because the crisis in Danzig-Polish relations nevertheless became more acute at the end of July, the sincerity of both Germany and Poland was really put to the test, a test aggravated by the desire of the National Socialist leadership in Danzig to use the situation to bring about annexation to Germany.[52]

At a conference in Danzig, the German state secretary, von Bülow, made it quite clear to the Danzig leaders that annexation to Germany was not yet possible. In order to annex Danzig, Germany would either have to fight—and for this it was not yet prepared—or give up its claims to the Polish Corridor—and this was out of the question. Danzig must, therefore, negotiate with Poland; and since the Poles were quite willing to talk, a settlement should be possible.[53] In spite of these instructions, the Danzig leaders moved forward ruthlessly until they were given unmistakable directives by Hitler and Göring to follow a conciliatory line; the abrupt change in policy produced agreement between Danzig and Poland on 9 August.[54]

Although lesser Polish officials as well as the National Socialist leaders in Danzig pushed forward recklessly, those at the top wished to avoid raising a basic political problem that could divide Germany and Poland. Once Hitler

49. Szembek, pp. 94–102.

50. *G. D.,* C, 4, No. 158; *Lipski Papers,* Nos. 46, 47; Szembek, p. 97.

51. *G. D.,* C, 4, No. 190; Nielsen (U. S. chargé a.i. Warsaw) dispatch 770 of 17 July 1935, State 760c.62/296.

52. *G. D.,* C, 4, Nos. 214, 215, 224, 226, 227; Szembek, 23 July 1935, p. 108.

53. *G. D.,* C, 4, No. 240. There is another, more detailed, memorandum on this meeting in Nuremberg document 3899–PS (National Archives). Roos (p. 186, n. 17, and elsewhere) refers to this document as coming from Schacht's files; I am of the opinion that it is from Göring's.

54. *G. D.,* C, 4, Nos. 240, 244, 245, 247, 250, 251, 254, 256; von Bülow to Lammers, 6 August 1935, T–120, 1468/3015/D 598332; Radowitz to von Bülow, 22 August 1935, 2387/4620/E 200851–852.

and Beck insisted on the implementation of their position the crisis passed; and the German government made the necessary arrangements to maintain Danzig's economic life without interfering with Poland's vital interests.[55]

The theory advanced by Beck at the time—and later by Hans Roos in his book[56]—that the German foreign ministry was pushing forward on its own, hoping to force Hitler's hand, is not borne out by the evidence now available. The effort to precipitate a more serious crisis originated in Danzig and can be understood on the basis of directives from Hitler to Forster and Greiser. In the spring, Hitler had cautioned the Danzig leaders not to allow the annexation question to arise in the election campaign or to permit the campaign to damage German-Polish relations.[57] As the economic crisis became more serious, however, Hitler approved in advance the exchange control regulations that precipitated the confrontation with Poland. He also urged the Danzig National Socialists to show "determination, energy, and toughness" in order to reassure the local population, frightened by devaluation and Polish pressure.[58] He left open the ultimate intentions and position of the German government, adopting, as he often did, a position that allowed him to decide at the last minute whether it was safe to move forward radically or wiser to defer action. The prompt and clear reaction of Poland showed Hitler, and Göring who handled the details for him, that there could be no fait accompli without drastic repercussions. Accordingly, Hitler promptly insisted that the Danzig leaders agree to a settlement regardless of their personal preferences and their earlier disregard of von Bülow's warnings.

The settlement of the Danzig currency dispute in August 1935 showed the effect of the determination that Hitler and Beck had expressed in the preceding month; no specific problem in German-Polish relations should be allowed to interfere with a continuation of the policy marked by the agreement of January 1934.[59] On the other hand, Göring's mission to Poland in January 1935 had shown that there were also limits beyond which that policy could not be extended. The discovery of this upper limit to German-Polish relations was also the result of a German probe of Poland's position. The parallel course of Germany and Poland in response to the proposed Eastern Locarno Pact has been described; it inspired Hitler to consider more far-reaching plans for German-Polish cooperation.

When the German-Polish agreement was first under consideration, Hitler explained to Rauschning the possibility of a joint German-Polish military

55. *G. D.,* C, 4, Nos. 258, 272, 358; *Lipski Papers,* pp. 215–17; Szembek, 6–9 August 1935, pp. 108–13; "Bestellung aus der Pressekonferenz, 9.8.1935," Bundesarchiv, Brammer, Z.Sg. 101/6, f. 50.

56. Roos, pp. 185–89.

57. This is clear from the reports on Forster's confidential briefing of German correspondents on 13 March 1935, in Bundesarchiv, Brammer, Z.Sg. 101/28, f. 97–109, and Bundesarchiv, Traub, Z.Sg. 110/1, f. 29–35.

58. *G. D.,* C, 4, No. 150.

59. On Beck's visit see Szembek, 2–3 July 1935, pp. 103–07; *G. D.,* C, 4, No. 190.

action against Soviet Russia. From his talk with Pilsudski in December 1933, Rauschning was convinced that the Poles would never agree to such a scheme.[60] Nevertheless, Hitler returned to this theme a year later. Around the first anniversary of the German-Polish agreement of 26 January 1934, the subject was apparently on Hitler's mind. He gave a pleasant public interview to the semiofficial *Gazeta Polska*[61] after discussing with Lipski, the Polish ambassador, the possibility of a joint German-Polish defense against the Soviet Union in preference to a German alliance with the Soviet Union, dividing Poland between them.[62] The new president of the Danzig Senate, Arthur Greiser, had just made a successful visit to Warsaw; now Göring was to go to Poland.[63] Hitler's instructions to Göring may well have reflected his exuberance as a result of the Saar plebiscite; in any case, Hitler and Göring spent several days together at the Obersalzberg near Berchtesgaden between the plebiscite and Göring's departure on his "hunting trip."[64] It would appear that Göring was to hunt for something other than wildlife.

The available evidence indicates that Göring was instructed to raise with the Polish government, and particularly with Marshal Pilsudski, the possibility of a German-Polish military alliance against Russia in which a successful war would lead to Polish expansion into the Soviet Ukraine and German expansion into the area of the Baltic states and North Russia. Such an arrangement might involve leaving the Polish Corridor unchanged, in which case Lithuania would go to Germany, or shifting the corridor by substituting Polish control of Lithuania for its present access to the sea, with Germany controlling the area beyond Lithuania.[65] The Poles were friendly and courteous, they extended themselves to make Göring's trip agreeable, and they assured their distinguished guest of their continued interest in amicable German-Polish relations. In spite of Göring's allusions to the alternative possibility of a German-Soviet agreement to partition Poland, however, the Polish leaders made it quite clear that they would not have any part in such an alliance. They knew that if such a scheme failed they would lose their independence to the Soviet Union; if it succeeded, they would lose their independence to Germany. The men who looked upon themselves as the architects of Polish independence were not interested in either pos-

60. See pp. 72–73, above.

61. *Polish White Book,* No. 14.

62. Ibid., No. 13; *Lipski Papers,* No. 33.

63. On Greiser's visit see Szembek, 9 January 1935, p. 16; Cudahy dispatch 561 of 15 January 1935, State 760c.60K/324.

64. Geist to Moffat, 26 January 1935, Moffat Papers, Vol. 8.

65. In addition to the evidence cited by Roos, pp. 208–12, I have used a report of 22 February 1935, on a discussion between General Schindler, German military attaché in Poland, and Defense Minister von Blomberg about Göring's visit in the papers of General Beck, Bundesarchiv, H 08–28/1, f. 54. The report was initialed by Beck on 22 February 1935; according to it, Hitler had explained the scheme discussed during Göring's visit to Poland in defensive terms and as proposed by the Poles. See also *G. D.,* C, 3, No. 474; Cudahy dispatches 583 of 29 January and 607 of 21 February 1935, State 760c.62/262 and 264.

sibility in 1935 any more than in 1939. They were prepared to go a considerable way in cooperation with Germany, even at the risk of annoying their French ally, but not to the extent of allying themselves with Germany and thereby throwing themselves upon the mercy of Berlin.[66]

This episode throws light both on German long-range goals and on the limits of German-Polish friendship. Evidence of later German approaches to Poland indicates that Hitler kept in mind the possibility of joint operations against Russia in spite of the fact that Göring had been politely waved off. With no wish simply to regain the German borders of 1914, Hitler was prepared to have Poland play some subordinate part in the schemes of territorial aggrandizement he visualized for the future. But while he found the Polish government unwilling to associate itself with such dangerous enterprise, he could see from the very mild Polish reaction to Germany's reintroduction of conscription in March 1935 that that country was still willing to operate diplomatically in concert with Germany and independently of France.[67] Because this was in any case the prime aim of Germany's policy toward Poland in the years when Germany was not yet ready for a major war, Hitler would continue to maintain the course of accommodation with Warsaw in spite of the rebuff to his more ambitious concepts.

The expansion of Germany's military might was, of course, of great concern to the other major powers, Italy, France, and Britain. The purge of 30 June 1934, the assassination of Dollfuss on 25 July and the assumption by Hitler of the presidency upon Hindenburg's death at the beginning of August strengthened Hitler's hold on Germany but did nothing to enhance Germany's reputation abroad. The general revulsion was compounded by two specific aspects of these events. The clumsy attempt to justify some of the murders of 30 June by reference to "a foreign power" with which the victims had allegedly conspired threw a temporary cloud over German relations with France, the country generally assumed to have been the one in contact with the "conspirators." If this matter was cleared up by subsequent explanations and reassurances to the French, the impact of the Vienna coup of 25 July on Germany's relations with Italy was far more lasting.[68]

The shock of the coup of 25 July for German-Italian relations has already

66. On Polish-French difficulties at this time, see Szembek, 23 January 1935, p. 26, 28 January, p. 31, 2 February, pp. 36–38; Laroche, pp. 191–95.

67. On Poland's mild reaction to the announcement of conscription see Szembek, pp. 46–49; *Lipski Papers,* Nos. 38, 39; *G. D.,* C, 3, Nos. 536, 553; U. S. 1935, 1:205–07; 2:311; Cudahy telegram 23 of 22 March 1935, State 862.20/767; Girsa (Czech minister Warsaw) report 27 of 18 March 1935, Czech document in T–120, 1041/1809/413562–563.

68. On the events of June 30 see Bracher, *Machtergreifung,* pp. 934ff. There are relevant documents in *G. D.,* C, 3, and *B. D.,* 2d, 6. The German foreign ministry was hardly touched directly by the purge; on 2 July K. A. Vicco von Bülow-Schwante and Attaché Lippert were arrested by Prince Waldeck, the party's representative in the Wilhelmstrasse, for the SS, but both were released by the Gestapo on the same day (Memorandum by von Bülow-Schwante, 2 July 1934, T–120, 2371/4601/E 188783–784).

been described. There followed a deterioration in that relationship that took a long time to mend.[69] There was a press feud of extreme violence that poisoned the atmosphere and continued well into the fall. A major factor that made a return to any degree of cordiality difficult was the continued activity of the National Socialists in Austria. Immediately after the failure of the 25 July coup, the German government made a public and spectacular show of changing its policy toward Vienna. This did not, however, entirely alleviate the situation because neither the person of the new ambassador to Vienna—von Papen—nor the sincerity of the shift was trusted abroad. The chief of the cabinet of the Italian foreign minister, Baron Pompeo Aloisi, commented in his diary that Germany, "having been conquered in the field of terrorism, now wants to triumph by diplomacy."[70] The appearance of the new German emissary to Vienna, therefore, was taken as a sign more of a shift in emphasis than in direction. Simultaneously, international awareness of the continued existence of the Austrian legion in Germany and of ties between the German and Austrian National Socialist parties gave the German assurances of a new policy a hollow ring indeed.[71] The complicated negotiations for a possible internal political truce in Austria conducted by the new Austrian chancellor, Kurt von Schuschnigg, and one of the more independent local National Socialists, Anton Reinthaller, in the fall of 1934 were unsuccessful and therefore led to no real easing of the situation.[72]

It is not surprising that under these circumstances the Austrian government did what it could to strengthen its international position by publishing a suitably edited and documented account of the 25 July coup, by maintaining close relations with Italy, and by appealing to Britain and France for continued support.[73] The Italians held to their position of reserve toward Germany and in fact expressed rather openly their continued suspicions of

69. The events as seen by an Italian official in any case not very favorable to national socialism may be followed in the entries for the second half of 1934 in Aloisi, *Journal*.

70. Ibid., 27 July 1934, p. 207.

71. On the Austrian legion and related activities in Germany after the July coup see *G. D.*, C, 3, Nos. 134, 135, 141, 165, 183, 174, n. 8, 179, 208, 337, 347, 362, 398, 424, 435; "Aktenvermerk über Besprechung österreich. Mil. Att. Gen.Maj. Jansa mit Obstlt. Böckmann am 13.IX.1934," T–120, 2890/6115/E 454920–921; Memorandum of Renthe-Fink "zu II Oe 3349," 8 December 1934, ibid., frame E 454949.

On the continued ties between the German and Austrian National Socialists see *G. D.*, C, 3, Nos. 116, n. 10, 173, 198, 398, n. 1; Memorandum by von Bülow, 19 November 1934, T–120, 909/1574/381349; inclosure to American Legation Vienna dispatch 183 of 19 October 1934, State 863.00/1104. It should be noted that the German military attaché in Vienna, General Muff, favored the continuation of German support, both in leadership and money, to the Austrian National Socialists (Bericht 25/34 geh. 323 of 10 September 1934, T–120, 2695/5705/E 414396–398).

72. On the Reinthaller negotiations see *G. D.*, C, 3, Nos. 198, 257; von Papen to Hitler, A 3264/34, 12 November 1934, T–120, 778/1549/376671. For informed and detailed analyses of these negotiations by the American minister in Vienna, George S. Messersmith, see his dispatch 202 of 7 November 1934, and his letters to Undersecretary of State William Phillips of 8 and 16 November 1934, State 863.00/1114, 1135, and 1136.

73. Osuský (Czech minister Paris) to Beneš, No. 376 of 23 August 1934, Czech document in T–120, 1143/2028/444313–315.

German motives toward Austria. To ease this situation, both von Papen and Ulrich von Hassell, the German ambassador to Rome, began to urge that Germany subscribe to some international statement on the integrity of Austria. The German government, however, declined whatever schemes along these lines von Papen, von Hassell, or the Italian or Hungarian governments proposed. Hitler, fully supported by von Neurath and von Bülow, believed that it was wiser for Germany not to tie its own hands by any meaningful agreement. Since it had no intention of moving openly against Austria right away, the international clamor would subside in time; Germany had only to wait. If Germany did not lose its nerve, it would emerge from the situation without having assumed any formal restraints. When Berlin accepted a commitment about Austria in 1936, it would be of a bilateral, not a multilateral, nature.[74]

In the face of this unwillingness to make any substantial gestures toward Austria and, by implication, toward Italy, German-Italian relations remained distant. The open hostility slowly subsided, but the period of cooperation on the international scene was replaced by one of coolness and latent hostility. In the eyes of the Italian government, German hegemony in Europe could be even more dangerous than French hegemony. By instructions to the press and by warning of French ambitions, the German government tried to deter Italy's turn toward France, but without success. Rome did not wish to destroy all ties with Germany and cultivated those with the German military on the assumption that only the National Socialist party was responsible for Germany's Austrian policy, but there was nevertheless an unmistakable reorientation of Italian policy to a closer relationship with France.[75] If Italy's support of the German position on the Saar question helped maintain a friendly tie with Berlin,[76] its developing interest in an aggressive policy in East Africa played a key part in Italy's rapprochement with France that was to culminate in Pierre Laval's visit to Rome in January 1935.[77]

Laval was in Rome 4–8 January 1935. He had paved the way by seeing to it that no blame was publicly attached to Italy for its role in supporting the Croatian terrorists responsible for the October 1934 assassination of Laval's predecessor, Barthou, and King Alexander of Yugoslavia.[78] If this regard for Mussolini's susceptibilities inclined the Italian leader to a friend-

74. *G. D.*, C, 3, Nos. 127, 161, pp. 338–41, Nos. 166, 167, 174, 230, n. 8, 241, 266, 267, 296, 317, 345, 380, 408, n. 1; 4, pp. 1227–29; *B. D.*, 2d, 6, Nos. 546, 548, 556, 560, 561; Memorandum of von Neurath, RM 1031 of 12 September 1934, T–120, 2383/4619/E 198016.

75. *G. D.*, C, 3, Nos. 118, 152, 222, 293, 303, 310, 352, 381, 383, 385, 406, 425; Memorandum of von Bülow, 12 December 1934, T–120, 784/1555/377605–606; Kausch, "Streng vertrauliche Anweisung über die Behandlung der österreichischen Probleme," 12 September 1934, Bundesarchiv, Brammer, Z.Sg. 101/4, f. 101.

76. *G. D.*, C, 3, Nos. 228, 299, 309, 318, 376; von Hassel report I 1366, 21 December 1934, T–120, 2700/5737/H 029165–168.

77. *G. D.*, C, 3, No. 230.

78. Miličevič, *Königsmord von Marseille*, p. 85.

lier regard for France, Mussolini's own interest in an African empire turned him in the same direction. The preparations for what eventually became the Italo-Ethiopian war were already under way; the first major incident, that at Wal Wal, had occurred on 4 December 1934.[79] Italy could not risk an advance in East Africa without some assurance from France. If France supported Italy, Britain would be unlikely to act alone.

In their talks, Mussolini and Laval came to a series of agreements.[80] The published agreements dealt with Italian rights in Tunisia, the cession of some African desert by the French to Libya and a tiny piece of coast to Italian Eritrea, and the turning over by France of some shares in the railway connecting Djibouti in French Somaliland with the Ethiopian capital of Addis Ababa. There was a further agreement to consult together if Austrian independence should be threatened, while any future danger to Austria was to be obviated by a Danubian Pact containing a pledge of noninterference into Austrian domestic politics to be signed by Austria, Germany, Czechoslovakia, Yugoslavia, Hungary, and Italy, with France, Rumania, and Poland also invited to adhere. A secret arrangement provided for French-Italian consultation if Germany assumed complete freedom to rearm in violation of the Versailles treaty. In addition, the French minister gave Mussolini a free hand to move forward in Ethiopia, a step leading to misunderstanding on both sides. Italy assumed that France really would support it and was, therefore, disappointed when France, however reluctantly, later joined in sanctions against Italy; while the French may not have expected Mussolini to move toward an outright military conquest of all Ethiopia and were therefore to find themselves in a position of having to choose between support of the League and their new-found friend.[81]

The German government was invited to sign the Danubian Pact, but Hitler was no more interested in tying his own hands in this way than in any others. On the basis of Laval's general policies there are good reasons for believing that he really hoped to combine a check to German ambitions—through the Franco-Italian alignment—with good Franco-German relations, but as the following account of those relations will show, it was a one-sided desire. In the meantime, Berlin rejected immediate adhesion to the Rome agreements and insisted on negotiations about German participation hedged about with conditions Germany confidently expected would

79. The origins and beginnings of Mussolini's aggressive policy toward Ethiopia are examined in George W. Baer, *The Coming of the Italian-Ethiopian War* (Cambridge, Mass.: Harvard University Press, 1967), chaps. 2 and 3.

80. See the summary in Scott, pp. 214–17 and Geoffrey Warner, *Pierre Laval and the Eclipse of France, 1931–1945* (New York: Macmillan, 1968), pp. 66–71. The agreements themselves, including the secret ones, are published and examined in Donald C. Watt, "The Secret Laval-Mussolini Agreement of 1935 on Ethiopia," *Middle East Journal,* 15 (1961), 69–78. In addition, see Norman Davis's report on a talk with Dino Grandi in the diary of William Phillips, 3 April 1936, Phillips Papers, Vol. 10; and von Papen to Hitler, telegram 3 of 5 January 1935, T–120, 2499/4939/E 271937.

81. Franklin D. Laurens, *France and the Italo-Ethiopian Crisis, 1935–1936* (The Hague: Mouton, 1967), chap. 2; Baer, chap. 4.

be rejected. As before, Germany would refuse all multilateral commitments.[82]

German-French relations from the summer of 1934 to early 1935 were dominated by three themes. There was the effort of France to revive the disarmament negotiations or to arrange a new security system like an Eastern Locarno that eventually became the Franco-Soviet alliance. There was the growing rapprochement between France and Italy, arising out of their common opposition to Germany's Austrian policy. Finally, there were the attempts to improve German-French relations directly by the official route of government negotiations and the unofficial method of contacts between veterans organizations, friendship societies, and so on, that had been inaugurated the previous winter and spring. In the background, there was the problem of the forthcoming plebiscite in the Saar as a possible source of conflict between the two powers, or alternatively, as a means of reconciliation by the cooperative removal of a troublesome issue in their relationship.

The efforts to revive disarmament negotiations were a failure, as could be expected in view of the German position. German rearmament was proceeding at a fairly rapid rate, and there was no reason for it to stop under circumstances where no one was willing to take any action to stop it. To avoid a major crisis before Germany was ready to face it, the foreign ministry restrained the pressures from the military for remilitarization of the Rhineland, but otherwise the only restraint still exercised was the temporary postponement of the reintroduction of conscription.[83] Otherwise, Germany rearmed without regard to protests or concern expressed by other countries.[84] The public atmosphere inside Germany was increasingly militarized, and foreign observers commented on the unprecedented indoctrination of the youth, in fact of the whole population, with a spirit of militarism and the expectation of victory in another war. In the focus on military rearmament with its emphasis on the training of soldiers and the production of arms, this facet—the rearmament of public opinion, so to speak—is often overlooked; but it went forward rapidly in the early years of the National Socialist regime as Hitler himself had indicated that it would as a prerequisite for the material rearmament of the country.[85]

82. *G. D.*, C, 3, Nos. 407, 411, 418, 423, 438–40, 456, 460, 461, 466; von Papen report A 53/35, T–120, 2757/5885/E 431254–259. It is worth noting that as late as 30 January 1935, Laval still professed to believe that there was a chance that Germany would sign a Danubian Pact (U. S. 1935, 1:182–84).

There is an apt retrospective view of Laval's 1935 policy in Sir G. Clerk's (Paris) dispatch 142 of 31 January 1936: "Two main characteristics inform M. Laval's character: a genuine horror of war and a natural inclination to double-dealing" (Foreign Office C 656/1/17).

83. *G. D.*, C, 2, Nos. 452, 487; 3, Nos. 2, 159, 170, 274, 369, 393; Liebmann Notes for 9 October 1934, ED 1, pp. 73–74.

84. *G. D.*, C, 3, Nos. 355, 356, 358.

85. See the very perceptive letter of the U. S. consul general in Berlin, Raymond Geist, to the chief of the Division of West European Affairs in the Department of

Germany and the European Powers

The abortive negotiations for an Eastern Locarno and the subsequent Franco-Soviet Pact have already been mentioned, as has the Franco-Italian rapprochement. If these developments did not lead to a substantial stiffening of French policy toward Germany, it was mainly due to other developments in the relations of these two powers. Although Laval's predecessor, Louis Barthou, wished to build up defenses against German aggression, he was by no means interested in having France follow an aggressively anti-German policy herself. He made every effort to maintain cordial relations with Germany and to surmount the incidents and problems that arose from time to time.[86] Through de Brinon, Barthou arranged for a friendly meeting with von Ribbentrop and attempted to combine a security system for France with good relations with Germany.[87] If Barthou was cool but friendly, his successor, Pierre Laval, was even more interested in improving German-French relations. The German government was happy to see him become foreign minister, and though never responding with any substantial gestures of its own, always listened with great pleasure to his protestations that he wanted to end the past hostility between the two countries.[88] This was particularly evident in regard to the forthcoming plebiscite in the Saar. Laval did everything possible to avoid incidents in anticipation of what was likely to be a heavy vote for reunion with Germany in the hope that this might pave the way for better relations thereafter.[89]

If there were some signs that official relations were improving slightly, at the same time unofficial contacts were being expanded. A speech by Rudolf Hess to the war veterans of the world on 8 July 1934 started a major German effort to utilize contacts between German and foreign veterans associations as a means of building up support for peaceful relations.[90] There

---

State of 15 September 1934, Moffat Papers, Vol. 5. In 1934, the APA began a major effort to have the iron ore shipments from Sweden rerouted through Lübeck instead of Rotterdam, Antwerp, and Emden in view of the prospect of future war (Daitz to Rosenberg, 6 November 1934, Nuremberg document 1356–PS, National Archives). During the same period, the German navy established contact with Estonia to try to secure oil from the Estonian oil shale works (Nuremberg document 984–PS, National Archives).

86. *G. D.*, C, 3, No. 31, n. 14; Memorandum of von Neurath, RM 478 of 26 April 1934, T–120, 2383/4619/E 197951–952.

87. *G. D.*, C, 3, No. 31; U. S. 1934, 1:122; *B. D.*, 2d, 6:454; von Ribbentrop to Hitler, 1 June 1934, T–120, 1784/3650/D 813444–445.

88. *G. D.*, C, 3, Nos. 240, 399; Memorandum of von Bülow, 7 November 1934, T–120, 2372/4602/E 189975–977; Mastný report 78 of 24 October 1934. Czech document in T–120, 1041/1809/413756–757 (parts in Berber, *Prager Akten*, No. 33).

89. *G. D.*, C, 3, Nos. 290, 297, 300, 306, 307, 328, 330, 335, n. 2, 340, 343, 344, 357, 363–65, 368, 370, 372, 375, 377, 396; *D. D. B.*, 3, No. 146; Eden, pp. 113–17; Warner, *Laval*, pp. 61–63.

90. Text in Rudolf Hess, *Reden* (Munich: Eher, 1938), pp. 39–48. See also *B. D.*, 2d, 6, No. 501; Gerl to Hess, 1 January 1938, Nuremberg document 3752–PS (National Archives); Köster telegram 946, 11 July 1934, T–120, 2696/5717/H 024391–392.

followed a series of direct contacts between German and French veterans organizations, personally encouraged by Hitler, including trips by leaders of various veterans groups. The foreign ministries on both sides attempted to restrain these activities, but their impact on the international atmosphere should not be underestimated. The sentiments of those involved were in most cases quite sincere, even if the German government planned to utilize them for far different purposes than the participants realized.[91]

The French were not the only ones who were building up hopes for a relaxation of tension after the Saar plebiscite. Most anxious for some agreement in 1934, and still hoping for an accommodation even after the shocks of early 1935, was Great Britain. British policy had been oriented toward an understanding with Germany based on some degree of German rearmament within the framework of a general settlement that included Germany's return to the League.[92] Beyond the continued unwillingness of Germany to agree to any such policies, there was a specific aspect of German rearmament as well as German policy in international trade that made for friction with London. As has already been mentioned, German rearmament in the air raised an immediate and strong reaction in Britain. If the French were alarmed at increases in the German army, the English were most sensitive to the possibility of war in the air. It was Stanley Baldwin who, in November 1932, made the statement: "The bomber will always get through." Under the impact of German air rearmament, Britain began to rebuild its own air force, if only on a small scale; and the accompanying debate in the House of Commons showed how fear of German strength influenced British policy.[93] If Baldwin now asserted that Britain's line of defense was on the Rhine, and if Ramsay MacDonald warned the German ambassador, Leopold von Hoesch, that an air arms race might play the same role that the naval race had played before World War I, these were ominous signs of danger ahead; but no serious concern about their long-range implications appear to have influenced the German government. In Berlin the main

91. *G. D.*, C, 3, Nos. 311, 321, 324, 359, n. 10, 367, 388; Paris telegram 1529, 3 December 1934, T–120, 2661/5669/H 014966; "Bestellungen a.d. Pressekonferenz, 30.11.34," Bundesarchiv, Brammer, Z.Sg. 101/4, f. 198; Domarus, 1:464. A number of documents on the veterans' contacts in November-December 1934 are in T–120, 2696/5717/passim. There is a summary of these projects and their general purpose and setting in Wilhelm Ritter von Schramm, "Hitlers psychologischer Angriff auf Frankreich," *Aus Politik und Zeitgeschichte*, Beilage zu *Das Parlament*, B 5/61, 1 February 1961. A contemporary survey that shows the role of Otto Abetz and the misuse of genuine goodwill on both sides is in Memorandum by von Rintelen, "II Fr. 414," 12 February 1935, T–120, 2696/5717/H 024647–649. For information from the French side, there are two interesting reports by the Czech chargé a.i. in Paris, Ibl, No. 30 of 3 December and No. 32 of 4 December 1934, Czech documents in T–120, 1041/1809/413752–753 (excerpts in Berber, *Prager Akten,* No. 36), and frame 413754.

92. *G. D.,* C, 2, No. 164; *B. D.,* 2d, 6, Nos. 161, 164.

93. *G. D.,* C, 3, Nos. 90, 98, 99, 138; cf. U. S. 1934, 1:76; *B. D.,* 2d, 6, No. 443.

emphasis remained on talking and stalling while rearming.[94] British protests and warnings were disregarded.[95]

The aspect of German international trade policy most upsetting to the British—as it was to the United States—was the handling of international payments. For a great trading nation, this was, of course, a matter of considerable public concern. A serious crisis in the summer of 1934 was met by forced clearing legislation in which Britain took advantage of its favorable situation to pressure Germany into substantial concessions. The whole development of German-British trade and payments was, nevertheless, a subject of continuing friction, and one that disillusioned many British officials about the possibility of dealing constructively with the whole range of British-German differences.[96] Since the German government could find foreign exchange to repurchase the bonds on which it had defaulted and to pay for imports connected with rearmament, there was an understandable annoyance among British negotiators over German claims of a lack of foreign exchange to pay for past obligations or current purchases of a non-military nature.[97] As in the case of German relations with the United States, such economic troubles were mainly important as symbols rather than causes of a process of deterioration of Germany's relations with other lands, though in London as in Washington the German tactics were also well calculated to engender maximum dislike and distrust on the part of those who had to deal with Berlin.

On the plane of official German-British relations, there was, thus, a clear and significant worsening of the situation, and the German diplomatic reports from London reflect that process quite accurately.[98] It was also

94. *G. D.*, C, 3, Nos. 154, 289; *B. D.*, 2d, 6, No. 547; Schweppenburg, *Erinnerungen eines Militärattachés*, p. 17; "Vertrauliche Informationen vom 9. November 1934," Bundesarchiv, Brammer, Z.Sg. 101/27, f. 439–41.

95. *G. D.*, C, 3, Nos. 355, 356, 358.

96. *G. D.*, C, 2, Nos. 193, 196, 197, 200, 204, 212, 231, 233, 426, 466, 471, 490; 3, Nos. 9, 12, 18, 20, 21, 29, 35–38, 42, 44, 46, 49, 53, 54, 58, 108, 130, 160, 175, 176, 185, 277, 278, 316; *B. D.*, 2d, 6, Nos. 386, 469; *TMWC*, 36:573; Note by von Ulrich, "W 8025," 17 September 1934, T–120, 2628/5622/E 404066–067; "Sitzung des Handelspolitischen Ausschusses vom 8. August 1934," 2612/5650/H 003919–20; "Bestellungen a.d. Pressekonferenz v. 4.12.34," Bundesarchiv, Brammer, Z.Sg. 101/4 f. 203–04.

97. See MacDonald's comments in *G. D.*, C, 2, No. 28, and those of the British negotiator, Sir Frederick Leith-Ross, in "Aufzeichnung über die 6. Sitzung der deutsch-englischen Wirtschaftsverhandlungen am 26. September 1934 vormittags," T–120, 2628/5622/E 404013–018.

The documentation on this subject in the British Foreign Office records is almost endless. For a reflection of the thinking in London see Wigram's minute of 25 October 1934 (Foreign Office C 7091/90/18); for the views of the British negotiator, Sir Frederick Leith-Ross, see Phipps's Berlin telegram 267 of the same date (Foreign Office C 7280/90/18). It should be noted that these documents relate to the British threat of a forced clearing system to secure German agreement to a new Anglo-German transfer agreement. A summary of the British-German negotiations is in Foreign Office C 646/25/18.

98. A detailed analysis is in Bismarck's report, A 3234 of 12 September 1934, T–120, 2628/5622/E 404078–102.

obvious to the Germans that Britain and France were moving more closely together in the military sphere and that Britain was as sensitive as ever toward any German threat to Belgium.[99] On the other hand, there seemed to be no reason for Berlin to fear a really drastic change in British policy.

Clearly the British government would take no great risks. This had been shown by its mild and anxious rather than vigorous reaction to Germany's departure from the League. Similarly, any concessions Britain might make to Japan to enable Britain to concentrate on Europe would be interpreted as a sign of weakness.[100] Hitler himself was receiving from Rosenberg indications of soundings in London that pointed toward a willingness to go far to meet Germany's wishes.[101] In late September 1934, he received a most interesting report, widely circulated, of a conversation between the counselor of the German embassy in London and Edgar Granville, private secretary to the British foreign secretary, Sir John Simon. Granville stressed that Britain was making progress in its rapprochement with Japan and he thought relations with Germany much improved. He emphasized Britain's policy of isolation and of accepting no commitments and made an assertion that could only have sounded like a go-ahead to Hitler: "No country, and especially not England, would ever go to war for the interests of other nations outside its own territory."[102] Such a statement could be interpreted to mean that Britain might go to war outside its own territory if it believed this to be in its own interests, but such was clearly not the interpretation Hitler placed on this or similar statements later. It suggested instead the possibility of a direct accommodation between the two countries, a subject on which von Ribbentrop touched while in London in November 1934 and toward which contacts between the Lord Privy Seal, Sir Anthony Eden, and Hitler might lead in the future.[103]

The Berlin government was further encouraged in its belief that there would be no serious resistance to its continental ambitions by the unofficial contacts from Britain that became more numerous at this time and that in turn inspired British officials to take an optimistic view of the future. An "Anglo-German Group" was formed in London at the end of 1934, and Lord Allen of Hurtwood visited Hitler on 25 January 1934 in its behalf to explore the possibility of German-British friendship.[104] A few days later

99. *G. D.,* C, 3, No. 47. There was a series of soundings about a German-Belgian nonagression pact that was badly mishandled by von Ribbentrop but showed both British sensitivity and German worry about any new multilateral commitments (*G. D.,* C, 2, Nos. 464, 467, 497, 502, 503; 3, Nos. 52, 71, 73, 94; *B. D.*, 2d, 6, Nos. 430–32, 450, 466; *D. D. B.*, 3, No. 97).

100. Feiling, *Life of Neville Chamberlain*, p. 253.

101. Rosenberg, *Tagebuch*, 11 July 1934, pp. 49–51; cf. ibid., September 1934, pp. 57–58.

102. Bismarck's report, "Unterredung mit dem Parlamentarischen Privatsekretär Sir John Simons über aussenpolitische Fragen," T–120, 2903/6161/E 461714–719. The date on the document is burned; it was received in Berlin on 29 September 1934 and given file number III E 2609.

103. *G. D.,* C, 3, Nos. 333, 334; T. Jones, 16 December 1934, p. 139.

104. *G. D.,* C, 3, Nos. 422, 463; Arthur Marwick, *Clifford Allen: The Open Conspira-*

Phillip Kerr, Lord Lothian, received assurances from Hitler of his great desire for peace. Through this meeting preparations were also begun for the subsequent visit to Berlin of Sir John Simon himself.[105] In his talks with German leaders, Lothian always insisted that the outstanding issues would have to be settled by peaceful negotiations, but there is nothing to indicate that his hosts took this point very seriously. It was in fact quite clear that at the beginning of 1935 the British government was determined to attempt a settlement with Germany and this attitude was both supported and pushed forward by the policy of England's leading newspaper, *The Times.*[106] Simultaneously, the campaign of those whose religious inclinations led them to imagine that they could appeal to the "good" in the leaders of National Socialist Germany helped to shape portions of British opinion in a direction favoring concessions to Germany. The honorable motives of these men evoked no response from the makers of German policy, but those who approached Germany with eyes focused on their own doctrines rather than German realities were slow to be disillusioned.[107]

The German response to all the overtures made to them was the opposite of what the British and French had hoped for. The desire for peace and friendship was always taken solely as a sign of weakness, as it may have been in part, but only in part. As Hitler explained to his ministers when triumphantly discussing the arrangements agreed upon for the Saar plebiscite, "The French have definitely missed the opportunity for a preventive war. This also explains France's effort for rapprochement."[108] In view of this German interpretation of friendly gestures from her neighbor in the West, the overwhelming vote for union with Germany in the Saar on 13 January and the subsequent transfer of the area to Germany produced the opposite effect in Berlin from what those outside Germany had hoped. Instead of clearing the air by removing a German grievance and a potential source of friction, it freed Germany from restraint and made the

---

tor (Edinburgh: Oliver & Boyd, 1964), pp. 159–62. See also Rosenberg, *Tagebuch,* 15 March 1935, p. 76 (should read Hurtwood, not "Mentwood"); Jacobsen, p. 335. There is a skeptical evaluation of this "marché des dupes" in Foreign Office C 2518/55/18.

105. *G. D.,* C, 3, Nos. 445, 468; J. R. M. Butler, *Lord Lothian, 1882–1940* (London: Macmillan, 1960), pp. 203–04, 330–37; Gärtner, p. 309.

106. *G. D.,* C, 3, Nos. 421, 469; Memorandum of von Neurath, RM 10, 10 January 1935, T–120, 2383/4619/E 198062–063; Rosenberg, *Tagebuch,* 21 January 1935, pp. 65–66. Sir John Simon's hopes are set forth in his letter of 14 January 1935, to King George V, quoted in Nicolson, *King George the Fifth,* p. 522. For the attitude of *The Times* see *The History of the Times,* 4: *The 150th Anniversary and Beyond, 1912–1948,* Part II (London: The Times, 1952), chap. 23; the excellent contemporary analysis in the letter of George S. Messersmith to Phillips of 6 June 1935, State 863.00/1203; and Mastný's report 57 of 7 June 1936, Czech document in T–120, 1040/1809/413136–138. See also Eden's complaints about *The Times* to the cabinet, 8 April 1935, Foreign Office C 2962/55/18.

107. A fine survey of the major elements and individuals in this movement for better British-German relations is in Donald C. Watt, "Christian Essay in Appeasement," *Wiener Library Bulletin,* 14, No. 2 (1960), pp. 30–31; for a broader analysis see the same author's *Personalities and Policies,* pp. 123–35.

108. *G. D.,* C, 3, No. 373. Hitler had by this time been confident for some time that France would not launch a preventive attack (ibid., Nos. 281, 283, 293).

German leaders more exuberant and determined. The world would soon find out in which direction Berlin would move.

Whatever new schemes in arms limitations the British and French governments might devise at their meeting early in February 1935, Germany was determined to go ahead on its own. The German strategy had been reconfirmed in January: there might be negotiations, but there would be no agreement in any way limiting the extent of German armaments or imposing international controls or inspection.[109] The negotiations on the proposals anyone might make would simply be used to cover the time while Germany rearmed.[110] The return of the Saar to Germany only made this policy more attractive. Hitler gave some reassuring public interviews, but his privately expressed sentiments were of a very different nature.[111]

In conference with Göring on the Obersalzberg before his trip to Poland, Hitler confirmed that Germany would sign none of the pacts then being pushed by France. Hitler indicated that in about two weeks Germany would take an important step in the field of armaments; the record we have does not indicate what that step was to be, but either the announcement of air rearmament or the reintroduction of conscription, or both, appears to have been discussed.[112] Germany would use the German minorities in neighboring states, including Lorraine, to secure territorial concessions. Hungary would become dependent on Germany, and a possible Habsburg restoration in Austria could be the first step "in the process of closing in on Czechoslovakia." In the meantime, Germany would continue its efforts to reduce the fears of France.[113] Such efforts, however, would in no way inhibit its far-reaching plans for expansion eastward.[114]

As Germany acted on these sentiments by a parallel course of public assurances of peaceful intent and continued rejection of all proposals for

109. Institut für Zeitgeschichte, Liebmann Papers, ED 1, pp. 79–82; *G. D.*, C, 3, Nos. 436, 437, 446; Memorandum of von Neurath, RM 41, 19 January 1935, T–120, 2383/4619/E 198071–072; Phipps telegram 24, 19 January 1935, Foreign Office C 507/55/18.

110. *G. D.*, C, 3, No. 454. The minutes of the Anglo-French discussions of 1–3 February are in Foreign Office C 893/55/18; see also C 1048/55/18.

111. Interview by Pierre Huss of the Hearst press on 16 January 1935, Domarus, 1:473–74; by Ward Price on 17 January, ibid., pp. 474–76. Huss gave a report on his days on the Obersalzberg to the U. S. consul general in Berlin, and the latter's letter to Jay Pierrepont Moffat of 26 January 1935 (Moffat Papers, Vol. 8) is the main source for the text that follows. See also Hitler's comments to Rosenberg on 8 February 1935, in Rosenberg's *Tagebuch,* pp. 69–70.

112. Göring may also have been authorized to inform the Poles of the forthcoming German step. There are both hints and denials of this to be found in the Czech diplomatic documents; Girsa (Warsaw) report 27 of 18 March 1935, T–120, 1041/1809/413562–563; Mastný report 21 of 20 March, ibid., frame 413507; Mastný's telegram of 22 March, ibid., frame 413428.

113. In the State Department, only the reference to a Habsburg restoration was questioned, on the assumption that it would hinder rather than help Germany's *Anschluss* ambitions (Moffat to Geist, 27 February 1935, Moffat Papers, Vol. 8).

114. For confirming indirect evidence on Hitler's exposition of his long-range intentions in late January 1935 see Mastný report 8 of 27 January 1935, and his memorandum of February 1935, Czech documents in T–120, 1040/1809/413228–230 and frames 413102–108.

substantive agreement, the stimulus events in the Saar had given to German intransigence began to be recognized abroad.[115] The disappointment of British hopes for a more reasonable attitude after the plebiscite might have been expected to dampen the enthusiasm for direct approaches to Berlin, but such was not the case.[116] The British were certainly aware that Germany might merely be trying to split them from France, but in spite of grave doubts among the permanent officials of the foreign office, plans were pushed for a visit to Berlin by Simon and Eden for discussions with Hitler.[117] The timing may have been good from the British point of view but was particularly bad for Germany. The British wanted to explore German reactions to various new proposals for an air pact and revised security arrangements, while the German government was planning to reveal publicly the existence of its air force. The secret decree on the air force was agreed upon in the cabinet in Berlin on 26 February just before the date of Simon's visit was announced.[118] Since the decree was to take effect on March 1 and announced to the governments of other countries a few days later, the German government wanted Simon's visit postponed. It found an excuse in a phrase in the British white paper calling for a slight measure of British rearmament in response to developments in Germany and promptly discovered that Hitler was too ill to receive visitors from England.[119]

While the British were puzzling out ways to arrange a visit after all, Hitler not only announced the existence of the German air force but planned further action to move rearmament forward during the expected international negotiations on new pact proposals until "after a year no one would dare attack us anymore."[120] In the days between 5 March and 13 March Hitler decided to announce the reintroduction of conscription in Germany. There is ample evidence that he had always intended to take this step; he had promised it to the military immediately after 30 January 1933; and he had been obliged to postpone it solely because of the international situation. He thought it safe now and wished to make the announcement of it before Simon came to Berlin. Hitler made the decision himself and only informed the German foreign ministry and his military leaders at the last moment. Von Blomberg was skeptical, but Hitler went ahead, supported it would appear by many of his military and civilian advisers and perhaps influenced by the

115. U. S. 1935, 1:5, 7, 185–87; *G. D.*, C, 3, Nos. 489, 490; *Lipski Papers,* No. 33; Eden, pp. 136–37; Phipps dispatch 60, 22 January 1935, Foreign Office C 623/55/18.

116. Moffat to Ray Atherton (London), 19 February 1935, Moffat Papers, Vol. 8.

117. *G. D.*, C, 3, Nos. 501–503; Cmd. 5143, Nos. 7, 8; for an excellent picture of the Foreign Office atmosphere in the early and mid-1930s, and especially the roles of Wigram and Vansittart, see Valentine Lawford, *Bound for Diplomacy* (London: John Murray, 1963). The minutes of Simon's Paris talks before his Berlin trip are in Foreign Office C 1657/55/18; his briefing memorandum in C 2696/55/18.

118. *G. D.*, C, 3, No. 507.

119. Ibid., Nos. 517, 519; Meinck, *Hitler und die deutsche Aufrüstung,* pp. 92–96; Beneš circular of 21 March 1935, Czech document in T–120, 1041/1809/413467–468 (parts in Berber, *Prager Akten,* No. 41).

120. Rosenberg, *Tagebuch,* 12 March 1935, pp. 74–75; *TMWC,* 34:44–46; *G. D.*, C, 3, No. 534.

lack of reaction to the announcement of air rearmament. The outside world was angry but confined itself to verbal protests. The British ministers, undaunted by reality, would visit Berlin all the same.[121] The trip might give both sides an opportunity to secure a clearer picture of the other's plans and intentions.

The conversations between Simon and Eden on the one hand and Hitler accompanied by von Neurath and von Ribbentrop on the other produced no agreement on any subject. The British exploration of the possibility of Germany's agreeing to a pact covering Austria, returning to the League, signing an Eastern Locarno, or making any other clear commitment was answered unmistakably in the negative.[122] The British ministers were disappointed by the realization that the settlement they had hoped for was unattainable. Eden appears to have drawn the conclusion that there was little prospect of this changing in the future. Simon, on the other hand, was to continue hoping for the best. There is nothing to suggest that Hitler was greatly impressed by either the talks or by such warnings as he received of a stiffening in British attitude as a result of his own actions or his announcement during the talks that Germany had reached parity in air power with Britain. This last boast was probably an exaggeration, but if so, it only added fear as a deterrent to the already existing reluctance of London to face the dangers ahead.[123]

Like the visit of the Soviet commissar for foreign affairs, Vyacheslav Molotov, to Berlin five-and-a-half years later, the visit of Sir John Simon gave the two sides an opportunity to size up each other. Hitler took the occasion to speak volubly of peace but made evident his intent to continue preparation for war; Sir John hoped that a combination of concessions to Germany with firmness unaccompanied by action might avert the possibility of war. The personal impressions received are of importance: Hitler gave an impression of deep sincerity, Sir John of weakness. Both were, in a way, misled. Hitler was sincere in not wanting a war with England, since he wished its acquiescence in his proposed eastern conquests; but just as Sir John failed to see clearly that Hitler wanted a certain kind of war—even if he did not wish to fight England as yet—so Hitler failed to understand that Sir John's sincere wish for peace did not mean that England would not fight under any circumstances. The subsequent course of German-English relations would only reinforce these mutual self-deceptions.

121. Meinck, pp. 97–99; Hossbach, pp. 94–96; Feiling, p. 255; *G. D.,* C, 3, Nos. 526, 528, 532, 539, 548, 550; U. S. 1935, 2:297; Rosenberg, *Tagebuch,* 16 March, pp. 76–77; Mastný report 19 of 17 March, Czech document in T–120, 1041/1809/413502–504; British cabinet conclusions of 18 March, Foreign Office C 2285/55/18.

122. On the talks see *G. D.,* C, 3, Nos. 528, 531, 537, 552, 555; U. S. 1935, 1:200–02; Simon, pp. 202–03; Eden, pp. 148–59; Černý (Czech chargé a.i. London) report 13 of 1 April 1935, Czech document in T–120, 1041/1809/413548–550 (excerpt in Berber, *Prager Akten,* No. 44); General R. van Overstraeten, *Albert I–Léopold III* (Bruges: Desclée de Brouwer, 1949), pp. 160–62. The British minutes are in Foreign Office C 2580/55/18; see also C 2797/55/18.

123. Butler, p. 204; T. Jones, 30 March 1935, p. 144.

9 From Stresa to the Remilitarization of the Rhineland

After the visit of the British ministers to Germany in late March 1935, Sir Anthony Eden continued to Moscow, Warsaw, and Prague, while Sir John Simon returned to London. Eden found the Soviet government anxious about Germany, the Polish leaders satisfied with their independent line, and the Czech government astonishingly confident about the future.[1] In the meantime, preparations were made for a meeting between the leaders of Britain, France, and Italy at Stresa prior to discussion by the League at Geneva of the German announcement of conscription.

The German government, having just raised major claims to further rearmament in the talks with Simon and Eden—right after the announcement of conscription—was at least a little concerned about the possibility of all the other European powers collaborating against it and followed the diplomatic situation with great care. For a short time, the tone from Berlin was more conciliatory, although no substantive concessions were offered in the continuing negotiations for an air pact, an Eastern Locarno, or a Danubian Pact.[2] The long-heralded meeting at Stresa took place on 11 April. As planned, the meeting led to the issuance of a joint communiqué expressing regret at the German unilateral action on conscription, reaffirming loyalty to Locarno, and insisting that the policy of the powers would continue to be inspired by the need to maintain Austria's independence

1. See Eden's own account in *Facing the Dictators* (Book One, chaps. 9 and 10), and Foreign Office C 2689/ C 2690/ C 2726/ C 2930/55/18.

2. *G. D.*, C, 3, Nos. 563, 564, 567; 4, Nos. 5, 9, 10, 17; Cmd. 5143, No. 12; Geyr von Schweppenburg, *Erinnerungen eines Militärattachés,* pp. 35–36. On the Danubian Pact see M. Sz-Ormos, "Sur les causes de l'échec du pacte danubien (1934–35)," *Acta Historica,* 14, No. 1–2 (1968), pp. 21–81.

and integrity.[3] The deliberate failure of the British prime minister and foreign secretary to bring up the subject of Ethiopia and their subsequent acquiescence in a formula referring to the maintenance of peace "in Europe"—with that restrictive phrase personally inserted by Mussolini—was not unreasonably taken by Mussolini as a green light for his East African venture. The pacific character of British policy, revealed to him by the leak of British diplomatic papers from the British embassy in Rome that lasted from 1935 until at least 1939, only confirmed him in his resolution. The effects of this were to become apparent in the summer and fall of 1935; at the moment, the solidarity of the three powers appeared to be complete, and at the subsequent meeting of the council of the League all joined in denouncing the recent German move.[4]

Some emphasis to the isolation of Germany was given by the signing on 2 May 1935 of the Franco-Soviet Pact of mutual assistance, followed by a Czech-Soviet Pact on 16 May.[5] If Berlin officials had anticipated these developments, they were somewhat surprised to see Poland join in the united front at Geneva. The Poles had been obdurate in the face of Eden's approach at the beginning of April—and had so informed the Germans—and they had been angry over the failure of Britain, France, and Italy to invite them to Stresa.[6] Warsaw's fear that Germany might make concessions at Poland's expense had been met by reassurances from Berlin.[7] In Geneva, however, the Polish government was not yet prepared to isolate itself as the spokesman for Germany, and in response to pressure from the Western powers had gone along with the resolution condemning Germany. Beck, the Polish foreign minister, was no doubt concerned that while no action of any sort would follow from passage of the resolution, the French government might well denounce the Franco-Polish alliance if Poland refused to

3. This statement was, however, far weaker than the Franco-Italian treaty exchanging military guarantees of the dimilitarized Rhineland and the independence of Austria that Mussolini, according to one source, had proposed to France before the meeting (Osuský reporting to Beneš on a conversation with Laval, 9 April 1935, Czech document in T–120, 1041/1809/413446).

4. On the Stresa conference and the subsequent council session see U. S. 1935, 1:212–16, 229–32, 244–46, 260–69; *G. D.*, C, 4, Nos. 24, 33, 36, 37, 46; Cmd. 5143, No. 13; Scott, pp. 240–43; Vansittart, *Mist Procession,* pp. 516–21; Colvin, *None so Blind,* pp. 60–61; Baer, chap. 6; Laurens, pp. 42–43; Geoffrey Thompson, *Front-Line Diplomat* (London: Hutchinson, 1959), pp. 96–99; Breckinridge Long Diary, 8 April 1935, p. 127, and 17 April, pp. 134–37, Library of Congress, Manuscript Division, Long Papers. The British briefing paper for Stresa is in Foreign Office C 3049/55/18; the minutes in C 3289/55/18.

On the Italian access to British diplomatic documents see Colvin, pp. 58–60; Mario Toscano, "Problemi particolari della storia della Secunda Guerra Mondiale," *Rivista di studi politici internationali*, 17, No. 3 (1950), pp. 388–98.

5. For the terms and final negotiations see Scott, pp. 243–50; *G. D.*, C, 4, No. 44. Excerpts from Soviet documents on the negotiations are in the series of articles by M. Andreyeva and L. Vidyasova in *International Affairs* (Moscow).

6. Szembek, 2 April 1935, pp. 52–56, 12 April, p. 61; *G. D.*, C, 4, Nos. 8, 11; U. S. 1935, 1:217–22.

7. *G. D.*, C, 4, Nos. 28, 30.

support the public gesture.[8] To Hitler, however, this action, coming between the Polish rejection of his overture for a military alliance against Russia and Laval's trip to Warsaw, may have looked like a warning of possible total isolation.[9] The opportunity to reestablish close German-Polish relations came sooner than expected: Marshal Pilsudski died on 12 May; the Poles reassured Berlin of their intention of continuing his policy toward Germany; and Göring was sent to the funeral ceremonies, using the opportunity to regale the Poles with promises of peace, tales of Soviet airfields in Czechoslovakia, and invitations to Berlin.[10]

Hitler himself contributed to calming the fears of other powers by a major foreign policy speech on 21 May 1935.[11] He offered bilateral nonaggression pacts to all neighbors except Lithuania (which was currently an object of German wrath); he assured the world that he wanted only peace; he promised to observe the Locarno Treaty including the demilitarization of the Rhineland; and he declared that Germany had no desire to interfere in the internal affairs of Austria or to secure its annexation to Germany. Since the evidence shows not only that each of these promises was later broken but that preparations to break a number of them were already under way, it may be asked why he would make them and why anyone believed him. The first question is easy to answer. He was concerned that the recent alliance between France and the Soviet Union together with the Stresa front might bring together all the other European powers against him in a mutual-assistance system of the type he never failed to denounce. The very alliance that he would use a year later as an excuse to break the Locarno Pact at first led him to promise adherence to that system so that he might reassure those who had been alarmed by his most recent step.

That anybody believed these pledges is more difficult to understand. Laval was as interested as ever in attaining an agreement with Germany, and he had so informed Göring when the two had had an opportunity to speak at the time of Pilsudski's funeral.[12] The British naval attaché in Berlin had told his American colleague that he would "feel more disposed to place reliance on German assurances, had he not been categorically told that no submarines were building, just prior to the announcement that twelve keels had been laid down."[13] His government, however, did not share this skepticism. Sir John Simon had come back from Berlin dubious about the possi-

8. Ibid., Nos. 41, 49; Szembek, 19–20 April, pp. 64–65, 29 April, p. 67; Krofta's comments to the section chiefs of the Czech foreign ministry, No. 14/35, 18 April 1935, Czech document in T–120, 1041/1809/414148–149.

9. Szembek, 10 May 1935, pp. 70–74; *G. D.*, C, 4, Nos. 88, 90.

10. Roos, pp. 218–19; *G. D.*, C, 4, Nos. 98, 115, p. 494; *Lipski Papers*, Nos. 43, 44; Szembek, 18 May, pp. 81–83, 87, 27 May, pp. 89–90.

11. Domarus, 1:505–14.

12. Szembek, 18 May 1935, pp. 81–83, 23 May, pp. 88–89; Strauss (Paris) dispatch 1905, 28 May 1935, State 862.20/1031. See also *G. D.*, C, 4, Nos. 127, 129; Cmd. 5143, No. 26; Warner, *Laval*, p. 83.

13. White (U. S. counsellor Berlin) dispatch 2016, 29 May, 1935, State 862.20/1040.

bility of agreement with Hitler; but after each encounter with reality, he returned to the attempt for a settlement with Germany.[14] Although willing to support a measure of British rearmament, Sir John always tried for some agreement with Germany, unwilling or unable to recognize that the attempts themselves only assured German intransigence because they were interpreted as signs of weakness.[15] Accordingly he continued talks with the Germans about the various pact proposals that had been under consideration before his trip to Berlin.[16] The one and only project that came to fruition, however, was not one of the international arrangements hitherto publicly endorsed by the British, French, or Italian governments but an Anglo-German naval agreement that provided for precisely the one thing the Stresa meeting had condemned: the repudiation of a treaty commitment without the consent of all the partners to that treaty.

The origins and nature of the Anglo-German naval agreement of 1935 are quickly told; its significance requires more extensive comment.[17] The naval limitations treaty in force in the early 1930s, the London Naval Treaty of 1930, was to expire in 1935, and a conference to determine the possibility of a new naval treaty was expected. In the summer of 1934 there was some consideration of Germany's policy toward participation in such a conference, and Hitler decided that, though not eager to join, Germany would play a part if invited.[18] It was, however, much easier to go ahead and build whatever warships Germany's shipyard capacity and raw material resources would allow.[19] The construction program already set up was carried forward; and, as Hitler explained to Admiral Raeder at the beginning of November 1934, no lack of money would be allowed to interfere with the progress of naval rearmament.[20] About the time of this discussion, Hitler decided that

14. Bingham (London) telegram 169, 10 April 1935, State 862.20/853; Emmet (The Hague) dispatch 191, 2 April 1935, State 862.20/914; von Papen telegram 33, 6 April 1935, T–120, 2499/4939/E 272003–04; Geyr report [5 April 1935], T–120, 2677/5576/E 400281–285.

15. U. S. 1935, 1:249–54; Atherton (London) dispatch 1389, 25 April 1935, State 862.20/980; "Vertraulicher Informationsbericht," 22 May 1935, Bundesarchiv, Brammer, Z.Sg. 101/28, f. 179–81.

16. Cmd. 5143, Nos. 19, 20, 22–25; *G. D.,* C, 4, Nos. 68, 77, 79, 82, 102, 106, 107, 113, 117, 122, 140, 151, 152; Long (Rome) dispatch 1111, 24 May 1935, and Bingham telegram 241, 27 May, State 862.20/1033 and 1020; Long Diary, 28 May 1935, pp. 149–50, Long Papers. For the skeptical comment of Jay Pierrepont Moffat see his letter to Hugh R. Wilson, the American minister in Switzerland, of 6 May 1935: "Unless there is a reasonable chance of success, negotiations (I fear) do more harm than good. To be concrete, I cannot help feeling that to maneuver Germany into talking or negotiating when she does not mean to abjure her ambitions or reach an agreement would not only *not* result in appeasement but might actually aggravate the situation" (Moffat Papers, Vol. 9).

17. The best treatment of the subject is Donald C. Watt's "The Anglo-German Naval Agreement of 1935: An Interim Judgement," *Journal of Modern History,* 28, No. 2 (June 1956), pp. 155–75. References to sources cited in that article are generally not repeated here.

18. *G. D.,* C, 3, Nos. 25, 32.

19. Ibid., No. 287.

20. Raeder-Hitler talk of 2 November 1934, *TMWC,* 34:775–76.

he would make his diplomatic demand for naval strength equal to one-third of the British navy and so inform the British government. There is little evidence of the precise origin of this figure.[21] There is, however, evidence, to be recounted presently, that in spite of being elaborately spelled out in the agreement between Germany and England, the figure was violated in a number of ways from the very beginning. Hitler's projection of this figure therefore must be taken as a facet of his political views of the moment rather than as a precise indication of his plans for naval construction.

Hitler wanted to build up a navy, and he wanted the friendship of Britain in the initial phases of his expansionist policy. He was determined to build up Germany's naval power, and he at no time hesitated to disregard his treaty commitments if they interfered with these plans. It was obvious, however, that the German navy would be relatively small to begin with, both because of the great time needed to build the larger warships and because the major emphasis in the allocation of Germany's resources would have to go to the army and air force. The navy that Germany would need for its first wars was the kind that would protect its access to Swedish iron ore, safeguard communications with East Prussia, ensure control of the Baltic against the Soviet Union, and give it the ability to threaten the oceanic supply routes of France. Such a navy would not have to be so large as to threaten England, and in view of Germany's unfortunate pre-1914 naval rivalry with England, why not say so? This was the concept Hitler had already set forth in *Mein Kampf,* and if agreement with England could be reached, it would serve to reassure that country while Germany moved forward in other areas on its target list, simultaneously dividing England from France. In this context, the ratio of one-third, or 35 percent, of British naval strength was an expression of an intent to build a substantial navy without (for the time being) threatening British naval supremacy—though on the assumption that Britain was prepared to forego its naval interests in such other parts of the world as the Far East. If Britain would agree to sanction such a German navy, the resulting treaty would be a major diplomatic triumph, a triumph requiring no concession that might interfere with Germany's plans. If Britain did not agree, Germany would continue to build such a navy all the same.

At the end of November 1934, the German government informed Great Britain of its interest in bilateral naval negotiations, its claim for an end to all restrictions on German naval construction such as those embodied in the peace treaty, and its willingness to restrict itself to 35 percent of British naval strength.[22] In the meantime, construction was pushed as rapidly as possible, so that the German navy might have attained the greatest possible strength by the time negotiations actually took place.[23] As the British and

21. *G. D.*, C, 3, No. 298. The figure may have originated with Admiral Raeder. A German Navy document of 4 June 1934 refers to his having ordered construction planning to be developed on the basis of "33⅓ percent of English tonnage" (Marineleitung "A IV a 2136/34 G. Kdos." of 4 June 1934, T–120, 3234/7792/E 565815).

22. *G. D.*, C, 3, Nos. 358, 360; Foreign Office C 841/55/18.

23. See Hitler's instructions to this effect of 16 January 1935, quoted in document 854–D, *TMWC*, 35:558 (cf. Bracher, p. 803, n. 267).

German naval authorities stayed in touch in the winter of 1934–35, the figure of 35 percent eventually leaked out, and the British asked that the subject be deferred until Simon's visit to Berlin in March.[24] On 26 March, Hitler personally told Sir John that the German demand was one he still insisted upon, claiming that its implicit acknowledgment of British naval superiority was a major concession. Although in Hitler's view the proposed ratio was a guideline he was already preparing to exceed in some areas, Sir John appears to have thought it a maximum demand from which the Germans might be persuaded to back down in the course of negotiations.[25] He was to be disabused of this notion at the naval talks in London to which he formally invited the Germans while in Berlin.

On the basis of von Ribbentrop's assignment to the disarmament negotiations and his participation in the meetings with Simon and Eden, Hitler decided in late March 1935 to entrust him with the conduct of the talks, insisting in the initial instructions that 35 percent be an irreducible minimum demand.[26] Just as the visit of Simon to Berlin had been put off until after the German government had announced the existence of its air force and the reintroduction of conscription, so now the naval talks were postponed until Germany could announce its naval rearmament and then calm the resulting flurry of excitement. In both cases, Hitler moved shrewdly to improve his bargaining position. In April 1935, the Germans informed the British of some of their naval construction plans, at first denying and subsequently affirming the inclusion of submarines.[27] The resulting uproar in Britain then provided the opportunity to delay actual talks until after Hitler's 21 May speech promising peace and goodwill to all. Once again the British were left with the choice of becoming involved in negotiations that would necessarily look like acquiescence in Germany's move—or sulk in their tents. Under these circumstances, the time for the negotiations was finally set for early June 1935.[28] The instructions to the German delegation were simply to insist on the 35 percent figure and leave all else as flexible as possible.[29] The British government may not have anticipated the signing of a formal document, and the German foreign ministry did not either, but the talks did in fact lead to an exchange of notes that had the effect of a treaty.[30]

From the first meeting on 4 June, von Ribbentrop insisted that preliminary to any discussion of details must be British agreement to the 35 percent

24. *G. D.*, C, 3, Nos. 416, 541.

25. Ibid., No. 555, pp. 1064–73; 4, No. 19.

26. Ibid., 3, No. 560.

27. Ibid., 4, Nos. 25, 51, 52.

28. On the background, see ibid., Nos. 50, 54, 55, 58–60, 66, 74, 104.

29. Ibid., No. 100.

30. Ibid., No. 114; Dodd telegram 114, 29 May 1935, State 862.34/120. The main German source for the talks is a file of the German naval staff in T–120, 3223/7790/passim; most of the relevant documents in *G. D.*, C, 4, are from this file which I have examined in full.

formula. He both refused to deviate from this minimum and pressured for its acceptance—the approach he came to take to most diplomatic problems. The British negotiators overcame their initial reluctance; the British cabinet agreed; and by the evening of 5 June the Germans had been told that the figure would be accepted.[31] It was only after Sir John Simon had officially confirmed acceptance of the figure on 6 June that the British government began to consult other interested powers.[32] This matter will be reviewed subsequently, but the sequence of events clearly shows British willingness to move rapidly to an agreement, if necessary disregarding the protests of others.

Once the British government had given way on the main point at issue, agreement on the other details was reached without great difficulty.[33] Because the Germans were already beginning a large program of submarine construction that would soon put them well in excess of the 35 percent limit, they insisted that in this category they be allowed a 45 percent figure for the time being, and parity, i.e., 100 percent of British strength in submarines in principle.[34] This meant that as soon as Germany's violation of this portion of the agreement became too obvious—as it did by the end of 1938—the German government could claim its privilege of parity and thus retroactively legitimize its treaty violations.[35]

The British government, in the middle of a change on 7 June in which Baldwin replaced MacDonald and Sir Samuel Hoare took over Simon's position, approved the agreement with Germany on the advice of its naval leaders, in response to the tremendous domestic political pressures for disarmament agreements, and in the hope of putting a limit on German rearmament in at least one field. It seemed to them that the French government had repeatedly caused them to miss opportunities for agreement with Germany; that the insistence of France on not agreeing formally to any degree of German rearmament in fact had led to unlimited German rearmament. The British may well have thought that failure to agree to 35 percent at the time would only lead, as in the case of German air armaments, to a subsequent claim for parity. London was, therefore, willing to go ahead, regardless of the views of others.[36]

31. *G. D.,* C, 4, Nos. 131, 132, 135–37.

32. Ibid., No. 141; U. S. 1935, 1:163–64. Sir Samuel Hoare in his memoirs claims that this was the second time that other powers were asked, but he is clearly in error (Viscount Templewood, *Nine Troubled Years* [London: Collins, 1954], pp. 141–42).

33. *G. D.,* C, 4, Nos. 154, 156, 165; but see the Krogmann diary entry for 23 June 1935, quoted in Jacobsen, p. 415, n. 7.

34. *G. D.*, C, 4, No. 148.

35. See the summary in document D–854, *TMWC,* 35:559. The description of the violations of the Anglo-German naval agreement in the area of submarines in this source must be discounted somewhat because its purpose was to defend the leadership of the German navy against subsequent charges that the submarine arm had been neglected in the years before World War II.

36. I cannot agree with the emphasis placed by Watt (p. 169) on the key role played by timing and the fact that Sir Robert Craigie, the Foreign Office representa-

These views were distinctively negative. The Italian government was unwilling to protest and presumably took the British action as confirming its previous assessment of British weakness. The French government was most disturbed by this breach of the Stresa front. The willingness of Great Britain to sanction German violations of the peace treaty, to make a bilateral "deal" with Germany, and to confront its erstwhile ally with a fait accompli aroused great bitterness in Paris.[37] The British readiness to disregard treaties and pledges in this case played a fateful role in the developing divergence between the policies of Britain and France in regard to Italy in 1935. As Donald C. Watt aptly characterized the posture of Britain after the naval agreement: "This was not, perhaps, the most suitable position from which to launch the crusade which occupied Britain's attentions for the second half of 1935 against Italy, the defiler of treaties, the breaker of covenants."[38] If the Soviet Union was alarmed[39] and Japan was pleased, the other major power, the United States, was most skeptical. In Washington, the agreement was thought to represent a shrewd move on Germany's part, one fraught with danger for the future.[40] The official American position was noncommittal, but State Department officials were clearly skeptical of the wisdom of the British action, a skepticism that would reinforce the isolationist tendency of American thinking.[41]

The effect of the agreement on Germany was most important. Von Ribbentrop's stock immediately rose tremendously; he obviously knew how to implement Hitler's ideas and have them accepted by the British. The possi-

---

tive in the British delegation, was the head of the American department in assessing the British decision to sign the naval agreement in June 1935. The German claim to 35 percent had been known to the British government for at least six months when the German delegation arrived in London; it is difficult to believe that there had been no discussion of the subject in the Foreign Office and the cabinet before the June talks. This aspect of the issue, as well as the relationship of British interest in the 35 percent figure to its desire for naval limitation vis-à-vis France and Italy, is examined in a Yale dissertation by Charles Bright.

37. The French memorandum in reply to the British request for comment is available in summary in Strauss telegram 511, 18 June 1935, U. S. 1935, 1:165–66. In March 1936, the French ambassador to Berlin commented that since Hitler was always saying that he would not agree to any unequal treaties, the Anglo-German naval agreement would surely go the way of Locarno (*D. D. F.*, 2d, 1, No. 435); see also Baer, pp. 184–87.

38. Watt, "The Anglo-German Naval Agreement," p. 174.

39. U. S. 1935, 1:168. The Soviets had been informed by Eden on 28 March that the German demand of 35 percent was regarded as "impossible" (Foreign Office C 2726/55/18, p. 3).

40. Memorandum of Noel H. Field (Division of Western European Affairs), 8 June 1935, State 862.34/146.

41. Hull telegram to Bingham No. 135, 11 June 1935, U. S. 1935, 1:164–65; Moffat to Atherton, 24 June 1935, Moffat Papers, Vol. 8.

For the negative impact of the Anglo-German naval agreement in Scandinavia, where it was seen as yielding control of the Baltic to Germany, see Nils Ørvik, "From Collective Security to Neutrality; The Nordic Powers, The League of Nations, Britain and the Approach of War, 1935–1939," in K. Bourne and D. C. Watt (eds.), *Studies in International History* (London: Longmans, 1967), p. 389.

bility of further German-British agreements loomed in the distance—if Germany could secure London's acquiescence in its own plans at no cost, there was no limit to the expressions of friendship that Hitler would utter. The proper instrument of such a policy, moreover, was obviously the man who had started it so successfully.[42] This impression, and the dangerously erroneous deductions Hitler made from it, was reinforced by simultaneous developments in the contacts between German and English war veterans. Here, too, von Ribbentrop's efforts appeared to be bringing about useful results.

Von Ribbentrop had made a number of useful contacts in England in November 1934[43] and had followed this up by establishing relations with the British Legion, the major British veterans' organization, in February 1935. Out of this grew an invitation to a delegation from the legion to visit Berlin. The British Foreign Office did not object to such contacts, and at the annual convention of the legion on 9 June 1935—during the naval talks—the president of the legion, General Sir Frederick Maurice, voiced his belief that a visit to Germany would be a good idea.[44] There followed the celebrated speech of Edward, Prince of Wales, on 11 June favoring contact between British and German veterans. In Britain, the fact that the officers of the British Legion, of which the future Duke of Windsor was the patron, had requested this speech was overlooked as the government became concerned over possible repercussions. The king reprimanded his son, and the British government reassured the French.[45] In Germany, however, the speech was interpreted in the light of earlier pro-German utterances made by the Prince of Wales and, combined with the subsequent visit of the legion group to Germany and their reception by Hitler, led to exaggerated views of pro-German feelings in England.[46] There can be little doubt that this exploitation of a genuine desire for peace and reconciliation enhanced the short-run pressures for concessions to Germany, but it also contributed to the unwarranted assumption by Berlin that there would be no limits to such concessions.

As for Germany's general diplomatic position, the advantages of the naval agreement were considerable. The Stresa front was broken; France

42. On this aspect see especially Erich Kordt, *Nicht aus den Akten,* pp. 108–12, and the incident recounted in Jacobsen, p. 79.

43. Kordt, pp. 81ff.

44. Wootton, pp. 173–76.

45. Ibid., pp. 176–82; *G. D.*, C, 4, No. 159; Bingham to Hull, 28 June 1935, State 740.00/38½, and Bingham to Roosevelt, 24 December 1935, Hyde Park, P. S. F. Bingham. An "Aktennotiz" of the APA of 20 February 1934, on a conversation with Prince Hohenlohe-Langenburg suggests that this relative of the British royal family may have played a part in laying the groundwork for the veterans' contacts and the Prince of Wales's speech (T–454, 86/21). See also Jan Masaryk's report 21 of 1 August 1935, Czech document in T–120, 1041/1809/413559–561.

46. *G. D.,* C, 4, No. 27; Wootton, pp. 183–87; Richard Meinertzhagen, *Middle East Diary 1917–1956* (London: Cresset Press, 1959), pp. 154–55; Helfferich, *1932–1946 Tatsachen,* pp. 143–44.

was isolated. The Italian government was pleased.[47] Germany's prestige had risen, and it had acquired the platform from which it could, as became evident very quickly, reject any and all efforts for international agreements and guarantees to secure the peace. Perhaps learning from this experience, the British government in subsequent years would always insist that agreements on specific subjects, such as colonies, be made only within a wider framework of arrangements to protect peace in Europe, but in this first and last experiment in a bilateral settlement the British had given Germany a decisive advantage in the diplomatic arena.

As far as naval construction was concerned, the agreement had no particular significance. Germany could and did develop its navy as it wished and to the extent that its resources permitted.[48] While the current construction program was largely within the limits of the naval agreement, Germany already had begun to inaugurate those naval schemes that looked to the distant future when Germany would want a navy able to cope with Britain's. The plans for the construction of the superbattleships needed for that purpose and the facilities required for that type of a navy were begun at the very time when Hitler celebrated his latest diplomatic triumph.[49] These preparations shed a revealing light on Hitler's sincerity. They also reveal the complete unreliability of the memoirs and statements of Admiral Raeder, the commander in chief of the German navy, who claims to have believed Hitler's public avowals of permanent friendship with Britain in the very years when his own headquarters was preparing the plans and initiating construction of a navy designed to challenge Britain on the high seas.

As the world looked with astonishment at the conclusion of the Anglo-German naval agreement, a crisis of even greater scope was occupying the center of attention. The imminent conflict between Italy and Ethiopia would benefit only the men in Berlin. The details of the diplomacy surrounding that conflict are not relevant here—though it may be worth recording that, of all those involved in that sordid episode, today only the chief victim, Haile Selassie, emperor of Ethiopia, sits in the seat of the mighty. For an understanding of the evolution of the international situation and Germany's place in it, however, certain aspects of that conflict must be reviewed.

Mussolini decided to push forward his plans for the seizure of Ethiopia in the fall of 1934. In view of the hostility between Germany and Italy over the Austrian question, the ruler of Ethiopia tried to secure arms from Germany as well as other sources. The Berlin government, however, had no wish to antagonize Italy over issues so remote from Germany's concerns. Germany

47. *G. D.,* C, 4, Nos. 199, 206.

48. Ibid., No. 275; *TMWC*, 41:3–5.

49. On this subject see the very important details in Paul W. Zieb, *Logistische Probleme der Kriegsmarine* (Neckargemünd: Vowinckel, 1961), pp. 140–44. For British credulousness on this subject see Sir Robert Craigie's minutes of 23 November 1936, Foreign Office A 9482/4671/45.

declined to help and set a neutral course in the developing confrontation.[50] In the manner previously described, the Italian African venture brought Italy and France closer together, an alignment cultivated by both powers in the first half of 1935 and hastened by the Anglo-German naval agreement. That agreement showed the French that they would have to work with Italy to prevent the annexation of Austria by Germany, and it is not entirely coincidental that the Franco-Italian military convention for cooperation against any German military move against Austria was signed on the day after the anniversary of the Battle of Waterloo that had been thoughtlessly picked for the signing of the naval agreement.[51] This alignment of Italy and France was very much on the minds of the leaders of Britain as they faced the crisis over Ethiopia.

The British government, having failed to warn Mussolini at Stresa and thus becoming responsible for his belief that he could move forward with impunity, made a number of last-minute attempts to dissuade the Italian leader from his aggressive designs. There was a scheme to recompense Ethiopia for making concessions to Italy by giving it an outlet to the sea through a part of British Somaliland; there was a special trip by Sir Anthony Eden, the British minister for League of Nations Affairs, to Rome; and there was a great deal of pleading and talking at Geneva. None of this had the slightest impact on Mussolini who by now was determined to go ahead. He felt that the status of his regime was committed to aggression once he openly started to move under the impression that he had France's approval and Britain's tacit consent.[52] Confronted by this determination, Britain and France adopted precisely those policies best calculated to harm their own interests and least likely to aid Ethiopia.

The British government, carried forward by a sudden outburst of popular support for the League, now advocated sanctions against Italy but was unwilling to risk a war that successful sanctions might well precipitate. They would annoy Italy by obstruction—and thus simultaneously rally the Italian people to Mussolini's venture while spoiling the prospect of a future common front against German aggression—but they would not push their measures to the risk of conflict. The British government was reasonably confident that they could defeat Italy, but they were worried about the future international situation if their navy had been weakened in a war in the Mediterranean; and they were worried about the evolution of Italy's domestic situation if they should defeat Italy and precipitate Mussolini's fall.

50. *G. D.*, C, 3, Nos. 280, 402, 403.

51. Baer, pp. 84–85; Laurens, pp. 52–53; Gamelin, *Servir,* 2:163–69; Gaetano Salvemini, *Prelude to World War II* (Garden City: Doubleday, 1954), p. 223; *G. D.*, C, 4:976, n. 5; Long to Roosevelt, 8 February 1935, Hyde Park, P. S. F. Long; Osuský's reports to Beneš of 27 June and 2 July 1935, Czech documents in T–120, 1041/1809/413466 and 1143/2028/444368–369.

52. The account in Baer, chaps. 7–10, is considerably more perceptive than Laurens, chaps. 4–6.

They thus antagonized Italy but without inflicting sufficient damage to reduce the potential danger that Italy might pose to Britain in the future.[53]

The French were amazed at the enthusiasm with which the British public endorsed in Africa the very principle of collective security they had hitherto rejected with such emphasis in Europe. The nation that had been unwilling to accept responsibility for the integrity of the East European allies of France suddenly seemed eager to support Ethiopia. Coming right after the British abandonment of the Stresa front in the naval treaty with Germany, the anti-Italian thrust of British policy was especially regretted by a French government that had apparently won over Italy to a common front of resistance to German aggressive moves in Europe. The reluctance of France, under these circumstances, to support Britain wholeheartedly on the Ethiopian question helped restrain the British from pushing forward with effective measures against Italy lest they be left facing Italy alone. This in turn meant, first, that Mussolini knew it was safe for him to go forward with his policy, and second, that the British would be angry with the French for not giving full support to the concept of collective security. This, in turn, would affect British policy on the question of supporting France in taking action against Germany in the March 1936 crisis over Germany's violation of Locarno in remilitarizing the Rhineland. The French, on the other hand, had seen little reason to support Britain's new crusade for the League, while London simultaneously refused to extend similar enthusiasm to its prospective obligation to assist France under the Locarno agreements. Forced by circumstances to choose between the League and Rome, Britain and France destroyed the League, alienated Rome, and drifted further apart themselves.

As this situation developed during the course of the summer and fall of 1935, it provided the German government with great benefits that may be divided into four general categories. First, it made it easy for Germany to postpone and eventually evade agreement on all of the various pact proposals that had once been the subject of such great international interest. The same reluctance of the Western powers to antagonize Germany while they were in difficulty with Italy also enabled Germany to proceed essentially undisturbed with the process of rearmament and military planning. A third benefit for Germany was that the concentration of Britain, France, and Italy on the Mediterranean gave Germany a greater opportunity to extend its influence in the Balkans, an opportunity enhanced by the imposition of sanctions on Italy which opened up new possibilities for German trade expansion. The fourth and in the long run perhaps most important result of the Ethiopian conflict was the rapprochement between Italy and Germany that would come to be known as the Axis.

The first of these themes need not be traced in detail. In tedious negoti-

53. It should be noted that the drain upon Italy by its involvement first in Ethiopia and then in Spain certainly affected its conduct of diplomacy in 1939 and of the war after 1940, but these long-range effects were of no help to England in the mid-1930s.

ations, the German government delayed and eventually rendered impossible any agreement on new security pacts. The Air Pact, the Eastern Locarno Pact, the Danubian Pact, all fell victim to Germany's unwillingness to accept multilateral restrictions on its freedom of action.[54] The final rejection of all new security pacts was given by Hitler to the British ambassador, Sir Eric Phipps, on 13 December 1935; and in that conversation Hitler alluded to the next step on the road: the demilitarized Rhineland.[55] By this time, Germany's departure from the League of Nations had become final, with the end of the two-year period after withdrawal specified in the covenant.[56] The British and French had, in fact, already dropped, at least for the time being, their request that Germany return to the League as part of the international agreements under consideration.

The French prime minister and foreign minister, Pierre Laval, had been prepared to go even further. In a lengthy series of negotiations in the summer and fall of 1935 he had attempted to secure a direct rapprochement with Germany. These negotiations, falling between the signing and the ratification of the Franco-Soviet alliance, were designed to bring about a harmonizing of that pact with better Franco-German relations, to reduce the importance of the pact with Russia, and to strengthen Laval's position in the quicksand of French politics. He clearly had in mind as a model his previous agreement with Italy—on which French policy continued to build[57]—and included in the concept personal contact with Hitler. Through official and unofficial channels, Laval attempted to bring about some agreement between the two neighbors, urging speed because his successor was unlikely to follow a similar policy, but hoping to commit the next French government to agreement with Germany just as his predecessors had committed his own government to the Soviet Union. To these overtures there was no positive response from Germany, and by the end of 1935 all these efforts, like their predecessors, had been thwarted by Berlin.[58] As the chief of the

54. These negotiations can be traced in Cmd. 5143 and *G. D.*, C, 4.

55. *G. D.*, C, 4, Nos. 460, 462; the reference to ending the demilitarization of the Rhineland is not included in the report of Sir Eric Phipps in Cmd. 5143, No. 46. See also *Lipski Papers*, No. 55.

56. See Gilbert (Geneva) telegram 503, 15 October 1935, State 500.C 001/1136. The German foreign ministry immediately pushed for the dissolution of the German Society for League of Nations Questions (Memorandum of von Bülow, 22 October T–120, 2371/4601/E 188839).

57. On Gamelin's visit to Rome in July and Badoglio's trip to Paris in September see *G. D.*, C, 4, Nos. 194, 373.

58. On the official negotiations see *G. D.*, C, 4, Nos. 225, 231, 235, 277, 287, 415, 418, 419, 423, 425, 426, 430, 435, 440, 467; Dodd, *Diary*, 22 May 1935, p. 247; Dodd dispatch 2492, 27 November 1935, State 751.62/327; Warner, *Laval*, pp. 84, 92–94, 110–111. On unofficial contacts involving the APA see Rosenberg to Lammers, 29 January 1936, Nuremberg document 274–PS (National Archives), and Jacobsen, p. 62, n. 17; on unofficial contacts involving de Brinon see *G. D.*, C, 4, No. 384; Szembek, 9 November 1935, pp. 130–31; Dodd telegram 217 of 7 November and dispatch 2450 of 8 November 1935, State 751.62/320 and 325; "Informationsbericht Nr. 53," 28 October and "Informationsbericht Nr. 56," of 11 November 1935,

west European section of Rosenberg's foreign policy office later expressed it, Laval's plans for agreement with Germany "could not be carried out because Germany turned them down."[59]

Postponing to the indefinite future any treaty arrangement like the proposed Eastern Locarno Pact implied not only an unwillingness on Germany's part to place its relationship with Britain and France on a new basis but had similar implications for its relations with the Soviet Union. The economic relationship of Germany and Russia was maintained under the terms of the new trade treaty of 9 April 1935 that provided for German credit to Russia of 200 million marks.[60] The hopes initially attached to the prospect of this agreement during the negotiations for it faded under the impact of an unfriendly speech by Vyacheslav Molotov on 28 January and the exceedingly uncooperative attitude of Schacht during the talks with David Kandelaki, the leader of the Soviet trade delegation to Berlin.[61] There is considerable evidence, all the same, that the continued worry of Soviet leaders about German intentions led them to hope that there was still some prospect of normalizing political relations. The Soviet Union entered upon its new treaty with France reluctantly and while still leaving open other possibilities; Soviet leaders repeatedly indicated as much to the Germans by expressions of fear of German intentions combined with hope for new agreements.[62] The German government displayed no interest in responding to these soundings, but in the summer of 1935 informal negotiations in

---

Bundesarchiv, Brammer, Z.Sg. 101/28, f. 317–19 and 335–37. On unofficial contacts that continued the use of war veterans see Forster (Paris) report B 2946 III, 4 July 1935, T–120, 2696/5717/H 024408–410; Krofta's comments to the section chiefs of the Czech foreign ministry, No. 25/35, 12 September 1935, Czech document in T–120, 1041/1809/414166–167.

In May 1937, Laval gave an interesting review of all his efforts to some unofficial German visitors; see the enclosure attached to Rosenberg's letter to Göring, 22 May 1937, Bundesarchiv, Stabsamt Göring, f. 134–145.

59. Georg Ebert to Rosenberg, 22 July 1937, T–454, 86/163.

60. *G. D.*, C, 4, Nos. 20, 21.

61. On the economic negotiations and on German-Soviet trade in this period see *G. D.*, C, 3, Nos. 494, 505, 514, 529, 546, 562; White (Berlin) dispatches 1640 of 5 January and 1715 of 29 January 1935, State 861.51–German credits/53 and 54; Russland-Ausschuss der Deutschen Wirtschaft circular to the members of its Vorstand, 11 January 1935, EAP 250–d–18–15/8 in T–81, roll 15, serial 36; Wiley (Moscow) dispatch 392 of 16 February and telegram 93 of 9 March 1935, State 861.51–German credits/57 and 58.

The turn in the negotiations can be seen by comparing the German foreign ministry's request to the Gestapo not to proceed with planned searches of Soviet agencies in Germany because of the negotiations on 25 January with the positive response when the Gestapo checked again on 14 February 1935 (Tippelskirch, Aufz. IV Ru 310, T–120, 2791/6025/H 047200–201 and IV Ru 636, T–120, 2792/6025/H 047222).

62. *G. D.*, C, 4, Nos. 2, 3, 7, 15, 23, 70, 78, 95, 180; Schulenburg's report of 9 January 1935, T–120, 1071/1906/429003; Schulenburg telegram 49, 22 March 1935, T–120, 2792/6025/H 047259. Note also the report of Trautmann on a conversation with the counselor of the Soviet embassy in Peking in report 527, 25 May 1935, T–120, 2792/6025/H 047280–287.

Berlin between Schacht and Kandelaki roused new hopes on the Russian side.

The details of the Schacht-Kandelaki talks of June and July 1935 are by no means clear as yet, but it appears that Schacht had substantially reversed his earlier attitude. The subsequent failure of the Germans to follow through on the talks as soon as their political implications became clear, and the eventual collapse of the more novel parts of even the economic portions of the proposed agreements, strongly suggests that Germany's raw material and foreign-exchange shortages were the dominant element in Schacht's initiative rather than any political directive from Hitler. It should be remembered, on the other hand, that the ideological preconceptions of the Soviet leaders inclined them to look upon Schacht as far more influential than he really was, to assume that he would be not only aware of the political implications of any major agreement but also able to insist on his policy regardless of doubts expressed elsewhere in the German government, and therefore to attach to the negotiations—and their eventual failure—an importance greater than the facts probably warranted.

In June 1935, Schacht suggested an expanded German-Soviet trade program which he hoped to make attractive to the Soviet government by offering a general credit of a very large sum, eventually defined as 500 million for a ten-year period. Kandelaki immediately went to Moscow to discuss this project. There the highest Soviet leaders, including Stalin, not unreasonably assumed that political as well as economic motives must lie behind any such German proposal. Kandelaki returned with the reply that the Soviet government would like to await the completion of the existing 200-million program before entering on bigger projects, but then immediately suggested that German-Soviet political relations might be improved.[63] The German government did not follow up on this hint—evidence that Schacht had moved on his own with economic rather than political objectives in mind—but when the economic discussions were resumed at the end of October 1935, the Soviet government returned to the political issue. The Russians were clearly angry over the French delay in ratifying the Franco-Soviet Pact; and just as the government of Pierre Laval made a last effort at accommodation with Germany before ratification, so now the Soviet government made what can only be interpreted as a last attempt to come to agreement with Germany before committing itself to a policy of collective security. In conversations in Moscow the Russians convinced German diplomats that they were seriously interested in exploring new approaches.[64] The Soviet leaders were encouraged by another conversation

63. *G. D.*, C, 4, No. 211. On the June talks see Bullitt (Moscow) telegram 255, 27 June 1935, State 861.51–German credits/68. The denial by Hilger (of the German embassy in Moscow) reported in Bullitt's telegram 257 of the same date (ibid./69) merely reflects the secrecy of the Schacht-Kandelaki talks; even the German foreign ministry appears to have found out about the credit offer only in December 1935.

64. *G. D.*, C, 4, Nos. 383, 387, 407.

between Schacht and Kandelaki on 30 October 1935 in which the long-term credit possibility was again ventilated, leading the Russians to think once again that there must be political intentions on the German side.[65] From mid-November to early December, the Russian government made a series of diplomatic probes of German intentions, trying to sound them out directly in Berlin and through the German embassy in Moscow as well as indirectly through the German consul general in Tiflis.[66]

Discussions between the Germans and Russians took place in Berlin during the negotiations for a new economic agreement in December of 1935 and January and February 1936. There was disagreement within the German government over the best course to follow. The German ambassador to Russia, Count Friedrich Werner von der Schulenburg, went to Berlin to confer with Hitler and with Germany's economic and military leaders.[67] The Russian requests for military equipment within the trade agreement framework as well as the long-term character of the trade credit both—perhaps intentionally—gave the trade negotiations a political aspect that Hitler, it soon become evident, did not want. The negotiations, therefore, were allowed to continue indecisively, and as the French government moved toward ratification of the Franco-Soviet Pact in late February, the Russians also lost interest.[68] The broader questions were removed from the talks and eventually a routine trade and payments agreement was signed on 29 April 1936.[69]

Hitler desired correct military relations with the Red army, and he preferred that mutually profitable trade relations continue, but he wanted nothing that would deprive him of an anti-Bolshevik propaganda line while Germany was building up its power in Central Europe.[70] He was also con-

65. Ibid., No. 386.

66. Ibid., Nos. 439, 453; Dienstmann (Tiflis) to German embassy Moscow, telegram 28, 16 November 1935, and Tippelskirch (Moscow) to Roediger (Berlin), 18 November 1935, T–120, 1071/1906/429127–129; Memorandum by Tippelskirch, 28 November, ibid., frames 429130–132; Hencke (Berlin) to Tippelskirch, 26 November, T–120, 1097/2082/450950–951, and Tippelskirch to Hencke, 28 November, ibid., frames 450956–960; Leibbrandt (APA) to Rosenberg, 25 November 1935, and Memorandum of Eugen Dürksen (APA), 13 November 1935, EAP 250–d–18–05/5, T–81, serial 32, roll 11. It should be noted that the representative of the Narkomindel in Tiflis who contacted the German consul general there was Georgei Astakhov, later a key figure in the 1939 German-Soviet negotiations.

67. *G. D.,* C, 4, No. 439; Hencke to Tippelskirch, 4 December 1935, T–120, 1097/2082/450965–969.

68. On these negotiations see Niclauss, pp. 187–91; *G. D.,* C, 4:968, Nos. 472, 483, 489, 490, 502, 505, 518, 524, 530, 565; *D. D. F.,* 2d., 1, Nos. 8, 21, 46, 364; U. S. 1936, 1:200–02, 212–13; Hencke (Berlin) to von Dirksen (Tokyo), 14 January 1936, T–120, 1097/2082/450885–890; Hencke to Schulenburg, 29 January 1936, ibid., frames 450919–921; Hencke to Schulenburg, 5 February 1936, ibid., frames 450926–927; Köstring (German military attaché Moscow), Beilage I zu Bericht 3/36, 3 February 1936, T–120, 2760/5892/E 433188–189. See also Chilston (Moscow) to Collier (London), 11 February 1936, Foreign Office N 911/187/38.

69. The text and relevant document in *G. D.,* C, 4, No. 302.

70. Interrogation of Köstring by Oron J. Hale, 30–31 August 1945, Office of the

cerned about the possible repercussions in Poland of a German-Soviet rapprochement since Poland's acquiescence was important for the remilitarization of the Rhineland; the Poles were reassured by Göring that the rumors of better German-Soviet relations were false.[71] Beyond the light they shed on both German and Soviet foreign policy in 1935, these negotiations by their interrelation of economic and political issues in the initial stages as well as the simultaneous negotiations with other powers foreshadow the German-Soviet discussions of 1939. But the difference should be clearly noted: Russia was interested in 1935, but Germany was not. Its primary interest was still in gaining time to rearm, not yet in Soviet acquiescence in an attack on other countries. When Germany actually contemplated war, its attitude toward the Soviet Union would change.

In the meantime, the Moscow government had directed the Comintern, the international organization of Communist parties subservient to the Soviet Union, to alter its policy of attacking the Socialists throughout the world as "Social Fascists" and thus the main enemies of the working class. Instead, in order to secure allies against a possible future German threat, the Communist parties abroad were reoriented toward a united front against fascism in alliance with other parties in their respective countries. This united front policy was developed during 1935, though its official endorsement at the Seventh Comintern Congress in August 1935 did not immediately end all doubts among the Communist faithful. In any case, it had not restrained Stalin from continuing to explore the possibility of a political agreement with Germany; the check to that had come from Berlin.[72]

German rearmament proceeded rapidly during 1935. After the reintroduction of conscription, both the military and civilian leaders of Germany were worried lest any activity in the demilitarized zone in the Rhineland provide France with an opportunity to claim a violation of the Locarno Pact that might justify military action. Great care was accordingly exercised to avoid such activity or at least to camouflage it or keep it to a minimum.[73] Such restrictions, however, did not substantially hinder the building up of Germany's armed forces. In fact, the year that brought conscription back into German life also saw the beginning of military planning going beyond the emergency defensive measures considered at the time Germany left the League. The details of this planning cannot yet be reconstructed, but there is enough evidence to indicate its general nature.

Chief of Military History, Foreign Studies Branch; Hencke (Berlin) to Tippelskirch (Moscow), 11 March 1936, T–120, 1097/2082/451002–005; Tippelskirch to Hencke, 16 March, ibid., frame 451008; Hencke to Tippelskirch, 18 March, ibid., frames 451009–012; Hencke to Tippelskirch, 25 March, ibid., frames 451014–017.

71. *G. D.*, C, 4, No. 591.

72. See Armstrong, *Politics of Totalitarianism*, pp. 33–38.

73. *G. D.*, C, 4, Nos. 32, 56, 57, 118, 147, 163, 242, 420; Fritsch on 24 April 1935, Liebmann Notes, Institut für Zeitgeschichte, ED–1. pp. 83–85; Reichenau on 26 June 1935, *TMWC*, 36:434–35.

Immediately following the promulgation of conscription, the German ministry of war initiated the process of revising the defense plans of October 1933.[74] The situation in which Germany might have to fight was defined in a directive of 30 March 1935 as one of warding off an attack by France and Italy. In this directive, the possibility of attacking Czechoslovakia was referred to, but there is explicit rejection of a surprise attack on that country; military action would be taken only if the Czechs had already taken aggressive action themselves.[75] Discussions by the Minister of War with the chiefs of the branches of the German armed forces during April, however, led to a reorientation of von Blomberg's thinking: on 2 May he asked the armed forces to prepare precisely for that surprise attack (*Überfall*) which his office had previously rejected.[76]

This suggestion of an attack on Czechoslovakia immediately provoked a violent rejoinder from the chief of staff of the German Army, General Ludwig Beck, who had apparently not taken part in the April discussions. He warned his commander in chief, General von Fritsch, that the attack on Czechoslovakia proposed in this directive would lead to a general war and to Germany's defeat and occupation with its army trapped in Bohemia. He declined to prepare the detailed suggestions von Blomberg had requested, and he asked to be relieved of his position if there were any serious intention of going forward with the project.[77] The subject of an attack on Czechoslovakia thereupon disappeared from the military records for two years—as far as one can tell at the moment—but there is nothing to suggest that this quiescence reflected any fundamental change in policy. Hitler himself indicated to some of his officers in the fall of 1935, after Mussolini's attack on Ethiopia, that a similar occasion might come for Germany.[78] As Viktor Brack of Hitler's staff explained to a member of the American embassy in Berlin in November 1935, Hitler would not undertake active steps in foreign policy until "the platform from which he can shoot has been firmly estab-

74. *G. D.,* C, 3, No. 540.

75. Ibid., No. 568.

76. Blomberg directive on "Schulung," 2 May 1935, *TMWC,* 34:485–86.

77. The full text of Beck's memorandum of 3 May in Beck's papers in the Bundesarchiv, H 08–28/2. Excerpts from the memorandum and the covering letter to Fritsch are printed in Foerster, pp. 31–32. The additional documents now available (see nn. 74 and 75) and the full text of Beck's memorandum support the interpretation in Boris Čelovsky, *Das Münchener Abkommen,* p. 91, against the fanciful efforts of Meinck, *Hitler und die deutsche Aufrüstung,* pp. 137–38. The formulation in Helmut Krausnick, "Vorgeschichte und Beginn des militärischen Widerstandes gegen Hitler," *Die Vollmacht des Gewissens,* 1 (Munich: Hermann Rinn, 1956), p. 263, is better than Meinck's but still does not face the issue as squarely as Beck himself did. Useful, but inconclusive, are the documents now printed in Voelker, *Dokumente und Dokumentarfotos,* pp. 445–50. There is a fine analysis of the relationship of Beck's protest to the conflict between the leadership of the German army and the leadership of the German armed forces as directed by von Blomberg in Klaus-Jürgen Müller, *Das Heer und Hitler* (Stuttgart: Deutsche Verlags-Anstalt, 1969), pp. 210–13, 229–31.

78. Görlitz, *Keitel,* pp. 80–81.

lished."[79] Until that moment came, Germany would concentrate on rearming.[80]

Southeast Europe was another area in which the show of great concern over Ethiopia enabled Germany to move forward in 1935–36. German military thinking was already being directed against Czechoslovakia, as has just been demonstrated; its diplomatic policy in this period was designed to lay the groundwork for steps against that country when Germany was ready and the situation favorable. It would be somewhat misleading to read into the events an interpretation based on the precise steps followed by Germany in 1938, but there were ample contemporary signs of the general orientation of German policy.

German policy toward the Czech state in 1935 and early 1936 may be described as falling into three separate categories. In international propaganda, Germany stressed the new treaty between Czechoslovakia and the Soviet Union in order to discredit the Czech state, implying that it was Russia's Central European aircraft carrier. In direct relations between Berlin and Prague, the Germans were mainly intent upon maintaining a generally hostile attitude, refraining from agreement on any specific issue outstanding between the two countries, the question of agitation against Germany by German émigrés living in Czechoslovakia being the most important of these at the time.[81] Looking to the future was the third theme of German policy: the financial and political support of Konrad Henlein's Sudeten German Front, later party, inside Czechoslovakia. While there were various crosscurrents within this movement, its growth in 1934 and early 1935 made it appear to Berlin as a suitable successor of the prohibited German National Socialist party as an instrument of German policy. Henlein received large financial subsidies from Berlin for the campaign preceding the May 1935 elections as well as for other activities of his party. For such operations, the needed foreign exchange could always be found. The German government, acting both through regular diplomatic channels and through the Society for Germandom Abroad (*Verband für das Deutschtum im Ausland*) began the operations that one day were destined to lead to disaster both the German and the Czech inhabitants of Czechoslovakia.[82]

79. Dodd dispatch 2470, 15 November 1935, State 860M.01–Memel/443; cf. Phipps dispatch 1160, 13 November 1935, Foreign Office C 7647/55/18.

80. See the minutes of the eleventh session of the Reichsverteidigungsausschuss of 6 December 1935, *TMWC*, 36:437–77.

81. On the general subject of German-Czech relations see *G. D.*, C, 3, No. 33; 4, Nos. 89, 105, 359, 429, 580. On the negotiations concerning émigrés see *G. D.*, C, 3, Nos. 477, 480, 511, 523; 4, Nos. 89, 128; Beneš to the Czech legation in Berlin, 3 June 1935, Czech document in T–120, 1041/1809/413480–481; Krofta's comments to the section chiefs of the Czech foreign ministry, No. 20/35, 6 June 1935, Czech document in T–120, 1041/1809/414158.

82. On the German subsidies to Henlein see *G. D.*, C, 3, Nos. 482, 509; 4, Nos. 119, 320, 357, 413, 512; a useful survey in Brügel, pp. 258–74. The author cannot accept Jacobsen's evaluation (pp. 162ff.) of the VDA's role in this regard.

Henlein's party won a great victory in the May elections, absorbing the majority of the German voters within the Czech state.[83] The financing of the Henlein party from Berlin was known to the Prague government, and Berlin in turn knew that the Czech government was aware of the facts.[84] None of this would prevent the German government, or certain postwar German writers, from stressing the wholly imaginary independence of Henlein and the obtuseness of the Czech government in not making greater concessions to him. The Czech government, understandably alarmed, continued to hope for an accommodation between the major powers as the best way to peace.[85] The only alternative for the Czech government would be direct agreement with Germany. As Eduard Beneš, the foreign minister and later president of Czechoslovakia, explained quite frankly to the American minister, Czechoslovakia had no alternative other than dependence on its principal allies if it were not to fall under Germany's influence.[86] After March 1936, Beneš was to try for a direct agreement with Germany, only to discover that this, too, was precluded by Berlin's policy. Germany's intentions ruled out any agreement; strengthening the Sudeten German party as a weapon for future use against the Czech state from within, Germany bent its diplomatic efforts to reorient Hungary's policy and sought to split the Little Entente as a means of pressuring Czechoslovakia from without.

In its dealings with Hungary, Germany attempted to focus the revisionist aspirations of Budapest on Czechoslovakia. On various occasions in 1934 and 1935, the German government emphasized to the leaders of Hungary that they should concentrate their revisionist demands in a single direction—northward—and improve their relations with Yugoslavia and possibly even with Rumania. If this were accomplished, joint German-Hungarian pressure could be brought to bear on the Czechs while Hungary would be free of threats from the other members of the Little Entente.[87]

83. *G. D.*, C, 3, No. 525; 4, No. 99; Krofta's comments to the section chiefs of the Czech foreign ministry, No. 19/35, 23 May 1935, Czech document in T–120, 1041/1809/414156.

For the election, the Sudeten German Front made an arrangement with the Carpathian German party under which the former subsidized the latter and arranged for Franz Karmasin, who was to play a significant role in later years, to be elected to the Czech parliament. The annex to the electoral agreement of 28 March 1935 is printed in Král, *Die Deutschen in der Tschechoslowakei,* p. 76.

The possible relationship of the Sudeten Germans to the Slovak nationalists at this time is not clear; see the letter of K. Hoffman of the Czech legation in Berlin to the Czech foreign ministry about Dr. Peter Bazovský, 8 July 1935, Czech document in T–120, 1143/2028/444500–501; Hoensch, *Slowakei,* p. 59. I am indebted to Professor Josef Anderle for information about Bazovský and his father based on Ivan Dérer, *Slovenský vývoj a ludácká zrada: Fakta, vzpomínky a úvahy* [Slovak development and the Populist Treason: Facts, Reminiscences and Reflections] (Prague: Kvasnička a Hampl, 1946), pp. 338–39.

84. Král, p. 82.

85. U. S. 1935, 1:227.

86. Wright (Prague) dispatch 131, 25 March 1935, State 862.20/920.

87. For German explanations of this policy see the Stülpnagel memorandum of 7 November 1934, Bundesarchiv, Beck, H 08–28/1; Rosenberg, *Tagebuch,* 2 Feb-

The Hungarian government was not entirely persuaded of the wisdom of this policy and particularly the reconciliation with Yugoslavia. They objected strenuously to the antirevisionist statements Hermann Göring was supposed to have made in Belgrade as he sought Germany's own rapprochement with Yugoslavia, and Göring himself had to urge the policy of concentrating on the Czechs and improving relations with Belgrade while in Budapest in May 1935.[88] The same theme was urged on the Hungarian chief of staff during his visit to Berlin in the following month.[89] When the Hungarian prime minister, Julius Gömbös, made his second pilgrimage to Berlin in late September, he spoke as if he were somewhat inclined to fall in with German wishes, but the Germans simply could not persuade Hungary to make a clean break with its past policies in this regard.[90] Whatever Gömbös may really have thought, his position in domestic Hungarian affairs was not firm enough to permit him to renounce any of Hungary's revisionist hopes. He may also have feared the future intentions of Germany itself because of other aspects of German-Hungarian relations.

The Germans had been most displeased when Hungary joined with Italy and Austria in the Rome protocol of March 1934 and continued to hold this deviation against Budapest.[91] The Hungarian and German governments also continued to spar at arm's length about the fate of the German minority in Hungary. Hungary still hoped for cooperation between the German and Magyar minorities in the successor states, but the Germans preferred to concentrate on the situation in Hungary. The contacts between German agencies and the minority inside Hungary aroused the suspicions of the

---

ruary 1935, pp. 67–69. Hitler assumed that this policy would also make Hungary totally dependent on Germany (Geist to Moffat, 26 January 1935, Moffat Papers, Vol. 8).

88. On the incident concerning Göring's alleged statements in Belgrade about Hungarian revisionist demands, see *G. D.*, C, 4, Nos. 291, 292, 305, 323, 336. This issue precipitated a German demand for the recall of the Yugoslav minister to Berlin, Constantin de Masirevich, who was replaced in August 1935 after considerable prodding from Berlin.

On Göring's trip to Budapest see *G. D.*, C, 4:291–92 and No. 146; *Horthy Papers*, No. 21 and p. 82; Masirevich report, ca. 22 May 1935, in Szinai and Szücs, p. 182; Beck memorandum on a conversation with von Bülow on 22 June 1935, Bundesarchiv, Beck, H 08–28/2; Montgomery (Budapest) dispatch 258, 10 June 1935, State 762.64/36.

89. Beck's notes on the meeting of 24 June 1935, in Bundesarchiv, Beck, H 08–28/2; excerpts in Foerster, p. 28.

90. *G. D.*, C, 4, Nos. 307, 311, 328, 344, 348; Magda Ádám, Gyula Juhász, and Lajos Kerekes (eds.), *Allianz Hitler-Horthy-Mussolini* (Budapest: Akadémiai Kiadó, 1966), No. 8. On Gömbös's visit to Berlin (and the almost simultaneous visit of German air force General Erhard Milch to Budapest) see also Messersmith to Phillips, 4 October 1935, State 863.00/1235; Dodd dispatch 2355, 2 October 1935, State 762.64/40; Riggs (Budapest) dispatch 287, 11 October 1935, State 762.64/44. Von Neurath declined a return invitation soon after (von Neurath telegram to Budapest No. 58, 6 November 1935, T–120, 1436/2980/D 580602).

91. *G. D.*, C, 2, Nos. 311, 313, 327, 341, 345, 346; Memorandum of von Bülow, 16 March 1934, T–120, 2372/4602/E 189882–883.

Budapest government; at the same time, the continued refusal of the Hungarian regime to grant the wishes of the minority agitated the Germans. Certainly in this sphere there was no sign of cooperation, although there was at least a frank exchange of views.[92] The Hungarians refused to be drawn into any treaty system that might require them to impose sanctions against Germany in support of Austrian independence, but Germany's continued interference into Austrian affairs did nothing to bring Berlin and Budapest closer together.[93] In the economic field, however, the close ties begun in 1933–34 were extended; and, within rigid limits, Germany began the delivery of weapons as part of the trade relations between the two countries.[94] Hungary became increasingly dependent on Germany economically; as the situation was described at a German government conference on 8 October 1935: "In the case of Hungary and Yugoslavia, the foreign ministry is of the opinion that the political considerations responsible for the special concessions made to these countries at the beginning of 1934 remain unchanged."[95]

Since Yugoslavia was the other country to which Germany's economic concessions were to be continued, and the repercussions of these and of other signs of a German-Yugoslav rapprochement within Hungary have already been mentioned, the continuation of that rapprochement in 1934 and 1935 deserves to be placed in the context of German advances in Southeast Europe. The economic relationship just referred to continued.[96] The willingness of Yugoslavia to follow Britain's lead in a policy of sanctions against Italy in the winter of 1935–36 was to provide a further opening to Germany. The disruption of Yugoslavia's very important trade with Italy was not compensated for by adequate concessions from Britain and France. By the time sanctions ended in July 1936, the road to further German economic penetration had been opened wider than ever, and no return to the trade pattern that existed before the sanctions occurred.[97]

A direct hand in the improvement of German-Yugoslav relations was taken by Hermann Göring. He had made a brief trip to Belgrade in May

92. *G. D.*, C, 2, No. 731; 3, Nos. 305, 400, 426; 4, Nos. 38, 139, 178, 233, 267, 274, 314, 337, 424, 527; Memoranda of von Bülow of 16 March and 28 August 1934, T–120, 1436/2980/D 580519 and 580551; Memorandum of von Bülow, 3 September 1934, T–120, 2372/4602/E 189895; Jacobsen, pp. 521–28.

93. *G. D.*, C, 2, Nos. 444, 455; 3, Nos. 150, 266, n. 3, 296; von Papen to Hitler, No. 50 of 8 May 1935, T–120, 2499/4939/E 272032–033. See also the report of Mackensen on the visit of the German Minister of Education Rust to Horthy and Gömbös, 16 October 1934, T–120, 2700/5737/H 029049–052.

94. *G. D.*, C, 4, Nos. 209, 307, nn. 2 and 10, 310, 316, 391.

95. "Sitzung des Handelspolitischen Ausschusses vom 8. Oktober 1935," T–120, 2612/5650/H 004051. Germany and Hungary were also cooperating directly on some police matters (Memorandum by von Bülow-Schwante, 14 March 1935, T–120, 2899/6141/E 459241–242).

96. *G. D.*, C, 4, Nos. 434, 447; "Sitzung des Handelspolitischen Ausschusses vom 26. April 1935," T–120, 2612/5650/H 004015.

97. Hoptner, pp. 98–102; *D. D. F.*, 2d, 1, No. 52.

1934.[98] The October 1934 murder of Yugoslav king Alexander I at Marseilles by Croatian terrorists supported by Mussolini provided the opportunity for a second trip by Göring.[99] While Laval saw to it that Italy was not compromised in the international uproar that followed the assassination, the German government not only made a genuine effort to help find the culprits[100] but capitalized on Yugoslav resentment over French negligence in security precautions by sending Göring, the Prussian minister president, to the funeral ceremonies in Belgrade. There he made a good personal impression, assured the Yugoslav leaders that Germany would not support any Hungarian effort at revision of the Hungarian-Yugoslav border by force of arms, and gave a general impetus to an era of improved relations between Germany and Yugoslavia.[101] He was to promote this trend further by a third visit to Belgrade in May 1935 on a combined honeymoon and goodwill tour. The friendly reception he received on this occasion made him an even more firm advocate of the line that saw Yugoslavia as a possible friend of Germany in the Balkans and a joint opponent of the Habsburg restoration in Austria that was again being discussed in the spring and summer of 1935.[102] Under the new government of Milan Stojadinovič, installed in Belgrade in July 1935, the policy of its predecessor was continued with the support of the regent, Prince Paul. By the spring of 1936, Yugoslavia was clearly realigning itself with Germany.[103] By that time, Göring was trying to mediate between Yugoslavia and Hungary, although it was by no means certain that Germany's aim of detaching Yugoslavia from the Little Entente could be achieved.[104] Moreover, a new, more pro-German minister to represent Yugoslavia in Berlin was appointed at the end of 1935; and the French government could recognize the signs that Belgrade was developing a policy closer and closer to that of the Third Reich.[105]

98. *G. D.*, C, 3, No. 27; Czech minister in Belgrade report of 14 May 1934, and Czech minister in Bucharest report of 17 May 1934, Czech documents in T–120, 1041/1809/413695 and 413678.

99. Salvemini, p. 169; von Hassell report I 1366, 21 December 1934, T–120, 2700/5737/H 029165–168.

100. Miličevič, pp. 78–79; *G. D.*, C, 2, Nos. 332, 354.

101. *G. D.*, C, 3, Nos. 263, 269, 319; Wilson (Belgrade) dispatch 204, 23 October 1934, State 760H.62/16.

102. *G. D.*, C, 4, Nos. 91, 93, 198, 261; von Papen to Hitler report A 1661, 13 July 1935, T–120, 2499/4939/E 27091–093; Jacobsen, p. 360.

For his dealings with Yugoslavia, Göring used Franz Neuhausen whom he had saved from a jail sentence in Bulgaria (Bodenschatz to Mackensen, 10 November 1938, Nuremberg document 1824–PS, National Archives). Neuhausen became consul general in Belgrade and official representative of the Four-Year Plan there. On Göring's trip to Belgrade and on other occasions, he acted as Göring's official representative (*G. D.*, C, 4:163; Faber du Faur, p. 220; scattered correspondence in Bundesarchiv, Stabsamt Göring). During World War II, he played a major role in the administration and looting of German-occupied Yugoslavia.

103. *G. D.*, C, 4, Nos. 191, 434, 446, 447.

104. Ibid., Nos. 444, 533, 550, 576.

105. *D. D. F.*, 2d, 1, No. 42.

In contrast to the willingness of Hungary at least to consider better relations with Yugoslavia, Germany's effort to bring Hungary and Rumania closer together was a complete failure.[106] This did not prevent Germany from endeavoring to increase both its trade and its influence in Rumania itself. In the fall of 1934 and the spring of 1935 there were negotiations that led to a new agreement expanding the level of trade between the two countries and preparing the way for even closer ties.[107] The foreign policy office of the National Socialist party tried to use these negotiations to further its own schemes for interfering with Rumanian domestic politics on behalf of movements that were pledged to domestic policies more akin to the National Socialist party and to foreign policies more responsive to German demands. These attempts appear to have had relatively little influence on the course of German-Rumanian economic relations, but they both aided the extremist elements inside Rumania and made the government in Bucharest—and especially King Carol—more suspicious of Germany.[108]

More important for the German government in these years than the internal politics of Rumania was that country's relationship with other major powers, and especially with the Soviet Union. German policy was concentrated on efforts to keep Rumania from joining the bloc forming against it, and particularly from granting the Soviet Union the right to move troops across Rumanian territory in case of German aggression against Czechoslovakia or any other country. If German policy had been completely successful in this regard by the spring of 1936, several factors had combined to make it so. The economic relations between Germany and Rumania surely played a part. The concern of Rumania lest it become the object of great power conflicts no doubt contributed a share. The unimpressive conduct of the Western powers in the face of German rearmament measures was not calculated to inspire confidence in Bucharest.[109] The manner in which Germany refused to give open support to Hungarian revisionist aspirations against Rumania was of some help.[110] A variety of German personal ties to the ruler of Rumania was also exploited. The most important factor

106. *G. D.,* C, 4, No. 576.

107. Ibid., 2, Nos. 285, 295, 302, 387, 543, 551, 556; 4, Nos. 6, 110, 297; "Sitzung des Handelspolitischen Ausschusses vom 13. September 1934," ". . . vom 8. Oktober 1934," ". . . . vom 11. Oktober 1934," ". . . . vom 15. Oktober 1934," ". . . vom 2. November 1934," ". . . vom 14. Juni 1935," T–120, 2612/5650/H 003936, 3952, 3954, 3961, 3968–69, 4022–23.

108. Copy of a memorandum by Duckwitz of the APA, 17 August 1934, Nuremberg document 1147–PS (National Archives); *G. D.,* C, 3, No. 285, n. 2; Rosenberg to Darré, 14 September 1934, 1147–PS; Rosenberg, *Tagebuch,* 21 January and 2 February 1935, pp. 65–67, 26 February 1935, pp. 73–74; Rosenberg memorandum for Hitler, 1 September 1935, 080–PS; von Neurath to Rosenberg, 7 September 1935, 027–PS; Wiedemann to Rosenberg, 14 February 1936, cited in *G. D.,* C, 4:1070, n. 5.

109. Šeba (Czech minister in Bucharest) telegram of 19 March 1935, Czech document in T–120, 1041/1809/413419–420.

110. See especially *G. D.,* C, 4, No. 514.

that kept Rumania from making the concession to the Soviet Union that Germany most feared was the realization of Rumania's leaders, including the foreign minister, Nicolae Titulescu, that in any new war between Germany and Russia any Southeast European country involved would lose its independence to the winner—which he expected would not be Germany—and that only the maintenance of peace could save them.[111] Thus the combination of German pressures and Rumanian fears kept Rumania out of any firm anti-German alignment.

While Germany kept Hungary within its orbit, made great strides toward drawing Yugoslavia into it, and kept Rumania from joining those opposed to Germany, its policy toward the other countries in the southeast was concentrated on economic arrangements. With Turkey, Greece, and Bulgaria, Germany developed stronger economic ties. It also initiated a small program of exporting armaments to those nations. Such arms exports violated German law, but no German official or officer of the period found that significant. More important in the long run was the fact that such economic ties and arms exports helped to displace Italian influence in the area and reestablish German standing and prestige.[112] By the beginning of 1936, Germany had attained an established position in Southeast Europe to the point where it could warn the countries of that area to take no steps and make no arrangements among themselves without considering German interests and respecting its role.[113]

Behind this new diplomatic position of Germany stood another factor: the continued strength and existence of Germany itself as a power that had chosen a path entirely different from that stamped as appropriate by the victors of the last war. Perhaps in Germany there was a new model to follow, one that retroactively placed the various new authoritarian systems of the East and Southeast European states in an entirely more favorable perspective—harbingers of the future rather than temporary aberrations

111. Note ibid., No. 205. On the discussions of German-Rumanian relations, Rumanian policy toward the Soviet Union, and German worry that Rumania might grant transit rights for Russian troops see *G. D.*, C, 2, Nos. 322, 387; 4, Nos. 64, 110, 153, 160, 175, 339, 353, 362, 385, 393, 401, 405, 427, 431, 478, 516, 535, 561, 577, 581; Pochhammer (Bucharest) telegram II Balk 1137g, 13 May 1935, T–120, 2758/5888/E 431675; von Papen to Hitler, No. 2644 of 11 November 1935, 2499/4939/E 272148; "Bestellung aus der Pressekonferenz vom 26. November 1935," Bundesarchiv, Brammer, Z.Sg. 101/6, f. 196; [Memorandum by Rosenberg on a conversation with Rumanian Minister Comnen on 29 February 1936], Nuremberg document 030–PS (National Archives). The account in Oprea, *Titulescu's Diplomatic Activity*, pp. 97–101, stresses Titulescu's willingness to sign with Russia, but fails to explain fully the failure of the negotiations.

112. For Turkey see *G. D.*, C, 3, Nos. 59, 353, n. 4, 371, 484; 4, Nos. 26, 144, 449. For Bulgaria see ibid., 3, No. 411, n. 3; 4, Nos. 14, 48, 481, 557; Dodd dispatch 2028, 5 June 1935, State 762.70/4; White (Berlin) dispatch 1539, 4 December 1934 and McArdle (Sofia) dispatch 150 of 31 May 1935, State 762.74/10 and 12. For Greece see *G. D.*, C, 3, No. 124; 4, Nos. 312, 369, 459; on Göring's trip to Greece see the volume "Studienfahrt 1934, Griechenland," in Library of Congress, Prints and Photographs Division, No. 3809.

113. *G. D.*, C, 4, Nos. 543, 558, 559.

in a time of economic and nationalistic crisis. The pompous façade of National Socialist Germany not only impressed its own population and gave them a secular substitute for a form of religious salvation but also radiated to the new and reorganized states to the East and Southeast the confident message that perhaps this was indeed the wave of the future.[114]

The last and perhaps most important benefit that Germany drew from the estrangement between Italy and the Western powers over Ethiopia was the slow reorientation of Italy from its close ties with France and England early in 1935 to a position more friendly toward, or at least more tolerant of, Germany. The major factor in the friction between Italy and Germany had been the Austrian question, and Italy had aligned itself with France partly in response to the danger of an *Anschluss*.[115] France in turn had been willing to make concessions to Italy to bring it more firmly into a position of defending the status quo in Europe and for that reason had been reluctant to oppose Italy's East African venture. As the Ethiopian question became increasingly acute in the spring and summer of 1935, Germany remained aloof and neutral, rejecting the possibility of embarrassing and weakening Italy in Europe by supporting Ethiopia.[116] The Italian government appreciated this attitude and in the face of the hardening opposition of the Western powers began to think of a rapprochement with Berlin.[117]

A key factor in any new development in German-Italian relations was the relationship of Germany to Austria. German interference in Austria's internal affairs continued in 1935; it was directed both to influencing public opinion in Austria and gaining an increasing control over Austrian economic life.[118] Furthermore, Germany refused to commit itself to any international agreement either against interference in Austria or affirming its independence.[119] Nevertheless, there were certain signs that German policy was shifting, from one looking to immediate control of Austria to a temporary accommodation that still, of course, left all possibilities open for the future. Hitler's views, as explained on 19 January 1935 in Berlin to a

114. This is, in essence, also the conclusion drawn by Martin Broszat in "Faschismus und Kollaboration in Ostmitteleuropa zwischen den Weltkriegen," *Vierteljahrshefte für Zeitgeschichte,* 14, No. 3 (July, 1966), p. 241.

115. An excellent summary of this development is in the report for the year 1934 of the German military attaché in Rome, General Fischer, 10 June 1935, T–120, 2676/5609/E 402176–181.

116. *G. D.,* C, 3, Nos. 403, n. 2, 557, 558; 4, Nos. 63, 83, 212; "Bestellungen aus der Pressekonferenz vom 27. Februar 1935," Bundesarchiv, Brammer, Z.Sg. 101/5, f. 64.

117. *G. D.,* C, 4, Nos. 63, 87, 109; *Lipski Papers,* No. 45; Baer, p. 159.

118. For German propaganda in Austria see *G. D.,* C, 4, No. 241; Memorandum of Altenburg II Oe 47, 5 January 1935, T–120, 2832/6077/E 450716–718; Memorandum of Köpke II Oe 1658, 27 June 1935, 2836/6111/E 453099. For German intervention into Austrian economic life in 1935 see *G. D.,* C, 3, No. 533; 4:346–47; *Der deutsche Imperialismus und der Zweite Weltkrieg,* 2:471, 486–87.

119. *G. D.,* C, 3, Nos. 410, 527, 530; Memorandum by von Papen, 16 February 1935, T–120, 2499/4939/E 271971–974; Diary of Breckinridge Long (on a talk with von Hassell), 16 April 1935, pp. 133–34, Long Papers.

group of Austrian National Socialist leaders including Alfred Frauenfeld, the former *Gauleiter* of Vienna, was that they should stay out of internal Austrian affairs. Germany would continue to provide financial support for the Austrian National Socialist party, but "the Austrian question could be solved only by means of foreign policy [as opposed to an internal coup]. This would take a period of three to five years until Germany had rearmed to a point where no one could interfere with it."[120] In the meantime, steps were finally taken to move the Austrian legion from Bavaria to northwest Germany where it would no longer be a sore point in relations with Austria.[121] The German press was instructed, apparently on direct orders from Hitler, that for a while there was to be no reporting whatsoever on Austria.[122] The leaders of the Austrian National Socialist party in Germany were directed to make themselves as inconspicuous as possible.[123] When there had been renewed agitation over a possible restoration of the Habsburgs in the spring of 1935 and the German position appeared temporarily weak because of the announcements of conscription and naval construction, Hitler tried to reduce foreign fear of Germany by promising in his speech of 21 May that he would respect the independence of Austria.[124]

The response of the Austrian government to this gesture was a friendly hint that bilateral German-Austrian talks might well lead to an agreement. This possibility had been canvassed earlier in the year in conversations between von Papen and the general secretary of the Austrian foreign ministry as well as the Austrian chancellor, Schuschnigg.[125] Schuschnigg had demonstrated his interest in some accommodation as early as the fall of 1934 in his talks with various Austrian nationalist and National Socialist leaders; and he now returned to the subject, replying to Hitler's speech with a conciliatory statement before the Austrian parliament. Under these circumstances, von Papen thought it advisable to confer with Hitler in person.[126] Germany's policies toward Austria and Italy were now under the

120. The report on Frauenfeld's talk was transmitted to Austrian police headquarters in Vienna by an Austrian informant and then in turn betrayed to the German legation in Vienna. See the German legation's report of 22 January 1935, in T–120, 2499/4939/E 271824. The speed with which such information was passed around is itself revealing—a four-day cycle from Berlin to Vienna and back.

121. *G. D.*, C, 3, Nos. 510, 522; but see the memorandum of Renthe-Fink II Oe 933, 13 April 1935, T–120, 2890/6115/E 455075–076.

122. "Bestellungen aus der Pressekonferenz vom 22. Januar 1935," Bundesarchiv, Brammer, Z.Sg. 101/5, f. 19.

123. *G. D.*, C, 4, No. 85; Memorandum of Altenburg II Oe 465, 15 February 1935, T–120, 2990/6115/E 455047–048.

124. On the talk about a Habsburg restoration in early 1935 see *G. D.*, C, 4, Nos. 34, 84, 96, 138; Long Diary, 10 April 1935, pp. 128–31, Long Papers (see also Long's dispatch 1042, 11 April 1935, State 862.20/952).

125. *G. D.*, C, 4, No. 111; von Papen's memoranda on his talks with Secretary General Peter on 15 February and with Schuschnigg on 10 April 1935, in T–120, 2499/4939/E 271971–974 and E 272006–013.

126. Gehl, p. 109; von Papen to Hitler A 1388, 13 June 1935, T–120, 2499/4939/E 272053–055 (note von Papen's reference to his plan to report orally on an important conversation with Starhemberg).

simultaneous review that their close interrelationship certainly warranted.

By this time—mid-June 1935—the first signs of better German-Italian relations were evident, in part in response to the relaxation in German-Austrian tensions. An effort was being made in both Rome and Berlin to restrain the press from the polemics that had characterized the latter part of 1934, and there were also attempts to improve the economic relations between the two countries.[127] Whatever Mussolini's suspicions of German long-term aims, his increasing concentration on Ethiopia persuaded him to adopt a friendlier attitude toward Germany, if only to offset the pressure from the League powers.[128] The German foreign ministry did not wish to respond in any immediate way to this opportunity for a rapprochement in spite of the urgings of the German ambassador, Ulrich von Hassell. Recognizing that it was Rome's concern over the Ethiopian question that made it suddenly so solicitous of Germany, the German foreign ministry preferred to wait, confident that increasing isolation would make Italy more willing to make concessions to Germany.[129] Hitler's attitude, however, was somewhat different. He evidently regretted the estrangement from the Italian leader, an estrangement that thwarted his basic approach to German-Italian relations. In order to bridge the gap, therefore, he turned to Mussolini's unofficial emissary in Berlin, Giuseppe Renzetti, as soon as the possibility of improving German-Italian relations appeared.

On 21 June 1935, Hitler explained to Renzetti that he wanted Rome to replace the Italian ambassador to Berlin, Vittorio Cerruti. Indirectly revealing that the Germans were reading at least some of the reports of the Italian ambassador, Hitler maintained that Cerruti did not report accurately to Rome, unlike the British, French, and Polish ambassadors who, regardless of their private views, reported exactly what Hitler told them. Just as he himself would recall von Hassell or anyone else from Rome within twenty-four hours if Mussolini so requested, and just as he would send to Rome as replacement anyone Mussolini desired—except von Ribbentrop for whom Hitler had other plans—so he expected Mussolini to replace Cerruti with someone more congenial (though apparently no specific names were mentioned). Hitler further argued that he wanted a return to better German-Italian relations. He disclaimed at length any responsibility for the Vienna coup of 25 July 1934, asserting that he did not want to annex Austria. All he was interested in was that some National Socialists be included in the

127. On the press see *G. D.*, C, 4, No. 124; General Fischer (Rome) annex 1 to report 12/35, 2 May 1935, T–120, 2676/5609/E 402244–247; "Bestellungen aus der Pressekonferenz vom 25. Mai 1935," Bundesarchiv, Brammer, Z.Sg. 101/5, f. 170. On trade see *G. D.*, C, 4, No. 67, n. 2; Memorandum of Clodius, II It 658, 18 April 1935, T–120, 2700/5737/H 029272–273.

128. Baer, pp. 160–61; *G. D.*, C, 4, Nos. 120, 121, 162; Dodd dispatch 2037, 6 June 1935, State 762.00/96. On Mussolini's long-term concerns see U. S. 1935, 1:188.

129. *G. D.*, C, 4, Nos. 164, 166, 194, 202. Again one cannot escape the impression that the personal element played a part: von Hassell was for, so von Neurath was against, better relations (cf. ibid., Nos. 5, 9).

Austrian government. In any case, Germany and Italy had too much in common to allow the Austrian problem to come between them, and proper diplomatic representation would facilitate better cooperation.[130]

This approach to Mussolini through Renzetti clearly reveals the continued link between Hitler's Austrian policy and his Italian policy in the summer of 1935. Mussolini responded promptly by transferring Cerruti to Paris and replacing him with Bernardo Attolico, hitherto the Italian ambassador in Moscow.[131] The day after Cerruti said farewell to von Bülow, the German ambassador to Moscow wrote von Bülow that Attolico was hurrying to Berlin at Mussolini's instructions so that he could attend the National Socialist party rally in Nuremberg in September as a demonstrative contrast to his predecessor who had acted in concert with the ambassadors of other major powers in declining to attend these annual spectacles.[132] The change of ambassadors was designed to create a change of atmosphere, in the hope of paving the way for a change of policies.[133]

Hitler had at first followed a rather cautious policy toward Italy's East African venture, perhaps in part out of regard for his relations with England that had been improved by the naval agreement. In spite of considerable anti-Italian and pro-Ethiopian sympathies among the German public, he held to a policy of neutrality in a form distinctly inclined in favor of Italy.[134] Once Italy actually initiated hostilities at the beginning of October,

130. Renzetti to Mussolini, 21 June 1935, T–586, 419/009445–450. On 28 June Renzetti sent additional comments on Cerruti coming from Hermann Göring (ibid., frames 009476–477). There is a detailed account of this incident in Jens Petersen, "Deutschland und Italien im Sommer 1935, Der Wechsel des italienischen Botschafters in Berlin," *Geschichte in Wissenschaft und Unterricht,* 20, No. 6 (June 1969), 330–41.

131. In her memoirs, Elisabetta Cerruti refers to hearing news of the impending transfer of her husband to Paris in May 1935 (*Ambassador's Wife,* pp. 189, 194). This is either an error in memory or an indication that Mussolini, who was aware of Cerruti's attitude toward the National Socialists, had already decided to move him before receiving Hitler's request. According to the diary of Baron Aloisi (p. 160), Göring had asked for Cerruti's recall when he was in Rome on 7 November 1933 to deliver Hitler's letter to Mussolini explaining Germany's departure from the League (cf. ibid., 4 February 1934, p. 177). Aloisi further records (18 November 1933, p. 162) that Mussolini did decide to recall Cerruti at that time. Mussolini changed his mind, however; the trip of Suvich to Berlin in December 1933 that Göring had requested at the same time as he had demanded Cerruti's recall may have looked like an adequate gesture.

132. Memorandum of von Bülow, 12 August 1935, T–120, 2373/4602/E 190090; Schulenburg to von Bülow, 13 August 1935, T–120, 2387/4620/E 200989–992; *G. D.,* C, 4, No. 265. Attolico was soon agitating for Italy's withdrawal from the League (*G. D.,* C, 4, No. 437).

133. Massimo Magistrati, "La Germania e l'impresa italiana di Etiopia (Ricordi di Berlino)," *Rivista di studi politici internationali,* 17, No. 4 (Oct.–Dec. 1950), pp. 588–90. Magistrati had served under Attolico in Rio de Janeiro; the article cited here may be considered Magistrati's memoirs for the period preceding his *L'Italia a Berlino, 1937–1939* (Rome: Mondadori, 1956).

134. There is considerable evidence that Hitler doubted the wisdom of Mussolini's attack on Ethiopia (see Meinertzhagen, pp. 154–55; *G. D.,* C, 4, No. 367), but as in other instances, was willing to work with him regardless of differences in judgment on specific issues.

the dangers to Germany of an Italian collapse in the face of Western sanctions were simply too great. It might well be to Germany's advantage for the war in East Africa to last a long time, but the defeat of Mussolini would isolate Germany and set a dangerous precedent among other major powers of resistance to aggression. Hitler was aware of these implications, so expressed himself, and directed German policy accordingly.[135]

At the same time Hitler requested Mussolini to replace Cerruti, he also authorized von Papen to continue the informal talks about a possible bilateral German-Austrian agreement.[136] Von Papen at first moved quickly. He was worried that the diplomatic focus of the great powers on East Africa and the temporary restraint that Henlein's electoral victory had imposed on Czechoslovakia would lead Schuschnigg to push for a Habsburg restoration as a safeguard of Austrian independence in accord with Schuschnigg's personal preferences, a move that might be safely attempted at that moment.[137] A German-Austrian agreement—or even serious negotiations for such agreement—would obviously forestall any such move, and on 11 July von Papen handed a draft proposal to the Austrian foreign minister.[138] It provided for a settlement of current differences in German-Austrian relations and looked forward to the close coordination of their policies. Negotiations on the proposal were hindered by division within the Austrian government, continued agitation over the restoration issue, and Schuschnigg's temporary absence from government affairs due to the automobile accident in which his wife was killed. From the German side, the unseemly anniversary celebration of the murder of Dollfuss hardly aided the progress of talks.[139] In spite of such difficulties, a little progress was made, leading to an agreement to restrain press attacks on each other, announced on 28 August 1935.[140] The Austrian foreign minister replied in a

135. For an expression of Hitler's views see Görlitz, *Keitel,* pp. 80–81; Wiskeman, p. 67. For the evolution of Germany's neutrality policy in a manner best calculated to protect its own interests while favoring Italy see *G. D.,* C, 4, Nos. 246, 261, 283, 298, 299, 313, 322–27, 333, 334, 343, 346, 350–52, 361, 364, 365, 371, 372, 382, 389, 394–400, 406, 408, 410, 438, 441; "Informationsbericht Nr. 55," 7 November 1935, Bundsarchiv, Brammer, Z.Sg. 101/28, f. 327–331.

For an excellent discussion of German opinion and government policy see the "Aufzeichnungen über Deutschlands aussenpolitische Lage," of 17 October 1935, Bundesarchiv, Brammer, Z.Sg. 101/28, f. 299–305.

For a report on Italy's use of Hamburg as a port for the transshipment of goods to evade the League's sanctions see Erhardt (U. S. consul general Hamburg) dispatch 583, 16 November 1935, State 765.84/2810; cf. *D. D. F.,* 2d, 1, No. 55.

136. *G. D.,* C, 4, No. 197. Germany knew of Italian-Austrian arrangements in case Germany invaded Austria (ibid., No. 296).

137. Von Papen to Hitler, A 1620 of 9 July and A 1685 of 16 July 1935, T–120, 2499/4939/E 272083–088, E 272089–090; *G. D.,* C, 4, Nos. 206 n. 6, 216, 228.

138. *G. D.,* C, 4, No. 203; *Guido Schmidt Trial,* pp. 474, 476–77; Messersmith dispatch 503, 25 July 1935, State 762.63/292.

139. Von Papen to Hitler, A 1451 of 22 June and A 1931 of 17 August 1935, T–120, 2499/4939/E 272056–059, E 272105–110.

140. *G. D.,* C, 4, Nos. 588–91; Memorandum of von Bülow, 18 July 1935, T–120, 2373/4602/E 190172–173; "Vertrauliche Bestellung an die Redaktion" [29 August

generally favorable manner to von Papen's general approach on 1 October; but in agreement with Hitler, von Papen handled the subsequent talks in a dilatory manner as internal changes in the Austrian government followed the outbreak of war between Italy and Ethiopia.[141]

While the British and French stumbled from bluster to blunder in the Ethiopian crisis, the Germans could afford to wait. Stanley Baldwin might be sure that Germany would start a war in two to four years; and on the eve of the Italian attack, Sir Samuel Hoare could talk of American cooperation in sanctions to bring down Mussolini; but Germany's only real concern was that Hoare's eloquent speech of 11 September in Geneva in favor of collective security might be followed by an accommodation between Italy and the League powers that would shift attention back to Europe.[142] For a moment it looked as if the Hoare-Laval proposals of early December 1935 might provide the basis for a settlement, but as the British public condemned in Ethiopia what they would later hail in Czechoslovakia, the war in East Africa ground on to the sole benefit of the Third Reich.[143] The esteem of the German government for British astuteness was not likely to be enhanced by this performance. They had known of prior British assurances to Mussolini that no serious steps would be taken against Italy.[144] The later policy of the British leaders may have been actuated by the best of motives, but it could only appear to Berlin in the worst possible light. London's concern over the danger from Germany if Britain became embroiled in war with Italy had played a part in the desire for compromise with Mussolini—a compromise that might save at least a bit of Ethiopia when no one was willing to fight to defend the whole country—but the turn to appeasement after a clarion call for determined action was guaranteed to destroy whatever opportunities might have existed in either direction. As the future British prime minister, Neville Chamberlain, had himself predicted in July 1935, either Mussolini had to be stopped completely or the League would be worthless—the small powers would race each other to Berlin.[145]

It would, in fact, be some time before the race of the small powers to

1935], Bundesarchiv, Brammer, Z.Sg. 101/6, f. 76; Messersmith dispatch 537, 30 August 1935, State 762.63/297.

141. Gehl, pp. 109–11; *G. D.*, C, 4, Nos. 319, 333, 335, 349, 368; "Informationsbericht Nr. 52," 22 October 1935, Bundesarchiv, Brammer, Z.Sg. 101/28, f. 309–11.

142. *G. D.*, C, 4, Nos. 308, 360, 366, 375, 404, 412; Memorandum of S. R. Fuller on a conversation with Stanley Baldwin, 30 September 1935, Hyde Park P. P. F. 2616.

143. On the Hoare-Laval plan see Laurens, chap. 11; Warner, pp. 115–26; Hoare, pp. 177ff.; Vansittart, *Mist Procession*, pp. 537–41; Maurice Peterson, *Both Sides of the Curtain* (London: Constable, 1950), pp. 116–22; T. Jones, pp. 158–61; U. S. 1935, 1:699–705, 711–13, and 1936, 3:100–02; *G. D.*, C, 4, Nos. 457, 458, 461, 465, 469; *FDR and Foreign Affairs*, 3:136–37; Bingham to Roosevelt, 24 December 1935, Hyde Park, P. S. F. Bingham; Memorandum of Breckinridge Long (Rome), 7 February 1936, Phillips Papers, Vol. 36.

144. *G. D.*, C, 4, Nos. 317, 321, 326, 329; General Fischer annex 2 to report 24/35, 11 October 1935, T–120, 2676/5609/E 402357.

145. Feiling, p. 265.

Berlin began, but the country that would lead the race and become Germany's first ally—Mussolini's Italy—was already beginning to gravitate in that direction. The failure of the Hoare-Laval plan made practically certain that there would be no return to the Stresa front. In spite of Laval's written plea to Mussolini after that failure and in contradiction of his own earlier promises, Mussolini denounced his agreement with France on 28 December 1935.[146] Italy would move forward to total occupation of Ethiopia under circumstances in which Germany would be its only potential ally.[147]

There were still points of friction between Germany and Italy, not only over Austria but also arising out of a heritage of mutual suspicion in the German and Italian diplomatic services.[148] Such continuing rumbling, however, could not obscure the fact that the whole world situation had changed greatly, to Germany's advantage. No one saw this more clearly than Hitler himself, who resolved to take advantage of it for his own next move. In any case, all danger to Germany had surely passed: as von Neurath wrote to the German ambassador to the Vatican on 13 November and as the commander in chief of the German army explained to a group of German generals soon after, there was no longer a danger of a preventive war because all feared the rising power of the new Germany.[149]

146. *D. D. F.,* 2d, 1, No. 145, n. 3.

147. Wiskeman, pp. 70–72; cf. *Lipski Papers,* No. 56.

148. *G. D.,* C, 4, Nos. 388, 408, 411, 414, 417, 463, 464, 469, 476, pp. 930–31; von Hassell report I 972, 19 December 1935, T–120, 2700/5737/H 029433–436. On the Austrian situation at this time see also *G. D.,* C, 4, Nos. 368 and 428.

149. *G. D.,* C, 4, No. 408; von Fritsch's comments on 18 November 1935, Liebmann Notes, Institut für Zeitgeschichte, ED–1, pp. 87–89.

10 The Remilitarization of the Rhineland

The Emperor [Haile Selassie] said he was perplexed by the strange maneuvers of European diplomacy and the half measures of the League. He realized of course that the stage was set for another European war and that in the present confusion arising from Germany's defiance of Locarno Ethiopia's fate is relegated to a secondary place. But he found it difficult to understand British inconsistencies and France's inability to see that if Italy had been checked in time Germany would never have dared to follow in her footsteps. (Engert telegram 259, 1 May 1936, U. S. 1936, 3:64)

The provision of the 1919 peace settlement requiring the demilitarization of the left bank of the Rhine and a strip fifty kilometers wide on the right bank had been reaffirmed in the Locarno Pact. It formed not only an integral part of those treaties but constituted the single most important guarantee of peace in Europe. Observance of this arrangement rendered any German attack on France or the Low Countries impossible, while the British and Italian guarantees of Locarno protected Germany against any possible French aggression. Furthermore, the fact that Germany was open to invasion in the West made her incapable of aggression in any other direction: any attack on Austria, Czechoslovakia, Poland, Lithuania, or Denmark might precipitate a French attack that Germany could not possibly ward off. The Locarno Pact thus provided stability in a Europe that, if organized on anything even remotely resembling the national principle, was certain to have a Germany potentially more powerful than any country other than the Soviet Union. The imposition of a demilitarized zone on Germany might seem to some a disproportionate German contribution to such stability, but the accompanying British guarantee against France had been welcome compensation for Germany two years after the French occupation of the Ruhr.

Moreover, it could be argued with considerable justice that an arrangement that restrained Germany from adventurous policies might be advantageous not only to the potential victims of such policies but to the Germans themselves. Although it was invariably assumed in Germany between the wars that any drastic revision of the territorial status quo initiated by Germany would unfailingly redound to Germany's advantage, there was no natural or divine law to this effect. The restraining influence of the demilitarized zone could thus be said to have favorable as well as unfavorable implications for Germany, but certainly this was not the German view. In Germany, the early evacuation of allied occupation troops from the Rhineland was soon forgotten, the restriction on the nation's sovereignty was considered an unreasonable and one-sided imposition, and German propaganda was often successful in making the subject appear to others in a light similar to the one in which the Germans themselves saw it.

For Hitler's government, the demilitarized zone was a particularly serious hindrance. It complicated the general progress of rearmament; more significantly, it precluded any really active foreign policy in the direction of expanding Germany's living space, the main aim of the Hitler regime. The National Socialist members of the Reichstag had voted against the Locarno agreement in 1925; in *Mein Kampf,* Hitler had contrasted that agreement as a sign of the continuing decay of the Weimar Republic with the recovery of Prussia after the defeat of 1806.[1] Once in power, however, Hitler recognized that it was very dangerous for Germany to tamper with this portion of the European order: France might move, and some or all of the other powers might back the French. In the early years of the National Socialist regime, therefore, care was taken not to provoke any concern about Germany's adherence to Locarno. On the contrary, Hitler repeatedly reaffirmed his intention of keeping the terms of that treaty and within Germany insisted that such preliminary steps as were taken toward remilitarizing the Rhineland be kept secret and to a minimum. Such caution, however, was dictated by the exigencies of the moment; Hitler would seize what looked to him like the earliest possible opportunity to cast off that restriction on his freedom of action. He had thought of introducing a demand for the abolition of the demilitarized zone into the disarmament negotiations in 1934 but had dropped the idea in the summer of that year because of Germany's difficult diplomatic situation. Had it not been included in the Locarno as well as the Versailles settlement, the demilitarized zone would in fact have been reoccupied in March 1935 when conscription was reintroduced.[2] Hitler was then still operating with the argument that Germany considered itself bound by agreements it had signed voluntarily but not bound by those imposed

1. *Mein Kampf,* 2:761–62; similarly in *Hitlers zweites Buch,* p. 114.

2. See the letter from Frohwein of the foreign ministry to Erbe of the Ministry of the Interior, "II Abr. 2075," 11 August 1934, T–120, 3289/7881/E 570604. *G. D.*, C, 4, No. 575; German text in Esmonde Robertson (ed.) "Zur Wiederbesetzung des Rheinlandes 1936," *Vierteljahrshefte für Zeitgeschichte,* 10, No. 2 (April 1962), p. 195.

upon it; and in the publicity of the day, the Versailles and Locarno treaties were allocated to these different categories.

There is some evidence that in the summer of 1935 Hitler referred to the future remilitarization of the Rhineland in conversations with his associates, although as yet in indefinite terms.[3] Whether the step would be taken as a result of negotiations with the other Locarno powers, especially France, or without such preliminaries, was still open; but the concept that the step would be taken in the spring of 1936 was already included in Hitler's consideration of the issue.[4] During 1935, the German government began to prepare a legal case against the continued validity of the Locarno agreement by claiming that the Franco-Soviet Pact was incompatible with it. This contention was not only rejected by other signatories, including Italy, but it is most doubtful that the Germans themselves seriously held to it. They carefully avoided recourse to the procedures that the Locarno Pact itself provided for precisely such a claim and eventually switched to other arguments. Although there is as yet no clear evidence on the issue, it would appear that the main purposes in raising this point were to prepare the ground for domestic propaganda solidifying German opinion and to raise the question of the demilitarized zone in international affairs, partly by clouding the legal aspect, partly by raising the Soviet threat. This, in turn, would give the German government some picture of likely foreign reaction to any actions violating the Locarno agreement. Under these circumstances, the willingness of the French government to submit the German legal claim to legal adjudication may well have served only to reinforce Hitler's belief that a dramatic step on his part would not be met by drastic countermeasures.[5]

In November and December of 1935 the possibility of German action in the Rhineland came increasingly to the fore. The French ambassador to Berlin, André François-Poncet, warned his government after meeting with Hitler on 21 November that the German government would soon either confront France with a fait accompli in the Rhineland—counting on French internal dissentions and love of peace to keep France from moving—or would propose negotiations to end the demilitarized zone.[6] When Hitler met

3. See the reports of Jean Dobler, French consul general in Cologne, of 30 May 1935, in *Les Évenements survenues en France de 1933 à 1945, Temoignages et documents recueillis par la Commission d'enquête parlementaire* (Paris: Presses Universitaires, 1947), 2:474–77, of 13 June 1935, cited in his report of 12 March 1936, ibid., pp. 483–84, and of 26 June 1935, in ibid., pp. 478–79. These reports are referred to in *D. D. F.*, 2d, 1:108, n. 1 and p. 142, No. 96, n. 2. The conversation between Hitler and Rudolf Diels about which the latter spoke with Dobler appears to be the meeting described in a confused manner, but with explicit reference to the demilitarized zone, by Diels in his memoirs, *Lucifer ante portas* (Stuttgart: Deutsche Verlags-Anstalt, 1950), pp. 80–85. Internal evidence shows that Diels was unaware of Dobler's reports and testimony when writing his own account.

4. Rumors in the German Ministry of War referring to March 1936 as the date for action are cited in Bella Fromm, *Blood and Banquets* (New York: Harpers, 1942), 28 October 1935, p. 209.

5. *G. D.*, C, 4, Nos. 72, 170; *D. D. F.*, 2d, 1, No. 227.

6. François-Poncet's report quoted in *D. D. F.*, 2d, 1, No. 37, p. 53.

with the British ambassador on 13 December and rejected renewed British overtures for an air pact, he himself referred explicitly to the need to end the demilitarized status of the Rhineland.[7] Hitler was by this time already discussing the details of reentering the Rhineland with his military advisers; around Christmas, the commander in chief of the German army, General von Fritsch, was reviewing Hitler's plan with the heads of the operations and organization sections of the army general staff and explaining to them his worries about possible foreign complications growing out of such a move.[8]

Diplomatic contacts with the other signatories of Locarno in January 1936 were marked by several clearly discernible characteristics. In those meetings which brought Hitler, von Neurath, and von Bülow together with French diplomats, the emphasis was on German complaints about the Franco-Soviet Pact that was about to go to the Chamber of Deputies for ratification.[9] The Germans also claimed to be greatly exercised over the Franco-British staff talks that were developing out of joint policies toward Italy and the danger of war in the Mediterranean. While the Germans professed to see in these talks a threat against themselves, they in fact expected no attack but were greatly concerned that the British and French might plan to ward off German aggression jointly while ostensibly coordinating plans against possible further Italian aggression. Similar complaints were launched in German conversations with the British who were scolded about their military talks with the French and given new excuses for Germany's un-

7. The German record in *G. D.*, C, 4, Nos. 460 and 462 makes this clear in spite of its absence from the report of Phipps published in Cmd. 5143, No. 46. The summary of the German record circulated to German embassies abroad is reflected in *D. D. F.*, 2d, 1, No. 160; it includes a reference to the demilitarized zone (cf. *G. D.*, C, 4, No. 462, n. 6). The British government knew of the German demand and began to consider the issue (see Foreign Office C 8329/55/18). The full report of Phipps is in C 8364/55/18; on the editing of Cmd. 5143 see C 2488/ C 2493/4/18.

8. Memorandum of Freiherr von Siegler on a conversation with General Otto Stapf (in 1936 head of the organization section) on 6 June 1952, Institut für Zeitgeschichte, Z.S. 152, pp. 7–8. In his memoirs, General Erich von Manstein, then chief of the operations section, claims that he heard nothing about any intended remilitarization of the Rhineland from von Fritsch at that time and claims that Beck, not von Fritsch, first told him and Stapf about the forthcoming events on the morning of 5 March 1936 (*Aus einem Soldatenleben* [Bonn: Athenäum, 1958], p. 236). The only way to reconcile the two accounts is to interpret the December meeting as one concerning the general problems of a Rhineland occupation, with the March one dealing only with implementation of an operation immediately ensuing. On the whole, Stapf's account appears more trustworthy than Manstein's, which is one long, almost whining, apologia. Manstein's account, if taken literally, is also incompatible with the memoirs of Friedrich Hossbach, then chief military adjutant of Hitler, who claims that Hitler discussed the intended reoccupation with von Fritsch in Berlin on 12 February (*Zwischen Wehrmacht und Hitler*, p. 97). It is difficult to believe that von Fritsch thereupon kept his chief of operations completely uninformed for three weeks.

9. Hitler-François-Poncet on 1 January in *D. D. F.*, 2d, 1, No. 1, and U. S. 1936, 1:180–81; von Bülow-François-Poncet on 10 January, in *D. D. F.*, 2d, 1, No. 30, and Memorandum of von Bülow, 10 January, T–120, 2373/4602/E 190273–274; Bülow-François-Poncet on 13 January in *D. D. F.*, 2d, 1, No. 49, and *G. D.*, C, 4, No. 494, with important additions noted on the copy filmed in T–120, 2373/4602/E 190275–279.

willingness to go forward as promised with negotiations for an air pact.[10] From these talks, both the British and French governments received the impression that the Berlin regime was looking for an excuse to justify reoccupation of the Rhineland, though the Germans invariably denied this assertion when confronted with it.

It was becoming obvious to the French government that some step in regard to the Rhineland was probably imminent and that whatever reluctance the German army might have about the risks involved, Hitler would disregard that reluctance if he decided to move.[11] The French military attaché in Berlin thought that action to remilitarize the Rhineland was impending but that the Germans would first try to find out what the French reaction would be and then act if it seemed safe to do so.[12] Precisely for this reason there were some in Paris who believed that France should warn Germany if military moves in answer to a German coup were in fact intended.[13] On this subject, French officials were in a largely self-created dilemma to which they never found a satisfactory solution. They were convinced on the one hand that once Germany remilitarized the Rhineland it would fortify its border with France and then destroy with impunity the Little Entente, France's allies; but they also had a ridiculously exaggerated view of German military strength and were therefore reluctant to become involved then and there in a conflict with Germany.[14] Thus, though recognizing the implications of a remilitarized Rhineland not only for France but for the whole of Europe, the French leaders were already so terrified of what they imagined to be German military strength as to make it unlikely that they would muster the needed energy to prepare any counteraction to a German fait accompli. In fact, as the evidence of French documents reveals to the incredulous observer, during the weeks of January and February 1936, as the issue of the Rhineland came to the fore, France not only lacked a previously prepared plan for a military countermove to remilitarization but did not even begin to prepare one while all its intelligence and diplomatic sources were telling them that such a step was impending.[15]

Since the French government on the whole was reasonably well-informed

10. Eden-Hoesch on 6 January in *G. D.*, C, 4, No. 484, Memorandum by Wenninger, II M 374g, 6 January, T–120, 2673/5578/E 400748, and Cmd. 5143, Nos. 47, 48; Neurath-Phipps on 14 January, in *G. D.*, C, 4, No. 496; von Neurath-Phipps on 17 January in *G. D.*, C, 4, Nos. 500, 501, von Neurath memorandum RM 40, 17 January, T–120, 2383/4619/E 198234–235, Cmd. 5143, No. 49, and *Diplomaciai iratok magyarország külpolitikájához 1936–1945,* 1 (Budapest: Akadémiai kiadó, 1962) (hereafter cited as *Hungarian Documents*, 1), No. 19.

11. *D. D. F.*, 2d, 1, Nos. 17, 24, 27, 36, 37, 59, 91.

12. Ibid., No. 63; cf. No. 76.

13. Ibid., No. 53.

14. Ibid., Nos. 82, 83.

15. The relevant documents may be found in *D. D. F.*, 2d, 1. The general situations described had already been clear from *Les Évenements* and from the second volume of the memoirs of General Maurice Gamelin, *Servir* (Paris: Plon, 1946). The problems of relationships between the French military commanders and civilian authorities are analyzed in Philip C. F. Bankwitz, *Maxime Weygand and Civil-Military Relations in Modern France* (Cambridge: Harvard University Press, 1967).

on the extent of German rearmament, the exaggerated view of German military strength in 1936, placing it ahead of France in trained men and about to pull ahead in matériel, may have been due to the psychological effect of Germany's paramilitary formations like the SA of whose utility in regular military operations the French had apparently convinced themselves, or to the belief that the secret rearmament of Germany in prior years had in fact extended much further than either French intelligence at the time or the facts known later indicated, or to a need to deceive oneself with good excuses for refraining from action—or to a combination of all three.[16] While holding to this overassessment of German might, the French government was also unwilling to raise the subject of the demilitarized zone in negotiations with Germany, fearful of opening up the very question they preferred not to face. In short, France was incapable of formulating any coherent diplomatic or military plan in the face of impending disaster.[17]

The Belgian government was as worried about the threats and rumors of an end to Locarno as the French, but they were even less eager than France to become involved in either diplomatic initiative or a military countermove. On the contrary, the possibility of complications about the demilitarized zone and Belgium's obligations in relation to it only reinforced those tendencies in Belgium that were already pressing it toward a neutralist position.[18]

As the British government faced the prospect of German moves on the demilitarized zone in the first weeks of 1936, disappointment over the refusal of Germany to agree to an air pact was mingled with reluctance to take any serious action against a German coup. Both the air pact and the demilitarized zone were discussed in London with German and French leaders when they arrived for the funeral of George V at the end of January 1936, but no firm British position emerged.[19] Proposals were discussed at that time within the British government in an attempt to come to a general agreement with Germany. These schemes envisaged using the Rhineland and the return of Germany's former colonies in Africa in bargaining for Germany's return "to Geneva disarmament and a formal renunciation of any territorial designs in Europe, including aims at absorption of Austria and Czechoslovakia."[20] But the British government neither decided to try

16. The picture of German rearmament shown in Castellan's book is confirmed and supplemented by the reports in *D. D. F.*, 2d, 1. The exaggerated view of German strength—which ignores the lack of arms and ammunition for the paramilitary formations—still echoes in General Maurice Gauché's book, p. 46. Similar views were expressed by the French Minister of War, General Louis Mourin, on 31 March 1936 (*D. D. B.*, 4, No. 62).

17. *D. D. F.*, 2d, 1, Nos. 125, 126, 170; *D. D. B.*, 4, No. 5.

18. *D. D. F.*, 2d, 1, Nos. 73, 123, 137, 146, 167; *D. D. B.*, 4, documents listed under chap. 1; *G. D.*, C, 4, No. 547.

19. *D. D. F.*, 2d, 1, Nos. 32, 112; *G. D.*, C, 4, Nos. 501, 523, 529, 547; Cmd. 5143, No. 50; Eden, pp. 364–65, 372–76; British documents in Foreign Office C 151/ C 418/ C 763/ C 796/4/18.

20. Memorandum of Vansittart of February 1936, quoted in Colvin, *None so Blind*, p. 55; Feiling, p. 300; Atherton (London) dispatch 2207, 22 May 1936, State 740.0011 Mutual Guarantees (Locarno)/700. See also *D. D. F.*, 2d, 1, No. 113. A similar

for such an agreement at the time nor tried to make such an effort jointly with the French.[21] What the Western powers would not do from a position of strength in 1936 they would subsequently try to do from a position of weakness in 1938—though then at the expense of others rather than themselves.

At this time, the French knew nothing of internal British discussions of a general approach to Germany. They accurately foresaw, however, that the British government would be only too glad to use as an excuse for evading action the same step—French ratification of the Franco-Soviet Pact of 1935—that the Germans would use as an excuse for their move. The French ambassador to London correctly anticipated that the British, who looked upon Locarno more as a guarantee of the existing borders than as a security for the demilitarized zone, would not be alarmed by any German move that involved no crossing of the Franco-German or Belgium-German border and that in their opinion the French would not act either. Britain and France both looked to the other for reinforcement of its own weakness rather than confirmation of a strong resolve, and both were well satisfied.[22]

In the meantime, the German government was preparing its move. There were the beginnings of a serious tightening of the economic situation as the German rearmament boom approached a state of full employment. Problems involving foreign exchange and raw materials allocation that were to eventuate in the launching of the Four-Year Plan later that year were not yet publicly evident in full detail. The situation was serious enough, however, to suggest a propaganda campaign to rally public opinion in Germany around new perspectives in the economy: the old slogan of the National Socialist party had been "Freedom and Bread"; on 17 January 1936, Goebbels launched a new slogan, "Guns or Butter."[23] Some observers ar-

---

course is advocated in effect in Dodd's dispatch 2651 of 8 February 1936, U. S. 1936, 1:189–95. British documents pertaining to these internal discussions may be found in Foreign Office C 7734/ C /7752 C 8523/55/18, N 518/187/38, N 833/20/38, N 855/427/59, C 663/97/18, C 7515/134/18, C 454/ C 585/ C 614/ C 750/ C 807/ C 880/ C 979/ C 998/ C 1028/ C 1353/4/18, C 400/99/18, W 1048/ W 1274/79/98. The close relationship of this discussion to the consideration of future British policy toward the League in view of the fiasco of British actions in the Ethiopian crisis may be followed in W 5075/79/98.

21. At about the same time that Vansittart was urging an effort using colonial concessions for a comprehensive settlement with Germany, President Roosevelt was arranging for a sounding of German officials on a scheme for leasing to Germany specific mining and other concessions in colonies to meet the supposed needs of the German economy (Hyde Park P. P. F. 2616; Roosevelt must have given Fuller instructions for his talk with Schacht of 1 April 1936, at their meeting on either 13 February or 6 March 1936).

On British consideration of a transfer of mandates to Germany in the spring and summer of 1936, ending in a negative decision in July, see Foreign Office C 4275/ C 5185/ C 5520/ C 5822/ C 5973/97/18.

22. *D. D. F.*, 2d, 1, Nos. 106, 163, 184. See also Sir Lewis Namier's essay on the Flandin memoirs, in *Europe in Decay* (London: Macmillan, 1950), pp. 9–33, and the British cabinet discussion of 5 March 1936 in Foreign Office C 1760/4/18.

23. See Arnold J. Toynbee, *Survey of International Affairs 1936* (London: Oxford University Press, 1937), p. 123; *D. D. F.*, 2d, 1, No. 80. This was the public manifestation of the difficulties alluded to in the conference between Hitler, Schacht, and

gued subsequently that one of the reasons for the timing of Germany's Rhineland action was to divert the attention of the German public by a spectacular coup from the economic difficulties of the winter of 1935–36, and certainly some of Hitler's diplomatic advisers were very much concerned by the extent to which such political considerations had influenced him to act.[24] More important in the circumstances under which Hitler made his decision in timing was the position of Italy.

The estrangement between Italy and the Western powers and the concomitant beginnings of a rapprochement between Italy and Germany as a result of the Italian attack on Ethiopia have already been examined. In the first months of 1936, these developments were coming to a head as a result of events in Geneva and in Ethiopia. In Geneva, after the failure of the Hoare-Laval plan, the sanctionist powers were again turning to the consideration of the possibility of including oil among the items not to be sold to Italy. It was recognized by both Britain and France that such a measure would mean a final rupture with Italy, and the Italian government assured them that Italy would leave the League if such sanctions were in fact decided upon.[25] The desire of the Italians to use this threat in their negotiations with Britain and France was to have unexpected repercussions in March; but when first raised, it helped restrain the Western powers who in any case were reluctant to push the sanctions policy further. The discussions in Geneva in January and February, however, were strenuous and bitter; and Rome could not yet be certain of their outcome.

While these arguments were going on in Geneva, the situation in East Africa was marked by a temporary stalemate during which the Italians prepared for new offensive moves against Ethiopia. Under these circumstances Rome was hardly inclined to take a strong line against Germany. It was this combination of factors that was of great importance to Hitler in making any decision. As long as the friction between Italy and the Western powers continued, he could hope that the Italian government would not look unfavorably on a German move that directed attention away from Italy. Certainly Italy would hardly participate in a policy of sanctions against Germany while itself the victim of sanctions, a point that was equally clear to all concerned.[26] Once the Italians had won their war in East Africa, however, a rapprochement between Italy and the British and French was always possible. The Italians might then trade support of sanctions against Germany for an end to sanctions against themselves. The Italian victories in East Africa in February 1936, may well have helped precipitate

---

others on 25 November 1935, and Schacht's letter to von Blomberg of 24 December 1935 (*TMWC*, 36:291–95). Cf. Meinck, *Hitler und die deutsche Aufrüstung*, pp. 160–62.

24. See von Hassell's subsequent private memorandum on the Rhineland coup, in Robertson, pp. 202–05.

25. *D. D. F.*, 2d, 1, No. 19.

26. Ibid., No. 142; U. S. 1936, 1:183–87; *G. D.*, C, 4, No. 519; cf. *Hungarian Documents*, 1, No. 3.

German action for which German-Italian conversations had already paved the way.

On 17 January 1936, the German ambassador to Italy, Ulrich von Hassell, had a conversation with Hitler in which the possibility of better German-Italian relations was canvassed. Hitler's comments show that he considered the German-Italian antagonism of 1934 a closed chapter and that, assuming Italy would not rejoin the Stresa front, he was prepared to continue a policy of benevolent neutrality toward Italy in its African venture. Furthermore, he was quite explicit on the point that Germany would not return to the League of Nations, so that the Italians could continue to use the threat of withdrawal, a threat that Ambassador Attolico strongly urged his government to carry out.[27] The Italian government indicated its willingness to push for a more accommodating course toward Germany in Vienna; the Germans soon followed up on these hints with the Austrians but deferred serious negotiations—which eventually led to the agreement of 11 July 1936—until after the more immediate goal of remilitarization had been attained.[28]

In the last days of January and the first days of February 1936, Hitler considered the question of reoccupying the Rhineland in the immediate future.[29] The submission of the Franco-Soviet Pact to the Chamber of Deputies for ratification, announced by the Laval government on 16 January and implemented by the new French government of Albert Sarraut on 11 February, would provide an appropriate excuse. On 12 February the German chargé d'affaires in Paris was summoned to a conference with Hitler, von Blomberg, von Neurath, and von Ribbentrop to report on possible French reactions to remilitarization.[30] The attitude of Italy was also of key importance at this juncture. The Italians themselves apparently expected a German move at this time,[31] as von Hassell explained to Hitler when they

27. *G. D.*, C, 4, No. 506; cf. "Information," 18 January 1936, Bundesarchiv, Brammer, Z.Sg. 101/29, f. 31.

28. *G. D.*, C, 4, Nos. 515, 525, 545; Robert H. Whealey (ed.), "Mussolini's Ideological Diplomacy: An Unpublished Document," *Journal of Modern History*, 39, No. 4, (Dec. 1967), 432–37; "Bestellung aus der Pressekonferenz," 22 January 1936, Bundesarchiv, Brammer, Z.Sg. 101/7, f. 57; *Hungarian Documents*, 1, Nos. 4 (German text in *Acta Historica*, 7, Nos. 3–4 [1960], 366–67), 17, 26, 27, 36, 42. On the postponement of serious negotiations see especially *G. D.*, C, 4, No. 586.

29. For a reflection of Hitler's having discussed the subject with Göring—who was to participate in all the key meetings on this question—before 10 February 1936 see *D. D. F.*, 2d, 1, No. 162; for a reference by von Papen to Hitler reviewing the issue at the time see the former's comments to the Hungarian foreign minister Kanya of 5 February, *Hungarian Documents*, 1, No. 27. For material on the preparations in the German foreign ministry in the first week of February 1936 see T–120, 3289/7881/E 570752–766.

30. Letter of Dirk Forster in *Wiener Library Bulletin*, 10 (1956), 48. Forster was chargé at the German embassy in Paris from the death of Roland Köster on 31 December 1935, to the appointment of Count Johannes von Welczek in April 1936. See also Max Braubach, *Der Einmarsch deutscher Truppen in die entmilitarisierte Zone am Rhein im März 1936* (Cologne: Westdeutscher Verlag, 1956), p. 14.

31. *G. D.*, C, 4, No. 553.

discussed the matter on 14 February.[32] Hitler had probably already decided to act, but he preferred to coordinate his denunciation of Locarno with Mussolini if at all possible, or at least to secure Mussolini's acquiescence.

The possibility of sending Göring as a special messenger to Rome was canvassed, but it had been dropped by the time von Hassell returned to Germany for further deliberations on 19 February.[33] By then, Hitler had not only decided to go ahead, he had rejected out of hand recent British approaches for some form of new agreement and was already working out the details of the speeches and proposals that would accompany his move into the Rhineland.[34] He would promise the French and British almost anything to keep them quiet for the moment; in spite of von Hassell's objections, he wanted to move right away, partly for the domestic reasons that have already been touched on. Von Hassell was to sound out Mussolini's attitude, while Göring would contribute his share to the preparations by a trip to Warsaw rather than Rome.

In Warsaw, Göring was to reassure the Poles that rumors of a German-Soviet rapprochement were false and to scout out their reaction to any German move against the Locarno agreement.[35] To the outside world, the visit, coming right after one by Hitler's legal expert, Hans Frank, demonstrated that German-Polish relations were good in spite of continued difficulties over the payments for Germany's railway traffic across the Polish Corridor and the excitement produced by a speech of Schacht calling for the return of Polish Upper Silesia.[36] In the preceding months, following the uncertainty after Pilsudski's death in May 1935, the combined efforts of the two governments had kept their friction points, especially in Danzig, at a minimum. The two powers had maintained reasonably good relations, in part at the expense of the democratic opposition in Danzig.[37] But this had not been a

32. Hossbach, p. 97; *G. D.,* C, 4, No. 564; Robertson, pp. 192–93, 202–03.

33. *G. D.,* C, 4, No. 575; Robertson, pp. 194–95, 203–05.

34. On these British approaches see U. S. 1936, 1:196–98; *G. D.,* C, 4, Nos. 562, 568, 583, 594; 5, No. 8; Cmd. 5143, Nos. 51, 57; Eden, p. 379. Von Hassell cites von Bülow as explaining Hitler's indifference toward the British overtures as due to the fact that they did not fit into his plans (Robertson, p. 204).

35. On Göring's visit see Szembek, 11 February 1936, pp. 159–60, 19 February, pp. 162–63; *G. D.,* C, 4, No. 591; *D. D. F.,* 2d, 1, Nos. 212, 221, 222; *D. D. B.,* 4, No. 17; Slávik (Czech minister in Warsaw) report 21, 29 February 1936, Czech document in T–120, 1040/1809/413313.

36. On the Corridor payments issue see p. 186, above, and *D. D. F.,* 2d, 1, Nos. 118, 148, 178, 179; Szembek, 22 December 1935, p. 144, 10 February 1936, p. 159. The subject was discussed when Beck was in Berlin at the end of January 1936 (*D. D. F.,* 2d, 1, Nos. 124, 128; Cudahy (Warsaw) dispatch 989, 30 January 1936, State 760c.62/310). On Schacht's speech at Beuthen on 28 January and the resulting difficulties see *G. D.,* C, 4, No. 591, n. 6; *D. D. F.,* 2d, 1, Nos. 127, 129; Szembek, 12 February, p. 161.

37. On German-Polish relations in 1935 and early 1936 see Szembek, pp. 89–90, 143–46, 149, 152–54, 162; *Lipski Papers,* Nos. 49, 55, 56; *G. D.,* C, 4, Nos. 142, 442, 443, 454, 468, 473, 474, n. 6, 492, 499, 500, 509, 520, 522, 546; Radowitz (Danzig) dispatch I.G. 722/35, 18 June 1935, T–120, 2787/6023/H 044646–648; Schliep (War-

simple operation. There were strong internal pressures for a policy closer to France and less cooperative toward Germany than the one followed by the Polish foreign minister, Josef Beck. Beck gambled on a double-track policy: he could pretend to agree with those in the Polish government who wished to stand by France in case of a reoccupation of the Rhineland although he believed that Poland was not obligated to do so[38] because he did not believe that France would really move when the time came. Göring could return to Germany reassured, while Beck was ready both to reassure the advocates of a firm common policy with France in resistance to Germany and to follow in practice a continued policy of aloof but effective cooperation with Germany.[39]

While Göring was sounding out the Polish government, von Hassell returned to Rome. He had already received an indirect indication from Mussolini, who was circumventing the Italian foreign ministry, that Italy would take no action if Germany broke with the Locarno Pact in response to the Franco-Soviet Pact.[40] This position was reiterated by Mussolini to von Hassell on 22 February. Mussolini still thought it likely that oil sanctions would be instituted—in which case he would leave the League and make Locarno "disappear of its own accord."[41] If the Germans, however, were to act before that time, Italy would not move against them, an assurance that was subsequently confirmed in spite of some efforts in the Italian foreign ministry to restrain the firm commitment Mussolini had made.[42]

Under these circumstances, Hitler felt that he could make his move, although some anxiety remained. Poland would be unlikely to act. Italy would certainly stand aside. The British government had shown by its own recent approaches that little strong action need be feared from that quarter. The new king, Edward VIII, was thought friendlier to Germany than had been

---

saw) report P VI 17, 22 November 1935, ibid., frames H 044685–687; Gallman (U. S. consul Danzig) dispatches 125, 31 August 1935, State 760K.62/45, 139 of 2 October, 162 of 19 November, 166 of 5 December, State 860K.00/183, 187, and 189; *D. D. F.*, 2d, 1, Nos. 84, 86, 89, 97.

38. Szembek, 4 and 26 February 1936, pp. 159, 163.

39. See the summary of the evidence in Roos, pp. 233–37. The newly published French documents add detail but support the interpretation of Roos (see below, pp. 255f.). A detailed attack on Beck's person and career by Poles opposed to his policies, possibly the Sikorski group, may be found in the Czech documents under 3 December 1935, T–120, 1143/2028/444370–378.

40. *G. D.*, C, 4, No. 574.

41. Ibid., No. 579 (German text in Robertson, pp. 196–99); von Hassell to von Neurath, 23 February 1936, Deutsches Zentral Archiv Potsdam, Büro RAM 60952 (hereafter cited as DZA Potsdam 60952).

42. *G. D.*, C, 4, Nos. 592, 598 (German text in Robertson, pp. 200–01), 603 (German text in Robertson, p. 202), pp. 1170–72; 5, No. 5. The key figure in opposition to Mussolini's new policy was Fulvio Suvich, the Undersecretary of State in the Italian foreign ministry. He not only tried to tone down Mussolini's statements to von Hassell but also reassured the French and American ambassadors about the significance of von Hassell's peregrinations (*D. D. F.*, 2d, 1, No. 211; Long Diary, 22 February 1936, pp. 315–16, Long Papers; U. S. 1936, 1:204–05).

George V; as the head of the department of the German foreign ministry dealing with Great Britain expressed it: "King Edward does not mistrust us."[43] A propaganda campaign against the Franco-Soviet Pact would weaken any resolve to act in both Britain and France; as von Hassell noted on 22 February, "it was quite clear that he [Hitler] really wanted the ratification to use as a platform for his action."[44] Hitler's interview with the French journalist Bertrand de Jouvenel on 21 February, not published in France until 28 February after ratification of the Franco-Soviet Pact in the Chamber of Deputies, has sometimes been taken as an honest effort by Hitler to forestall ratification; but since Hitler expressly rejected warnings to London and Paris to prevent ratification, the friendly statements in that interview can now be seen as merely the last in a series of propaganda moves toward the French. It almost misfired by stimulating the French to inquire what new plans for better German-French relations Hitler might have in mind, but Hitler put off answering such embarrassing questions until his troops could give the reply.[45]

If the French were to be assuaged by sweet words, more spectacular balm would soothe the English: Hitler would offer to return to the League just when the British had indicated that such a return was no longer a prerequisite for an Anglo-German rapprochement. Confronted by the dazzling prospect of receiving even more than they dared hope for, the British government and the British public would surely be entranced into acquiescence. This particular concession had not been included among the list of diversionary offers Hitler had sketched out on 19 February.[46] In fact, Hitler had just reassured the Italians that he had no intention of returning to Gen-

43. U. S. 1936, 1:188. Dieckhoff was summarizing the import of a conversation von Neurath had had with the new king in London at the time of the funeral of George V. Von Neurath had expressed similar views to the Hungarian foreign minister Kanya when they were both in London (*Hungarian Documents,* 1, No. 19). Cf. *G. D.,* C, 4, Nos. 507, 510; 5, 316. For other contemporary indications of a pro-German attitude of Edward VIII see also *G. D.,* C, 4, No. 531; Phillips Diary, 29 January 1936, Phillips Papers, Vol. 9, p. 1271. Edward VIII was to be treated well in the German press, as were the exchange of German and British war veterans occurring simultaneously in part in line with his previously discussed speech as Prince of Wales (Wotton, pp. 194–99; "Bestellung aus der Pressekonferenz," 18 January 1936, Bundesarchiv, Brammer, Z.Sg. 101/7, f. 43).

44. Von Hassell's notes in Robertson, p. 204. The full sentence reads: "Bezeichnend ist, dass er ausdrücklich ablehnte, durch Warnungen in Paris und London die Ratifikation zu verhindern: es war ganz klar, dass er die Ratifikation geradezu wünschte, nämlich als Plattform für seine Aktion." On the propaganda campaign preceding the remilitarization see *D. D. F.*, 2d, 1, Nos. 95, 104, 172, 193, 204, 205, 208; Domarus, 1:565–68; Cmd. 5143, No. 52; Hitler's decree about the press of 29 January 1936, in *Anordnungen des Stellvertreters des Führers* (Munich: Eher, 1937), pp. 244–49.

45. On the Jouvenel interview and the resulting French inquiries see Domarus 1:579–81; Cmd. 5143, Nos. 54–56; *D. D. F.*, 2d, 1, Nos. 255, 265, 272, 281, 293, 349; *G. D.,* C, 4, No. 604; Long Diary, 23 March 1935, pp. 328–29, Long Papers; Osuský (Czech minister Paris) telegram of 29 February 1936, Czech document in T–120, 1040/1809/413087.

46. *G. D.,* C, 4, No. 575 (German text in Robertson, p. 195).

eva and knew that the Italians were using the threat to leave the League in their attempts to prevent oil sanctions. Why then this added offer with its possible disadvantages along with its assumed benefits?

The evidence for Hitler's last-minute change of plans leading to the inclusion of an offer to return to the League is scanty and indirect. The doubts and hesitations expressed by all of his military and some of his diplomatic advisers may have suggested the need to dangle additional concessions before the Western powers; certainly a return to Geneva would be the most spectacular of these, and there is evidence that Hitler discussed it with von Neurath on 27 February.[47] In the second place, the sanctions committee of the League was scheduled to meet on 2 March; and Italian threats to leave the League were important because they seemed to be having the desired effect of frightening France and England out of supporting oil sanctions.[48] In a short time, however, Britain and France would be unlikely to become further entangled in trouble with Italy once Germany had moved into the Rhineland; they would hardly turn to oil sanctions then, and Italy's threat to leave Geneva would become irrelevant. Still another factor minimized the possibility of Germany antagonizing Italy by offering to return to the League at precisely the moment that Italy was threatening to leave: nothing in the record suggests that Hitler was in any way serious about the offer. Once it had served its purpose of confusing opinion abroad, Germany would have no more interest in it. Any Italian objection would then wither automatically. It should be noted, however, that in this case as in others Hitler was inclined to take extreme steps or make major additional concessions in a crisis, leaving the possible repercussions to be dealt with later. As in 1933 he had been willing to risk temporary Italian displeasure by leaving the League without prior warning to Rome, so now he would use the promise to return to Geneva under circumstances certain to be offensive to Mussolini. The key matter in Hitler's eyes was the Rhineland action itself. He would find ways to take care of other problems later.

On 2 March 1936, the military directives for the reoccupation of the Rhineland were issued; on 5 March the date for the action was set as 7 March, a Saturday, in the hope of gaining a weekend's respite before any

47. Memorandum of Dodd, 29 February 1936, Dodd Papers, folder 1936–D. A summary of this memorandum is in *Dodd Diary*, pp. 314–16, and his account of the meeting to François-Poncet in *D. D. F.*, 2d, 1, No. 292. Von Neurath's own memorandum on his meeting with Dodd on 29 February is short and uninformative (RM 162, T–120, 2383/4619/E 198262–263).

Von Papen subsequently claimed credit for having talked Hitler into his offer to return to Geneva in a conversation with Sir Walford Selby, British minister to Austria, when the latter was about to return to London for consultation on 12 March (*D. D. F.*, 2d, 1, No. 420). Von Papen's own report on this conversation (*G. D.*, C, 5, No. 90) refers to the German offer in general terms. The British ambassador to Germany claimed to know that the German foreign ministry was opposed to the idea and that von Bülow had not been told about it until the last moment (*D. D. B.*, 4, No. 74).

48. See especially *D. D. F.*, 2d, 1, Nos. 218, 224, 239; *G. D.*, C, 5:1; Eden, pp. 367–69. A summary of the evidence in Laurens, pp. 324–33.

counteraction could be taken. On the day of the reoccupation, the Locarno powers were to be informed and the Reichstag would meet to hear Hitler explain his move while promising peace and goodwill to all.

German military plans provided for small German units to move into the Rhineland, joining the local militarized police (*Landespolizei*) and staging a fighting withdrawal if there were a military counteraction from the West.[49] The story that the German troops had orders to withdraw if France moved against them is partially correct but essentially misleading; the withdrawal was to be a tactical defensive move, not a return to the earlier position. The possibility of a war was thus accepted by Hitler, but he clearly did not think the contingency very likely. There were some last-minute conferences in Berlin, especially on 2 March, and rumors of some impending move circulated in the German capital; but when Hitler summoned his cabinet on 6 March, orders had been given and the troops were already on the move.[50]

In the last days before the German move, rumors and warnings had not been lacking. It was quite clear to the British and French governments that something might be done by the Germans, using the ratification of the Franco-Soviet Pact as an excuse, and that the German step might well involve the demilitarized zone. The two governments had begun to discuss this problem, and the French government, at least, was warned by its representatives of a possibly imminent move.[51] This danger, however, only led the French to a more accommodating attitude toward England in regard to the prospect of including Germany in a new naval agreement growing out of the London Naval Conference.[52] By deferring somewhat to British wishes for good relations with Germany, the French government hoped to keep England cooperative in case of any drastic German move, but it may be doubted that such a course had much substantive value. As for direct action in response to any German move, the French no more planned this now than before. They awaited the worst, unwilling and unable to cope with the clear dangers ahead.[53] They knew that, largely because of domestic pressure from the Flemish element, Belgium was trying to loosen its military ties to

49. The evidence is ably summarized in Donald C. Watt, "German Plans for reoccupation of the Rhineland: A Note," *Journal of Contemporary History*, 1, No. 4 (Oct. 1966), pp. 193–99. See also *D. D. F.*, 2d, 1, No. 320.

50. Minutes of the council of ministers of 6 March 1936, in *G. D.*, C, 5, No. 9. On the meetings of 2 and 3 March I have been unable to find official contemporary records, but see Dertinger's "Abendmaterial," 2 March 1936, and "Informationsbericht Nr. 12," 5 March 1936, in Bundesarchiv, Brammer, Z.Sg. 101/29, f. 81–91; *D. D. F.*, 2d, 1, Nos. 272, 531.

51. *D. D. F.*, 2d, 1, Nos. 175, 180, 188, 200, 242, 287, 288.

52. The relationship of Germany to the later stages of the London naval conference is not reviewed here because of its relative unimportance. On this subject, especially as it affected Franco-British relations see ibid., Nos. 120, 155.

53. Ibid., Nos. 186, 187, 196, 203, 241, 269, 283. The French government was aware of the fact that the French general staff had no plans whatever for coping with a German remilitarization of the Rhineland; see especially ibid., No. 223. On similar British indecision see U. S. 1936, 1:213. Flandin told Eden on 3 March that France would not act alone (Foreign Office C 1386/4/18).

France.[54] The French government also knew that their eastern allies could be depended upon only as long as France could aid them by threatening Germany's open western border.[55] The leaders of the Little Entente, in turn, recognized that if Germany moved west it would be only so that subsequently it could move east and southeast. Once Germany had fortified its western border, France would be incapable of preventing Germany from taking any action it might decide upon in regard to them, and the countries of Southeast Europe would have to draw the consequences.[56] The only way the French could console themselves was with the notion that a German move into the Rhineland would be likely to lead France to a firmer alliance with England, including plans for common defense against any further German aggression westward. This purely defensive perception of the issues reflected the self-assessment of France as incapable of maintaining the status quo in Europe. Its view of the future in regard to Franco-British relations was largely correct. The two points together constituted France's abdication from any significant role in European diplomacy. The initiative would pass to Germany, checked if at all by Britain.[57]

On 7 March, German troops moved into the demilitarized zone, the German foreign minister, von Neurath, informed the ambassadors of the major foreign powers about the German move, and Hitler spoke to the assembled Reichstag. The initial troop deployment was kept small, establishing remilitarization while simultaneously showing that no attack across the French or Belgian border was intended.[58] Hitler had a last-minute attack of nerves,[59] but he then issued the final orders and the troops marched. When the news reached Paris and London on the morning of 7 March, there was shock but no immediate action. The German notification with its accompanying offers of peace had been designed primarily to ward off any dangerous repercussions. Since France was both most affected by the German step and potentially most dangerous to Germany, every effort was made to urge the British government to restrain the French. That the British and French would object to what Germany had done was taken for granted, but the real issue was whether any action would accompany or follow their anticipated complaints.[60]

The initial situation was all that Germany could hope for. In London,

54. The negotiations over officially announcing the termination of the Franco-Belgian military convention of 1920 may be followed in *D. D. B.*, 3. Agreement was registered on 6 March 1936!

55. *D. D. F.*, 2d, 1, No. 156.

56. Ibid., Nos. 256, 270.

57. The French general staff memorandum of 18 February 1936 on Franco-British cooperation if Germany reoccupied the Rhineland clearly points in this direction (ibid., No. 202).

58. The military moves are summarized in Braubach, p. 19; notifications, sent to Germany's diplomats on 5 March for delivery on 7 March, in *G. D.*, C, 5, Nos. 3, 4, 7.

59. Hossbach, pp. 97–98.

60. On the initial notifications and protests see *D. D. F.*, 2d, 1, Nos. 298, 307; Cmd. 5143, No. 58; Eden, pp. 380–82; *G. D.*, C, 5, Nos. 12–16, 21; U. S. 1936, 1:208.

Sir Anthony Eden immediately acted as the Germans had hoped by trying to restrain the French, and the French in turn suggested that there was not much sense in considering new peace proposals from Berlin when those that Germany had signed voluntarily could be tossed aside so casually.[61] But whatever response the French ambassador in London or foreign minister in Paris might give to English suggestions, the fact was that the British government's first inclination as expressed on 7 March was that there had been a deplorable breach of international behavior but that no immediate counteraction was called for. As the British Foreign Office informed the American chargé d'affaires, "England would make every endeavour to prevent the imposition of military and/or economic sanctions against Germany."[62]

The French could have acted alone, however, had they had the will to do so and had this will infused into its military leadership an interest in planning for such a contingency. In spite of some courageous voices in the cabinet, the lack of determination of the majority of the ministry, reinforced by the hesitations of the military, carried the day. The political factor of an election two months off, a public fearful of war and willing to fight only in defense of France's own frontiers, and a military program that contained no plan whatsoever for any relevant countermove combined to force a diplomatic rather than a military rejoinder to Germany.[63] The implications of this policy were clear to the French foreign minister; the next day Flandin told the American ambassador to Paris that the Germans would first fortify the Rhineland and then turn east.[64]

In an attempt to avert such grim prospects, Flandin attempted in the days immediately following to recover by diplomacy what had been lost by inaction. René Massigli of the French foreign ministry had armed him with a clear prognosis of what would happen if France yielded on this occasion: the Poles would draw the logical consequences in determining their future policy, the pro-German line would come to the fore in Yugoslavia and Rumania, the Czechs would settle for the best terms they could get, and Austria would clearly be next on the list.[65] In a series of conversations and conferences, Flandin now attempted to persuade the other Locarno powers

61. *D. D. F.*, 2d, 1, Nos. 301, 316, 317; see also ibid., No. 520; *D. D. B.*, 4, No. 21; Eden, pp. 383, 388.

62. Atherton (London) telegram 92, 9 March 1936, State 740.001 Mutual Guarantee (Locarno)/381. See also the telegrams 187 and 190 of Strauss from Paris, 10 March, ibid., /401 and 402 (item 406 in this file is identified in U. S. 1936, 1:232–33 as item 460 by mistake). The reaction of the Belgians was similar to that of the British (*D. D. F.*, 2d, 1, No. 330).

63. The evidence is summarized in Braubach, pp. 26–28; *D. D. F.*, 2d, 1, No. 334. Note that French army plans required mobilization of the whole French army to chase three German regiments across the Rhine (ibid., No. 393; *Les évenements* 1:62, 65), and that Gamelin seriously doubted that France could break through in the Rhineland and defeat Germany (*D. D. F.*, 2d, 1, Nos. 334, 525).

64. U. S. 1936, 1:216–17.

65. This accurate prediction of the events of the subsequent two years may be found in *D. D. F.*, 2d, 1, No. 407.

to take some sort of drastic action against Germany. The terms of the Locarno Treaty gave him a strong position to argue for British support unless either Great Britain wished to break its own treaty commitments or was prepared to see France act on its own. For a short time it looked as if Flandin and those in England like Winston Churchill who thought action was needed, were making headway.[66]

Following a stormy meeting of the Locarno powers in Paris, another conference was held in London the weekend after the German coup. By this time, the concern felt in the British Foreign Office over a possible breach with France as well as the more critical attitude of many people in British public life toward the German move were beginning to make themselves felt.[67] Flandin now took a stronger line and began to get some British support. He could point to assurances of cooperation from at least some of France's allies. The Czech and Rumanian governments had promised to side with France;[68] the case of Yugoslavia was more doubtful, but at least that country's government sounded encouraging.[69] Since none of these powers could afford to participate in economic sanctions against Germany, the value of their support was by no means very great—that is, unless France and England were willing to turn to military action. The position of the other East European allies of France was even more dubious. The Soviet Union might argue against appeasement and its leaders denounce Germany's actions, but neither wanted nor expected France to march.[70] Poland was simultaneously assuring the French of loyalty to the alliance and assuring the Germans that since Germany was not planning to attack France there was no occasion for the alliance to become effective. Beck reassured the French while expressing to the Germans some concern that their offer of a twenty-five-year pact in the west and the south contrasted strangely with the ten-year term of the German-Polish agreement.[71] He thus satisfied

66. See *D. D. F.*, 2d, 1, Nos. 322, 328, 380; U. S. 1936, 1:228–29; *G. D.*, C, 5, Nos. 27, 35, 37, 43, 47, 50, 58; *D. D. B.*, 4, Nos. 41–44; Geyr von Schweppenburg, pp. 83–86; Eden, pp. 390–99.

From the British records, however, it would appear that on the evening of 13 March Flandin agreed to legalize remilitarization *after* negotiations (see Foreign Office C 1996/4/18, p. 232).

67. *D. D. F.*, 2d, 1, Nos. 363, 410; *G. D.*, C, 5, Nos. 66, 73; U. S. 1936, 1:232–33; Winston S. Churchill, *The Gathering Storm* (Boston: Houghton Mifflin, 1948), pp. 195–97.

68. Czechoslovakia: *D. D. F.*, 2d, 1, Nos. 385, 402; *G. D.*, C, 5, Nos. 70, 86, 120. Rumania: U. S. 1936, 1:227–28.

69. *D. D. F.*, 2d, 1, Nos. 360, 377; but see *G. D.*, C, 5, Nos. 48, 56; *Hungarian Documents*, 1, No. 40; Hoptner, *Yugoslavia in Crisis*, p. 45.

70. *D. D. F.*, 2d, No. 366; U. S. 1936, 1:212.

71. *D. D. F.*, 2d, 1, Nos. 303, 324, 325, 327, 408; *G. D.*, C, 5, Nos. 19, 61, 82, 106; Szembek, 7, 10, 11 March 1936, pp. 166–70; U. S. 1936, 1:230, 239–41; Slavik report 25, 9 March, and report 28, 14 March 1936, Czech documents in T–120, 1040/1809/413319–324 (excerpt from latter report in *Prager Akten*, No. 59); Gotthold Rhode, "Aussenminister Josef Beck und Staatssekretär Graf Szembek," *Vierteljahrshefte für Zeitgeschichte*, 2, No. 1 (Jan. 1954), pp. 90–93; Cudahy dispatch 1078, 2 April 1936, State 740.0011 Mutual Guarantee (Locarno)/616 (the

Polish Marshal Rydz-Smigly who believed that France would indeed move against Germany, without jeopardizing his own policy based on the assumption that no drastic action would in fact ensue.[72] That such procedures did nothing for Beck's personal reputation and involved enormous risks will be obvious; that the French government could draw from such duplicity a reinforcement for its own weakness and thereby in turn confirm Beck in his course is equally clear. Whatever judgment one might subsequently make of the wisdom of such policies, Flandin must have realized that all he could expect from Warsaw was a vote for some pious resolution in the council of the League.

As for Italy, with Britain one of the two guarantor powers of the Locarno Pact, even such a vote could not be counted on, to say nothing of any meaningful steps against Germany. Still the object of sanctions, Italy was not about to join in sanctions against Germany. The Italian government was indeed upset over the way in which Germany had acted; as in 1933 Hitler had warned Mussolini that Germany would leave the disarmament conference but had not indicated that he also planned to leave the League, so now he had informed Rome of the planned remilitarization of the Rhineland but not his intention to offer to return to Geneva. For reasons previously explained, this shocked the Italian government and momentarily strengthened the pro-French elements in the Italian foreign ministry. Mussolini himself, after a few days of sulking, returned to his line of tacit support for Germany. The advantages to Italy of Germany's coup were too obvious to overlook: attention shifted from Ethiopia to the Rhineland; as for Germany's return to the League, it would soon become apparent that it was scheduled for the Teutonic Calends.[73] Under these circumstances, the key to the situation, which on the first days had been in Paris, now shifted to London. If Britain were willing to act, something would be done; if not, there would not only be no action at all but there might well be a real breach between London and Paris.

The British government was aware of this fact and attempted to secure some concessions from Germany to use in restraining the French demands for joint action. They hoped for some reduction in the German troops in the Rhineland—or at least a promise of no further increases—and some com-

---

section omitted from U. S. 1936, 1:275, dealing with Beck's conversation with Flandin in London in which Beck had categorically refused to back France in military action against Germany).

72. *D. D. F.*, 2d, 2, Nos. 71, 214; *D. D. B.*, 4, No. 14. For a different view, defending Polish policy, see Waclaw Jedrzejewicz (ed.), *Diplomat in Paris 1936–1939, Memoirs of Juliusz Lukasiewicz, Ambassador of Poland* (New York: Columbia University Press, 1970) (hereafter cited as *Lukasiewicz Papers*), pp. 8–11.

73. *G. D.*, C, 5, Nos. 11, 18, 26, 28, 41, 45, 54, 75, 330, 350; U. S. 1936, 1:210; *D. D. F.*, 2d, 1, Nos. 378, 396; Laurens, pp. 343–44. The real meaning of Germany's offer should have been clear to all when the German government insisted on 8 March that Eden strike the phrase "She wished to return [to the League] now" from his statement in the House of Commons (*G. D.*, C, 5, No. 31).

mitment not to fortify the area.[74] Berlin had been anxiously watching the reactions of the other powers. Observers in the German capital noted the widespread anxiety; behind the scenes Hitler followed the reports from abroad with great care and examined the British request with his advisers. At first he was quite worried and inclined to offer concessions, but he recovered his firmness and declined to make any concessions beyond a temporary halt in further increases in troops in the Rhineland.[75] The Germans gave out a little information on their troop strength in the former demilitarized zone to show that they were not about to attack France or Belgium, but the details revealed were not specific enough to be considered an explicit commitment.[76] The German people were whipped into ecstatic enthusiasm by a propaganda campaign for the new "elections" Hitler had decreed;[77] simultaneously, Hitler attempted to soothe opinion abroad, especially in England, by murmuring sweet assurances to the noted English correspondent, Ward Price, on 9 March.[78]

With no substantial concession from Germany to use in negotiations with the other Locarno powers in London on 12–13 March, the British leaders, already moving toward a more serious view of the situation, began to stiffen their resolve in response to Flandin's arguments. During these two days, the possibility of drastic action against Germany again came to the fore; for a short time it seemed as if Great Britain either would give its blessings to a French move of some sort or join France in sanctions itself. The choice for Britain appeared to be between a breach with France and the likelihood of further German aggression or some drastic response to the occupation of the Rhineland with some risk of immediate conflict with Germany. For a

74. *G. D.*, C, 5, No. 81. The idea may have originated with Lord Lothian; see ibid., No. 74, and Butler, *Lord Lothian,* pp. 212–13.

75. *G. D.*, C, 5, No. 84. Because of the inaccessibility of the contemporary documentation at the time various early accounts of these events were written, the chronology has frequently been confused; it can now be clarified. There were three crises in Berlin: the first, recorded by Hossbach and referred to above, occurred on 5 March, before the final orders to the troops to move. The second took place right after the 8 March speech of the French prime minister, Sarraut, and is the one referred to in the text here. It preceded the crisis of the weekend of 12–14 March, related to the well-known telegram sent by the three German service attachés in London that will be examined shortly. For referral to Hitler of the diplomatic reports during the crucial days see the notes in *G. D.*, C, 5. For the crisis of nerves in Berlin on 8–10 March see, in addition to the evidence summarized in Braubach, pp. 21–23, *G. D.*, C, 5, Nos. 76; *D. D. F.*, 2d, 1, Nos. 337, 394, 395; Görlitz, *Keitel,* p. 91 (Keitel has reversed the sequence of the second and third crises but is nevertheless useful as a source because he took von Blomberg's place at a conference held on either 9 or 10 March).

76. *G. D.*, C, 5, Nos. 23, 65.

77. See the "Richtlinien für den Wahlkampf," of 10 March 1936 in Bundesarchiv, Brammer, Z.Sg. 101/29, f. 101–05. Excerpts from Hitler's speeches in Domarus, 1:603–16. See also *D. D. F.*, 2d, 1, Nos. 456, 457, 543.

78. Domarus, 1:598–601; *D. D. F.*, 2d, 1, No. 383; Arnold J. Toynbee (ed.), *Documents on International Affairs 1936* (London: Oxford University Press, 1937), pp. 57–61; George Ward Price, *I Know these Dictators* (New York: Holt, 1938), p. 179.

moment it looked as if the British government inclined to the second alternative.[79]

Reports on this threatening development reached Berlin on 12–13 March, accompanied by hints that Italy was weakening in its support of Germany and accentuated by warnings from Germany's military attachés in Paris and London that there was an imminent possibility of war.[80] It was in the face of these serious contingencies that von Blomberg, the war minister, apparently urged Hitler to make some significant concessions, possibly the withdrawal of those units that had been moved furthest west.[81] Von Neurath opposed any such concessions, and Hitler after some wavering agreed with him.[82] Hitler was to hold these warnings and worries against the military; the fact that he himself eventually remained firm and came through the crisis successfully was to have later significance. The one token move that Hitler did authorize was a more precise statement of the size of German forces in the Rhineland to combat both press exaggerations of their size and any fears of a possible German attack.[83]

The crisis ebbed as quickly as it had arisen. The British government eventually agreed to certain gestures toward Paris in order to please the French, but all sanctions or other drastic measures against Germany were rejected. What caused this rapid turn away from a firm stand? Three factors stand out. In the first place, it was clear from the beginning of the crisis and had been made increasingly explicit by 13 March that the British Dominions, especially the Union of South Africa and Canada, would not stand with England if it came to war. The South African government in particular was busy backing the German position in London and with the other Dominion governments.[84] Second, Britain's own leaders were unwilling to risk war, and they recognized that such a risk was indeed present. Nothing in the record suggests that Prime Minister Baldwin had any clear idea of the issues involved. He was being advised by his friend Thomas Jones to take Hitler's offers at face value and otherwise do nothing, advice in which Lord Lothian, Vincent Massey, the Astors, Sir Thomas Inskip (who was about to be appointed minister for the coordination of defense), Arnold Toynbee (who

79. There is an excellent summary of the crisis in *G. D.*, C, 5:236–37. See also ibid., Nos. 85, 91, 92, 127; U. S. 1936, 1:235–36, 241–44; *D. D. F.*, 2d, 1, Nos. 414, 425; Eden, pp. 399–403.

80. *G. D.*, C, 5, Nos. 87–89, 94, 98 (the famous telegram of the three service attachés in London), 113; *D. D. F.*, 2d, 1, No. 405; Geyr von Schweppenburg, pp. 86–88; Fitz-Randolph, *Frühstücks-Attaché*, pp. 31–35. See also *G. D.*, C, 5, Nos. 96, 102.

81. Testimony of Jodl, *TMWC*, 15:352; Görlitz, *Keitel*, p. 91; Kordt, *Nicht aus den Akten*, p. 134.

82. See *G. D.*, C, 5, No. 98, n. 2, 109; Affidavit of Schmidt (the interpreter), *TMWC*, 10:218–19; Testimony of von Neurath, *TMWC*, 17:41–42.

83. *G. D.*, C, 5, Nos. 104, 112, 145, 222.

84. Ibid., Nos. 95, 118, 127, 175, 262; *D. D. F.*, 2d, 1, No. 346; U. S. 1936, 1:244. There is a brief discussion of this episode in Donald C. Watt, "South African Attempts to Mediate between Britain and Germany 1935–1938," Bourne and Watt, *Studies in International History*, pp. 406–07.

had just returned from meeting Hitler), and Norman Davis (who was in London for the naval negotiations) joined wholeheartedly.[85] Not only members of the cabinet but the king himself urged a peaceful settlement, and his intervention was known to the German government.[86] Most important, however, was the pressure of British public opinion, influenced not only by the feeling that the demilitarization of the Rhineland had been an unjust portion of the peace settlement but seeing no good reason for risking war over an action that, however reprehensible, did not itself involve an attack on another country—unlike the Italian attack on Ethiopia in the preceding year. As the British Secretary of State for War explained to the German ambassador in London on the evening of 8 March, "though the British people were prepared to fight for France in the event of a German incursion into French territory, they would not resort to arms on account of the recent occupation of the Rhineland. The people did not know much about the demilitarization provisions and most of them probably took the view that they did not care 'two hoots' about the Germans reoccupying their own territory."[87]

Once this point was clear on 14 March, the denouement of the crisis was as expected. The Germans were invited to send a representative to a meeting of the League council in London, where the council members listened to von Ribbentrop imitate his master's voice before voting that Germany had indeed broken its treaty commitments.[88] To calm the French, the British in a meeting of the Locarno powers on 19 March agreed to a stiff note

85. See T. Jones, 8 March 1936, pp. 179–81. Norman Davis's account of the same discussion is in the Phillips diary for 3 April 1936, Phillips Papers, 10:1420. Toynbee had just lectured in Germany at the invitation of Hans Frank's Academy for Germanic Law in favor of revising the peace settlement in regard to South Tirol, Austria, the Sudetenland, Eupen, Memel, and so on, and had been to see Hitler who gave him an outline of Germany's expansion plans for the next few years (in addition to the record of Jones already cited, see *D. D. F.*, 2d, 1, No. 250; *The Times* of London, 29 February 1936; Frank, *Im Angesicht des Galgens*, pp. 216–18; Memorandum of Toynbee, 8 March 1936, Foreign Office C 1814/4/18; and the not very informative section 22 in Toynbee's memoirs, *Acquaintances* [London: Oxford University Press, 1967]). On Lord Lothian at this time see also *D. D. F.*, 2d, 1, Nos. 436, 438.

86. While the extravagant tales of Fritz Hesse, *Das Spiel um Deutschland* (Munich: Paul List, 1953), pp. 59ff., have been effectively demolished by Helmut Krausnick, "Legenden um Hitlers Aussenpolitik," *Vierteljahrshefte für Zeitgeschichte*, 2, No. 3 (July 1954), p. 220 and n. 10, there is ample evidence for a less spectacular role by Edward VIII (*G. D.*, C, 5, Nos. 77, 147, 178). The British cabinet discussions of 13–16 March may be traced in Foreign Office C 1996/4/18.

87. *G. D.*, C, 5, No. 33; Duff Cooper, pp. 196–97. Other comments to the same effect in the memoirs of Churchill, Eden, and others. The subsequent development of British opinion, especially among the general staff, can be traced in the reports of the German military attaché in London, Geyr von Schweppenburg, in T–120, 2673/5576/passim, summarized in his memoirs, pp. 88–95.

88. On the invitation to von Ribbentrop and his stay in London see *G. D.*, C, 5, Nos. 119, 121, 123, 124, 126, 134, 135, 138, 152, 154, 157; *D. D. F.*, 2d, 1, Nos. 429, 437, 444; Schmidt, *Statist auf diplomatischer Bühne*, pp. 320–24; Kordt, pp. 136–44, 192; Jan Masryk (Czech minister London) report 5, 27 March 1936, Czech document in T–120, 1040/1809/413088–093 (some rearranged excerpts in *Prager Akten*, No. 62).

to Germany and military staff conversations if no immediate satisfactory settlement were reached; but though the staff talks that eventually did take place annoyed the Germans, there was no real substance to this British gesture of consolation for France, and the Germans knew it.[89] On the other hand, the Germans used the firm tone that the British had agreed to as an occasion for righteous indignation, rejection of all the major proposals made to them, and further delay, delay being the main object of German policy during the last half of April and the month of May.[90]

It was in part to make it easier to secure these delays in international action by continued negotiations that counterproposals accompanied Berlin's rejection of the London proposals of 19 March when that rejection was made official.[91] By that time it was evident to all that there would be no drastic action against Germany and that even economic sanctions had been ruled out.[92] The German government was forced to be cautious; every effort had been made to avoid incidents that might lead to new complications.[93] Berlin had also had some anxious moments about the attitude of Italy. For a moment it looked as if Mussolini might consider withdrawing support from Germany in return for the dropping of League sanctions against Italy, but by late March he had returned firmly to a pro-German position in the negotiations.[94] Even Belgium was becoming increasingly reluctant to stand by France and under German pressure turned increasingly toward a neutral position.[95] All Europe could see that the German triumph was complete. This triumph was symbolized by Berlin's refusal to answer a series of questions about its counterproposals presented by the British government on its own behalf and that of France.[96] The one thing Germany did not want was a set of new fixed obligations; once the various offers made by Berlin

89. *G. D.*, C, 5, Nos. 162, 163, 168, 199; U. S. 1936, 1:263–64; *D. D. F.*, 2d, 1, Nos. 454, 481, 483, 484, 498. The proposals of 19 March are summarized in *G. D.*, C, 5:208–14. On the military staff talks see *D. D. F.*, 2d, 1, Nos. 492, 493; 2, Nos. 4, 5, 19, 92, 97, 217; Eden, pp. 415–17; *D. D. B.*, 4, Nos. 53, 63, 64, 72, 76, 99; *G. D.*, C, 5, Nos. 122, 227, 236, 251, 259, 290, 303, 340; see also Foreign Office C 2305/ C 2361/ 4/18.

90. *G. D.*, C, 5, Nos. 176, 182, 183, 186–88, 285, 286; *D. D. F.*, 2d, 1, No. 521.

91. *G. D.*, C, 5, Nos. 200, 207, 208, 211, 242–44, 247; *D. D. B.*, 4, Nos. 57, 58; *D. D. F.*, 2d, 1, No. 517. It should be noted that the German military was more willing to be conciliatory than the foreign ministry (see *G. D.*, C, 5, Nos. 230, 233).

92. *G. D.*, C, 5, No. 214; *D. D. F.*, 2d, 1, No. 538.

93. *G. D.*, C, 5, Nos. 136, 137, 160, 218, 240.

94. Ibid., Nos. 117, 146, 149, 161, 164, 174, 177, 180, 184, 185, 219, 252, 255; *D. D. F.*, 2d, 1, Nos. 442, 518, 526; 2, No. 17.

95. *G. D.*, C, 5, Nos. 143, 167; *D. D. F.*, 2d, 1, No. 469; 2, No. 27. The Dutch had made it clear from the beginning of the Rhineland crisis that they would stay out of everything—until swallowed up (*G. D.*, C, 5, Nos. 83, 128, 190, 193).

96. On the early history of the "Questionnaire" and the German handling of it see Eden, pp. 416–19; *D. D. F.*, 2d, 1, No. 539; 2, Nos. 6, 103, 125, 126, 134, 140, 147, 162, 187; *D. D. B.*, 4, Nos. 74, 78, 82; *G. D.*, C, 5, Nos. 248, 266, 267, 272, 279, 280, 310, 313, 317; Mayer (Berlin) telegram 136, 7 May 1936, State 740.0011 Mutual Guarantee (Locarno)/688; Phipps telegrams 114 of 7 May and 175 of 14 May 1936, Foreign Office C 3458/C 3662/4/18.

during the crisis had served their purpose of confusing public opinion abroad and deterring any military countermeasures, all German interest in them vanished.

Collapse of the post-World War I security system in the face of German action was certain to lead to a complete reorientation of the policies of most of the European powers. Some of the resulting changes would take more time to make themselves felt, but immediate repercussions affected more than the European atmosphere. Each country was forced into a re-examination of the situation. Turkey could take advantage of the precedent created by Germany to end the regime of the Straits included in the Lausanne Convention.[97] Others were not so fortunate. Austria, which appeared to be next on Hitler's list, could only watch and hope for the best while making an effort to appease Germany.[98] Czechoslovakia, which had gone furthest in assuring France of support in the crisis, was both the most disappointed and the most threatened of France's allies. Horrified by the complaisance of the Western powers at Germany's coup and knowing that the fortifications Germany would soon build in that area would cut off the possibility of effective aid from other countries, the Czech government was compelled to reappraise the European situation and give serious consideration to a rapprochement with Germany.[99] The implications for Rumania were similar if less urgent. Its government had long tried to keep on friendly relations with Germany along with its alliance with France, but now there were increasing signs of a willingness to move closer to the Third Reich.[100] The economic factor that played some part in Rumania's relations with Germany was of greater importance in Yugoslavia. Its government was worried about the relief that Germany's coup provided for Italy, the prime concern of Yugoslavia's leaders; but certainly no steps would or could now be taken by Belgrade that would in any way antagonize its most important partner in trade.[101]

When the chiefs of staff of the Little Entente met in Bucharest on 15–20 June 1936, they maintained their military plans, especially vis-à-vis Hungary; but they agreed that the attitude of France would be the key to the

97. For the conference at Montreux, held in June and July 1936 in response to a Turkish note circulated about a month after the Rhineland occupation, see U. S. 1936, 3:503–28; *G. D.*, C, 5, No. 277; *D. D. F.*, 2d, 2, passim.; Eden, pp. 471ff. The German government, in turn, was happy to have the Turks divert attention away from the Rhineland (Memorandum of von Bülow, 17 April 1936, T–120, 2373/4602/E 190256; *D. D. F.*, 2d, 2, No. 77).

98. *D. D. F.*, 2d, 1, Nos. 308, 332; 2, No. 18. For the negotiations leading to the Austro-German Agreement of 11 July 1936 see chap. 11.

99. For the first repercussions on Prague and the earliest signs of a possible new policy toward Germany see *D. D. F.*, 2d, 1, Nos. 373, 423, 424, 476; *G. D.*, C, 5, Nos. 55, 148, 256, 258. The Germans were not yet interested in a special agreement with the Czech government (ibid., No. 268); for the negotiations for such a treaty, see chap. 12.

100. *G. D.*, C, 5, Nos. 39, 131, 142; *D. D. F.*, 2d, 1, No. 494. The removal of Titulescu as Rumanian foreign minister later in 1936 must be seen in this context.

101. *G. D.*, C, 5, Nos. 202, 216; *D. D. F.*, 2d, 1, No. 510.

future conduct of each country. If France withdrew its promise of protection from Central Europe, the allies there would be forced to choose between the two great powers—Germany and the Soviet Union—that flanked the region.[102] Their fears would have been confirmed had they known that the French service chiefs had concluded at the end of April that if Germany proceeded to fortify the Rhineland and did not attack through the Low Countries, France could help its East European allies only by an operation similar to that staged at Salonika in World War I.[103] France, as these ideas showed, was determined to fight only a defensive war, defensive in both strategy and tactics. This limited its choices; those of its allies were more restricted still.[104] In fact, it could be said that they were even more restricted than anyone as yet realized: only the sight of the French dozing in the Maginot Line while Poland was being overrun in 1939 would reveal to all that promises of assistance from Paris had been worthless since 1936, if not before.

Pope Pius XI told the French ambassador to the Vatican on 16 March 1936 that if France had immediately sent 200,000 soldiers into the Rhineland all would have been well. He recognized that it was France's love of peace that had restrained it but added that such an attitude would hardly prevent Germany from next taking steps against Austria and Czechoslovakia.[105] This aspect of the crisis—that the wish for peace might most dramatically undermine the prospects for it—was most evident within Germany itself. The absence of drastic foreign reaction to Germany's move following upon a period of anxious waiting in Germany only encouraged the government to take risks and the German people to allow Hitler to take those risks since he seemed to come out all right. The German public had been greatly alarmed, and now their relief and joy were all the greater.[106]

Hitler, who had acted against the counsel of his military advisers, was now all the more confident that he could assume even greater risks, disregard cautious advice, and triumph by bluff until he could conquer by force. His one worry at the beginning of his rule had been that France might be led by statesmen who would act before he could take the road of military conquest; he was now confident that there was no such danger. He knew as well as foreign observers that for some time at least Germany could only grow stronger and less vulnerable as it continued to rearm and fortify its western border. Its position, it seemed, could only get better, its risks decrease, as the war France and Britain had been unwilling to chance when they were in a

102. *D. D. F.*, 2d, 2, No. 365; Rudolf Kiszling, *Die militärischen Vereinbarungen der Kleinen Entente* (Munich: Oldenbourg, 1959).

103. *D. D. F.*, 2d, 2, No. 138; cf. ibid., No. 23; 3, Nos. 9, 38, 67, 394.

104. Ibid., 2, Nos. 369, 375.

105. Ibid., Nos. 441, 447. The Vatican had kept silent for fear of jeopardizing the rights of Catholics in Germany (ibid., No. 342; *D. D. B.*, 4, No. 45).

106. *D. D. F.*, 2d, 1, Nos. 458, 467, 513; Dodd, *Diary,* 18 March 1936, pp. 323–24.

strong position would become more and more dangerous for them.[107]

Neville Chamberlain recorded in his diary for 12 March 1936 that he had emphasized in his talk with Flandin "that public opinion here would not support us in sanctions of any kind. His [Flandin's] view is that, if a firm front is maintained by France and England, Germany will yield without war. We cannot accept this as a reliable estimate of a mad dictator's reactions."[108] Both Chamberlain and Flandin were partially right and partially wrong. Chamberlain was probably correct in his assessment of British opinion when that opinion had never been informed as to the significance of the demilitarized zone, and we now know that Hitler at least would have tried to fight—he was quite mad enough for that. Flandin was probably correct in the assumption that a firm front presented by Britain and France would suffice to win out, but he was wrong in thinking that it could be done without war and in his fear that France could not take care of the situation by itself. Where there was no will, all were determined to make certain that they would not find a way.

107. For excellent analyses of the situation see *D. D. F.*, 2d, 1, No. 439; U. S. 1936, 1:219–27, 258–60. For German awareness of the key issue of France's future inability to aid its allies see *G. D.*, C, 5, No. 189. On Hitler's attitude, see Braubach, pp. 38–40; Frank (talk with Hitler on 28 March 1936), p. 211.

108. Feiling, p. 279.

11 Germany Ascendant: The Power Shift of 1936

The German-Austrian Agreement; German Relations with Italy, England, and France; Outbreak of the Spanish Civil War

The evident success of Germany in not only remilitarizing the Rhineland but securing tacit international acquiescence to this step inaugurated a drastic and obvious shift in the whole international situation. The estrangement of Italy from the Western powers had made that country more friendly to Germany, a change that affected both barriers to German expansion of which Italy was the guarantor. Italy was, *de jure,* one of the guaranteeing powers of Locarno; it abandoned this role in favor of Germany's demolition of the Locarno system under the circumstances just described. *De facto,* Italy was the protector of Austrian independence, and Mussolini was turning away from that role at the same time. In January 1936, Mussolini had indicated to the German ambassador, Ulrich von Hassell, that the time for an Austro-German agreement had come and that he would simultaneously urge such a course on the Austrian government.[1] The Berlin government had noted this Italian shift with pleasure but preferred to postpone further exploration of the possibility of an agreement with Austria until after the remilitarization of the Rhineland when, presumably, better terms could be secured from Austria.[2]

The shift in Italy's position, growing out of its East African venture, was no secret or surprise in Vienna. Under these circumstances, the possibility of a return to more democratic governmental procedures to improve the prospects of support from the British and French public was apparently considered in Vienna.[3] Aware

1. *G. D.,* C, 4, Nos. 485, 486.

2. Ibid., Nos. 487, 497, 545.

3. See the Austrian memorandum of 18 December 1935, in Braunthal, *Tragedy of Austria,* p. 209.

of Italy's waning interest, the Austrian government, however, preferred to look around for diplomatic support elsewhere in preference, or in addition, to London and Paris.[4] A rapprochement with Czechoslovakia—and through it with the Little Entente—was one such possibility, and the Austrian chancellor, Kurt von Schuschnigg, made efforts in this direction on a visit to Prague in January 1936.[5] Although the Czech government was in principle quite sympathetic to Austria's needs, especially in terms of improved economic relations, attempts to secure an alternative form of international support for Austria with the Little Entente powers failed in spite of French support. The renewed agitation for a Habsburg restoration was certainly in part responsible for this failure. The Austrian government was unwilling to hazard the risks attendant upon such a restoration and was equally unwilling to renounce restoration permanently. It therefore had to forego the advantages a renunciation might have brought if it had extended beyond the purely temporary restraint pressed upon Vienna by friend and foe alike.[6] Austria, accordingly, had neither the possible benefits in terms of the recognized independent status and stability of a restoration nor of the renunciation of restoration; leaving the question open may have been wise in regard to domestic affairs but it was hardly productive in international affairs.

Nor could the Austrian government place reliance upon Hungary. The established Rome protocols association of Italy, Hungary, and Austria provided no basis for an Austrian policy independent of German influence. As Schuschnigg told the Hungarian prime minister, Gömbös, and the foreign minister, Kanya, in mid-March, he wanted better relations with Germany, but a pact restricted to the topic of external aggression would not suffice; he needed an agreement against intervention in internal affairs. To the insistence of the Hungarians that trade treaties with any Little Entente powers was one thing but that no Southeast European treaty system of an economic or political nature could be established without the immediate participation of Germany, Schuschnigg could only reply, with a smiling reference to the Rhineland occupation, that apparently Berlin reserved to itself the sole right to confront the world with a fait accompli.[7] When the Rome protocol powers met in Rome on 21–23 March 1936, both the Italian and Hungarian leaders urged the Austrian chancellor to come to a prompt agreement with Germany, making such domestic concessions as might be necessary. Mussolini suggested that internal opposition in Austria to such

4. *D. D. F.*, 2d, 1, No. 5.

5. Ibid., Nos. 74, 88; *G. D.*, C, 4, No. 488 and p. 1043; *Hungarian Documents*, 1, Nos. 3–7, 8 (German text in *Acta Historica*, 7, Nos. 3–4 [1960], pp. 368–69), 9–13, 16, 23–25, 28, 33, 38, 60; U. S. 1936, 1:181–83; Schuschnigg, *Austrian Requiem*, chap. IX.

6. *D. D. F.*, 2d, 1, Nos. 34, 60, 164; *Hungarian Documents*, 1, Nos. 2, 14, 15, 18, 20, 22, 29, 37, 43; *G. D.*, C, 4, Nos. 526, 542, 544, and pp. 1102, 1106.

7. *Hungarian Documents*, 1, No. 62 (German text in *Acta Historica*, 7:369–72); cf. ibid., Nos. 64, 68; *G. D.*, C, 5, No. 129; U. S. 1936, 1:495–96.

a course, hitherto provided by Starhemberg and the *Heimwehr,* need no longer be feared, a hint that Schuschnigg—who knew that the *Heimwehr* depended on Italian subsidies—doubtless understood.[8]

Under these circumstances Schuschnigg moved toward a resumption of the tentative negotiations he had held with von Papen in the preceding year. During the early months of 1936, recriminations in German-Austrian diplomatic contacts slowly gave way to consideration of a possible agreement.[9] Even the galling affront to Austria implicit in the inclusion of such Austrian National Socialists as Theo Habicht in the German National Socialist party list of candidates for the Reichstag in the "elections" of 29 March caused no change in either Austrian or Italian calculations. Though a clear indication of Germany's ultimate aims, the gesture provoked only oral protests.[10] Starhemberg, aware of Mussolini's shift of policy, made a last-minute attempt to arrange the German-Austrian agreement himself, using the former Austrian minister of justice, Franz Hueber, who was a *Heimwehr* member and a brother-in-law of Göring, as a go-between; but Schuschnigg outmaneuvered his rival and succeeded in removing him from political influence in the middle of May.[11]

A direct, personal contact between the leaders of Germany and Italy smoothed the way for the German-Austrian negotiations. In late March, Hans Frank, the attorney who had defended Hitler in court cases during the 1920s and after 1933 was charged by Hitler with reorienting German law according to National Socialist precepts, saw Hitler before going to Rome to lecture. Hitler asked him to deliver a friendly message of solidarity to Mussolini, assuring him of Germany's sympathy in his Ethiopian venture and in the joint struggle against both bolshevism and the democracies. Frank talked with Mussolini on 4 April, delivered the message, and in turn received assurances of Italian support in the current negotiations growing out of Germany's reoccupation of the Rhineland. Mussolini's resentment toward England and France over sanctions was still a major factor motivating Italian policy.[12] The spring of 1936 was to see a number of

8. Gehl, pp. 125–26; *G. D.,* C, 4, Nos. 569, 597; 5, Nos. 165, 171, 204, 226, 253; *D. D. F.,* 2d, 1, No. 499; 2, No. 110; *Hungarian Documents,* 1, Nos. 41, 48, 51, 53–55, 70, 71 (German text in *Acta Historica,* 7:372–73), 72, 74, 76.

9. Memorandum of von Bülow, 27 January 1936, T–120, 2373/4602/E 190398–400; *G. D.,* C, 4, No. 586; 5, Nos. 80, 226; *Hungarian Documents,* 1, Nos. 19, 21, 27, 45, 52, 56, 58.

10. *D. D. F.*, 2d, 1, No. 502; von Papen telegram 35, 23 March 1936, T–120, 2499/4939/E, 272276; Memorandum of von Bülow, 26 March, 2373/4602/E 190331; von Bülow to Hess, 2 April, 778/1549/376262–263.

11. Gehl, pp. 126–29, summarizes the evidence and the events. See also *G. D.,* C, 4, No. 556; 5, Nos. 90, 246, 311; *Hungarian Documents,* 1, Nos. 69, 89, 99; Renthe-Fink to Mackensen, II Oe 1418 of 14 May 1936, T–120, 2832/6077/E 450726.

12. On Frank's Rome trip see *G. D.,* C, 5, No. 255; Hans Frank, *Im Angesicht des Galgens,* pp. 220–33; Aloisi, 4 April 1936, p. 366. Frank's account is marred by obvious inaccuracies—e.g., the reference to the civil war in Spain that had not yet started (p. 229)—but the sarcastic picture of Frank in Filippo Anfuso, *Rom-Berlin im diplomatischen Spiegel* (Trans. by Egon Hyman; Essen: Pohl, 1951), p. 23, is not

exchange visits between Berlin and Rome, culminating in that of Mussolini's daughter, Edda Ciano, who went to Berlin in June.[13] Such special personal diplomacy was equally important for the short-term accommodation between Germany and Austria and for the long-term rapprochement between Germany and Italy. That Hitler, not Mussolini, would set the tone for their common fate could be seen in a secondary aspect of Frank's trip: Mussolini's advice against conflict with the Christian churches was the only specific recommendation Frank took back to Hitler. Hitler was happy to see relations with Italy improve, but as for religious policy he would go his own way.

In the spring and early summer of 1936, the German government prepared the way for an agreement with Austria not only by improving the atmosphere in German-Italian relations but also by increasing domestic pressure on the Austrian government. On the recommendation of von Papen, the Germans subsidized the militant Right wing of the Austrian trade union movement, the *Freiheitsbund*. Suitably violent in its anti-Semitism and pronounced in its pro-National Socialist sympathies, this organization would pressure the government for concessions from the streets.[14] Simultaneously, on the diplomatic level von Papen would urge the Austrian chancellor to accept into the government men who were referred to as representatives of the "national opposition." These men were ostensibly respectable elements in Austrian public life who could be depended upon to move Austria into close subservience to and eventual annexation by Germany. Those Austrians most prominent in this category—Edmund Glaise-Horstenau, the officer and military historian, General Carl von Bardolff, who headed the German club in Vienna, and Heinrich Ritter von Srbik, the noted historian—were all eventually rewarded with places on Hitler's list of National Socialist Reichstag deputies. Their opportunity to earn this honor was provided by the 1936 negotiations.[15] To avoid incidents that might interfere with the diplomatic talks and negotiations among the Austrians, those

---

warranted. Frank's account of Hitler's message to Mussolini (Frank, p. 221) corresponds closely with contemporary sources on Hitler's views. For Frank's trips to Italy in the 1920s and his temporary withdrawal from the NSDAP over the South Tirol question see Hoepke, pp. 310, 327.

13. For the careful way in which the French government observed such signs of a German-Italian rapprochement see *D. D. F.*, 2d, 2, Nos. 127, 239, 218, 278, 325, 334, n. 1; Drummond (Rome) dispatch 658 of 5 June 1936, Foreign Office R 3302/341/22.

14. *G. D.*, C, 5, Nos. 172, 319 (also in *TMWC*, 31:200–02). It should be noted that as shrewd an observer of the Austrian scene as G. E. R. Gedye did not realize that von Papen was paying for the *Freiheitsbund* (*Betrayal in Central Europe* [New York: Harper, 1939], pp. 176–77).

15. Bardolff had been refused an interview with Hitler in 1933 (*G. D.*, C, 1, No. 497, n. 2) but was considered the future National Socialist leader of Austria (*B. D.*, 2d, 6, No. 300). Von Srbik gave lectures in support of national socialism in Berlin in early 1936 (*D. D. F.*, 2d, 1, No. 243). Biographies of Glaise-Horstenau, von Bardolff, and von Srbik may be found in the Reichstag handbook.

Austrians identified as National Socialists were given strict orders from Berlin to keep quiet and refrain from terrorist acts.[16]

In May and June of 1936 the talks between Schuschnigg and von Papen moved rapidly toward a conclusion. Schuschnigg, for reasons still not quite clear, appears to have believed that a German promise to respect Austria's independence and refrain from interfering in internal affairs would be kept and thus agreed to make concessions. In part he appears to have felt that his own position might be strengthened by a rapprochement with Berlin that would calm the situation inside Austria and that in any case he could not afford to reject an opportunity to secure Hitler's public recognition of the independence of Austria. If Germany adhered to its promise to respect that independence and to refrain from internal intervention, it would be all to the good. If, however, Germany violated its freely given pledge, it would show up Hitler's duplicity once and for all. However dubious the logic of this approach—very similar to the Vatican's in the 1933 concordat negotiations—it sufficed for the Austrian chancellor.[17]

Hitler was interested in an amnesty for his followers in Austria and the entrance of representatives of the "national opposition" into the Austrian government. Obviously an agreement could only strengthen Germany's position in Vienna, in part at the expense of Italy. The Italian government not only acquiesced but even urged agreement on Schuschnigg. Mussolini told him to settle with Germany when the two met early in June. Furthermore, on 10 June the Italian dictator dismissed Fulvio Suvich as undersecretary in the foreign ministry and gave up the office of foreign minister to his son-in-law, Galeazzo Ciano. Suvich had been a strong defender of Austrian independence, while Ciano, whatever his later views, started out determined to do everything differently.[18] In the field of German-Austrian relations this policy would quickly bear fruit; under Italian urging and German pressure, Schuschnigg moved toward a settlement with Berlin.[19]

Only two possible obstacles still stood in the way of agreement. German demands might be so high as to scare off the Austrian government, which was then likely to turn to a Habsburg restoration as the only alternative support of Austrian integrity.[20] German willingness to make some minor

16. *G. D.*, C, 5, No. 297; Memorandum of Renthe-Fink, 4 May 1936, T–120, 2838/6112/E 453702; *Anordnungen des Stellvertreters des Führers*, 3 June 1936, p. 297.

For the negotiations up to the Hitler-von Papen meeting of 10 May see *G. D.*, C, 5, Nos. 288, 294, 304; *Hungarian Documents,* 1, Nos. 91, 94, 96.

17. *D. D. F.*, 2d, 2, Nos. 108, 225, 241, 380.

18. *G. D.*, C, 5, No. 381; cf. Neurath Memorandum RM 356, 25 April 1936, T–120, 2383/4619/E 198289.

19. A summary of the negotiations is in Gehl, pp. 129–31. Published documents in *G. D.*, C, 5, Nos. 321, 325, 343, 344, 351, 357, 360, 369, 371; *D. D. F.*, 2d, 2, Nos. 327, 371; *Hungarian Documents,* 1, Nos. 101, 103–105. See also von Papen's reports to Hitler A 2734 of 20 May, T–120, 778/1549/376292–296, and A 3154 of 11 June, 2499/4939/E 272370–372.

20. *G. D.*, C, 5, No. 393; *D. D. F.*, 2d, 2, No. 347; *Hungarian Documents,* 1, Nos. 106, 110–12, 116; von Papen to Hitler, A 3281 of 17 June 1936, T–120, 2499/4939/E 272373–380; Messersmith telegram 30, 18 June, State 863.01/354.

concessions in the talks sufficed to avert that possibility, although Schuschnigg rejected a German demand for a Berlin veto on any restoration. The other threat to German success lay in a possible last-minute shift in Italian policy due to a rapprochement with Britain and France.

The Italian conquest of Ethiopia in the spring of 1936 rendered the policy of sanctions meaningless. The same fear of the impact on the European balance of a permanent realignment of Italy had previously tempered their willingness to make sanctions really effective and now hastened the desire of the Western powers to abandon sanctions lest Italy adopt a different policy in Europe when able to shift the emphasis of its influence from the African continent. In June and early July of 1936, France and Britain made an attempt to restore their earlier relationship with Italy, but this attempt failed completely, only underlining the extent to which Mussolini had already shifted toward Germany.

Future historians with full access to the Italian archives may come to the conclusion that whatever chance there might have been for a return to Stresa had been lost in April and May of 1936 when French efforts to hasten a rapprochement with Rome were wrecked by the interaction of the continued reluctance of the British public to abandon its attachment to the League's policy in Africa with the exaltation of the Italians over their final triumph in Ethiopia, a triumph involving a large-scale use of poison gas. Mussolini would not by some moderate gesture build a bridge over the gulf that the British did not yet care to cross. Once more the Western powers chose the worst of alternatives: they would neither prevent an Italian victory that effectively destroyed the League[21] nor quickly make the best of a bad situation by abandoning a lost policy at a time when such a shift might still have influenced the Italian government.[22] Perhaps Mussolini was merely holding out a return to Stresa as bait designed to gain him an early end to sanctions and possibly even recognition of his African empire while actually intending to move toward Germany all along. The Western powers would never find out as they allowed the critical weeks to go by. Neville Chamberlain's speech of 10 June, referring to hopes placed in the continuation of sanctions as the "very midsummer of madness," was criticized by some as made too soon when in fact it came too late to have any significant effect on the international situation.[23]

21. See Stanley Baldwin's statement on 13 April that he would not allow the African situation to lead to war; Germany was the greater danger but had to be dealt with softly until Britain rearmed (*D. D. F.*, 2d, 2, No. 63).

22. Laurens, pp. 354–56, places a major part of the responsibility for the failure to conciliate Italy on Léon Blum, but partly contradicts himself by stressing Mussolini's own intransigeance.

23. Chamberlain had himself opposed the lifting of sanctions earlier; see his diary entry for 2 May 1936, in Feiling, p. 281; cf. Eden, pp. 432–34. The negotiations of April-May 1936 can best be traced in the French diplomatic documents, 2d series, 2, esp. Nos. 46, 73, 90, 111, 112, 133, 144, 149, 150, 173, 233, 234, 245, 248, 262, 265, 271, 272, 286, 293, 294. See also Vansittart's memorandum of 21 May in Colvin, pp. 105–06.

At almost the same time as Suvich's dismissal, the Popular Front under Léon Blum came to power in France. Given Mussolini's animosity toward Eden, this combination of government changes made any rapprochement between France, England, and Italy unlikely. However strongly Léon Blum might wish to work for peace, there would be no early echo of his hopes from Rome.[24] By the time Mussolini might have reevaluated his policy, the outbreak of the Spanish civil war and Italian intervention in that conflict had already confirmed his new course. The choices made in Rome in the winter of 1935–36 proved to be even more far-reaching than anyone in Italy may have realized at the time.[25]

Under these circumstances, the German-Austrian negotiations proceeded rapidly to a successful conclusion. The agreements signed on 11 July, after von Papen and Glaise-Horstenau had secured Hitler's approval, provided for German recognition of Austrian independence and for Austria to follow a course closer to Germany in international affairs. A variety of other provisions covered both some accommodation on outstanding issues and mechanisms for the preparation of further economic and cultural agreements, but the real significance of the event is not evident from the texts to which Schuschnigg affixed his name.[26] The Austro-German agreement marked a major triumph for Hitler in supplanting Italian influence in Vienna and in heralding a new role for Germany in Southeast Europe. In a more technical diplomatic context, here was another victory for bilateral over multilateral negotiations.[27] The signing of the agreement in the same week that marked the official burial of sanctions against Italy by the League symbolized the demise of the concept of collective security.

As for German adherence to the promise not to interfere in Austrian internal affairs, that would continue only as long as Germany found it in its own interests to do so, regardless of any agreement. The secretary general in the Austrian foreign ministry expressed Austrian worries over this question the day before the agreement was signed.[28] An internal political measure of the Austrian government would eventually be used by Hitler as the occasion for annexing that country; if he paid some attention for a short time

24. *D. D. F.*, 2d, 2, No. 275.

25. The last efforts to divert Italy from its pro-German course and thus to reorient its Austrian policy are summarized in Gehl, pp. 131–32. See also *G. D.*, C, 5, Nos. 410, 415; *D. D. F.*, 2d, 2, Nos. 311, 312, 332, 417.

26. Texts in *G. D.*, D, 1, Nos. 152, 153. On the concluding stages of the negotiations see *G. D., C*, 5, Nos. 389, 395, 401, 407, 408, 415, 423, 424, 447; *D. D. F.*, 2d, 2, Nos. 388, 422; *Hungarian Documents,* 1, Nos. 121–23, 125–27; von Papen to von Neurath telegram 79, 23 June 1936, T–120, 2499/4939/E 272382; Messersmith telegram 36, 9 July, State 863.01/369; Messersmith dispatches 823, 10 July and 833, 17 July, State 863.00/1295 and 1296; Messersmith to Hull, 20 July 1936, Library of Congress, Cordell Hull Papers, Folder 91. See also the reference to the last stages of the negotiations in Seyss-Inquart to Glaise-Horstenau, 9 October 1936, PS–3623 (National Archives).

27. *D. D. F.*, 2d, 2, Nos. 432, 455.

28. U. S. 1936, 1:317. Cf. *D. D. F.*, 2d, 2, Nos. 439, 440, 474; *Hungarian Documents,* 1, Nos. 143, 144.

to his promise of noninterference in Austrian internal affairs, it was because he had already decided to build up fortifications in the Rhineland and continue rearmament before turning to new adventures to the south and east.[29] On 16 July Hitler explained this rationale to Austrian National Socialist leaders: they would have to keep quiet until Germany was ready to move. Incidents that endangered Germany's relations with Britain and France and threatened the developing friendship with Italy would only interfere with the ultimate aims of German policy. However disappointed for the moment, the Austrian National Socialists would have to work quietly and wait.[30] In the meantime, Hitler could wave off British concerns about his aggressive intentions and move forward with the improvement of relations with Italy. In the one area where the two prospective partners might clash, Mussolini had yielded to Germany; perhaps Hitler thought it only fair that Italy should thus repay his renunciation of South Tirol. As Jürgen Gehl put it: "Hitler had postponed the *Anschluss,* which he could not achieve anyhow for the time being, and gained Mussolini's friendship in return; Mussolini had renounced a policy which he had found impossible to continue and maintained Austria's independence at the same time."[31] Von Papen had attained the first major goal of his mission and offered to give up his post; but when Hitler talked to him at Bayreuth on 20 July, he decided to keep von Papen in Vienna and promote him to ambassador. It was in those same days at Bayreuth that Hitler made two other fateful decisions: to intervene in the Spanish civil war and to appoint Joachim von Ribbentrop as ambassador to Great Britain.[32] These decisions involved Germany's policies in the summer of 1936 toward Britain, Spain, and, by implication, toward Italy. The Austrian question occupied Hitler only briefly as his attention was demanded by other concerns.

In Germany's policy toward Great Britain, the naval aspect played a role in 1936 as it had in 1935, though in nowhere near as spectacular a manner. The British government wished to associate the Germans with the London Naval Conference in the early months of 1936 and eventually overcame French reluctance in this regard; but the conference—primarily because of Japan's departure from the naval limitations program—led to no significant results, and only a limited agreement between Great Britain, the

29. This is reflected in Bullitt's report on his talk with von Neurath on 18 May 1936 in U. S. 1936, 1:300–03. The Austrian minister to Germany had come to the same conclusion (*D. D. F.,* 2d, 2, Nos. 69, 121).

30. See the account of Friedrich Rainer, given in 1942, in 4005–PS, *TMWC,* 34:16–17. Paul Bargeton, political director at the Quai d'Orsay, predicted that this was the road to the *Anschluss* in April 1936 (*D. D. F.,* 2d, 2, No. 113); the chief of the Austrian general staff, General Jansa, also expected the Germans to wait until 1938 (ibid., No. 116). For an assessment by the Hungarian chargé in Vienna see *Hungarian Documents,* 1, No. 129.

31. Gehl, pp. 133–34. See also U. S. 1936, 1:322–25; *G. D.,* C, 5, No. 457.

32. *G. D.,* C, 5, Nos. 455, 475; D, 1, Nos. 158, 159.

United States, and France was signed on 25 March.[33] On the German side, the talks of February and March had shown that, in regard to procedure, Hitler wanted von Ribbentrop to handle formal political negotiations; Germany would push for maximum construction for itself, using the alleged danger from the Soviet Union as the handiest excuse of the moment. A brief ruckus with the British over cruiser types was smoothed over by nominal concessions from the German side, but the course of the German-British negotiations on naval questions from May to October 1936 reveals the public posture of Germany, as set by Hitler in accordance with Admiral Raeder's advice, as being entirely uncompromising on any matters that touched the building program the German navy was developing.[34] That program was designed to build up a force to fight France; the German navy still hoped that Britain would be neutral in such a conflict. The general thrust of the naval planning for war with France, however, was offensive, not defensive, in character and looked toward attacks on French shipping connections across the Atlantic as well as to North Africa.[35] The types of ships—heavy cruisers and aircraft carriers—that Germany was starting to build in pursuance of that strategy were, of course, the very ones that could be used for a similar conflict with England, a conflict for which the longer-range preparations of the German navy inaugurated in 1935 were also preparing the Third Reich.

Important influences were being brought to bear on the English government to keep open a line to Germany and perhaps work out a better relationship. A combination of German wooing and English interest was at work. With Stanley Baldwin as prime minister, ineffectual pessimism in foreign affairs had succeeded the ineffectual optimism of Ramsay Macdonald at 10 Downing Street. As Baldwin told his friend Thomas Jones: "With two lunatics like Mussolini and Hitler you can never be sure of anything. But I am determined to keep the country out of war. . . . You will not get our people for a long time yet to be willing to pledge themselves to go to war for objects in the east of Europe."[36] It was in this atmosphere that in May and June 1936 Baldwin considered a personal meeting with Hitler, and the British government suggested that the Germans invite a British minister,

33. The relationship of Germany to the conference can be traced in U. S. 1936, 1:40–42, 58–60, 63–64, 68, 71, 73, 78–81, 88, 94; *G. D.*, C, 4, Nos. 555, 584, 585, 589, 596, 599, 601, 605; 5, Nos. 6, 10, 46, 144; *D. D. F.*, 2d, 1, Nos. 90, 141, 153, 198, 500.

34. The negotiations may be followed in *G. D.*, C, 5, Nos. 309, 323, 331, 336, 337, 355, 361, 366, 402, 421, 431, 445, 448, 456, 459, 470, 486, 496, 529, 560, 563, 564, 571; *D. D. F.*, 2d, 2, No. 301; Kordt, *Nicht aus den Akten*, pp. 145–46. During these negotiations, the Germans also acknowledged that they were again fortifying the island of Heligoland in violation of Article 115 of the Treaty of Versailles (*G. D.*, C, 5, No. 418; "Anweisung Nr. 598," 19 June 1936, Bundesarchiv, Brammer, Z.Sg. 101/6, f. 391).

35. For details see Gemzell, pp. 42–50, 82.

36. T. Jones, 30 April 1936, p. 191. For recognition of British unwillingness to assume new continental commitments see *Hungarian Documents*, 1, Nos. 32, 35, 95.

possibly Lord Halifax, to Berlin. Nothing came of either scheme.[37] On the British side, there was suspicion and eventually disillusionment as Berlin refused even to answer the British questionnaire concerning a possible new set of international agreements to replace the destroyed Locarno system.[38]

From the German side, there was a willingness to exchange pleasant words, but adamant refusal to come to any concrete—and thus limiting—definition of German demands and possible concessions. Von Ribbentrop, therefore, could not repeat his triumph of the preceding summer as London increasingly recognized that the offers made by Hitler at the time of the remilitarization of the Rhineland in fact had never been intended seriously.[39] The sentiments voiced to von Ribbentrop by important people in England, however, can only have convinced him that Germany need not be concerned about Britain's European policy. Lord Lothian was preaching British agreement to the German annexation of Austria, Danzig, and Memel, while Sir Thomas Inskip, whom no one ever accused of either great energy or great competence, had been appointed to coordinate Britain's defense establishment.[40] The privately expressed suspicions of Neville Chamberlain that Germany would not act in good faith[41] and the public speech of Duff Cooper, Secretary of State for War, emphasizing the continued association of France and England were harbingers of a distant future rather than significant events of the time.[42] The current situation was affected more by the change of government in France.

The electoral victory of the Popular Front in France, the wave of strikes immediately following, and the subsequent formation of the government of Léon Blum had the paradoxical effect of bringing closer together the leaders

37. On the proposed Hitler-Baldwin meeting and the proposed trip of Lord Halifax see T. Jones, pp. 194–224 and 251–59, passim; U. S. 1936, 1:304, 332; *G. D.*, C, 5, Nos. 322, 326, 367, 379, 384; *D. D. F.*, 2d, 2, No. 283. The entries in Eden's diary for 20 May and 3 June, quoted in Eden, p. 421, belong in this context. See also Annelies von Ribbentrop (ed.), Joachim von Ribbentrop, *Zwischen London und Moskau* (Leoni: Druffel, 1954), pp. 67–68. The imagination boggles at the effort to visualize Baldwin and Hitler conversing.

38. On the protracted British efforts to secure an answer to their questions about German policy see *D. D. F.*, 2d, 2, Nos. 187, 194, 298, 309; *D. D. B.*, 4, No. 83; *G. D.*, C, 5, Nos. 322, 348, 359, 375, 379, 412, 416; *History of the Times*, p. 902; Eden, p. 420; Mayer (Berlin) telegram 199, 26 June 1936, State 740.0011 Mutual Guarantee (Locarno)/713; and Foreign Office C 3829/4/18.

It is not surprising that the British were upset by Germany's using the publication of the questionnaire as an excuse for not answering since they believed a leak in Berlin had forced publication on them (Atherton [London] dispatch 2207, 22 May 1936, State 740.0011 Mutual Guarantee (Locarno)/700).

39. *G. D.*, C, 5, No. 405; Dertinger's "Informationsbericht Nr. 21," 19 June 1936, Bundesarchiv Brammer, Z.Sg. 101/29, f. 241–51; British Foreign Office minutes on Phipps telegram 183 of 26 May 1936, Foreign Office C 3879/4/18.

40. Butler, *Lord Lothian*, pp. 213–15, 354–62; T. Jones, pp. 214–16; *D. D. F.*, 2d, 2. No. 243; Foreign Office C 4184/4/18.

41. Butler, p. 215.

42. Duff Cooper, *Old Men Forget*, pp. 202–04; *D. D. F.*, 2d, 2, No. 387.

while separating even further the followers of the British and French governments. Anthony Eden, who directed British foreign policy during the semiretirement of Baldwin in the late summer of 1936, found Blum and his foreign minister, Yvon Delbos, vastly more congenial than their predecessors, Albert Sarraut and Pierre-Etienne Flandin.[43] The shift to the left represented by developments in France, however, could be and was exploited by the German government as an ideological supplement to the Franco-Soviet Pact and as grist for anti-Communist propaganda that was being intensified in 1936 and was correctly assumed to have some influence on the conservative followers of the British government.[44] The German government preferred to exploit the possibility of dividing the two Western powers rather than to respond positively to the friendly approaches of the new French government.

Though aware of the fact that, in spite of its anti-National Socialist inclinations and the presence of Léon Blum, a Jew, as prime minister, the new government of France wanted good relations with Germany in continuation of the traditional anti-Versailles proclivities of the French Left, Berlin carefully turned a deaf ear to all approaches from Paris.[45] Under these circumstances, the British, French, and Belgians discussed with each other what to do about a replacement for the Locarno Treaty and after much irresolute deliberation decided to call for a new Five-Power conference in the fall of 1936. By that time Germany and Italy in concert were refusing to participate in any new security scheme, though couching their declinations in polite, ever-ingenious excuses for postponement of discussions.[46]

Of fateful long-range importance for Germany's relations with the Western powers was the appointment of von Ribbentrop as ambassador to London in the summer of 1936. The appointment was initially designed in part to appease von Ribbentrop by giving him a significant appointment when

43. The views of Eden emerge clearly from his memoirs. He comes down very hard on Flandin (see esp. pp. 423–25) and comments on Blum: "I rejoiced at the improvement he would be on his predecessors" (p. 429). A careful reading of the French diplomatic documents suggests that the feelings were reciprocal.

44. *D. D. F.*, 2d, 2, Nos. 230, 231, 297, 317, 323; "Bestellungen aus der Pressekonferenz vom 2. September 1936," Bundesarchiv Brammer, Z.Sg. 101/8, f. 131.

45. *G. D.*, C, 5, Nos. 314, 345, 350, 358, 387, 388, 411, 414, 422, 499, 521; *D. D. F.*, 2d, 2, Nos. 352, 379; U. S. 1936, 1:315–16; Memorandum of von Bülow, 25 May 1936, T–120, 2373/4602/E 190290–291.

46. No useful purpose would be served by reviewing these negotiations. They may be traced in: *D. D. F.*, 2d, 2, Nos. 324, 377, 386, 405, 407, 411, 414, 431, 450, 464, 468, 470, 473, 478; 3, passim.; *G. D.*, C, 5, Nos. 391, 417, 425, 428, 435, 446, 463, 466, 471, 474, 475, 477, 478, 484, 487–89, 515, 530–33, 541, 546–48, 552, 558, 561, 585, 596, 601, 607, 617, 631, 632; D, 3, Nos. 66, 85; Eden, p. 439; U. S. 1936, 1:327–28, 347, 353–55, 384–87; *D. D. B.*, 4, Nos. 86, 87, 89–91, 93–98, 100–102, 105–11, 124, 125, 127, 141, 143, 152, 155, 162–64, 169, 171–73, 180, 185; *Ciano's Diplomatic Papers* (ed. Malcolm Muggeridge, trans. Stuart Hood; London: Odhams, 1948), pp. 19, 20–21, 22; "Vertrauliche Bestellung für die Redaktion," 9 October 1936, Bundesarchiv Brammer, Z.Sg. 101/8, f. 219; Dodd telegram 305, 17 October 1936, State 740.0011 Mutual Guarantee (Locarno)/825; Foreign Office C 4721/C 5228/C 7712/4/18.

von Neurath displayed unaccustomed energy in opposing von Ribbentrop's appointment to the post of Secretary of State vacated by the sudden death of Bernhard von Bülow.[47] Initially expected to improve relations between Germany and England, the new ambassadorial appointment was to have the opposite effect. Von Ribbentrop would leave England convinced of British opposition to Germany and equally convinced of its inability to do so with any real danger to Germany.[48] He approached his task with what can only be called idiotic ideas about bribing his way to success in London.[49] He returned an advocate of war against Great Britain.[50] The impression he himself made in England was most unfavorable. His long delay in going to London to assume his post, his lengthy absences from his assignment there, and his general demeanor made few friends.[51] The implications of all this would become evident in later years when von Ribbentrop became German foreign minister.

Hitler's own attitude toward negotiations for any new treaties with the Western powers was made crystal clear by an incident relating to what was essentially a minor point but a most revealing one all the same. Part XII of the Treaty of Versailles had contained a number of provisions for international regulation of certain rivers and canals in Germany.[52] There had been some negotiations about revising these provisions in accordance with German wishes, but at the time of the crisis over the Rhineland the German government had denied any intention of denouncing this part of the treaty or even making amicable revision a prerequisite for Germany's return to the League.[53] A variety of negotiations took place during the summer of 1936, and tentative agreements satisfactory to Germany were initialed on 4 May concerning the Rhine and on 5 October concerning the river Elbe. The issue was obviously on the road to an amicable solution.[54] When Hitler

47. *TMWC,* 40:472–73; Jacobsen, pp. 301–02. See also *G. D.*, C, 5, No. 601, on von Ribbentrop's view of his assignment, and Szembek's diary, 14 August 1936, pp. 201–02, for von Ribbentrop's reaction to his appointment.

48. Johnson (U. S. chargé a.i. London) dispatch 3879, 8 February 1938, State 862.00/3745.

49. He had originally wanted a million Reichsmark in pounds in 1935 ("Notiz für den Führer," 29 October 1935, 1169–PS, National Archives), and then tried again in 1936 (Note by Ritter, 5 November 1936, DZA Potsdam, 60964, f. 29). He discussed the subject with the press attaché of the German embassy in London (Fitz-Randolph, *Frühstücksattaché aus London,* pp. 80–81).

50. See *G. D.*, D, 1, No. 93, and the comments of Hewel about von Ribbentrop's views in Picker, *Hitlers Tischgespräche*, pp. 238–39.

51. U. S. Undersecretary of State Sumner Welles reporting on his talk with King George VI and Queen Elizabeth on 11 March 1940, wrote: "Both the King and Queen spoke with vehement detestation of Ribbentrop. . . ." The report is at Hyde Park; other parts are printed in U. S. 1940, 1:21–117.

52. The provisions themselves and a summary of their history in the interwar years may be found in U. S. 1919, 13:647–91.

53. *D. D. F.*, 2d, 1, Nos. 237, 382, 398; *G. D.*, C, 5, Nos. 3, 69.

54. *G. D.*, C, 5, Nos. 497, 614, p. 1113 and n. 11; Dertinger, "Informationsbericht Nr. 22," 23 June 1936, Bundesarchiv, Brammer, Z.Sg. 101/29, f. 253–59; "Bestellungen aus der Pressekonferenz vom 13. August 1936," ibid., Z.Sg. 101/8, f. 97.

was informed that Germany's demands had been met and a new treaty—this one for the Elbe—was to be signed on 24 November, he decided that Germany would under no circumstances agree to revision of the peace treaties by mutual consent. Instead, Germany would unilaterally denounce the relevant sections of the peace treaty, and do so in time to prevent an agreed solution.[55] The denunciation was made on 14 November. It could hardly be considered a good omen for peaceful revision or a model procedure encouraging Germany's neighbors to strive for new agreements. But few took notice.[56]

Aside from the international complications growing out of the Spanish civil war, soon to be discussed, German relations with the Western powers in the summer and fall of 1936 saw some spectacular but actually not very significant visits and an unspectacular trend that produced a major diplomatic shift in Germany's favor. The visits that attracted much attention were those of Hjalmar Schacht to Paris in August and that of David Lloyd George to Hitler in September, but the move that counted was made by Belgium in October.

Schacht's visit to Paris must be seen as the temporary interaction of two otherwise unrelated developments: Germany's interest in colonies and Schacht's declining influence in German affairs. The colonial question had played no special role in German foreign policy in the preceding years; to clarify its more prominent appearance at this time, a brief review of the subject and its earlier treatment in National Socialist Germany is necessary.

In *Mein Kampf,* as in his second book, Hitler had condemned the colonial policy of the Second Reich, primarily because it was not a colonial policy at all in the sense that he wished the term used. Colonialism to him meant the acquisition of territories suitable for German settlement after the expulsion, extermination, or enslavement of the local population. Lands suitable for such treatment were in his opinion available only in Eastern Europe—those suitable for European settlement outside the European continent having been preempted by others before Germany appeared on the colonial

55. The documents recording Hitler's decision will be published as *G. D.,* C, 6, Nos. 18, 25. For information that Hitler's personal reversal of the German foreign ministry's policy was known outside Germany at the time see report No. 32 of 26 November 1936, by Krno, the Czech minister at The Hague, Czech document in T–120, 1040/1809/413247–248.

56. For the German step and its repercussions see U. S. 1936, 1:372–74; *D. D. F.,* 2d, 3, No. 491; *D. D. B.,* 4, No. 180; "Bestellung vertraulich und sehr wichtig!" 14 November 1936, Bundesarchiv, Brammer, Z.Sg. 101/8, f. 315; Krno (Czech minister at The Hague) report 30, 17 November 1936, Czech document in T–120, 1040/1809/413245–246; Künzl-Jizerský (Czech minister Bern) report 27, 26 November 1936, Czech document in T–120, 1040/1809/413358–362; and the documents collected in Germany, Auswärtiges Amt, *Aussenpolitische Dokumente 1936,* Heft 2: *Aussenpolitische Vorgänge im zweiten Halbjahr 1936* (Nur für Dienstgebrauch; Berlin: Reichsdruckerei, 1937) (copy in Institut für Zeitgeschichte, Munich). The whole incident is reviewed briefly in Kordt, *Wahn und Wirklichkeit,* p. 79, n. 2. Ironically, the Poles immediately used the German action to reverse a Hague Court decision against them and favoring Germany in regard to the Oder River and its tributaries (cf. U. S. 1919, 13:662, and Szembek, 14 November 1936, p. 217).

scene. From this perspective, the acquisition of Germany's colonial empire in the last two decades of the nineteenth century had been merely a facet of Germany's trade policy with harmful effects on Germany's diplomatic position in the world and no compensating benefits in terms of land suitable for settlement. During the 1920s, the National Socialist party paid relatively little attention to the continuing agitation by colonial enthusiasts in Germany; but with the seizure of power, the party inherited the German colonial movement and "coordinated" it, a process that was simplified by the strongly rightist character of the members and leaders of colonial societies.[57]

In view of the low priority then assigned to the colonial issue by Hitler, those who were interested in the subject were allowed some time to work out a reconciliation between the policy of *Lebensraum* in Europe and colonial aspirations elsewhere. By 1936–37 this synthesis was developing; it is presented most succinctly by Hermann Behrens in an article appropriately entitled "Eastern and Colonial Policy—Their Complementary Necessity" in the October 1937 issue of *Deutscher-Kolonial-Dienst.*[58] Behrens, the associate editor of this organ of the colonial policy office of the National Socialist party, asserted that Germany needed both land for settlement and raw materials in which it was deficient. While Eastern Europe was suitable for settlement, it lacked many of the raw materials Germany required; conversely, colonial territories in Africa would provide the raw materials but were unsuitable for settlement. Germany obviously had to have both.

While organizational and ideological questions of colonial policy were being considered inside Germany with the bureaucratic infighting characteristic of the Third Reich, little had been done in the diplomatic field.[59] There was a brief flurry in the press about the former German possessions under

57. The survey by Mary E. Townsend, "Hitler and the Revival of German Colonialism," *Nationalism and Internationalism, Essays Inscribed to Carlton J. H. Hayes* (Edward M. Earle, ed.; New York: Columbia University Press, 1950), pp. 399–430, has now been replaced by Wolfe W. Schmokel, *Dream of Empire: German Colonialism, 1919–1945* (New Haven: Yale University Press, 1964), a useful but in many ways inadequate book. From East Germany, there is Horst Kühne, "Zur Kolonialgeschichte des faschistischen deutschen Imperialismus (1933–1939)," *Zeitschrift für Geschichtswissenschaft,* 9 (1961), 514–37. The best treatment is Klaus Hildebrand, *Vom Reich zum Weltreich, Hitler, NSDAP und koloniale Frage 1919–1945* (Munich: Wilhelm Fink Verlag, 1969). For the most active period of German colonial preparations, see Gerhard L. Weinberg, "German Colonial Plans and Policies 1938–1942," *Geschichte und Gegenwartsbewusstsein, Festschrift für Hans Rothfels* (Göttingen: Vandenhoeck & Ruprecht, 1963), pp. 462–91.

58. "Ost- und Kolonialpolitik: ihre ergänzende Notwendigkeit," *Deutscher Kolonial-Dienst,* 2, No. 10 (Oct. 1937), 1–8.

59. The account in Schmokel, chap. 1, is useful; but for von Ribbentrop's role earlier than 1937 (Schmokel, p. 30), see von Ribbentrop's letter of 3 July 1935, claiming control of colonial policy, quoted in Horst Kühne, "Die Fünfte Kolonne des faschistischen deutschen Imperialismus in Südwestafrika (1933–1939)," *Zeitschrift für Geschichtswissenschaft,* 8 (1960), 778, n. 48; von Ribbentrop's Minute for Hitler of 28 August 1936, *G. D.*, C, 5, No. 520; and Jacobsen, pp. 296–98. Very detailed is Hildebrand, pp. 248–451.

Japanese mandate in 1933 when Japan left the League and in 1935 when its withdrawal became final, but the only result of this was to point up the sensitivity of the Japanese government in regard to these Pacific islands.[60] In the spring of 1933 there were some discussions of colonial problems between Germany and Italy, but nothing came of them either.[61] Caution was the order of the day; Hitler authorized a little colonial propaganda, but it was all to be in low key, stressing Germany's rights but not attacking anyone.[62] Hitler touched on the colonial question in his conversation with Sir John Simon in the spring of 1935, tying the colonial issue to any German return to the League of Nations, possibly in response to a suggestion from the head of the Reich Colonial League; but he drew back as soon as Simon indicated opposition.[63]

The obvious British reluctance to move on this issue at a time when Hitler still thought of himself as wooing that country and the difficulties experienced by the National Socialists in former German Southwest Africa in the face of the determined opposition of the South African government which did not wish its platonic expressions of friendship for Germany converted into substantive concessions at its own expense led Hitler to maintain a most cautious attitude in 1935 and to keep German colonialist propaganda within bounds.[64] In an interview with the president of United Press in November 1935, Hitler said that Germany would never renounce its colonial demands, but he assured his listener that he would never make war on that account, an assurance that von Ribbentrop removed from the official text of the conversation.[65] As Germany grew stronger, Hitler appears

60. Gerhard L. Weinberg, "Deutsch-japanische Verhandlungen über das Südseemandat, 1937–1938," *Vierteljahrshefte für Zeitgeschichte,* 4, No. 4 (Oct. 1956), 391 and n. 4; see also German foreign ministry, "Stichworte für die mündliche Information der Presse," 18 March 1933, T–120, 2998/6694/H 099788; von Dirksen (Tokyo) report 1169, 29 March 1935, T–120, 2673/5575/E 400034–037; *G. D.,* C, 4, No. 73; and J. Reimers's Göttingen 1936 dissertation, "Das japanische Kolonialmandat und der Austritt Japans aus dem Völkerbund." Schmokel (pp. 140–41) appears to have missed most of the material relevant to this issue.

61. *G. D.,* C, 1, Nos. 171, 172, 176, 181.

62. "Bestellung aus der Pressekonferenz vom 8.2.34," ". . . vom 7. Mai 1934," ". . . vom 7. Februar 1935," Bundesarchiv, Brammer, Z.Sg. 101/3, f. 63, 215, and 101/5, f. 36; Rosenberg, *Tagebuch,* 4 May 1934, p. 28.

63. *G. D.,* C, 3, No. 555, pp. 1062–64. Hitler had noted with interest Schnee's memorandum on the colonial question of 20 March 1935 (ibid., No. 549), but the date leaves uncertain whether he saw it before or after the talk with Simon (see T–120, 3611/9785/E 687259).

Hildebrand argues that until 1935 Hitler used restraint in colonial questions as a means of trying for England's agreement to German eastward expansion, while afterward he used the colonial demand as a threat to secure such agreement. I am not convinced that the evidence supports such a clear line, at least for the mid-1930s.

64. *G. D.,* C, 4, Nos. 47, 263; "Bestellung aus der Pressekonferenz vom 26.8.1935," ". . . vom 7.9.1935," ". . . vom 29. Januar 1936," Bundesarchiv, Brammer, Z.Sg. 101/6, f. 70, 94, and 101/7, f. 69. See also the excerpts from a letter of Lammers to several state and party agencies of November 1935, quoted in Kühne, "Südwestafrika," p. 766; and the last paragraph of *D. D. F.,* 2d, 1, No. 181.

65. Domarus, 1:557–59; Dodd telegram 229, 30 November 1935, State 765.84/2809.

to have thought that at some time the Western powers would give Germany a mandate without concessions on his part except, conceivably, a return to the League.[66] Comments to this effect began to appear in Germany's diplomatic conversations and in its press in the early months of 1936, and Hitler himself referred to it in his Reichstag speech of 7 March about the Rhineland.[67] The triumph of Italy in East Africa contributed its share to accentuating the colonial question.[68] The subject was clearly in the air and was beginning to play a greater role in the thinking of the Berlin government. This may explain why Hitler allowed Schacht to try his hand at securing a return of colonies to Germany in August 1936.

Schacht had long been interested in the question of colonies for Germany, primarily as a source of raw materials; and he appears to have seriously believed that some of Germany's economic problems could be solved by the return of the colonies lost at the end of World War I. In his years as Hitler's economic assistant, he would bring up the colonial subject whenever possible.[69] He urged upon Hitler the need for colonies in Africa, arguing that expansion in Eastern Europe led into areas as densely populated as Germany itself (and not realizing that Hitler expected to depopulate them by force).[70] In September 1935 he had impressed upon S. R. Fuller, President Roosevelt's unofficial emissary, the importance he attached to Germany's securing colonies for economic reasons. Fuller's report to Roosevelt in October obviously made a considerable impression on the president.[71] At another meeting Roosevelt suggested that Fuller sound out the Germans about the idea of leasing mines and other economic concessions in colonies to meet their economic needs. When Fuller raised this possibility with Hitler and Schacht, the reception was interested rather than enthusiastic, although Schacht himself had had similar ideas a decade before.[72] Before the meeting with Hitler, Schacht urged Fuller to impress upon Hitler the

66. The account of a supposed meeting of Hitler with an old friend in December 1935 in which this assertion is attributed to him rings true (*D. D. F.*, 2d, 1, Nos. 15, 157).

67. Von Neurath mentioned it to the Rumanian minister, Comnen, on 24 February 1936 (*D. D. F.*, 2d, 1, No. 237); Rosenberg mentioned it to Comnen soon after (ibid., No. 267); for the press campaign, see ibid., Nos. 15, 134, 181, 233, 234; 2, No. 128; for the reception of this campaign in Japan see *G. D.*, C, 5, Nos. 195, 196; for the reference in Hitler's speech of 7 March see Domarus, 1:595 and *G. D.*, C, 5, No. 3.

68. *D. D. F.*, 2d, 2, No. 208.

69. See, e.g., U. S. 1933, 1:532–33; *G. D.*, C, 1, No. 222; Hildebrand, pp. 204ff.

70. *G. D.*, C, 3, No. 544. Hildebrand (pp. 228–29, 263–64) extends this distinction to other conservative supporters of Hitler who saw colonies as sources of raw materials in contrast to Hitler's schemes of eastward settlement.

71. U. S. 1935, 2:282–86 (Schmokel mistakenly identifies Fuller as American consul general and does not cite the relevant documents from Hyde Park); Fuller to Roosevelt, 11 October 1935; Roosevelt to Hull, 28 October; Roosevelt to Fuller, 14 November, all in Hyde Park, P. P. F. 2616.

72. Fuller memoranda of his talks with Hitler and Schacht on 1 April 1936, are in Hyde Park, P. P. F. 2616; cf. Schmokel, p. 85. See above, p. 156, for Roosevelt's authorization.

great cost of armaments as an argument for reducing the rearmament program in Germany. In this manner, Schacht was trying to enlist Fuller in his own struggle for policy and power in the German economy.

In the winter of 1935–36, the German economy began its shift from a rearmament boom in which unutilized resources were put to work into a period of economic crisis with competing priorities during which Schacht struggled with party leaders, especially Göring, over the control and direction of the German economy.[73] Eventually he was to lose that struggle, out of which the Four-Year Plan would emerge as the symbol of his failure; but while engaged in it, better relations with the western powers looked to Schacht like a way to cut armament costs and bring relief to Germany's raw material shortages by securing colonies.[74] He wanted to try his hand at negotiations to accomplish such gains for Germany; and although there is no direct evidence on the subject, it appears that he consulted Hitler, who authorized him to go ahead. Since Hitler planned to make no concessions in return for colonial gains, presumably he felt that there was nothing to be lost by allowing Schacht to make the effort.

Schacht went to Paris in August 1936 and discussed the colonial question with Léon Blum.[75] Blum, who was most interested in some permanent accommodation with Germany if that was at all possible and who was prepared to pay a price for it, was apparently favorably inclined to the idea of returning some colonies to Germany. In any such program, the Cameroons would be the obvious contribution of France. Though any definite steps toward actually handing over territories, even if a mandate of France, would be subject to agreement by the British, the impression Berlin received from the Paris talks was that a positive response would be forthcoming.[76] For the time that the German government thought that there was such a possibility, the German press was instructed to keep quiet on the subject.[77] Hitler touched on the topic briefly in his opening proclamation to the

73. Schweitzer, *Big Business in the Third Reich,* pp. 537–47.

74. *D. D. F.*, 2d, 2, Nos. 352, 355.

75. Schmokel, pp. 97–99; Earl R. Beck, *Verdict on Schacht* (Tallahassee: Florida State University, 1955), pp. 106–9; Joel Colton, *Leon Blum, Humanist in Politics* (New York: Knopf, 1966), pp. 213–15; Farnsworth, *Bullitt,* p. 159; Wilson (U. S. chargé in Paris) telegram 797, 26 August 1936, State 862.2222/25; Dodd telegram 270, 2 September 1936, State 751.62/336; Wilson telegram 832, 4 September 1936, State 751.62/367; Dodd to Moore, 28 August 1936, Hyde Park, R. Walton Moore Papers; *D. D. F.*, 2d, 3, Nos. 63, 196, 211, 213, 229; the key British documents are in Foreign Office C 7626/5740/18, C 6637/C 6639/C 7159/C 7461/C 7500/97/18.

76. See especially von Neurath's comments to the Hungarian foreign minister, Csaky, while in Budapest in late September 1936, reported in Stewart (Budapest) telegram 40 of 22 September and dispatch 475 of 24 September 1936, State 762.64/52 and 54; also Schacht's comments at the Bank for International Settlements' meeting in December 1936, reported in Bullitt telegram 1255, 15 December 1936, State 462.00 R 296 B.I.S./521.

77. "Bestellungen aus der Pressekonferenz vom 8. September 1936," ". . . vom 19. September 1936," ". . . vom 29. September 1936," Bundesarchiv, Brammer, Z.Sg. 101/8, f. 143, 169, 193.

Nuremberg party rally on 9 September, but in the most general terms.[78] Early in October, however, the Germans were to learn that they were not to receive any presents of colonies. The British government had gone the way of unilateral concessions once in the Anglo-German naval agreement of 1935; they were not about to repeat that performance. They now reinforced the inclination of the French government, hinted at by Blum to Schacht and subsequently indicated by François-Poncet to Hitler, not to discuss any colonial concessions to Germany except within the framework of a general European settlement. The Franco-German talks were, therefore, interrupted.[79] When the French tried to reopen the colonial question within the kind of general framework London had suggested, it would quickly become apparent that Germany was not interested.[80] Schacht's star continued on its declining path, a path that was not interrupted by any gratuitous colonial concessions to Germany.

The visit of David Lloyd George to Germany shortly after Schacht's trip to Paris was equally spectacular, equally fruitless. The former British prime minister had repeatedly spoken in Parliament in favor of concessions to Germany and continued to do so after Hitler came to power, most recently after the remilitarization of the Rhineland. He planned a trip to Germany to look at the social and economic experiments of the National Socialist regime and asked for an interview with Hitler. On 4–5 September 1936 the two met at Berchtesgaden and talked at length about the war in which they had played such different roles.[81] They also discussed German-English relations and the problem of a new Locarno, the whole visit having been urged by von Ribbentrop as a part of his efforts to secure British acquiescence in German policies. No concrete results were expected or attained; both men came from the meeting confirmed in their views and prejudices. Lloyd George was more enthusiastic about Hitler and concessions to him than ever; Hitler delighted in this confirmation of his hope that England could be lulled by pleasant assurances and anti-Communist effusions into a policy of detachment.[82]

Considerable reinforcement was also given to the positive image that Hitler wanted to project at this time by the staging of the Olympics. Held in elaborate surroundings in Berlin, attracting tourists and the attention of the entire world, the whole spectacle served as ideal propaganda for the

78. The full text of Hitler's proclamation in NSDAP, Reichsleitung, *Der Parteitag der Ehre vom 8. bis 14. September 1936* (Munich: Eher, 1936), pp. 30–47. Hildebrand ties Hitler's reticence to his reluctance to have colonial agitation disturb von Ribbentrop's mission to England.

79. *G. D.*, C, 5, No. 574; D, 1, No. 56; Eden, p. 568; *D. D. F.*, 2d, 3, Nos. 276, 334, 354, 393; Memorandum of Wigram, 29 October 1936, Foreign Office C 6701/97/18.

80. I will examine these negotiations in a subsequent book.

81. *G. D.*, C, 5, No. 526; T. Jones, pp. 243–51; Schmidt, *Statist auf diplomatischer Bühne,* pp. 336–40; Martin Gilbert and Richard Gott, *The Appeasers* (Boston: Houghton Mifflin, 1963), p. 36.

82. Hitler kept Lloyd George in fond memory; see, e.g., his comments on 20 May 1942, in Picker, p. 361, and 22 August 1942, in Trevor-Roper, p. 657.

new Germany. Every effort was made to avoid incidents and unfavorable publicity; Hitler even agreed to allow Jews to participate in the competition.[83] Foreign diplomats in attendance were entertained lavishly, and other visitors were suitably impressed. Such graciousness even extended to Sir Robert Vansittart, the permanent undersecretary in the British Foreign Office, who was generally thought to be unfriendly to Germany.[84] Rarely had Germany looked more contented and prosperous to the outside world. The struggle for the direction of Germany's economy was hidden from the view of those who could see a Germany in which there were jobs for all, even if they were in the army—in which the term of service was increased from one year to two years some ten days after the Olympics ended.

While public attention was focussed on the speculations and negotiations for a new Locarno, the travels of Schacht and Lloyd George, the Olympic games, and, soon after, the romance of Edward VIII and Wallis Warfield Simpson, a shift was quietly under way in the foreign policy of Belgium. There were two major issues in Germany's relations with Belgium: the territory of Eupen-Malmédy, ceded to Belgium under the Treaty of Versailles, and the general problem of political relations as defined by the Treaty of Locarno. Since the German government expected to secure the return of Eupen-Malmédy at some time in the future, Hitler and his diplomats were careful to remind the Belgians from time to time that Hitler's periodic assurances to the world that he had no further territorial demands beyond whichever one he was insisting on at the time did not in fact apply to that territory.[85] The German government followed developments in Eupen-Malmédy with great interest, though unwilling to enter into any comprehensive discussion of that issue because such discussions would force its real aims into the open.[86] To calm the Belgians and perhaps wean them away from their close relationship with France, the Berlin government made

83. See the reports of August-September 1935, of Charles H. Sherrill, member of the International Olympic Committee (including a report on a talk with Hitler on 24 August 1935), to Miss LeHand for President Roosevelt, in Hyde Park, P. S. F. File Germany, Confidential. Sherrill, who had been U. S. minister in Argentina and ambassador in Turkey, died shortly before the Olympic games. For references to him in Roosevelt's published correspondence see *F.D.R., Personal Letters 1928–45,* 1:436, 452.

84. On the effort to impress Sir Robert Vansittart see Colvin, pp. 108ff.; *G. D.,* C, 5, Nos. 489, n. 2, 510; *D. D. F.,* 2d, Nos. 85, 100. Vansittart's comments on his conversation with Hitler may be found in Mastný's report 79, 11 August 1936, Czech document in T–120, 1040/1809/413202–203; Phipps telegrams 251 of 6 August and 211–Saving of 13 August 1936, Foreign Office C 5750/C 5871/4/18.

85. *G. D.,* C, 1, No. 142; 2, No. 310; 4, Nos. 108, 381, 403, 471. Count Davignon, before moving from Warsaw to his new post as Belgian minister in Berlin, had expressed the view that Belgium ought to return Eupen-Malmédy—but that it would be a bad precedent (Szembek, 22 January 1936, p. 151).

86. *G. D.,* C, 4, Nos. 342, 477, 491, 508, 534; *D. D. B.,* 3, No. 164; 4, No. 2; Jaques Davignon, *Berlin 1936–1940, souvenirs d'une mission* (Paris-Brussels; Éditions Universitaires, 1951), pp. 43–46; German foreign ministry to Richthofen (Brussels), 12 May 1936, T–120, 2742/5864/E 429973.

several informal approaches to Brussels, primarily through von Ribbentrop, in 1934 and 1935.[87] It may be doubted that such gestures reassured the Belgians, especially since Germany was suspected, and quite correctly, of dealing with the Belgian Rexist opposition, a Fascist party established in 1935.[88]

From the point of view of the Belgians, the growing strength of Germany presented a serious menace and most difficult policy problems. Belgium's close relationship with France was a source of anxiety in domestic affairs because of the division between the Flemish and Walloon elements, the former engaging in vehement anti-French agitation. The failure of France to act decisively when Germany remilitarized the Rhineland suggested that the Belgian tie to Paris was no longer the great source of strength in foreign affairs that the government in Brussels had once thought it to be. Under these circumstances, Belgium looked for new approaches to the problem of maintaining its security. In the summer of 1936, there began a drift toward a neutral position in which Belgium would accept from others guarantees of its independence but would refuse to obligate itself to aid them in turn. In short, Belgium would only be guaranteed, not a guarantor. The government still hoped that the negotiations for a new Locarno would in fact produce a treaty providing Belgium with a substitute for the lost assurances of the past; but as the obduracy of Germany made that prospect ever more unlikely, the Belgian government leaned increasingly in the direction of neutrality, with Germany naturally urging it on.[89]

The decisive turn in Belgian policy came in October, signalized by a speech of the king to the cabinet and subsequently confirmed in public statements by the government. The new policy in effect cut Belgium lose from its Western allies by restricting itself to the defense of its own territory. It would rearm for that purpose, and getting domestic support for rearmament had been an important factor in leading to the new policy, but it would not engage itself further. Domestic pressures as well as foreign dangers had moved Belgium out of the Locarno framework. Since the Germans could be and were confident that France and Britain would not violate Belgian neutrality, they no longer needed to worry about a broad assault in the west if Germany moved east. Conversely they could be reasonably certain that Belgium would have no help until it was too late if the Germans themselves moved in the west. It was not until April 1937 that Britain and

87. *G. D.*, C, 2, No. 443; 3, No. 336, n. 3; *B. D.*, 2d, 4, No. 421; Morris (U. S. minister Brussels) dispatches 579 of 2 October and 636 of 16 November 1935, State 755.62/11 and 14; White (counselor Berlin) dispatch 2358, 4 October 1935, State 755.62/13.

88. *G. D.*, C, 5, Nos. 460, 507, 527, 543, 582, 604, 629. Louis De Jong, *The German Fifth Column in World War II* (trans. C. M. Geyl; Chicago: University of Chicago Press, 1956), p. 199, is mistaken in thinking Degrelle received financial support only from Italy; at least as of September 1936, his group was getting help from Berlin (*G. D.*, C, 5, No. 582).

89. *D. D. B.*, 4, Nos. 77, 88, 92, 103, 120–23, 126; *D. D. F.*, 2d, 1, No. 282; 2, Nos. 260, 362, 416; 3, Nos. 14, 47, 97, 128, 172, 287, 296, 300, 307, 325, 344; *G. D.*, C, 5, Nos. 349, 391, 444, 494; van Overstraeten, pp. 212–14, 225–26, 229–30.

France formally released Belgium from its obligation to provide mutual assistance under the Locarno agreements, but the real shift was by then already an accomplished fact.[90]

Overshadowing all other events in the summer of 1936 and dominating world attention for long thereafter were the outbreak of civil war in Spain and the intervention of various European powers in that conflict.[91] Hitler himself had paid little attention to Spain. As he saw Spain, its neutrality in World War I had confirmed its unimportance in international affairs; Spain's supposed antagonism to France in North Africa suggested it might become a possible secondary ally against France in the future.[92] During the early years of National Socialist rule in Germany, the problems of Spain attracted little attention in Berlin.[93] An extensive apparatus of National Socialist organizations was developed in the German colony in Spain to assure their subservience to the regime in Berlin and help to advance German interests abroad. In this regard Spain was not unique, though the seizure of relevant archives in the early stages of the civil war in 1936 has made such activities in Spain better known than most.[94] Though individuals from the foreign

90. The best available survey of Belgian policy, though written before the publication of the Belgian documents, is still Jane K. Miller, *Belgian Foreign Policy between Two Wars, 1919–1940* (New York: Bookman, 1951). There is a good account in Toynbee, *Survey of International Affairs 1936,* pp. 351–60. A useful analysis that stresses the internal political and military factors in the change of Belgian policy is Pierre Henri Laurent, "The Reversal of Belgian Foreign Policy 1936–1937," *Review of Politics,* 31, No. 3 (July 1969), 370–84. See also *G. D.,* C, 5, Nos. 606, 610, 634; *Lipski Papers,* No. 63. A British review may be found in Foreign Office C 8323/4/18.

In assessing French reaction to the Belgian step, it must be noted that on the day before the king's speech the Belgian ambassador in Paris had assured the French foreign minister that no decision had yet been taken (*D. D. B.,* 4, No. 126). The repercussions of the Belgian step and the negotiations that followed can be traced in ibid., Nos. 129ff. and *D. D. F.,* 2d, 3, Nos. 346ff. The full explication of the king's position may be found in van Overstraeten, pp. 230–34, 237–39.

91. A recent survey of the literature in Rainer Wohfeil, "Der spanische Bürgerkrieg 1936–1939, Zur Deutung und Nachwirkung," *Vierteljahrshefte für Zeitgeschichte,* 16, No. 2 (April 1968), 101–19.

92. *Hitlers zweites Buch,* pp. 140, 217.

93. There is some useful information on German-Spanish relations in the period before 1936 in Marion Einhorn, *Die ökonomischen Hintergründe der faschistischen deutschen Intervention in Spanien 1936–1939* (Berlin: Akademie-Verlag, 1962), chap. 2.

94. The documents were seized in July 1936 in Loyalist Spain, and some of them appeared in *Schwarzrotbuch, Dokumente über den Hitlerimperialismus,* published by the Deutsche-Anarcho-Syndikalisten (Barcelona: Asy-Verlag, 1937). The author knows of no serious evaluation of this material. The comments on this publication in the otherwise often useful book by Manfred Merkes, *Die deutsche Politik gegenüber dem spanischen Bürgerkrieg 1936–1939* (Bonn: Röhrscheid, 1961), pp. 15–17, are even sillier than those to which he takes exception. Merkes's assertion that the document on p. 318 of the *Schwarzrotbuch* is a forgery is unproved and most unlikely. Since those publishing the *Schwarzrotbuch* clearly had access to supplies of letterhead stationery of various National Socialist agencies in Spain, it is striking that the only document in the collection said—without the slightest proof—to be forged should be one of the very few not on letterhead stationery and with contents that only tangentially support the assertion of German relations with the rebels. Had the edi-

organization of the NSDAP, the AO (*Auslandsorganisation*), were to play an especially prominent part in German aid to Franco, there is nothing to suggest that the AO in Spain differed greatly from similar establishments among Germans in other countries. In Spain, as elsewhere, the AO was in an uneasy relationship with the regular German diplomatic service, the two cooperating but often in conflict with one another at the same time.[95] At least as significant as both these arms of German policy in the actual conduct of relations between Germany and Spain were the official and unofficial dealers in weapons.

Some German firms had long been interested in arms sales to Spain.[96] Of greater importance, because of the contacts developed through them, were the attempts to include German military equipment in the German-Spanish trade balance in the year preceding the civil war. Efforts on the part of rightist elements within the governing coalition in Spain to use a tie to German suppliers of weapons for their own purposes met with German interest in arms exports. Nothing concrete came of this scheme, but in the course of trying to make it work, the then chief of staff, General Francisco Franco, developed—if he did not already have—a great interest in German weapons for the Spanish army.[97] Not only had the talks involved Franco personally as well as the sending of Spanish officers to Berlin, subsequently there were other contacts of a less formal and official nature that are still shrouded in doubt because of the lack of adequate documentation. The importance of those contacts lies in the fact that they took place in the period between the Spanish elections of 18 February and the military uprising of 17 July 1936.

The February elections in Spain brought victory to the Left, which was, however, not sufficiently united to establish a Popular Front government. The moderates attempted to steer the Spanish republic through the storms; the radical Left was divided between those who wanted a Socialist state and those who, as anarchists, were not sure they wanted a state at all. The radical Right, which had tried to dismantle the republic from the inside during the preceding years, now turned to the idea of overturning it by force.

---

tors of the *Schwarzrotbuch* wished to forge evidence, they could easily have done much better. The contents of the document, furthermore, are in accord with information to be found in the German foreign ministry files in a general way.

The book by Franz Spielhagen (pseud.?), *Spione und Verschwörer in Spanien* (Paris: Édition du Carrefour, 1936), is based on the same collection of documents (not the same manuscript as Merkes states), and includes important items not printed in the *Schwarzrotbuch*. For a discussion of the Éditions du Carrefour, a Comintern publishing firm in Paris, see Babette Gross, *Willi Münzenberg, eine politische Biographie* (Stuttgart: Deutsche Verlags-Anstalt, 1967), pp. 253–58, 276–78.

95. A detailed study of the AO is badly needed; the best available survey is in Jacobsen, pp. 90–160.

96. Some relevant information may be found in the *Schwarzrotbuch,* pp. 297–313.

97. The negotiations can be followed in *G. D.,* C, 4, Nos. 303, 330, 445, 450; 5, Nos. 133, 215; von Bülow memorandum of 20 August 1935, T–120, 2373/4602/E 190194–195.

The government tried to protect itself by transferring Franco and other generals opposed to the republic to less sensitive posts but was reluctant to arm the workers lest they overturn rather than defend republican institutions.

The official discussions of German arms deliveries to Spain had ceased by the spring of 1936, but now unofficial ones were held. One document of 17 June 1936 alluding to this subject was published by the Loyalists after it was seized in a Spanish office of the German Labor Front.[98] Another of 6 July is included in the postwar publication of German foreign ministry documents. Of special interest is the suggestion in this document that the German who figured prominently in the operation was a "Herr Feltjen" who was in the aircraft industry and was identified in the German Ministry of War as a zealous gunrunner.[99] This indicates the at least extremely likely possibility that the man referred to was Colonel Josef Veltjens, a retired World War I air ace whom Hermann Göring regularly employed for officially sponsored missions that were too shady or "undiplomatic" to be exposed to the light of day.[100] Certainly the evidence is clear that Veltjens played a role in certain arms deliveries to Franco during the civil war, arms deliveries that were kept separate from the bulk carried through regularly organized channels and, unlike that bulk, were regularly paid for in foreign exchange.[101] Either through Veltjens or someone in a very similar position

98. See *Schwarzrotbuch*, picture 183 on p. 318 (see above, n. 94). Other documents are quoted in Spielhagen, pp. 138–42.

99. *G. D.*, C, 5, No. 433. The relevant portion of the document has been printed in German in *G. D.*, D, 3:3, n. 1. The translation of the key words: "wie ich bei meinen Freunden im anderen Hause erfahren habe," into "as I have heard from friends of mine elsewhere" is inaccurate. The author of the letter was liaison man from the foreign ministry to the Ministry of War, and it is to contacts in the latter agency that the passage obviously refers. Possibly the weapons deals referred to were with the Carlists, a monarchist group also plotting against the Spanish republic (see Hugh Thomas, *The Spanish Civil War* [New York: Harper & Rowe, 1963], who had access to the Carlist archives).

100. On Veltjens's World War I career see Walter A. Musciano, *Eagles of the Black Cross* (New York: Ivan Obolensky, 1965), pp. 183–85. According to this source, Veltjens died in October 1943.

101. On Veltjens's activities during the Spanish civil war see the following documents: Sonderstab Wilberg to Ministry of Finance, 2344/37 g.Kdos. of 9 August 1937, in Bundesarchiv, RFM, R 2/20, f. 73; 2541/37 g.Kdos. of 24 August 1937, ibid., f. 100; 4969/39 g.Kdos. of 17 January 1939, ibid., R 2/23, f. 35; 6822/39 g.Rs. of 9 June 1939, ibid., f. 207. The references to "Velschen" and "Vetschew" in the diary of Alfred Jodl for 27 and 30 March 1937 refer to these activities (*TMWC,* 28:353). For a picture of the Veltjens business in the total delivery system in 1937 see the "Bericht nebst Anlage der Deutschen Revisions- und Treuhandaktiengesellschaft Berlin über die bei der ROWAK Handelsgesellschaft m.b.H., Berlin vorgenommenen Prüfung des Jahresabschlusses zum 31. Dezember 1937" (hereafter cited as *Rowak Report*), p. 8, in Bundesarchiv, RFM, R 2/27, f. 46. There are indications that Veltjens may also have been involved in German schemes to supply defective weapons to the Loyalists in Spain (Thomas, p. 296; Ian Colvin, *Chief of Intelligence* [London: Gollancz, 1951], pp. 33–34; Jakob Leonhard, *Als Gestapoagent im Dienste der Schweizer Gegenspionage* [Zurich; Europa-Verlag, 1946], p. 11; but see Merkes, p. 67). The book by Glenn T. Harper, *German Economic Policy in Spain during the Spanish Civil War, 1936–1939* (The Hague: Mouton, 1967), is based solely on published material; Veltjens is not mentioned.

In August 1940, Veltjens served as Göring's agent for arms sales to Finland

there were some contacts; in addition, General Sanjurjo, the most prominent, though not necessarily the most important, of the Spanish plotters, had visited Germany in February 1936.[102]

Such contacts may have encouraged some among the Spanish conspirators to hope for aid from Germany in a coup, but they went forward for reasons of their own, expecting to win quickly. Had those expectations been fulfilled, the new regime in Madrid would presumably have turned to Berlin for the military supplies needed to keep in subjection a largely hostile population; but nothing suggests that Franco and the other enemies of Spanish democracy expected a difficult struggle in which outside assistance would be vital to them. After all, they controlled or expected to control the military forces of Spain. Nor did the plotters look to national socialism for political inspiration. Determined to return Spain to an ancient form of government uncontaminated by any ideology stemming from the preceding two or three centuries, the officers cooperated with but looked down upon the minuscule Spanish Fascist party, the Falange, whose insignificance at the time was matched only by that of the Spanish Communist party—even though in the blaze of battle these splinter groups were later to cast their shadows over the contending parties.[103] Had the coup been successful, it would have affected the international balance by one single and significant change: the replacement of a Spanish regime friendly to France by one antagonistic to it. It was the partial success and partial failure of the coup that set the stage for massive intervention by other nations.

The first onslaught of the military uprising succeeded in many cities in Spain and Spanish Morocco, but several setbacks suggested the possibility of imminent failure. In some cities the coup failed in its initial stages, in others armed workers rallying to the defense of the republic recaptured key centers. The prospective new chief of state, General Sanjurjo, lost his life when his plane crashed because it was overloaded with the general's gorgeous uniforms. The air force and the navy rallied to the side of the government. Only in northwest Spain and Morocco could the conspirators consolidate their initial success; in Morocco they had the one real army, the Army of Africa with its Moroccan troops, under General Franco who was newly flown in but well-known to it as its former leader. But if Spain was to be conquered from North Africa in 1936 as it had been in 711, then that army had to be transported across the Straits to the Spanish mainland. Since the government forces controlled the air and sea and Franco himself had

(Weinberg, *Germany and the Soviet Union,* p. 127). Göring later placed him in charge of German purchasing operations in the black market in Western Europe (see Göring's order of 13 June 1942 and Veltjens's report of 15 January 1943, quoted in *TMWC,* 5:525–31, and Göring's testimony in ibid., 9:331).

102. Thomas, p. 101.

103. A useful account of the civil war's origins and course may be found in the book by Hugh Thomas cited above. Dante A. Puzzo, *Spain and the Great Powers, 1936–1941* (New York: Columbia University Press, 1962), is good but not sufficiently critical of its sources. Donald S. Detwiler, *Hitler, Franco und Gibraltar, Die Frage des spanischen Eintritts in den Zweiten Weltkrieg* (Wiesbaden: Steiner, 1962), chap. 1 and notes, is very helpful.

had to be flown to Morocco by a plane secretly chartered in England, only foreign assistance in the form of air transport could save the uprising. For such aid, Franco turned to Hitler and Mussolini.

The Italian dictator had recently successfully concluded his conquest of Ethiopia in defiance of the League and was looking for new adventures. He had followed up his association with the Spanish dictator Primo de Rivera by a secret arrangement promising support to the Spanish monarchists against the republic in March 1934.[104] Once assured that the present uprising was supported by the elements he had promised to aid, Mussolini decided to send some airplanes as the first installment of what was to become a major commitment. The German response to Franco's plea, however, was made quite independently, though the parallel policies of the two dictators were to play a powerful role in bringing their countries closer together, a theme mentioned earlier and to reappear frequently hereafter.

The appeal for German aid was taken to Hitler by two officials of the AO in Morocco, Adolf Langenheim, who as head of the Tetuán party local (*Ortsgruppe*) was the highest National Socialist dignitary in Spanish Morocco, and Johannes Bernhardt, the economic expert of the local National Socialists. Bernhardt, who during his years as a businessman in Morocco had developed contacts with the officers of the Spanish army there, was the moving spirit.[105] Carrying letters from Franco to Hitler and Göring, Langenheim and Bernhardt, accompanied by a Spanish officer, flew to Germany where the head of the AO, Ernst Wilhelm Bohle, arranged for them to confer with Rudolf Hess, who in turn saw to it that they were sent to Bayreuth to meet Hitler, there for the annual Wagner festival.[106] The German foreign ministry favored a neutral attitude, wanted to reject Franco's request for planes—a request which had also been made through diplomatic channels—and had nothing but discouraging advice for Bohle.[107] The officials of the foreign ministry, with whose views von Neurath concurred after he returned to Berlin from Bayreuth, thought it risky for Germany to become involved in an internal dispute in Spain when such aid was sure to come to public attention. Hitler would decide otherwise.

In the key conferences with Hitler at Bayreuth on 26 July, neither von Neurath nor von Ribbentrop were consulted. Present were Göring, von Blomberg, the minister of war, and Admiral Canaris, the chief of the German armed forces intelligence office. Canaris had been in Spain repeatedly since he first worked there in espionage activities during World War I. He

104. *Journal of Modern History,* 24 (1952), 181–83; U. S. 1937, 1:294; Puzzo, p. 42.

105. On Bernhardt, unless otherwise noted, see Merkes, p. 19; Harper, pp. 12–13; and the sources cited by them. Spielhagen, pp. 120–29, passim, and in three unnumbered photocopies, brings information on the activities of Bernhardt and Langenheim in prior years.

106. Merkes, p. 20; Interrogation of Bohle, 5 November 1946, *Deutsche Bank Investigation, Annex,* Exhibit 404. The letters of Franco have not been found; that he wrote to Göring as well as Hitler would fit in with knowledge on Franco's part of earlier arms deliveries via Veltjens.

107. *G. D.,* D, 3, Nos. 2, 5, 10.

spoke the language fluently, had kept up his contacts, and knew Franco. It is probable that he advised support of the insurgents; he certainly was to play a key role in pushing for German support of Franco thereafter and became, if he was not already, a valued friend of the Spanish leader.[108] There is no evidence of von Blomberg's views at that time.[109] Göring subsequently claimed that he himself had strongly urged aid be given; and since he was not only a close friend of Hitler—and quite probably the backer of Veltjen's or others' arms deals—but also the chief of the air force that would provide the planes Franco was requesting, his advice no doubt carried weight. Göring asserted that he used as arguments the need to prevent the spread of communism and the desire to test his air force.[110] The supposed danger of communism may well have influenced Hitler even though in reality the military revolt in Spain gave the Communists their first real influence.

There is important circumstantial evidence that military arguments of an economic nature were advanced and played an important role in the German decision to aid Spain. Göring had been placed in charge of raw material imports and was soon after given control of the Four-Year Plan to make Germany economically ready for war. Hitler subsequently referred to the importance of Spanish raw materials to Germany.[111] Göring was to occupy a key role in German-Spanish economic relations with Bernhardt as his main agent. Certainly no one could then have predicted that in 1937 Germany would import from Nationalist Spain alone about as much as it had imported from all of Spain in 1935, would shift the bulk of these imports into categories useful for rearmament, and would be able to avoid paying foreign exchange for any of them;[112] but it is surely likely that Göring and Bernhardt urged on Hitler the possible advantages to Germany of access to Spain's important mineral resources on terms congenial to Germany's rearmament needs. It is significant that the earliest contemporary document I have found that deals with the actual organization of aid to Franco is a report on a conference between Göring and his associates on 30 July in which the two subjects discussed were the Spanish situation and the problem of raw materials and foreign exchange.[113] Intertwined in the discussion

108. Colvin, *Chief of Intelligence,* pp. 30–34; Karl Heinz Abshagen, *Canaris, Patriot und Weltbürger* (Stuttgart: Union Deutsche Verlagsgesellschaft, 1950), pp. 159–64. The most reliable information on Canaris is in Helmut Krausnick (ed.), "Aus den Personalpapieren von Canaris," *Vierteljahrshefte für Zeitgeschichte,* 10, No. 3 (July 1962), 280–310.

109. Merkes (p. 24) claims that von Blomberg was opposed to aid, citing Hossbach, pp. 41–42, as his source. Hossbach, however, expressly states that he was on leave at this time; the cited passage deals with the later request for German divisions. For this issue, raised in December 1936, see pp. 297–98, below.

110. *TMWC,* 9:280–81.

111. See his speech of 13 September 1937, in Raoul de Roussy de Sales (ed.), *Adolf Hitler, My New Order* (New York: Reynal & Hitchcock, 1941), pp. 425–27.

112. *Rowak Report,* pp. 3–8, R 2/27, f. 41–46.

113. "Aktenvermerk über die Besprechung beim Herrn Generaloberst am 30.7.36," 1 August 1936, Nuremberg document 3890–PS (National Archives).

were the special staff Wilberg had set up to handle aid to Spain, the training of air force personnel in long-distance flying, the sending of an expeditionary force and transports, the problem of raw materials and foreign exchange, the plans for the forthcoming Nuremberg rally, and the need to discuss with Hitler the use of the rally for propaganda about Germany's problems in obtaining raw materials. If all these issues were interrelated on the afternoon of 30 July, there is little reason to doubt that they were equally related in the late evening of 25 July.[114]

There is later evidence in 1936 that Hitler wished to keep the attention of the Western powers focussed elsewhere; that was, as will be shown, a motive for German action in continuing a policy of limited aid to Franco during a lengthy struggle. There is nothing to suggest this as an original motive, since the whole concept of transporting Franco's army across the Straits into Spain was designed to bring a quick victory. If that came as expected, then it was hoped Franco would remember where his help had come from. The fact that German aid was from the first—even before the establishment of formal nonintervention machinery—placed in the hands of special and partially camouflaged organizations suggests that Hitler had given himself an out in case the whole enterprise should fail. Certainly a government on the other side of France that was friendly to Germany would be of advantage to Hitler's plans. Common action with Mussolini's Italy would bring Italy and Germany closer together, but there is no evidence that this was apparent when Hitler first acted. It was clear that the Spanish rebels would fail if they could not move their army, and Hitler decided to help them do so.[115]

It has often been said—and correctly—that Hitler postponed decisions; he certainly did not do so in this case. The military dependence of Franco would provide a lever for German influence in Spain, but it should not be thought that the Spanish leader was in any way prepared to become a conscious tool of foreign powers. Perhaps precisely because he knew how much he needed the assistance of Hitler and Mussolini, Franco was as sensitive and prickly as any Spaniard in upholding his own honor and dignity. Hitler and Mussolini would find Franco as difficult as Winston Churchill and Franklin Roosevelt later found Charles de Gaulle; in the same years that Churchill was to complain about having to bear the Cross of Lorraine, Hitler might have voiced similar sentiments about the Yoke and Arrows of Franco's Spain.

114. Additional indirect confirmation can be seen in the fact that Rowak, the firm set up to handle deliveries to and from Franco from the German end, was entrusted later in 1936 and in 1937 by Göring with assignments designed to lead to raw materials imports from Norway, Bulgaria, Chile, and Peru (see *Rowak Report*, passim), and in 1938 was being assigned similar responsibilities in North China, Iran, Afghanistan, and Portugal (Reichsfinanzministerium, Abt. I, to Abt. V, Wi 3735–405 I geh. of 27 July 1938, Bundesarchiv, RFM, R 2/22, f. 75).

115. I disregard the postwar comments of Joachim von Ribbentrop on this subject as not sufficiently reliable to be of use.

Not only would the requested planes be sent from Germany but contingents of German forces as well. In Berlin, a special staff under air force General Helmuth Wilberg was created in the Ministry of War, where it started to function formally on 1 August 1936, although it was already operating on 26 July, the day after Hitler's decision.[116] Simultaneously Franco and Bernhardt established an agency to handle the Spanish end of the special relationship between Germany and the insurgents. This organization, of which Bernhardt was the sole director, was called Hisma for short (Compañia Hispano-Marroqui de Trasportes), served as cover for the transportation of Franco's troops, handled German supplies in Spain, arranged the repayments Franco would make, and became the major agent for German penetration of the Spanish economy.[117] Under the auspices of Hisma, the Germans were ferrying Franco's troops by 28 July. The first installment of the German expeditionary corps left Hamburg on the night of 31 July-1 August under Major Alexander von Scheele and began operations in Spain a week later. Other air force units soon followed. Their dispatch, the subsequent sending of armored units, and the provision of military supplies to Franco's own forces were to lead to the creation of a German trading company to parallel Hisma. This organization, called Rowak (Rohstoffe- und Waren-Einkaufsgesellschaft), was also directed by Bernhardt in accordance with Göring's orders. Bernhardt thus controlled both ends of the economic transactions, drew munificent sums for himself, and bribed his way through the Spanish economy.[118] With the special staff of Wilberg and Rowak in Germany and the military headquarters under Scheele and Hisma in Spain, the institutional framework for German support of Franco had been created in a few days. It soon became apparent that Franco's victory would take far longer.

The transport of Franco's army by German and Italian planes made it possible for the insurgents to join their Moroccan holdings to the area in northwest Spain that had fallen under the control of General Mola upon the capture of Badajoz on 14 August, thus enabling the rebels to organize and maintain a position against the republic. But in the very days that the first German aid was being given, it became increasingly evident that the strength of the republic was vastly greater than its opponents had antici-

116. The financial accounts of Sonderstab Wilberg always refer to 1 August 1936 as the beginning date; see Bundesarchiv, RFM, R 2/19, passim.; Merkes, p. 28. General Schweickhard replaced Wilberg in 1938; the earliest document on which the author has seen his name is dated 28 April (R 2/21, f. 219).

117. A good summary of its history to 1940 is the report of the German Ministry of Economics, "Entstehung, Entwicklung, und gegenwärtiger Stand des Rowak/Sofindus Konzerns," 15 March 1940, T–71, roll 32, frames 426049–70. Sofindus (Sociedad Financiera Industrial Ltda.) was a holding company established by Hisma for its Spanish subsidiary interests.

118. See Herbert Feis, *The Spanish Story* (New York: Knopf, 1948), pp. 280–82; *Rowak Report,* pp. 23 and 27, R 2/27, f. 85 and 89; Deutsche Revisions- und Treuhandaktiengesellschaft to Ministry of Finance, "Betrifft Rowak," 2 June 1938, p. 13, Bundesarchiv, RFM, R 2/27, f. 113.

pated. Though this was not immediately recognized in Germany, the Nationalists, as they came to be called, had in fact been losing ground while German help was being organized.[119] Additional German and Italian support would be needed if Franco were to win what in August and September of 1936 looked increasingly like a civil war rather than a quick coup.

During August and September German supplies and personnel were sent to Spain in small but still significant quantities. This was in pursuit of Hitler's original decision, reaffirmed on 24 August.[120] By then General Wilberg had conferred with Franco, and a special German military representative was now appointed in the person of Lieutenant Colonel Walter Warlimont.[121] Warlimont joined Admiral Canaris on his second trip to Rome to coordinate German and Italian aid policies before continuing on to Spain. Just before Canaris and Warlimont left for Rome, Hitler sent a secret emissary to Mussolini, Prince Phillip of Hessen, instead of von Neurath, who did not wish to attract attention to Germany's policy. The prince—whose marriage into the Italian royal family made his trip seem natural—was to become Hitler's emissary to Rome on a number of occasions; this time he was to assure Italy of Germany's intentions in Spain, preclude German-Italian rivalry there, and suggest that both powers be represented to General Franco by special liaison officers. Mussolini immediately agreed to the German suggestions.[122] The close contacts between Germany and Italy on this matter were to become an increasingly important facet of the diplomacy of the period; suffice it to say that at no time since 1933 had the two worked together so harmoniously.[123]

In Spain Warlimont conferred with Franco and other leaders while the German commitment slowly increased. There were the usual frictions between the Germans in Spain and between German and Spanish officials; but these problems had no influence on policy formulation.[124] The series of decisions about Spain that Berlin had to make in the last four months of 1936 grew not out of such squabbles but out of diplomatic repercussions and

119. The German chargé in Madrid reported on 23 and 25 July on the trend against the insurgents, but nothing suggests that this was known to Hitler when he made his decision (*G. D.*, D, 3, Nos. 4, 11).

120. Merkes, p. 30; Einhorn, pp. 90–93. On the aid to Franco at this time by the German navy see *G. D.*, D, 3, No. 27; *D. D. F.*, 2d, 3, No. 84; and the report by Admiral Carls on the activities of the German naval detachment in Spanish waters in July and August 1936 in the Deutsche Zentralarchiv Potsdam, cited by Einhorn, e.g., on pp. 91 and 119.

121. For this and other evidence of Warlimont subsequently cited see the statements of Warlimont, 17 September 1945, to Harold Deutsch, in National Archives, DeWitt C. Poole Mission materials.

122. Von Neurath to Dieckhoff, 24 August 1936, DZA Potsdam, Büro RAM, 60 951, f. 71–72 (this is the full text of the letter from which an excerpt is in *G. D.*, D, 3, No. 55); von Neurath to Dieckhoff, 27 August 1936, DZA Potsdam, 60 951, f. 74.

123. See Merkes, pp. 30–32; *D. D. F.*, 2d, 3, Nos. 81, 179.

124. Thus other firms tried unsuccessfully to break Bernhardt's monopoly; this appears to me to be the main thrust of the lengthy report by Willy Messerschmidt in *G. D.*, D, 3, No. 80.

military developments of the conflict. These decisions, in the order in which the occasion for them arose, may be listed as, first, the response to the Franco-British proposal for a nonintervention agreement; second, the problem of further military commitment to Spain; third, the timing of recognition of the Franco regime; and fourth, the level of German commitment as it became clear that without major deployment of German and Italian troops in Spain the triumph of Franco would be long delayed.

The proposal of France and Britain of an international policy of nonintervention in the civil war was designed to keep that war from spreading to the rest of Europe and to minimize its impact on their own domestic situation, a motive especially strong in bitterly divided France. In view of the weakening Italy had suffered as a result of its military investment in the Ethiopian venture and the unready state of Germany, this policy in reality warded off nonexistent dangers at the expense of the legal government of Spain, but this miscalculation was not readily apparent to the British and French at the time. The British, who were most insistent on this policy, were no doubt influenced by their own experiences with Spain which suggested that a victory for the insurgents would in fact not be likely to lead to the domination of Spain by foreign powers; but the unwillingness of the democratic states to assist the Spanish republic was to make that republic increasingly dependent on Russian assistance, which in turn provided a further argument against support by the Western powers for their potential friends on the peninsula.[125] During negotiations, both the Germans and Italians delayed in order to make sure that their first assistance reached Franco. Germany eventually agreed to the nonintervention agreement on 24 August 1936, the same day that Hitler decided to send further military aid to Spain.

A nonintervention committee was established in London in September 1936, and Germany was to play its role in that melancholy farce until 1939. In view of the large number of Italian soldiers in Spain and in order to keep friction with England within tolerable limits, the Germans generally allowed Italy to take the lead on the committee's stage. In the wings, Germany went forward in disregard of whatever platitudes were currently being recited to an increasingly skeptical world audience. But the role of the committee cannot be dismissed entirely. It provided a face-saving device for France and England. It also helped to convince von Ribbentrop and Hitler that they could disregard British and French susceptibilities as long as those two countries were not themselves the object of attack—and by the time Germany was ready for that, they would hardly be in a position to defend themselves effectively.[126]

125. As Mussolini told Göring on his visit to Rome in January 1937: "The English Conservatives have a great fear of Bolshevism, and this fear could easily be exploited politically. This task would fall principally on Germany, since it is rather difficult for Italy to convince the English Conservatives in view of events in the Mediterranean" (Ciano, *Diplomatic Papers,* p. 87; German text in DZA Potsdam, 60 951, f. 88).

126. There is no study of the nonintervention committee as such, but extensive

A second substantive question for Germany in the fall of 1936 was whether it should make further military contributions to the insurgents for control of Spain against a government that was receiving public support in many parts of the world and was beginning to obtain some aid from France and, as yet indirectly, from the Soviet Union.[127] Germany's most important and spectacular aid to Franco in the fall of 1936 was the Condor Legion, a special air force that became the major instrument of tactical air support for the Nationalists during the civil war. There is at this time no available evidence as to when the decision to send this force was made and how that decision was arrived at. The first commander of the legion, General Hugo Sperrle, went to Spain by way of Rome on 31 October accompanied by the Prince of Hessen and carrying general instructions for the new program dated 30 October.[128] The legion itself became operational early in November, absorbing the air force units sent earlier.[129]

The decision to send the Legion, a force consisting of four to five thousand men, with planes, antiaircraft guns, and related equipment, was presumably taken sometime during October. When the Italian foreign minister Galeazzo Ciano, met first with von Neurath and later with Hitler on 21 October and 24 October, additional military effort in Spain on the part of both countries was mentioned. It is not certain whether the decision to send the legion had been taken just before or followed after, perhaps as a result of these talks.[130] The text of the general directive for the legion's commander

discussion of it may be found in the works of Thomas, Merkes, and Puzzo, the memoirs of Anthony Eden, and the books of David I. Catell, *Soviet Diplomacy and the Spanish Civil War* (Berkeley: University of California Press, 1957), and P. A. M. van der Esch, *Prelude to War, The International Repercussions of the Spanish Civil War* (The Hague: Mouton, 1951). Important additional information on the policy of France may be found in *D. D. F.*, 2d, 3, and in David W. Pike, *Conjecture, Propaganda, and Deceit and the Spanish Civil War, The International Crisis over Spain, 1936–1939, as seen in the French Press* (Stanford: Institute of International Studies, 1968). The parallel policy of the United States is covered by F. Jay Taylor, *The United States and the Spanish Civil War, 1936–1939* (New York: Bookman, 1956), and Richard P. Traina, *American Diplomacy and the Spanish Civil War* (Bloomington: Indiana University Press, 1968).

127. On aid from the Soviet Union, see the works of Thomas and Catell as well as Armstrong, *Politics of Totalitarianism*, pp. 38–45.

128. *G. D.*, D, 3, No. 113. Merkes (p. 33) has reversed the chronology. He suggests that the Condor Legion was sent in response to Soviet aid to the republic, especially the international brigades which he himself states first appeared in the fighting on 8 November. The instructions of 30 October in fact refer to possible future rather than past assistance by Russia. A British assessment of German, Italian, and Soviet aid in Foreign Office W 16391/9549/41.

129. The financial accounts use 7 November 1936, as the beginning date. In an interrogation of 18 October 1945, now in the National Archives, Sperrle gave 1 November 1936 as the beginning date for the Condor Legion; that may refer to the day on which he arrived in Spain from Rome and assumed command of the German air force units in the area. On the composition and activity of the legion see Karl-Heinz Völker, *Die Deutsche Luftwaffe 1933–1939* (Stuttgart: Deutsche Verlags-Anstalt, 1967), pp. 149–54; Merkes, pp. 33–36.

130. Ciano's account of these talks is in his *Diplomatic Papers*, pp. 52–60; the German record is in *G. D.*, C, 5, No. 618.

stresses the need to speed up operations in Spain in order to bring about the prompt capture of Madrid, which in turn would justify diplomatic recognition of Franco by Germany and Italy and thus pave the way for the tendering of greater aid. This suggests that dissatisfaction with the slow progress of operations was an important factor in Hitler's decision to dispatch the legion to Spain. The close connection of this problem with that of diplomatic recognition raises the third of the policy questions that Berlin faced in its handling of developments in Spain.

The issue of which group, Loyalists or Insurgents, was to be considered the legal government of Spain was precipitated by the failure of the Insurgents to seize the whole country either in the initial uprising or in the fighting that ensued. In the period of warfare from August 1936 on, the sympathies of Germany were obviously with Franco, but as yet its formal diplomatic relations were with the government of the republic. In view of Germany's preference, recognition of the Franco government, installed in Burgos at the end of September, was largely a matter of timing. To avoid needless provocation of Britain and France, to assure adequate cover for the early shipments of aid to Franco, to secure information from the Republican side, and to protect the large number of Germans still living in the area controlled by the government in Madrid, the Germans continued official relations with that government for some time. During that period, the only activities of the German diplomatic service, beyond those implied in the reasons for maintaining relations, were to handle various incidents mainly resulting from German intervention and to make trouble for Spanish diplomats in Germany.[131]

As Franco's African legions approached Madrid during October, the Berlin government first decided to extend recognition to Franco when he took the capital, and they coordinated this policy with Rome.[132] When the Insurgents were held at bay by Madrid's defenders, Hitler changed his mind. Again there is no direct evidence to explain Hitler's reasons. Hitherto the Germans had tried to use the promise of diplomatic recognition as an incentive for Franco in the hope of speeding up the tempo of his campaign—not for the last time to be a major concern in Berlin and Rome. As Franco's offensive became stalled in street fighting in the capital, however, this may have seemed an increasingly pointless condition. Awareness of the fact that in any case the struggle in Spain would go on for a long time may well have impelled Hitler to make his formal commitment. It was announced on 18 November, with Germany and Italy acting at the same time.[133] The prestige of the two dictators was now tied to Franco's fate; they could hardly afford

131. Merkes, pp. 45–47.

132. *G. D.*, D, 3, Nos. 95, 109; and the sources cited in n. 130, above.

133. Merkes, pp. 47–67. Merkes argues that Berlin and Rome acted out of excessively optimistic assessments of the situation in Spain. I believe he has missed the evidence which shows the two powers aware of the slow progress of the Insurgents. Furthermore, Hitler's December decision on troop shipments, reviewed below, certainly reveals him speculating on a long conflict on the Iberian peninsula.

to see him lose; they would soon face the question of whether they wished merely to prevent such an eventuality or whether they would move beyond that goal to help him win quickly and decisively.

The fighting in Spain in November and early December 1936 showed the strength but also the weakness of the two sides. With Germany and Italy providing air support, and later armored support as well, the trained Army of Africa could make substantial progress against the militia of the Republic. As the forces of the Republic gained experience and discipline and as arms purchased in France and Russia arrived, the pace of Franco's progress was slowed. Furthermore, the casualties among his experienced soldiers could not be replaced readily from the part of Spain he occupied in view of the antipathy of the local population. The addition of small but effective international brigades to the Republican side in the struggle for the capital helped to bring the Insurgents' offensive to a halt. As it became clear that the Republic would hold Madrid and the Nationalists faced a continuing struggle, morale in the Franco camp began to sag and the spirits of the Loyalists rose. Under these circumstances, Germany and Italy were confronted with the question of what to do. They could hardly let Franco fail without great loss of prestige as well as the loss of all they had invested. If they provided a great deal of assistance to Franco, they could help him win quickly but at great cost to themselves and at the risk of major international complications. The third possibility was to provide Franco with enough help to carry on but not enough to finish the war quickly.

Under these conditions, the Italian government decided to send large contingents of Italian soldiers, after first assuring themselves of future political collaboration by a secret agreement dated 28 November 1936.[134] Although Admiral Canaris as representative of the German Minister of War informed a special Italian conference on 6 December that it was most unlikely that Germany would send regular units of the German army to Spain, Mussolini decided to send Italian soldiers by the thousands.[135] He felt committed and believed the outcome of the struggle in Spain of great importance for Italy's future.

Similar action had been urged on the German government by General Wilhelm Faupel, the new German representative to Franco. Faupel, who spoke fluent Spanish as the result of his work with the Argentinian and Peruvian armies after his service in World War I, had been charged by Hitler to represent German interests in Nationalist Spain. A strong sympathizer with national socialism, he had directed the Ibero-American Institute in Berlin and had had close ties with the party's foreign organization before going to Spain.[136] There he quickly recognized the military inadequa-

134. Text in *G. D.*, D, 3, No. 137; and *Documents secrèts de la 2e guerre mondiale, La politique allemande en Espagne (1936–1943)* (Paris, 1946), No. 1.

135. *G. D.*, D, 3, Nos. 133, 136, 139, 151, 156. The reference by Mussolini to von Blomberg's views in the last of the documents cited must be based on statements by Canaris on 6 December. Von Blomberg had seen Hitler on 3 December (*TMWC*, 32:335).

136. Merkes, pp. 68–69; Einhorn, pp. 125–30; Jacobsen, p. 474.

cies of the Insurgent forces and suggested on 4 December that a German division and an Italian division be sent to Spain, that German officers train a portion of Franco's army, and that the resulting force make a concerted push to break the front of the Republic. It was his view that unless this were done the war would drag on and the Insurgents might lose.[137] Although the evidence is not quite conclusive, it would appear that Franco himself expressed similar views.[138]

The reaction in the German foreign ministry to these calls for help was extremely negative. There the officials had been opposed to German intervention in Spain from the beginning. They were now faced with the problem of warding off a British-French effort to initiate a multilateral approach to mediation in the Spanish civil war.[139] At the same time, the special treaty Franco had signed with Italy provided an excellent excuse for allowing Italy to play a leading role in the whole dangerous enterprise.[140] Furthermore, the well-known xenophobia of the Spaniards was certain to hurt any power intervening in Spain on such a scale, while the perils of complications with France and Britain looked enormous.[141] In the face of this situation, Faupel returned to Germany to argue the issue in person.[142]

A conference was held in the chancellery in Berlin on 21 December. Present were Hitler, Göring, von Blomberg, von Fritsch, the commander in chief of the German army, Hossbach, the chief representative of the military to Hitler, General Faupel, and Colonel Warlimont, who had just returned from his tour of duty as German military representative at Franco's headquarters.[143] Von Neurath was either present at this meeting or had a separate

137. *G. D.*, D, 3, Nos. 144, 148. Cf. the conference of Göring with a number of high-ranking Luftwaffe officers on 2 December 1936 (*TMWC*, 32:334–36).

138. This would seem to have been the thrust of Faupel's telegram 592 of 9 December 1936, which has not turned up (see *G. D.*, D, 3, No. 148, n. 1, and 151, n. 1). Some details of Franco's plea for help and the negative reaction in Berlin leaked out at the time; see Dertinger's "Informationsbericht Nr. 55," 17 December 1936, in Bundesarchiv, Brammer, Z.Sg. 101/29, f. 543–47.

Ronald Strunk, who had earlier reported on the Italo-Ethiopian war for the *Völkische Beobachter* and was now in Spain, appears to have had views similar to those of Faupel and may have supported his pleas in Berlin; see the reports of the U. S. consul at Seville on Strunk's statements reported in telegrams of 29 November and 11 December 1936, U. S. 1936, 2: 582–83, 611.

139. On Germany's unwillingness to participate in mediation see *G. D.*, D, 3, Nos. 146, 147, 152.

140. Ibid., No. 142.

141. Ibid., Nos. 145, 155. Cf. also the first sentence of ibid., No. 169.

142. The precise dates of Faupel's stay in Germany are not known. Hassell's telegram of 17 December refers to the possibility of Faupel's stopping in Rome on his return trip to Spain (ibid., No. 156). Faupel had written from Spain on 10 December (No. 148) and was back by 30 December (No. 172). Merkes does not mention Faupel's trip. See also Phipps telegram 442–Saving, 19 December 1936, Foreign Office W 18547/62/41.

143. The main source for this conference is Warlimont's statement cited in n. 121, above. He has alluded briefly to the meeting in his published memoirs, *Im Hauptquartier der deutschen Wehrmacht 1939–1945* (Bonn: Athenäum, 1964), p. 26. Hossbach refers to it in his memoirs, *Zwischen Wehrmacht und Hitler*, p. 42. The allusion in the memoirs of Ernst von Weizsäcker, *Erinnerungen* (Munich: Paul List, 1950),

session with Hitler about the same time.[144] By then Faupel had decided to ask for three German divisions, not one. Von Blomberg strongly opposed sending them, as did von Fritsch, Hossbach, and Warlimont. It is not certain what Göring's views were, though apparently he too objected.[145] The arguments were obvious: the great risks of war with the Western powers, problems of supply, interference with the progress of Germany's own rearmament program. Either at the same or another meeting, von Neurath urged the arguments of the foreign ministry. Hitler may have made up his mind earlier;[146] he now formally decided against sending German troops on a large scale. He stated that he was interested in focussing European attention on Spain for a long time, not a quick victory for Franco, especially if it endangered Germany's own rearmament program. Continuation of the civil war would divert attention from Germany. To make sure Franco was not defeated, the Germans would send additional help; and preparations were to be made to increase that aid if disaster threatened the Nationalist cause. But Faupel would have to return to Spain without the promise of German divisions. The bigger costs, especially in troops, the Germans would gladly leave to Italy.

The Germans themselves would draw from the bloody turmoil in Spain three enormous advantages—important raw materials for themselves,[147] the immobilization of the Western powers during their preoccupation with Spanish problems, and the inability of Italy to return to cooperation with those powers while intervening heavily in the civil war. That war would thereby continue the process begun by the Italian war against Ethiopia. The more deeply Italy was committed, the closer it would become to Germany. The longer the civil war lasted, the more difficult it would be for Italy to leave the German orbit again.[148]

Germany would help to keep Franco from losing, but if his victory were long-postponed that would help rather than hurt the Third Reich. Almost a

---

pp. 129–30, is based on discussions by Faupel with the foreign ministry. The statement made to the U. S. military attaché in Berlin at the Ministry of War on 14 December (U. S. 1936, 2:612) is important confirmatory evidence on the views held there. See also Dodd, *Diary,* 25 December 1936, p. 374; Pike, p. 79.

144. See the letter of von Neurath to von Hassell of 22 December 1936, DZA Potsdam, 60 964, f. 41.

145. Warlimont asserts that Göring opposed, Weizsäcker that he favored the dispatch of troops. Since Warlimont was present and Weizsäcker almost certainly was not, Warlimont is more likely to be correct.

146. See above, n. 135. The indirect evidence on the Hitler-Blomberg meeting of 3 December 1936, suggests that at that time Hitler was disinclined to send further troops.

147. On the earliest shipments see Einhorn, pp. 117–19.

148. Von Hassell had made this argument in a detailed report of 18 December which reached Berlin on 19 December (*G. D.,* D, 3, No. 157). He had asked von Neurath to show this report to Hitler (letter of 18 December, DZA Potsdam, 60 964, f. 40), and von Neurath on 22 December wrote him that he had done so (DZA Potsdam, 60964, f. 41).

A fine summary of the policy of Mussolini in 1936 and its implications for Italy's relations with the Western powers and with Germany is in Ferdinand Siebert, *Italiens Weg in den Zweiten Weltkrieg* (Bonn: Athenäum, 1962), pp. 48–53.

year after the meeting on 21 December 1936, Hitler was to repeat his views as to the advantages for Germany of a lengthy conflict in Spain at the notorious conference on 5 November 1937 recorded in the Hossbach Memorandum.[149] German policy toward the Spanish civil war had stabilized in accordance with that view by the end of 1936 and was to remain essentially unchanged until the war burned itself out in 1939. The implementation of that policy cannot be examined here; its foundations had been laid by the decisions of the last months of 1936.

The process of decision-making in the case of Spain shows two simultaneous transitions in the development of German foreign policy between 1933 and 1939. As German strength increased, Hitler was more willing to become involved in adventures beyond the borders of the Reich. For the first time since the disastrous course of events in Austria in 1934, German prestige was committed to a cause in another country. Surely the Rhineland triumph bolstered Hitler's confidence in this regard. Yet, in the very process of foreign adventure, Hitler was still mindful of the handicaps under which Germany labored. The inadequacy of its armaments and raw materials still suggested caution; Spanish ores might help with both, but the risks and costs had to be kept within limits.

The other shift clearly evident in Germany's Spanish adventure is the eclipse of the foreign ministry. For Hitler, that ministry was not the control agency for the management of Germany's foreign affairs—he would perform that role himself—but merely one possible instrument to be used or not as the exigencies of the moment suggested. The foreign organization of the party, the chief of military intelligence, the air ministry—any one of them could serve as an instrument when the occasion suited. If using all of them at the same time led to squabbles between them, that was no substantial problem if Hitler's policy was served. In that policy and its implementation, the interaction between short-term opportunism and long-term consistency comes out clearly. No one should underestimate the shrewdness with which Hitler seized on the opportunity that Franco's uprising provided and with which he limited German involvement to maximize the advantages and minimize the risks of intervention.

149. Since Merkes does not understand the general line of German policy in this matter, he asserts (pp. 127–28) that those who accept the statement in the Hossbach memorandum have been misled; in fact it is Merkes who has misled himself as has already been pointed out by Detwiler (pp. 141–42, n. 31).

12 The Consolidation of Germany's Position in Central and Eastern Europe in 1936

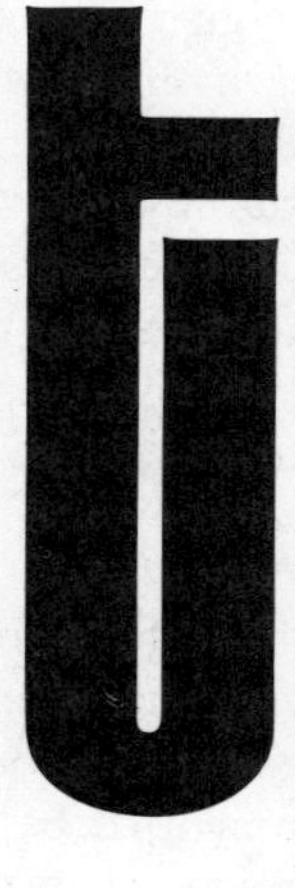

he general shift in the world situation that took place in 1936 due to Germany's spectacular success in the Rhineland influenced its relationship with most countries. The reverberations of the new situation could be felt in the smallest country and the furthest part of the globe. An examination of Germany's relations with a number of countries both inside and outside Europe will show how the common theme of recognition of Germany's actual or at least potential predominance in Europe transcends the peculiar circumstances growing out of the specific issues of each relationship. In every case, the issues remain, but—like the colored pieces of a kaleidoscope—once severely disturbed, they fall into an entirely new pattern even though it contains the same pieces that were there earlier.

Perhaps because the trend toward a rapprochement with Germany was already under way early in 1936, this is especially obvious in the case of Lithuania. In his speech of 21 May 1935 Hitler had expressly excluded Lithuania from the countries with which Germany would sign a nonaggression pact, and he had repeated his strictures at the gathering of the Reichstag in Nuremberg on 15 September of that year.[1] This vehement antagonism was ostensibly based on the interference of Lithuania in the rights of the Memel Germans assured them by the Memel Statute.[2] It is interesting how concerned Hitler became about democratic procedures in countries other than Germany; the "benefits" of ending democracy were obviously to be reserved to the inhabitants of the Reich. Hitler did not appreciate the irony in his denouncing the Lithuanian government for allegedly

1. Texts in *G. D.*, C, 4:171–72 and 632–33; Domarus, 1:510–11, 536.
2. See above, pp. 82–85.

mistreating Germans just because they were Germans at the same session of the Reichstag which passed the infamous Nuremberg laws against German Jews because they were Jews.

The actions of the Lithuanian government, culminating in the prosecution of many Memel Germans in the Kovno trial of 1934–35, had aroused objections both inside and outside Germany at the severity of the sentences imposed on those convicted at the end of March 1935. In the spring and summer of 1935, as the Germans maintained economic pressures against Lithuania, the signatory powers of the Memel Statute repeatedly intervened with the Lithuanian government to urge a more concilatory course.[3] The British consistently took the lead in these representations, which eventually bore fruit in a relatively free election held in the Memel area in September. A united front of the German parties won an overwhelming victory in these elections; and, under further pressure, primarily from the British, the Lithuanian government entrusted the direction of local affairs to the United German front.[4]

British attempts to promote a German-Lithuanian rapprochement in the winter of 1935–36 were not so successful to begin with.[5] Two factors—one acting on the Germans and the other on the Lithuanians—were to bring the two together. The Germans were increasingly concerned about the impact of the economic measures they were using against Lithuania. These measures, in practice, bore most heavily on the Memel Germans, while the Lithuanian government was finding new trade partners to offset the impact of Germany's steps on the rest of the economy.[6] The Lithuanian government, for its part, was obviously impressed by Germany's great success in the Rhineland. In his speech of 7 March 1936, Hitler acknowledged the political concession Lithuania had made in the September election and the

3. *G. D.*, C, 4, Nos. 13, 39, 42, 62; U. S. 1935, 1:249–54. The pressures on the Lithuanian government, especially by the British, can be followed in the reports by the U. S. chargé a.i. in Kovno (Kaunas), C. Porter Kuykendall: dispatches 199 of 18 March 1935 (State 860 M.01-Memel/346), 221 of 23 April (ibid., /361), 230 of 29 April (ibid., /368), 235 of 6 May (ibid., /369), 267 of 25 June (ibid., /387), 276 of 12 July (ibid., /390), and 283 of 24 July (State 760M.62/108).

4. *G. D.*, C, 4, Nos. 239, 255, 300, 305, 345, 356; Plieg, chap. X; Gentzen, pp. 88–90; Memorandum of von Neurath RM 710, 23 September 1935, T–120, 1468/3015/D 597747; Kuykendall dispatches 335 of 17 October 1935 (State 860 M.01-Memel/434), 343 of 24 October (State 760M.62/113), 365 of 18 November (State 860 M.01-Memel/446), 370 of 22 November (ibid., /447), 373 of 29 November (ibid., /448), and enclosure 6 to dispatch 380 of 5 December (ibid., /450).

5. *G. D.*, C, 4, Nos. 377, 378, 422, 456 (on the meeting mentioned in this document see also Kuykendall dispatch 435 of 24 February 1936, State 860 M.01/462); Dodd dispatch 2470, 15 November 1935, State 860 M.01-Memel/443; Kuykendall dispatches 385 of 12 December 1935 (ibid., /451), 392 of 28 December 1935 (ibid., /452), 402 of 3 January 1936 (ibid., /455), and 424 of 4 February 1936 (State 760M.62/118).

6. *G. D.*, C, 4, Nos. 495, 548, 549, 554, 578; Gentzen, pp. 81–82; Memorandum of Grundherr IV Ba 367/36, 21 January 1936, T–120, 3611/9798/E 687675–677; Memorandum of Roediger, 31 January 1936, T–120, 3070/6606/E 496493–494; Memorandum of von Neurath RM 93, 7 February 1936, T–120, 2383/4619/E 198244.

formation of the local Memel government by dropping his previously voiced objections to treaties with Lithuania.[7] In the following months, the Lithuanians reluctantly came to agree to a new economic treaty with Germany that could be used to benefit the Memel Germans.[8] The differences between Germany and Lithuania were by no means settled definitively, but the uneasy truce of 1936 surely reflected the stronger international position of Germany as compared with the preceding years. Furthermore, the Germans, in the future, could expect more support on the Memel question from Italy, the one signatory power that had been most unwilling to insist on Lithuania's observance of the Memel Statute.[9] When Ciano was in Berlin in October 1936, von Neurath reminded him of the fact that "Italy's attitude has so far been far from friendly toward us" and secured Ciano's promise that Italy would mend its ways in this regard.[10]

As for Germany's long-run aims in regard to Memel, they were best served by the maintenance of an uneasy status quo; Germany, in Hitler's eyes, was not yet ready for the international repercussions of the forcible seizure of Memel. But he did not want the future possibility of such a seizure deprived of its excuse by a truly effective international guarantee of the rights of the Memel Germans.[11] Such a guarantee, Hitler feared, would probably be implemented by the appointment of an international commissioner who would see to it that the Memel Germans were accorded in real life the rights guaranteed them by international agreement. Such an arrangement was the last thing Germany wanted. In fact, in Danzig, another area Germany had lost after World War I, Berlin was trying very hard to have the international commissioner removed precisely because his protection of the rights of the Danzig Germans was too effective.

The problem of Danzig was to dominate German-Polish relations in 1936 as the Germans worked, eventually successfully, to demolish the League of Nations' guarantee of the constitutional rights of the Germans in the free city; but before the course of that campaign is traced, a word must be said about other issues affecting German relations with Poland.

The long-standing feud over the transfer into foreign exchange of the German payments to Poland for railway transportation across the corridor had apparently been settled by the agreement of 7 April 1936.[12] That settlement had been reached through the personal intervention of Hitler and

7. The reference to Lithuania and the possibility of a German-Lithuanian nonaggression pact—subject to rather elastic conditions—was included as part 6 of the German proposals read by Hitler to the Reichstag and delivered to the Locarno powers.

8. The negotiations and their difficulties may be followed in *G. D.*, C, 5, Nos. 329, 441, 512; U. S. 1936, 1:266; Kuykendall dispatch 460, 6 April 1936, State 760 M.62/120.

9. *G. D.*, C, 4, Nos. 306, 308. The reluctance of Italy to pressure Lithuania on the Memel issue was probably not unrelated to Italy's own policies in the Tirol area.

10. *G. D.*, C, 5, No. 622.

11. Hitler's views as expressed to the German consul general in Memel on 23 October 1935 are recorded in the latter's memorandum of that date (ibid., 4, No. 378).

12. See above, pp. 186, 248.

Göring at a time when the Rhineland crisis made concessions to Poland appear desirable in the broader context of European affairs. As difficulties arose in the implementation of the new payments system, the Germans became less accommodating; as Hermann Göring expressed it in late May, "It is, however, no longer so necessary as it seemed to be a few weeks ago, on account of considerations of foreign policy, to meet the Polish desires to so great an extent."[13] The remaining financial problems of the transit traffic were eventually settled by agreement on 31 August 1936; and by that time the other major economic issue between Germany and Poland, the fate of the industrial complex in Polish Upper Silesia known as I. G. Kattowitz/Laura, had also been settled. The bargaining had been hard, but these running sores in German-Polish relations were finally treated.[14]

More important than these questions were the general problems of the relationship between Germany and Poland in a Europe transformed by the remilitarization of the Rhineland. The refusal of France to move in the face of this German step had been expected by the Polish foreign minister, Beck, but not by some of Poland's military leaders. Poland now followed a carefully balanced policy. While willing to work with Germany to prevent the creation of a new security system including the Soviet Union and while also endeavoring to avoid having to side against Germany in the negotiations for a new Locarno, the Warsaw government simultaneously wanted reassurances from France that its alliance with that country was still effective. In addition, the weakening of any French assistance because of the remilitarized Rhineland suggested the need for greater Polish military strength. Beyond formal reassurances from France, therefore, Poland wanted French financial aid. Both the formal assurances and funds were forthcoming from Paris; the summer of 1936 saw France and Poland drawing closer together and exchanging visits of their leading military figures. Most of the concessions, however, were made by France: Poland would neither draw closer to Czechoslovakia nor abandon its policy of cautious friendship with Germany.[15] In fact, in order to reassure Germany that Poland was not drifting into the hostile camp, the Polish undersecretary for foreign affairs, Jean Szembek, was sent on a special mission to Berlin in August 1936. By that time, the Danzig problem had entered a new stage as a result of German moves.

In mid-June 1936, Hitler decided to reopen the Danzig question. The precise timing, causes, and purposes of this decision are shrouded in se-

13. *G. D.*, C, 5, No. 356.

14. Ibid., No. 491, p. 942. For restraints on the German press in this regard see "Bestellungen aus der Pressekonferenz vom 4. April 1936," Bundesarchiv, Brammer, Z.Sg. 101/7, f. 243.

15. Roos, pp. 237–73. In addition to the sources cited there, see *G. D.*, C, 5, Nos. 139, 173, 245, 293, 308, 332, 518; *D. D. F.*, 2d, 1, Nos. 445, 455, 487, 488, 497; 2, Nos. 35, 118, 215, 170, 349, 364; 3, Nos. 153, 158, 169, 259, 271, 275, 301, 308, 326, 451; U. S. 1936, 1:356–57; Smutný (Czech chargé a.i. Warsaw) report 69, 22 August 1936, Czech document in T–120, 1040/1809/413347–349 (changed excerpts in *Prager Akten*, No. 71); *Lukasiewicz Papers*, pp. 7–8, 12–21.

crecy,[16] and scholars who have worked on this subject have turned up little new evidence. With or without Hitler's prior authorization, in early June 1936 the National Socialists in Danzig under the leadership of Gauleiter Albert Forster stepped up dramatically their campaign against the surviving opposition parties in the free city. Since the failure of the National Socialists to gain a two-thirds vote in the elections precluded legal steps against opponents under an enabling law, terror and propaganda were the instruments of Forster's policy.[17] The president of the Danzig Senate, Arthur Greiser, was both Forster's rival in Danzig and uncertain about the policy Hitler wanted followed. He had written Sean Lester, the League high commissioner, on 3 June congratulating him on the extension of his term and expressing Greiser's "especial pleasure at the appointment."[18] As late as 16 June, as the incidents in Danzig increased, Greiser tried to secure a letter from Lester to use in Berlin in an effort to have Forster either removed or at least curbed.[19] This effort to calm the situation, though for the moment supported by the German foreign ministry and Göring, was soon reversed.

When Forster saw Hitler on 19 June he not only must have received approval of his course, but, in view of what followed, Hitler either reaffirmed or newly approved a policy of further provocation in Danzig.[20] Perhaps the League's recent humiliation in the Ethiopian case suggested to Hitler that this was a propitious time to move against that hated institution at another point. Perhaps the internal turmoil in France in the first days of the Popular Front government suggested that Poland's reactions to changes in the free city would be restrained by awareness of the weakness of its principal ally. Perhaps Hitler simply acted in response to Forster's urgings, allowing him to make another attempt at the destruction of the opposition parties in Danzig now that the situation that had imposed caution six months earlier had passed. Whatever the reason, Forster was authorized to move ahead in a program calculated to provoke trouble.

The new provocation in Danzig took the form of an intentional slight to the high commissioner by the officers of the visiting German cruiser *Leipzig* together with an inflammatory attack on the high commissioner and the League by Forster, an attack whose text, significantly, was published in Germany before it appeared in Danzig on 27 June.[21] Furthermore, when

16. On the secrecy at the time see the perceptive report by Dertinger, "Informationsbericht Nr. 24," 6 July 1936, Bundesarchiv, Brammer, Z.Sg. 101/29, f. 265–69.

17. Leonhardt, pp. 226–30; *G. D.,* C, 5, Nos. 373, 394; Szembek, 20 June 1936, p. 182. The account in Breyer, pp. 202ff. is quite superficial.

18. Gallman (U. S. consul Danzig) dispatch 258, 7 August 1936, State 860K.00/237. This letter was subsequently quoted by Lester in his 12 September report to the council of the League of Nations (League of Nations, *Official Journal,* November 1936, pp. 1359–62).

19. Gallman dispatch 269, 9 September 1936, State 860K.00/240.

20. *G. D.,* C, 5, No. 373.

21. On the Danzig crisis see ibid., Nos. 417, 419, 429; *D. D. F.*, 2d, 2, Nos. 390–96; 3, Nos. 11, 15.

Lester's complaints were discussed by the League council in Geneva on 4 July, Greiser, who had previously been carefully coached in Berlin, delivered himself of a tirade against Lester, the institution of the high commissioner, and the League and showed his best party manners by thumbing his nose and sticking out his tongue at the journalists reporting the council session. With the League deflated by the setback on Ethiopia, Greiser could be most heroic by contrast with his more subdued appearance the preceding January. He returned in triumph to Danzig by way of Berlin, while the Polish government, as the legal representative of Danzig in international affairs, was asked by the council to settle the dispute over the *Leipzig* incident.

It is abundantly clear from the record that the Germans wanted Lester removed; from Hitler on down, all German officials parroted this demand for months to all diplomats and to the world. Lester's defense of the rights of the Danzig opponents of national socialism in accordance with the League's guarantee of the constitution of the free city stood in the way of complete nazification of the area and was, therefore, to be terminated. There was also some thought of ending the position of the high commissioner, but on that point—as well as the further thought of perhaps annexing Danzig to the Reich—the reaction of Poland would be decisive. Germany would push, but not too far.

Berlin could find out just how far it was safe to push in Danzig by watching the reaction inside Poland and by talking with Beck. Greiser spoke with Beck at Geneva and invited him to speak with Göring on his way back to Warsaw through Germany.[22]

The Polish government had been warned beforehand of both the *Leipzig* incident and the Forster speech, but they were not ready for Greiser's frontal assault on the League's position in Danzig. Both the personal position of Beck as the foreign minister identified with the policy of cooperation with Germany and the basic position of Poland in Danzig were at stake. Beck's policy of working with Germany appeared to have blown up in his face, while the removal of the League from Danzig was bound to threaten Poland's rights in the free city. Unlike the Germans, who did not recognize the advantages of the institution of the high commissioner until the German population had been expelled from Danzig after another war, the Poles saw quite clearly the dangers of a direct confrontation between Germany and Poland in Danzig. They believed that they had no interest in protecting the Germans opposed to national socialism in Danzig, but they were very much concerned about the protection of their own interests; and they thought, probably erroneously, that the two issues could be separated. The leading figure in Poland after Pilsudski's death, General Edward Rydz-Smigly, had expressed the view on 30 June that when Germany was ready for war in two or three years, that war would start over Danzig.[23] In the crisis at Geneva,

22. *G. D.*, C, 5, No. 430.
23. Szembek, 30 June 1936, p. 185.

Beck warned Warsaw to take precautions and cautioned the Germans that Poland would react immediately to any unilateral German step changing the status of the free city.[24]

The clear Polish response was immediately recognized in Berlin; obviously a change in the person, not the institution, of the high commissioner was all that Poland would tolerate. Göring first reassured the Polish ambassador, Lipski, and then Beck on 5 July that nothing would be done to interfere with Polish rights in Danzig and did not push the subject when Beck maintained a reserved view of any institutional alterations.[25] Under these circumstances, the alarm expressed over the crisis by Britain and France only provided German diplomats with opportunities to denounce Lester, while Beck found a quiet way to dispose of the *Leipzig* incident and National Socialists in Danzig were instructed not to interfere with Polish rights.[26] Some tension remained, however, because Polish public opinion had been greatly disturbed, and all of Beck's enemies used the Danzig uproar against him. Just as Greiser had tried to redeem himself for his prior friendship with Lester by taking an extreme position at Geneva,[27] so Beck had to stand firm lest he be accused of allowing his German policy to injure Poland's vital interests at a most sensitive point.[28]

When Szembek visited Germany in August, therefore, he could assure his German hosts of Polish willingness to let changes be made in Danzig as long as Polish interests were not affected. Furthermore, he had been instructed to explain that the exchanges of visits of the leading French and Polish military figures, General Gamelin and General Rydz-Smigly, did not imply that Poland was drawing closer to France or abandoning its policy of working with Germany. In any case, Poland would not help the Czechs. He was to make clear, however, that Poland would protect its own interests in Danzig, as elsewhere, peacefully and in cooperation with Germany if possible, but by fighting if it became necessary. In his conversations with Hitler, von Ribbentrop, Göring, von Neurath, and others in Berlin, Szembek poured forth reassuring comments while declining to pursue hints of possible changes in the status of Danzig or any future replacement for the Upper Silesian Minorities Statute scheduled to expire in 1937.[29] The Germans for

24. *Lipski Papers,* No. 57; Szembek, 5 July 1936, p. 186; cf. *D. D. F.,* 2d, 2, Nos. 396, 410.

25. *G. D.,* C, 5, Nos. 434, 438; *Lipski Papers,* No. 58; Szembek, 6 July 1936, p. 186.

26. *G. D.,* C, 5, Nos. 436, 437, 443, 467; *Lipski Papers,* Nos. 59, 60; *D. D. F.,* 2d, 2, Nos. 401, 413, 427, 430.

27. Cf. Leonhardt, p. 222.

28. *G. D.,* C, 5, Nos. 458, 472, 473, 476; *D. D. F.,* 2d, 3, Nos. 16, 32, 44, 126, 139; Schliep (Warsaw) report PV 17/7–36, 21 July 1936, T–120, 1315/2371/D 495821–823, and "Vermerk Pol V 2151: Unterredung Greiser-Papeé," 27 July, ibid., frames D 495835–837; Slávik (Czech minister Warsaw) report 62, 14 July, Czech document in T–120, 1040/1809/413341–342 (excerpt in *Prager Akten,* No. 68).

29. Szembek's account of his talks is in his *Journal,* pp. 188–203; German accounts in *G. D.,* C, 5, Nos. 506, 513; see also von Papen to Hitler, 21 August 1936, *Guido Schmidt Trial,* p. 407; *D. D. F.,* 2d, 3, No. 159.

their part all reassured him of their lasting devotion to the German-Polish Pact, promised not to interfere with Polish rights in Danzig, and urged the removal of Lester. Though warned by the well-informed Belgian minister in Berlin that the Germans had in no way really given up their territorial claims on Poland, Szembek returned to Warsaw greatly pleased and reassured. Germany in the weeks of the Olympics had been impressive indeed, and the protestations of friendship had sounded sincere, underlined as they were by the calm German reception of the exchange of French and Polish military visits. Szembek, at least, was convinced.[30]

Neither Rydz-Smigly nor Beck, however, were as certain of German sincerity as Szembek. Though as enthused as Szembek by the anti-Soviet and anti-Communist tirades that he recounted having heard in Berlin, the other Polish leaders were suspicious that these were, as Rydz-Smigly put it, merely "a camouflage and pretext for the pursuit of a policy of aggression."[31] Though more perceptive than the undersecretary, the inspector-general of the Polish army did not quite recognize that the tirades were *both* sincere and a pretext; that the National Socialist leaders both detested communism and the Soviet Union and used anti-Bolshevik slogans to cover aggressive policies they intended to pursue in any case. The events in Danzig in the fall of 1936 certainly removed some of the cover from German policy.

As the National Socialists in Danzig took advantage of the situation to move more drastically against the opposition, Lester prepared his last report, filed on 12 September, and resigned in view of the obvious determination of the powers at Geneva to pay no attention to the violations of the Danzig constitution. The League heard Beck's report on his handling of the *Leipzig* incident, entrusted him with settling the problems between the high commissioner and the Danzig Senate, and generally turned its back on internal developments in the free city, though without abandoning the formal presence of the League and its theoretical rights.[32] The Germans now had a free hand inside Danzig, and a new high commissioner had to be located who would mediate between Germany and Poland without interfering with the illegal measures taken against the opposition and the Jews. This task was eventually accomplished by the designation of Carl J. Burckhardt as high commissioner in February 1937 with the clear understanding that his role would be strictly limited.[33] The report circulated to its missions abroad by

30. Szembek, 23 September 1936, p. 204; *Lipski Papers,* No. 61; *G. D.*, C, 5, No. 551; von Papen to Hitler telegram 115, 8 September 1936, T–120, 2500/4939/E 272464.

31. Szembek, 30 September 1936, pp. 206–08. The issue is summarized well by Roos, pp. 257–59.

32. Leonhardt, pp. 260–64; *G. D.*, C, 5, Nos. 524, 557, 566, 573; Szembek, 30 September 1936, p. 206, 7 October, pp. 208–09; Memorandum of Greiser, 6 October 1936, T–120, 1315/2371/D 495841–844. The basis on which the powers excused their policy was that the original basis for the establishment of the free city had been the protection of Poland's access to the sea, not the defense of some Germans against other Germans (Gordon [Geneva] telegram 45, 27 January 1937, State 860 K.00/276).

33. Burckhardt's own account may be found in his *Meine Danziger Mission, 1937–1939* (Munich: Callwey, 1960). Some devastating comments in Johann W. Brügel,

the German foreign ministry on 11 February 1937, summarizing the League's handling of the Danzig issue just before Burkhardt accepted the appointment, appropriately commented that "although Danzig had originally set itself further goals, the settlement arrived at in Geneva can surely be considered progress."[34]

What was meant by "progress" had been evident in Danzig in the interim. Immediately after the League decision formally turning the problem over to Poland, the Poles had begun to examine the next steps.[35] They preferred to have a high commissioner in Danzig to keep from confronting Germany directly over every incident affecting Polish interests in Danzig. Little did they realize how quickly this issue would arise. Forster received Hitler's approval on 12–13 October to outlaw the Danzig Socialist party and to proceed against the other remaining non-National Socialist parties as well. He was told by Hitler not to rush things too much during these violations of the constitution, and he was given similar cautions by von Neurath.[36] The National Socialist gauleiter of Danzig was, however, not the type of person to go about his business quietly and carefully. Greiser had put on a show in Geneva; he would top that by a performance where it really counted, in Danzig.

Forster immediately moved rapidly against the opposition by a series of drastic measures and also told his followers that the disappearance of the Poles would follow that of the opposition parties from Danzig. Once before, in November 1935, Forster had allowed his enthusiasm to unveil Germany's real aims, thereby alarming Poland and forcing Hitler to tell his trusted but overexuberant aide to restrain himself.[37] Now, after his triumph over Lester, Forster outdid himself. The Four-Year Plan then being proclaimed in Germany would prepare the country for war. Germany would take Danzig first, and the rest would follow. The League had no business in Danzig, nor had the Poles. Forster told his party followers that Hitler wanted them to be quiet and careful, but he can hardly have expected them to listen quietly—or the Poles to pay no attention—when he also told them that Hitler would be entering Danzig in a few months and when the district party chief in

---

"The Neutral Appeaser," *Wiener Library Bulletin,* 14, No. 3 (1960), 56. The negotiations are covered by Gallman (Danzig) dispatch 324, 13 January 1937 and Cudahy (Warsaw) dispatch 1480, 29 January 1937, State 860 K.00/274 and 280. See also memorandum of Skrine Stevenson (London), 15 October 1936, Foreign Office C 7282/33/55.

34. "Pol V V635/37," 11 February 1937, T–120, 1315/2371/D 495896.

35. *G. D.,* C, 5, Nos. 575, 579; Szembek, 8 October 1936, pp. 209–10.

36. On Forster in Germany see *G. D.,* C, 5, Nos. 584, 594, 609, 605. This last document is a memorandum by Weizsäcker of which much has been made by Burckhardt and Denne (pp. 115–17). Denne, whose research is often careless, has a distorted account of the whole crisis of October 1936, ignoring the Polish protests (p. 74). See the comments by Fritz T. Epstein, *Jahrbuch für die Geschichte Mittel- und Ostdeutschlands,* 11 (1962), 475.

37. *G. D.,* C, 4, No. 454; Schliep (Warsaw) report P VI 17/11.35, 3 December 1935, T–120, 2787/6023/H 044685–687.

introducing Forster proclaimed that Poland would have to be eliminated altogether.[38]

It is hardly surprising that an uproar in German-Polish relations ensued, with Berlin hard put to calm the aroused suspicions of Warsaw. Since the German government was indeed not yet ready to move toward the "further goals" alluded to in these undiplomatic speeches, Hitler eventually agreed to restrain Forster once again. Appropriate assurances were given to the Polish government, and the Polish protests were answered by suitably accommodating replies. While the Germans would not allow any increase in Polish rights in Danzig, they promised scrupulously to observe the existing ones; and, like the Poles, the Germans for their part now saw some usefulness in the high commissioner as a buffer against the extension of the other power's influence in the free city.[39] A major threat to German-Polish relations was averted, but if anyone in Warsaw still had illusions, they must have been both blind and deaf; for the benefit of the latter, Göring explained to Ambassador Lipski that Hitler would someday demand an extraterritorial passage across the Polish Corridor in exchange for unspecified compensation elsewhere.[40]

The summer and fall of 1936 thus saw German relations with Poland enter a new phase. While Germany still wanted to maintain the truce entered in the first year of National Socialist rule, was generous with soothing assurances and ceremonial courtesies,[41] and would restrain the more exuberent advocates of expansion when their excessively frank statements aroused Polish ire, the consolidation of German power in Europe provided the basis for a more aggressive policy. Still unwilling to challenge Poland at points where the Poles made their resistance firm and obvious, the National Socialist leaders were now more willing to try for gains. Though in retrospect the removal of Lester from Danzig symbolized the disastrous fate awaiting both Germans and Poles, the triumph of the National Socialists over the representative of the League with Polish connivance in 1936 certainly marks the end of an epoch. The Germans in the Saar had ended their own freedom when they cast their votes for union with Germany in 1935; those in Danzig lost it in 1936. Poland would have to look to its interests as best it could. With any prospective French aid held off by the remilitarized Rhineland—to say nothing of the defensive strategy of Paris—this would be no easy task.

Another way in which Danzig illustrates the changing situation in 1936 is

38. Text in Emessen, pp. 123–26. The reference to the Four-Year Plan will also be examined in the following chapter.

39. Szembek, pp. 211–216; *G. D.*, C, 5, Nos. 623, 628, 630, 635, 636, 639; 6, Nos. 4, 5, 12, 13, 43, 45, 61; *D. D. F.*, 2d, 3, Nos. 387, 465, 466, 470, 488, 494, 514. A detailed exposé of the Polish position by Count Josef Potocki, chief of the western department of the Ministry of Foreign Affairs, in dispatch 1355 from the U. S. Chargé a.i., Rose, of 2 November 1936, State 860 K.00/263.

40. Szembek, 3 November 1936, p. 214; *Lipski Papers,* p. 270.

41. See material on the reception in Berlin in October 1936 of a delegation of Polish veterans by the head of the German veterans organization, Hanns Oberlindober, and the chief of the German-Polish Institute, SA-Brigadeführer Prof. Achim von Arnim, in EAP 250–d–18–20/2, T–81, roll 17, serial 38.

that, as in the case of German policy toward the Spanish civil war, the key decisions were made by Hitler without consultation with the German foreign ministry. Hitler either gave Forster instructions himself or allowed Göring to handle the issues. The foreign ministry could only plead for information. What makes this particularly interesting is that in the case of German-Polish relations, Hitler had no need to worry about "softness" in the foreign ministry. On the contrary, as he well knew, the policy of cooperation with Poland was quite unpopular in the Wilhelmstrasse, and any tightening in the relationship would only be welcomed there. Nevertheless, he found it more congenial to his work habits to meet party cronies in Munich than to carry forward the business of government in the Berlin chancellery. His self-confidence, not surprisingly, had grown, and he would conduct Germany's affairs as he saw fit.

As applied to the Soviet Union in 1936, such conduct meant primarily the use of real or imagined Soviet actions as excuses for whatever he planned to do. The Franco-Soviet Pact had provided the pretext for remilitarizing the Rhineland; in August 1936, Russian moves were cited to explain the extension of the term of service in the German army; and at the Nuremberg party rally in September denunciations of the Soviet Union filled the autumn air. At all times, the supposed use of Czech airfields by the Russian air force provided a fine talking point for Germany's political and diplomatic leaders. The contemporary evidence, however, shows that the fairy tales about the "Soviet aircraft carrier in Central Europe" were never believed by those who assiduously spread them and that German military planning was at no time seriously concerned about the Soviet menace that was supposedly keeping the German general staff awake at night.[42]

Behind the fury and the fancy, German-Soviet relations in 1936 proceeded in essentially the same manner that they had before. From the German side, the fulminations in public were not allowed to interfere with trade relations between the two countries. The more extensive schemes that Schacht and Soviet trade representative David Kandelaki had talked about had foundered early in 1936. A routine trade agreement providing for a continuation of the former level of exchange was worked out instead and finally signed on 29 April.[43] In subsequent months, the German interest in raw materials needed for rearmament, especially manganese—an alloy used in making steel of which 50 per cent of the world's production was mined in the Soviet Union—led the Berlin government to consider more extensive trade arrangements. Hermann Göring, whose Four-Year Plan set up later in the year was ostensibly directed against the Soviet Union, was especially interested in better economic relations with Russia in view of Germany's

42. On the German use of the Soviet menace while disbelieving it see *G. D.,* C, 5, Nos. 141, 205, 392, 427, 517; *D. D. F.,* 2d, 2, Nos. 3, 361; U. S. 1936, 1:303; Brügel, *Tschechen und Deutsche,* pp. 354–55; Mastný report 31, 13 March 1936, Czech document in T–120, 1040/1809/413199–201.

43. *G. D.,* C, 5, No. 302; Hencke (Berlin) to Tippelskirch (Moscow), 25 March and 8 April 1936, T–120, 1097/2082/451014–17 and 31–32.

shortage of foreign exchange. He began to take a direct part in pushing for a higher volume of trade and provided the political cover for his cousin, Herbert Göring of the Reich Ministry of Economics, who played an active part in informal efforts to accomplish that purpose. While the Germans wanted raw materials, the Soviets wanted military equipment, especially for their navy. Very little came of the whole project, but this episode is deserving of comment because of the light it sheds on the foreign policies of both countries.[44]

On the German side, the priority of the economic needs of the armaments program is obvious. Equally obvious is the assumption that the use of the armaments—at least against the Soviet Union—was not expected immediately; hence the willingness to supply some military equipment to Russia. The Soviet interest in naval equipment was simultaneously being expressed to the United States where the Russians wished to buy a battleship.[45] During the period of the nonaggression pact with Germany, Moscow would again solicit German aid in building up the Red navy; this was a field of armaments in which the Soviet Union looked abroad longer than any other. What is more interesting is the repeated hints made by Russian diplomats during the course of the economic talks, and even aside from them, especially in the fall of 1936, suggesting that better economic relations might lead as well to better political relations with Germany.[46]

The German remilitarization of the Rhineland and the fact that Germany could now build fortifications there obviously increased Russia's danger by vitiating any value that the Franco-Soviet Pact might have had. There were, in any case, no military arrangements between France and the Soviet Union to provide for the pact's implementation, and it became increasingly clear that there would be none.[47] It is hardly surprising that Maxim Litvinov, the People's Commissar for Foreign Affairs, was quoted as denouncing the Blum government for being much too willing to mollify Germany.[48] The shift in Soviet instructions to the French Communist party, directing them not to oppose armaments expenditures, the implementation of the policy of the Popular Front against fascism promulgated at the Seventh Congress of the Comintern in August 1935, the efforts to maintain reasonably good relations with Italy during the period of sanctions,[49] and the instructions to the Com-

44. On these talks see *G. D.,* C, 5, Nos. 312, 341, 342, 347, 535, 549, 590, 591, 615; *D. D. F.,* 2d, 2, No. 269; Niclauss, pp. 190–93.

45. See U. S. Soviet Union 1933–1939, pp. 458ff.

46. In addition to the sources cited in n. 44, above, see the Memorandum by Dürksen, head of the eastern section of the APA, of 12 October 1936, in EAP 250–d–18–05/4, T–81, roll 11, serial 32; "Informationsbericht Nr. 38," 13 October 1936, "Privater Sonderbericht," 17 October 1936, Bundesarchiv, Brammer, Z.Sg. 101/29, f. 375–79, and 385–93; Excerpt from a Memorandum by Tippelskirch (Moscow), 28 November 1936, T–120, 2792/6025/H 047369; *D. D. F.,* 2d, 3, No. 292; Hilger, p. 265.

47. U. S. 1936, 1:358–59.

48. Ibid., pp. 345–46.

49. See *G. D.,* C, 5, No. 334; evidently based on intercepted documents.

munists in Spain to restrain radical social experimentation on the Republican side, all point to an essentially defensive posture against any threat from Germany combined with a casting about for possible allies. In the year that the great purge was beginning to shake the whole structure of the Soviet Union, it is hardly surprising that Stalin should be most cautious in foreign affairs. The best explanation of the friendly hints to Germany would appear to be that, in this context, direct reassurance might be one good way to avert any danger from Germany.[50]

The Soviet hints were never taken up in Berlin, and in response to Hitler's speeches wistfully commenting on the wonders he could do for Germany if he had Russia's major agricultural and industrial areas, the Soviets could only reply with the comment that they were ready to defend themselves. But just as the Germans were not nearly as alarmed by the Soviet Union as they pretended, so the Russian government was not nearly as unwilling to accommodate itself to Germany as it claimed. Both powers were playing for time.

The country most frequently attacked in German propaganda, especially in 1936, as a tool of Soviet policy was Czechoslovakia. It was pictured as a threat to Germany's heart. As previously indicated, the German government and military never believed in the reality of these dangers, but once the temporary calm enjoined by the risks of the Rhineland occupation had passed, the press campaign against Prague was renewed vigorously.[51] Simultaneously, the appearance of members of the Sudeten German party on the National Socialist list of candidates for the Reichstag in the "election" that was to ratify Hitler's Rhineland move suggested to the Czech government the long-term implications of Germany's continued relationship with that political party allegedly loyal to Czechoslovakia.[52]

The Czech government, however, did not really need such intimations of danger from Germany. The geographic and military realities were sufficiently obvious without them. Seen from Prague, the remilitarization of the Rhineland was an obvious prelude to German advances in Central and Southeast Europe. Any failure of the Western powers to react vigorously would both embolden Germany to move rapidly and, by enabling it to establish a fortified barrier against France, made future help from the West even more problematical. Recognizing these dangers, the Czech leaders reassessed

50. Note Molotov's interview of 12 March, published in *Pravda* on 24 March 1936, Beloff, 2:54.

51. See *D. D. F.*, 2d, 1, No. 512; 2, Nos. 39, 343.

52. On the Reichstag election list and Czech protests about it see *D. D. F.*, 2d, 1, No. 502; Mastný report 36 of 25 March and report 39 of 31 March 1936, Czech documents in T–120, 1040/1809/413123–125 and 118; von Bülow to Lammers, 31 March 1936, T–120, 3469/8911/E 622094–096; Lammers to von Neurath, 7 April 1936, ibid., frames E 622105–106. On German government and party relations with the Sudeten German party in early 1936 see *G. D.*, C, 4, No. 285; 5, Nos. 44, 284; Král, *Die Deutschen in der Tschechoslowakei*, Nos. 36, 38, 39, 41; Krofta's comments to the section chiefs of the Czech foreign ministry, No. 6/36, 20 February 1936, Czech document in T–120, 1041/1809/414084.

their situation.[53] They believed that Hitler would move against Austria first and then turn on them, an assessment as logical as it was accurate.[54] Where could they turn for help or for a reduction of hostile pressures? The other hostilities that Czechoslovakia faced were those of Hungary and Poland. Hungary was simply unapproachable from Prague.[55] Since Poland was an ally of Czechoslovakia's own ally, France, it might have been possible to persuade the Poles that the German threat to Czechoslovakia ultimately menaced Poland as well, but the Polish foreign minister, Beck, too much influenced by his anti-Czech proclivities and the hope of possible territorial gain in Teschen and elsewhere at Czechoslovakia's expense, would not be swayed. Neither French nor Czech efforts in 1936 produced any change in either the policy or personnel in Warsaw.[56] Where else could help come from? As might be expected, the Czech leaders thought of their allies of the Little Entente, Rumania and Yugoslavia, but quickly discovered that though still willing to stand together against Hungary—which presented no real threat to any of them—these countries could not be persuaded to assume the risk of opposing Germany. This was especially true of Yugoslavia which was steadily moving toward the German orbit.[57] Help would have to come from a greater distance.

The possibility of help from England was realistically judged remote by the Czech leaders. Still reasonably confident that France would come to their aid if they were attacked by Germany, they were fairly certain that England would not fight in that contingency unless it were clearly a part of a broader German offensive.[58] The question of how England regarded the role of Czechoslovakia in Europe was thus of the greatest importance, and it was in this context that the issue of the Sudeten Germans assumed significance. If the British government and public could be reassured that the

53. *D. D. F.*, 2d, 1, No. 256; 2, Nos. 84, 182; U. S. 1936, 1:290–95; *Hungarian Documents,* 2, Nos. 28, 32; Krofta circular to all Czech mission, 9 March 1936, Czech document in T–120, 1040/1809/413214–215; Krofta's comments to the section chiefs of the Czech foreign ministry Nos. 8/36, 11/36 (excerpt in *Prager Akten,* No. 63), 15/36, of 12 March, 2 April, and 3 June 1936, Czech documents in T–120, 1041/1809/414086, 414089–090, 414096; Mastný report 28, 12 March 1936, Czech document in T–120, 1040/1809/413128–130.

54. *D. D. F.*, 2d, 2, No. 175; Krofta's comments, No. 23/35 of 11 July 1935, Czech document in T–120, 1041/1809/414163.

55. The most recent summary in Hoensch, *Ungarische Revisionismus,* Part I, Sections A and B. For Beneš's similar evaluation see his comments to the German minister on 16 October 1936, in *G. D.*, C, 5, No. 614, p. 1110. See also *Hungarian Documents,* 1, Nos. 59, 81, 84, 98, 145, 194; 2, Nos. 54, 55.

56. Čelovsky, pp. 77–79; Szembek, 11 May 1935, p. 77, 26 February 1936, p. 163, 21 December 1936, p. 220; *D. D. F.*, 2d, 2, Nos. 25, 75; 3, No. 215; *Hungarian Documents,* 2, Nos. 39, 49. Only in July, at the time of the crisis over Danzig, was Beck a little more friendly (Krofta's comments, No. 17/36, 9 July 1936, Czech document in T–120, 1041/1809/414098–099).

57. Čelovsky, pp. 72–73; *G. D.*, C, 5, Nos. 374, 540; U. S. 1936, 1:368–70; *Hungarian Documents,* 1, Nos. 44, 50, 57, 67, 113.

58. *D. D. F.*, 2d, 2, No. 475; U. S. 1936, 1:339–42.

Sudeten Germans were treated decently and had no just grievances, London might be induced to look at the broader significance of Czech-German relations. If, on the other hand, the leaders of the Sudeten German party and the German government could convince the British that Sudeten German grievances were the real issue, then the aims of Germany might be successfully hidden behind the slogan of self-determination. The year 1936 therefore saw the beginning of a race between these two views of the Sudeten question: a pretext for aggression or a grievance to be corrected.

The British would urge the Czechs to make concessions to the German minority, and the Prague government was increasingly inclined to make them; but the longer the discussion of such concessions, the more they appeared to be the kernel when they were really only the shell.[59] Simultaneously, the Sudeten German party, seconded by Berlin, made every effort to stimulate British concern about the internal development of Czechoslovakia. This meant trips to London by Konrad Henlein and other Sudeten German leaders to assure the British of their loyalty to the Czech state and their sole interest in the welfare of the Sudeten Germans within Czechoslovakia, while in fact the internal affairs of the Sudeten German party were being supervised from Berlin with the German government picking the leaders, setting the policy lines, and giving or withholding financial support as the situation appeared to dictate.[60] Henlein, nevertheless, was a convincing advocate in London; the process of obscuring the fact that Hitler was not the least bit interested in the Sudeten Germans was well under way by the fall of 1936.

In addition to its relations with France and England, Czechoslovakia had an alliance with the Soviet Union on the one hand and faced the alternatives of fighting Germany or trying to reach an accommodation with it on the other. This complex of questions was seen by the Czech leaders, especially by Beneš himself, as a whole; and Czech foreign policy in the mid-1930s can be analyzed intelligently only if Beneš's perception of the situation is clearly understood. Explained in detail to Anthony Eden on his visit to Prague in April 1935, it was to be repeated with only slight variations on subsequent occasions, variations that can be accounted for by changed circumstances. The basic view, however, remained unchanged.[61]

59. On British efforts to get the Czechs to make concessions see *D. D. F.*, 2d, 2, Nos. 110, 255; 3, No. 505; Brügel, *Tschechen und Deutsche,* p. 288; Mastný report 79, 11 August 1936, Czech document in T–120, 1040/1809/413202–203.

60. For Henlein's related propaganda efforts in England see Král, Nos. 47, 49, 54 (*G. D.*, C, 5, No. 465), 66 (will be *G. D.*, C, 6, No. 228); Foreign Office R 7511/234/12. The record of Vansittart's talk with Henlein on 20 July 1936 is in Foreign Office R 4395/32/12. For German direction of the Sudeten German party in 1936, especially during its internal troubles in the summer, see *G. D.*, C, 5, Nos. 353, 364, 372, 480, 505, 508, 559, 579 (Král, No. 58); Král, Nos. 45, 46, p. 93, Nos. 55, 56; *Germany and Czechoslovakia, 1918–1945*, pp. 29, 94–95.

61. The memorandum on Beneš's talk with Eden on 4 April 1935, Czech document in T–120, 1143/2028/444408–418; summarized by Krofta in his comment No. 13/35, 11 April 1935, ibid., 1041/1809/414146–147. Beneš's views expressed to the French minister Lacroix, reported by the latter on 28 May 1936, *D. D. F.*, 2d, 2, No. 255, and Lacroix's analyses of the views of Beneš and Krofta in ibid., Nos. 351 and 475. Similar views were later expressed by Beneš to the U. S. minister Carr on 28 February 1938

As Beneš saw it, Czechoslovakia had to follow and depend on France, but it could not and would not fight Germany by itself. For centuries the Czech people had lived in the same political structure with the Germans. They had survived German control. If they had to, they would survive German control again. But German control of Bohemia—and such steps leading toward that control as the German annexation of Austria—would threaten the status of France, Italy, and Great Britain as great powers in Europe. Because the Czechs could survive as a people but the other three nations could not survive as great powers if Germany were allowed a free hand in Central Europe, the other three had an enormous stake in Czech independence. It was they who were, therefore, threatened most by Germany's advance. If they recognized this fact and helped Czechoslovakia, Czechoslovakia would certainly defend itself. If they did not, they would suffer as seriously, if not more seriously and permanently, than the Czechs. Furthermore, it was in this context that Beneš saw the Czech alliance with the Soviet Union.

Beneš had no admiration for communism and no special affection for the Soviet Union, but he thought it essential that Russia be brought into the picture. Preoccupied with its internal development and worried by the possibility of German and Japanese aggression, the Soviet Union would be a threat to others only if it were *not* brought into an alliance with the Western powers and Czechoslovakia; for it would then align itself with Germany at the expense of the countries that lay between. As a result of such an arrangement, Germany would dominate Central Europe, and all the dangers for the other powers would result as if Germany had secured that domination by itself.

From all this Beneš concluded that it made sense for Czechoslovakia to have a defensive alliance with the Soviet Union, that the Franco-Soviet Pact was equally important, and that Italy and Britain both should recognize that German policy toward Austria and Czechoslovakia threatened them at least as much as the two countries menaced directly. If, however, others did not see the dangers, then Czechoslovakia, which could not act by itself, would have to make at least an attempt to come to some arrangement with Germany. The situation in the summer and fall of 1936 suggested that the three Western powers did not see the dangers: Italy was moving closer to Germany, while France and Britain were unwilling to act decisively against the German threat. Czechoslovakia therefore would explore the possibility of a new agreement with Germany that did not run counter to Czechoslovakia's existing treaty commitments but would render them less vital by reducing the threat from Germany that was supposed to make them operative.[62]

(U. S. 1938, 1:410–14; noted by Čelovsky, p. 69). See also the analyses by the German minister Eisenlohr of 16 April 1936, *G. D.*, C, 5, No. 284, and the minutes of Eden's visit in Foreign Office C 2930/55/18.

62. In retrospect, Beneš's view was certainly more perceptive than that of most contemporaries. The only point he overlooked was the possibility that another period of German control, if of the National Socialist variety, might include the physical ex-

The explorations of Germany's attitude made by the Czech government during the spring and summer of 1936 through the official diplomatic channels produced formal German affirmations that the German-Czech arbitration treaty of 1925 was still in effect and that Hitler's speech at the time of the remilitarization of the Rhineland offering nonaggression pacts to Germany's neighbors applied to Czechoslovakia. The German diplomats, however, clearly did not wish to enter into detailed negotiations; furthermore, they wanted any new German-Czech treaty to eliminate Czechoslovakia's alliance system.[63] There appeared to be little promise for the Czechs in this approach. The real issue was whether there were possibly other elements in the German government that preferred a different policy and could obtain Hitler's approval. A conversation between Göring and Vojtéch Mastný, the Czech minister in Berlin, on 29 February 1936, apparently suggested to Beneš that there might be other currents in Berlin and thus helped pave the way for the secret feelers put forth several months later.[64]

The informal negotiations between Germany and Czechoslovakia began in August 1936 and ended in January 1937.[65] One of von Ribbentrop's assistants in his *Dienststelle* office, Albrecht Haushofer, son of the famous geopolitician, had urged in April 1936 that Germany take advantage of its strengthened position after the Rhineland occupation to attempt a settlement with Czechoslovakia that would exchange German recognition of the boundary for Czech concessions to the Sudeten Germans. There would be an increase of trade—which had fallen off drastically in the preceding years—and a newspaper truce. Such a settlement, publicly heralded as a broadening of the 1925 arbitration treaty, would pave the way for a loosening of Czechoslovakia's ties to France and the Soviet Union.

---

termination of his own people. In pre-World War II Europe, that omission is hardly surprising. On this issue see my "Germany and Czechoslovakia, 1933–1945," in *Czechoslovakia Past and Present,* 1 (The Hague: Mouton, 1969), pp. 765–67.

63. *G. D.,* C, 5, Nos. 268, 515; 6, No. 62; *D. D. F.,* 2d, Nos. 26, 182, 442, 475; U. S. 1936, 1:326–27, 339–42; Mastný telegram of 12 March 1936, Czech document in T–120, 1040/1809/413072, and Mastný report 77, 23 July 1936, ibid., 413195–196.

64. There is a brief discussion of the Göring-Mastný talk on which Mastný reported only orally to Beneš on 9 March 1936, in a lengthy retrospective analysis of German-Czech relations by Mastný of 23 March 1938; this report No. 52 is in T–120, 1040/1809/412815–818, and has been published in Václav Král (ed.), *Das Abkommen von München 1938* (Prague: Academia, 1968), No. 55. It should be noted that Mastný thought that although Hitler's long-term aims were anti-Czech, he would abstain from war in the short run because time was working for him (see Mastný's report 48, 25 May 1935, Czech document in T–120, 1041/1809/413521–528 [excerpts in *Prager Akten,* No. 50]).

65. I published an account of the "Secret Hitler-Beneš Negotiations in 1936–37," in the *Journal of Central European Affairs,* 19, No. 4 (Jan. 1960), 366–74. There are additional details from the Czech archives in Robert Kvaček and Václav Vinš, "K Německo-Ceskoslovenským sondážím ve třícatých letec (Concerning the German-Czech soundings in the 1930s)," *Československý Časopis Historicky,* 14 (1966), 887–96, and Robert Kvaček, "Československo-německá jednáni v roce 1936 (Czech-German negotiations in 1936)," *Historie a Vojenství,* 5 (1965), 721–54. There is a detailed account in Brügel, pp. 355–61. Sources cited in these accounts will not be referred to in the notes unless quoted or also published in a Western language elsewhere.

Haushofer was authorized to proceed; the way for him to discuss the matter with Mastný was prepared by a meeting between Mastný and Count Maximilian Karl zu Trauttmannsdorff, another dabbler in diplomacy, on 14 August 1936.[66] Haushofer talked with Mastný about a possible German-Czech understanding on 18 October. After Mastný had conferred with Beneš, he repeated his earlier invitation to Haushofer to come to Prague to meet with Beneš. With the authorization of Hitler and von Ribbentrop, Haushofer and Trauttmannsdorff went to Prague where, on 13–14 November, they met with Beneš as well as the foreign minister, Krofta. These discussions had been kept secret from the German foreign ministry, but the German secret police were kept informed, in part because the SS through the *Volksdeutsche Rat* was playing an important role in Germany's contacts with German minorities abroad.[67] Though insisting on this secrecy, Beneš himself had hinted to the German minister in Prague that he would like some special treaty with Germany as it was evident that the negotiations for a new Locarno were not leading anywhere.[68]

The discussion in Prague indicated that an agreement was theoretically possible. The fears of the Germans over Czech-Soviet relations were countered by Beneš—an important point because the German negotiators appear to have been seriously influenced by German propaganda on this question.[69] On the other side of the same issue, Beneš made it clear that Czechoslovakia would abide by its two defensive alliances. An agreement with Germany would take the form of a nonaggression pact with a Czech reservation about its obligations under the League covenant; such a treaty would remove Czech fears of an attack by Germany and German fears of Czechoslovakia joining the Soviet Union in an attack on Germany. The settlement would also provide for increased trade, a common policy on the Habsburg question, a press truce, and restrictions on the political activities of émigrés. The increase in trade would be so handled as to benefit the Sudeten areas—a process similar to that followed in the trade settlement between Germany and Lithuania to provide relief for the Memel Germans. Furthermore, the agreements arrived at could enable the German government to push for improvements in the status of the Sudeten Germans. Haushofer and Trauttmannsdorff returned to Germany to lay these plans

66. Trauttmannsdorff had been involved in unofficial negotiations in German-Austrian relations in 1933 (see *G. D.*, C, 2, Nos. 49, 71). In the fall of 1934 he was in charge of foreign affairs for Franz Seldte's Stahlhelm veterans organization (see Ministry of the Interior to foreign ministry, I A 965/372, 11 December 1934, T–120, 2696/5717/H 024508) when Seldte tried unsuccessfully to secure a position for him in the foreign ministry (Memorandum of von Bülow, 25 October 1934, 2371/4601/E 188795). In 1936 he was an aide of the Minister of Labor (also Seldte); in World War II he served for a time as head of the Berlin office of the Colonial Policy Office of the NSDAP.

67. On the Volksdeutsche Rat see Jacobsen, pp. 176–225, 605–07.

68. *G. D.*, C, 5, No. 614. See also Krofta's policy directive of 16 September 1936, Czech document in T–120, 1040/1809/413231; *D. D. F.*, 2d, 3, Nos. 154, 167.

69. In this connection see *D. D. F.*, 2d, 2, Nos. 376, 425, 446; 3, Nos. 320, 352; *G. D.*, C, 5, Nos. 550, 587.

before Hitler on 25 November. In the interim, the Czech government had asked the Austrian secretary of state for foreign affairs, Guido Schmidt, who was in Berlin on 19–21 November, to sound out the German government about the possibility of a German-Czech agreement and had also raised the possibility of a press truce with Goebbels through Mastný.[70]

Now that the real possibility of a German-Czech agreement loomed out of the mist of generalities, what would Hitler do? He had always held out hope of agreement; later he was to complain that no one had ever taken him up on his offers. For once a country was doing what Ambassador Dodd had suggested in the spring: ". . . that the best present chance is to call Hitler's bluff for peace, since the powers concerned do not seem willing or capable of calling his bluff for war."[71] The auspices were not particularly favorable. Göring had shifted from his earlier views—if those had been sincere in the first place. While in Budapest for the funeral of the Hungarian prime minister, Gömbös, Göring had told the Hungarian foreign minister that the conquest of Czechoslovakia would be easy. The Czech fortifications "would slow down the German troops, but they would in no way alter Germany's plans against Czechoslovakia."[72] The German foreign minister, von Neurath, was continuing to take a hard line: Germany would sign a nonaggression pact with Czechoslovakia only if it ended its alliances;[73] and the foreign ministry was doing its best to keep the Sudeten Germany party functioning according to German directives.[74] Hitler himself had indicated to Guido Schmidt that German relations with Czechoslovakia could be improved only if the Czechs gave up their relationship with the Soviet Union, a condition he had not included in his earlier offer of a nonaggression pact with Czechoslovakia.[75]

Under these circumstances it is not surprising that Hitler when confronted with Haushofer's proposals struck out the suggested nonaggression pact and entirely ignored the possibility of using German influence to improve the lot of the Sudeten Germans. He was interested in an increase in trade, he would have liked to neutralize Czechoslovakia in case of a Soviet attack, and he wanted émigré activities restricted. Cooperation on the Habsburg issue only raised a question in his mind. Clearly Hitler could not care less about the Sudeten Germans; any satisfaction they received would only undermine his

70. For Guido Schmidt's action in Berlin in behalf of the Czech government see *G. D.,* D, 1, No. 188, p. 293. For the Goebbels-Mastný talk see Krofta comments, No. 24/36, 26 November 1936, Czech document in T–120, 1041/1809/414117; *G. D.,* C, 6, No. 78. For British views of a possible Czech-German agreement at this time see Foreign Office R 7381/1799/12.

71. U. S. 1936, 1:278.

72. *Hungarian Documents,* 1, No. 158 (German text in *Acta Historica,* 7, Nos. 3–4 [1960], p. 374).

73. *G. D.,* D, 1, No. 188, and C, 6, No. 11.

74. Král, *Die Deutschen in der Tschechoslowakei,* Nos. 58 (*G. D.,* C, 5, No. 578), 60; *G. D.,* C, 6, No. 31.

75. *G. D.,* D, 1, No. 181, p. 283.

case against Czechoslovakia as a whole. He was interested primarily in settling the side issues in German-Czech relations. He would have liked to neutralize Czechoslovakia—it would fall all the more easily under German control once it broke its alliances—but the price of a nonaggression pact that would limit his own options was more than he would pay. Knowing that Germany was in no danger of attack itself, he saw no reason to tie his own hands. Furthermore, he was not about to alienate Hungary to whom he was urging the concentration of revisionist desires against Prague. As for the negotiations, if Haushofer could secure everything Germany wanted without significant concessions, he was welcome to try again.

Haushofer and Trauttmannsdorff, after giving Mastný what appears to have been an expurgated account of the meeting with Hitler, returned to Prague for another talk with Beneš on 18 December 1936.[76] The discussion concentrated on the Sudeten German question and on Czech-Soviet relations and then turned to the contents of a possible agreement. Haushofer presented Hitler's refusal of a nonaggression pact as a refusal to conclude such a pact unless Czechoslovakia gave up its rights and obligations under the League covenant, something the Czechs obviously would not do. Beneš, therefore, prepared a treaty that merely reaffirmed the 1925 arbitration treaty and provided for nonintervention into each other's internal affairs, an expansion of trade, and assurances that outstanding questions would be settled in a friendly way through diplomacy. There might also be some sort of police agreement against subversion, although Beneš insisted that he would not join the Anti-Comintern Pact. Though stating that they would have to check with Hitler again, Haushofer and Trauttmannsdorff agreed that both sides should now prepare drafts and then confer again, with other government agencies (including eventually the regular diplomats) being brought in. The evidence suggests that the German emissaries were sincere in their optimism, though they would soon be disillusioned.

Beneš believed that definitive agreement was imminent and prepared a draft agreement and accompanying communiqué.[77] The atmosphere in the Czech foreign ministry had been optimistic for some time, and both Beneš and Mastný thought that only minor details needed to be worked out.[78] Trauttmannsdorff made another trip to Czechoslovakia early in January 1937 and then helped Haushofer to prepare a draft treaty for Hitler whom

76. English text of Beneš's memorandum in *Germany and Czechoslovakia 1918–1945*, No. 28 (note the omission on p. 105); cf. Edmund A. Walsh, *Total Power* (Garden City, N.Y.: Doubleday, 1948), pp. 31, 53.

77. The English text of the draft agreement only is in ibid., No. 29; German texts of both plus accompanying remarks by Beneš are among the Czech documents in T–120, 1040/1809/412843–847. The date of 9 March 1936, under which this item was filed in the Czech archives, may have been taken from the date of Mastný's report to Beneš on his talk with Göring (see n. 64).

78. A good view can be obtained from the report of the U. S. minister in Prague, J. Butler Wright, on a conversation with Ferdinand Veverka, previously Czech minister in the U. S. and then minister in Vienna, on 7 December 1936, in U. S. 1936, 1:375–79.

Haushofer saw again in that month, probably around the 15th. Haushofer presented a draft treaty along the lines he had discussed with Beneš and very similar to the treaty prepared by Beneš. Hitler was not interested and told Haushofer to draw out the negotiations, in effect dropping them. Other than reproaches from von Neurath about going behind his back, never again would the Czechs hear about this subject from the Germans.[79]

What had happened and what does it reveal about German policy toward Czechoslovakia? Hitler was willing to have explored the topic of German-Czech relations, but his offer to sign a nonaggression pact with Czechoslovakia was as false as his offer to return to the League.[80] If there were short-range gains to be secured as a result of Germany's strengthened position, well and good. But unworried about attacks by others, he was not about to restrict his own freedom of action. Haushofer and Trauttmannsdorff might be sincerely concerned about the problems of the Sudeten Germans; Hitler was not. Haushofer recognized this and saved his records of the episode as evidence of Hitler's perfidy; he showed them to a friend while working in the opposition to Hitler that would eventually cost him his life.[81] Ironically, Hitler followed only one piece of advice given him by Haushofer, and that was to continually raise Sudeten German demands as a means of aborting any German-Czech agreement if that suited Germany.[82] Along that road no new agreement with Czechoslovakia could be signed, and even public reaffirmations or extensions of old agreements like the 1925 arbitration treaty could only increase the danger of action by Britain and France when the time came for Germany to break such a treaty.

For the Czechs, the only other conceivable approach was to reassure the Western powers by concessions to the Sudeten Germans. This meant, eventually, direct negotiations with Konrad Henlein and his associates, a route that the Czech government was most reluctant to follow. At the same time as the informal negotiations recounted above were taking place, Beneš was in indirect contact with Henlein through an intermediary; but these feelers

79. *Germany and Czechoslovakia 1918–1945,* No. 32 (*G. D.*, C, 6, No. 288); Wiedemann, pp. 125–26. For subsequent Czech reference to these negotiations as having been broken off in January 1937 by the Germans see Beneš's comments to Hugh Wilson, the U. S. ambassador to Germany, on 6 August 1938, in U. S. 1938, 1:540–41; Mastný's general report of 23 March 1938, cited in n. 64; Krofta's comments in *Germany and Czechoslovakia 1918–1945,* No. 34, and *Hungarian Documents,* 2, No. 63. On French knowledge of the secret negotiations see *D. D. F.,* 2d, 3, Nos. 448, 460, 464.

80. An assurance to this effect had been given to the Hungarians in May 1936; see *Hungarian Documents,* 2, No. 20.

81. Rainer Hildebrandt, *Wir sind die Letzten; aus dem Leben des Widerstandskämpfers Albrecht Haushofer und seiner Freunde* (Neuwied/Berlin: Michael, 1949), pp. 22–23, 51–52.

82. This was the way Hitler instructed Henlein in March 1938 (*G. D.*, D, 2, Nos. 107, 109; note that Haushofer was present as a representative of the Volksdeutsche Mittelstelle at the second of these meetings). Hitler is also supposed to have broken off the negotiations because he expected a change in the leadership of the Soviet Union; I can find no contemporary evidence to support this thesis from the German side.

did not lead to direct talks until the fall of 1937.[83] Perhaps out of hope for direct German-Czech negotiations at some time in the future, or out of fear of weakening their alliances, or out of concern about internal political repercussions—or all three—the Prague government never used the 1936–37 negotiations as a sign of their own good will and good faith in an appeal to the Western powers. That field would be left mainly to Henlein and his mentors in Berlin.[84]

To the other countries of East Central and Southeast Europe the growing strength of Germany's position as a result of the remilitarization of the Rhineland was to become obvious in the summer and fall of 1936. The history of the German-Austrian agreement of July has already been told. The relations between Germany and Hungary continued to be marked by a certain closeness as in previous years, but Germany's far stronger position led it to subordinate its policy toward Hungary first to its interest in wooing Yugoslavia and subsequently, especially after the fall of the Rumanian foreign minister, Titulescu, to a rapprochement with Rumania. In the case of all three countries, as well as Bulgaria and Greece, Germany continued to use economic policy as a handmaiden of both domestic rearmament and foreign political influence.

The Hungarian government was worried lest Germany's offers of nonaggression pacts at the time of the Rhineland coup might actually lead to some sort of Eastern Locarno that would blunt Hungary's revisionist aspirations toward Czechoslovakia. The Germans reassured them on this point, particularly in regard to any German-Czech agreement, though they refused to agree to any special formal ties to Hungary.[85] As a matter of fact, throughout 1936 the Germans continued to urge the Hungarians to concentrate on Czechoslovakia as their main enemy and to arrive at an accommodation with Yugoslavia.[86] When the Hungarian regent, Admiral Horthy, met Hitler in August 1936, this was the main topic of their conversation, with Horthy explaining the difficulty of coming to any arrangement with the Serbs who controlled Yugoslavia and Hitler urging him in this direction anyway.[87] Both expressed their antipathy to Czechoslovakia,

83. The intermediary, Prince Max of Hohenlohe-Langenburg, was to play an important role in Henlein's activities in 1937–38; for his activities in the winter 1936–37 see *G. D.,* C, 6, Nos. 76, 96; D, 2, No. 1. For his earlier activities in German-British relations see above, p. 215, n. 45.

84. There is no major study of Czech propaganda abroad in the 1930s. A very one-sided account, using Czech documents captured by the Germans in 1939, is Rudolf Urban, *Demokratenpresse im Lichte Prager Geheimakten* (Prague: Orbis, 1943).

85. *G. D.,* C, 5, Nos. 63, 130, 296, 305, 320; *Hungarian Documents,* 1, Nos. 87, 90, 118; 2, Nos. 5, 6, 8, 13, 18, 20, 37; *D. D. F.,* 2d, 3, Nos. 181, 205, 208, 220. The Hungarians, of course, were in principle pleased over Germany's gaining "equality of rights" and hoped to imitate it with German support (*D. D. F.,* 2d, 1, No. 466; *G. D.,* C, 5, No. 305, n. 5, 413; *Hungarian Documents,* 2, Nos. 15, 19).

86. *G. D.,* C, 5, Nos. 49, 171; *Hungarian Documents,* 1, No. 135; 2, Nos. 3, 4, 7, 53; Hoensch, *Ungarische Revisionismus,* pp. 41–45.

87. On the Hitler-Horthy meeting see Miklos Horthy, *Ein Leben für Ungarn* (Bonn:

and Horthy indicated his approval of the annexation of Austria by Germany.

Such exchanges were all very general and very pleasant; when von Neurath visited Budapest in September, however, the atmosphere was not quite so friendly. Each country was afraid that the other might under some circumstances drag it into war, but a more immediate difficulty was the resumption of German complaints about the treatment of Hungary's German minority and Hungary's dissatisfaction with the German minister in Budapest, an especially touchy point since the latter was von Neurath's son-in-law.[88] At the time of von Neurath's visit, the man who had come in a way to be the symbol of German-Hungarian friendship, the Hungarian prime minister, Julius Gömbös, lay fatally ill in a Munich sanatorium. His death on 6 October provided an occasion not only for a great display of official mourning in Munich but also for Göring's trip to Hungary for the funeral.[89] While in Budapest, Göring explained to the Hungarian foreign minister that Germany would annex Austria and that Czechoslovakia would be occupied as well, expressed some reservations about Rumania, and waxed enthusiastic about Yugoslavia, while Kanya attempted to reassure him that the policies of Gömbös would be continued. Göring also devoted considerable attention to trade relations between Germany and Hungary, relations which were becoming quite a problem for the Hungarians because of the large debts Germany was running up.[90] This trade question and the German remonstrances about the German minority were of serious concern to the Hungarians, but Germany's turn toward Yugoslavia and Rumania worried them even more.[91]

Before death removed him from the scene, Gömbös had expressed the notion that Germany was friendliest when it was weak, but now that it was growing stronger and its friendship was desired by others, Hungary was no longer important to it; for this reason Germany was playing up to Yugoslavia and Rumania.[92] This trend in German policy became startlingly

Athenäum-Verlag, 1953), pp. 178–80; *Hungarian Documents,* 1, Nos. 148 (*Allianz,* No. 13), 151–53; 2, No. 31 (*Horthy Papers,* No. 22); *G. D.*, C, 5, No. 516; Macartney, p. 150.

88. On von Neurath's visit see *Hungarian Documents,* 1, No. 156; *G. D.,* C, 5, Nos. 555, 556; Stewart (U. S. chargé a.i. Budapest) telegram 40 of 22 September and dispatch 475 of 24 September 1936, State 762.64/52 and 54.

89. Material on the ceremonies in Munich, involving Hitler himself as well as other dignitaries, may be found in the Ritter von Epp papers, "Beilagen zum Tagebuch vom 1.VII.36 bis 31.XII.36, Band 6," Bundesarchiv, Epp 18/4.

90. On the Göring visit see *Hungarian Documents,* 1, No. 158 (*Allianz,* No. 14); *G. D.,* C, 5, No. 589. Schacht had dealt with the economic matters when in Budapest on 19 June (U. S. 1936, 1:488–89, 494–95).

91. On the economic situation see *G. D.,* C, 5, No. 612; 6, Nos. 22, 51, 60, 70. On the negotiations in late 1936 about the German minority see *G. D.,* C, 6, Nos. 71, 97, 98; "Bestellungen aus der Pressekonferenz vom 17. Dezember 1936," Bundesarchiv, Brammer, Z.Sg. 101/8, f. 427.

92. Stewart dispatch 409, 9 June 1936, State 762.64/48; cf. *Hungarian Documents,* 2, No. 61.

apparent in November when German press attacks on the new Hungarian government of Kálmán Darányi culminated in an article in the *Völkische Beobachter* on 15 November that suggested Germany would not support revision of all aspects of the peace treaties. Simultaneously, rumors circulated suggesting that Hitler had inspired this article by Rosenberg and that the Hungarian-Rumanian territorial dispute over Transylvania was the one referred to as perhaps not in need of revision.[93] Since Hitler, as we now know, expressed precisely these views to a prominent Rumanian politician on the following day, the rumors were accurate indeed.

Rumanian foreign policy had been directed by Nicolae Titulescu since 1933. He had played a leading role on the European scene as an outspoken advocate of collective security, a position most recently exemplified by his strong support of sanctions against Italy. He had been very much concerned as German power increased that if Germany and the Soviet Union ever went to war with each other, Rumania would be crushed between them. He was, therefore, torn between the desire for a treaty with the Soviet Union similar to the Czech-Soviet treaty which might keep the danger of war away from Rumania and the fear that if war came and Soviet aid were provided, the Russians would keep Bessarabia—as they had in 1878—or for that matter, never leave Rumania at all. As the Rhineland occupation both dramatized and further increased the weakness of France, this issue became pivotal in Rumanian policy. Titulescu toyed with the idea of trying for a treaty of mutual assistance accompanied by Soviet recognition of the Rumanian possession of Bessarabia, but nothing came of this concept. There was strong domestic opposition to a treaty with Russia. King Carol of Rumania was opposed, and Titulescu himself was never quite certain it was a good idea.[94] When the Rumanian government was reconstructed during Titulescu's absence at the end of August 1936, he was dropped from his post as foreign minister. Even if his successor, Victor Antonescu, pleaded loyalty to France and the Little Entente, there can be no doubt that, both symbolically and politically, Rumania had abandoned a long-trodden path even if it had not yet firmly decided on a new course.[95]

The German government had been relatively unfriendly toward Rumania because of its foreign policy, and Germany was not yet a major importer of

93. Macartney, pp. 177–78. In the winter of 1936–37, the Hungarians also had some information about the secret German-Czech negotiations, which naturally alarmed them (*Hungarian Documents,* 2, Nos. 59, 63).

94. On Titulescu's policy in 1936 see *G. D.,* C, 5, Nos. 53, 300, 380, 385, 396, 397, 399, 432; *D. D. F.,* 2d, 2, Nos. 159, 160; U. S. 1936, 1:368–70; *Hungarian Documents,* 1, Nos. 4, 6; 2, Nos. 9, 26, 29; Šeba (Czech minister Bucharest) telegram of 8 March 1936, Czech document in T–120, 1040/1809/413079–080. An interesting report on Titulescu's views in January 1935 is quoted in M. Andreyeva and L. Vidyasova, *International Affairs* (Moscow), 9, No. 7, 123.

95. The change in Rumania is analyzed very well in Toynbee, *Survey of International Affairs 1936,* pp. 517–24. For German views of it see *G. D.,* C, 5, Nos. 528, 576; for Polish rejoicing see *Hungarian Documents,* 2, Nos. 42, 43. Cf. *D. D. F.,* 2d, 3, Nos. 228, 362. For a recent Rumanian account, see Oprea, *Titulescu's Diplomatic Activity,* pp. 102–6, 158–68.

Rumanian oil.[96] The occasional dabbling of National Socialist agencies in the internal politics of Rumania had hindered rather than helped relations between the two countries, and these activities continued to disturb the picture in 1936.[97] Rosenberg, the head of the APA, was using his other position as editor of the *Völkische Beobachter* to funnel money to supposedly sympathetic politicians in Rumania through Radú Lecca, a shady figure in the extremist Christian National party who would become notorious as the leading figure in Rumania's anti-Semitic activities during World War II. Lecca was to provide support for Octavian Goga, Germany's favorite among those on the Rumanian lunatic fringe; but though formally received by Hitler and von Neurath in August 1936, Goga was not to play any significant role until the end of 1937. The most important individuals in the 1936 rapprochement were King Carol himself and Georges Bratianu, a Rumanian political leader whose family had long played an influential role in that nation's history.

Bratianu had been in Germany in January 1936 in pursuit of his own policy of closer relations with Germany and opposition to ties with the Soviet Union. In Berlin he met von Neurath; and the Polish ambassador, Jósef Lipski, arranged for him to meet Göring as well.[98] Göring was taking some interest in Rumanian affairs,[99] and he saw Bratianu again on his visit to Berlin in November 1936. Bratianu then went to Paris for a few days and on his return to Berlin had meetings with von Neurath and Hitler, the reception having been arranged by Göring. In these conversations, Bratianu received assurances from both Göring and Hitler that Germany would oppose Hungarian revisionist aspirations as long as Rumania was not tied closely to the Soviet Union. Von Neurath was less friendly, but Bratianu could tell who formulated German policy. Hitler referred to Rosenberg's *Völkische Beobachter* article as an indication of German policy. The personal inclination of Bratianu toward a rapprochement with Germany and a general position not unlike Poland's was only reinforced by his visits to Paris and Brussels.[100]

King Carol as well as the new leaders of the Rumanian government were most pleased by the signs of better relations with Germany. Though they would not abandon their ties with France or turn openly against the Soviet Union, the Rumanians were gratified by Germany's announced unwillingness to support Hungarian revisionism and looked to better trade relations

96. On German petroleum imports in the early and mid 1930s see Hillgruber, pp. 81, 248–51.

97. See *G. D.*, C, 5, Nos. 397, 440, 492, 497, 498, 576.

98. *D. D. F.*, 2d, 1, No. 102; Lipski's report of 27 January 1936 has not been published; see *Lipski Papers,* p. 273.

99. *D. D. F.*, 2d, 1, Nos. 93, 149.

100. Documents on Bratianu's visits to Berlin from the German archives will appear as *G. D.*, C, 6, Nos. 36 and 38 (part already in *G. D.*, D, 5, No. 228, n. 3). Most important are *Lipski Papers,* Nos. 62 and 63. Cf. *D. D. F.*, 2d, 3, No. 372.

as well as better political relations with as much enthusiasm as Berlin.[101] From the perspective of Germany, another breach had been made in both the Little Entente and France's influence in Europe. The burial of collective security proceeded apace. While the Hungarians were being urged ever more insistently to concentrate all their revisionist aspirations against Czechoslovakia, the Czech's Rumanian ally was being directed toward the German orbit.[102]

During 1936, it increasingly seemed as if Yugoslavia were already within that orbit. The rapprochement between Yugoslavia and Germany was to make further progress in 1936. In the crisis over the Rhineland, Yugoslavia leaned to the British rather than the French view of the situation but could not in any case join in sanctions against Germany. Yugoslavia's participation in sanctions against Italy had severely damaged its foreign trade and had helped open the way for Germany to take first place as Yugoslavia's trade partner. For Yugoslavia to drop its trade with Germany under these circumstances—while sanctions against Italy were still in effect—would lead to absolute disaster for the company. Belgrade did not want to give up ties to Paris but could not be expected to join any measures against Germany.[103]

The economic ties that bound Yugoslavia to Germany were strengthened during 1936. Göring appointed his associate Franz Neuhausen as his special representative for Southeast Europe with headquarters in Belgrade.[104] Göring's interest in Yugoslavia was heightened by the responsibilities he was assuming in the field of foreign exchange and raw materials. In view of Yugoslavia's mineral resources—especially the Bor copper mines—Göring redoubled efforts to develop economic relations with Belgrade. In this regard he saw eye to eye with Hjalmar Schacht who toured the capitals of Southeast Europe in June 1936 and whose efforts were concentrated on Yugoslavia with Göring's blessings.[105] There could be no doubt that Germany was not only acquiring a predominant influence in Yugoslavia's foreign trade but was also beginning to play a greater role in its domestic

101. *G. D.*, C, 5, No. 576 and pp. 1003–4; 6, Nos. 42, 80, 82, 83, 92; *Hungarian Documents,* 2, Nos. 47, 50. See also Jan Masaryk to Krofta, 28 November 1936, Czech document in T–120, 1143/2028/444464.

102. For German pressure on Hungary to follow an exclusively anti-Czech policy in the winter 1936–37 see *G. D.*, C, 6, Nos. 53, 98, 145. It should be noted that the dates of these talks bracket the German-Czech soundings discussed above.

103. *G. D.*, C, 5, No. 114; *D. D. F.*, 2d, 1, No. 432; 2, No. 120; *Hungarian Documents,* 1, Nos. 40, 57, 139; Girsa (Czech minister Belgrade) telegram of 10 March 1936, Czech document in T–120, 1040/1809/413078.

104. *G. D.*, C, 5, Nos. 105, 224.

105. On Schacht's visit to Belgrade, as well as his general aims, see Hoptner, pp. 46–47, 98–100; U. S. 1936, 1:500–02; *G. D.*, C, 5, No. 376 (excerpts in Auswärtiges Amt, *Dokumente zum Konflikt mit Jugoslawien und Griechenland,* No. 21); *D. D. F.*, 2d, 2, Nos. 300, 302; "Informationsbericht Nr. 19," 3 June 1936, Bundesarchiv, Brammer, Z.Sg. 101/29, f. 225–29.

economy. Efforts were even being made to use German-Yugoslav trade for the support of the Far Right in Yugoslav internal politics, especially the Zbor organization of Dimitrije Ljotić.[106] The Yugoslav government was beginning to see that all was not necessarily perfect in an economic tie to the Third Reich, but by late 1936 there was little that could be done about that.[107]

Perhaps even more worrisome for the Yugoslavs was the rapprochement between Germany and Italy. The Belgrade government which had once looked to Paris for protection against Italy had found France immobilized by Germany. The Soviet Union hardly provided an alternative protector against either Italy or Germany for a country that did not even have diplomatic relations with Moscow.[108] Under these circumstances, and with German prodding, Yugoslavia turned toward a rapprochement with its traditional enemies, Italy and Bulgaria; and by the end of 1936 that shift was very largely completed.[109] Here was another reorientation in alignments following upon Germany's ascendancy. From Belgrade, neutrality looked like the only way out of the dilemma; for Yugoslavia as for other European countries, if they would not pool their strength, each would be forced to rely on its own isolated weakness. From the German point of view, this meant Yugoslavia's acquiescence in the annexation of Austria and in whatever Berlin might have in mind for Czechoslovakia. The French recognized the danger, but their efforts in late 1936 failed to reverse the tide in Southeast Europe by promises of assistance in return for expressions of solidarity against any enemy. Of the countries directly affected by this plan, Yugoslavia was strongest in its objections.[110] The Little Entente had become almost meaningless.

While German relations with Yugoslavia were growing closer in 1936, those with Bulgaria had already reached a stage where Germany dominated Bulgaria's foreign trade, and some Bulgarians were becoming alarmed about the extent of their country's dependence on the Third Reich. When Schacht was in Sofia on his Balkan tour, there was some resentment of his complacent assumption that Bulgaria was in effect a German colony, but there were no subsequent signs of any change in the situation.[111] The supply

106. Hoptner, p. 103. These negotiations were handled by the National Socialist gauleiter of East Prussia, Erich Koch. Relevant documents of the foreign trade section of the APA are memoranda of 17 and 18 August 1936, by its chief, Malletke, in Nuremberg document 912–PS (National Archives); *G. D.*, C, 6, Nos. 91, 104. See also Hory and Broszat, p. 30.

107. See *G. D.*, C, 5, No. 592.

108. A brief survey in Hoptner, pp. 173–76.

109. *G. D.*, C, 5, Nos. 449, 452, 534, 538, 586; 6, Nos. 20, 27; *D. D. F.*, 2d, 3, No. 299; *Allianz*, No. 16; Hoptner, pp. 43–45, 62–63; Campbell (Belgrade) dispatch 274, 20 November 1936, Foreign Office R 7105/1627/92.

110. *G. D.*, C, 5, No. 540; 6, No. 19; *Hungarian Documents*, 2, Nos. 36, 40, 48, 51; *D. D. F.*, 2d, 2, No. 418; 3, Nos. 448, 457, 467, 468; U. S. 1936, 1:383–84; Hoptner, pp. 55–58.

111. U. S. 1936, 1:491–92.

of arms to Bulgaria was playing an increasing role in the tightening of Germany's hold on that country, while that hold was being utilized to direct Bulgarian agriculture toward those crops and its mining toward minerals, most useful to Germany's war-directed economy.[112]

Arms exports by Germany also played a part in its relations with Greece.[113] Germany occupied an increasing role in Greek foreign trade, especially in taking Greek tobacco exports, and Schacht stopped in Athens on his tour in order to help that process along.[114] As yet, however, Greece was too remote from Germany's immediate concerns to call for attention to the problems and attitudes of that country.[115] Of far greater importance to Germany was its effort to reestablish a major role for itself in Turkey. Exchanges of diplomatic pleasantries in the first years of the Hitler regime gave way in 1936 to a very definite process of economic alignment.[116] In this process, the secretary general of the Turkish foreign ministry, Numan Menemencioğlu, played as active a part as the German negotiators, offering to turn over to Germany the import quotas of other countries like the United States.[117] The course of negotiations for new agreements, however, did not turn out to be so smooth in spite of a visit by Numan to Berlin in May and a trip by Schacht to Ankara in June 1936. The British did what they could to counter the German efforts; and the Turks themselves began to have reservations about the foreign trade practices of Hitler's Germany.[118] The new convention governing the Straits that Turkey secured in the summer of 1936 also raised some questions about German-Turkish relations, though these were soon smoothed over.[119] The real diplomatic tug-of-war over Turkish policy still lay in the future; in 1936 both the Germans and the Turks were content to move slowly toward improved trade relations.

112. *D. D. F.*, 2d, 1, No. 171; *Rowak Report*, 31 December 1937, p. 12, and Anhang, p. 3, Bundesarchiv, Reichsfinanzministerium, R 2/27, f. 50 and 65. On the German-Bulgarian arms trade and efforts to counter it by other countries see *D. D. F.*, 2d, 1, No. 240; *G. D.*, C, 4, No. 557, n. 1; *Hungarian Documents*, 1, No. 138; Krofta to Beneš, 25 September 1935, and Czech foreign ministry circular of 14 December 1935, Czech documents in T–120, 1041/1809/413485 and 413495.

Klaus Sohl's polemic, "Die Kriegsvorbereitungen des deutschen Imperialismus in Bulgarien am Vorabend des zweiten Weltkrieges," *Jahrbücher für Geschichte der UdSSR und der Volksdemokratischen Länder*, 3 (1959), 91–119, contains information primarily on the period from 1937 on.

113. *G. D.*, C, 4, No. 539.

114. U. S. 1936, 1:489–91; *G. D.*, C, 5, No. 383; *D. D. F.*, 2d, 2, No. 428; Dimitri Kitsikis, "La Grèce entre l'Angleterre et l'Allemagne de 1936 à 1941," *Revue Historique*, 238 (July-Sept. 1967), pp. 91–95.

115. For German-Greek relations in 1936 see *G. D.*, C, 5, Nos. 110, 482, 501.

116. *G. D.*, C, 1, No. 394; 4, Nos. 566, 572; 5, No. 100.

117. Ibid., 5, No. 287.

118. *D. D. F.*, 2d, 2, No. 316; 3, No. 203; Hans Kroll, *Lebenserinnerungen eines Botschafters* (Cologne; Kiepenheuer & Witsch, 1967), pp. 97–100; "Sitzung des Handelspolitischen Ausschusses vom 27. April 1936," T–120, 2612/5650/H 004078–079; Rahn (Ankara) to Pilger (Berlin), 15 and 22 April 1936, T–120, 3391/8632/E 604860–874.

119. *G. D.*, C, 5, Nos. 328, 462, 464, 468, 481, 483, 493, 633.

While Germany's reoccupation of the Rhineland by diverting attention elsewhere and forcing a revision of the peace settlement had greatly facilitated the realization of Turkey's ambition to revise the Straits regime, the rapprochement of Germany with Italy—Turkey's potential enemy in the Mediterranean—cast a shadow over German-Turkish relations.

Germany's interests in the Middle East beyond Turkey were of small significance before 1937. There was some trade, especially with Egypt, but it had declined during the depression and was not yet receiving the attention it would in the years just prior to the outbreak of war.[120] German efforts over a two-year period to develop an oil concession in Iraq were dropped in 1936 when a German government guarantee was refused because Germany would soon be producing enough synthetic oil of its own.[121] The attention paid to occasional incidents only confirms the general picture of disinterest. The assassination of the Afghan minister to Berlin by an Afghan student in June 1933 naturally caused considerable excitement—especially since the victim was a brother of the king of Afghanistan, and a prominent Afghan exile intervened on behalf of the assassin—but did not substantially affect the slow development of closer relations between Germany and Afghanistan.[122] Rosenberg's APA was playing a part in this process, but his role did not become important until 1937 and 1938. Almost as spectacular as the assassination would have been the return to the Egyptian government of the world-famous head of Nefretete which had been brought years before to the State Museum in Berlin under rather dubious circumstances. Though favored by Göring and Goebbels, this propaganda gesture was vetoed by Hitler himself.[123]

120. On German economic interests in the Middle East see Lukasz Hirszowicz, *The Third Reich and the Arab East* (London: Routledge & Kegan Paul, 1966), pp. 15–17. The Berlin Free University dissertation of Mohamed-Kamal El Dessouki, *Hitler und der Nahe Osten* (Berlin: Ernst-Reuter-Gesellschaft, 1963), does not deal with the years before 1937. Heinz Tillmann, *Deutschlands Araberpolitik im Zweiten Weltkrieg* (Berlin: Deutscher Verlag der Wissenschaften, 1965), is very useful for the period after 1937 in spite of its polemical tone but has little to add to Hirszowicz for the pre-1937 period.

121. The account in Hirszowicz should be supplemented by Oberkommando der Marine, "Ölversorgung der Kriegsmarine," 29 April 1940, pp. 3–5, Nuremberg document 984–PS (National Archives); Fritz Grobba, *Männer und Mächte im Orient* (Göttingen: Musterschmidt, 1967), pp. 91–94, 157–58; Foreign Office E 708/708/65.

122. On the assassination see Gordon (Berlin) dispatch 2464 of 7 June and Dodd dispatch 1054 of 21 July 1933, State 701.90H62/7 and 9; Memorandum of von Bülow, 10 January 1935, T–120, 1522/3088/D 625157; Note of 14 January 1935, T–120, 2389/4621/E 202263; Memorandum by Malletke of the APA, 11 January 1937, p. 3, Nuremberg document 1360–PS (National Archives). See also Malletke's notes on Afghanistan of 17 January 1936, Nuremberg document 1354–PS (National Archives); Grobba, p. 56. There is a good survey of German-Afghan relations as of December 1936 in Foreign Office N 6271/593/97.

123. On this incident see Memorandum by von Bülow, 4 October 1933, T–120, 2374/4603/E 191014; Memorandum by von Bülow, 9 October 1933, 1522/3088/D 625373–374; Stohrer (minister in Egypt) telegram 82, 13 December 1933, ibid., D 625376, and his note on a meeting with Hitler on 7 March 1934, ibid., D 625378–379. There is a characteristically distorted reference to the incident in Hanfstaengl, pp. 222–23.

The Consolidation of Germany's Position

The measures taken in accordance with National Socialist racialist views certainly did nothing to assist the slow development of better relations with Iran and the building up of German cultural and economic influence there.[124] A trade consortium agreement signed with the Iranian government on 30 March 1936 on behalf of several German firms by Ferrostaal A. G. was to open the way for German economic penetration of Iran. The first deliveries were signed for in December 1936; they were to be locomotives and freight cars for the new Trans-Iranian Railway.[125] This route would become a major avenue for American supplies to the Soviet Union in World War II; the official history of that operation refers to the first American railway troops riding to Tehran "on a train drawn by a little prewar Ferrostaal locomotive" and having "to get out and push the train up the more difficult grades."[126]

None of these matters could compare in importance with the impact on the Middle East caused by that aspect of National Socialist racial policies that went beyond prohibiting a minute number of Iranians and other so-called "non-Aryans" from marrying "Aryan" Germans to a policy of forcing the emigration of Jews from Germany. Some of these Jewish refugees would no doubt have gone to Palestine in any case, but the pressure of Jewish migration to the mandated territory was increased by the German policy of using Jewish migration to Palestine as a device for expanding German foreign trade and countering the threat of a world-wide Jewish boycott of German goods. Special agreements that evidently had Hitler's support were arrived at in the summer of 1933 under which Jews who left Germany for Palestine were accorded less onerous conditions for the transfer of their property abroad by way of an agreement providing for additional German exports to Palestine.[127] Thus, as an unintended by-product of National Socialist persecution of the Jews, the Third Reich was strengthening the Jewish position in Palestine, a development that affected both the Arabs and the Germans in that country. The latter, a small group of the Templar religious sect who had migrated to Palestine in the nineteenth century, were not likely to cause much trouble—whatever the sentimental concerns of

124. On a dispute over racial matters with Iran in 1936 see the notes by Hermann von Harder of the APA's foreign trade section of 11 and 13 July and 24 August 1936, Nuremberg document 913–PS (National Archives). On the growth of German-Iranian trade see Tillmann, pp. 18–19.

125. For relevant documents from the files of the German Ministry of Economics see T–71, roll 84, frames 587557ff. From these papers, which deal with the covering of deficits German firms expected to incur from deliveries to Iran, one can obtain a general idea of the program.

126. T. H. Vail Motter, *The Persian Corridor and Aid to Russia* (Washington: Government Printing Office, 1952), p. 347.

127. On the agreement and the attendant policies and practices see *G. D.*, C, 1, Nos. 369, 399; D, 5, No. 575; T–120, 3404/8817/E 613758–890, passim; Hirszowicz, pp. 26–27; Raul Hilberg, *The Destruction of the European Jews* (Chicago: Quadrangle, 1961), p. 95; Jacobsen, pp. 156–57; Jacob Robinson, *And the crooked shall be made straight* (New York: Macmillan, 1965), p. 95. A copy of the German ministry of economics circular of 28 August 1933 implementing the agreement is in Foreign Office C 8300/6839/18.

German party and diplomatic officials—but the Arabs were in a very different situation.

Increasingly worried by the increases in Jewish migration to the Holy Land, the majority coming from countries other than Germany, the Arab leaders were beginning to think about Germany as a possible ally both against the Jews and against the British and French mandatory authorities in the Middle East. The Arab uprising in Palestine which began in April 1936 and led the Peel Commission to advocate the partition of Palestine in the summer of 1937 would precipitate new policy questions for Berlin. When that time came, the German government would have to weigh such factors as the friendship of its new Axis partner, the possibility of antagonizing Britain by close association with the Arabs, interest in expanding foreign trade and hurrying Jewish emigration, the possibility of a Jewish state, and the potential assistance to Germany from Arab states and national movements. The Germans were to find the problems of the Middle East no easier, even if more remote, than anyone else.

The Third Reich, however, did have a major potential asset in its efforts to penetrate the Middle East after the initial consolidation of its power in Europe by the end of 1936. This asset was its enmity to Britain, France, and the Jews; in other words, its enmity to all the presumed enemies of the Arabs with the possible exception of Italy. The widespread assumption that Germany was one country that though friendly to Italy did not aspire to political control in the Middle East and was actually or potentially hostile to the British and French whose rule was the main object of Arab nationalist hostility provided Germany with a possible welcome in the Arab world. The developments of subsequent years would show how Germany could and would take advantage of that situation and how the other major powers would respond to this new factor in a part of the world from which they had thought Germany expelled with the defeat of its Ottoman ally.[128]

128. There is a story in the memoirs of Fritz Grobba (pp. 94–95) that in the spring of 1933 Hitler turned down the possibility of an oil concession in Saudi-Arabia because of Germany's inability to protect it in case of war. In view of Grobba's unreliability—he confuses the diplomatic crises of 1938 and 1939 (pp. 182–83)—this account cannot be accepted without confirming evidence.

13 On to War: The Axis, The Anti-Comintern Pact, and the Four-Year Plan

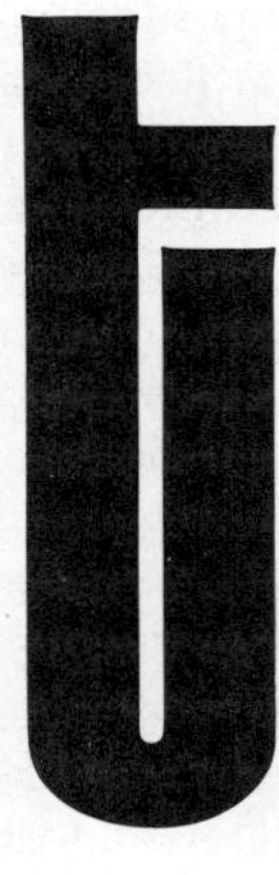

he halting steps in the direction of a rapprochement between Italy and Germany in the first half of 1936 have already been traced. The slowness of the process and the periodic recurrence of suspicion and friction must not be allowed to obscure the importance of the shift in the European balance implied by the new alignment. If the conversion of Italy from a barrier to a reluctant supporter of German expansion was less speedy and spectacular than the similar shift of the Soviet Union in 1939, it was no less significant. At the level Germany's strength had reached in 1936, the influence of Italy—however much the product of imagination rather than reality—immeasurably facilitated the creation of that image of power Hitler needed to frighten off potential challenges abroad and hesitations at home. If historians have found it proper to point to the difficulties that marked German-Italian relations after the formation of the Axis, as they have found it necessary to call attention to the inner contradictions of the "hollow alliance" between Germany and Japan,[1] we must remember that the observer of the international scene in the 1930s was influenced more by the image of strength and health than by the postmortem discovery of all manner of congenital defects in those alignments. Policy was made on the appearance of the day rather than the archival research of subsequent decades, and few modern leaders understood this more clearly than Adolf Hitler. If the landmarks along the road to a German-Italian alliance were marked more by bombast than by substance, this was not necessarily unintentional; both parties were often more interested in impressing other powers with the strength that the appearance of solidarity provided than in tying their own hands by detailed treaties or dovetailed policies. The Axis in the pre-

1. Johanna M. Meskill, *Hitler and Japan: The Hollow Alliance* (New York: Atherton Press, 1966).

World War II period, therefore, must be seen both from the point of view of diplomacy and as it presented itself by means of propaganda; its importance resulted from the existence of both, even though they might at times be in conflict with each other.

If the Ethiopian conflict had pulled Italy away from an alignment with Britain and France while pushing it closer to Germany, the end of that war in Africa ought to have allowed a return to the earlier relationship. This was not to be. Mussolini's vanity had been wounded by the imposition of sanctions; it annoyed him at the same time as its eventual ineffectiveness influenced his negative assessment of British will and power. In his hour of triumph, the delays in ending sanctions angered him. At the same time, the German-Austrian agreement that he himself had urged now operated to reduce a most, if not the most, important barrier to agreement with Germany. Moreover, the new officials Mussolini had appointed to high positions in the Italian foreign ministry, Count Ciano and Undersecretary Bastianini, were sympathetic to a policy more closely attuned to Berlin.[2]

The triumph in Ethiopia led Mussolini to create an issue made to order for trouble with the Western powers and friendship with Germany. The king of Italy was proclaimed emperor of Ethiopia on 9 May 1936, and the countries of the world were expected to recognize him as such. Recognition became increasingly a matter of prestige in Mussolini's eyes, assuming a political importance out of all proportion to its actual significance.[3] With or without the formal title, Italy would exercise control over that part of Africa only as long as its military forces occupied it; but as in his decision to move forward in East Africa in the preceding year, Mussolini had engaged his prestige, a dictator's most precious possession. The importance of the issue must also be seen in an international context in which the Japanese puppet state of "Manchukuo" was not recognized by the powers as an independent country and in which Franco would have to wait almost three years for recognition from major powers other than Germany and Italy.

It was precisely in this field that a concession by Britain was psychologically most difficult to obtain. London might quietly acquiesce in events that could not be changed without war, but the extension of formal recognition was more than the British public could be expected to accept. At the same time, however, this was also one field where Germany could easily afford to be gracious. Recognition of Italy's rule in Ethiopia cost Germany nothing; and the more noise was made about the whole question, the more valuable the German gesture could be made to appear in Mussolini's eyes. Berlin's willingness to accede to Italy's desire for recognition at a time and under circumstances of Italy's choosing was, therefore, made known to

2. See *D. D. F.*, 2d, 2, No. 338.

3. Documents on the recognition question, especially as it related to the accreditation of diplomats, may be found in ibid, 3.

Rome with Hitler's approval in late June 1936.[4] The fact that Germany asked for no concessions in return sweetened the gesture and made it easier for the German ambassador, Ulrich von Hassell, to coordinate with Mussolini and Count Ciano during the following weeks a joint policy of Germany and Italy toward the abortive negotiations for a new Locarno.[5] The common aversion of the two powers toward any new system of security in Western Europe would provide a platform for diplomatic contact and cooperation for the balance of 1936.[6]

The Spanish civil war not only afforded another common bond between Germany and Italy but, as already indicated, inhibited a return of Italy to closer relations with Britain and France. This became particularly obvious as Italy engaged itself in Spain more directly and extensively than Germany was prepared to do. Furthermore, this Italian policy implied a deterioration in Italian-Soviet relations, which had been rather good in preceding years. Although Mussolini always recognized the anti-Bolshevik explanations of Axis policy a propaganda façade for steps Italy and Germany wished to take in any case, his joining in this chorus in 1936 affected Italy's relations with the Soviet Union, then just beginning the process of liquidating its own Communist party with a ruthlessness that Mussolini and Hitler could envy. It is not surprising, therefore, that as Italy cut itself off from possible alternative associations in the West and the East, the coordination of its policies with those of Germany should be increasingly noted by the world at large.[7] This coordination was heralded by a visit of the new Italian foreign minister —Mussolini's son-in-law—to Berlin.

The question of a formal visit by Ciano to Berlin had been ventilated in a most informal and still partially unclarified manner in late July 1936 by an unofficial emissary of Hans Frank. The current excitement over the situation in Spain and, it would appear, the hostility of the German foreign minister, von Neurath, had led to a postponement of the proposed venture.[8] Although Hitler stressed his good relations with Mussolini in his meeting with Horthy on 22 August, von Neurath was still exerting a delaying influence on the rapprochement with Italy.[9] The trip of the prince of Hessen

4. *G. D., C,* 5, Nos. 390, 409, 479; Ciano, *Diplomatic Papers,* pp. 8–9; *D. D. F.,* 2d, 3, Nos. 114, 118; *Hungarian Documents,* 1, Nos. 108, 115.

5. *G. D., C,* 5, No. 442; D, 1, No. 155; Ciano, *Diplomatic Papers,* pp. 13–14; *D. D. F.,* 2d, 3, No. 6.

6. See p. 274.

7. U. S. 1936, 1:335–38, 350–53; 2:447; *Hungarian Documents* 1, No. 140.

8. This incident is not mentioned in Frank's memoirs. The sources used are a somewhat dubious account in Anfuso, pp. 22–23, and von Neurath's memorandum of 4 August 1936, in *G. D., C,* 5, No. 554, n. 2. The third edition of Anfuso's memoirs, published by Cappelli in 1957 under the title *Da Palazzo Venezia al lago di garda (1936–1945),* contains additional material for the last years of the war but not for the period covered here.

9. On the Horthy visit see pp. 321f., above; on von Neurath's views at this time see *G. D., C,* 5, No. 523.

to Rome at the end of August 1936 to coordinate German and Italian policy in Spain and the repeated appearances of Admiral Canaris in Italy on similar missions have already been alluded to. They helped pave the way for an exchange of unofficial visits in late September. Hans Frank went to Rome again, and Filippo Anfuso, Ciano's secretary, who had previously served as vice-consul in Munich and in the Italian embassy in Berlin, was introduced to Hitler by the prince of Hessen.[10] In these informal contacts, Mussolini and Hitler reassured each other's emissaries of their dislike, distrust, and lack of regard for Great Britain—a common bond that needed expression since each was suspicious of possible flirtations with England by the other. The road was to be prepared for an eventual visit of Mussolini to Germany—Hitler having been in Italy in 1934—but there was agreement that Ciano would go first. By this time it was already evident that the war in Spain was likely to continue for some time, keeping the two powers closely aligned in a common enterprise. Ciano's trip would not only afford him an opportunity to meet with Germany's leaders but would signal the creation of a new relationship. What precisely that relationship might be and how it could be most appropriately presented to the world, remained to be discussed before Ciano and his entourage headed north.

For four weeks the German and Italian governments exchanged views about the agreements to be reached in the forthcoming meeting, hoping to straighten out all differences of opinion beforehand.[11] Disregarding minor details, one can see in these preliminary negotiations both those interests that drew the two countries together and those that kept them apart. They were both opposed to a new Locarno agreement that went beyond a simple promise of nonaggression between Germany and France—anything else would restrict Germany's freedom of action in Central and Eastern Europe. Both were willing to support Franco, though Italy more so than Germany; at the same time, both recognized that any request for territorial concessions from Franco would be fatal to his reputation and prospects in Spain. The two countries agreed that bolshevism was an abomination. Both were pleased that the German-Austrian Agreement of 11 July had removed a major source of friction between Berlin and Rome, and both hoped that improvements in Italian-Yugoslav relations would assist the breakup

10. On Frank's trip see his *Im Angesicht des Galgens,* pp. 233–34; *G. D.,* C, 5, No. 553; Ciano, *Diplomatic Papers,* pp. 43–48. On Anfuso's trip see his *Rom-Berlin im diplomatischem Spiegel,* pp. 23–29; Magistrati, "La Germania e l'impresa italiana di Etiopia," pp. 602–03.

11. *G. D.,* C, 5, Nos. 554, 562, 568, 572, 583, 585, 586, 588, 593, 595, 597, 599, 600, 602, 603, 608, 613, pp. 1122–24; *D. D. F.,* 2d, 3, No. 330; Ciano, *Diplomatic Papers,* pp. 49–50; Dertinger's "Informationsbericht No. 39," 21 October 1936, Bundesarchiv, Brammer, Z.Sg. 101/29, f. 399–407.

It should be noted that Italian sources available for the second half of 1936 are very meager: Aloisi's diary ends in June 1936; the memoirs of Magistrati and the diary of Ciano both begin with 1937. The eighth series of the publication of Italian documents will eventually cover this period, but the editors decided to begin with the last rather than the first volumes of this series in order to document the events of the spring and summer of 1939.

of the Little Entente. With Germany willing to recognize the Italian empire in Ethiopia, Italy was prepared to be gracious about Germany's minute economic interests there. The two were now also in agreement as to their policy toward the League of Nations: Italy would sabotage its operations as long as it stayed inside, and when Italy left the League the German offer to return to Geneva, once made to delude the British but long since consigned to oblivion, would be withdrawn formally as well. Pleasant but hardly very meaningful words would be exchanged about economic cooperation and Italian diplomatic support for a return of colonies to Germany.

At the same time, the record of the preliminary talks illuminates some divergencies between Germany and Italy. Each had its own ideas about the tactics to be followed in the negotiations with Britain and France about a new Locarno, and each adhered to its own procedure. More important, neither was prepared to defer to the interests of the other in its general policy toward the Balkans. Here in particular the Germans wanted to be quite certain not to restrict their own ambitions in any way. The strong position Italy had secured through the Rome protocols was being undermined by the growth of German influence in Southeast Europe, and Berlin was not about to give up the advantages it expected to harvest from that trend. The two nations would also follow different routes in their policies in East Asia. Italy was willing to go further toward at least de facto recognition of Manchukuo than was Germany, while the Germans, as they explained to Ciano after his arrival, had decided to negotiate a different set of agreements with Japan. As for the formal aspects of the visit, there is something of the unconscious humor that dogged the whole Axis relationship in the fact that beforehand Ciano wanted his visit trumpeted about in a big way while von Neurath preferred a more subdued staging; but by the time it was all over, Ciano was tired and annoyed by the extensive ceremonies.[12] Since both parties were greatly interested in the propaganda effect of their relationship on other powers, especially England, all had to smile for the photographers.

While Ciano was in Germany he met with von Neurath, Göring, and Hitler.[13] With Göring's role confined on this occasion primarily to economic issues, von Neurath canvassed with Ciano in their talks on 21–22 October a wide range of topics in addition to those foreshadowed by the preparatory negotiations. Agreement being reached without much difficulty, von Neurath went on to explain Germany's reluctance to recognize Manchukuo lest its interests in China be jeopardized. He urged Italian support in the dispute over Lithuania's administration of Memel and also asked that Italy recall

12. Compare *G. D.*, C, 5, No. 562, with Anfuso, pp. 35 and 38, and Dertinger's "Informationsbericht Nr. 41," 26 October 1936, Bundesarchiv, Brammer, Z.Sg. 101/29, f. 415–17.

13. *G. D.*, C, 5, Nos. 618, 620–22, 624; D, 3, No. 106; Dodd *Diary*, 26 October 1936, p. 359; Ciano, *Diplomatic Papers*, pp. 52–60; Anfuso, pp. 30–38; Frank, p. 234; *Hungarian Documents,* 1, Nos. 161, 164, 168; *D. D. F.*, 2d, 3, Nos. 395, 408, 410, 412, 413; Kitsikis, p. 104.

Eugenio Morreale from Vienna. Morreale had acted for Mussolini in the Austrian capital when Italy still maintained its opposition to any form of German influence there; he was now to be removed as Cerruti had been and as von Hassell and Attolico were in later years.[14] Like the Minotaur, the Axis claimed victims each year. Had Ciano been more perceptive, he might have recognized that the Axis would some day claim far greater sacrifices: von Neurath explained to him that while the time to take Danzig and the corridor from Poland had not yet arrived, the Germans "wished to wait for the propitious moment and to settle our differences with the Poles as far as possible in a peaceful manner."[15] The record does not divulge Ciano's thoughts on this subject; he merely referred to Italy's good relations with Poland. In line with the exchanges that had preceded his journey, he asked Germany to help Italy improve its relations with Yugoslavia, a prospect that fitted in well with German policy at the time.

The meeting between Hitler and Ciano provided an opportunity for mutual admiration. Matching this admiration in intensity was their common dislike of Britain. Ciano fed Hitler's antagonism by giving him some British diplomatic documents, stolen in Rome, that contained nasty but accurate evaluations of the National Socialist regime, its leaders, and its aims. The German dictator and the Italian foreign minister agreed not only in their hostility to the English but on the use of antibolshevism as a screen for the process of rallying other countries to them, thereby paralyzing England while the two powers continued their armament programs. The suggestion Hitler made for coordinating German and Italian policy toward Yugoslavia complemented Ciano's requests; Germany and Italy would jointly urge Hungary to concentrate its revisionist aspirations against Czechoslovakia, thereby facilitating Belgrade's alignment with themselves. The one potential stumbling block to German-Italian cooperation was brought in by Hitler in a manner as spectacular as it was discreet: he showed his Italian guests the window of his Berchtesgaden residence through which one could see Austria clearly and close by. But nothing was allowed to spoil the exchange of pleasantries.

A common front was shown to the world. Mussolini might subsequently negotiate with the British,[16] but he thought of himself as allied to Germany by ties that were real even if not concrete. The term may have originated elsewhere and earlier, but it was Mussolini who in his speech in Milan on 1 November 1936 gave the term "Axis" its public definition. He expected to play a major role in shaping the policy and reaping the benefits of this combination. Like Hitler's domestic German allies before 30 January 1933, Mussolini could not afterward complain that he had been misled about Hitler's intentions. As Ciano recorded in his report on the conversation at

14. Mussolini had alluded to the possibility of demanding the recall of von Hassell on 19 February 1936 (Aloisi, p. 351).

15. *G. D.*, C, 5, No. 620.

16. Eden, pp. 478ff.

Berchtesgaden, Hitler had told him: "In three years Germany will be ready, in four years more than ready; if five years are given, better still."[17]

For Germany, the association with Italy had both short- and long-range advantages. In the immediate situation it meant that Germany could safely continue to disregard the British and French suggestions for a new Locarno. The slow but perceptible growth of German influence in Central and Southeast Europe could continue unchecked, especially in Austria. In a broader perspective, the Axis provided Germany full assurance that it could move forward with its rearmament program without fear of anyone taking preventive action. As its potential enemies slowly awakened to the danger that faced them, that danger was magnified automatically by the junction, however tenuous, of Italy to Germany. The economic problems of German rearmament, signalized by the establishment of the Four-Year Plan simultaneously with the creation of the Axis, could not be taken advantage of by others had they been so minded. It was this same deterrent effect on potential resistance to the growth of German power that lay behind the other international association into which Germany entered in the fall of 1936. On 23 October 1936, the same day on which Ciano and von Neurath signed a confidential protocol embodying the policies on which they had agreed in the German foreign ministry at Wilhelmstrasse 74, across the street in the Dienststelle Ribbentrop at Wilhelmstrasse 64 Joachim von Ribbentrop and the Japanese ambassador, Mushakoji Kintomo, initialed the Anti-Comintern Pact.[18]

If German policy toward East Asia had been subject to various crosscurrents in the first part of the National Socialist regime, that confusion was compounded in subsequent years. In China during 1935 and 1936, the German military advisers continued their work of trying to assist Chiang Kai-shek in the formation of a modern army. Military equipment from Germany was reaching the Chinese Nationalist government, and when the quality of that equipment left something to be desired, General von Faulkenhausen, the chief of the advisory staff, did what he could to have the situation mended. As Chiang consolidated his power, the possibility of his extending government control to the Canton area suggested that the German military advisers there as well as the industrial projects of Hans Klein would be included in his orbit. Germany might lose repayment from the local warlord, but its influence would continue.[19]

17. Ciano, *Diplomatic Papers,* p. 58. See also Wiskemann, chap. IV, and Mario Donosti (pseud. of Mario Lucciolli), *Mussolini e l'Europa; la politica estera fascista* (Rome: Leonardo, 1945), part 2, chap. 1.

18. Gerhard L. Weinberg (ed.), "Die geheimen Abkommen zum Antikominternpakt," *Vierteljahrshefte für Zeitgeschichte,* 2, No. 2 (April, 1954), 201.

19. On the military advisers in Nanking and in Canton in 1935 see Altenburg (German consul general Canton) report 564, 3 June 1935, T–120, 2988/6681/H 096433; Plessen (German legation Nanking) report 701, 10 July 1935, ibid., frame H 096438; von Falkenhausen to Brinckmann, 13 August 1935, T–120, 2988/6680/H 096326–330.

What most interested Berlin, and especially the Ministry of War, about Klein's projects, however, was neither influence nor payment but return shipments of raw materials from China. These materials, especially the tungsten needed for Germany's armaments industry, provided the incentive to support Klein and to clear up the difficulties with Chiang and other elements in China—including German diplomats and businessmen there—that Klein generated in his never-ending feuds.[20] In the process of supporting him, the German government agreed to move its legation from Peiping to Nanking and subsequently to raise its status to that of an embassy.[21] When the Chinese government was particularly obliging in the dispatch of tungsten, the Germans were first moved to send thank-you telegrams and then special gifts—a ceremonial sword for Chiang from Hitler and a special car for him from von Blomberg.[22] The Nanking authorities may have been reminded of gifts exchanged with barbarians in bygone days.

The exchange of Chinese raw materials for German military supplies became a subject of increasing importance for both parties in 1936. Chiang sent a special mission to Germany to discuss the trade program. This mission, which was received by Hitler on 27 February just before he met the new Chinese ambassador, Tien Fong, was to place orders in Germany within the framework of a 100 million mark revolving credit that would be repaid by Chinese raw materials.[23] As Rowak and Hisma had been organized to handle the sending of German military supplies in exchange for raw materials from Spain, so a special company, the Hapro (Handelsgesellschaft für industrielle Produkte m. b. H.) was created for analogous trade with China.[24] Klein expected to play the same role in Hapro that Bern-

20. *G. D.*, C, 4, Nos. 338, 432, 517, 552, n. 1; German Ministry of Education to the foreign ministry, 20 August 1935, T–120, 2988/6680/H 096323–324. For Rheinmetall and Solothurn deliveries in this period see German legation Nanking report 259, 17 March 1936, 2991/6691/H 098691–693.

For an excellent survey of Germany's increasing dependence on imports of tungsten from China during the 1930s see Jörg-Johannes Jäger, *Die wirtschaftliche Abhängigkeit des Dritten Reiches vom Ausland dargestellt am Beispiel der Stahlindustrie* (Berlin: Berlin Verlag, 1969), pp. 156–58.

21. Rabenau, *Seeckt; Aus seinem Leben,* p. 713; von Neurath memorandum RM 540, 27 June 1935, T–120, 2383/4619/E 198120–121; U. S. 1935, 3:523.

22. German Ministry of Economics to foreign ministry, Nr. 3866/35 geh. Ausl. VII, 11 November 1935, T–120, 2988/6680/H 096333; foreign ministry to Nanking telegram 32, 13 November, ibid., frame H 096334; German Ministry of War to foreign ministry, Nr. 4406/35 geh. Ausl. VII, 14 December 1935, T–120, 2991/6691/H 098586; telegrams of Kung and Chiang to Blomberg, 20 November 1935, T–77, 81/804743–744.

23. Rabenau, p. 717; Meier-Welcker, pp. 687, 691–92, 696; Karl Drechsler, *Deutschland-China-Japan 1933–1939, Das Dilemma der deutschen Fernostpolitik* (Berlin: Akademie Verlag, 1964), pp. 15–18; *G. D.*, C, 5, Nos. 64, 156, 254, 270; Seeckt to Blomberg, 8 January 1936, T–77, 81/804745–746; Memorandum of Voss, IV Chi 356, 29 February and 4 March 1936, T–120, 2988/6680/H 096355–360; Trautmann telegram 54, 19 March 1936, ibid., frames H 096383–384, and following documents on serial 6680.

24. Hapro was placed under the general jurisdiction of the Four-Year-Plan in October 1937. For information about it see esp. T–77, rolls 123–24, which contain

hardt performed in Rowak and Hisma, but von Blomberg exercised a closer supervision, using his economic expert Colonel Thomas to keep an eye on developments. In view of the grave doubts of German diplomats in China and the foreign ministry in Berlin about the whole operation, the German shipments were sent in stages to make certain that Chinese payments in foreign exchange or raw materials did not get too far behind.[25]

As a counterpart to the special Chinese trade mission to Germany and to make sure that the projects moved forward reasonably well in the complicated situation in East Asia, von Blomberg sent General von Reichenau to China in late May 1936.[26] Von Reichenau had moved from his position in the armed forces office (Wehrmachtsamt) in Berlin to head military district VII in Munich in October 1935, but military missions with a political flavor appear to have interested him more than the routine work of building up Germany's army. In spite of the misgivings of the German foreign minister and the German ambassador to Tokyo, Herbert von Dirksen, then home on leave in Germany, von Reichenau went out for several months, seeing Chiang Kai-shek, the German diplomats in China, and, of course, his brother who was working with Klein.[27]

The reason for von Neurath's and von Dirksen's objections to this trip by von Reichenau, beyond their general distrust of Klein's projects, was the fear that so spectacular an action as the dispatch of a famous general on the active list to China, coming on top of a German credit agreement giving China terms more favorable than those accorded China by any other country, would seriously imperil Germany's relations with Japan.[28] Out of fear of such repercussions, the diplomats had been successful in persuading von Blomberg to order a German general in Peiping to cancel his acceptance of a position as military adviser to General Sung Che-yuan, the key figure in the Hopei-Chahar political council governing parts of North China. Any German role there would have looked like participation on the Chinese side in the complicated tug-of-war over Japan's efforts to extend its influence from Manchuria southward. Here the clash between China and Japan was too obvious and clear-cut for Germany to take sides.[29] The hopes for delivery

---

Hapro's reports for 1941–43. For Klein's views see his telegram to the Ministry of War of 20–21 November 1935, in T–77, 81/804741–742.

25. *G. D.,* C, 5, Nos. 217, 235, 238, 239, 281; *D. D. F.,* 2d, 2, No. 246; Blomberg to Falkenhausen, W.Stb. 2688/36 geh., 25 March 1936, T–120, 2988/6680/H 096411–412. A detailed account on Klein's projects may be found in a report by an official of the Reichsbank, Rosenbruch, who was a member of the Kiep mission discussed in the text, of 3 April 1936, T–120, 2787/6022/H 044486–492.

26. *G. D.,* C, 5, No. 306.

27. On Reichenau's activities in China and German-Chinese trade problems in the summer of 1936 see *G. D.,* C, 5, Nos. 386, 461, 495, 502, 504, 536; *D. D. F.,* 2d, 2, No. 476; Dertinger, "Informationsbericht Nr. 37," 10 October 1936, Bundesarchiv, Brammer, Z.Sg. 101/29, f. 373.

28. *G. D.,* C, 4, No. 433; 5, Nos. 238, 239, 306, 338, 346; von Dirksen, *Moskau-Tokio-London,* p. 185.

29. The relevant exchanges for the period 25–29 February 1936 may be found in

of key raw materials from China, however, were evidently too strong to be sacrificed to the objections of Japan when they concerned an area not as exposed as the provinces of China adjacent to Manchukuo.

The relationship of Germany's need for raw materials for its armaments program and its lack of foreign exchange for purchasing them to its policy in East Asia was brought out particularly clearly in a ministerial conference in Berlin on 27 May 1936.[30] With Göring, Schacht, and von Blomberg for once in agreement, von Blomberg stated: "Certain hopes for the future can be placed in China. Anything that antagonizes it politically must therefore be avoided. [We] must proceed with caution in the rapprochement with Japan; recognition of Manchukuo at this time would destroy the current operations of Klein in China." When Göring responded with the comment that a common front involving China and Japan against the Soviet Union could probably be created, he added to the issues of recognition of Manchukuo and rapprochement with Japan the third of the themes interacting in German activities in the Far East in 1935–36 beyond the developing interest in the raw materials of China.

Germany's concern with Manchukuo growing out of its need to import soybeans and soybean products has already been discussed in Chapter 5. The import and foreign-exchange crisis of 1935–36 suggested to Berlin the wisdom of following up on the ill-fated adventures of Ferdinand Heye by a more orthodox approach. A special trade mission was planned in the summer of 1935, and to avoid antagonizing the Chinese the "study commission" headed by Minister Kiep was to go to China, Japan, and Thailand as well as Manchuria, though its main focus of attention would be on the Manchurian soybean trade.[31] The mission's primary purpose, in fact, was to arrange a trade and compensation agreement with the Manchukuo authorities, satisfying Japan by dealing with those authorities and thereby recognizing them de facto, while minimizing Chinese objections by avoiding any legal recognition of the puppet regime the Japanese had installed in Hsinking.[32] The commission spent several months in East Asia, eventually arriving at an agreement with the Manchukuo authorities on 30 April 1936.

Where Germany's rearmament program was even indirectly involved, Germany would ignore Chinese protests over its dealing with the puppet regime of Manchukuo just as it had ignored Japan's objections to the Hapro

---

T–120, 2988/6681/H 096489–494. Lindemann, the German general involved in the incident, has given his version in his memoirs, *Im Dienste Chinas,* pp. 502–05.

30. A record of the conference, by Lieutenant Colonel Wilhelm Löb, in 1301–PS, *TMWC,* 27:144–48. Löb was an air force officer who played an important role in Göring's economic projects in 1936–37 (see Berenice A. Carroll, *Design for Total War, Arms and Economics in the Third Reich* [The Hague: Mouton, 1968], pp. 125ff.).

31. Trautmann telegram 105, 22 July 1935, T–120, 2992/6692/H 098833.

32. *G. D.,* C, 4, p. 782; U. S. 1935, 3:374; Reichsstelle für Devisenbewirtschaftung (Wohlthat) to Kiep, 20 September 1935, T–120, 2612/5650/H 004047; "Instruktion für die Wirtschaftliche Studienkommission für Ostasien," 24 September 1935, ibid., frame H 004048.

trade agreement with Chiang Kai-shek. In each case, the Berlin government gave priority to the foreign trade requirements of its rearmament program while attempting to keep to a minimum the political effects of such measures upon its relations with China and Japan.[33] As the Germans themselves saw their foreign economic policy, they had concentrated on the Danubian area in 1933–34, on Latin America in 1934–35, and on the Far East in 1935–36.[34]

In view of the repercussions that Germany's relations with China and Japan always had on the attitude of the other, it is not surprising that some of the more adventurous elements involved in National Socialist foreign policy should have attempted to mediate the differences between Nanking and Tokyo, thereby eliminating the constant problems of choice between the two. This first German effort at mediation in the Far East, which foreshadows that of 1937–38, cannot yet be traced in detail, but there is enough information to provide an outline of the affair. The key figures were Hermann Kriebel and Edmund Fuerholzer, both examples of the amateur in diplomacy upon the National Socialist scene. Kriebel began as a Bavarian staff officer, served in the China expedition in 1900–1901 at the time of the Boxer Rebellion, and after occupying prominent staff positions during and after World War I organized in Bavaria paramilitary units associated with Hitler. Together the former corporal and the retired lieutenant colonel had played key roles in the attempted putsch of November 1923 and together they served their jail terms in Landsberg. Kriebel had later joined those German officers who worked with Chiang Kai-shek. He remained in touch with Hitler and in 1934 became German consul general in Shanghai. His long acquaintance with Hitler gave him direct access to the dictator, and he used it when the possibility of a special diplomatic scheme arose in the fall of 1935.[35] Fuerholzer, like Kriebel, had been involved in the ultranationalist movements of post-World War I Bavaria but had gone to the United States in 1926 where he dabbled in German-American political activity while keep-

33. *G. D.*, C, 4, Nos. 448, 479, 552; 5, Nos. 195, p. 499, No. 537; Weinberg, "Recognition of Manchoukuo," pp. 154–55; "Bestellungen aus der Pressekonferenz vom 30. April 1936," ". . . vom 2. Juni 1936," ". . . vom 25. Juni 1936," Bundesarchiv Brammer, Z.Sg. 101/7, f. 285, 353, 403; Memorandum of Gaus, zu IV Chi 5136 II, 21 January 1936, T–120, 2992/6692/H 098837; Memorandum of von Bülow, 4 May 1936, T–120, 2373/4602/E 190263–264.

34. See the foreign ministry's circular of 17 August 1936, *G. D.*, C, 5, No. 511.

35. On Kriebel's career see Albrecht von Thaer, *Generalstabsdienst an der Front und in der O.H.L.* (ed. by Siegfried A. Kaehler) (Göttingen: Vandenhoeck & Ruprecht, 1958), p. 190, n. 119; Heinrich Bennecke, *Die Reichswehr und der Röhm-Putsch* (Munich: Olzog, 1964), p. 9; Jacobsen, p. 27. From April 1939, Kriebel served as the chief of the personnel and administrative section of the foreign ministry until his death in February 1941. Hitler later remembered him as a diplomat who though "one of our men" was still ignorant enough to write him that the Japanese were not strong enough to settle with the Chinese (*Hitler Table Talk,* Trevor-Roper edition, 2 February 1942, p. 277; similarly, Wiedemann, pp. 174–75). In earlier years, Hitler had paid more attention to Kriebel's views on East Asia (see the report on the Hitler-Strasser talk of 22 May 1930, in Otto Strasser, *Aufbau des deutschen Sozialismus* [2d ed., Prague: Heinrich Grunov, 1936], p. 132).

ing in touch with the National Socialist party in Germany. He worked from 1933 on in the German news service, Transocean, mainly as its Far Eastern chief with headquarters in China.[36]

In mid-October 1935, Fuerholzer had a conversation with the Chinese prime minister, Wang Ching-wei, who requested on behalf of himself and Chiang Kai-shek that Hitler help arrange for a compromise between China and Japan, a compromise that would lead to cooperation between the three countries in economic matters as well as in the struggle against communism. Kriebel was in Berlin at that time, and Fuerholzer flew to Germany so that they could jointly approach Hitler.[37] In Germany, this scheme was brought to the attention of Hitler and von Ribbentrop at a time when von Ribbentrop was already working on an anti-Comintern agreement with the Japanese military attaché, Oshima Hiroshi. Oshima indicated that his superiors in Japan were indeed interested in an agreement with China, and Hitler thereupon gave his approval in principle to the concept of German mediation. While Kriebel was on his way back to East Asia, however, relations between China and Japan over Japanese intrigues in North China had deteriorated to such an extent that Berlin decided that nothing could be done for the time being after all.[38] The wounding of Wang Ching-wei in an assassination attempt had removed him from the scene during the key part of the negotiations, a factor of great importance in view of his favorable attitude toward the idea of an accommodation with Japan. Although the subject appears to have been touched on again subsequently, the German government maintained its reserve in view of the obvious lack of any Japanese interest in better relations with the Nanking government.[39] Berlin was interested in aiding a Chinese-Japanese rapprochement, but only if there appeared to be some chance of success.

The Fuerholzer-Kriebel soundings had come into tangential relations with another set of informal discussions: the von Ribbentrop-Oshima talks about an anti-Comintern pact. There are still gaps in the record of those negotiations, because they too were conducted through special channels and largely behind the backs of the foreign ministries in both Berlin and Tokyo. The picture in this case, however, is much clearer than in regard to the attempted German mediation.[40] In May or June of 1935, at the same time

36. On Fuerholzer's career see his papers in T–81, Serials 53 and 185–89. He was subsequently active in various German foreign propaganda operations in Europe and the United States.

37. *G. D.*, C, 4, No. 416; Chinese ambassador Berlin to Kriebel, 18 October 1935, T–120, 2991/6691/H 098604; Lammers to Kriebel, St.S. Nr. 3445/35, 19 October 1935, ibid., frame H 098605; Fuerholzer to Trautmann, 21 October 1935, T–81, Roll 32, Serial 53, frame 28931, and Fuerholzer's letter to Hitler's adjutant, Captain Wiedemann, 1 October 1938, ibid., frame 29257; Memorandum by Fuerholzer on a conversation with an unidentified Japanese official on 9 and 10 August 1935, T–81, roll 33, frames 29810–812.

38. *G. D.*, C, 4, Nos. 433, 451, 452.

39. For further documentation on the episode see ibid., Nos. 466, 479, 493.

40. There is an excellent account in Sommer, pp. 23–42. The account here is based on Sommer and the sources he lists unless otherwise noted.

that von Ribbentrop was negotiating the naval agreement with England, he made contact with Oshima through an intermediary, Friedrich Wilhelm Hack, who had once worked for the South Manchurian Railway Company —the key instrument of Japanese expansion on the mainland of Asia—and had met the Japanese military attaché in Germany through his subsequent activities in the arms trade.[41] Von Ribbentrop appears to have been interested in some agreement of an anti-Soviet character; but Oshima delayed any response until von Ribbentrop at his first personal meeting with Oshima in October 1935 insisted that the Japanese general staff be asked its views as to the attitude either Germany or Japan should take in case the other were involved in war with the Soviet Union. Oshima thereupon secured instructions from the Japanese general staff that the idea of cooperation against Russia deserved investigation and was told that a representative of the general staff would be sent to Berlin to look into the matter.

Up to this point, von Ribbentrop may not have had Hitler's full approval of his ideas, though it is difficult to imagine that he would have acted at all had he thought that the Führer would be opposed. While Oshima and von Ribbentrop awaited the Japanese emissary, a project for a pact with Japan was worked out in the Dienststelle Ribbentrop by Hermann von Raumer, its Far Eastern specialist. To avoid an open breach with the Soviet Union, the pact with Japan would ostensibly be directed against the Comintern. Hitler approved the idea on 25 November 1935, a few days after he had also agreed to try to secure the adherence of China to this scheme in the course of German mediation between that country and Japan. With the Japanese emissary in Berlin conferring with Oshima, von Ribbentrop, and von Blomberg, and with everyone in agreement on an anti-Comintern Pact that Britain and Poland would be asked to join, all seemed to be going forward to a formal agreement.[42] Immediately thereafter, however, there was a setback in the negotiations.

In the first place, von Neurath argued strongly against tying Germany to Japan.[43] He was greatly concerned about the repercussions of a German alignment with Japan on its relations with England. It was von Neurath's view that Japan really had nothing to offer Germany, and for a while he appears to have cooled Hitler's receptivity to von Ribbentrop's brainstorm. At the same time, there is evidence that—possibly under the influence of General Beck, the German army chief of staff, and General Ott, the German military attaché in Tokyo—Minister of War von Blomberg began to have

41. For some of Hack's later adventures, especially his role in Japanese peace feelers in 1945, see Robert J. C. Butow, *Japan's Decision to Surrender* (Stanford: Stanford University Press, 1954), pp. 104–8; cf. Heinkel, p. 373.

42. *G. D.*, C, 4, No. 416; 5:271, 273; Testimony of Wakamatsu Tadaichi, International Military Tribunal for the Far East, Proceedings, pp. 33700–713.

43. Sommer is incorrect in thinking that the German foreign ministry did not know about the von Ribbentrop-Oshima negotiations until informed by von Dirksen in the summer of 1936 (Sommer, pp. 28–30). See especially von Dirksen's letter of 1 January 1936 which refers to a discussion of the subject between von Neurath and Hitler before 9 December 1935 (*G. D.*, C, 4, No. 479).

second thoughts. Berlin was willing to let the project languish for a while; only the German ambassador in Tokyo, Herbert von Dirksen, was still pushing.

If there was reluctance in Berlin, equal hesitation could be seen in Tokyo. There the Japanese foreign ministry did its best to restrain the enthusiasm aroused among the military by the special emissary from Berlin. The military revolt in Tokyo on 26 February 1936 would eventually give the more adventurist element in the Japanese government an opportunity to push forward with the pact, but the confusion attendant upon the revolt and its suppression contributed to a temporary delay. Equally important in reinforcing doubts in both Berlin and Tokyo was the general concern aroused in the world by a Soviet-promoted leak of information about the negotiations.

There had been rumors about fabricated and real leaks concerning the German-Japanese negotiations all through 1935.[44] Then, in December 1935 and January 1936, the Soviet government, which had learned of the negotiations through its espionage apparatus,[45] began to release reports about them to the world press, presumably with the hope of preventing any agreement. There was an immediate flurry of press reports, diplomatic inquiries, and carefully worded denials. Though the denials were, particularly those of von Neurath, more a product of hope than of honesty, the international uproar caused by the rumors of a German-Japanese alliance resulted in greater caution by both prospective allies.[46] In Berlin, both Göring and von Blomberg voiced reservations about Japan at the conference on 27 May 1936, discussed previously.[47] The German foreign ministry, in fact, would have preferred to drop the whole idea, although Ambassador von Dirksen still argued for continuation of the negotiations.[48]

The summer and fall of 1936, on the other hand, saw both Japan and Germany once again interested in an agreement. In Japan, the influence of the military was stronger than ever after the immediate repercussions of the February incident had passed. That incident, one of a long series in which Japanese ultranationalists hoped to demonstrate their superior ability to direct Japan's domestic and foreign policies by the murder of—they hoped—large numbers of high government officials, left the Japanese foreign ministry more intimidated than ever while simultaneously impressing on the

44. Presseisen, p. 77; *G. D.,* C, 4, No. 238; U. S. 1935, 3:481–82; note on a conversation with Otto Strasser on 4 March 1935, from the political archive of the Czech foreign ministry, Czech document in T–120, 1143/2028/444433.

45. Walter G. Krivitsky, *In Stalin's Secret Service* (New York: Harper, 1939), chap. 1; F. W. Deakin and G. R. Storry, *The Case of Richard Sorge* (London: Chatto & Windus, 1966), p. 162.

46. *G. D.,* C, 4, Nos. 475, 479, n. 6, 504, 511; 5, No. 155; *D. D. F.,* 2d, 1, No. 62; U. S. 1936, 4:19–20, 31–32, 93; Dodd, *Diary,* 26 February 1936, pp. 315–16; Memorandum of Dodd, 29 February 1936, Dodd Papers, folder 1936–D.

47. *TMWC,* 27:147. Cf. *G. D.,* C, 5, No. 306, where von Blomberg is reported as having told von Reichenau that a rapprochement with Japan was out of the question and that von Ribbentrop's negotiations had been broken off.

48. *G. D.,* C, 4, Nos. 479, 573; 5, No. 197.

leaders of Germany the idea that Japan was at least on the way to a form of government as fine as their own.[49] The Soviet agreement with Outer Mongolia, published on 8 April, coming after the French ratification of the Franco-Soviet Pact also increased the attractiveness of Germany to the Japanese leaders as a possible restraining influence on Soviet policy in the Far East, which in those years was directed toward the containment of Japanese expansion on the mainland of Asia.[50] Hack was sent by the Germans to Tokyo in the spring of 1936 to help revive the negotiations there as he had helped start them the year before—and he unwittingly kept the Soviet Union informed of their progress by confiding in Richard Sorge, a key agent of Moscow in Japan.[51]

Hitler himself considered the whole problem of German policy toward Japan in June and July of 1936. In the context of his decision to intervene in Spain and to move closer to Italy, he also saw Japan as possibly associated in some way with Germany. He discussed this possibility with von Ribbentrop and Oshima at Bayreuth in late July when the decisions to aid Franco and to send von Ribbentrop to London were made, and it is clear from subsequent events that Hitler decided to go forward with the negotiations at that time. There was some thought of including England in whatever arrangements might be concluded, but this idea fell by the wayside as the negotiations for a German-Japanese agreement went forward in the fall of 1936.[52] Hitler disregarded those, especially the German ambassador to China, who warned against relying on Japan; on the other hand, he would not yet commit himself to Japan to such an extent as to cut off the economic relations with China that the Germans hoped would help their armament program.[53] To protect the economic relationship with China, Germany would not allow its negotiations with Japan to include the recognition of Manchukuo.[54] The Japanese, for their part, wanted to keep their commit-

49. *D. D. F.*, 2d, 1, No. 244; see also "Bestellungen aus der Pressekonferenz vom 27. Februar 1936," Bundesarchiv, Brammer, Z.Sg. 101/7, f. 139.

50. *G. D.*, C, 5, Nos. 59, 196; *D. D. F.*, 2d, 2, No. 13.

51. Deakin and Storry, pp. 182–85. The special messages to Berlin mentioned in this account that Sorge helped encipher for General Ott, the German military attaché in Tokyo, appear to be those referred to in *G. D.*, C, 5, No. 197. The mission of Hack is not discussed in Chalmers Johnson, *An Instance of Treason, Ozaki Hotsumi and the Sorge Spy Ring* (Stanford: Stanford University Press, 1964). It should be noted that Sorge's photocopying of German embassy Tokyo documents starting early in 1936 presumably enabled the Soviet government to decipher the German diplomatic codes. The leaks referred to by Krivitsky may have done so in 1935.

52. *G. D.*, C, 5, Nos. 362, 509; von Dirksen, p. 186. For the Hitler-Oshima-von Ribbentrop meeting of 22 July 1936 see Sommer, p. 34.

53. *G. D.*, C, 5, Nos. 363, 461, 495, 502; Dertinger's "Informationsbericht Nr. 37," 10 October 1936, Bundesarchiv, Brammer, Z.Sg. 101/29 f. 373. The volume of these trade relations was to play a major role in the resistance to a switch of German policy toward full support of Japan in 1937–38; in 1936 Germany sent over 23 million marks and in 1937 over 82 million marks worth of military supplies to China (*G. D.*, D, 1, No. 576; see also Drechsler, pp. 51–53).

54. Weinberg, "Recognition of Manchoukuo," p. 156; *G. D.*, C, 5, Nos. 608, 621, 637.

ments to Germany from antagonizing the Russians to an extent that would interfere with the economic interest most important to Japan—the fisheries negotiations with the Soviet Union. Within these limitations, what sort of agreement could Germany and Japan work out, and what would be its meaning?

The text of the treaty, initialed on 23 October and formally signed on 25 November 1936, provided merely for cooperation between the two powers in opposing the Communist International, opened this cooperation to other countries that might wish to join, and set a five-year term to the treaty. A supplement called for a police commission to implement the cooperation. Since it was well known that the Communist parties of Germany and Japan had been effectively suppressed long before, it is not surprising that secret agreements in addition to the published ones were immediately suspected. The German government had acknowledged the truth to Ciano when he visited Germany in October, but otherwise Berlin and Tokyo publicly denied the existence of secret agreements. There was, in fact, a whole series of them.[55] By these additional agreements, Germany and Japan promised to do nothing that might in any way assist Russia in case of an unprovoked attack or threat of attack by the Soviet Union on the other partner and agreed to sign no political treaty with the Soviet Union not in accord with the anti-Comintern Pact without the consent of the other. These secret commitments, however, were modified by equally secret reservations. The Japanese, with German consent, excluded from the scope of their obligations any treaties on fisheries concessions or border questions—precisely the subjects of greatest immediate importance in Japanese-Soviet relations. The Germans, on the other hand, responded with a tortuous explanation superficially reconciling the new agreement with the German-Soviet treaties of Rapallo and Berlin which governed German-Soviet relations but were now declared in accordance with the new pact as they were no longer effective insofar as they diverged from it. Another secret exchange papered over this curious piece of logic.

The immediate international repercussions of the anti-Comintern Pact were very negative. The Soviet Union broke off the fisheries negotiations with Japan in spite of Tokyo's reassurances. The British government was affronted by the spectacle of the German ambassador to London spending most of his time on projects that seemed to be directed as much against England as anyone else. In Japan, the international uproar over the agreement strengthened the hand of those opposed to a closer alignment with Germany. There was alarm everywhere about the secret agreements all suspected existed but only the Soviet government knew in authoritative detail.[56] Certainly the Chinese government was alarmed by what appeared to it to be

55. Texts published in Weinberg, "Abkommen zum Antikominternpakt," pp. 197–201, and Sommer, pp. 494–99.

56. U. S. 1936, 1:392–405, passim; *G. D.*, C, 6, No. 105; Dertinger's "Informationsbericht Nr. 46," 19 November 1936, Bundesarchiv, Brammer, Z.Sg. 101/29, f. 479–81; Foreign Office files F 7223 and F 7504/303/23.

a radical departure in German policy, and the German diplomatic and military representatives had to exert considerable effort to calm the anxieties of Chiang Kai-shek.[57]

The German-Japanese agreements were, as has been shown, not nearly as extraordinary as was suspected. They constituted a form of anti-Soviet alliance, but simultaneously converted that alliance into an association of dubious strength by a variety of reservations. This self-mutilation of the alliance was indicative of the nature of the relations between Germany and Japan and of each to the Soviet Union. On the basis of the agreement they could move jointly; on the basis of the reservations, each could go its own way. There were other possibilities as well. As many opponents of the pact in Japan feared, it could very easily be made into an alliance against the Western powers, and Germany was to attempt that in 1938–39. The confusion in the policy directions, especially of Germany, was involuntarily revealed by von Ribbentrop himself when he told Stalin in August 1939, at the time of the signing of the German-Soviet Non-Aggression Pact, that the current joke in Berlin was that Stalin himself would join the anti-Comintern Pact.[58]

Such reflections on the tenuous nature of the German-Japanese alignment must not be allowed to obscure its real importance in other respects. In Berlin, von Ribbentrop had again triumphed over the doubts of the foreign ministry; he would look upon the association with Japan as his special contribution to the world's wisdom.[59] As in the case of the alliance between Germany and Italy, the will of Hitler rather than the terms of any agreement defined German policy; and since he thought of the pact as an option for Japan, he would eventually sacrifice Germany's position in China to that option. Similarly, in its repercussions on the outside world, the propagandistic effect, the images produced, and the fears created were perhaps more significant than the textual contradictions. The most powerful disturbers of the peace of Europe and Asia had drawn together, with Italy associated with them. England, France, the Soviet Union, the United States, all had to remember that if they were involved in difficulties on one side of the globe, they were threatened on the other side as well. The alliance of the victors of World War I had fallen apart soon after the Armistice; whatever the internal frictions in that association, it dominated world events as long as it held to-

57. Sommer, p. 57; Drechsler, pp. 25–26; and documents to be published as *G. D.*, C, 6, Nos. 15, 56, 64, 66, 74, 75. The Chinese for a moment considered replacing the German military and Italian air advisers with British officers (Foreign Office F 7567/166/10).

The decision of Hitler to break the agreements with China for the exchange of military supplies for raw materials did not come until 1937; General Georg Thomas confused this with 1936 in his memoirs, "Gedanken und Ereignisse," *Schweizer Monatshefte,* 25 (December 1945), 537–58.

58. *G. D.,* D, 7, No. 213, p. 191.

59. The foreign ministry maintained its frigid distance from the anti-Comintern Pact; von Neurath's assistant von Kotze acknowledged receipt of the originals of the signed documents and appended documents in a cooly formal note to von Ribbentrop of 29 January 1937 (DZA Potsdam, Büro RAM 60964, f. 57).

gether even superficially. Now a new globe-spanning alliance was obviously in the process of formation; who could predict with assurance whether it would lead to joint control of world affairs or joint suicide in a disaster brought on by the confident advocates of the new dispensation?[60]

Repeated reference has been made in this and preceding chapters to the relationship of internal economic problems in the winter of 1935–36 to the timing of Hitler's decision to remilitarize the Rhineland and to the role of trade questions in Germany's relationship with the United States, the Far East, Spain, and Southeast Europe in 1936. These economic issues were, as has been shown, generally facets of Germany's rearmament policy, that is, they concerned the problem of importing those materials Germany needed for rearmament. This problem became particularly acute in 1936 for several reasons.

By 1936, the boom in the German economy that had been produced by the government's enormous deficit spending for armaments and investment in armaments and related industries had led to full employment in the German economy. Under such circumstances, further expansion of government expenditures for arms could easily lead to inflationary pressures. Countering such pressure, the maintenance of the deflationary tax program of the Brüning government during the National Socialist period helped restrain consumption; the restrictions on dividends and private investment reserved the flow of capital to those industries involved in rearmament; and the enforced investment of all accumulating savings in government bonds served the same purpose.[61] The destruction of the trade unions meant that the workers could not take advantage of the improved employment situation to press for higher wages. The control of foreign trade was used not only to conserve foreign exchange but to make certain that the available foreign exchange was utilized for such imports as the government thought wise and to subsidize such exports as seemed likely to produce additional foreign exchange in those markets where it was most needed. This policy had been complicated by the devaluation of the pound and the dollar in earlier years, a difficulty accentuated by additional devaluations in Europe in 1936. Hitler, however, was determined to avoid devaluation for political and psychological reasons; and although the possibility of devaluation of the mark was apparently considered seriously in the summer of 1936, no steps in that direction were allowed.[62] The various manipulations used in the preceding

60. The joint suicide concept was mentioned by one of the strongest Japanese advocates of an alliance with Germany, Matsuoka Yosuke, then president of the South Manchurian Railway, in a speech on 23 December 1936 (cited in Sommer, p. 53, and Gordon A. Craig and Felix Gilbert [eds.] *The Diplomats* [New York: Athenaeum, 1963], p. 619).

61. An excellent survey of the fiscal policies of National Socialist Germany may be found in René Erbe, *Die nationalsozialistische Wirtschaftspolitik 1933–1939 im Lichte der modernen Theorie* (Zurich: Polygraphischer Verlag, 1958), chaps. 2, 3, and 4.

62. Ibid., p. 189; Dieter Petzina, *Autarkiepolitik im Dritten Reich, der nationalsozialistische Vierjahresplan* (Stuttgart: Deutsche Verlags-Anstalt, 1968), p. 44.

years to assist Germany's foreign trade program were, however, no longer so useful; there was increasing resistance abroad and fewer resources at home for use in that program.

The serious difficulties in Germany began with a crisis over food imports in the winter of 1935–36, continued with raw materials shortages in the spring and summer of 1936, and came to a head in decisions that focused attention on the whole structure of the German economy. The scholarly dispute over the nature of that economy, between those who argued that it was organized for total war and those who pointed to the fact that it was not fully mobilized until the latter part of World War II, has been resolved by the thoughtful analysis of Berenice Carroll who has shown how the National Socialist economy was geared to war from the beginning, how substantial and steady increases in its orientation toward armaments continued year by year, and why total mobilization was postponed until Germany was faced by precisely that type of war Hitler had most wanted to avoid.[63]

Impressed by the immense problems Germany had faced during the stalemate of World War I because of its enemies' access to and its own lack of key raw materials, Hitler looked toward war in the future not as a long wearying struggle but as a quick series of strong blows bringing down one enemy, to be followed by a subsequent repetition of that process with another enemy. Such a strategy—encapsulated in the term *Blitzkrieg,* "lightning war"—presupposed not the total mobilization of all of a nation's resources but a substantial headstart over potential enemies who would be knocked out before either side had been forced into total mobilization by a drawn-out conflict. Such a strategy was cumulative, in a manner of speaking, because its success in the first instance would give Germany control of added territory and resources and thus a better chance for success the next time. It would also avoid the imposition on the home front of such sacrifices as might remind the population of the rigors—and hence the ultimate outcome—of the last war. On the contrary, success would further consolidate support at home for the next successful war.[64] A rapidly built air force as well as what came to be known as psychological warfare and fifth-column activities would all play important roles in putting the lightning into the expected wars.[65]

As shown in the first chapter, such wars would be fought for land on which the Germans could grow the food they needed to support themselves independently of any imports; the bread crisis of the winter of 1935–36 reinforced Hitler's fixation on this primitive concept of the need for greater land area in the struggle for survival. He had made this point in his talk to the German generals right after his accession to power.[66] He had repeated

63. *Design for Total War,* especially preface and chaps. I, IV, V, and X.

64. See the somewhat similar analysis in Alan S. Milward, *The German Economy at War* (London: Athlone Press, 1965), pp. 7–14.

65. It should be noted that the French air attaché in Berlin clearly perceived this strategy of rapidly building up an air force that could win a short, violent conflict for a country lacking the resources to fight a long war (*D. D. F.,* 2d, 2, No. 252).

66. See above, pp. 26–27.

essentially the same point a year later in a speech to the generals and high SA and SS officers on 28 February 1934.[67] It would reappear in Hitler's memorandum on the Four-Year Plan. Furthermore, the conquests that brought Germany agricultural land would provide other raw materials that it lacked, a point of which Hitler must have been reminded by observing the difficulties that even limited sanctions had caused for Italy.

As the German economy moved into a foreign exchange and resource allocation crisis in 1936, therefore, Hitler had to define his policy as against alternative solutions. There was the possibility of leaving the military forces at approximately the levels planned for 1936–37. From a purely economic standpoint, such a policy would take care of the crisis. The financial needs, as Schacht pointed out, could be covered at a substantial level, with the increased tax revenue from a growing economy being used to retire some of the Mefo-bills originally printed to pay for rearmament. The level of arms production could be maintained, with exports taking up the slack after an army of fixed size had been adequately equipped and sufficient stockpiles of weapons and munitions created.[68] The problem of foreign exchange could be dealt with successfully because Germany could earn enough for the imports needed to sustain an army of about forty divisions. Furthermore, in one key area in which imports for the military services were essential, that of petroleum products, Germany was approaching self-sufficiency in 1936. Facilities for the production of petroleum products from coal were reaching the levels needed for a very large proportion of Germany's requirements if it did not expand its forces—and hence its needs.[69] But it was precisely in this area that the requirements of a further rapid expansion of Germany's military forces would precipitate drastic changes in the organization of the German economy.

Still another possibility would have been a total economic mobilization with a drastic shift of economic resources to military production. Such a policy of preparing Germany by arming in depth for a war of attrition like the preceding conflict had long been urged—though unsuccessfully—by General Georg Thomas, the key person in military-economic planning in the

67. Bracher, *Nationalsozialistische Machtergreifung,* pp. 749–50.

68. Note the comment by the deputy director of department IV of the German foreign ministry inserted into his memorandum of 14 February 1935, "that it was extremely desirable to provide opportunities for export for our armaments industry against a slackening in the home demand from about 1937 onward" (*G. D.,* C, 3, No. 491).

69. See Wolfgang Birkenfeld, *Der synthetische Treibstoff 1933–1945, Ein Beitrag zur nationalsozialistischen Wirtschafts- und Rüstungspolitik* (Göttingen: Musterschmidt, 1964), p. 50; Annex 1 to "Aufzeichnung über die Versorgungslage auf dem Betriebsstoffgebiet und ihre Auswirkungen für die Wehrmacht," 9 March 1936, in 1301–PS, *TMWC,* 27:132. In this table, the percentage figures on production in the 1938 column apply to the need estimated for the military as expanded by 1938; when the figures are adjusted in relation to the needs of military forces at the 1936 level, they range from 33 percent to 100 percent coverage of the estimated need in each category.

German military hierarchy.[70] While the restriction of armaments expansion necessarily implied that over a period of time Germany would lose its military headstart over other countries and could not attack them with hope of quick success, the policy advocated by Thomas implied a drastic reordering of the German economy preparatory to fighting the kind of all-encompassing war of attrition Hitler hoped to avoid by a sequence of brief, victorious wars. It is hardly surprising that as he faced the economic choices of 1936 Hitler should follow the advice neither of Schacht nor of Thomas.

In the fall of 1935 Hitler had turned to Göring to decide a dispute between Schacht and the Minister of Agriculture, Darré, concerning the use of foreign exchange for food purchases. Göring decided in favor of Darré.[71] When it became evident early in 1936 that there would be shortages of oil—or the foreign exchange needed to pay for importation—to cover the needs of an expanding military force, Hitler was asked to step into the bureaucratic infighting over the issue. Again Hitler turned to Göring, placing him in charge of fuel in March and giving him broad authority over the whole field of raw materials and foreign exchange in April.[72] Göring was a personal associate who could be expected to carry out Hitler's ideas ruthlessly; he was directly involved in the oil question in his role as air minister and commander in chief of the German air force; and he was close to Wilhelm Keppler, Hitler's economic adviser, who had been especially interested in the development of the synthetic oil industry.[73] Under these circumstances, Göring began to build up his position in the economic sphere, creating and absorbing agencies and feuding with other agencies for both policy and power.[74] The immediately pressing gap in the foreign-exchange situation in the summer of 1936 was met by an emergency measure requisitioning the foreign-exchange holdings and claims of German individuals and companies; the needs for the next few years were to be covered by more basic changes in economic policy.[75]

70. On Thomas see his *Geschichte der deutschen Wehr- und Rüstungswirtschaft (1918–1943/45)* (ed. by Wolfgang Birkenfeld; Boppard-am-Rhein: H. Boldt, 1966); and Carroll, chap. II.

71. For a view of this crisis considerably more favorable to Darré than that taken by other historians see Petzina, pp. 31–33.

72. Carroll, pp. 122–25; Birkenfeld, pp. 79–81; Beck, *Schacht,* pp. 84–85; Petzina, pp. 36–48.

73. Carroll, p. 124; Birkenfeld, p. 36; Memorandum by Wilhelm Keppler, 2 November 1934, Nuremberg document NI–15655. Note the report that Keppler at a conference on 25 March 1936 opposed financial requests of the German navy connected with developing oil sources in Iraq on the grounds that Germany would soon cover its requirements from home production (OKM, "Ölversorgung der Kriegsmarine," 29 April 1940, p. 3, Nuremberg document 984–PS).

74. Carroll, pp. 125–27; Meinck, *Hitler und die deutsche Aufrüstung,* pp. 157–73; *G. D.,* C, 5, No. 260; *D. D. F.,* 2d, 2, No. 130; von Neurath's memoranda RM 384, 4 May 1936, and RM 418, 12 May 1936, T–120, 2383/4619/E 198300–301, 304–305.

75. Petzina, pp. 46–47.

The internal feuds of the summer of 1936 were, in one way, nothing unusual in the National Socialist system; rather, they were typical of the government of the Third Reich. If they provoked a redefinition of policy in explicit terms by Hitler himself, it was because they touched on the basic direction of the German economy—a subject that interested him greatly—rather than the usual bureaucratic squabbling that he tolerated or perhaps even enjoyed as a means of keeping full control of basic policy while others worried and argued about the details.[76] Schacht had not given up hope; his trip to Southeast Europe in the summer of 1936 may be seen as an effort on his part to show that the maintenance and extension of his trade policy could best serve the interests of the Reich, while his attempts to secure colonial concessions from the Western powers pointed to what he considered a reasonable way to obtain access to raw materials (as an unconscious alternative to Hitler's view of East European conquests). The new organization Göring was setting up was having its troubles, and Germany's foreign-exchange situation was at its most difficult in the days just before the opening of the Olympics on 1 August. The crisis is reflected by a circular sent to all German missions abroad by the foreign ministry on 30 July.[77] On the same day, at a conference in Göring's office, there was a discussion of the raw materials and foreign-exchange situation, the forthcoming annual Nuremberg party rally, and Göring's plan to discuss both subjects with Hitler, primarily to urge Hitler as well as Göring to speak on economic problems at the rally.[78] During August the crisis came to a head: Hitler and Göring discussed the subject at least once and probably more often than that.[79] On one of these occasions, on or before 26 August, Hitler handed Göring a memorandum embodying his views on the situation and containing his policy directives.

Years later, on the night of 13–14 October 1941, Hitler referred to having written memoranda on only a few questions of vital importance such as the Four-Year Plan.[80] When several years after that occasion he gave a copy of the Four-Year Plan memorandum to Albert Speer, then Minister of

76. The most detailed survey of this crisis is in Arthur Schweitzer, "Foreign Exchange Crisis of 1936," *Zeitschrift für die gesamte Staatswissenschaft,* 118, No. 2 (April 1962), 243–77.

77. *G. D.,* C, 5, No. 485.

78. "Aktenvermerk über Besprechung beim Herrn Generaloberst am 30.7.36," Nuremberg document 3890–PS (National Archives).

79. It should be noted that Göring requested a memorandum on the foreign exchange and raw materials question from former Price Commissar Goerdeler on 7 August, enclosing with his request memoranda by Thomas and State Secretary Trendelenburg of the Ministry of Economics (Gerhard Ritter, *Carl Goerdeler und die deutsche Widerstandsbewegung* [Stuttgart: Deutsche Verlags-Anstalt, 1955], p. 76).

80. Trevor-Roper, *Hitler's Table Talk,* p. 57; Wilhelm Treue (ed.), "Hitlers Denkschrift zum Vierjahresplan 1936," *Vierteljahrshefte für Zeitgeschichte,* 3, No. 2 (April 1955), 184, n. 2. An English text of the memorandum is in *G. D.,* C, 5, No. 490, with a memorandum by Speer of 22 August 1945, concerning Hitler's giving him the original memorandum in 1944. On Hitler's memorandum see also Carroll, p. 95, n. 8; Petzina, p. 49.

Armaments and War Production, he still thought of it as evidence of the lack of understanding of Schacht and the opposition of the German business community to his own far-sighted plans. The text of the memorandum shows Hitler's memory accurate in this regard; it also shows his negative reaction to a memorandum on the proper way to deal with the economic crisis written by Carl Goerdeler, former price commissar and later leader of the opposition to Hitler.[81] The proposals of others that Germany restrict the further expansion of its armaments to fit its means provide a part of the background against which Hitler reasserted his views and his plans.

The memorandum was prepared by Hitler in Berchtesgaden right after the Olympic games. During those August days, he received Horthy, von Blomberg, and von Neurath as well as Göring. It was at this time, on 24 August, that he signed the law extending the term of compulsory military service from one to two years; in *Mein Kampf* he had referred to such a term as the absolute minimum for turning out really trained soldiers.[82] In his memorandum, he referred to making the German army the first in the world in the shortest possible time—the days when for propaganda purposes he talked about Germany's *Gleichberechtigung* (equality of rights) were long since past. How was this army to be used and how could the German economy equip and sustain it? With attacks on the doubters and the skeptics, he set forth the same doctrines to be found in *Mein Kampf* and in his second book in terms attuned to the situation of the moment.

The armed forces of Germany were to be made stronger, they were to be ready for war within four years, and they were to be used for a war in which Germany would solve its long-term needs for food and raw materials by territorial expansion. This irreversible goal dictated the means to be taken in the interim to take care of the short-term deficiencies. If foreign exchange was in short supply, whatever there was must be used for the importation of raw materials needed for armaments. Furthermore, the raw materials should be used immediately for war production, not stockpiled for some future contingency.[83] There was no point to major efforts to expand exports to areas Germany could not control politically. Under no circumstances could the armaments program be restricted to make foreign exchange available for foodstuffs or other imports not related to the armaments program. The way to conserve foreign exchange even within the armaments category was the same as the way to protect Germany against the effects of blockade once it was ready to attack: by rapid development of the synthetic industry,

81. The author shares the doubts of Treue (p. 192, n. 16) that Hitler directed his polemics as strongly and personally against Goerdeler as Ritter supposed.

82. *Mein Kampf,* 2:604–05. For contemporary French perceptions of this step see *D. D. F.,* 2d, 3, Nos. 192, 198, 200. For another report on Hitler's views at this time see Rost van Tonningen's letter to Mussert of 20 August 1936, in his *Correspondentie,* 1:321–22.

83. This point is of some importance since it suggests that Hitler expected to fight with the weapon types then already in production or about to go into production.

first in regard to petroleum products, second with synthetic rubber, and finally with any other materials that could be synthesized inside the Third Reich. No financial considerations of competitive prices were to be allowed to play a role in decisions of this sort—the dominating consideration would be that something could be produced at home, not that it might be purchased more cheaply abroad. This same standard was to be applied to such raw materials as iron and steel, in which the exploitation of low-grade domestic ores would require enormous capital investment and result in products of very high cost—but *domestic* high-cost products that would be financed by the state if private industry should prove recalcitrant.

The basic thrust of this policy was clear, and it is hardly surprising that its implementation should have been turned over to Göring, a man with political and military interests, rather than Schacht or Thomas with their fiscal and technical preoccupations.[84] Hitler wanted a domestic economy geared to a series of wars of short, hard blows during which any threatened blockade would not prevent Germany's military forces, with overwhelming first-line strength but few or no reserves, from crushing its enemies. The Four-Year Plan would make this possible by increasing domestic production of synthetics and products from low-grade ores. This would simultaneously conserve the limited foreign exchange available to Germany to be used for those imports that were essential to the armaments industry and simply could not be produced at home, while it would also reduce Germany's vulnerability to blockade when war came. When presented to the German people in Hitler's proclamation and speeches at the Nuremberg rally, his decree on the Four-Year Plan of 18 October, and Göring's speech of 28 October, the whole project was wrapped up in the anti-Bolshevik propaganda that Hitler was simultaneously recommending to Count Ciano as the screen behind which Germany and Italy would unite against England. The real nature of both Hitler's aims in war and his intended use of the coming victory was revealed in his speech of 12 September, in which he visualized a Russia freed of bolshevism, no longer ruled by Russians but rather exploited by Germans. In this perspective, the relationship of an uneconomic forcing of the German economy in the Four-Year Plan can be seen as integrally related to a policy of ruthless exploitation of future conquests made possible by that plan's execution.[85]

The one aspect of the Four-Year Plan that remains to be discussed is the reference to time limits—four years in both the title of the plan and the text of the memorandum and eighteen months for self-sufficiency in gasoline

84. This is confirmed by the references to Hitler's memorandum in Göring's lengthy exposé of his policy to Schacht of 22 August 1937, Nuremberg document 493–EC, *TMWC,* 36:554, 563.

85. This point is explained in considerable detail in Bracher, *Nationalsozialistische Machtergreifung,* pp. 752–56 (Petzina's critique of this interpretation [p. 194] is totally mistaken as it attributes to Sauer, the author of this part of the book, the belief that the Four-Year Plan involved total mobilization of the economy, something Sauer does not claim). The speech of Gauleiter Forster in Danzig on 20 October 1936, cited in the preceding chapter, reflects Hitler's comments to him at this time (see especially Emessen, p. 125).

that also appears in the text. What did these time limits mean? The beginning of the new time span is provided by Hitler's initial request in 1933: "give me four years and you will not recognize Germany"; a request to which National Socialist propaganda made repeated reference during the mid-1930s as the rearmament boom brought the appearance of prosperity to the country, and which Allied soldiers derisively chalked on the ruins left standing in 1945. After 1933, Hitler made several references to the time limits of a second period at the end of which he would be ready for war. On 24 September 1935, after the party rally of that year at which he had already referred to the need for building up the synthetics industry, Hitler told the leaders of the party that he needed about four years until he would be ready to make war.[86] On 24 October 1936, he told Ciano that Germany would be ready for war in three years but would prefer to have four or five years for preparation.

When these and other time estimates are examined, they might be shown to be inconsistent, unrealistic, and therefore insignificant or at least evidence for a lack of planning. The more reasonable deduction to make would be that Hitler was determined to launch the first of a series of wars in a few years but was not going to tie himself down to precise dates and enemies until the last minute. This combination of long-range planning with opportunism in detail, of a fanatically held goal with a flexibility of means, fits with all his other activities and all the available evidence. It was certainly in these terms that Göring, the confidant entrusted with the implementation of Hitler's schemes, understood the commission given him. When he read Hitler's memorandum to a council of ministers on 4 September 1936, Göring explained that Goerdeler's proposal as well as any other proposals to limit the armaments program had to be rejected. On the contrary, the arms program had to be accelerated. In this circle, which included Schacht, there was still a little of the camouflage to be found in the memorandum and speeches: the inevitable war is specified as being against Russia and the current situation is referred to in the terminology applied before World War I to the days immediately preceding the formal orders for mobilization (*drohende Kriegsgefahr*).[87] When Göring discussed such matters in the more intimate circle of his air force generals on 2 December 1936, he could be more explicit. "We are already at war; only the shooting has not yet started."[88]

86. See Lösener's report in *Vierteljahrshefte für Zeitgeschichte*, 9, No. 3 (July 1961), 281. (The date of 29 September is in error; see Domarus, I: 542, and Sekretär des Führers, "Daten aus alten Notizbüchern," p. 8.)

87. Text of the minutes by Löb as 416–EC in *TMWC*, 26:488–91. The significance of Göring's use of the term "drohende Kriegsgefahr" has been overlooked by other commentators; it was widely known at the time because of its role in the extensive debate about the circumstances surrounding the outbreak of World War I.

88. Memorandum by Bodenschatz, 2 December 1936, 3474–PS, *TMWC*, 32:335 (The German reads: "Wir befinden uns bereits im Kriege. Nur wird noch nicht geschossen"). The same document records Göring's insistence on a speed-up in airplane production; on 11 November Raeder had ordered more rapid building of submarines (806–D, *TMWC*, 35:529–30).

The years after 1936 would be devoted to building up Germany's military might until it was ready to start shooting.[89]

Combined planning of the German army, navy, and air force for the moment when Germany was at the point of launching hostilities had been inaugurated before 1936 but really developed in that year for the first time. The army continued its concentration on Czechoslovakia. The navy argued for its previously developed plan for a war in the Atlantic Ocean from bases on both sides of the Atlantic to be secured by negotiations—with Franco—or to be seized from France in the Western Hemisphere and from Norway to prevent any blockade of Germany.[90] Göring's phraseology on 2 December should be read in connection with his proposal of 23 November that Germany could win only if it began hostilities by a surprise attack on the enemy's air force and its bases.[91] But the time for executing any such plans was not yet at hand, and Hitler would delay his choice in the interim. The most important issue as he saw it was the acceleration of Germany's armament program, and he believed that the directives and powers he had given to Göring with the Four-Year Plan would assure that program's completion. While the Four-Year Plan prepared the basis for the wars Hitler intended to wage, there would be, as he assured the world on 30 January 1937, no more surprises.[92]

89. The character of the Four-Year Plan as pointing to a war launched by Germany was recognized by François-Poncet at the time; see his report of 28 October 1936, in *D. D. F.,* 2d, 3, No. 417, esp. p. 648.

90. The best account of these plans at present is in Gemzell, pp. 45–57, 156

91. Ibid., p. 175.

92. Domarus, 1:668.

Conclusion

In a few years the whole European and world situation had changed. At the beginning of the 1930s, world attention had been focused on the Great Depression and the settlement of problems still remaining from what was generally called the Great War or the World War. In spite of the aggression of Japan against China in the fall of 1931, nothing was further from most minds than the possibility of another world-wide conflict of the great powers, partly because in the thinking of most such a conflict could only be perceived in terms of the immense casualties and costs of the last war. By the end of 1936, it still appeared unbelievable and inconceivable to most people that anyone or any group could *want* to bring about such a conflict, but the possibility of its taking place now loomed as a distinct reality. That possibility was associated in the thinking of most with the growing might of Hitler's Germany.

The interaction of three factors may be seen as responsible for this revolutionary change in the international situation. In the first place, the peace settlement at the end of the war had left a Europe that was in reality quite different from what many imagined. It was widely believed that Germany had been disproportionately weakened by the peace settlement, with its former enemies left in control of the continent. The reality was otherwise. Having accepted the principle of nationality as the basis for the organization of Europe, the victors of 1918 necessarily created a Europe—insofar as their influence reached—in which the Germans were the most numerous people after the Russians and in which by virtue of its skills and resources Germany remained potentially a most powerful country. The prior defeat of Russia had both removed the danger against which Otto von Bismarck had tried to protect Germany by an alliance with Austria-Hungary—the dismemberment of Austria-Hungary by an all-powerful Russia—and had simultaneously helped open the way for the appearance of a large number of new or newly enlarged states in East and Southeast Europe that, whatever the rights and wrongs of their respective external boundaries and internal institutions, were all certain to be far weaker than Germany. In recognition of these facts, the Treaty of Versailles had placed a number of restrictions on Germany, but these restrictions neither altered the basic realities nor eliminated the drastic weakening that Germany's enemies had suffered in four years of bitter war.[1] Self-deception and propaganda had obscured these facts from the eyes of many; but once the last of the major restrictions on German power had been eliminated with the remilitarization of the Rhineland, the hard realities returned the illusions of prior years to the shadowy dream-world whence they had sprung, though some still failed to perceive this. Germany had emerged from the World War *relatively* at least as powerful if not more powerful than when it entered that conflict, with its erstwhile enemies relatively weaker than in 1914 and in any case divided among themselves.

The historical importance of Adolf Hitler lies precisely in the fact that a country of such potential might took him as its leader and gave him its support. This was no case of a skillful prince leading a small state to new heights or laying the foundation for some successor's mighty adventures. Rather it was the assumption of authority in one great power that already had the potential for vastly greater power by a man determined to consolidate and increase the strength already there for great adventures that would enable him to dominate the globe.

The nature and practical implementation of that ambition, insofar as they relate to foreign policy, have been the subject of this book. The second factor in the reversal of the world situation in the 1930s, then, is the policy of Adolf Hitler, and I have tried to show how the traditional separation of foreign from domestic policy cannot be applied. From the military indoctrination of youth to the creation of a vast synthetic oil industry, from arithmetic examples that show how much mental defectives cost society—with the implication that therefore they should be killed—to the preparation of shipyards for the building of super-battleships to challenge England's supremacy on the seas, all aspects of the Third Reich must be seen as an integral whole. The emphasis here has been on the development of Germany's position in Europe because it was in that development that the path to the future was delineated most clearly.

And Hitler trod that path with a combination of caution and bravado, of opportunism and consistency, that leaves the observer torn between wonder and fear. Some outside observers thought he might founder in the con-

1. The author discussed this matter at greater length in a paper read at the 1968 meeting of the American Historical Association, "After 50 Years, the Defeat of Germany and the European Balance," published in *Central European History,* 2, No. 3 (Sept. 1969), 248–60.

flicting currents of German politics or succumb to the economic problems of an unorthodox fiscal system, while some inside Germany hoped that they could contain or restrain his wilder plans; but all such speculations proved false. In the first year and a half of his rule, Hitler ruthlessly gathered power into his own hands while at the same time beginning the military preparations for the wars he planned to wage, thereby binding to himself the military leaders of Germany who were the only possible challengers to his control of the country. In this initial period, the danger of foreign reaction to his enterprises was still such as to deter him from excessive risks, but even as he exercised caution he also moved boldly in some fields. The concordat with the Vatican and the new relationship with Poland both represented shrewd applications of his principle of trying for bilateral agreements for immediately useful objectives, agreements that could and would be broken as soon as it suited him. The departure from the League of Nations and the disarmament conference at the earliest possible moment pointed to the consistency of his long-term objectives. And he would never risk compromising those objectives by entering any new multilateral agreements, whether asked by other powers or urged by his own associates. At times Hitler would let others go ahead on some more risky venture and see how well they could do; both in Austria in 1934 and in Danzig on several occasions he allowed his underlings to test the ground. When they failed or if the risks turned out to be too great, he would pull back temporarily and try another approach. Having seized the initiative, he could always produce a relaxation of international tension by simply holding back for a while.

Unwilling to submit to routine, Hitler developed a personal style of government that was clear in its ends but entirely flexible in its means and instruments. Whatever and whoever could deliver the goods was fine with him. The bureaucrats of the foreign ministry whom he had inherited could work for him though he despised them; the most unlikely adventurer could get a hearing and a chance to try his hand at foreign policy if his scheme appeared plausible. His own associates could feud with each other and build up rival organizations as long as each would follow their leader's commands on such topics and at such times as he chose to issue them. Sometimes orders were not issued at all, or not for a long time. The multiple confusions in German policy toward East Asia in the early years of National Socialist rule can be explained in large part by the fact that Hitler had as yet no clear idea of what he wanted in regard to that distant area and that under such circumstances every German agency and ministry could have its own policy or even several. But such drifting was carefully circumscribed: when a question needed prompt action, like the request of Franco for help in July 1936, then Hitler made his decision; and any agency that did not want to carry out his plan soon found that another agency had been assigned the implementation of that particular policy.

What counted most in Hitler's eyes was the rearmament of Germany which would enable it to move forward by threat or by force. He would accept no external limits on the expansion of Germany's forces, and he would launch the Four-Year Plan when the strictures of Germany's economy threatened to impose internal limits. Shrewdly taking advantage of the love of peace and fear of war in other countries in those years when war would have been most dangerous for Germany, he built up Germany's strength to the point where others could no longer contemplate war as an answer to German aggression except as a most dangerous undertaking. And there could be no doubt of the popularity of this policy inside Germany. The plebiscites held in 1933, 1934, and 1936 cannot be taken as an accurate gauge of public opinion, but all German and foreign observers agreed as to Hitler's popularity within the country, a popularity that would in turn enable him to demand greater exertions from the people in the future.

The development of German might and a generally united German population under Hitler's leadership has to be seen against a third element, the weak and disunited powers threatened by Germany. The new nations created out of the wreckage of the Austro-Hungarian and Russian empires were all too small and too weak, either alone or together, to play a really significant role in restraining German ambitions. Poland could take temporary advantage of its powerful neighbors in the years of their travail; but once Germany and Russia had recovered even a part of their strength, either the enmity or the friendship of those great powers could be fatal to Poland. Czechoslovakia had secured defensible boundaries at the peace conference and the comparative stability of its democratic institutions could put some strength behind them, but even then it could not be expected to stand up to Germany alone. Any serious danger to the European order could be held off only by the great powers. Of these, Italy had been so torn by the war that its fragile institutions had crumbled before the blaring trumpets of Mussolini's Blackshirts, and he was more interested in upsetting than maintaining the status quo. There may have been a real possibility of rallying Italy to an anti-German coalition, because its fear of an *Anschluss* and its desire for influence in the Balkans collided with Hitler's policies, but whatever the chance for such a development, Britain and France had ruined it forever by wavering between firmness and complaisance toward the Ethiopian conflict. Every concession made to Mussolini after that fiasco only confirmed his assessment of the weakness of the Western democracies and increased his admiration for the way Hitler took advantage of it—along with a desire to do likewise.

The Soviet Union had been slow to recognize the danger of national socialism and, once it realized the threat, wavered between attempts to rally all other possible enemies of Germany to its side and efforts to make a direct arrangement with Hitler himself. Neither policy could be implemented with success in the years reviewed here; Hitler was not yet interested in an alliance with the Soviet Union, and many of the potential allies of Russia were as fearful of it as they were of Germany. Weakened domestically by the upheavals accompanying the second Five-Year Plan and the beginning of the great purge, weakened externally by threats from Japan in the Far East and poor relations with most countries that might be aligned against Germany, the government in Moscow could only view with alarm a rising menace in Central Europe that had declared the seizure of vast parts of Russia to be its avowed objective.

The United States had compounded its isolationist proclivities with a single-minded preoccupation with the Depression, regrets over its entrance into the last war, and a determination to stay out of the next one. The economic part of the new administration's foreign policy, the reciprocal trade agreements program, found considerable support among the American public; but the moment the administration gingerly tried steps on the political road, the reaction was very different, as shown by the defeat of the effort to have the United States join the World Court. The American public was certainly disenchanted with Germany and becoming alarmed by developments in Europe, and the American government was perhaps better informed than any other; but neither the anguish of American newspaper readers nor the papers gathering dust in the State Department and White House files could affect the situation in Europe. On the contrary, the absence of any active American role and the general expectation that that absence would continue could only encourage German adventures and discourage any thoughts of resistance.

Great Britain and France had gone their own ways after the great war had seen them fighting alongside each other for over four years. The British thought themselves secure after exertions so great and so costly that it seemed unbelievable that they had actually made them and inconceivable that they could ever make them again. Having become certain that neither they nor anyone else had really wanted the last war, they were all the more certain that no one could possibly want another. With such perspectives, differences and difficulties among nations were by their very nature calls for negotiations in which the British expected to contribute their part, assuming that others would do likewise. When the French refused to follow this prescription in the disarmament negotiations, the British would go ahead and do it on their own in the Anglo-German naval agreement, only to find that with the government of National Socialist Germany this approach did not work. But thereafter domestic concerns would distract British attention for some time; Wallis Simpson seemed much more interesting than Adolf Hitler.

That left France as the sole watcher at the gate. But France was both internally divided and externally impotent. Existing internal divisions were exacerbated by the impact of the depression which came later in France than in most other countries and, therefore, more nearly coincided with the first years of Hitler's rule in Germany. The great bitterness associated with these internal divisions broke into riots several times in the 1930s and confronted the changing governments in Paris with serious difficulties in governing the country at home, to say nothing of taking bold steps in foreign affairs.[2] Whatever the wisdom of French policy toward Germany in the years right after the war, by the 1930s the energy and decisiveness for a firm policy were no longer present. The evidence of French unwillingness to take even the smallest risks of military action has been cited at several points. By way of summary, it may be said that there was no plan at all to maintain the most important guarantee for the safety of France and the smaller countries of East and Southeast Europe, the demilitarized zone in the Rhineland. Furthermore, French contingency planning for any aggressive move by Germany was of an essentially defensive nature, and this proclivity toward withdrawing into a shell was accentuated by the anticipation of the French that their unwillingness to do anything about the remilitarization of the Rhineland opened up the prospect that Germany would soon construct fortifications there. Although they did not yet know it, France's Eastern allies had already been practically written off in 1936. The most they could hope for in the way of help from France was an expedition to Salonika on the pattern of the Allied effort in that theater in World War I.[3]

This fixation on the military strategy of the earlier conflict is of broader significance than its relevance to the peripheral operation at Salonika that the French general staff pondered in 1936 and would propose in a slightly different form in the winter of 1939–40. It illuminates the nature of the French position in Europe. A victor in the war, it had won only in the company of allies who were now either distant or hostile in attitude toward France. And for itself, victory had been so costly as to seem unrepeatable. But even if repeatable, the strategy of victory had been essentially defensive; the Germans had been defeated by the successful crushing of their offensive. The importance of this fact has generally been discussed from the German side; that is, for its implications as support for the stab-in-the-back legend and for the inability of the German people to perceive and assimilate the reality of their defeat in the war. The ending of the war in the downfall of German hopes of entering Paris rather than an Allied march to Berlin, however, had implications for French attitudes as well. It seemed to suggest that defensive rather than offensive strategy would win out in modern war.[4]

The defensive approach was confirmed for the French by another aspect of that defensive victory which symbolized for France its triumph in the war—Verdun. The calamitous casualties suffered in that battle, as well as the rest of the war of course, paralyzed French military and diplomatic thinking. In a sense, the German strategist of that operation, Erich von

2. A doleful report on French conditions may be found in the letter of Jesse Strauss (U. S. ambassador Paris) to Franklin D. Roosevelt of 20 January 1936 (Hyde Park, P. S. F. France: Jesse Strauss; in *FDR and Foreign Affairs,* 3:166–70). Roosevelt's answer of 13 February is printed in *FDR, Personal Letters*, 2:555–56.

3. This summary is based on *D. D. F.*, 2d, 2, No. 23; 3, Nos. 9, 38, 67, 394. On this French military abdication in Europe see also *Lipski Papers,* p. 275.

4. The arguments of some German generals with Hitler about strategy during the winter of 1939–40 as well as earlier suggest that not only French military thinking was affected by this line of reasoning.

Falkenhayn, had been proved correct in the belief that if you were once caught in a war of attrition, the way to win was to utilize acts of attrition more effectively than the other side. The change in German military leadership in the summer of 1916 meant that the evidence of the French mutinies in 1917 and the near-collapse of the French armies in the early summer of 1918 failed to make much of an impact on a German leadership that looked for victory in spectacular breakthroughs, but the reality of French enfeeblement was there all the same. It would weigh like lead on the French themselves, leading them to rash use of what strength they had in the 1920s and to abdication from a leading role in Europe in the 1930s.

Hitler shrewdly recognized that the key question he faced was whether France would or would not move quickly. If it did not move quickly, its opportunity for easy victory would pass; and then he could pick the time to attack and defeat the French. Since his early years in power coincided with the years of French retreat from a vigorous policy, he could take advantage of the situation to accentuate and reinforce the French unwillingness to risk war. Until 1936, France could act alone if it wished to; thereafter it, it would feel unable to move without allies. Hitler knew that a direct attack on France would bring it such allies, Great Britain if no other, but nothing suggested that other steps of his would bring about such a danger for Germany. It is not surprising that by May 1936 German diplomats were confidently predicting that before long—after beginning the fortification of its western border—Germany would take over Austria and that no one would try to stop it.[5]

The pattern of German policy and foreign reaction was well established. Germany would move aggressively, accompany each move by new assurances and promises, and hope that others could be lulled into acquiescence. This process would continue—with Germany taking and keeping the initiative—until one of two contingencies occurred. The increasingly aggressive moves of Germany might eventually either so arouse the British and French as to lead them to resist or to help the desperate resistance of one of the victims.[6] The other possibility was that Britain and France might acquiesce in every move of Germany until Hitler was ready to attack them at a time or times of his own choosing. There was, of course, always the theoretical possibility that the Germans themselves might get rid of him, but in 1936 nothing looked less likely.

5. So von Neurath to Bullitt on 18 May 1936 (U. S. 1936, 1:300–01; note von Neurath's comment at the same time "that the German government knew just as well as the Russian that all talk of Russian military assistance to Czechoslovakia at the present moment was nonsense" ibid., p. 303). Similarly Herbert Scholz, secretary of legation at the German embassy in Washington, on about the same date (*Hungarian Documents*, 1, No. 97).

6. For analyses along these lines see François-Poncet's report on the German situation of 25 March 1936 (*D. D. F.*, 2d, 1, No. 503) and Alexis Leger's comments to Bullitt on 21 May 1936 (U. S. 1936, 1:308–09). See also Vansittart's memorandum on "The World Situation and British Rearmament," 16 December 1936, Foreign Office A 9996/9996/51.

In the face of this situation, fear of war seemed not only sure to lead to war but even to make it more devastating when it finally did come. But lives lost in a preventive war are lost as surely as those lost in a war started by others; and without the most obvious and dire dangers, democracies will never find preventive war a readily trod path. To open the gates of Janus because someone else is certain to do so later looked like an unconscionable risk. Perhaps things would somehow change; perhaps the dictator would die and his successors follow other policies. We now know that none of this happened, but who could know it then—and know it surely enough to gamble lives on that knowledge? In 1938, as we now also know, Hitler was so worried about his health that he wrote his last will.[7] On the other hand, we know, too, that in 1939 his fiftieth birthday suggested to him that he ought to start a war soon while he was still in his prime. But who could make judgments on the basis of such facts, even had they been available elsewhere in the world of the 1930s? The answer is, of course, that those who aspire to positions of national leadership must be prepared to make precisely such judgments and to stake their reputations and the lives of their people upon them. There are no policies without risks. But those who take the greater when they think they are taking the lesser risk may still be accorded the charity of compassion for having listened in their hearts to the sentiment King George V voiced to his ministers, that having taken his people through one war he could not bear to lead them into another. That lead would have to come from elsewhere. And it did.

7. See Gerhard L. Weinberg (ed.), "Hitler's Private Testament of May 2, 1938," *Journal of Modern History,* 27, No. 4 (Dec. 1955), 415–16.

Bibliography

Introductory Comments on Archives

German Archives

Extensive parts of the German archives were microfilmed after World War II; the most comprehensive collection of such films is in the National Archives in Washington. Such microfilms are cited in this study by their National Archives microcopy number. The microfilmed records used originate primarily from the foreign ministry, chancellery, naval headquarters, and party offices. The National Archives also holds important German documents collected for, but not used at, the Nuremberg trials as well as postwar interrogations of German officials. Related materials were in the Foreign Studies Branch of the Office of the Chief of Military History at the time the author did his research. There are also some German documents in the Manuscript and Prints and Photographs Divisions of the Library of Congress. Microfilms from the Berlin Document Center are largely in the National Archives, but a group of materials from the NSDAP Hauptarchiv was microfilmed—though rather poorly—for the Hoover Institution. Among the records held at the German Federal Archives in Koblenz that were not processed by the various filming operations, those most important for this study were the collections of instructions for the German press, the papers of General Ludwig Beck, and the records of the Ministry of Finance. There are small groups of papers as well as considerable postwar interrogations at the Institute for Contemporary History in Munich. German records that fell into Soviet hands and are now for the most part in East Germany are generally cited only at second hand from publications by East German scholars.

Italian Archives

The Italian archives for the 1930s are still closed to scholars, but an important group of papers was microfilmed by the Allies in World War II; and these films have been used at the National Archives where they are listed as microcopy T–586. The other Italian films at the National Archives (T–821) pertain principally to the period of World War II and to prewar military affairs. The microfilm of Count Ciano's papers contains no documents for the years before 1938.[1]

1. Howard M. Smyth, *The Ciano Papers: Rose Garden* (Washington: Howard M. Smyth, 1969), p. 60.

Czechoslovak Archives

The Czech archives were seized practically intact in 1939 by the Germans, who had a team that prepared and sent to Berlin translations of many documents. Those translations that were found after the war in the German foreign ministry archives were microfilmed and are described in detail in the data sheets covering them that were prepared by Fritz T. Epstein.[2] This collection includes both copies of diplomatic dispatches and telegrams and the summaries of periodic briefing reports given by the Czech foreign minister, Kamil Krofta, to the section chiefs of the Czech foreign ministry. Documents of this type, available at the National Archives, are cited as "Czech document in T–120" with specific container, serial, and frame numbers. The internal evidence as to their authenticity and the general reliability of the translations is now confirmed by the fact that those translations are being used as the textual basis for the majority of the items in a document collection published under the auspices of the present Czech government.[3] Doctoring of the translated documents for political purposes had been left to von Ribbentrop's propagandist, Friedrich Berber, more recently professor at the University of Munich.[4]

American Archives

United States archives have proved unusually valuable in the preparation of this work. American diplomats in the 1930s were often exceedingly well informed—even if the government in Washington did little with their reports except file them. Many European officials entrusted Americans with information very difficult or impossible to find elsewhere, and the Central Files of the Department of State in the National Archives are as a result not only important for German-American relations but also the depository of all manner of fascinating details about such subjects as the Danzig issue, German relations with Lithuania, and the foreign policies of France and Austria. The papers of the special State Department mission to Germany under DeWitt C. Poole are also useful. The records of the American War Department include in addition to what one might expect such special items as copies of papers of the German military advisers to Chiang Kai-shek.

Materials at the National Archives must be supplemented by important collections elsewhere. The Franklin D. Roosevelt papers at Hyde Park contain much of interest; the R. Walton Moore and Clairborne Pell papers

2. T–120, 1039/1809/411884–927; 1143/2028/444168–183; 1316/2376/D 496875–880.

3. Václav Král (ed.), *Das Abkommen von München 1938, Tschechoslowakische diplomatische Dokumente 1937–1939* (Prague: Academia, 1968), p. 43.

4. Friedrich Berber (ed.), *Europäische Politik 1933–1938 im Spiegel der Prager Akten* (3d ed.; Essen: Essener Verlagsanstalt, 1942). Crossreferences have been provided in the footnotes where a document on microfilm can be compared with what appears in this collection.

there are less important. The significance of the Jay Pierrepont Moffat and William Phillips papers at Harvard can be seen from the many references to them in the notes. At the Library of Congress, I have consulted the papers of Wilbur J. Carr, Norman H. Davis, William E. Dodd, Cordell Hull, Breckinridge Long, and Laurence A. Steinhardt. The George S. Messersmith papers are at the University of Delaware.

Other Archives

The British archives were opened too late for the author to use at the Public Records Office. Copies of individual documents selected on the basis of the published index to the Foreign Office records were ordered from the P.R.O. The French and Soviet archives are closed. Publications of documents from them as well as from other archives are listed in the bibliography.

No effort has been made to make this bibliography exhaustive. The literature on the general subject is so vast that only works actually cited in this book are included, together with a small number of other works whose general ideas, organizing concepts, or supplementary detail were of real significance in shaping my views. The bibliographies listed in Part I, as well as some of the secondary works in Part IV, provide additional listings.

I. Bibliographies, Guides, Archives Inventories, and Other Reference Works

American Historical Association, Committee for the Study of War Documents, and National Archives and Records Service. "Guides to German Documents Microfilmed at Alexandria, Va." Washington: National Archives, 1958–.

Bibiliothek für Zeitgeschichte, Stuttgart (formerly the Weltkriegsbücherei). *Jahresbibliographie* (formerly *Bücherschau der Weltkriegsbücherei*). The most important bibliographic tool for twentieth-century European history.

Billig, Joseph. *Alfred Rosenberg dans l'action idéologique, politique et administrative du Reich hitlérien.* Paris: Éditions du Centre, 1963. Inventory of the Rosenberg papers at the Centre de Documentation Juive Contemporaine, Paris.

Das Deutsche Führerlexikon 1934/1935. Berlin: Stollberg, 1934.

Facius, Friedrich; Booms, Hans; Boberach, Heinz. *Das Bundesarchiv und seine Bestände*. Boppard: Harald Boldt, 1961.

Great Britain, Foreign Office. *Index to the Correspondence of the Foreign Office.* 1933–1936, 4 vols. per year. Nendeln/Liechtenstein: Kraus Reprint, 1969.

Heinz, Grete, and Peterson, Agnes F. *NSDAP Hauptarchiv, Guide to the Hoover Institution Microfilm Collection.* Stanford: Hoover Institution, 1964.

Kent, George O. *A Catalog of the Files and Microfilms of the German Foreign Ministry Archives 1920–1945*. 3 vols. Stanford: Hoover Institution, 1962–66.

Lötzke, Helmut. *Übersicht über die Bestände des Deutschen Zentralarchivs Potsdam.* Berlin (East): Rütten & Loening, 1957.

Neuburger, Otto. *Official Publications of Present-Day Germany*. Washington: Government Printing Office, 1944.

Robinson, Jacob, and Friedman, Philip. *Guide to Jewish History under Nazi Impact*. New York: Yivo, 1960. Very broad bibliographic coverage.
Schulthess europäischer Geschichtskalender. 1933–1936.
Statistisches Jahrbuch für das Deutsche Reich. 1933–1941/42.
Toynbee, Arnold J. (ed.). *Survey of International Affairs*. 1933–1936.
Weinberg, Gerhard L., *et al. Guide to Captured German Documents*. Montgomery: Air University, 1952. *Supplement*. Washington: National Archives, 1959.
Wiener Library. *From Weimar to Hitler, Germany 1918–1933*. 2d ed. London: Vallentine, Mitchell, 1964.

II. Publications of Documents, Speeches, etc.

A. Major collections, organized by country

AUSTRIA

Beiträge zur Vorgeschichte und Geschichte der Julirevolte. Vienna: Bundeskommissariat für Heimatdienst, 1934.
Red-White-Red Book. Vienna: Austrian State Printing House, 1947.

BELGIUM

Documents diplomatiques belges 1920–1940. Ch. de Visscher and F. Vanlangenhove (eds.). *La Politique de sécurité extérieure. 1931–1937*. Vols. 3 and 4. Brussels: Académie royale, 1964–65.

FRANCE

Documents diplomatiques français 1932–1939. 1st series, 1932–1935, Vol. 2; 2d series, 1936–1939, Vols. 1–3. Paris: Imprimerie Nationale, 1963–67.
Les Évenements survenues en France de 1933 à 1945, Temoignages et documents recueilles par la commission d'enquête parlementaire. 9 vols. Paris: Presses Universitaires, 1947.

GERMANY

Documents secrets du ministère des affaires étrangère de l'Allemagne. 2. *Hongrie, La politique allemande 1937–1943*. 3. *La politique allemande en Espagne 1936–1943*. Trans. by Madeleine and Michel Eristov. Paris: 1946.
Documents on German Foreign Policy 1918–1945. German edition: *Akten zur Deutschen Auswärtigen Politik 1918–1945*. Series B, 1925–1933, is cited from the German edition, Göttingen: Vandenhoeck & Ruprecht, 1966–. Series C, 1933–1937, is cited from the English-language edition, Washington: Government Printing Office, 1957–. Series D, 1937–1945, is cited from the German edition, Baden-Baden: Imprimerie Nationale, later P. Keppler, 1950–. For the period covered by this book, only vol. 6 of Series C remains to be published.
United States Office of Military Government for Germany, Finance Division. "Report on the Investigation of the Deutsche Bank." 4 vols. OMGUS, 1946. Annex. OMGUS, 1947.

GREAT BRITAIN

Documents on British Foreign Policy 1919–1939. 2d series, 1930–1937. Vols. 4–6, 1933–1934. London: H. M. Stationery Office, 1950–57.
Parliamentary (Command Papers): Cmd. 5143. *Correspondence showing the course of certain Diplomatic Discussions directed towards securing an European Settlement, June 1934 to March 1936*. Miscellaneous No. 3 (1936). London: H. M. Stationery Office, 1936.

HUNGARY

Diplomáciai iratok magyarország külpolitikájáhaz 1936–1945. Vols. 1–2. Budapest: Akadémiai kiadó, 1962–66. These volumes contain German-language summaries of each document. In cases where the full text of the document has appeared elsewhere in a western language, that is indicated in the footnote where the document is cited from this collection.

Allianz Hitler-Horthy-Mussolini: Dokumente zur ungarischen Aussenpolitik (1933–1944). Budapest: Akadémiai kiadó, 1966.

The Confidential Papers of Admiral Horthy. Budapest: Corvina Press, 1965.

ITALY

I Documenti diplomatici italiani. 7th series, 1922–1935; 8th series, 1935–1939. Rome: Libreria dello stato, 1952–.

Ciano, Galeazzo. *Ciano's Diplomatic Papers*. Ed. by Malcolm Muggeridge. Trans. by Stuart Hood. London: Odhams, 1948.

POLAND

Weissbuch der Polnischen Regierung. Basel: Birkhäuser, 1939. Important corrections in the *Lipski Papers*, see below under Jedrzejewicz, Waclaw (ed.).

PORTUGAL

Dez anos de política externa (1936–1947). Lisbon: Impresa Nacional, 1961–. Documents on 1936 only about the Spanish civil war.

UNION OF SOVIET SOCIALIST REPUBLICS

The major Soviet collection of documents, *Dokumenty vneshney politiki SSSR*, has not yet reached 1933. From the Soviet side, there is the publication:

"The Struggle of the U.S.S.R. for Collective Security in Europe during 1933–1935." Edited by M. Andreyeva and L. Vidyasova. *International Affairs* (Moscow). Vol. 9 (1963), No. 6, 107–16; No. 7, 116–23; No. 8, 132–39; No. 10, 112–20. See also:

Soviet Documents on Foreign Policy, 1917–1941. Edited by Jane Degras. 3 vols. London: Oxford University Press, 1951–53.

UNITED STATES

Foreign Relations of the United States. Washington: Government Printing Office, 1861–. All the volumes for the years covered by this book have appeared, as have several supplementary volumes. The latter all include the title of the main series in their respective titles, with the exception of:

Peace and War, United States Foreign Policy 1931–1941. Washington: Government Printing Office, 1943.

Important documentary collections from the Roosevelt papers are:

F.D.R.: His Personal Letters, 1928–1945. Edited by Elliot Roosevelt. 2 vols. New York: Duell, Sloan and Pearce, 1950.

Franklin D. Roosevelt and Foreign Affairs, January 1933—January 1937. Edited by Edgar B. Nixon. 3 vols. Cambridge: Harvard University Press, 1969. Serious questions have been raised about this publication.

THE VATICAN

The Vatican series, *Actes et documents du Saint Siège relatifs à la seconde guerre mondiale,* starts with March, 1939. For the earlier period, there is:

Der Notenwechsel zwischen dem Heiligen Stuhl und der Deutschen Reichsregierung. Vol. 1. *Von der Ratifizierung des Reichskonkordats bis zur Enzyklika "Mit brennender Sorge."* Mainz: Matthias-Grünewald-Verlag, 1965.

B. Other documents and collections, organized by editor

Anordnungen des Stellvertreters des Führers. Munich: Eher, 1937.

Askew, William C. (ed.). "Italian Intervention in Spain: The Agreements of March 31, 1934 with the Spanish Monarchist Parties." *Journal of Modern History*. 24, No. 2 (June 1952), 181–83.

Auerbach, Hellmuth (ed.). "Eine nationalsozialistische Stimme zum Wiener

Putsch vom 25. Juli 1934." *Vierteljahrshefte für Zeitgeschichte.* 12, No. 2 (April 1964), 201–18.

Baynes, Norman H. (ed.). *The Speeches of Adolf Hitler, April 1922—August 1939.* 2 vols. London: Oxford University Press, 1942.

Berber, Friedrich (ed.). *Europäische Politik 1933–1938 im Spiegel der Prager Akten.* 3d edition. Essen: Essener Verlagsanstalt, 1942.

Boepple, Ernst (ed.). *Adolf Hitlers Reden.* Munich: Deutscher Volksverlag, 1934.

Braunthal, Julius. *The Tragedy of Austria.* London: Gollancz, 1948. Contains a collection of documents edited by Paul R. Sweet: "Mussolini and Dollfuss, An Episode in Fascist Diplomacy."

Deuerlein, Ernst (ed). *Der Hitler-Putsch, Bayerische Dokumente zum 8./9. November 1923.* Stuttgart: Deutsche Verlags-Anstalt, 1962.

———. "Hitlers Eintritt in die Politik und die Reichswehr." *Vierteljahrshefte für Zeitgeschichte.* 7, No. 2 (April 1959), 177–227.

Domarus, Max (ed.). *Hitler, Reden und Proklamationen 1932–1945.* 2 vols. Neustadt a.d. Aisch: Verlagsdruckerei Schmidt, 1962.

Emessen, Theodor R. (ed.). *Aus Görings Schreibtisch.* Berlin: Allgemeiner Deutscher Verlag, 1947.

France, Centre Nationale de la Recherche Scientifique. *Les Relations militaires franco-belges de mars 1936 au 10 mai 1940.* Paris: Éditions du Centre Nationale de la Recherche Scientifique, 1968.

Gajan, Koloman, and Kvaček, Robert (eds.). *Germany and Czechoslovakia, 1918–1945.* Prague: Orbis, 1965.

Germany, Foreign Ministry. *Aussenpolitische Dokumente 1936.* Heft 2. *Aussenpolitische Vorgänge im zweiten Halbjahr 1936.* Berlin: *Reichsdruckerei,* 1937. A copy of the "For official use only" publication is in the Institut für Zeitgeschichte, Munich.

———. *Zweites Weissbuch der Deutschen Regierung.* Basel: Birkhäuser, 1939.

———. *Weissbuch 7. Dokumente zum Konflikt mit Jugoslawien und Griechenland.* Berlin: Eher, 1941.

Görlitz, Walter (ed.). *Keitel, Verbrecher oder Offizier?* Göttingen: Musterschmidt, 1961.

Hess, Rudolf. *Reden.* Munich: Eher, 1938.

Der Hochverratsprozess gegen Dr. Guido Schmidt vor dem Wiener Volksgericht. Vienna: Österreichische Staatsdruckerei, 1947.

Hooker, Nancy Harvison (ed.). *The Moffat Papers: Selections from the Diplomatic Journals of Jay Pierrepont Moffat, 1919–1943.* Cambridge: Harvard University Press, 1956.

International Military Tribunal. *Trial of the Major War Criminals.* 42 vols. English edition. Nuremberg, 1946–48.

Jedlicka, Ludwig (ed.). *Die Erhebung der österreichischen Nationalsozialisten im Juli 1934, Bericht der Historischen Kommission des Reichsführers SS.* Vienna: Europa-Verlag, 1965.

Jedrzejewicz, Waclaw (ed.). *Diplomat in Berlin, 1933–1939, Papers and Memoirs of Józef Lipski, Ambassador of Poland.* New York: Columbia University Press, 1968.

———. *Diplomat in Paris 1936–1939, Memoirs of Juliusz Lukasiewicz, Ambassador of Poland.* New York: Columbia University Press, 1970.

Jochmann, Werner (ed.). *Im Kampf um die Macht, Hitlers Rede vor dem Hamburger Nationalklub von 1919.* Frankfurt/M: Europäische Verlagsanstalt, 1960.

———. *Nationalsozialismus und Revolution, Ursprung und Geschichte der*

NSDAP in Hamburg, 1922–1933. Frankfurt/M: Europäische Verlagsanstalt, 1963.

Jullien, Albert (ed.). *Le vrai visage des maitres du IIIe Reich, Les instructions secrètes de la propagande allemande*. Paris: Petit Parisien, 1934.

Karsai, Elek (ed.). "The Meeting of Gömbös and Hitler in 1933." *New Hungarian Quarterly*. 3, No. 5 (Jan.-Mar. 1962), 170–96.

Kerekes, Lajos (ed.). "Akten zu den geheimen Verbindungen zwischen der Bethlen-Regierung und der österreichischen Heimwehrbewegung." *Acta Historica*. 11, Nos. 1–4 (1965), 299–339.

———. "Akten des ungarischen Ministeriums des Äusseren zur Vorgeschichte der Annexion Österreichs." *Acta Historica*. 7, Nos. 3–4 (1960), 355–90.

Kiszling, Rudolf. *Die militärischen Vereinbarungen der Kleinen Entente*. Munich: Oldenbourg, 1959.

Král, Václav (ed.). *Das Abkommen von München 1938, Tschechoslowakische diplomatische Dokumente 1937–1939*. Prague: Academia, 1968.

———. *Die Deutschen in der Tschechoslowakei, 1933–1947*. Prague: Nakladatelstvo Československé Akademie Věd, 1964.

Krausnick, Helmut (ed.). "Aus den Personalpapieren von Canaris." *Vierteljahrshefte für Zeitgeschichte*. 10, No. 3 (July 1962), 280–310.

Kursell, Otto von (ed.). *Adolf Hitlers Reden*. Munich: Deutscher Volksverlag, 1925.

Phelps, Reginald H. (ed.). "Hitler als Parteiredner im Jahre 1920." *Vierteljahrshefte für Zeitgeschichte*. 11, No. 3 (July 1963), 274–330.

Picker, Henry, *et al.* (eds.). *Hitlers Tischgespräche im Führerhauptquartier 1941–1942*. Stuttgart: Seewald, 1965. A better edition than the one by Ritter, but marred by numerous errors and the failure to take into account the texts available at the Library of Congress.

Preiss, Heinz (ed.). *Adolf Hitler in Franken, Reden aus der Kampfzeit*. Nuernberg: [Verlag der Stürmer?], 1939.

Les procès de collaboration, Fernand de Brinon, Joseph Darnand, Jean Luchaire, compte rendu stenographique. Paris: Albin Michel, 1948.

Ritter, Gerhard (ed.). *Hitlers Tischgespräche im Führerhauptquartier 1941–1942*. Bonn: Athenäum, 1951. The first, and worst, edition of this source.

Ritthaler, Anton (ed.). "Eine Etappe auf Hitlers Weg zur ungeteilten Macht, Hugenbergs Rücktritt als Reichsminister." *Vierteljahrshefte für Zeitgeschichte*. 8, No. 2 (April 1960), 193–219.

Robertson, Esmonde (ed.). "Zur Wiederbesetzung des Rheinlandes 1936." *Vierteljahrshefte für Zeitgeschichte*. 10, No. 2 (April 1962), 178–205.

Sales, Raoul de Roussy de (ed.). *Adolf Hitler, My New Order*. New York: Reynal and Hitchcock, 1941. A collection of speeches.

Schmidt, Richard, and Grabowsky, Adolf (eds.). *Disarmament and Equal Rights*. Berlin: Carl Heymanns, 1934.

Schwazrotbuch, Dokumente über den Hitlerimperialismus. Deutsche-Anarcho-Syndikalisten. Barcelona: Asy-Verlag, 1937. Documents seized from German agencies in Spain in July 1936.

Szinai, Miklos, and Szücs, László (eds.). "Horthy's Secret Correspondence with Hitler." *New Hungarian Quarterly*. 4, No. 11 (1963), 174–91.

Rost van Tonningen, Mednoud Marinus. *Correspondentie van M. M. Rost van Tonningen*. The Hague: Nijhoff, 1967–.

Treue, Wilhelm (ed.). "Hitlers Denkschrift zum Vierjahresplan 1936." *Vierteljahrshefte für Zeitgeschichte*. 3, No. 2 (April 1955), 184–210.

Trevor-Roper, Hugh R. (ed.). *Hitler's Table Talk, 1941–1944*. London: Weidenfeld and Nicholson, 1953.

United States, Mixed Claims Commission. *Final Report of H. H. Martin.* Washington: Government Printing Office, 1941.

Die Verschwörung gegen Österreich, Dokumente und Akten. Vienna: Reichspost, 1933.

Vogelsang, Thilo (ed.). "Neue Dokumente zur Geschichte der Reichswehr, 1930–33." *Vierteljahrshefte für Zeitgeschichte.* 2, No. 4 (Oct. 1954), 397–436.

Voelker, Karl-Heinz (ed.). *Dokumente und Dokumentarfotos zur Geschichte der deutschen Luftwaffe; aus den Geheimakten des Reichswehrministeriums, 1919–1933, und des Reichsluftfahrtministeriums, 1933–1939.* Stuttgart: Deutsche Verlags-Anstalt, 1968.

Watt, Donald C. (ed.). "The Secret Laval-Mussolini Agreement of 1935 on Ethiopia." *Middle East Journal.* 15 (1961), 69–78.

Weinberg, Gerhard L. (ed.). "Die geheimen Abkommen zum Antikominternpakt." *Vierteljahrshefte für Zeitgeschichte.* 2, No. 2 (April 1954), 193–201.

———. "Hitler's Private Testament of May 2, 1938." *Journal of Modern History.* 27, No. 4 (Dec. 1955), 415–19.

———. "National Socialist Organization and Foreign Policy Aims in 1927." *Journal of Modern History.* 36, No. 4 (Dec. 1964), 428–33.

Whealey, Robert H. (ed.). "Mussolini's Ideological Diplomacy: An Unpublished Document." *Journal of Modern History.* 39, No. 4 (Dec. 1967), 432–37.

III. Diaries, Memoirs, Collected Papers, and Other Works by Key Participants

Abetz, Otto. *Das Offene Problem, Ein Rückblick auf zwei Jahrzehnte Deutscher Frankreichpolitik.* Cologne: Greven-Verlag, 1951.

Aloisi, Pompeo. *Journal (25 juillet 1932–14 juin 1936).* Trans. by Maurice Vaussard. Paris: Plon, 1957.

Anfuso, Filippo. *Rom-Berlin im diplomatischen Spiegel.* Trans. by Egon Hyman. Essen: Pohl, 1951.

Aretin, Erwin von. *Krone und Ketten.* Munich: Sueddeutscher Verlag, 1955.

Beck, Joseph. *Dernier rapport, politique polonaise, 1926–1939.* Neuchâtel: Éditions de la Baconnière, 1951.

Bennecke, Heinrich. *Die Reichswehr und der "Röhm Putsch."* Munich: Olzog, 1964.

Blücher, Wipert von. *Gesandter zwischen Diktatur und Demokratie, Erinnerungen aus den Jahren 1935–1944.* Wiesbaden: Limes, 1951.

Blum, John Morton (ed.). *From the Morgenthau Diaries.* 3 vols. Boston: Houghton Mifflin, 1959–67.

de Brinon, Fernand. *Frankreich-Deutschland 1918–1934.* Trans. by Albert Koerber. Essen: Essener Verlagsanstalt, 1935.

———. *Mémoires.* Paris: L. L. C., 1949.

Burckhardt, Carl J. *Meine Danziger Mission, 1937–1939.* Munich: Callwey, 1960.

Cerruti, Elisabetta. *Ambassador's Wife.* New York: Macmillan, 1953.

Chatfield, Admiral Sir Ernle. *The Navy and Defence.* 2: *It might happen again.* London: W. Heinemann, 1947.

Cooper, Alfred Duff. *Old Men Forget.* New York: E. P. Dutton, 1954.

Davignon, Jacques. *Berlin 1936–1940, souvenirs d'une mission.* Paris, Brussels: Éditions universitaires, 1951.

Diels, Rudolf. *Lucifer ante portas, es spricht der erste Chef der Gestapo.* Stuttgart: Deutsche Verlags-Anstalt, 1950.

Dietrich, Otto. *12 Jahre mit Hitler*. Cologne: Atlas, 1955.

Dirksen, Herbert von. *Moskau-Tokio-London, Erinnerungen und Betrachtungen zu 20 Jahren deutscher Aussenpolitik 1919–1939*. Stuttgart: Kohlhammer, 1950.

Dodd, William E. Jr. and Martha (eds.). *Ambassador Dodd's Diary*. New York: Harcourt Brace, 1941.

Eden, Anthony. *The Memoirs of Anthony Eden, Facing the Dictators*. Boston: Houghton Mifflin, 1962.

Ernst, Robert. *Rechenschaftsbericht eines Elsässers*. 2d ed. Berlin: Bernard & Graefe, 1955.

Faber du Faur, Moriz von. *Macht und Ohnmacht, Erinnerungen eines alten Offiziers*. Stuttgart: Hans E. Günther, 1953.

Feis, Herbert. *1933, Characters in Crisis*. Boston: Little, Brown, 1966.

Fitz Randolph, Sigismond-Sizzo. *Der Frühstücks-Attaché aus London*. Stuttgart: Hans Riegler, 1954.

Flandin, Pierre-Étienne. *Politique française, 1919–1940*. Paris: Éditions nouvelles, 1947.

François-Poncet, André. *Als Botschafter in Berlin 1931–1938*. Trans. by Erna Stübl. Mainz: Florian Kupferberg, 1949.

Frank, Hans. *Im Angesicht des Galgens*. Munich: Friedrich Alfred Beck, 1953.

Frick, Wilhelm. *Die Nationalsozialisten im Reichstag*. Munich: Eher, 1928 and 1932.

Fromm, Bella. *Blood and Banquets, A Berlin Social Diary*. New York: Harper, 1942.

Gärtner, Margarete. *Botschafterin des guten Willens, Aussenpolitische Arbeit 1914–1950*. Bonn: Athenäum, 1955.

Gamelin, Maurice. *Servir*. 2 vols. Paris: Plon, 1946.

Gauché, Maurice. *Le deuxième bureau au travail (1935–1940)*. Paris: Amiot-Dumont, 1953.

Gedye, G. E. R. *Betrayal in Central Europe, Austria and Czechoslovakia: The Fallen Bastions*. New York: Harper, 1939.

Grobba, Fritz. *Männer und Mächte im Orient, 25 Jahre diplomatische Tätigkeit im Orient*. Göttingen: Musterschmidt, 1967.

Guariglia, Raffaelo. *Ricordi, 1922–1946*. Naples: Edizioni scientifiche italiane, 1949.

Hanfstaengl, Ernst. *Hitler, The Missing Years*. London: Eyre & Spottiswoode, 1957.

Heinkel, Ernst. *Stürmisches Leben*. Stuttgart: Mundus-Verlag, 1953.

Helfferich, Emil. *1932–1946 Tatsachen, Ein Beitrag zur Wahrheitsfindung*. Jever (Oldenbourg): C. L. Mettcker & Söhne, 1968.

Hentig, Werner Otto von. *Mein Leben eine Dienstreise*. Göttingen: Vandenhoeck & Ruprecht, 1962.

Herriot, Édouard. *Jadis*. 2: *D'une guerre à l'autre, 1914–1936*. Paris: Flammarion, 1952.

Hesse, Fritz. *Das Spiel um Deutschland*. Munich: Paul List, 1953.

Hildebrandt, Rainer. *Wir sind die Letzten; aus dem Leben des Widerstandskämpfers Albrecht Haushofer und seiner Freunde*. Neuwied/Berlin: Michael, 1949.

Hilger, Gustav. *Wir und der Kreml, Deutsch-sowjetische Beziehungen 1918–1941*. Bonn: Athenäum, 1964.

Hitler, Adolf. *Mein Kampf*. 2 vols. Munich: Eher, 1933 edition.

Hitlers zweites Buch, Ein Dokument aus dem Jahr 1928. Ed. by Gerhard L. Weinberg. Stuttgart: Deutsche Verlags-Anstalt, 1961.

Horthy, Miklos. *Ein Leben für Ungarn*. Bonn: Athenäum, 1953.

Hossbach, Friedrich. *Zwischen Wehrmacht und Hitler 1934–1938*. Wolfenbüttel: Wolfenbütteler Verlagsanstalt, 1949.

Hull, Cordell. *Memoirs*. 2 vols. New York: Macmillan, 1948.

Jones, Thomas. *A Diary with Letters 1931–1950*. London: Oxford University Press, 1954.

Kaeckkenbeek, Georges. *The International Experiment of Upper Silesia, A Study in the Workings of the Upper Silesian Settlement, 1922–1937*. Oxford: Oxford University Press, 1942.

Kessler, Harry Graf. *Tagebücher 1918–1937*. Frankfurt/M: Insel-Verlag, 1961.

Kleist, Bruno Peter. *Zwischen Hitler und Stalin*. Bonn: Athenäum, 1950.

Kordt, Erich. *Nicht aus den Akten*. Stuttgart: Deutsche Verlags-Anstalt, 1950.

Krebs, Albert. *Tendenzen und Gestalten der NSDAP*. Stuttgart: Deutsche Verlags-Anstalt, 1959.

Krivitsky, Walter G. *In Stalin's Secret Service*. New York: Harper, 1939.

Kroll, Hans. *Lebenserinnerungen eines Botschafters*. Cologne: Kiepenheuer, Witsch, 1967.

Lang, Serge, and Schenck, Ernst von (eds.). *Memoirs of Alfred Rosenberg*. Trans. by Eric Posselt. Chicago: Ziff-Davis, 1949.

Langoth, Franz. *Kampf um Österreich: Erinnerungen eines Politikers*. Wels: Welsermühl, 1951.

Laroche, Jules. *La Pologne de Pilsudski, souvenirs d'une ambassade 1926–1935*. Paris: Flammarion, 1953.

Lawford, Valentine. *Bound for Diplomacy*. London: John Murray, 1963.

Leonhard, Jakob. *Als Gestapoagent im Dienste der Schweizer Gegenspionage*. Zurich: Europa-Verlag, 1946.

Lindemann, Fritz. *Im Dienste Chinas, Erinnerungen aus den Jahren 1929 bis 1940*. Peking: Selbstverlag, 1940.

Lüdecke, Kurt G. W. *I knew Hitler*. New York: Scribner's, 1937.

Luther, Hans. *Politiker ohne Partei*. Stuttgart: Deutsche Verlags-Anstalt, 1960.

———. *Vor dem Abgrund, 1930–1933, Reichsbankpräsident in Krisenzeiten*. Berlin: Propyläen Verlag, 1964.

Magistrati, Massimo. "La Germania e l'impresa italiana di Etiopia (Ricordi di Berlino)." *Revista di studi politici internationali*. 17, No. 4 (Oct.–Dec. 1950), 563–606.

Manstein, Erich von. *Aus einem Soldatenleben*. Bonn: Athenäum, 1958.

Meinertzhagen, Richard. *Middle East Diary 1917–1956*. London: Crescent Press, 1959.

Miličevič, Vladeta. *Der Königsmord von Marseille*. Bad Godesberg: Hohwacht, 1959.

Nadolny, Rudolf. *Mein Beitrag*. Wiesbaden: Limes, 1955.

van Overstraeten, General R. *Albert I–Léopold III, Vingt ans de politique militaire belge 1920–1940*. Bruges: Desclée de Brouwer, 1949.

Papen, Franz von. *Der Wahrheit eine Gasse*. Munich: Paul List, 1952.

Paul-Boncour, Joseph. *Entre deux guerres*. 2. New York: Brentano's, 1946.

Peterson, Maurice. *Both Sides of the Curtain*. London: Constable, 1950.

Phillips, William. *Ventures in Diplomacy*. London: John Murray, 1952.

Price, George Ward. *I know these Dictators*. New York: Holt, 1938.

Raeder, Erich. *Mein Leben*. 2 vols. Tübingen: Schlichtenmayer, 1956.

Rauschning, Hermann. *Die Revolution des Nihilismus*. Zurich: Europa-Verlag, 1938.

———. *The Voice of Destruction*. New York: Putnam, 1940.

Rheinbaben, Werner Freiherr von. *Viermal Deutschland*. Berlin: Argon-Verlag, 1954.

Ribbentrop, Annelies von (ed.). *Joachim von Ribbentrop, Zwischen London und Moskau*. Leoni: Druffel, 1954.
Rintelen, Anton. *Erinnerungen an Österreichs Weg*. Munich: Bruckmann, 1941.
Rosenberg, Alfred. *Der Zukunftsweg einer deutschen Aussenpolitik*. Munich: Eher, 1927.
Schmidt, Paul. *Statist auf diplomatischer Bühne, 1923–45*. Bonn: Athenäum, 1950.
Schuschnigg, Kurt von. *Austrian Requiem*. Trans. by Franz von Hildebrand. New York: Putnam, 1946.
———. *My Austria*. Trans. by John Segrue. New York: Knopf, 1938.
Schweppenburg, Leo Geyr von. *Erinnerungen eines Militärattachés, London 1933–1937*. Stuttgart: Deutsche Verlags-Anstalt, 1949.
Selby, Sir Walford. *Diplomatic Twilight, 1930–1940*. London: John Murray, 1953.
Seraphim, Hans-Günther (ed.). *Das politische Tagebuch Alfred Rosenbergs 1934/35 und 1939/40*. Munich: Deutscher Taschenbuch Verlag, 1964.
Shirer, William L. *Berlin Diary 1934–1941*. New York: Knopf, 1942.
Simon, Sir John. *Retrospect*. London: Hutchinson, 1952.
Strasser, Otto. *Ministersessel oder Revolution*. Berlin: Kampf-Verlag, 1930. Reprinted in his *Aufbau des deutschen Sozialismus* (2d ed.; Prague: Heinrich Grunov, 1936).
Szembek, Jean. *Journal 1933–1939*. Paris: Plon, 1952. This is only a selection from the diaries; a complete edition in Polish is in the process of publication.
Szymánski, Antoni. "Als politischer Militärattaché in Berlin (1932–1939)." *Politische Studien*. 13, No. 141 (1962), 42–51.
Temperley, Arthur C. *The Whispering Gallery of Europe*. London: Collins, 1938.
Templewood, Viscount (Sir Samuel Hoare). *Nine Troubled Years*. London: Collins, 1954.
Thomas, Georg. "Gedanken und Ereignisse." *Schweizer Monatshefte*. 25 (Dec. 1945), 537–58.
Thompson, Geoffrey. *Front-Line Diplomat*. London: Hutchinson, 1959.
Toynbee, Arnold J. *Acquaintances*. London: Oxford University Press, 1967.
Vansittart, Sir Robert. *The Mist Procession*. London: Hutchinson, 1958.
Warlimont, Walter. *Im Hauptquartier der deutschen Wehrmacht 1939–1945*. Bonn: Athenäum, 1964.
Weizsäcker, Ernst von. *Erinnergungen*. Munich: Paul List, 1950.
Wiedemann, Fritz. *Der Mann der Feldherr werden wollte*. [Dortmund?]: Blick und Bild Verlag, 1964.
Winkler, Franz. *Die Diktatur in Österreich*. Zurich: Orell Füssli, 1935.
Zieb, Paul W. *Logistische Probleme der Kriegsmarine*. Neckargemünd: Vowinckel, 1961.
Ziehm, Ernst. *Aus meiner politischen Arbeit in Danzig 1914–1939*. 2d ed. Marburg: Herder-Institut, 1960.
Zuylen, Baron Pierre van. *Les mains libres, politique extérieure de la Belgique, 1914–1940*. Paris: Desclée de Brouwer, 1950.

IV. Secondary Works

Absolon, Rudolf. *Wehrgesetz und Wehrdienst, 1935–1945*. Boppard: Harald Boldt, 1959.
———. *Die Wehrmacht im Dritten Reich*. 1: *30. Januar 1933 bis 2. August 1934* Boppard: Harald Boldt, 1969.

Abshagen, Karl Heinz. *Canaris, Patriot und Weltbürger*. Stuttgart: Union Deutsche Verlagsgesellschaft, 1950.

Adler, Selig. "The War-Guilt Question and American Disillusionment, 1918–1928." *Journal of Modern History*. 23, No. 1 (March 1951), 1–28.

Aigner, Dietrich. *Das Ringen um England, Das deutsch-britische Verhältnis, Die öffentliche Meinung 1933–1939, Tragödie zweier Völker*. Munich: Bechtle, 1969.

Aretin, Karl Otmar Freiherr von. "Kaas, Papen und das Konkordat von 1933." *Vierteljahrshefte für Zeitgeschichte*. 14, No. 3 (July 1966), 252–79.

Armstrong, John A. *The Politics of Totalitarianism, The Communist Party of the Soviet Union from 1934 to the Present*. New York: Random House, 1961.

———. *Ukrainian Nationalism, 1939–1945*. 2d ed. New York: Columbia University Press, 1963.

Baer, George W. *The Coming of the Italian-Ethiopian War*. Cambridge, Mass.: Harvard University Press, 1967.

Baldwin, Arthur Windham. *My Father: The True Story*. London: Allen & Unwin, 1955.

Bankwitz, Philip C. F. *Maxime Weygand and Civil-Military Relations in Modern France*. Cambridge, Mass.: Harvard University Press, 1967.

Bay, Achim. *Der nationalsozialistische Gedanke der Grossraumwirtschaft und seine ideologischen Grundlagen*. Erlangen-Nürnberg Diss. Nuernberg, 1962.

Beck, Earl R. *Verdict on Schacht*. Tallahassee: Florida State University, 1955.

Beloff, Max. *The Foreign Policy of Soviet Russia*. 2: *1936–1941*. London: Oxford University Press, 1949.

Bennecke, Heinrich. "Die Memoiren des Ernst Röhm." *Politische Studien*. 14, No. 148 (1963), 179–88.

Bennet, Benjamin. *Hitler over Africa*. London: T. Werner Laurie, 1939. Contains an appendix of German documents seized at the National Socialist headquarters in Windhoeck in July 1934.

Bensel, Rolf. *Die deutsche Flottenpolitik von 1933 bis 1939*. Beiheft 3 der *Marine-Rundschau*. Frankfurt/M: Mittler, 1958.

Berend, Tibor Iván, and Ránki, György. "German-Hungarian Relations Following Hitler's Rise to Power." *Acta Historica*. 8 (1961), 313–46.

Bernhardt, Walter. *Die deutsche Aufrüstung 1934–1939, Militärische und politische Konzeptionen und ihre Einschätzung durch die Alliierten*. Frankfurt/M: Bernard & Graefe, 1969.

Bierschenk, Theodor. *Die deutsche Volksgruppe in Polen*. Kitzingen: Holzner, 1954.

Birkenfeld, Wolfgang. *Der synthetische Treibstoff 1933–1945, Ein Beitrag zur nationalsozialistischen Wirtschafts- und Rüstungspolitik*. Göttingen: Musterschmidt, 1964.

Birkenhead, Earl of. *Halifax, The Life of Lord Halifax*. Boston: Houghton Mifflin, 1966.

Bleyer, Hans. "Die ungarländische Deutschtumsfrage im Spiegel der diplomatischen Gespräche zwischen Budapest und Berlin." In *Gedenkschrift für Harold Steinacker (1875–1965)*. Munich: Oldenbourg, 1966, pp. 297–327.

Bloch, Charles. *Hitler und die europäischen Mächte 1933/34, Kontinuität oder Bruch?* Hamburg: Europäische Verlagsanstalt, 1966.

———. "La Grande-Bretagne face au réarmament allemand et l'accord naval de 1935." *Revue d'histoire de la deuxième guerre mondiale*. 16, No. 63 (July 1966), 41–68.

Bloch, Kurt. *German Interests and Policies in the Far East*. New York: Institute of Pacific Relations, 1940.

Bolloten, Burnett. *The Grand Camouflage: The Spanish Civil War and Revolution, 1936–39*. New York: Praeger, 1968.

Bibliography

Borkenau, Franz. *The Spanish Cockpit.* Ann Arbor: University of Michigan Press, 1963.

Bourne, Kenneth, and Watt, Donald C. (eds.). *Studies in International History.* London: Longmans, 1967.

Bracher, Karl Dietrich; Saur, Wolfgang; and Schulz, Gerhard. *Die nationalsozialistische Machtergreifung.* 2d ed. Cologne: Westdeutscher Verlag, 1962.

Bonnell, Allen T. *German Control over International Economic Relations, 1930–1940.* Urbana: University of Illinois Press, 1940.

Bradley, Pearle E. Q. *The National Socialist Attack on the Foreign Policies of the German Republic 1919–1939.* Ann Arbor: University Microfilms, 1954.

Braubach, Max. *Der Einmarch deutscher Truppen in die entmilitarisierte Zone am Rhein im März 1936.* Cologne: Westdeutscher Verlag, 1956.

Breyer, Richard. *Das Deutsche Reich und Polen 1932–1937, Aussenpolitik und Volksgruppenfragen.* Würzburg: Holzner, 1955.

Brook-Shepherd, Gordon. *Dollfuss.* London: Macmillan, 1961.

Broszat, Martin. "Deutschland-Ungarn-Rumänien, Entwicklung und Grundfaktoren nationalsozialistischer Hegemonial- und Bündnispolitik 1938–41." *Historische Zeitschrift.* 206, No. 1 (Feb. 1968), 45–96.

———. "Faschismus und Kollaboration in Ostmitteleuropa zwischen den Weltkriegen." *Vierteljahrshefte für Zeitgeschichte.* 14, No. 3 (July 1966), 225–51.

———. "Die Memeldeutschen Organisationen und der Nationalsozialismus." *Vierteljahrshefte für Zeitgeschichte.* 5, No. 3 (July 1957), 273–78.

———. *Nationalsozialistische Polenpolitik, 1939–1945.* Stuttgart: Deutsche Verlags-Anstalt, 1961.

Brügel, Johann W. *Tschechen und Deutsche, 1918–1938.* Munich: Nymphenburger Verlagshandlung, 1967.

Buller, Ernestine Amy. *Darkness over Germany.* London: Longmans, 1943.

Bullock, Alan. *Hitler, A Study in Tyranny.* London: Odhams Press, 1952 and later editions.

Butler, J. R. M. *Lord Lothian, 1882–1940.* London: Macmillan, 1960.

Butow, Robert J. C. *Japan's Decision to Surrender.* Stanford: Stanford University Press, 1954.

Cameron, Elizabeth R. *Prologue to Appeasement. A Study in French Foreign Policy 1933–1936.* Washington: American Council on Public Affairs, 1942.

Campus, Eliza. "Die Hitlerfaschistische Infiltration Rumäniens, 1939–1940." *Zeitschrift für Geschichtswissenschaft.* 5 (1957), 213–28.

Carroll, Bernice A. *Design for Total War, Arms and Economics in the Third Reich.* The Hague: Mouton, 1968.

Cassels, Alan. "Mussolini and German Nationalism, 1922–25." *Journal of Modern History.* 35, No. 2 (June 1963), 137–57.

Castellan, Georges. *Le réarmament clandestin du Reich 1930–1935.* Paris: Plon, 1954.

Catell, David I. *Soviet Diplomacy and the Spanish Civil War.* Berkeley: University of California Press, 1957.

Čelovsky, Boris. *Das Münchener Abkommen von 1938.* Stuttgart: Deutsche Verlags-Anstalt, 1958.

———. "Pilsudskis Präventivkrieg gegen das nationalsozialistische Deutschland (Entstehung, Verbreitung und Widerlegung einer Legende)." *Die Welt als Geschichte.* 14, No. 1 (1954), 53–70.

Černý, Bohumil. "Der Parteivorstand der SPD im tschechoslowakischen Asyl (1933–1938)." *Historica.* 14 (1967), 175–218.

Churchill, Winston S. *The Second World War.* 1: *The Gathering Storm.* Boston: Houghton Mifflin, 1948.

Colton, Joel. *Leon Blum, Humanist in Politics.* New York: Knopf, 1966.

Colvin, Ian. *Chief of Intelligence.* London: Gollancz, 1951.

———. *None so Blind*. New York: Harcourt, 1965.

Compton, James V. *The Swastika and the Eagle; Hitler, the United States and the Origins of World War II*. Boston: Houghton Mifflin, 1967.

Craig, Gordon, and Gilbert, Felix (eds.). *The Diplomats*. Princeton: Princeton University Press, 1953.

Daim, Wilfred. *Der Mann, der Hitler die Ideen gab*. Munich: Isar, 1958.

Dallek, Robert. *Democrat and Diplomat, The Life of William E. Dodd*. New York: Oxford University Press, 1968.

d'Amoja, Fulvio. *Declino e prima crisi dell'Europa di Versailles, Studio sulla diplomazia italiana ed europea, 1931–1933*. Milan: D. A. Giuffré, 1967. Important for use of the Aloisi papers.

Deakin, Frederick William, and Storry, G. R. *The Case of Richard Sorge*. London: Chatto & Windus, 1966.

Debicki, Roman. *The Foreign Policy of Poland 1919–1939*. New York: Praeger, 1962.

Denne, Ludwig. *Das Danzig-Problem in der deutschen Aussenpolitik 1934–39*. Bonn: Röhrscheid, 1959.

Detwiler, Donald S. *Hitler, Franco und Gibraltar, Die Frage des spanischen Eintritts in den Zweiten Weltkrieg*. Wiesbaden: Steiner, 1962.

Deuerlein, Ernst. *Das Reichskonkordat*. Düsseldorf: Patmos-Verlag, 1956.

Der deutsche Imperialismus und der Zweite Weltkrieg. 2. Berlin (East): Rütten & Loening, 1961. An important collection of studies.

Dickmann, Fritz. "Machtwille und Ideologie in Hiters aussenpolitischen Zielsetzungen vor 1933." In *Spiegel der Geschichte, Festgabe für Max Braubach*. ed. by Konrad Repgen and Stephan Skalweit. Muenster: Aschendorf, 1964, pp. 915–41.

Divine, Robert A. *The Illusion of Neutrality*. Chicago: University of Chicago Press, 1962.

Donosti, Mario (pseud. of Mario Lucciolli). *Mussolini e l'Europa; la politica estera fascista*. Rome: Leonardo, 1945.

Dorpalen, Andreas. *Hindenburg and the Weimar Republic*. Princeton: Princeton University Press, 1964.

Drechsler, Karl. *Deutschland-China-Japan 1933–1939, Das Dilemma der deutschen Fernostpolitik*. Berlin (East): Akademie-Verlag, 1964.

Duroselle, Jean-Baptiste (ed.). *Les relations germano-soviétiques de 1933 à 1939*. Paris: Armand Colin, 1954.

Eichstädt, Ulrich. *Von Dollfuss zu Hitler*. Wiesbaden: Steiner, 1955.

Einhorn, Marion. *Die ökonomischen Hintergründe der faschistischen deutschen Intervention in Spanien 1936–1939*. Berlin (East): Akademie-Verlag, 1962.

Epstein, Fritz T. "National Socialism and French Colonialism." *Journal of Central European Affairs*. 3, No. 1 (April 1943), 52–64.

Erbe, René. *Die nationalsozialistische Wirtschaftspolitik 1933–1939 im Lichte der modernen Theorie*. Zurich: Polygraphischer Verlag, 1958.

Erickson, John. *The Soviet High Command*. New York: St. Martin's Press, 1962.

Esch, P. A. M. van der. *Prelude to War, The International Repercussions of the Spanish Civil War*. The Hague: Mouton, 1951.

Europäische Publikation. *Die Vollmacht des Gewissens*. 1. Munich: Hermann Ring, 1956.

Fabry, Philip W. *Der Hitler-Stalin Pakt, 1939–1941*. Darmstadt: Fundus, 1962.

Farnsworth, Beatrice. *William C. Bullitt and the Soviet Union*. Bloomington: Indiana University Press, 1967.

Feiling, Keith. *The Life of Neville Chamberlain*. London: Macmillan, 1946.

Feis, Herbert. *The Spanish Story*. New York: Knopf, 1948.

Foerster, Wolfgang. *Ein General kämpft gegen den Krieg. Aus den nachgelas-*

senen Papieren des Generalstabchefs Ludwig Beck. Munich: Münchener-Dom Verlag, 1949.

Foertsch, Hermann. *Schuld und Verhängnis, Die Fritschkrise im Frühjahr 1938*. Stuttgart: Deutsch Verlags-Anstalt, 1951.

Fox, John P. "Japanese Reaction to Nazi Germany's Racial Legislation." *Wiener Library Bulletin*. 23, Nos. 2 & 3 (1969), 46–50.

Fraenkel, Ernst. *Amerika im Spiegel des deutschen politischen Denkens*. Cologne: Westdeutscher Verlag.

Frye, Alton. *Nazi Germany and the American Hemisphere, 1933–1941*. New Haven: Yale University Press, 1967.

Gasiorowski, Zygmunt J. "Did Pilsudski Attempt to Initiate a Preventive War in 1933?" *Journal of Modern History*. 27, No. 2 (June 1955), 135–51.

———. "The German-Polish Nonaggression Pact of 1934." *Journal of Central European Affairs*. 15, No. 1 (April 1955), 3–29.

Gatzke, Hans W. "Russo-German Military Collaboration during the Weimar Republic." *American Historical Review*. 43, No. 3 (April 1958), 565–97.

Gehl, Jürgen. *Austria, Germany, and the Anschluss, 1931–38*. London: Oxford University Press, 1963.

Gemzell, Carl-Axel. *Raeder, Hitler und Skandinavien, Der Kampf für einen maritimen Operationsplan*. Lund: Gleerup, 1965.

Gentzen, Felix-Heinrich. "Die Rolle der 'Deutschen Stiftung' bei der Vorbereitung der Annexion des Memellandes im März 1939." *Jahrbuch für Geschichte der UdSSR und der Volksdemokratischen Länder*. 5 (1961), 71–94.

George, Margaret. *The Warped Vision, British Foreign Policy 1933–1939*. Pittsburg: University of Pittsburgh Press, 1965.

Geschichte des Grossen Vaterländischen Krieges der Sowjetunion. Vol. I. *Die Vorbereitung und Entfesselung des Zweiten Weltkrieges durch die Imperialistischen Mächte*. Berlin (East): Deutscher Militär-Verlag, 1962. The first volume of the Soviet official history of World War II in its German edition. Contains references to Soviet archives.

Gilbert, Martin, and Gott, Richard. *The Appeasers*. Boston: Houghton Mifflin, 1963.

Glaser, Hermann. *Spiesser-Ideologie, Von der Zerstörung des deutschen Geistes im 19. und 20. Jahrhundert*. Freiburg: Rombach, 1964.

Gross, Babette. *Willi Münzenberg, Eine politische Biographie*. Stuttgart: Deutsche Verlags-Anstalt, 1967.

Gruchmann, Lothar. *Nationalsozialistische Grossraumordnung*. Stuttgart: Deutsche Verlags-Anstalt, 1962.

Hagemann, Walter. *Publizistik im Dritten Reich*. Hamburg: Hamburger Gildenverlag, 1948.

Harper, Glenn T. *German Economic Policy in Spain during the Spanish Civil War 1936–1939*. The Hague: Mouton, 1967.

Harrigan, William M. "Nazi Germany and the Holy See, 1933–1936: The Historical Background of *Mit brennender Sorge*." *Catholic Historical Review*. 47, No. 2 (July 1961), 164–73.

Harris, Brice. *The United States and the Italo-Ethiopian Crisis*. Stanford: Stanford University Press, 1964.

Hart, B. H. Liddell. *The German Generals Talk*. New York: William Morrow, 1948.

Heiber, Helmut. *Joseph Goebbels*. Berlin: Colloquium Verlag, 1962.

Heiden, Konrad. *Adolf Hitler*. Zurich: Europa-Verlag, 1936.

Heineman, John L. "Constantin von Neurath and German Policy at the London Economic Conference of 1933: Background to the Resignation of Alfred Hugenberg." *Journal of Modern History*. 41, No. 2 (June 1969), 160–88.

Heinrichs, Waldo. *American Ambassador: Joseph C. Grew and the Development of the United States Diplomatic Tradition.* Boston: Little, Brown, 1966.

Helmreich, Ernst C. "The Arrest and Freeing of the Protestant Bishops of Württemberg and Bavaria, September–October 1934." *Central European History.* 2, No. 2 (June 1969), 159–69.

Hilberg, Raul. *The Destruction of the European Jews.* Chicago: Quadrangle, 1961.

Hildebrand, Klaus. *Vom Reich zum Weltreich, Hitler, NSDAP und koloniale Frage, 1919–1945.* Munich: Wilhelm Fink Verlag, 1969.

Hillgruber, Andreas. *Hitler, König Carol und Marschall Antonescu, Die deutsch-rumänischen Beziehungen 1938–1944.* Wiesbaden: Steiner, 1954.

Hirszowicz, Lukasz. *The Third Reich and the Arab East.* London: Routledge & Kegan Paul, 1966.

The History of the Times. 4: *The 150th Anniversary and Beyond, 1912–1948, Part II.* London: The Times, 1952.

Höltje, Christian. *Die Weimarer Republik und das Ostlocarno-Problem, 1919–1934.* Würzburg: Holzner, 1955.

Hoensch, Jörg K. *Die Slowakei und Hitlers Ostpolitik.* Cologne: Böhlau, 1965.

———. *Der ungarische Revisionismus und die Zerschlagung der Tschechoslowakei.* Tübingen: Mohr, 1967.

Hoepke, Klaus-Peter. *Die deutsche Rechte und der italienische Faschismus.* Düsseldorf: Droste, 1968.

Hofer, Walter. *Die Entfesselung des Zweiten Weltkrieges, Eine Studie über die internationalen Beziehungen im Sommer 1939.* 3d ed. Frankfurt/M: S. Fischer, 1964.

Hoggan, David L. *Der erzwungene Krieg.* Tübingen: Verlag der Deutschen Hochschullehrerzeitung, 1961.

Hoptner, Jacob B. *Yugoslavia in Crisis, 1934–1941.* New York: Columbia University Press, 1962. Important for the access of the author to Yugoslav materials.

Hory, Ladislaus, and Broszat, Martin. *Der kroatische Ustascha-Staat, 1941–1945.* Stuttgart: Deutsche Verlags-Anstalt, 1964.

Hughes, William R. *Indomitable Friend, The Life of Corder Catchpool 1883–1952.* London: Allen & Unwin, 1956. Important on Quaker contacts in German-English relations.

Institut für Zeitgeschichte, Munich. *Gutachten des Instituts für Zeitgeschichte.* 1. Munich: Selbstverlag, 1958.

Jacobsen, Hans-Adolf. *Nationalsozialistische Aussenpolitik 1933–1938.* Frankfurt/M: Alfred Metzner, 1968.

Jäckel, Eberhard. *Frankreich in Hitlers Europa.* Stuttgart: Deutsche Verlags-Anstalt, 1966.

Jäger, Jörg-Johannes. *Die wirtschaftliche Abhängigkeit des Dritten Reiches vom Ausland dargestellt am Beispiel der Stahlindustrie.* Berlin: Berlin Verlag, 1969. A most informative study.

Jarausch, Konrad. *The Four Power Pact 1933.* Madison: State Historical Society of Wisconsin, 1965.

Jetzinger, Franz. *Hitlers Jugend.* Vienna: Europa-Verlag, 1956.

Johnson, Chalmers. *An Instance of Treason, Ozuki Hotsumi and the Sorge Spy Ring.* Stanford: Stanford University Press, 1964.

deJong, Louis. *The German Fifth Column in World War II.* Trans. by C. M. Geyl. Chicago: University of Chicago Press, 1956.

Kerekes, Lajos. *Abenddämmerung einer Demokratie; Mussolini, Gömbös und die Heimwehr.* Trans. by Johanna Till. Vienna: Europa-Verlag, 1966.

Kimmich, Christoph M. *The Free City, Danzig and German Foreign Policy, 1919–1934.* New Haven: Yale University Press, 1968.

Kitsikis, Dimitri. "La Gréce entre l'Angleterre at l'Allemagne de 1936 à 1941." *Revue Historique*. 238 (July-Sept. 1967), 85–116. Very important because based on Greek archives.

Kluke, Paul. "Nationalsozialistische Europa-Ideologie." *Vierteljahrshefte für Zeitgeschichte*. 3, No. 3 (July 1955), 240–75.

Kochan, Lionel. "Russia and Germany 1935–1937, A Note." *Slavonic and East European Review*. 40 (1962), 518–20.

———. *Russia and the Weimar Republic*. Cambridge: Bowes & Bowes, 1954.

Koerner, Ralf Richard. *So haben sie es damals gemacht, Die Propagandavorbereitungen zum Österreichanschluss durch das Hitlerregime, 1933–1938*. Vienna: Gesellschaft zur Förderung Wissenschaftlicher Forschung, 1958.

Kordt, Erich. *Wahn und Wirklichkeit, Die Aussenpolitik des Dritten Reiches*. 2d ed. Stuttgart: Union Deutsche Verlagsgesellschaft, 1948.

Krausnick, Helmut. "Legenden um Hitlers Aussenpolitik." *Vierteljahrshefte für Zeitgeschichte*. 2, No. 3 (July 1954), 217–39.

Krecker, Lothar. *Deutschland und die Türkei im Zweiten Weltkrieg*. Frankfurt/M: Klostermann, 1964.

———. "Die diplomatischen Verhandlungen über den Viererpakt vom 15. Juli 1933." *Die Welt als Geschichte*. 21 (1961), 227–37.

Kühne, Horst. "Die fünfte Kolonne des faschistischen deutschen Imperialismus in Südwestafrika (1933–1939)." *Zeitschrift für Geschichtswissenschaft*. 8 (1960), 765–90.

———, *et al.* (eds.). *Interbrigadisten, Der Kampf deutscher Kommunisten und anderer Antifaschisten im national-revolutionären Krieg des spanischen Volkes 1936 bis 1939*. Berlin (East): Deutscher Militärverlag, 1966.

———. "Zur Kolonialpolitik des faschistischen deutschen Imperialismus (1933–1939)." *Zeitschrift für Geschichtswissenschaft*. 9 (1961), 514–37.

Kvaček, Robert. "Československo-německá jednáni v noce 1936 (Czech-German negotiations in 1936)." *Historie a Vojenství*. 5 (1965), 721–54.

———, and Vinš, Václav. "K Německo-Československým sondážým ve tričatých letec (Concerning the German-Czech soundings in the 1930's)." *Československý Časopis Historický*. 14 (1966), 887–96.

Langer, William L. and Gleason, S. Everett. *The Challenge to Isolation, 1937–1940*. New York: Harper, 1952.

Laqueur, Walter. *Russia and Germany, A Century of Conflict*. London: Weidenfeld & Nicolson, 1965.

Latour, Conrad F. *Südtirol und die Achse Berlin-Rom, 1938–1945*. Stuttgart: Deutsche Verlags-Anstalt, 1962.

Laurens, Franklin D. *France and the Italo-Ethiopian Crisis, 1935–1936*. The Hague: Mouton, 1967.

Laurent, Pierre Henri. "The Reversal of Belgian Foreign Policy 1936–1937." *Review of Politics*. 31, No. 3 (July 1969), 370–84.

Leonhardt, Hans L. *Nazi Conquest of Danzig*. Chicago: University of Chicago Press, 1942.

Leverkuehn, Paul. *Posten auf ewiger Wache*. Essen: Essener Verlagsanstalt, 1938.

Lewy, Guenter. *The Catholic Church and Nazi Germany*. New York: McGraw-Hill, 1964.

Liu, Chih-pu. *A Military History of Modern China, 1924–1949*. Princeton: Princeton University Press, 1956.

Loebsack, Wilhelm. *Danzigs Gauleiter Albert Forster*. Hamburg: Hanseatische Verlagsanstalt, 1934.

Macartney, Carlyle A. *October Fifteenth, A History of Modern Hungary*. 2 vols. Edinburgh: University Press, 1956.

Macleod, Iain. *Neville Chamberlain*. New York: Atheneum, 1962.

Marwick, Arthur. *Clifford Allen: The Open Conspirator*. Edinburgh: Oliver & Boyd, 1964.
Mason, John Brown. *The Danzig Dilemma*. Stanford: Stanford University Press, 1946.
McRandle, James. *The Track of the Wolf*. Chicago: Northwestern University Press, 1965.
Meier-Welcker, Hans. *Seeckt*. Frankfurt/M: Bernard & Graefe, 1967.
Meinck, Gerhard. *Hitler und die deutsche Aufrüstung, 1933–1937*. Wiesbaden: Steiner, 1959.
———. "Der Reichsverteidigungsrat." *Wehrwissenschaftliche Rundschau*. 6, No. 8 (Aug. 1956), 411–22.
Merkes, Manfred. *Die deutsche Politik gegenüber dem spanischen Bürgerkrieg 1936–1939*. Bonn: Röhrscheid, 1961.
Meskill, Johanna M. *Hitler and Japan: The Hollow Alliance*. New York: Atherton Press, 1966.
Miller, Jane K. *Belgian Foreign Policy between Two Wars, 1919–1940*. New York: Bookman, 1951.
Milward, Alan S. *The German Economy at War*. London: Athlone Press, 1965.
Moltmann, Günter. "Weltherrschaftsideen Hitlers." In *Europa und Übersee, Festschrift für Egmont Zechlin*. Ed. by Otto Brunner and Dietrich Gerhard. Hamburg: Hans Bredow-Institut, 1961, pp. 197–240.
Mosse, George L. *The Crisis of German Ideology, The Intellectual Origins of the Third Reich*. New York: Grosset & Dunlap, 1964.
Motter, T. H. Vail. *The Persian Corridor and Aid to Russia*. Washington: Government Printing Office, 1952.
Mueller-Hillebrand, Burkhart. *Das Heer 1933–1945*. 1: *Das Heer bis zum Kriegsbeginn*. Darmstadt: Mittler, 1954.
Müller, Klaus-Jürgen. *Das Heer und Hitler, Armee und nationalsozialistisches Regime 1933–1940*. Stuttgart: Deutsche Verlags-Anstalt, 1969.
Namier, Sir Lewis. *Europe in Decay*. London: Macmillan, 1950.
———. *In the Nazi Era*. London: Macmillan, 1952.
Niclauss, Karlheinz. *Die Sowjetunion und Hitlers Machtergreifung, Eine Studie über die deutsch-russischen Beziehungen der Jahre 1929 bis 1935*. Bonn: Röhrscheid, 1966.
Nicolson, Harold. *King George V*. London: Constable, 1952.
Offner, Arnold A. *American Appeasement, United States Foreign Policy and Germany, 1933–1938*. Cambridge, Mass.: Harvard University Press, 1969.
———. "William E. Dodd: Romantic Historian and Diplomatic Cassandra." *The Historian*. 34 (Aug. 1962), 451–69.
Oprea, I. M. *Nicolae Titulescu's Diplomatic Activity*. Trans. by Andrei Bantas. Bucharest: Academy of the Socialist Republic of Romania, 1968.
Orlov, Dietrich. *The Nazis in the Balkans*. Pittsburgh: Pittsburgh University Press, 1968.
Paikert, Geza Charles. *The Danube Swabians, German Populations in Hungary, Rumania and Yugoslavia and Hitler's Impace on Their Patterns*. The Hague: Nijhoff, 1967.
Perman, Dagmar H. *The Shaping of the Czechoslovak State*. Leyden: Brill, 1962.
Pese, Walter Werner. "Hitler and Italien." *Vierteljahrshefte für Zeitgeschichte*. 3, No. 2 (April 1955), 113–26.
Petersen, Jens. "Deutschland und Italien im Sommer 1935, Der Wechsel des italienischen Botschafters in Berlin." *Geschichte in Wissenschaft und Unterricht*. 20, No. 6 (June 1969), 330–41.
Peterson, Edward N. *Hjalmar Schacht, For and Against Hitler*. Boston: Christopher Publishing House, 1954.

Petwaidic, Walter. *Die autoritäre Anarchie*. Hamburg: Hoffman und Campe, 1946.

Petzina, Dieter. *Autarkiepolitik im Dritten Reich, Der nationalsozialistische Vierjahresplan*. Stuttgart: Deutsche Verlags-Anstalt, 1968.

———. "Hauptprobleme der deutschen Wirtschaftspolitik, 1932–1933." *Vierteljahrshefte für Zeitgeschichte*. 15, No. 1 (Jan. 1967), 18–55.

Pike, David Wingeate. *Conjecture, Propaganda, and Deceit and the Spanish Civil War: The International Crisis over Spain, 1936–1939, as seen by the French Press*. Stanford: California Institute of International Studies, 1968. Important for the author's access to French departmental archives.

Plieg, Ernst-Albrecht. *Das Memelland 1920–1939*. Würzburg: Holzner, 1962.

Pohle, Heinz. *Der Rundfunk als Instrument der Politik*. Hamburg: Hans Bredow-Institut, 1955.

Post, Gaines, Jr. "German Foreign Policy and Military Planning, The Polish Question, 1924–1929." Stanford University diss. 1969.

Presseisen, Ernst L. *Germany and Japan, A Study in Totalitarian Diplomacy 1933–1941*. The Hague: Nijhoff, 1958.

Puchert, Berthold. "Die deutsch-polnische Nichtangriffserklärung und die Aussenwirtschaftspolitik des deutschen Imperialismus gegenüber Polen bis 1939." *Jahrbuch für Geschichte der UdSSR und der Volksdemokratischen Länder Europas*. 12 (1968), 339–54.

———. *Der Wirtschaftskrieg des deutschen Imperialismus gegen Polen 1925–1934*. Berlin (East): Akademie-Verlag, 1963.

Pulzer, Peter G. J. *The Rise of Political Anti-Semitism in Germany and Austria*. New York: Wiley, 1965.

Puzzo, Dante A. *Spain and the Great Powers, 1936–1941*. New York: Columbia University Press, 1962.

Rabenau, Friedrich von. *Seeckt, Aus seinem Leben, 1918–1936*. Leipzig: Hase & Koehler, 1940.

Rauschning, Hermann. *The Conservative Revolution*. New York: Putnam's, 1941.

Remak, Joachim. " 'Friends of the New Germany': The Bund and German-American Relations." *Journal of Modern History*. 29, No. 1 (March 1957), 38–41.

Rhode, Gotthold. "Aussenminister Josef Beck und Staatssekretär Graf Szembek." *Vierteljahrshefte für Zeitgeschichte*. 2, No. 1 (Jan. 1954), 86–94.

Ritschel, Karl Heinz. *Diplomatie um Südtirol, Politische Hintergründe eines europäischen Versagens*. Stuttgart: Seewald, 1966.

Ritter, Gerhard. *Carl Goerdeler und die deutsche Widerstandsbewegung*. Stuttgart: Deutsche Verlags-Anstalt, 1955.

Robertson, Esmonde M. *Hitler's Pre-War Policy and Military Plans, 1933–1939*. London: Longmans, 1963.

Robinson, Jacob. *And the crooked shall be made straight*. New York: Macmillan, 1965.

Roos, Hans. *Polen und Europa, Studien zur polnischen Aussenpolitik 1931–1939*. Tübingen: Mohr, 1957.

———. "Die Präventivkriegspläne Pilsudskis von 1933." *Vierteljahrshefte für Zeitgeschichte*. 3, No. 4 (Oct. 1955), 344–63.

Rosinski, Herbert. *The German Army*. London: Hogarth, 1940.

Ross, Dieter. *Hitler und Dollfuss*. Hamburg: Leibniz-Verlag, 1966.

Salvemini, Gaetano. *Prelude to World War II*. Garden City: Doubleday, 1954.

Sanke, Heinz (ed.). *Der deutsche Faschismus in Lateinamerika, 1933–1943*. Berlin (East): Humboldt-Universität, 1966.

Sasse, Heinz Günther. "Das Problem des diplomatischen Nachwuchses im Dritten

Reich." In *Forschungen zu Staat und Verfassung, Festgabe für Fritz Hartung*. Ed. by Richard Dietrich and Gerhard Oestreich. Berlin: Duncker & Humblot, 1958, pp. 367–84.

Schechtman, Joseph B. *The Mufti and the Fuehrer, The Rise and Fall of Haj Amin el-Husseini*. New York: Yoseloff, 1965.

Schilling, Alexander. *Dr. Walter Riehl und die Geschichte des Nationalsozialismus*. Leipzig: Forum, 1933.

Schlesinger, Arthur M. Jr. *The Age of Roosevelt*. 2: *The Coming of the New Deal*. Boston: Houghton Mifflin, 1959.

Schmitz-Esser, Winfried. "Hitler-Mussolini: Das Südtiroler Abkommen von 1939." *Aussenpolitik*. 13, No. 6 (June 1962), 397–409.

Schmokel, Wolfe W. *Dream of Empire: German Colonialism, 1919–1945*. New Haven: Yale University Press, 1964.

Scholder, Klaus. "Die evangelische Kirche in der Sicht der nationalsozialistischen Führung bis zum Kriegsausbruch." *Vierteljahrshefte für Zeitgeschichte*. 16, No. 1 (Jan. 1968), 15–35.

Schramm, Wilhelm Ritter von. "Hitlers psychologischer Angriff auf Frankreich." Aus Politik und Zeitgeschichte, Beilage zu *Das Parlament*. B 5/61. 1 February 1961.

Schubert, Günter. *Anfänge nationalsozialistischer Aussenpolitik*. Cologne: Verlag Wissenschaft und Politik, 1963.

Schweitzer, Arthur. *Big Business in the Third Reich*. Bloomington: Indiana University Press, 1964.

———. "Foreign Exchange Crisis of 1936." *Zeitschrift für die gesamte Staatswissenschaft*. 118, No. 2 (April 1962), 243–77.

———. "Der ursprüngliche Vierjahresplan." *Jahrbücher für Nationalökonomie und Statistik*. 168 (1957), 348–96.

———. "Die wirtschaftliche Wiederaufrüstung Deutschlands von 1934–1936." *Zeitschrift für die gesamte Staatswissenschaft*. 114, No. 4 (1958), 594–637.

Scott, William E. *Alliance against Hitler, The Origins of the Franco-Soviet Pact*. Durham: Duke University Press, 1962.

Seabury, Paul. *The Wilhelmstrasse*. Berkeley: University of California Press, 1954.

Siebert, Ferdinand. *Italiens Weg in den Zweiten Weltkrieg*. Bonn: Athenäum, 1962.

Smith, Arthur L. *The Deutschtum of Nazi Germany and the United States*. The Hague: Nijhoff, 1965.

Sodeikat, Ernst. "Der Nationalsozialismus und die Danziger Opposition." *Vierteljahrshefte für Zeitgeschichte*. 14, No. 2 (April 1966), 139–74.

Sohl, Klaus. "Die Kriegsvorbereitungen des deutschen Imperialismus in Bulgarien am Vorabend des zweiten Weltkrieges." *Jahrbücher für Geschichte der UdSSR und der volksdemokratischen Länder*. 3 (1959), 91–119.

Sommer, Theo. *Deutschland und Japan zwischen den Mächten, 1935–1940*. Tübingen: Mohr, 1962.

Sontag, Raymond J. "The Origins of the Second World War." *Review of Politics*. 25, No. 4 (Oct. 1963), 497–508.

Spielhagen, Franz (pseud.?). *Spione und Verschwörer in Spanien*. Paris: Éditions du Carrefour, 1936.

Sprenger, Heinrich. *Heinrich Sahm, Kommunalpolitiker und Staatsmann*. Cologne: Grote, 1969.

Stehlin, Paul. *Témoignage pour l'histoire*. Paris: Robert Laffant, 1964.

Stephan, Werner. *Joseph Goebbels, Dämon einer Diktatur*. Stuttgart: Union Deutsche Verlagsgesellschaft, 1949.

Sz-Ormos, M. "Sur les causes de l'échec du pacte danubien (1934–35)." *Acta Historica.* 14, No. 1–2 (1968), 21–81.

Taylor, Alan J. P. *The Origins of the Second World War.* London: Hamilton, 1961.

Taylor, F. Jay. *The United States and the Spanish Civil War, 1936–1939.* New York: Bookman, 1956.

Teske, Hermann. *General Ernst Köstring, Der militärische Mittler zwischen dem Deutschen Reich und der Sowjetunion 1921–1941.* Frankfurt/M: Mittler, 1966.

Thomas, Georg. *Geschichte der deutschen Wehr- und Rüstungswirtschaft (1918–1943/45).* Boppard: Harald Boldt, 1966. This volume, edited by Wolfgang Birkenfeld, is a combination memoir and study written during World War II.

Thomas, Hugh. *The Spanish Civil War.* New York: Harper & Row, 1963.

Tillmann, Heinz. *Deutschlands Araberpolitik im zweiten Weltkrieg.* Berlin (East): Deutscher Verlag der Wissenschaften, 1965.

Toscano, Mario. "Eden's Mission to Rome on the Eve of the Italo-Ethiopian Conflict." In *Studies in Diplomatic History and Historiography in Honor of G. P. Gooch.* New York: Barnes & Noble, 1961, pp. 126–52.

———. *Le origini del patto d'acciaoi.* Florence: Sansoni, 1948.

———. "Problemi particolari della storia della Secunda Guerra Mondiale." *Rivista di studi politici internationali.* 17, No. 3 (1950), 388–98.

Traina, Richard P. *American Diplomacy and the Spanish Civil War.* Bloomington: Indiana University Press, 1968.

Treue, Wilhelm. "Das Dritte Reich und die Westmächte auf dem Balkan." *Vierteljahrshefte für Zeitgeschichte.* 1, No. 1 (Jan. 1953), 45–64.

Trevor-Roper, Hugh R. "Hitlers Kriegsziele." *Vierteljahrshefte für Zeitgeschichte.* 8, No. 2 (April, 1960), 121–33.

Truchanovskii, Vladimir G. (ed.). *Geschichte der internationalen Beziehungen, 1917–1939.* Trans. by Peter Hoffmann and Gabriele and Günter Rosenfeld. Berlin (East): Rütten & Loening, 1963.

Truckenbrodt, Walter. *Deutschland und der Völkerbund, Die Behandlung reichdeutscher Angelegenheiten im Völkerbundsrat von 1920–1939.* Essen: Essener Verlagsanstalt, 1941.

Urban, Rudolf. *Demokratenpresse im Lichte Prager Geheimakten.* Prague: Orbis, 1943.

Völker, Karl-Heinz. "Die Entwicklung der militärischen Luftfahrt in Deutschland, 1920–1933." *Beiträge zur Militär- und Kriegsgeschichte.* 3 (1962), 121–292.

———. "Die geheime Luftrüstung der Reichswehr und ihre Auswirkung auf den Flugzeugsbestand der Luftwaffe bis zum Beginn des Zweiten Weltkrieges." *Wehrwissenschaftliche Rundschau.* 12 (1962), 540–49.

———. *Die Deutsche Luftwaffe 1933–1939.* Stuttgart: Deutsche Verlags-Anstalt, 1967.

Waite, Robert G. L. *Vanguard of Nazism, The Free Corps Movement in Postwar Germany, 1918–1923.* Cambridge, Mass.: Harvard University Press, 1952.

Walsh, Edmund A. *Total Power.* Garden City: Doubleday, 1948.

Warner, Geoffrey. *Pierre Laval and the Eclipse of France, 1931–1945.* New York: Macmillan, 1968.

Watt, Donald C. "The Anglo-German Naval Agreement of 1935: An Interim Judgement." *Journal of Modern History.* 28, No. 2 (June 1956), 155–75.

———. "Christian Essay in Appeasement." *Wiener Library Bulletin.* 14, No. 2 (1960), 30–31.

———. "German Plans for Reoccupation of the Rhineland: A Note." *Journal of Contemporary History*. 1, No. 4 (Oct. 1966), 193–99.

———. *Personalities and Policies. Studies in the Formulation of British Foreign Policy in the Twentieth Century*. Notre Dame: University of Notre Dame Press, 1965.

———. "The Rome-Berlin Axis, 1936–1940, Myth and Reality." *Review of Politics*. 22, No. 4 (1960), 519–43.

Weinberg, Gerhard L. "The Defeat of Germany in 1918 and the European Balance of Power." *Central European History*. 2, No. 3 (Sept. 1969), 248–60.

———. "Deutsch-japanische Verhandlungen über das Südseemandat, 1937–1938." *Vierteljahrshefte für Zeitgeschichte*. 4, No. 4 (Oct. 1956), 390–98.

———. "German Colonial Plans and Policies, 1938–1942." In *Geschichte und Gegenwartsbewusstsein, Festschrift für Hans Rothfels*. Göttingen: Vandenhoeck & Ruprecht, 1963, pp. 462–91.

———. "German Recognition of Manchoukuo." *World Affairs Quarterly*. 28, No. 2 (July 1957), 149–64.

———. "Germany and Czechoslovakia, 1933–1945." In *Czechoslovakia Past and Present*. Ed. by Miloslav Rechcigl. The Hague: Mouton, 1969, 1:760–69.

———. *Germany and the Soviet Union, 1939–1941*. Leyden: Brill, 1954.

———. "Hitler's Image of the United States." *American Historical Review*. 69, No. 4 (July 1964), 1006–21.

———. "A Proposed Compromise over Danzig in 1939?" *Journal of Central European Affairs*. 14, No. 4 (Jan. 1955), 334–38.

———. "Schachts Besuch in den USA im Jahre 1933." *Vierteljahrshefte für Zeitgeschichte*. 11, No. 2 (April 1963), 166–80.

———. "Secret Hitler-Beneš Negotiations in 1936–37." *Journal of Central European Affairs*. 19, No. 4 (Jan. 1960), 366–74.

Wheeler-Bennet, John W. *The Nemesis of Power*. London: Macmillan, 1954.

Whiteside, Andrew G. *Austrian National Socialism before 1918*. The Hague: Nijhoff, 1962.

Wiskemann, Elizabeth. *The Rome/Berlin Axis*. 2d ed. London: Collins, 1966.

Woerden, A. V. N. van. "Hitler Faces England: Theories, Images and Policies." *Acta Historiae Neerlandica*. 3 (1968), 141–59.

Wohlfeil, Rainer. "Der spanische Bürgerkrieg, 1936–1939, Zur Deutung und Nachwirkung." *Vierteljahrshefte für Zeitgeschichte*. 16, No. 2 (April 1968), 101–19.

———. "Zum Stand der Forschung über Hauptprobleme des Spanischen Bürgerkrieges." *Militärgeschichtliche Mitteilungen*, 2 (1969), 189–98.

Wolfers, Arnold. *Britain and France between Two Wars*. New York: Harcourt, Brace, 1940.

Wootton, Graham. *The Official History of the British Legion*. London: Macdonald & Evans, 1956.

Wuescht, Johann. *Jugoslawien und das Dritte Reich*. Stuttgart: Seewald, 1968.

Index

Index